T[illegible] t

Ca[illegible] I

The Good Fight

Canadians and World War II

Edited by

J.L. Granatstein

and Peter Neary

Copp Clark Ltd.

Toronto

ISBN: 0-7730-5458-8

Executive editor: Jeff Miller
Managing editor: Barbara Tessman
Editor: Melanie Sherwood
Proofreader: Beverley Sotolov
Designer: Gordon Robertson
Cover photograph: Steve Payne
Typesetting: Carol Magee
Printing and binding: Metropole Litho Inc.
Cover illustration: The Canadian Volunteer Service Medal was awarded to members of the fighting services and nurses who died while on active service, completed eighteen months voluntary service, or had been honourably discharged before this service was complete. Seven figures representing nurses and the three fighting services are depicted on the medal, which was designed by Canadian Army war artist Charles Comfort.

Canadian Cataloguing in Publication Data

Main entry under title:
The good fight: Canadians and World War II
Includes bibliographical references.
ISBN 0-7730-5458-8

1. World War, 1939–1945 - Canada. 2. Canada -History - 1939–1945. I. Granatstein, J.L. 1939– . II. Neary, Peter, 1938– .

D768.15.G66 1995 940.53'71 C94-932822-7

Copp Clark Ltd.
2775 Matheson Blvd. East
Mississauga, Ontario
L4W 4P7

Printed and bound in Canada

1 2 3 4 5 5458-8 99 98 97 96 95

For Carole Granatstein and Nicholas and John Neary
who have thrived in peace and freedom
thanks to the sacrifices of those who fought and won the Second World War

And in memory of Arthur Patrick Bates and Jimmy Keshen
who played their parts in that conflict

Contents

V The Return

Introduction

Going to War

IN THE SUMMER OF 1939 there was scant enthusiasm in Canada for the prospect of another war against Germany. The memory of the horrible casualties in France and Flanders during the Great War was still fresh, and French and English Canadians still felt antagonistic toward each other over the issue of conscription, which had so divided the nation and its political parties in 1917 and 1918. Public debate during the 1930s had seemed, at times, to be sharply polarized, with League of Nations collectivists battling against imperialists and neutralists, while the great majority of Canadians struggled simply to survive a grinding, endless economic depression at a time when government social programs did not exist and public charity had given out under the strain.

What was different in 1939 was that Canada's constitutional position had changed. In 1914, the Dominion was a colony, legally bound by Britain's decision to fight; in 1939, thanks to the Statute of Westminster of 1931, Canada had full independence in foreign policy and, although there were differing views on the question, had the right to stay out of war if it so chose. In fact, there was no real choice. The Canadian humorist and university economist Stephen Leacock put it brilliantly in an article in *The Atlantic Monthly* in June 1939:

> If you were to ask any Canadian, "Do you have to go to war if England does?" he'd answer at once, "Oh, no." If you then said, "*Would* you go to war if England does?" he'd answer, "Oh, yes." And if you asked, "Why?" he would say, reflectively, "Well, you see, we'd *have* to."[1]

That was precisely the case. The legal obligation was gone, but for most English-speaking Canadians—the majority in the nation—the moral obligation and the wish to help Britain in any major war were still so powerful that Canada *had* to fight. The federal government simply had to recognize this fact of life. Certainly Mackenzie King and most of his cabinet and caucus did.[2]

By and large, French Canadians did not. To Québécois, Canada was *their* country, and it owed nothing to Britain or, for that matter, to France. European quarrels should be resolved by Europeans, and Canada's primary task was to stay clear. Realists in Quebec such as Justice Minister Ernest Lapointe, however, recognized that English Canada would insist on participation. That was permissible, they said, providing no one tried to force Quebeckers overseas. No conscription, no compulsory military service, no war to the last gasp this time. Still, the issue had to be managed carefully, and King and Lapointe cautiously played with public opinion through 1939, the prime minister sounding neutralist one day, while the justice minister was bellicose the next. But conscription was the shibboleth, the word no one could utter except to denounce.[3]

The politicians read and understood the national mood. In March 1939, both Prime Minister Mackenzie King and Conservative Party leader Robert Manion pledged themselves against conscription for overseas service in the event of war, pledges that King repeated solemnly in the Commons in September when the government honoured its promises to allow Parliament to decide Canada's course. Germany had invaded Poland on 1 September, and Britain and France had declared war on the 3rd. Although Canada had already begun to mobilize, technically the nation remained at peace, or so King told President Franklin Roosevelt, encouraging the American leader to send every possible weapon north while Canada remained neutral. After a debate in the House, King was able to bring Canada into the war without a recorded vote in Parliament, although there was a handful of opponents to participation. Given the nature and history of the country, the prime minister's achievement was a remarkable one. Canada was at war once again, but those promises against compulsory military service, those hostages to fortune, would not be forgotten in Quebec.

Men and Women in Uniform

THE ARMED FORCES scarcely existed at the beginning of the war. After two decades of low budgets and stagnation, Canada militarily began the Second World War from scratch. The Permanent Force, the "professional" army, numbered some 4500 all told, with about 450 officers. Many of the latter group were overage or unfit for active service. The Non-Permanent Active Militia, the reserve force, nominally amounted to 50 000 men, but training was notional; so was that strength figure. Just as critical was the lack of modern weapons: no tanks, no up-to-date artillery, and scarcely any trucks.[4]

The condition of the other services was no better. The Air Force, except for a few Hurricane fighters, had no modern aircraft. Its strength was less than the Army's, and markedly so where the reserve forces were concerned. The Royal Canadian Navy (RCN) had only 3500 officers and ratings, regular and reserve, but it did have a handful of modern destroyers divided between the coasts, and there was a reserve of trained seamen in fishing and merchant fleets that could be taken into service.[5]

In truth, no one anticipated a huge war effort. The government's policy, mirroring that of Great Britain, was one of "limited liability," a business term that suggested that Canada was not to be wholly responsible for the war's results. The blitzkrieg against Poland, over in a few weeks, was followed by a prolonged period of inaction, and that seemed to justify Canada's lackadaisical preparations. The Navy mobilized at once, as convoys immediately began to form in Halifax harbour for protection against Nazi U-boats. The Army announced plans to send a division of infantry overseas and to raise a second. The Royal Canadian Air Force (RCAF), much to its own and the nation's surprise, soon found itself committed to running a huge air-training plan.

Canada's wide-open spaces, far removed from the battlefields, seemed a perfect locale for the training of pilots, and the British had long realized this. In mid-September, prompted by the Australian and Canadian high commissioners in London, they asked Canada to direct the scheme, soon dubbed the British Commonwealth Air Training Plan (BCATP). Difficult, even bitter, negotiations ensued over the funding, but in December the plan was in place. Initially, it was to graduate just over a thousand pilots and another 900 aircrew each month for an initial total cost of some $650 million, of which Canada was to pay almost half. The tiny RCAF struggled to get the BCATP under way, enlisting civilian flying schools in the process, and developments were delayed by the sudden change in the war's course after May 1940. The first classes graduated in late 1940, and by 1942 BCATP schools in Canada had begun to pour forth pilots, navigators, wireless operators, and bombardiers in an extraordinary flood. Over 11 000 aircraft were used, and 104 000 men and women kept the BCATP flying. By war's end, the plan had trained 131 553 aircrew from all parts of the British Commonwealth (and not a few Americans, too). In all, 72 835 Canadians passed through the BCATP's air stations all across Canada. Arguably, the BCATP, its final cost to Canada $1.6 billion of a $2.2 billion total, was Canada's most important contribution to the war.[6]

Those trained aircrew were to be desperately needed after the disasters that befell Britain and France in the spring of 1940. The Germans had seized Denmark and Norway in April, and the panzers moved against the Low Countries and France in May. The French army crumbled, and the British Expeditionary Force (BEF) reeled back to the coast. Only a miracle allowed the BEF to be saved. There were feeble attempts to recreate another front in France: although two barely trained brigades of the 1st Canadian Division went to France, they escaped back to England almost without loss. Britain and its Dominions were alone; astonishingly, Canada, scarcely in the war as yet, was England's ranking ally, although only a handful of Canadian fliers helped win the Battle of Britain.

At last the stops were pulled out on the war effort at home, and "limited liability" went out the window. Recruiting stepped up and new formations took shape. By 1942, the Army overseas had three infantry and two armoured divisions plus two tank brigades organized after April 1942 into the First Canadian Army. The commander, Lieutenant-General Andrew G.L. McNaughton, was enormously popular with the troops and with Mackenzie King because he opposed conscription and wanted to keep the Army together. To point to McNaughton's prescience, in December 1941 an under-strength brigade that had been sent to Hong Kong from Canada was lost when the Crown Colony—along with a host of other Dutch, British, and American possessions—fell to Japanese attackers. The war had expanded to the Pacific, and there were pressures from British Columbia for stronger defences against a feared Japanese invasion. Troops and aircraft went to battle stations but, other than to occupy the Aleutian Islands off Alaska in June 1942 (from which they were eventually driven out in 1943), Japan never launched its forces against the West Coast.

The main theatre for Canada was Europe. The Army in Britain spoiled for a fight, but McNaughton's policy and government concurrence kept it defending the British Isles and in training. In August 1942, most of the 2nd Canadian Infantry Division took part in a disastrous attack on the French port of Dieppe. The slaughter on the pebbled beaches overlooked by high cliffs was terrible. Meanwhile, British forces had taken beatings in Greece and, after early successes against the Italians in Ethiopia and the North African desert, against General Erwin Rommel's Afrika Korps. The war was not going well for the Allies, though Hitler's invasion of the Soviet Union in June 1941 and the entry of the United States into the war in December 1941 put huge industrial and manpower resources at the Allies' command. Victories at Stalingrad and El Alamein began to turn the tide before the end of 1942.

At sea, the Royal Canadian Navy struggled to master the art of combatting German submarines. Shortages of suitable ships and deficiencies of equipment compounded the difficult task of turning yacht captains and city boys into efficient seamen. But the job had to be done: a huge percentage of Britain's supplies of food, raw material, and munitions came by sea. If the lifeline was cut, the war could be lost, and the German navy turned to the task with a will and new tactics. Wolfpacks of U-boats, sophisticated torpedoes, and skillful leadership almost brought the Allies to their knees. The RCN, struggling to learn its job in a navy equipped with corvettes—small under-armed vessels—saw convoys under its protection sadly battered and, for a time at the height of the Battle of the Atlantic in early 1943, the Canadian escort ships were pulled out of the line for retraining and refits.[7] But the Allied effort overcame the crisis, the German codes were finally cracked, the use of antisubmarine airpower became both more sophisticated and more widely available, and the RCN, refurbished and refreshed, was in at the kill. The Canadian ships and antisubmarine aircraft sank 52 U-boats, and the RCN provided a quite astonishing 50 percent of escorts for most of the North Atlantic convoys. By war's end, the RCN had aircraft carriers, cruisers, and an array of other vessels that operated in every theatre of war from the D-Day landings to the Pacific. The Navy's strength during the war reached 106 000 men and women, and incredibly the fleet was the third largest among the Allies by war's end.

The Royal Canadian Air Force underwent an even larger expansion, its total strength approximating a quarter million men and women in the BCATP and in 88 squadrons at home and overseas. Under the BCATP's terms, thousands of Canadian aircrew also served in Royal Air Force squadrons. In this way, the government reduced its expenditure on servicemen's salaries, but the RCAF lost track of some of its own men and received no credit for their service. A long struggle for "Canadianization" ensued as Ottawa tried to regain control over its pilots and aircrew, and the process was only partly successful. Still, RCAF bomber squadrons in No. 6 Group played a major role in the nighttime destruction of German cities and war potential, and the bomber crew fatalities, totalling just under ten thousand men, were horrific. Losses in some raids neared 10 percent of participating aircraft, and 5 percent was almost the norm, thus giving aircrew statistically insignificant chances of finishing their allotted thirty sorties. RCAF fighters and fighter bombers played major roles in Britain, North West Europe, the Middle East, and in the defence of Canada, while transport and maritime squadrons served around the world.[8]

For the Army, the disasters of Hong Kong and Dieppe aside, the years of training in England passed with excruciating slowness. McNaughton continued to fight to keep his Army together, but in 1943 finally, Ottawa overrode him and agreed to send the 1st Division to participate in the invasion of Sicily. Led by Major-General Guy Simonds, the division acquitted itself well and, joined by the 5th Canadian Armoured Division and I Canadian Corps headquarters, soon was advancing up the Italian boot. The fighting was fierce, most notably around Ortona at Christmas 1943, and the Canadians played a notable part in cracking the Hitler and Gothic lines. Before I Canadian Corps was pulled out of Italy in February 1945, 92 757 Canadians had served there; 5399 were killed in action, just under 20 000 were wounded, and 1004 became prisoners of war. The Italian sideshow had proved costly.[9]

For First Canadian Army, now led by General H.D.G. Crerar after McNaughton's sacking at the end of 1943, the main battleground was to be North-West Europe. The 3rd Canadian Infantry Division played its part on D-Day, successfully storming the Normandy beaches. Then the 2nd and 4th divisions joined, and the II Canadian Corps, led by Simonds, had a critical role in trapping the bulk of the German armies in France in the Falaise Gap. The Army, its ranks swelled by British, Polish, Belgian, and other formations, then cleared the French coast and plunged—all too literally—into the cold waters of the Scheldt estuary in the struggle to clear the approaches to the vital port of Antwerp. By the end of 1944, casualties were outrunning reinforcements, and wounded men were being put back into the line. Crerar's First Canadian Army, I Canadian Corps joining it in March, participated in the final great battles of the war in the spring of 1945, liberating the Netherlands and fighting across the Rhine. In all, the Army suffered 44 339 casualties in this eleven-month campaign; the war cemeteries scattered across France, Belgium, and Holland hold 11 336 who died in action. Plans to send a division to participate in the invasion of Japan, an assault expected to be very costly, were rendered unnecessary when Japan surrendered after A-bombs were used against Hiroshima and Nagasaki in August 1945.[10]

Considering the low military estate at the onset of war, Canada's record was a proud one. In all, more than 1.1 million men and women served in the Forces, a simply astonishing record for a nation of just over ten million people and one that simultaneously was exerting every effort in industrial and agricultural production. The war's cost to Canada in dollars has been estimated at $16 billion in 1995 dollars; the cost in lives was 42 042 dead and 54 414 wounded, numbers that do not and cannot include the lives blighted by grief and shock.

The Home Front

POLITICALLY, THE COMMANDING PERSONALITY of the war period was the Liberal prime minister, William Lyon Mackenzie King. His political career predated the Great War, and he had learned the hard lessons of that divisive conflict. Not surprisingly, he gave priority as party leader and prime minister to national unity. He had a long memory and could be very unforgiving. In his conduct of Canada's affairs he sought above all to avoid the mistakes of the past.

King turned sixty-five in December 1939 and often complained in his diary about a lack of vigour. But what he sometimes lacked in energy he more than made up for in experience. He was a strange mixture of a man, combining deep-seated insecurity with a profound sense of public mission, and self-pity with clinical calculation. The diplomat and diarist Charles Ritchie once described him as a "fat little conjurer with . . . flickering, shifty eyes and appliqué smile."[11] King sought guidance in spiritualism, but in reality used the spirits (of his mother, Sir Wilfrid Laurier, and others) as a cheering section for what his razor-sharp, partisan political instincts sensed to be the main chance.

In the seven months after the emergency session that brought Canada into the war in September 1939, King recorded a series of further political triumphs. In October 1939, Premier Maurice Duplessis of Quebec called a provincial election and challenged Canada's commitment to the war. Led by Justice Minister Ernest Lapointe, King's Quebec ministers threw themselves into the campaign. Quebeckers were told that their ministers would have to resign from cabinet if Duplessis was reelected. This in turn might clear the way for conscription. Conversely, the repudiation of Duplessis would strengthen their position in Ottawa and seal the existing bargain of participation without conscription. The Liberals won handsomely, but at the price of reaffirming a difficult promise.

In January 1940, Premier Mitchell Hepburn of Ontario, a Liberal but a King-hater, pushed a resolution through his legislature that criticized the Dominion government for not pursuing the war effort vigorously enough. King seized on this challenge to call a general election for 26 March 1940. The Conservatives campaigned for government above politics and called themselves the National Government Party. This name reminded Quebec of the despised Union government formed in 1917 by Conservatives and conscriptionist English-speaking Liberals after the introduction of compulsory military service. The Conservative approach assured King of another sweep in Quebec, but he also won big elsewhere with the argument that the government that had successfully led Canada into the war should be allowed to get on with the job of winning it.

The Liberals won the biggest majority that any party had obtained to that time in a national election. King had a majority of the seats in seven of the nine provinces and strong representation in New Brunswick and Alberta.[12] Unusually, he also commanded a majority in the country as a whole, even without the big bloc of seats with French-speaking majorities he had won in Quebec. His victory ensured that there would be no repeat in World War II of the khaki election of World War I. King had a freer hand than ever before, but he remained a consensus builder. On Friday, 1 September 1939, Governor General Lord Tweedsmuir had asked his prime minister whether he should wear a uniform or a morning suit to the opening of Parliament should war break out. King advised the morning suit on the grounds that the Canadian people would prefer "the quieter way of proceeding unless the other were absolutely necessary." This oily phrase neatly summarized King's general philosophy of wartime administration. Canada's best war effort would be achieved through compromise rather than confrontation.

King's delicate handling of the conscription issue after the 1940 election is the obvious case in point. With the fall of France in June 1940, he had to acknowledge the need for a stepped-up war effort. His answer was the National Resources Mobilization Act of 21 June 1940, which permitted the conscription of men but only for home service. Henceforth there were two categories of men in the Canadian Armed Forces:

general service volunteers and home service conscripts, who were popularly known as "zombies." When Camillien Houde, the mayor of Montreal, advised noncompliance with the registration that preceded this limited measure of conscription, he was interned.

By the time Japan attacked the United States in December 1941 and the European war became a world war, King was facing mounting pressure for full and unrestricted conscription. In response to this, the government announced in January 1942 that the people would be consulted on the issue in a plebiscite. When the vote was taken on 27 April, however, voters were not asked their opinion on conscription as such, but whether they would release the government from any promises it had made restricting the methods of raising men for military service. An affirmative answer would free the government to act but would not dictate any particular course of action. In this way King outflanked his critics, while leaving himself ample room to manoeuvre once the vote was taken. So clever was his question that all the opposition parties in Parliament advised a "yes" vote, which is what King also wanted. In the view of the Conservatives, the Co-operative Commonwealth Federation (CCF), and Social Credit, there was no need for the government to hold a plebiscite to get on with the job that needed to be done. But if a "yes" vote would finally get King to do his duty, so be it. In the event, large affirmative majorities were recorded in every province except Quebec. There, 71.57 percent of those who voted said "no" to the government. The view of Quebec nationalists, moreover, was that since the promises in question had been made to Quebec, only that province could release the government from them.

All this left King in a quandary. French Canada had given a firm "no," but English Canada had delivered a resounding "yes" and now expected something to be done. King responded by introducing Bill 80 to amend the National Resources Mobilization Act to give the government authority to deploy conscripts without geographical limitation. The fact that the government would have this power, King told his French-Canadian members, would not necessarily mean the power would be used. This would be done only as a last resort. But this time he failed to carry his Quebec caucus with him. Thus, when the vote was taken on second reading (agreement in principle) of Bill 80, a large majority of the French-Canadian members voted against it. Nonetheless, thanks in part to Conservative support, the bill carried 158 to 54. King had prevailed, but at a significant cost to party and national unity. While 1942 was not 1917, it left scars in Quebec just the same.

Recognizing the minority's hurt and anguish, King did not actually order conscripts overseas until November 1944, after the Normandy campaign and the Battle of the Scheldt, when Canadian forces were suffering heavy casualties. In announcing this decision, moreover, he appealed to Quebec for understanding and forbearance: he had held back from using his full powers as long as possible and eventually acted only because there was no other choice.

In June 1941, Charles Ritchie had made this astute observation about the prime minister in his diary: "Much as one would enjoy putting a spoke in the old hypocrite's wheel, the fact remains that there is no one who could take his place with anything like the same chance of keeping the country together. He is easy to rail at but not easy to replace."[13] Something like this latter sentiment probably served King well in Quebec in 1945. In the election of that year his government won a bare majority—125 of 245 seats—but in Quebec the Liberals carried 53 of 65 seats. Quebec had saved King, but was this only because he was the least of the evils? Certainly, the other national parties had competed with one another in pressing conscription on King and thereby put themselves out of contention in that province. In any event, his 1945 win, impressive as it was, must be measured against the return to office in 1944 of the militant autonomist Maurice Duplessis. Quebec may have delivered its true verdict about the events of the war on that occasion. This much at least is certain: another generation of French Canadians—the generation of the future advocate of sovereignty-association, René Lévesque—had been given a practical demonstration of the limits of minority influence within the Canadian federal system. Interestingly, Lévesque himself went overseas as a military war correspondent, but with American rather than Canadian forces.

Long-term consequences were, of course, easily overlooked in the euphoria of 1945. The coming of war in 1939 had quickly pulled Canada out of the lingering effects of the Great Depression and had set the country on the road to unprecedented production and prosperity. Naturally, Canadians looked to Ottawa to lead in mobilizing the resources of the country, and the Dominion government was soon enjoying an authority and prestige it had not known since the war of 1914–18. Canadians were given their first taste of big government in the Great War. In World War II big government came to stay. Technological change had made it possible for Ottawa to take charge as never before, and King and his ministers did not hesitate to do so. The day of indicative planning, survey research, mass personnel counselling, psychological testing, social science ideology, machine-driven administration, atomic development, and much else had arrived. Government had new means and could reach where it had not reached before. In these circumstances Canada came to exhibit many of the characteristics of a centralized state and a command economy.

C.D. Howe, minister of munitions and supply, personified wartime business and production success. He recruited some of the top businessmen in the country to direct the war economy and paid them a dollar a year. Service and heavy but fair taxation were the order of the day. Machines were soon humming as the industrialization of the country proceeded apace. In April 1941, to the great advantage of Canadian business and industry, Ottawa and Washington reached an agreement (the Hyde Park Declaration) whereby goods imported from the United States for incorporation into munitions destined for the United Kingdom could be charged to Britain's Lend-Lease account. Earlier Canada had linked up militarily with the United States through the Ogdensburg Agreement, which provided for the establishment of the Permanent Joint Board on Defence between the two countries. The new arrangements with the United States ensured continued growth and development in Canada, albeit with the consequence of closer ties with the behemoth to the south. By 1942 Canada had advanced to the point where Ottawa could make a billion-dollar gift to the hard-pressed British, for whom the war signified the beginning of a long downward slide in global influence.

As the grip of government tightened, Canadians were subjected to various regulatory regimes: blackouts, censorship, wage and price controls, rationing, and currency restrictions. But these were scarcely comparable to the hardships many Canadians had known in the 1930s. In *A Life in Our Times: Memoir*, John Kenneth Galbraith wrote that "never in the long history of human combat have so many talked so much about sacrifice with so little deprivation as in the United States in World War II."[14] Much the same was true of Canada. The war revived the Canadian economy, ended unemployment, and turned tens of thousands of Canadians into savers through the many victory bond campaigns. Among those who went overseas, the war cost many lives and involved great sacrifice. On the home front, it improved the social order and made it more stable.

In building the regulatory state, the government had a powerful instrument at its command in the War Measures Act of 1914. The Defence of Canada Regulations issued under this act came close to permitting government by fiat. In June 1940, the Communist Party and various Fascist organizations were banned. More controversially, in 1942 thousands of Japanese Canadians were removed from the Pacific coast. Eventually, in one of the most shameful episodes of the 1940s, their property was sold without their consent at fire-sale prices.

Canadians generally got a practical demonstration of how powerful their national government had become when, in March 1942, it introduced an extended plan of National Selective Service. The purpose of this change was to allocate an enlarged labour force to produce with maximum efficiency. Total war, the Canadian people were told by Elliott M. Little, the newly appointed director of National Selective Service, required that "every citizen must subordinate every other interest to the essential job of beating the enemy."[15] In practice, this meant an improved scheme of national registration, bringing many more women into the labour force, reconditioning the physically unfit, and restricting employment in certain jobs and industries. In its full elaboration, the National Selective Service scheme, administered by the Department of Labour, meant regimentation on a scope and scale that Canadian workers had never known before, and have never known since.

The remarkable demand for labour that came with the war also led to other fundamental changes. Women moved into the factories, shipyards, and munitions plants by the tens of thousands, filling spaces left by those men who had joined up and taking new jobs created by wartime expansion. The women workers were mostly single, often from rural Canada, but demand soon led married women into wartime work. As a result, and as an enticement to mothers, large munitions plants set up day-care centres. The country's need for workers was so great that old ideas about a woman's place and a mother's role were set aside, at least temporarily. Moreover, union membership expanded rapidly after 1939, and labour militancy with it. One of the biggest strikes occurred at Kirkland Lake, Ontario, during the winter of 1941–42. In 1943 there were more strikes and lockouts than in any previous year. A major issue in wartime labour unrest was union recognition. On 17 February 1944, the government acted to deal with this disruptive item by issuing Privy Council Order 1003 under the War Measures Act. PC 1003 introduced compulsory collective bargaining over a wide sphere of activities and established the Wartime Labour Relations Board. The new regulations were designed to meet the specific war need but, once established, collective bargaining soon became a permanent feature of the Canadian social landscape. If there were any doubts about this, they were laid to rest by the 99-day strike at the Ford Motor Company in Windsor, Ontario, in 1945. This strike produced a classic Canadian compromise, the Rand formula, named for Justice Ivan Rand, who arbitrated the dispute. Under the Rand formula a worker did not have to join the union as a condition of employment with the company, but everyone had to pay dues to the union because the agreement it negotiated applied to all and everyone benefited from it.

Another significant development for labour came in 1943 when the Canadian Congress of Labour, which had been formed in 1940, endorsed the CCF, Canada's democratic socialist party. The CCF had to battle with Communists as well as free enterprisers, and it enjoyed a surge of support as employment and prosperity expanded. Opinion polls, another new feature of Canadian life, showed this clearly. So, too, did election results. In 1942 Joe Noseworthy, a Newfoundland-born schoolteacher, defeated Arthur Meighen, freshly restored to the leadership of the Conservative Party and the personification of conscription, in a federal byelection in York South, Ontario. The next year, the CCF won 34 seats in the Ontario provincial election to 38 for the Progressive Conservatives, and 15 for Harry Nixon's Liberals, who were swept from power.[16] In 1944 Tommy Douglas led the CCF to power in Saskatchewan. In the 1945 Dominion election, although the CCF did not live up to its earlier polling promise and won only 28 seats (18 of them in Saskatchewan), it stood first among those members of the Armed Forces who voted in the United Kingdom and North-West Europe, and came second to the Liberals in the overall military vote.

Why did the CCF become so popular during the war? Many factors worked to its advantage. The contrast between the dirty thirties and the wartime economic boom was stunning. Government action had revived the economy, just as the CCF had always said it would. War and bureaucracy go hand in hand in the modern world, and planning, which was CCF gospel, was indispensable. So, too, was the idea of the efficacy of collective as opposed to individual effort, another piece of CCF holy writ. "War," George Orwell wrote in his celebrated essay "The Lion and the Unicorn," "is the greatest of all agents of change. It speeds up all processes, wipes out minor distinctions, brings realities to the surface. Above all, war brings it home to the individual that he is *not* altogether an individual."[17] This psychology, which applied in Canada as well as in the United Kingdom, helped clear the way for the CCF message. The party likewise benefited from the fact that in order for the democratic countries to mobilize their full strength, the war had to be fought *for* something as well as *against* somebody. Hitlerism would be destroyed and there would be, as the song said, "love and laughter and peace ever after, tomorrow, when the world is free."[18] Orwell discerned this reality when he wrote in 1940:

> The war and the revolution are inseparable. We cannot establish anything that a western nation would regard as Socialism without defeating Hitler; on the other hand we cannot defeat Hitler while we remain economically and socially in the nineteenth century. The past is fighting the future and we have two years, a year, possibly only a few months, to see to it that the future wins.[19]

The CCF was tailor-made for times like these; it claimed to have a blueprint for the Canadian revolution. Lastly, the party had a compelling cause in advocating the conscription of wealth, as well as of people. There was a bad memory in Canada of profiteering in World War I and, with it, a determination that this must not be allowed to happen again. Money must not be made at the price of blood, and the CCF played the potent appeal of this message for all it was worth.

The Return

THE OTHER PARTIES had cause to sit up and take notice of the advance of the CCF, but King had another good reason for quickening the pace of reform. He had lived through the social and economic upheaval that followed the Great War, and had become leader of the Liberal Party in the year of the Winnipeg General Strike, when the postwar Red Scare was at its height. Nothing like this could be allowed to happen again. In 1940, King was able to secure an amendment to the British North America Act that permitted the introduction of a limited scheme of unemployment insurance. In 1943, the *Report on Social Security for Canada* by McGill University professor Leonard Marsh was published. This document, Canada's equivalent of the famous report of Sir William Beveridge in the United Kingdom, called for the speedy introduction of a variety of welfare-state measures. In January 1944, in the speech from the throne opening a new session of Parliament, the government pronounced that plans for "the establishment of a national minimum of social security and human welfare should be advanced as rapidly as possible."[20] The "national minimum" included "useful employment for all who are willing to work; standards of nutrition and housing adequate to ensure the health of the whole population; and social insurance against privation resulting from unemployment, from accident, from the death of the bread-winner, from ill health and from old age." Later in 1944 the government introduced legislation providing for the payment of "family allowances." Significantly, the family allowance bill passed second reading 139–0, showing how reform had become the order of the day.

Capitalism was modified in Canada during World War II both to fight the war and to prepare for a smooth transition to peacetime conditions. Elaborate plans were made for demobilization and for the shift away from war production, and a comprehensive benefit and reestablishment program was worked out for veterans. Known as the Veterans Charter, this scheme went far beyond what had been done for veterans of World War I.

In September 1944, Walter Woods, deputy minister of the newly created Department of Veterans Affairs, wrote a complaining but revealing note to his minister after hearing on one of the stations of the Canadian Broadcasting Corporation an episode of the Johnson Wax program, an American show hosted by Clifton Fadiman.[21] In Woods' view the program had been "designed to reflect a disgruntled, bellicose attitude on the part of the United States service man." The soldier was characterized as "a ruthless individual" determined "to blast out of society" what he considered "to be his rights." No mention had been made of what his government had done for him. Rather, "the whole trend" had been to emphasize grievance and promote the idea that the soldier had "a chip on his shoulder" that he would do something about when he returned. From Woods' perspective, "this type of broadcast" did "incalculable harm" by implanting "in the minds of serving soldiers" that they were "a terribly wronged group" and that they should take "the law into their own hands." The program was in "bad taste" and "tended to create uneasiness, suspicion and antisocial attitudes." It also belied the fact that Canada had ready "the most comprehensive programme in the world for rehabilitation of her service men," and that they wanted only "a job and security."

Woods' letter reflected a general feeling in Ottawa that, by this time, the government was ready and able to do the big job that would have to be tackled when the victory was won. The plans were ready, the administrative machine was well oiled, and there was every reason to be optimistic and confident. These fine sentiments, it turned out, were not misplaced. The Canadians who went overseas in World War II came back to a better country than the Depression-scarred land of 1939. And the war was followed not by a social and economic *débâcle* but by the baby boom and growing general prosperity.

Canada went to war in 1939 because the United Kingdom went to war. Loyalty was the motivating force. But the Canadians who slogged their way up the Italian Peninsula and landed on the beaches of Normandy and helped to liberate the French and Dutch peoples understood that the war was about much more than connection to a "mother country." It really was about basic human rights and dignity and freedom from tyranny and persecution. Both at home and abroad, Canadians fought the good fight between 1939 and 1945. Their country was a willing and able participant in what has been called the last just war.

Notes

1. Stephen Leacock, "Canada and Monarchy," *Atlantic Monthly* (June 1939), 735.
2. On King's position, see H.B. Neatby, *William Lyon Mackenzie King*, vol. 3, *The Prism of Unity 1932–1939* (Toronto, 1976), chaps. 10, 15, 16.
3. See J.L. Granatstein and J.M. Hitsman, *Broken Promises: A History of Conscription in Canada* (Toronto, 1985), chap. 4.
4. J.L. Granatstein, *The Generals: The Canadian Army's Senior Commanders in the Second World War* (Toronto, 1993), chap. 1.
5. See, on the RCAF, W.A.B. Douglas, *The Creation of a National Air Force*, vol. 2, *The Official History of the Royal Canadian Air Force* (Toronto, 1986); on the RCN, see J.A. Boutilier, ed., *The RCN in Retrospect 1910–1968* (Vancouver, 1982), esp. chap. 5.
6. See Douglas, *Creation*, part II.
7. Marc Milner, *North Atlantic Run: The Royal Canadian Navy and the Battle for the Convoys* (Toronto, 1985).
8. See Brereton Greenhous et al., *The Crucible of War 1939–1945*, vol. 3, *The Official History of the Royal Canadian Air Force* (Toronto, 1994).
9. Daniel Dancocks, *The D-Day Dodgers: The Canadians in Italy, 1943–1945* (Toronto, 1991).
10. C.P. Stacey, *The Victory Campaign: The Operations in North-West Europe 1944–1945*, vol. 3, *Official History of the Canadian Army in the Second World War* (Ottawa, 1960).
11. Charles Ritchie, *The Siren Years: Undiplomatic Diaries 1937–1945* (London, 1974), 187.
12. In New Brunswick the Liberals won 5 of 10 seats. In Alberta, where Social Credit held the majority, the Liberals won 7 of 17 seats.
13. Ritchie, *The Siren Years*, 110–11.
14. John Kenneth Galbraith, *A Life in Our Times: Memoir* (Boston, 1981), 73.
15. Speech by Elliott M. Little, director of National Selective Service, to the convention of the Canadian Daily Newspaper Association, *The Labour Gazette*, April 1942, 10.
16. The Conservatives adopted the party name Progressive Conservative in 1942 when John Bracken replaced Arthur Meighen as party leader.
17. Sonia Orwell and Ian Angus, eds., *The Collected Essays, Journalism and Letters of George Orwell*, vol. 2 (Harmondsworth, 1970), 117.
18. William L. Simon, ed., *Reader's Digest Festival of Popular Songs* (Pleasantville, NY, 1977), 84.
19. Orwell and Angus, eds., *The Collected Essays, Journalism and Letters of George Orwell*, vol. 2, 113.
20. House of Commons, *Debates*, 1944, vol. 1, 4.
21. Department of Veterans Affairs, Veterans Affairs Canada, Charlottetown, Prince Edward Island, file 32-3-3, Woods to Minister, 8 Sept. 1944.

I

Going to War

Prime Minister Mackenzie King faithfully kept a diary for most of his life. Every day he recorded his conversations and meetings, his dreams and fears, and the resulting "record" (as he called it) is one of the great diaries left by a national leader. This excerpt conveys King's ruminations as this most unwarlike of men had to gird his loins to take Canada into war in September 1939.

Mackenzie King's Diary, 1–10 September 1939

Friday, 1 September 1939

I . . . WENT TO SEE THE G.G.[1] . . . I . . . said to him there was one thing that I felt very proud of, which was that . . . I had been able to bring Canada to the aid of Britain as a united country and with a unanimous Cabinet. The Governor said that that was a very great achievement; that I had done many things, but that this would remain as the greatest thus far. . . .

Saturday, 2 September 1939

Left for Kingsmere[2] about 3.30. . . . After dinner, I got J.[3] to walk with me around by the Sanctuary and we sat for a time on the verandah at Moorside.[4] McLeod[5] has had many of the things moved into town, carpets rolled up, etc. One felt the sadness of the empty house, particularly as one thought of the many homes that will become vacant in the event of war. I keep believing in peace as if not to was to lose one's faith and believing that Faith alone could conquer in the end. I felt there was still a slender thread, as if having occupied Danzig, and become possessed of part of Poland, some truce might be called before the time limit given by Britain to Germany would have expired.

I went to bed, however, feeling we were at the most critical moment of all, and that Sunday would disclose whether there would be peace or war. I have mentioned to J. at different times how the actions alike of the German and Italian dictators seem to have been of a character revealing a sort of contempt of Sunday. The real issue:—Christ vs. anti-Christ. . . .

Sunday, 3 September 1939

I awoke this morning between 5 and 6. Looked out and saw mist everywhere, and moonlight shining through it. Felt that, at that time, the fateful decision was being made. I felt it was best to try and get all the rest possible, so did not seek to waken for the broadcast from England.

Awakened, however, at 7. Took the phone in hand at 7.30. Got Turnbull[6] at the office and asked him quietly what word had come in. He told me that Britain was at war; that Chamberlain[7] had spoken to this effect in the House. I told him to arrange to have the Cabinet come together at 10.

I then dressed and had little Pat[8] come for his walk with me to our little trysting place on the moor. As I could just see his little form on the roadway, I whistled as sharply as I could, and out of the mist came a voice "I am here." It was J. who had come over from Shady Hill,[9] as she had promised last night to do, to give me the word which would come over the radio this morning. This was shortly after 8. . . .

I left the Farm[10] for the city about 9.30; reached the office a few minutes before 10. Press men, photographers, and others were waiting at the door, taking pictures of ministers as they were going in. All that aspect of it was abhorrent to me. I went straight to my office, talked with Skelton[11] and Heeney[12] about the most recent despatches, and began the preparation of something to say over the radio. . . . [I]t was arranged to have the broadcast at 5.30, and that Lapointe would read in French what I had said. . . . It was almost a quarter past five when I left L.H.[13] with the text of the speech in my hand. Fortunately I read it over on the way to the Chateau.[14] Just as I was nearing the Chateau entrance I found that page five was missing. . . . To my horror, before the missing page had reached me, Gladstone Murray[15] told me that this was to be the largest broadcast that had ever been made from Canada; that it was a world-wide broad-cast. . . . [T]he statement was my own and not manufactured. It contained my beliefs. I confess I had a real time in my hour of fatigue in so phrasing what I was saying as to avoid giving ground for discussion of the constitutional issue as to whether we were at war because Britain was at war, or because of action on our own part. It gave me an immense satisfaction to be able to say that I had kept Parliament in being that it might decide. . . .

I had a cup of tea at L.H. before motoring out to Kingsmere. . . .

Came up to bed a little before ten. As Roosevelt[16] was broadcasting at ten I sat in my pyjamas and listened to what he had to say. I came away from the radio feeling an almost profound disgust. It was all words, words, words. . . . I was more thankful than ever that my radio address came out before Roosevelt spoke, and that Canada had put herself on record as to where she stood on a purely voluntary basis. I am afraid a very bitter feeling will develop between our country and the States, and Great Britain and the States, as the result of their attitude in this crisis. . . .

To bed at 10.45 p.m. . . .

Thursday, 7 September 1939

Parliament re-assembled today. Throughout the morning I devoted time largely to today's proceedings, to make sure no slip would occur at any stage. I found it pretty difficult to concentrate, but managed to keep fairly calm and to get all my papers in proper order. . . .

When I went into the Commons, I was given a real ovation by the members, practically on all sides. I was really surprised when I got up to speak, to find how calm and collected I was. . . .

Friday, 8 September 1939

There were crowded galleries this afternoon. Every member seems to have been able to get to Ottawa in time. There has been general appreciation of the rapidity with which the Government has moved, and also of the manner in which we have been able to hold to our promise to let Parliament decide. Hamilton[17] and Blanchette,[18] the mover and seconder of the Address,[19] made exceptionally fine speeches. I was delighted with them. Manion[20] spoke also very well and at some length. I kept noting the various points that he brought up. Just a few minutes before I got up to speak, thoughts came to me quickly as to how best to introduce what I had to say. I started in very quietly and, I thought, felicitously. I recognized at once that I was going to be in good form and that strength and power were being given to me. I decided to go right ahead and use Manion's various topics as headings for my own speech; to say what came into my mind at the moment, as I dealt with each one in turn. The result was that I expressed my very soul. Did not keep back any thought or feeling which I had been cherishing in the last few days. . . .

Came back to L.H. about 6.15. Had a bath, and a rest of about an hour and then a little meal. This morning, in weighing, I found I had come down to 170. I had been 178 at Kingsmere. I am sure tonight, after speaking, I must have been below 170.

I got back into the House just at 8 o'clock, and concluded the speech about 9.30. . . . I was greatly pleased to gather from what one or two said that they felt my speech had helped to change votes and to lessen materially the opposition we were likely to meet with from some in our own group. With the exception of about six or seven men from Quebec, everyone seems to be of one mind with respect to Canada's duty at this time. I remained in the House until eleven, listening to Woodsworth[21] and Blackmore.[22] The former, I thought, was far from showing toward myself the appreciation of the words that I had spoken on his behalf. I realize Woodsworth is getting older and is in an extremely difficult position; that he is fighting alone against terrible odds. I shall not be surprised if, before this war is over, his day will have come.[23] . . . Immediately after the House adjourned, I began the revision of the speech. This kept me at the office until 4.30, when I returned to L.H. . . .

When I got back to L.H., little Pat and I had a lovely time. His little head looked up out of the basket, as I came in the room, and later he jumped out and we had biscuits and ovaltine together on the floor. To bed about 5 a.m. . . .

Saturday, 9 September 1939

I . . . went . . . to G.H.[24] H.E.[25] spoke of my speech last night saying he was glad I had spoken out about profiteering and also about giving relatives and friends positions. . . . I . . . said to him that the purpose of my call was to show him the statement I proposed to make on the orders of the day, and to tell him of the procedure the Cabinet felt it would be most advisable to adopt with respect to the proclamation to be issued. I then said we felt that it would be desirable to have the proclamation signed by H.M.[26] with respect to Canada in the same manner and much in the same terms as the proclamation made at Westminster, on Sunday last. H.E. instantly agreed. . . . H.E. . . . said that he was only H.M.'s representative with respect to those matters which the King himself was not in a position to perform. I said to him that it would stimulate I thought the pride of the country in its nationhood. It also would make clear the voluntary nature of the effort we were making. . . . He agreed completely and, in fact, was quite enthusiastic. . . .

On the orders of the day, I read the statement to the House, which I had prepared. It was received with very general applause from our own men, in particular, and some of the Conservatives. . . . I stayed in the House throughout the afternoon, listening first to Coldwell[27] and other speakers, and then enjoying, in particular, Lapointe's[28] speech. It was a very noble utterance throughout, very brave and truly patriotic. When he sat down, I clasped his hand with the warmest friendship and agreement in all he had said. . . .

Learned from our men that a word from me to Maxime Raymond might help to prevent him moving an amendment to the address. I had a talk with him in the lobby. Pointed out that I thought any amendment regarding a referendum at this stage would react against himself very strongly as it would be a ridiculous step to suggest in the existing circumstances. . . . I felt it would help materially the cause not to have any amendment if possible moved from our side of the House. . . .

One of the French members urged me very strongly to not have a vote forced on the division. Cardin[29] had evidently come to the conclusion that we had better find out who our friends were at once. If they did not vote with us, to cast them out. That, while preserving one end, was helping to defeat the same end in another direction. It was making it very difficult for many of the French members who felt that, at the present stage in their constituency, they might be strongly criticized for not having voted with the few who were opposing participation in the war. I seemed to be guided by some power in this matter, and when I went into the lobby and found Cardin talking very strongly to Lacroix,[30] who is a good fellow, but very difficult. I drew him to one side and pointed out how some of the others were feeling. He gave me his views but said he would do as I wished. I told him he knew his own Province better than I; that I would not restrain him if he thought best the course he was proposing. He said he would do as I wished.... As Cardin and I were talking, I noticed the lobby gradually clear though no bells were rung. I hastened into the House, not thinking that the question was being put by the Speaker, but thinking that the members had gone in to listen to some person who might be speaking. . . . I asked Lapointe quietly whether the question had been put, and he said yes, that we were ready for the next stage. . . . I then moved the adjournment of the House.

It was rather significant that neither Manion nor myself were in the House at the moment the division came. . . .

I then advised all the Cabinet to come at once to my room upstairs—401. . . .

When I went in to my office, the members of the Cabinet were seated around the 3 sides. The room seemed rather dark with only the one light in the ceiling above. All seemed to be in a deeply serious mood though quite calm and collected. When Lothrop[31] came over with the order,[32] I read it through and signed it in the presence of all. As I was about to sign, I suddenly lifted my eyes off the paper and was surprised to see my grandfather's bust immediately opposite, looking directly at me—the eyes almost expressing a living light. He was the one person in my thoughts as I affixed my signature to the order-in-council. Later, Coleman[33] came with the Proclamation[34] which required the signature of the Minister of Justice and myself as well as of the G.G. I read the Proclamation over and asked Lapointe to sign. He said to me to sign first which I did, and he then signed. I offered him my seat for him to affix his name. He did so leaning over without taking the seat. I then had Coleman take the document to town to the G.G. at G.H. who awakened from his slumbers to sign both the order-in-council and the Proclamation.

It was about half past twelve, when I said to the Ministers that that was all we should attempt at that meeting. As they went out of the door, practically all turned back and said goodnight. I was rather surprised at this evidence of their thoughts of myself. I was regretting very much throughout the evening that I felt I had not had the rest I needed to be able to deal with these matters in the quick and active fashion in which they should have been dealt with. . . . As I came down from the room, I walked through the Liberal lobby to my smaller office and said to A.H.,[35] who was with me, "How strange life is!" That, as regards my own life there could be no denying a certain destiny—meaning: "Obvious destiny." I remarked on how strange it was that I should have, hanging on my walls at L.H., the proclamation in the name of [the] Queen, putting a bounty on my grandfather's[36] head, in his leadership in a struggle for greater freedom, and that I, this very night had been the one to sign an order in Council as Prime Minister of

Canada, recommending immediately the entry of Canada into the war for the larger freedom of the world. When I came back to L.H. late in the evening, I looked at my mother's picture, and the pictures of other members of the family on the little table in my library. All I could say was—and I could not help saying it—"The names *Mackenzie* and *King* will have an honoured place in the records of our country." That we had played our part. I thought as well of others who had shared the lives of my parents, and their parents before them. The little family circle was all very much in my thoughts. . . .

With the issuance of the Proclamation of the state of war in the name of the King on identical terms with the Proclamation issued on behalf of the U.K. and with all action taken voluntarily on Canada's part, it may now be said that from now on Canada stands as a nation not only among the nations of the British Commonwealth, but as a nation among the nations of the world—a young nation with a bright light in her eyes and the spirit of idealistic youth. A Sir Galahad among other nations. . . .

It was nearly two when I got back to L.H. Roused little Pat out of his slumbers, and we shared a biscuit and some Ovaltine together. I was particularly struck with his having given up his little basket and slept at the side of my bed at night. He was first on the one side and later I found him sleeping on the other. He seems completely conscious of what is going on. When I put him back into his basket last night, I patted his little head for a few minutes, and he went off peacefully and quietly to sleep.

Before going down to my bed-room, I knelt and prayed that I might be able to renounce anything that would stand in the way of a complete surrender of self to God and my country, and that I might be given strength and guidance to carry on. . . .

Sunday, 10 September 1939

It was after two when I got to bed. Very tired. Bed seemed wonderfully comfortable and restful particularly with a warm blanket. The weather has changed. It is much colder today. Apart from that, I have perspired so freely and am so fatigued that I feel the cold more than I should. I would I think have slept comfortably had word come that our communications to Massey[37] and the King had been received.

I had left word for the Code Room to telephone Laurier House, and told the policeman at the House to waken and deliver to me any message that might come during the night. At 20 past 4, I awakened and got up. No message had been received up to that time. I went back to bed and rested. Slept off and on. When I next turned the light on, the clock by my bedside was exactly at 7. I took that exact hour and figure to mean that I was being told that all was all right. The subsequent telegram from Massey showed that H.M.'s permission was being given at 1.08 p.m. at Windsor. There being five hours difference with London, this would mean that Massey was, at that moment, receiving the King's approval. . . .

I breakfasted in the sun-room, enjoying first taste of the Kingsmere honey. . . . After breakfast, I came to the Library and began reading. . . .

'Phoned the office to see if 'phone connection had been established with England; then learned from S.[38] that a message had just that minute come in to the Code Room, which was being deciphered. . . .

"No. 367. Following for Prime Minister begins: Your telegrams 301 and 306 and unnumbered of the 9th of September. Have just returned from Royal Lodge, Windsor, where H.M. the King received me and gave his approval to your submission at 1.08 p.m."

This was exactly at five minutes to eleven. The two hands of the clock were over each other, just as they are, as I am dictating, at about 27 minutes past 5.

I spoke to S. about reserving for Parliament the story of happenings since it adjourned, and give only the bare facts to the Press. We discussed the exact moment at which we should regard a state of war existing, and agree that it should be the moment of the publication of the Proclamation in the Canada Gazette—the time being its receipt at the office of the Secretary of State for External Affairs. . . .

I had just been reading my Bible when this word of the King's approval came. I knelt and prayed for my country and for the cause of freedom, for strength and guidance in these times of need. I confess I have felt in the whole week no particular change of feeling at any moment, save one of immense relief this morning when I knew that the King's approval had come. I kept fearing that the jingo elements in the country would again be finding fault with me for not getting into the war as soon as we could. There will, I fear, be plenty of war before the end comes. S.'s own reaction was the same as mine. He expressed how great the relief was that "at last" all uncertainty had been removed. . . .

At a quarter to two, despatches came from E.A.,[39] at the top of which was the Extra of the Canada Gazette containing the Proclamation. I read it aloud to Handy[40] and said I would frame the copy and place this Proclamation beside the one offering a thousand pounds on my grandfather's head. It is not without significance and I believe without Divine purpose that it carries the name "William Lyon Mackenzie" as well as the name "King."

I was very tired when I went to rest at 2. I soon fell off to sleep and though called at intervals, intending to rest only a short time, found immense relief to my brain in getting a fairly sound sleep up until half past four.

Then had lunch, and later continued dictation of this diary reaching this point at six o'clock.

Dr. S.[41] has just 'phoned about the detention of the German Consuls, Windels and Schafhausen, and their wives. He agrees with me that they are fine people, and that we should deal with them as carefully as we can. He has written a letter informing Windels of the state of war existing, and to advise him to stay in his own house, and has had a Mounted Policeman in plain clothes staying in the house. I agreed that younger men, of military age, should be interned, and we will consider whether it would be better to let Windels and Schafhausen go to the States or intern them as well. I am inclined to think the former policy is best. The British Government seem anxious that we detain them here until the British Consuls get out of Germany. We will settle the matter tomorrow. How excruciatingly cruel a thing war is!

Concluded diary at 7.20 p.m. The little Church bells opposite were playing "Saviour, to Thy dear name we raise, with one accord our evening Hymn of praise." Just as this morning, the first Hymn I heard was "Holy, holy, holy"—mother's favourite Hymn. . . .

Left about 7.30 for Kingsmere. J. and G. joined me at dinner. We had a quiet and pleasant hour or two together, though I felt too tired to do much in the way of conversation. Got to bed about 10.30 p.m.

Notes

1. Governor General (Lord Tweedsmuir).
2. His country estate in the Gatineau Hills.
3. His close friend, Joan Patteson.
4. Summer house on the Kingsmere property.
5. Member of his household staff.
6. Walter J. Turnbull of the Prime Minister's Office.
7. Neville Chamberlain, the British prime minister.
8. His dog.
9. The summer house of Godfroy and Joan Patteson.
10. Kingsmere.
11. Oscar Douglas Skelton, the undersecretary of state for external affairs.
12. Arnold Heeney, King's principal secretary.
13. Laurier House, his Ottawa residence.
14. The Château Laurier hotel.
15. General manager of the Canadian Broadcasting Corporation.
16. Franklin D. Roosevelt, president of the United States.
17. Henry S. Hamilton, the Liberal member of Parliament for Algoma West, ON.
18. Joseph-Adéodat Blanchette, the Liberal member of Parliament for Compton-Frontenac, PQ.
19. The address in reply to the speech from the Throne.
20. Robert Manion, the Conservative leader.
21. James Shaver Woodworth, the leader of the Co-operative Commonwealth Federation (CCF), member of Parliament for Winnipeg North Centre, MB.
22. John H. Blackmore, the Social Credit leader, member of Parliament for Lethbridge, AB.
23. He died on 21 March 1942.
24. Government House.
25. His Excellency (Governor General Lord Tweedsmuir).
26. His Majesty (King George VI).
27. M.J. Coldwell, the CCF member for Rosetown-Biggar, SK.
28. Ernest Lapointe, the minister of justice and member of Parliament for Quebec East, PQ.

29. Pierre-Joseph-Arthur Cardin, the minister of public works and member of Parliament for Richelieu, PQ.
30. Wilfrid Lacroix, Liberal member of Parliament for Quebec-Montmorency, PQ.
31. H.W. Lothrop, assistant clerk of the Privy Council.
32. On 11 September, King described the sequence of events to the House of Commons as follows: "The cabinet met immediately after the adjournment of the house, and a report was made to council recommending that on the advice of the King's Privy Council for Canada a petition should be submitted to His Majesty the King with a view to the authorization by him of the issue of a proclamation forthwith to be published in the *Canada Gazette*. . . . The committee of the privy council concurred in the recommendation and it received the approval of His Excellency the Governor General. The Canadian High Commissioner was immediately instructed by telegram to submit to His Majesty the petition of the King's Privy Council for Canada that His Majesty would approve the issuing of a proclamation in his name embodying the declaration set forth in the order in council. It was added that a formal submission in writing would follow. At 11.15 a.m. on September 10, that is yesterday, the Secretary of State for External Affairs was informed by the high commissioner that His Majesty had given his approval to the submission. A special issue of the *Canada Gazette* was published at 12.40 noon containing the proclamation as duly signed."
33. E.H. Coleman, undersecretary of state.
34. This specified "that a State of War with the German Reich exists and has existed in Our Dominion of Canada as and from the tenth day of September, 1939."
35. Arnold Heeney.
36. William Lyon Mackenzie, one of the leaders of the rebellion of 1837 in Upper Canada.
37. Vincent Massey, Canadian high commissioner to the United Kingdom.
38. O.D. Skelton.
39. Department of External Affairs.
40. J.E. Handy, member of his personal staff.
41. O.D. Skelton.

The public mood in Canada was far from unanimous about the necessity or desirability of going to war again. There were pacifists who considered any war by definition unjust, and the leader of the Co-operative Commonwealth Federation, J.S. Woodsworth, spoke for them. Many French Canadians believed the war to be Britain's, not Canada's, a view expressed by Quebec Liberal Maxime Raymond. But Raymond's was not the only Quebec view, as Justice Minister Ernest Lapointe's emotional speech demonstrated.

Speeches in the House of Commons

J.S. Woodsworth, 8 September 1939

IT IS ONLY A FEW MONTHS since we erected in Ottawa a memorial to the poor fellows who fell in the last war; it is hardly finished before we are into the next war.

After the last war many of us dreamed a great dream of an ordered world, a world to be founded on justice. But unfortunately the covenant of the League of Nations was tied up with the Versailles treaty, which I regard as an absolutely iniquitous treaty. Under that treaty we tried to crush Germany. We imposed indemnities which have been acknowledged by all to be impossible. We took certain portions of territory. Even French black troops were put into the Rhineland—an indignity much resented at the time by the Germans. We took away colonies, sank ships, and all the rest of it. We know that long, sordid story. To no small extent it was this kind of treatment which created Hitler. I am not seeking to vindicate the things that Hitler has done—not at all. He may be a very devil incarnate, and the Prime Minister might have read a great deal more than the extracts he read tonight. But you cannot indict a great nation and a great people such as the German people. The fact is we got rid of the kaiser only to create conditions favourable to the development of a Hitler. Of course Canada had her responsibility. But the great nations did not take the League of Nations very seriously. I sat in as a temporary collaborator during one entire session of the league at Geneva, and I am afraid it was a disillusioning experience, as I found British delegates—and no doubt the same thing took place among the other delegates—acting in the league very much as I have seen members acting in this house. They talked and voted with an eye to British interests and to the elections. Even in Canada we did not take the league very seriously.

Further than that, there was a steady refusal of the nations to go to the help of the countries whose nationality was violated. It is all very well to talk about the sacredness of our treaty obligations. It is all very well to say that Hitler has broken treaties. Well what about France and Great Britain? It is a sad story. Think of Manchuria and Ethiopia and Spain and Czechoslovakia. And now it is Poland. Modern Poland undoubtedly was one of the nations set up as a result of the treaty. We remember also that Danzig formerly belonged to Germany; its population is something like 90 percent German. We know that there is a Corridor there which is undoubtedly very valuable to Poland but which is a bar to communications and the unity of Germany. All this is the result of the Versailles treaty. The free city of Danzig was a legal expedient. Lloyd George and others at the time warned the world that if the Polish Corridor were established in this way and the arrangement made as it has been with respect to Danzig, unquestionably the world was in for trouble in the days to come. I am not sure how far the question could have been settled peaceably; certainly it could not have been so settled at the very last. But efforts should have been made at an earlier stage to do justice. . . .

I would ask, did the last war settle anything? I venture to say that it settled nothing; and the next war into which we are asked to enter, however big and bloody it may be, is not going to settle anything either. That is not the way in which settlements are brought about. While we are urged to fight for freedom and democracy, it should be remembered that war is the very negation of both. The victor may win; but if he does, it is by adopting the self-same tactics which he condemns in his enemy. Canada must accept her share of responsibility for the existing state of affairs. . . .

Why cannot we have the same kind of courage and the same venturesome spirit during peace-time? When the call came for us to come to Ottawa, I was staying at a little summer resort near the international boundary south of Vancouver. Near Blaine there is a peace arch between the two countries. The children gathered their pennies and planted a rose garden, and they held a fine ceremony in which they interchanged national flags and sang songs and that kind of thing; a beautiful incident. Well, that is a part of our unguarded border. Ceremonies of that kind are possible in America because there is an unguarded border. If we had not had the Rush-Bagot treaty a hundred years ago we should have had many incidents of a very different character along the border. I have sometimes thought, if civilization goes down in Europe, as it may go down, that in America there may at least be the seeds left from which we can try to start a new civilization along better lines.

I take my place with the children. I know it seems very foolish, but as I talked the other day with a young woman whose proposed marriage was about to be postponed because her prospective husband might be called to the colours—he was a Canadian-born German and would have to fight his German cousins over there—I thought that for her the possibilities of life were fading away. Again I recall a talk the other day in my own city of Winnipeg to a group of young men who came to see me, some of whom have been unemployed for months past, who were wondering whether they should jump at this opportunity of getting a job. I do not care whether you think me an impossible idealist or a dangerous crank, I am going to take my place beside the children and those young people, because it is only as we adopt new policies that this world will be at all a livable place for our children who follow us. We laud the courage of those who go to the front; yes, I have boys of my own, and I hope they are not cowards, but if any one of those boys, not from cowardice but really through belief, is willing to take his stand on this matter and, if necessary, to face a concentration camp or a firing squad, I shall be more proud of that boy than if he enlisted for the war.

Mr. Tustin [Prince Edward-Lennox]: Shame!

Mr. Woodsworth: The hon. member can say "shame," but that is my belief, and it is the belief of a growing number of Canadians. I said I wanted to state my conviction. Now you can hammer me as much as you like. I must thank the house for the great courtesy shown me. I rejoice that it is possible to say these things in a Canadian parliament under British institutions. It would not be possible in Germany, I recognize that, but it is possible here; and I want to maintain the very essence of our British institutions of real liberty. I believe that the only way to do it is by an appeal to the moral forces which are still resident among our people, and not by another resort to brute force.

Maxime Raymond, 9 September 1939

Before embarking on a war whose consequences will be ruinous, to say the least, we should be entitled to ask ourselves why we should fight, for what purpose and in whose interest. Why would we be fighting? Not to defend Canada's territory. It is neither attacked nor threatened. Not to repel an attack on England, for it is England that has declared war on Germany.

We would be fighting to defend the territory of Poland, because Great Britain, "in order to honour her guarantees and her treaty obligations," decided to declare war upon Germany following the invasion of Poland.

But are we obliged to fight every time that England sees fit to go to war? Assuredly not. We have been told again and again that we are a sovereign nation. Where then is the justification?

We have no commitments with respect to Poland. If England guaranteed the frontiers of that country, including Teschen which was taken by Poland from Czechoslovakia at the time of the dismemberment of that country last October, violating the Munich pact after the manner of Germany—that does not concern us; and I do not see why we should be called upon to pay a debt incurred by England, without our consent, for certain considerations of interest to her. And what a debt! . . .

But, we are told; this is the fight for civilization, for our freedom.

Was it to this end that an alliance was sought with barbaric Russia, where every vestige of freedom has been suppressed?—Ideological wars, as I have amply demonstrated in this house, are a myth. The only wars ever fought are clashes of interests which end in treaties—for instance, the treaty of Versailles—allowing the victors to divide the spoils without giving a thought to the economic, financial, social or political consequences of their action, while the vanquished dream of revenge. Whence the expression: "war is the result of treaties." The war of 1914 is the most striking example of this nature. . . .

We shall hear clever speakers tell us with a voice full of humanitarian quavers that we must fight for democracy, liberty and a Christian social order. Those are words which are but too often misused. A short time ago, England and France endeavoured to conclude a mutual assistance pact with Russia, that antichristian and materialistic state, which is dreaded because of her perfidious doctrines, and is a hot-bed of revolutionary propaganda.

No one can pretend that the Soviets are interested in the welfare of democracy in the world after having destroyed it in their own country. Stalin himself said that outside war could have but one aim: world revolution. Stalin who, two years ago was responsible for the execution or the disappearance of two sovietic marshals and forty generals. And had France and England succeeded, we would have fought with the Russians as allies, under the pretence of defending liberty and democracy. What a spectacle!

A coalition of democratic countries with a view to holding Germany in check is being mooted. An amusing thing to note is that the countries which would form such a coalition: Poland, Rumania, Turkey, and Greece, are anything but democracies.

We are being asked to fight for the defence of liberty, when, in this very Canada of ours, it is being proclaimed in parliament that when England is at war Canada is at war—in other words, we have not even the liberty of living in peace, when no one is doing anything to disturb it. . . .

It is said that we must help the empire because the empire protects us. The empire has not created the oceans which surround our country and protect us against any effective attack. It is not the empire which is responsible for our proximity to the United States. We cannot credit the empire for the declaration made at Lima and Roosevelt's assurances of protection.

When policing the high seas, Britain is protecting herself against famine, she is protecting her own interests. The high seas everywhere provide Britain's means of communication and supply!

When has England taken up arms in our behalf? Never has she done so. Whereas we have twice engaged in war in America against the Americans in the United States, in 1775 and in 1812, to preserve Canadian soil for the British crown, and should the occasion arise we would not now hesitate to fight again to preserve it for Canadians and the King of Canada. We have also fought for Britain in the Boer war. No one will suggest that that war was waged for an ideal. Whatever may be the mistakes made by democracies and the Hitlerian methods which we all deprecate, we must consider our own interests.

What would our participation lead to? Politically, in the first place, it would mean a formal recognition of the formula resorted to by the Prime Minister, with all its consequences, namely "When Britain is at war, Canada is at war."...

A third consequence of our participation would be disunion within the country.

Are we to take such a risk? The Canadians of Quebec are attached to their land; they love it and stand ready to defend it at all times and better than anyone else, but they refuse to sacrifice their life, their property, the future of their children to help some other country to increase or conserve its wealth. They are too enlightened not to know that so-called ideological wars are just a snare. To seek to impose upon them a sacrifice which they are under no obligation to make is simply provocation.

The agreement of 1867 made no provision for defending the countries of Europe, and the Canadians of Quebec do not recognize any other military duty than that of defending their country, which is Canada. Let us not incite them to put an end to that agreement by imposing upon them other obligations than those which derive from it. . . .

Ernest Lapointe, 9 September 1939

I HATE WAR WITH ALL MY HEART and conscience, but devotion to peace does not mean ignorance or blindness. The Prime Minister (Mr. Mackenzie King) hates war and has devoted much of his time and energy to promoting the instruments of peace. Indeed, until the very last moment, when clouds hung heavily over the world, he was sending messages beseeching the dictators and the president of Poland to try to find means of avoiding this tremendous catastrophe. England has worked for peace. I know it; I have attended many of the conferences since the end of the great war, both in Geneva and in London. It is a base calumny to say that England is responsible for anything that has led to the present conflict. France has worked continuously for peace, and it is a slander to say that France is responsible in any way for the conflict. These nations have gone so far in their efforts to preserve peace that they have been the subject of strong and bitter criticism on the part of many people in their respective countries because of what was called, with derision, the "appeasement" policy. . . .

I gave last session, and I will not repeat them today, some of the reasons why it is impossible, practically, for Canada to be neutral in a big war in which England is engaged. We have a common national status; a British subject in Canada is a British subject in London or anywhere in the commonwealth, and a British subject in England is a British subject in Canada. We are using the diplomatic and consular functions of Great Britain throughout the world. Some of the most important sections of our criminal code are predicated on the absence of neutrality in the relations between Canada and Great Britain. The Foreign Enlistment Act, which we enacted only a year or so ago, indicates that Canada cannot be neutral, at least without repealing that legislation. I wish those who express great sentiments and views would answer me once on these matters; I should like it. Our shipping legislation is predicated on our alliance with Great Britain and our relations with her. If we had neutrality all Canadian ports would be closed to all armed vessels of Britain, and in time of war merchant ships have to arm themselves in order to travel over the ocean. As I said last year, the citizens of my city of Quebec would have to prevent the *Empress of Britain* from coming to Quebec harbour during a war, because she would have guns to protect her when travelling on the ocean. We would have to prevent enlistment on Canadian soil for the army or navy of Britain. Still some of the agitators who spoke at meetings last week said: "Let Britain come and enlist people; we have no objection; they will go and be paid by England." But this could not be done. If they do not know it, will they please learn it from me today? We would have to protect our neutrality against British vessels; Canadians would have to fight British vessels, if they wanted to be neutral during a war. We would have to intern British sailors who came to take refuge in any of Canada's ports. Does any hon. member believe that Canadians would permit British sailors to be interned anywhere in this country?

We have contracts and agreements with Britain for the use of the dry docks at Halifax and Esquimalt; we are bound by contracts. That is not neutrality. Of course we could change that; we could cancel and break all those contracts and engagements, but does my hon. friend think that the majority of Canadians would stand for it at this time?

I have given the definition of neutrality, the recognized definition, which is that of Oppenheim, the authority on international law:

> Neutrality may be defined as the attitude of impartiality adopted by a third state towards belligerents and recognized by belligerents, such attitude creating rights and duties between the impartial state and the belligerents.

Could such an attitude of impartiality be possible in Canada during a war, having regard to the present international situation? Could Canadians in one section of the country compel other Canadians in other sections to remain neutral and to enforce such neutrality even against their own king, if that should be necessary? . . .

I will go further; neutrality on the part of Canada at this time could not be other than a move favourable to the enemies of England and France. With the possible exception of the Soviet Union we have perhaps the greatest store and widest range of raw materials necessary for the carrying on of a war. This war, more particularly in its initial stages, will be largely in the air. Planes will do their utmost to destroy the industries and aviation centres of the enemy. Industry may become so crippled in the countries at war that replacements will become slow and difficult; and do not forget that Russia seems disposed to place her resources at the disposal of Germany. Britain and France will need our resources as a matter of life or death; and, sir, any such so-called favourable neutrality would be directly to the disadvantage of Britain and France. I say to every member of this house and to every citizen of Canada that by doing nothing, by being neutral, we actually would be taking the side of Adolf Hitler. . . . The whole province of Quebec—and I speak with all the responsibility and all the solemnity I can give to my words—will never agree to accept compulsory service or conscription outside Canada. I will go farther than that: When I say the whole province of Quebec I mean that I personally agree with them. I am authorized by my colleagues in the cabinet from the province of Quebec—the veteran leader of the senate, my good friend and colleague, the Minister of Public Works (Mr. Cardin), my friend and fellow townsman and colleague, the Minister of Pensions and National Health (Mr. Power)—to say that we will never agree to conscription and will never be members or supporters of a government that will try to enforce it. Is that clear enough?

I ask you, Mr. Speaker, is it not worth while to the Canadian nation, when the nation is at war, to preserve unity on the side on which Canada will be—this unity which is represented by the province of Quebec in the government—behind the measures being taken to help our mother country and France?

May I add that if my hon. friends and myself from Quebec were forced to leave the government I question whether anyone would be able to take our place. If my hon. friends in the far corner of the house opposite: if the Ottawa *Citizen*, which just now is waging a campaign for conscription, think they are serving Canada by splitting it at the very outset of the war, then I say they are gravely and seriously wrong.

Provided these points are understood, we are willing to offer our services without limitation and to devote our best efforts for the success of the cause we all have at heart. And those in Quebec who say that we will have conscription, in spite of what some of us are saying, are doing the work of disunity, the work of the foe, the work of the enemy. They weaken by their conduct and their words the authority of those who represent them in the government. So far as the insults and abuses of agitators are concerned—I disdain them! They will not deter me from the path of duty, as God gives me light to see it. I will protect them against themselves. I believe the majority in my province trust me; I have never deceived them, and I will not deceive them now. I have been told that my present stand means my political death. Well, at least it would not be a dishonourable end, and I am ready to make sacrifices for the sake of being right. But let me assure you, Mr. Speaker, that if only I can keep my physical strength, fall I shall not; and my friends shall not fall, either. . . .

I desire to conclude my remarks by referring to what was said by our gracious queen at Halifax when she was leaving Canada to return to the homeland. Her words in French went to the heart of every man, woman and child in my province. She said, "Que Dieu bénisse le Canada." God bless Canada. Yes, God bless Canada. God save Canada. God save Canada's honour, Canada's soul, Canada's dignity, Canada's conscience.

God give Canadians the light which will indicate to them where their duty lies in this hour of trial so that our children and our children's children may inherit a land where freedom and peace shall prevail, where our social, political and religious institutions may be secure and from which the tyrannical doctrines of nazism and communism are forever banished. Yes, God bless Canada. God bless our queen. God bless our king.

What of the militiaman, the Saturday-night soldier who, faced with war, had to decide if he would leave his family to go off to fight? Howard Graham was a small-town lawyer who had had his fill of fighting in Flanders, but in the interwar years he served in the local regiment and, as he recounted, went to training courses and, inevitably, to war. Graham did well in action in Sicily, and after the war became Chief of the General Staff.

Citizen and Soldier

Howard Graham

NEAR THE END of that beautiful August day, as I was clearing my desk to go to the cottage with the feeling that a difficult task had been accomplished, the phone rang. My secretary said, "Colonel Young is on the line."

I picked up the receiver and said, "Hello, Sherman, what's new?"

His reply was short and shattering. "We are mobilized as of one minute past midnight tonight. Get into your uniform."

Colonel Young's telephone call took me by surprise. My involvement with the Militia went back to World War I. Early in 1923, as I was leaving the Hotel Gilbert in Trenton after a Rotary luncheon with Arthur Baywater, a fellow Rotarian, he said: "Howard, why don't you come into the new regiment that I am just getting organized? I would be glad to have you and there would be no problem in getting you a commission."

"That sounds interesting, Arthur," I replied. "I'll think it over and give you a call."

A.E. Baywater was a veteran of World War I and had been severely wounded. After the war the Non-Permanent Active Militia, as it was called, was reorganized. Before the war almost every county in Ontario had a County Regiment. The number of regiments was in 1920 reduced by a program of disbanding or amalgamating units. So it was that the 16th Prince Edward (County) Regiment and the 49th Hastings Rifles were amalgamated to form the Hastings and Prince Edward Regiment, and Major Baywater, as he then was, was promoted to the rank of lieutenant-colonel to command the new unit.

It did not take me long to think it over. If I was going to be a "joiner," why not join the local regiment and be, for the first time, a commissioned officer and get to know and be associated with others of my own vintage from all sections of the two counties? So I called the Colonel, told him of my decision, and on 13 May 1923, was gazetted a provisional lieutenant on the strength of the Hastings and Prince Edward Regiment. In August of the following year, in Picton, I took a short course of instruction and became a full lieutenant. Five years later, after attending a camp school of instruction at Barriefield near Kingston, I passed the required examination and became a captain in January 1930.

In order to qualify as a "field officer," i.e., a major and above, it was necessary in those days to pass a Militia Staff Course. Thus I attended a course of evening lectures throughout the winter of 1931–32 given by a permanent force officer who came from Kingston to Belleville one night each week. By 1931, the road from Trenton to Belleville was paved and kept reasonably clear of snow, so that each Thursday, after an early evening meal, I drove along the twelve miles to the Belleville Armoury to join some twenty or thirty Militia officers from my own and other regiments and heard lectures on such military subjects as organization, administration, military law, tactics, map reading, and training. After a day's work at the office or in court, it was something of an ordeal. On some winter nights, when it was snowing and blowing and drifting, it was a most tiresome journey to Belleville and home again near midnight. However, I persisted, and in early spring spent two days in Kingston writing examinations on what was termed the theoretical part of the staff course. These tests were not difficult and I had no trouble passing.

The next stage of the staff course, called the practical phase, involved attending a two-week course at Petawawa Camp during the following summer. Since I was travelling in Europe in 1932, I deferred taking the practical phase until 1933. Then I attended and, as my certificate states, "having passed the required tests, is qualified for appointment to the staff of the NPAM of Canada in all grades up to and including Brigade Major." Hence, on 23 August 1934, I was gazetted major after ten years Militia service and after passing the Militia Staff Course.

I learned a little lesson at Petawawa from Major Bradbrooke. One of the tests on the practical side of the staff course was to prepare a plan to carry out successfully a military operation based on certain facts given to us by our instructor. For example, it might be for a withdrawal of a brigade while in contact with the enemy, or it might be to prepare orders for an attack over certain terrain against an enemy position. In this instance, we were a syndicate, a group of eight officers, and I was the syndicate leader. The problem was to prepare an operation order for a battalion attack on enemy positions. We gave the problem much thought, and I wrote the order in great detail with their help. In due course we presented it to "Brad." He read it over carefully, thought for a few moments, and then gave one of the best critiques I had ever heard. "Um," he said. "Very good gentlemen, it might work. But, you know, it reminds me of a whisky and soda with a hell of a lot of soda and very little whisky!" And I must confess he was quite right. He taught me that in preparing and giving orders, it was quite unnecessary to embellish them with flowery phrases. There should be no unnecessary verbiage to clutter up the essence of the subject. In later years I heard the story that General George Marshall, when he was American Chief of Staff, would return to a subordinate officer any appreciation or opinion on a particular subject or situation if it covered more than one foolscap sheet.

Before I received the certificate referred to above, I had to pass a test on equitation, or horsemanship. As a boy I had ridden any number of horses at the walk, trot, gallop, and even jumped low fences, but always bare-backed. Now, with two fellow officers, I had to go to Kingston, where the Military Riding School was located, and do a few turns aboard a horse with saddle. Very slippery it was! The examining officer was Captain (later Major-General) Churchill Mann, an expert in riding who was for several years a member of Canada's international jumping team. "Church" had us go through the various gaits with and without stirrups, but put us over no jumps, thank goodness! At the finish he said, "Well done, gentlemen. I am glad to say all of you have passed and shortly you will receive a certificate saying you are proficient in equitation. But one word of advice, never show it to a horse!" Such was the state of Canadian Militia thinking as late as 1933. Instead of riding horses, we should have been taking tests in driving and servicing motor vehicles. . . .

In 1935, the Department of Defence had instituted an Advanced Militia Staff Course for a limited number of Militia officers, a dozen or so for all of Canada. This course was intended to equip those who passed it for senior staff or command positions in the event of war, just as the Militia Staff Course qualified graduates for appointments only up to brigade major. In the fall of 1936, a second advanced course was authorized and units of the Militia were invited to submit names of proposed candidates. My regimental commander urged me to allow my name to be submitted. He argued that it would be advantageous not only to me personally but also to my regiment. It was a distinction to have one's name on the Militia List of Officers followed by the letters m.s.c. to indicate a pass in the ordinary staff course. But it was of much greater importance to have the MSC in capital letters to show a pass in the advanced course.

I was loath to spend more time than I was already on military affairs, as it was at the expense of my profession, my livelihood. But I finally agreed to have him submit my name. I was accepted, and during the winter of 1936–37 I would receive every two or three weeks a large bundle of magazines and papers that were to be perused. On the basis of information contained therein, candidates were to submit articles in which they would comment, agree, or disagree with what we had read. The material to be read covered international political situations, natural resources of various countries, forms of governments, and, of course, the organization and command of large military formations. I did the reading in the evening and found it all very interesting. I sent in my articles as prescribed to the director of the course, Colonel Ken Stuart, who was later to become Chief of the General Staff.

Being a lawyer with some experience in clear expression of arguments, and in putting them on paper, I rather enjoyed reading and certainly learned a great deal about international affairs. I did not mind disagreeing with some of the views expressed in the material that came to me. For example, I recall learning about a Canadian proposal to recruit, arm, train, and equip a number of divisions and put them in the field as had been done in World War I. My response to this was that from my impression of the public's attitude toward defence, such a program would not be feasible unless conscription was introduced as soon as war was declared, unless industry was mobilized at the same time, and unless money was made available to equip and train the Militia with the modern weapons, equipment, and vehicles that would be required in mobile warfare as opposed to the fixed lines of trench warfare we had seen in World War I. In 1936–37 we had a permanent, full-time army of only some 4000 to 4500, all ranks.

The outcome of the winter correspondence course was that twelve officers from across Canada were chosen to take the practical portion of the Advanced Staff Course to be held at Royal Military College in Kingston in the summer of 1937. I was one of the chosen few who came from across Canada. Of the twelve candidates, five were lawyers, and of these one from Halifax was a Rhodes Scholar and another became a Justice of the Supreme Court of Alberta. The course lasted a month. There was a directing staff of three officers. One, Colonel Stuart, became Chief of the General Staff; another, Major Burness, was lost at sea in 1940 when the SS *Nerissa* was sunk by U-boats; and the third, an English officer, Colonel Bucknall, then in Canada on exchange, became a British Corps Commander under Montgomery in World War II. I mention these names to indicate that I was in good company. We had first-class instruction and, as a result, much stimulative discussion.

So much about the courses of instruction in qualifying for senior army rank. But what of my regiment during the years from 1922 to 1939 and my part in its development? Colonel Baywater got us off to a good start by recruiting a full slate of officers from all parts of the counties of Hastings and Prince Edward. Some were farmers, some were young businessmen, and others came from the professions. Almost without exception in the early 1920s, all officers had served in France in the 1914–18 conflict. As the years passed, many of these men became too old for service and were replaced by younger men, but still, when mobilization came on 1 September 1939, the commanding officer and three or four others, including myself, were "veterans." Money was scarce and, as is always the case, as the period of peace after 1918 grew longer, the populace became less interested in matters military. Governments, yielding to the feelings of the voters and being exceedingly short of funds during the Depression years, cut the defence budget to the bone. Summer camps for the Militia at Barriefield and other central areas across Canada, where units from the various military districts had assembled for combined training, were discontinued for several years. Each unit, working on a very restricted budget, had to arrange for local camps. For example, one year the Hastings and Prince Edward Regiment had a camp on the fairground at Picton, in Prince Edward County, and another year at Madoc, in Hastings County, and others in Trenton and Cobourg. These were the only times that the members of a rural Militia unit like ours saw their fellows. In those days the officers brought their own uniforms and turned their pay over to the regimental fund. I can never recall drawing a cent of pay for time spent in regimental training.

We tried to keep the unit active and before the public in many ways. For example, in the 1930s we had several officers who were past masters of their respective lodges through the regimental area. When one of our officers was due for installation as master of his Masonic lodge, he and those of us who were past masters dressed in mess kit and we conducted the installation ceremony. On another occasion, an officer and his wife were having a baby christened in the Anglican church at Picton. We dressed in blue uniforms, complete with swords (all of which we bought out of our pockets), and, accompanied by our wives, attended the ceremony and afterward had a grand tea party in the Picton Armoury. I mention these affairs as examples to show how this regiment, and I am sure many others across Canada, kept the spirit and morale high in those difficult years, so that when the time came (as many of us were sure it would), this regiment would be able to take its appointed place in the mobilization plans. In a goodly number of years, the Hasty P's, as they came to be known, won the Infantry Association Cup for general efficiency in our Militia district.

What part did I play in this program? After qualifying as a lieutenant, I was posted to "A" Company of the regiment, centred in Trenton. Within two or three years, because of retirement or removal from the area of officers senior to me, I found myself commanding the company and continued to do so as I progressed in rank and qualifications. It was not until the late 1930s that I left "A" Company to become senior major and second in command of the regiment. I do not want to give the impression that commanding a company was a very onerous task. The company at any one time would not exceed a strength of forty. Trenton had no armoury, as such, but the Department of Defence leased a large barn, or shed, which had been used as a factory. Iron baffles were installed in one end, so that during the winter we could do "miniature rifle practice" using .22 ammunition fired from rifles that had been fitted with barrels with a .22 bore in place of the regular .303 bore. One corner of the shed was partitioned off as an office and a store room for uniforms and weapons. The bolts for rifles I kept in my office safe. I usually supplied the kindling wood for the stove, which burned soft coal, and often on a cold winter night in those distressing days of the

Depression, Jean would make a basket of sandwiches, and with these and a handful of tea leaves we helped to keep up the morale. In the summer I might take as many as thirty-five men to camp, and since many had only well-worn canvas sneakers, I arranged with a local shoe merchant to provide a pair of shoes where needed on the receipt of a chit from me, on credit until after the camp and the men had received their pay. In many cases, of course, I ended up paying for the boots, but they cost only $1.50 or $2 a pair. These economies were observed at the time when Agnes MacPhail, a socialist member of Parliament, rose each year and vehemently and, I suppose, conscientiously argued that the Defence budget be one dollar per annum.

In the summer of 1938, the practical portion of the Militia Staff Course was held in Port Hope, where the facilities of Trinity College School were used to house and feed the candidates. For some reason, the regular force lacked sufficient instructors for the large number of Militia officers in attendance and asked a few of us who had taken the Advanced Staff Course to act as instructors. I was one of these, and through acting as an instructor I benefited greatly from the discussions with such excellent permanent force officers as Colonel Tommy Burns, later lieutenant-general in command of the United Nations forces in Egypt. . . .

It is difficult to find words to express my feelings after I replaced the phone receiver that Friday afternoon of 31 August 1939. Colonel Young informed me that the regiment was being mobilized. When I had enlisted in 1916, it was with excitement and enthusiasm; the sense of adventure was in the air. I was leaving my family, but they were not dependent on me. I had no business to abandon. I was young and the future was mine. There were new countries to see, new friends to be made. Now, twenty-three years later, I was in my forty-second year and all was different. I hated the very thought of leaving my wife and son of six years and the home we had made and enjoyed together. Leaving a legal practice I had worked hard to develop and facing the thought of a substantial financial loss and going abroad now held no attraction for me.

What a fool I had been to spend time and money these past seventeen years on military affairs! Yet, I thought, I must be honest. I was only one of hundreds of Militia officers with families across Canada who would be feeling the same unhappy situation. We were not under any legal obligation to serve outside Canada until we signed an undertaking to do so. But to refuse to do that would have been in my opinion morally wrong and disloyal to the regiment and to the establishment that had trained me to carry out the duties I would now be required to perform. About these matters Jean agreed with me, though with sadness and reluctance. And so it was that I signed up for overseas service. Allan McNab and Isabel Hinds carried on the law practice. I went to war.

Busy days followed. Recruits appeared at first in great numbers. We had only World War I uniforms, old Ross rifles with bayonets, and no other weapons. Indeed, it was weeks and even months before all recruits could be properly outfitted from head to toe. And, sad to say, it was soon evident that my contention, written in the papers I had submitted on the Advanced Staff Course, was correct. The attitude of the people of Canada was such that a large army of four or five divisions in the field could not survive unless conscription was introduced at the very onset of hostilities. There was little of the enthusiasm for "the cause" in 1939 that there had been in 1914. No parson was dismissing his congregation after only a few chosen words so that they might attend a recruiting meeting in a local opera house. The result of this lukewarm or even antagonistic approach to supporting any war effort was quickly felt in our regimental area. The first spate of volunteers soon dried up, and we were hard put to reach our established strength of almost one thousand. However, by means of advertising and holding meetings in neighbouring counties, we did by near the end of October attain our objective and the whole regiment for the first time was assembled in Picton. Here the troops were accommodated in the basement of the armoury and in an old canning factory made habitable by installing makeshift heating, washing, and latrine facilities. The next six weeks were spent in "basic" military training at the nearby Picton Fairground and in route marches and other exercises to toughen up the troops.

We were frequently visited by officers from District Headquarters in Kingston, and I must acknowledge that they were most helpful in advising on training programs and in getting supplies and equipment to meet our needs. One day in late November, we received word that Major-General McNaughton, the General Officer Commanding the 1st Canadian Division, would arrive from Ottawa at Picton Fairground at 1400 hours to meet and inspect the regiment. On the appointed day, which was bitterly cold but sunny, we were duly mustered, more than nine hundred strong, and made a brave showing at about 1330 hours. We must not be late to greet the General! 1400 hours arrived but no General. The troops were getting very cold in a bitter wind, so the commanding officer had them march around for a few minutes and then form up again, expecting the General at any minute. This sort of activity went on all afternoon—march around, form up, march around, form up. At last, at 1600 hours, the General arrived. The compliments were paid, the inspection completed just before dark. It was a day long to be remembered by the troops, and the General was terribly embarrassed. What had happened? His staff officer was new to the job, and when he was told by the General to arrange for his visit for 4:00 p.m., he had mistranslated it to be 1400 hours and had so advised us, instead of converting it to 1600 hours!

Predictably, Quebec's mood was different from that of the rest of Canada. The memories of conscription from 1917 remained strong, and there was no love for Britain or France. What, then, could drive men to enlist? Gabrielle Roy, the distinguished Franco-Manitoban novelist who lived in Montreal after 1939, offered her interpretation in a famous passage from her best-known novel, *The Tin Flute*.

A New Life Was Beginning for Them All

Gabrielle Roy

KHAKI-CLAD FIGURES were rolling toward the Bonaventure Station in waves, carrying with them the bright colors of women's dresses, the sound of laughter and singing, of sobbing and sighing, the strong smell of rum, all the hubbub of an excited crowd.

Arriving early, Emmanuel and Florentine had found seats in the waiting-room. They sat talking, their hands clasped over the duffle bag that lay across their knees. Sentences were begun and never finished, last-minute instructions were exchanged between them, but their words were drowned in the tread of heavy boots and their private grief merged in the thousands of sighs that floated up to the vaulted ceiling.

Emmanuel stared with astonishment as his regiment appeared. Almost every face was lit up with joy. One of his comrades staggered in, held upright by two other soldiers who were laughing uproariously. Behind them came another, shouting drunkenly: "We're going to see the world! We're going to see the world!" Everyone was pretending to be hilarious, but the merriment had unhealthy overtones. Emmanuel turned his eyes away and embraced Florentine.

He had expected that it would be easier to leave her once they were married, that this bid for future happiness would bring him more confidence. But he realized now that happiness weakens a man's will. In this short interval certain ties had been forged, certain habits had been formed, not to be broken without a wrench. He saw Florentine trying on the dresses and hats he had bought for her twenty times a day; or else always impatient to go out and parade through the streets, stopping at every shop-window!

At times so full of coquetry, and at times so sad and bitter! And then there were rare moments of tenderness when she would take his hand and say: "Oh dear, I'll be so lonely and bored when you're gone!" The days had slipped by like minutes, like a dream, like a flash of lightning, he thought. Men who go away to war ought not to form attachments.

The crowd was singing and laughing all around them. Why were they singing? Why were they laughing? What was so joyous about their departure?

They rose in silence. Florentine helped him lift his duffle bag to his shoulder, then they walked out toward the train platform, their arms around each other's waists, like a hundred other couples. As the milling crowd threatened to tear them apart, they clasped each other more closely.

At the main gate giving on the tracks they spied a large group of people from Saint-Henri. Emmanuel and Florentine went over to join them.

Sam Latour was there, shaking hands all around, with a paternal and comical air. His placid ruddy face, with its broad smile, was completely out of harmony with the flood of invective that poured from his mouth: "That dog Hitler!" he was saying. "One of you be sure to bring me back three hairs from his mustache. Or I'll tell you what I'd like even better. Bring me the whole damn thatch and I'll make a little scrubbing brush of it."

But stronger and more persuasive than all the others, rose the voice of Azarius Lacasse. As brassy as a sergeant, he went among the soldiers and harangued them. "Tell them to hold fast in France till we get there." He pulled out a newspaper and opened it wide, to show the headline: *The Allies Fall Back on Dunkirk.* Azarius smashed his fist into the sheet.

"Tell them not to give up till we come!" he cried. "That's all I ask! Tell them the Canadians are coming! And maybe the Americans too before long." He caught sight of a boy in uniform, a little fellow who seemed quite bewildered, and tapped him on the shoulder: "You there," he said, "you're good for thirty Germans, aren't you?" Then he added, laughing: "But don't kill them all, leave a couple for me. Don't end the war too fast!"

Behind him shone the face of Pitou. And behind Pitou there were other faces with the same look of exaltation. Emmanuel felt as if he were dreaming. Were these the unemployed of yesterday? Were these the fellows he had known when they were forlorn and browbeaten, down in the mouth? Could that be Pitou, the musician, who had beguiled his years of idleness with songs from his guitar?

His eyes returned to Azarius, and he was even more troubled. Was this the man he had seen so crushed, only a week ago? Was this Rose-Anna's husband?

Azarius seemed no older than Emmanuel today. Strength seemed to flow from him in an irresistible stream. His desire for action, so long repressed, had found an outlet at last. He felt himself a man again.

And so the men of Saint-Henri had found their salvation!

Salvation through war!

Emmanuel looked at Florentine questioningly. There was a hollow feeling in his chest at first, and then he felt a storm seething within him. He was torn and shaken with uncertainty. The torments he had suffered that night alone on the mountain seized him again. The problem had changed from "Why am I going to war?" to "Why are we all going to war? We're going together . . . we ought to be going for the same reason."

It was not enough for him to know his own personal reasons; he also must know the fundamental truth that was guiding them all, the prime impulse that had urged on the soldiers in the last world war too. Without some such guiding light their departure made no sense, it was only a monstrous repetition of the same mistake.

He leaned toward Florentine and put the question to her.

"Why do you suppose we are going off to war, your father, your brother and I?" he asked.

She looked at him in surprise.

"You mean why did you enlist?"

"Yes."

"Well, I can see only one reason," she said soberly. "It's because there's something in it for all of you in the army."

He studied her for a long time. Yes, he should have thought of that sooner. She was much closer to the people than he; she knew them better. Her answers were the right ones. He looked around at the crowd. And he seemed to hear the same answer that Florentine had just given him on thousands of lips. Behind the crowd's deep breath of liberation he thought he could hear the sound of money clinking.

They, too, he mused. They too have been bought, as much as anybody, more than anybody!

And it seemed to him that with his own eyes he was witnessing the final bankruptcy of humanity. Wealth had spoken the truth on the mountain.

But after a moment he took himself to task. He went on to think: But no, that's not the whole truth. Those who fight profit least from the war. There are ever so many Léon Boisverts and Jean Lévesques who will rise in the world and perhaps make a fortune, thanks to the war, without taking any risks.

But then why were armies on the march? There must be some underlying truth that few were able to grasp, even those who had fought in the last war. Perhaps under a thick layer of human ignorance there was some obscure purpose that man could not express in words.

Suddenly Emmanuel heard rising above the uproar a metallic, arrogant voice in English:

"We'll fight to the last man for the British Empire!"

The Empire! thought Emmanuel. Are we fighting to hold on to territory? To keep the world's wealth for ourselves and bar the others out?

Now a whole group was singing: "There'll always be an England."

Yes, but how about me and Pitou and Azarius? wondered Emmanuel. Are we to fight for Merry England and the Empire? At this moment soldiers in other lands are singing their national anthem with the same enthusiasm. They're singing everywhere, in Germany, in Italy, in France. We French-Canadians ought to be singing "O Canada!" I suppose. No, no, he said to himself sternly, I refuse to be limited by a narrow patriotism. . . But am I the only one?

He tried to squirm away from the only explanation that was left. And yet it took a firm hold on his mind: none of them were going off to war for the same purpose. Some were going to the ends of the earth to preserve their empire. Others were going to the ends of the earth to shoot off a gun and receive a bullet, and that was all they knew. There were still others who were going away to earn bread for their families. But what would they find at the ends of the earth, aside from death, that could enlighten men on their common destiny?

At this point the gates opened wide and the crowd spilled over on the platform. All the rest was a nightmare to Emmanuel. He kissed his mother, his sister and his father. Then he embraced Florentine. In their brief life together he had discovered that she was vain, nervous, and sometimes irritable. He knew now that she was frivolous and weak, but he only loved her the more for it. He loved her like a child who needs protection.

As he put his arms around her he saw the tears streaming down her face. In the course of the last few days he had been mystified by her changing moods. Her coldness had often repelled him; her sudden outbursts of tenderness and her moments of reticence had perplexed him. Her tears now troubled him.

She stood there weeping on his shoulder. He could not know that she was crying with relief. But underneath her vanity there was also a vague feeling of sorrow. She was extremely impressionable. The whole scene of leave-taking, the tears and hand-waving, affected her superficial nature even more than the drama they symbolized. But Emmanuel, believing that at last she was deeply moved, almost broke down when he saw her tears.

He leaped on the moving train. For a moment he hung there on the step, clutching the hand-bar, his head bent forward in a pose that made him look as if he were faring forth on some heroic expedition. But still his internal torment, his burning question found no answer. He was leaving and still he knew not why.

And then, suddenly, the answer came to him in a flash . . . It came to him unexpectedly, not from Florentine, who stood there waving her hand, not from his mother, hardly visible now in the crowd, not from Azarius, who was swinging along beside the train. It came to him, like a miracle, from a stranger.

She was a tiny, shrunken, fragile old woman with a look of gentle resignation on her face, alone among strangers.

For one moment their glances crossed. And at that moment Emmanuel understood. The humble little woman was moving her lips as if to give him one last message. The words did not reach Emmanuel, but he could see by the movement of her lips that she was saying something that only he understood: "This will end. One day it will end. One day it will all come to an end."

And Emmanuel saw the light. This was the hope, so ill understood by most men, that was uplifting mankind once again: to do away with war.

Florentine was only a bright spot now. He saw her take out her powder puff and remove the traces of tears from her cheeks. Closing his eyes, he clung to the image of Florentine powdering her face as if he were already far, far away. Then he searched the crowd again for her thin little face, her burning eyes. But even before the train disappeared, she had turned her back and moved away.

She felt tired and nervous. Without waiting for her father she pushed her way through the crowd, and walked quickly to the station entrance.

The heat and the excitement had disturbed her, but she felt sad and oppressed too. It was not that Emmanuel's departure caused her any great pain, but she had a vague sense of loss, the extent of which she was only beginning to judge.

When she reached the lobby she stopped a moment to regain control of herself. What was troubling her? She had taken Emmanuel's sweetness and kindness for granted. These qualities had not surprised her. But his generosity had affected her deeply. Before he left, Emmanuel had turned over to her almost all of his last pay, in addition to his savings, which he had deposited in the bank to her account.

Florentine opened her handbag and fingered her checkbook and a roll of bills with a quiver of pleasure. Then she felt ashamed, and darted off into the street.

At the curb she just missed colliding with some young men who were getting out of a car. A woman had put out her hand to protect her. She was a tiny old woman, very frail and thin, all dressed in black.

"You've been seeing someone in your family off?" she asked. "Your father or your boy-friend?"

"My husband," said Florentine.

But she said the word with a feeling of dignity of which she became conscious only after she had spoken.

"You may be proud of him," said the old lady before she slipped away.

Florentine stood there dreamily for a moment. Then a timid smile, a new kind of smile came to her weary face. She had just remembered how people had looked at her in the last few days whenever she had appeared in public on Emmanuel's arm. And yet despite this pleasant memory there was a strange ache in her heart.

She did not love Emmanuel. At least she did not love him as she had once expected to love someone. But she was grateful to him, as if his love for her had evened the balance of her wrongs; and she had a sincere desire to return his affection. . . .

She walked up St. Jacques Street as night began to fall, and her practical little brain busied itself with the only thing she enjoyed thinking about: the future. All sorts of plans suggested themselves, all sorts of charming perspectives opened up. With the allowance that she and her mother received, they could live very well from now on. Emmanuel had begged her to stop working, but she was greedy for the money. I'll continue as long as I can, she thought. We'll have that much more. . . .

We're going to live well at last, she kept repeating to herself. Papa did the right thing, he did the right thing to enlist. It's the finest thing he ever did in his life. And Mamma, oh well, Mamma has to be miserable about something. I wonder why she takes it so hard. She never had so much money before!

She walked rapidly, calculating the sum of their combined incomes. And she was delighted to see how well everything had worked out. To plan their life in a sensible way required some presence of mind, and the responsibility was quite new to her. Their troubles were over, they were far away now. Yes, a new life was beginning for them all.

And yet at times she felt a pang as she thought of all the money that would be given to them, the women, while their men risked their lives. But not relishing such thoughts, she returned to her calculations. Good gracious, she was rich! There were so many things she could buy for her mother and the children as well as for herself. At heart she rejoiced at the course of events, for without the war where would they all be?

The troop train meanwhile was running through Saint-Henri, and Emmanuel leaned out of the window. . . . .

The railroad barriers, the bronze Sacred Heart, the church and the signal tower slipped past one by one. His final picture of the quarter was of a tree deep in a courtyard, its foliage drooping with fatigue before it had come into full leaf, its twisted branches pushing bravely up through a network of electric wires and clotheslines toward the sky.

Low on the horizon, a bank of heavy clouds foretold a storm.

Those who go off to fight leave their families and friends behind to wait and worry. Particularly hard hit were the children, whose feelings of desertion and bewilderment can only be imagined. Fortunately, the well-known Canadian writer Timothy Findley's short story encapsulates precisely those emotions.

War

Timothy Findley

THAT'S MY DAD IN THE MIDDLE. We were just kids then, Bud on the right and me on the left. That was taken just before my dad went into the army.

Some day that was.

It was a Saturday, two years ago. August, 1940. I can remember I had to blow my nose just before that and I had to use my dad's hankie because mine had a worm in it that I was saving. I can't remember why; I mean, why I was saving that worm, but I can remember why I had to blow my nose, all right. That was because I'd had a long time crying. Not exactly because my dad was going away or anything—it was mostly because I'd done something.

I'll tell you what in a minute, but I just want to say this first. I was ten years old then and it was sort of the end of summer. When we went back to school I was going into the fifth grade and that was pretty important, especially for me because I'd skipped grade four. Right now I can't even remember grade five except that I didn't like it. I should have gone to grade four. In grade five everyone was a genius and there was a boy called Allan McKenzie.

Anyway, now that you know how old I was and what grade I was into, I can tell you the rest.

It was the summer the war broke out and I went to stay with my friend, Arthur Robertson. Looking back on it, Arthur seems a pretty silly name for Arthur Robertson because he was so small. But he was a nice kid and his dad had the most enormous summer cottage you've ever seen. In Muskoka, too.

It was like those houses they have in the movies in Beverly Hills. Windows a mile long—pine trees out-side and then a lake and then a red canoe tied up with a yellow rope. There was an Indian, too, who sold little boxes made of birch-bark and porcupine quills. Arthur Robertson and I used to sit in the red canoe and this Indian would take us for a ride out to the raft and back. Then we'd go and tell Mrs Robertson or the cook or someone how nice he was and he'd stand behind us and smile as though he didn't understand English and then they'd have to buy a box from him. He certainly was smart, that Indian, because it worked about four times. Then one day they caught on and hid the canoe.

Anyway, that's the sort of thing we did. And we swam too, and I remember a book that Arthur Robertson's nurse read to us. It was about dogs.

Then I had to go away because I'd only been invited for two weeks. I went on to this farm where the family took us every summer when we were children. Bud was already there, and his friend, Teddy Hartley.

I didn't like Teddy Hartley. It was because he had a space between his teeth and he used to spit through it. Once I saw him spit two-and-a-half yards. Bud paced it out. And then he used to whistle through it, too, that space, and it was the kind of whistling that nearly made your ears bleed. That was what I didn't like. But it didn't really matter, because he was Bud's friend, not mine.

So I went by train and Mr and Mrs Currie met me in their truck. It was their farm.

Mrs Currie got me into the front with her while Mr Currie put my stuff in the back.

"Your mum and dad aren't here, dear, but they'll be up tomorrow. Buddy is here—and his friend."

Grownups were always calling Bud "Buddy." It was all wrong.

I didn't care too much about my parents not being there, except that I'd brought them each one of those birch-bark boxes. Inside my mother's there was a set of red stones I'd picked out from where we swam. I thought maybe she'd make a necklace out of them. In my dad's there was an old golf ball, because he played golf. I guess you'd have to say I stole it, because I didn't tell anyone I had it—but it was just lying there on a shelf in Mr Robertson's boathouse, and he never played golf. At least I never saw him.

I had these boxes on my lap because I'd thought my mum and dad would be there to meet me, but now that they weren't I put them into the glove compartment of the truck.

We drove to the farm.

Bud and Teddy were riding on the gate, and they waved when we drove past. I couldn't see too well because of the dust but I could hear them shouting. It was something about my dad. I didn't really hear exactly what it was they said, but Mrs Currie went white as a sheet and said: "Be quiet," to Bud.

Then we were there and the truck stopped. We went inside.

And now—this is where it begins.

After supper, the evening I arrived at the Curries' farm, my brother Bud and his friend Teddy Hartley and I all sat on the front porch. In a hammock.

This is the conversation we had.

BUD: (to me) Are you all right? Did you have a good time at Arthur Robertson's place? Did you swim?

ME: (to BUD) Yes.

TEDDY HARTLEY: I've got a feeling I don't like Arthur Robertson. Do I know him?

BUD: Kid at school. Neil's age. (He said that as if it were dirty to be my age.)

TEDDY HARTLEY: Thin kid? Very small?

BUD: Thin and small—brainy type. Hey, Neil, have you seen Ted spit?

ME: Yes—I have.

TEDDY HARTLEY: When did you see me spit? (Indignant as hell) I never spat for you.

ME: Yes, you did. About three months ago. We were still in school. Bud—he did too, and you walked it out, too, didn't you?

BUD: I don't know.

TEDDY HARTLEY: I never spat for you yet! Never!

ME: Two yards and a half.

TEDDY HARTLEY: Can't have been me. I spit four.

ME: Four YARDS!!

TEDDY HARTLEY: Certainly.

BUD: Go ahead and show him. Over the rail.

TEDDY HARTLEY: (Standing up) Okay. Look, Neil . . . Now watch . . . Come on, WATCH!!

ME: All right—I'm watching.

(Teddy Hartley spat. It was three yards-and-a-half by Bud's feet. I saw Bud mark it myself.)

BUD: Three yards and a half a foot.

TEDDY HARTLEY: Four yards. (Maybe his feet were smaller or something.)

BUD: Three-and-foot. Three and *one* foot. No, no. A *half*-a-one. Of a foot.

TEDDY HARTLEY: Four.

BUD: Three!

TEDDY HARTLEY: Four! Four! Four!

BUD: Three! One-two-three-and-a-half-a-foot!!

TEDDY HARTLEY: My dad showed me. It's four! He showed me, and he knows. My dad knows. He's a mathematical teacher—yes, yes, yes, he showed me how to count a yard. I saw him do it. And he knows, my dad!!

BUD: Your dad's a crazy man. It's three yards and a half a foot.

TEDDY HARTLEY: (All red in the face and screaming) You called my dad a nut! You called my dad a crazy-man-nut-meg! Take it back, you. Bud Cable, you take that back.

BUD: Your dad is a matha-nut-ical nutmeg tree.
TEDDY HARTLEY: Then your dad's a . . . your dad's a . . . your dad's an Insane!
BUD: Our dad's joined the army.

That was how I found out.

They went on talking like that for a long time. I got up and left. I started talking to myself, which is a habit I have.

"Joined the army? Joined the army? Joined the ARMY! Our dad?"

Our dad was a salesman. I used to go to his office and watch him selling things over the phone sometimes. I always used to look for what it was, but I guess they didn't keep it around the office. Maybe they hid it somewhere. Maybe it was too expensive to just leave lying around. But whatever it was, I knew it was important, and so that was one thing that bothered me when Bud said about the army—because I knew that in the army they wouldn't let my dad sit and sell things over any old phone—because in the army you always went in a trench and got hurt or killed. I knew that because my dad had told me himself when my uncle died. My uncle was his brother in the first war, who got hit in his stomach and he died from it a long time afterwards. Long enough, anyway, for me to have known him. He was always in a big white bed, and he gave us candies from a glass jar. That was all I knew—except that it was because of being in the army that he died. His name was Uncle Frank.

So those were the first two things I thought of: my dad not being able to sell anything any more—and then Uncle Frank.

But then it really got bad, because I suddenly remembered that my dad had promised to teach me how to skate that year. He was going to make a rink too; in the back yard. But if he had to go off to some old trench in France, then he'd be too far away. Soldiers always went in trenches—and trenches were always in France. I remember that.

Well, I don't know. Maybe I just couldn't forgive him. He hadn't even told me. He didn't even write it in his letter that he'd sent me at Arthur Robertson's. But he'd told Bud—he'd told Bud, but I was the one he'd promised to show how to skate. And I'd had it all planned how I'd really surprise my dad and turn out to be a skating champion and everything, and now he wouldn't even be there to see.

All because he had to go and sit in some trench.

I don't know how I got there, but I ended up in the barn. I was in the hayloft and I didn't even hear them, I guess. They were looking all over the place for me, because it started to get dark.

I don't know whether you're afraid of the dark, but I'll tell you right now, I am. At least, I am if I have to move around in it. If I can just sit still, then I'm all right. At least, if you sit still you know where you are—but if you move around, then you don't know where you are. And that's awful. You never know what you're going to step on next and I always thought it would be a duck. I don't like ducks—especially in the dark or if you stepped on them.

Anyway, I was in that hayloft in the barn and I heard them calling out—"Neil, Neil"—and "Where are you?" But I made up my mind right then I wasn't going to answer. For one thing, if I did, then I'd have to go down to them in the dark—and maybe I'd step on something. And for another, I didn't really want to see anyone anyway.

It was then that I got this idea about my father. I thought that maybe if I stayed hidden for long enough, then he wouldn't join the army. Don't ask me why—right now I couldn't tell you that—but in those days it made sense. If I hid then he wouldn't go away. Maybe It would be because he'd stay looking for me or something.

The trouble was that my dad wasn't even there that night, and that meant that I either had to wait in the hayloft till he came the next day—or else that I had to go down now, and then hide again tomorrow. I decided to stay where I was because there were some ducks at the bottom of the ladder. I couldn't see them but I could tell they were there.

I stayed there all night. I slept most of the time. Every once in a while they'd wake me up by calling out "Neil! Neil!"—but I never answered.

I never knew a night that was so long, except maybe once when I was in the hospital. When I slept I seemed to sleep for a long time, but it never came to morning. They kept waking me up but it was never time.

Then it was.

I saw that morning through a hole in the roof of the hayloft. The sunlight came in through cracks between the boards and it was all dusty; the sunlight, I mean.

They were up pretty early that morning, even for farmers. There seemed to be a lot more people than I remembered—and there were two or three cars and a truck I'd never seen before, too. And I saw Mrs Currie holding onto Bud with one hand and Teddy Hartley with the other. I remember thinking, "If I was down there, how could she hold onto me if she's only got two hands and Bud and Teddy Hartley to look after?" And I thought that right then she must be pretty glad I wasn't around.

I wondered what they were all doing. Mr Currie was standing in the middle of a lot of men and he kept pointing out the scenery around the farm. I imagined what he was saying. There was a big woods behind the house and a cherry and plum-tree orchard that would be good to point out to his friends. I could tell they were his friends from the way they were listening. What I couldn't figure out was why they were all up so early—and why they had Bud and Teddy Hartley up, too.

Then there was a police car. I suppose it came from Orillia or somewhere. That was the biggest town near where the farm was. Orillia.

When the policemen got out of their car, they went up to Mr Currie. There were four of them. They all talked for quite a long time and then everyone started going out in all directions. It looked to me as though Bud and Teddy Hartley wanted to go, too, but Mrs Currie made them go in the house. She practically had to drag Bud. It looked as if he was crying and I wondered why he should do that.

Then one of the policemen came into the barn. He was all alone. I stayed very quiet, because I wasn't going to let anything keep me from going through with my plan about my dad. Not even a policeman.

He urinated against the wall inside the door. It was sort of funny, because he kept turning around to make sure no one saw him, and he didn't know I was there. Then he did up his pants and stood in the middle of the floor under the haylofts.

"Hey! Neil!"

That was the policeman.

He said it so suddenly that it scared me. I nearly fell off from where I was, it scared me so much. And I guess maybe he saw me, because he started right up the ladder at me.

"How did you know my name?"

I said that in a whisper.

"They told me."

"Oh."

"Have you been here all night?"

"Yes."

"Don't you realize that *everyone* has been looking for you all over the place? Nobody's even been to sleep."

That sort of frightened me—but it was all right, because he smiled when he said it.

Then he stuck his head out of this window that was there to let the air in (so that the barn wouldn't catch on fire)—and he yelled down, "He's all right—I've found him! He's up here."

And I said: "What did you go and do that for? Now you've ruined everything."

He smiled again and said, "I had to stop them all going off to look for you. Now,"—as he sat down beside me—"do you want to tell me what it is you're doing up here?"

"No."

I think that sort of set him back a couple of years, because he didn't say anything for a minute—except "Oh."

Then I thought maybe I had to have something to tell the others anyway, so I might as well make it up for him right now.

"I fell asleep," I said.

"When—last night?"

"Yes."

I looked at him. I wondered if I could trust a guy who did that against walls, when all you had to do was go in the house.

"Why did you come up here in the first place?" he said.

I decided I could trust him because I remembered once when I did the same thing. Against the wall.

So I told him.

"I want to hide on my dad," I said.

"Why do you want to do that? And besides, Mrs Currie said your parents weren't even here."

"Yes, but he's coming today."

"But why hide on him? Don't you like him, or something?"

"Sure I do," I said.

I thought about it.

"But he's . . . he's . . . Do you know if it's true, my dad's joined the army?"

"I dunno. Maybe. There's a war on, you know."

"Well, that's why I hid."

But he laughed.

"Is that why you hid? Because of the war?"

"Because of my dad."

"You don't need to hide because of the war—the Germans aren't coming over here, you know."

"But it's not that. It's my dad." I could have told you he wouldn't understand.

I was trying to think of what to say next when Mrs Currie came into the barn. She stood down below.

"Is he up there, officer? Is he all right?"

"Yes, ma'am, I've got him. He's fine."

"Neil dear, what happened? Why don't you come down and tell us what happened to you?"

Then I decided that I'd really go all out. I had to, because I could tell they weren't going to—it was just *obvious* that these people weren't going to understand me and take my story about my dad and the army and everything.

"Somebody chased me."

The policeman looked sort of shocked and I could hear Mrs Currie take in her breath.

"Somebody chased you, eh?"

"Yes."

"Who?"

I had to think fast.

"Some man. But he's gone now."

I thought I'd better say he was gone, so that they wouldn't start worrying.

"Officer, why don't you bring him down here? Then we can talk."

"All right, ma'am. Come on, Neil, we'll go down and have some breakfast."

They didn't seem to believe me about that man I made up.

We went over to the ladder.

I looked down. A lot of hay stuck out so that I couldn't see the floor.

"Are there any ducks down there?"

"No, dear, you can come down—it's all right."

She was lying, though. There was a great big duck right next to her. I think it's awfully silly to tell a lie like that. I mean, if the duck is standing right there it doesn't even make sense, does it?

But I went down anyway and she made the duck go away.

When we went out, the policeman held my hand. His hand had some sweat on it but it was a nice hand, with hair on the back. I liked that. My dad didn't have that on his hand.

Then we ate breakfast with all those people who'd come to look for me. At least, *they* ate. I just sat.

After breakfast, Mr and Mrs Currie took me upstairs to the sitting room. It was upstairs because the kitchen was in the cellar.

All I remember about that was a vase that had a potted plant in it. This vase was made of putty and into the putty Mrs Currie had stuck all kinds of stones and pennies and old bits of glass and things. You could look at this for hours and never see the same kind of stone or glass twice. I don't remember the plant.

All I remember about what they said was that they told me I should never do it again. That routine.

Then they told me my mother and my dad would be up that day around lunch time.

What they were really sore about was losing their sleep, and then all those people coming. I was sorry about that—but you can't very well go down and make an announcement about it, so I didn't.

At twelve o'clock I went and sat in Mr Currie's truck. It was in the barn. I took out those two boxes I'd put in the glove compartment and looked at them. I tried to figure out what my dad would do with an old box like that in the army. And he'd probably never play another game of golf as long as he lived. Not in the army, anyway. Maybe he'd use the box for his bullets or something.

Then I counted the red stones I was going to give my mother. I kept seeing them around her neck and how pretty they'd be. She had a dress they'd be just perfect with. Blue. The only thing I was worried about was how to get a hole in them so you could put them on a string. There wasn't much sense in having beads without a string—not if you were going to wear them, anyway—or your mother was.

And it was then that they came.

I heard their car drive up outside and I went and looked from behind the barn door. My father wasn't wearing a uniform yet like I'd thought he would be. I began to think maybe he really didn't want me to know about it. I mean, he hadn't written or anything, and now he was just wearing an old blazer and some grey pants. It made me remember.

I went back and sat down in the truck again. I didn't know what to do. I just sat there with those stones in my hand.

Then I heard someone shout, "Neil!"

I went and looked. Mr and Mrs Currie were standing with my parents by the car—and I saw Bud come running out of the house, and then Teddy Hartley. Teddy Hartley sort of hung back, though. He was the kind of person who's only polite if there are grownups around him. He sure knew how to pull the wool over their eyes, because he'd even combed his hair. Wildroot-cream-oil-Charlie.

Then I noticed that they were talking very seriously and my mother put her hand above her eyes and looked around. I guess she was looking for me. Then my dad started toward the barn.

I went and hid behind the truck. I wasn't quite sure yet what I was going to do, but I certainly wasn't going to go up and throw my arms around his neck or anything.

"Neil. Are you in there, son?"

My dad spoke that very quietly. Then I heard the door being pushed open, and some chicken had to get out of the way, because I heard it making that awful noise chickens make when you surprise them doing something. They sure can get excited over nothing—chickens.

I took a quick look behind me. There was a door there that led into the part of the barn where the haylofts were and where I'd been all night. I decided to make a dash for it. But I had to ward off my father first—and so I threw that stone.

I suppose I'll have to admit that I meant to hit him. It wouldn't be much sense if I tried to fool you about that. I wanted to hit him because when I stood up behind the truck and saw him then I suddenly got mad. I thought about how he hadn't written me, or anything.

It hit him on the hand.

He turned right around because he wasn't sure what it was or where it came from. And before I ran, I just caught a glimpse of his face. He'd seen me and he sure looked peculiar. I guess that now I'll never forget his face and how he looked at me right then. I think it was that he looked as though he might cry or something. But I knew he wouldn't do that, because he never did.

Then I ran.

From the loft I watched them in the yard. My dad was rubbing his hands together and I guess maybe where I'd hit him it was pretty sore. My mother took off her handkerchief that she had round her neck and put it on his hand. Then I guess he'd told them what I'd done, because this time they *all* started toward the barn.

I didn't know what to do then. I counted out the stones I had left and there were about fifteen of them. There was the golf ball, too.

I didn't want to throw stones at all of them. I certainly didn't want to hit my mother—and I hoped that they wouldn't send her in first. I thought then how I'd be all right if they sent in Teddy Hartley first. I didn't mind the thought of throwing at him, I'll tell you that much.

But my dad came first.

I had a good view of where he came from. He came in through the part where the truck was parked, because I guess he thought I was still there. And then he came on into the part where I was now—in the hayloft.

He stood by the door.

"Neil."

I wasn't saying anything. I sat very still.

"Neil."

I could only just see his head and shoulders—the rest of him was hidden by the edge of the loft.

"Neil, aren't you even going to explain what you're angry about?"

I thought for a minute and then I didn't answer him after all. I looked at him, though. He looked worried.

"What do you want us to do?"

I sat still.

"Neil?"

Since I didn't answer, he started back out the door—I guess to talk to my mother or someone.

I hit his back with another stone. I had to make sure he knew I was there.

He turned around at me.

"Neil, what's the matter? I want to know what's the matter."

He almost fooled me, but not quite. I thought that perhaps he really didn't know for a minute—but after taking a look at him I decided that he did know, all right. I mean, there he was in that blue blazer and everything—just as if he hadn't joined the army at all.

So I threw again and this time it really hit him in the face.

He didn't do anything—he just stood there. It really scared me. Then my mother came in, but he made her go back.

I thought about my rink, and how I wouldn't have it. I thought about being in the fifth grade that year and how I'd skipped from grade three. And I thought about the Indian who'd sold those boxes that I had down in the truck.

"Neil—I'm going to come up."

You could tell he really would, too, from his voice.

I got the golf ball ready.

To get to me he had to disappear for a minute while he crossed under the loft and then when he climbed the ladder. I decided to change my place while he was out of sight. I began to think that was pretty clever and that maybe I'd be pretty good at that war stuff myself. Field Marshal Cable.

I put myself into a little trench of hay and piled some up in front of me. When my dad came up over the top of the ladder, he wouldn't even see me and then I'd have a good chance to aim at him.

The funny thing was that at that moment I'd forgotten why I was against him. I got so mixed up in all that Field Marshal stuff that I really forgot all about my dad and the army and everything. I was just trying to figure out how I could get him before he saw me—and that was all.

I got further down in the hay and then he was there.

He was out of breath and his face was all sweaty, and where I'd hit him there was blood. And then he put his hand with my mother's hankie up to his face to wipe it. And he sort of bit it (the handkerchief). It was as if he was confused or something. I remember thinking he looked then just like I'd felt my face go when Bud had said our dad had joined the army. You know how you look around with your eyes from side to side as though maybe you'll find the answer to it somewhere near you? You never do find it, but you always look anyway, just in case.

Anyway, that's how he was just then, and it sort of threw me. I had that feeling again that maybe he didn't know what this was all about. But then, he had to know, didn't he? Because he'd done it.

I had the golf ball ready in my right hand and one of those stones in the other. He walked toward me.

I missed with the golf ball and got him with the stone.

And he fell down. He really fell down. He didn't say anything—he didn't even say "ouch," like I would have—he just fell down.

In the hay.

I didn't go out just yet. I sat and looked at him. And I listened.

Nothing.

Do you know, there wasn't a sound in that whole place? It was as if everything had stopped because they knew what had happened.

My dad just lay there and we waited for what would happen next.

It was me.

I mean, I made the first noise.

I said: "Dad?"

But nobody answered—not even my mother.

So I said it louder. *"Dad?"*

It was just as if they'd all gone away and left me with him, all alone.

He sure looked strange lying there—so quiet and everything. I didn't know what to do.

"Dad?"

I went over on my hands and knees.

Then suddenly they all came in. I just did what I thought of first. I guess it was because they scared me—coming like that when it was so quiet.

I got all the stones out of my pockets and threw them, one by one, as they came through the door. I stood up to do it. I saw them all running through the door, and I threw every stone, even at my mother.

And then I fell down. I fell down beside my dad and pushed him over on his back because he'd fallen on his stomach. It was like he was asleep.

They came up then and I don't remember much of that. Somebody picked me up, and there was the smell of perfume and my eyes hurt and I got something in my throat and nearly choked to death and I could hear a lot of talking. And somebody was whispering, too. And then I felt myself being carried down and there was the smell of oil and gasoline and some chickens had to be got out of the way again and then there was sunlight.

Then my mother just sat with me, and I guess I cried for a long time. In the cherry and plum-tree orchard—and she seemed to understand because she said that he would tell me all about it and that he hadn't written me because he didn't want to scare me when I was all alone at Arthur Robertson's.

And then Bud came.

My mother said that he should go away for a while. But he said: "I brought something" and she said: "What is it, then?" and now I remember where I got that worm in my handkerchief that I told you about.

It was from Bud.

He said to me that if I wanted to, he'd take me fishing on the lake just before the sun went down. He said that was a good time. And he gave me that worm because he'd found it.

So my mother took it and put it in my hankie and Bud looked at me for a minute and then went away.

The worst part was when I saw my dad again.

My mother took me to the place where he was sitting in the sun and we just watched each other for a long time.

Then he said: "Neil, your mother wants to take our picture because I'm going away tomorrow to Ottawa for a couple of weeks, and she thought I'd like a picture to take with me."

He lit a cigarette and then he said: "I would, too, you know, like that picture."

And I sort of said: "All right."

So they called to Bud, and my mother went to get her camera.

But before Bud came and before my mother got back, we were alone for about ten hours. It was awful.

I couldn't think of anything and I guess he couldn't, either. I had a good look at him, though.

He looked just like he does right there in that picture. You can see where the stone hit him on his right cheek—and the one that knocked him out is the one over the eye.

Right then the thing never got settled. Not in words, anyway. I was still thinking about that rink and everything—and my dad hadn't said anything about the army yet.

I wish I hadn't done it. Thrown those stones and everything. It wasn't his fault he had to go.

For another thing, I was sorry about the stones because I knew I wouldn't find any more like them—but I did throw them, and that's that.

They both got those little boxes, though—I made sure of that. And in one there was a string of red beads from Orillia and in the other there was a photograph.

There still is.

II

Men and Women in Uniform

The novelist Hugh Garner was noted for the gritty realism of his tales about ordinary Canadians. His wartime service on cramped, crowded, sometimes unseaworthy corvettes during the Battle of the Atlantic gave him ample experience to draw upon for *Storm Below,* the 1949 novel from which this excerpt is drawn.

A War of Strangers

Hugh Garner

THE WEATHER, which had closed in several times during the day, finally shut in completely with the setting of the watery sun. The convoy moved ahead quietly through the shrouding mantle of darkness, the parabolas of its threescore wakes lit with the phosphorescence of the icy sea.

Those upon the bridge took hold of something steady and stared into the murk. The Captain and Mr. Allison, the navigating officer, stood together conversing in low voices, their coat collars turned up against the freezing wind. "If they're waiting for us, we should be abeam of them before long," said the Captain.

"I think so, sir. Of course, they may have lost us since it began to blow."

"They might." They stood together in silence, staring into the darkness.

There was a camaraderie between these two, which while not overly apparent to the casual observer, held them together, to the exclusion of the other officers. Being former Merchant Navy men they had more in common than did the others, who had followed many professions, and they had an equal respect for each other's knowledge and seamanship.

"How is Moody making out on the asdic plot?" asked the Captain. Moody was one of the coders, whose job during action was to help Allison on the plotting table where the maze of anti-submarine runs were charted, so that the position of the submarine, in relation to the ship, was always known.

"He's a good boy. He's learning fast," answered Allison.

The Captain walked across to the port side of the bridge and stood behind the look-out, staring into the darkness. The sea ran past the ship at express speed, the corvette's fourteen knots being magnified by the illusion of the tumbling water.

He turned around and glanced for a moment at a small group of figures standing in the lee of the funnel. He thought, some of the crew have anticipated action stations tonight. It was remarkable how the news got around the ship. Probably the telegraphists and coders spread it—or, more than likely, the stewards. Farther aft, on the quarter-deck, three or four seamen were struggling with a depth charge which they were hoisting into one of the stern rails.

There was no noise save the wind brushing through the ship's upper works and the faint hum of the engines from below. The voices of those standing around the funnel were driven across the stern by the wind.

He felt his way again to the starboard side and paused there, able now to hear the dit-da-da-dit-dit of the telegraph keys from the wireless cabin below. The starboard look-out and the signalman on watch were standing together, hands deep in pockets, their faces half turned from the searing wind.

The Captain walked forward again, skirting the Oerlikon platform, and rejoined the navigating officer against the forward dodger. He glanced at the compass needle before turning his face to stare out into the darkness.

He thought, it is a silent war out here. A war of ambush and shooting fish in a barrel. Jerry lies out here somewhere, knowing that we are approaching him; able to hear us with his sound-gear. He sits just above the surface of the water, his tubes trained on a ship in the convoy, and he waits until he can't miss, before he fires his torpedoes. We in turn try to pick him up on our radar, or sight him; then we attack, with gun-fire if he is above water, and with depth charges if he is below. If he dives we follow him with the asdic, and we plot all his turns and evasions. The hunter becomes the fox, and his manoeuvrability is limited by the element in which he must hide. We, in turn, are being plotted by him and he knows where we are lying also. He can hear our screw churning up the water above his head, while we can tell where he is lying or moving by the magic of a detection gear which sends us his position as though we were probing for him with a pole.

His job is completed when he has fired his torpedoes, and all he wants to do then is hide. But our job is only starting and we follow him, if we can, relentlessly, as though he were a cockroach running evasive action beneath a human boot. When we find ourselves above him we drop our charges and hope that he will be destroyed.

There is no human element in submarine warfare. It is submarine against ship, then ship against submarine. It is a fourteen charge pattern of depth charges, each containing three hundred and fifty pounds of high explosive, being dropped in the area in which the submarine is believed to be lying. It is the explosive war-head of a torpedo ripping to shreds the boiler-room or the fo'castle of a plodding ship.

It is only after the battle that the human element is apparent at all. It is only when the stunned, frozen and oil-smeared survivors are lifted from the boats and rafts; only when the sullen, deafened Jerry prisoners are hoisted aboard in their lifebelts that the thought occurs that there were men on these steel things which were fighting one with the other.

It is a war of strangers, friend and foe alike. A mile to starboard lay the convoy. There are men aboard all the ships, and they have been travelling with us for eleven days, and yet they are perfect strangers to us. Just as much strangers as are the men who are lying in wait in the submarines somewhere ahead.

It was a mean, sneaking way to wage a war. Indian warfare carried from the forest into the width and depth of the ocean; no preliminary barrages, no attacks over the top of a trench, no infiltration. It was a war of deceit and deception; a battle of the sharpest eyesight, both human and mechanical.

If it belongs to the enemy, sink it without warning. Blow the guts out of it. Kill every man aboard with hot steel and concussion; with the caress of live steam from his blown-up boilers; with the slow strangulation of the Atlantic; with the zut-zu-ut of small-arms fire as he tries to surface and swim for his life. Ram him if he is smaller than you are; cut him in half.

If a handful of Laskar seamen scramble into a floating raft, shoot them like vermin for the glory of the Third Reich. If fifty men are floating on the surface in their life jackets and a submarine is hiding beneath them, fire your charges and sink him, even though it means the death and rupturing of the fifty swimmers above. Even though it means the tremendous shock of sea-water through every pore and orifice of their bodies, and they scream to you to pick them up . . .

"There it goes, sir!" cried Allison, pointing to a flash of flame to starboard. A dull thud floated across the water, followed almost immediately by a long, low, frightened hoot of a ship's whistle.

Before Allison had finished speaking, the Captain had his thumb jammed down on the button of the Action Station bell.

Frenchy Turgeon stood on the deckplates in No. 1 stokehold, engaged in a shouted conversation with his watch-keeping mate, First Class Stoker Wally Crabbe, in the No. 2 boiler-room.

Beneath the bright electric bulbs on the bulkhead, the valve wheels, pumps, gauge glasses and oil feed pipes were a devil's workshop which supplied the steam to run the engines of the *Riverford*. The fuel was pumped from tanks, situated below decks throughout the ship, and was carried by means of fuel lines, through pumps, into the fire-boxes beneath the boilers. It ignited, and sent its thermal power above to heat the water in the boiler tubes. This was boiled into steam, which in turn passed back through lines to the reciprocating engine, where it pushed the pistons, turning the shaft, which spun the propeller.

Through the open, watertight door between the two boiler-rooms, Frenchy caught occasional glimpses of Wally as he went about his work. Above him, the boiler face sloped toward the bulkhead at his back, as though ready to topple forward, and cut him off forever from the air and night sky which lay hidden in the higher gloom, beyond the stokehold hatch. It seemed to French that the stokehold was a vibrating steel cavern, into which he had been lowered to do penance for his sins. Now and again he glanced into the white, shimmering heat of the fires, turning his face away quickly from their searing blast. The voice of the other stoker was distorted and magnified, as it reverberated in the confined, steel-lined space.

During the past three or four days, since the convoy had left the warm waters of the Gulf Stream, the boiler-room had cooled, and the temperature on the deck, differing from that higher up the ladders, was cool enough to warrant the wearing of a shirt or sweater.

The oddly distorted echo of Crabbe, singing one of his ribald songs, bounced from the steel plates.

"The French . . . a funny race, parley voo,
  The French they . . . race, parley voo;
The French they . . . a funny race,
  They fight with their feet . . . with their FACE,
Inky, dinky . . . ley voo!"

"You shut your mout', you *maudit* baskerd!" Frenchy shouted back. His voice reverberated above the roar of the fires, and the vibrations of the ship.

"What . . . you say?" came back the question from Wally.

"You watch dem fire, dat's all you can do. You t'ink you smart fella wit' your song. You make a noise like a *cochon*—like a beeg pork!"

"Work! Who don't work?" asked the other, purposely misconstruing Frenchy's last sally.

Frenchy ignored him and wiped his hands on some waste, and sat down on an oil-stained butter box which served as a bench. He glanced at his gauges before taking a package of cigarettes from his back pocket and extracting a smoke. His hand left black fingerprints on the clean whiteness of the paper.

Back home in Montmagny the maple sap would be running soon, and the Young Peoples Society at the church would be organizing sugar parties into the maple woods south of town. The night shift would be at work in the foundry, and M. Revillon, the foreman of the plate shop, would be shouting at Chasson or Jean-Claude Boucher to stop their chatter and get on with their work. His girl friend Gabrielle would be sitting in Mme. Robichaud's *Chez Cecille* toying with a Coca-Cola, while she read his last airgraph letter to her friends.

He grew sad when he thought of Gabrielle. Though she had not mentioned it outright, several times during the last few months there had been half-concealed hints that Paul Gregoire, who had found a job as a provincial motorcycle policeman, had asked her to go out with him. When he pictured the tall, moustached figure of Gregoire, and remembered how far *he* was away from Gabrielle, he wished sometimes that he had stayed on at the stove company and got his draft deferments like the others.

How far away was he now, he wondered? Geography was not one of his strong points, and the Atlantic Ocean to him was a square body of water, eleven to fourteen days' sailing time across, in which were scattered such exotic places as Newfoundland, Ireland, Gibraltar, Iceland and the Azores. The Azores was the only place he had visited which seemed to him to be islands. Though they said that the other places were also islands, with the exception of Gibraltar, he did not believe them. An island to Frenchy was a piece of land lying in the water, both ends of which could be seen from a few miles distance.

"Frenchy!" rumbled the voice of Wally.

"W'at you want?" he shouted back.

"Nothing. I thought . . . dead, that's all."

Frenchy's reply was halted in his throat by a noise which sounded like the ship's bottom being struck by a gigantic padded hammer. It was followed immediately by the clamour of the Action Station gong. He jumped to his feet and ran to the connecting doorway between the stokeholds.

The vibrations on the deck-plates were suddenly increased, and from the engine-room came the accelerant shug-shug of the steam through the pistons as the engine was revved up. The ship heeled to port, and there was the clatter of small gear on the plates as everything movable shifted with centrifugal force. He grasped at the bulkhead for support, and shouted to the other stoker, who was making his way across the canting deck, "What is it, a dep' charge?"

The face that Wally turned to him was chalk white beneath its streams of oil, and he shouted back above the incessant ringing of the bell, "That was no depth charge . . . torpedo . . . something's been fished!"

He turned from the doorway, fighting back the panic which gripped him at the other's words. There was the noise of heavy boots on metal, and he looked above him to see the weaving form of Stoker Petty Officer Collet coming down the ladder.

The Royal Canadian Navy's role in the battle against the U-boats was, by any measure, a distinguished one. But there were difficulties resulting from a lack of experience, obsolescent equipment, and, sometimes, weak leadership at the top. The first professional historian to explore these difficult questions that boiled to the surface in 1943 was Marc Milner of the University of New Brunswick.

Royal Canadian Navy Participation in the Battle of the Atlantic Crisis of 1943

Marc Milner

It is generally conceded that the Royal Canadian Navy made a vital contribution to the Allied victory in the Battle of the Atlantic, September 1939 to May 1945. Yet no attempt has been made to explain the role of the service in the final crisis of 1943, when the German U-boat wolfpack campaign against the main North Atlantic convoy routes was finally and decisively beaten. This apparent oversight is disturbing, particularly since historians assure us that the RCN [Royal Canadian Navy] was a major participant in the struggle. However, this gap in our knowledge of RCN operations with the Mid-Ocean Escort Force (MOEF) may stem not from neglect but perhaps from a conspiracy of silence—early 1943 was a very trying time for the RCN. The ability of Canadian escorts to carry on operations in the mid-Atlantic had been brought into question by the convoy battles of late 1942; mounting losses to Canadian-escorted convoys led the British to propose, in early December, that the RCN component of the MOEF be withdrawn until such time as its training could be improved. The Naval Staff in Ottawa reacted bitterly to this proposal in light of the British allegation that poor training was largely at fault. However, as the Canadians mustered their case the disastrous battle of convoy ONS 154, in which the RCN escort proved incapable of preventing the loss of fifteen ships, eliminated all hopes of successfully challenging the British. In early 1943 Canada's MOEF escorts were quietly transferred to a British command, and the role of the RCN in the North Atlantic over the following months was much reduced. In short, Canada's most prestigious naval commitment collapsed as the battle reached its climax. With it fell all chance of active participation in the great destruction of the wolfpacks in April and May, 1943, a goal toward which the RCN's unbending efforts, the source of its ultimate shortcomings, had been directed.

While the role of the Royal Canadian Navy in the Battle of the Atlantic is of immense importance to the battle generally, and to the history of the RCN in particular, the record of the Canadian service—its problems, accomplishments, and failings—has not been analysed thoroughly. There are two predominant themes in the existing literature. Canadian historians quite rightly lay emphasis on the size of the Canadian forces committed. Indeed, in naval terms alone, by early 1943 no less than 48 percent of the escorts assigned to the main North Atlantic convoys were Canadian.[1] This theme, heavily laced with the pride of accomplishment, colours the works of the official historians Gilbert Tucker and Joseph Schull.[2] Unfortunately, Tucker's penchant for detail and analysis is not found in Schull's operational history. In fairness to Schull, detailed analysis was not his mandate. His history is really a survey of notable RCN adventures, enjoyable anecdotes designed more to foster a national following for the navy than to satisfy historians; it does not place peculiarly Canadian problems and achievements in fighting the Battle of the Atlantic in context. Schull's account of the ten-month period from July 1942 to May 1943, about which so much has been written, is a case in point.

That period was one of sharp contrasts for the Battle of the Atlantic. The U-boat campaign had gained momentum all through the latter half of 1942, and in November Allied shipping losses reached 807 754 tons, a new wartime high.[3] Foul weather in December and January gave the Allies some respite, but the increasing number of U-boats being deployed in the mid-ocean made it painfully clear that the worst was yet to come. Only good intelligence kept losses down in February 1943, but when the Germans changed their codes in early March, the wolfpacks achieved their greatest successes of the war. During the first three weeks of that month 22 percent of all the ships sailing in the main trans-Atlantic convoys failed to reach their destination. The British, in desperation, considered abandoning the convoy system, a desperate move indeed since there was no viable alternative. The situation was only restored by the timely repenetration of the German U-boat cypher, "Triton," later in the month. In April and May the combination of excellent intelligence, recently arrived support groups, and extended aircover dealt a death blow to the German wolfpack campaign and eliminated the serious threat to the main North Atlantic convoys for the rest of the war.

If the RCN was a major participant in this phase of the battle, as both Tucker and Schull would have us believe, that cannot be gathered from the history of the operations in which neither large scale participation nor successes are documented. In fact, Tucker, whose interest in operations at sea in volume two of *The*

Naval Service of Canada was peripheral, mentions without qualification that a disproportionate number of Canadian escorts were in refit in early 1943. While he states that four RCN escort groups doing "coastal" work were to be assigned to the MOEF in the months of March and April 1943,[4] he does not disclose which coast, nor does he account for the four groups apparently already assigned to MOEF.[5] Unfortunately, it is not clear if Tucker intended to sort out these unexplained remarks in his unpublished third volume. Certainly Schull did not.

In the section of Schull's *The Far Distant Ships* dealing with this period, the small role of the Royal Canadian Navy in the crisis of 1943 is apparent.[6] Schull recounts at length the RCN convoy battles of 1942 but says little of the first five months of 1943. At a time when other historians focus on the exploits of embattled escorts and support groups, Schull writes in general terms about the course of events at sea. His main stress is on the establishment of the Canadian North West Atlantic Command, in itself no mean achievement. Yet he almost suggests that there was really nothing left to say about Canadian operations in early 1943, despite the fact that the battle was passing through its most crucial phase.

That the Canadian side of the story of these months has been inadequately told is clear from its lack of impact on foreign accounts. General accounts of the Battle of the Atlantic treat the RCN tersely. Reference to the Canadians is usually limited to one or two paragraphs that note the rapid expansion from six prewar destroyers in 1939 to over two hundred warships of all types by the end of 1942 and comment on the fact that the expansion caused some problems.[7] It may be expected that chauvinism among the larger powers would deny the RCN a proper place in the history proportionate to its actual role. In fact, the fault lies with the Canadians, who have simply not put their own house in order, for from the outset, the inadequacies of the operational history left the field open for others to speculate and hypothesize on the merits of Canada's contribution. Nowhere is this more apparent than in the works of Captain Donald Macintyre.[8] Macintyre wrote several books about the Battle of the Atlantic, all of which were published after the official Canadian histories in the early 1950s. It is obvious that Macintyre was unimpressed by the RCN. His vehement attack on the RCN, in the first five pages of chapter seven in *U-Boat Killer*, is the most damning criticism of the Royal Canadian Navy in print.[9] The gist of the Macintyre thesis is simply that Canada's wartime fleet expanded too quickly and as a result was utterly inefficient. Macintyre suggests that the RCN should have swallowed its national pride and contributed men and ships directly to the Royal Navy, where the cadre of experienced personnel would have softened the effects of expansion. The very things which Canadians regard highly about their World War II achievement—its tremendous growth and subsequent participation in important tasks—are the very things which Macintyre abhors.

One may ascribe Macintyre's opinions to the British attitude toward "colonials." Indeed, the opinion that Canadians were rowdy, ill-disciplined frontiersmen was widely held by the British. Even Admiral Sir Max Horton's biographer, Rear-Admiral W.S. Chalmers, RN [Royal Navy], who was generally sympathetic to the Canadians, equated the makeshift nature of the wartime RCN and its conduct at sea to the frontier spirit.[10] Clearly, the British never appreciated the RCN's desire to assert itself as an independent service. Nor did the British outgrow their first impressions of Canada's expanded navy, which were formulated during the winter of 1941–42 in the Western Atlantic. At no other period in the war was the overall efficiency and appearance of the RCN at so low an ebb. The first construction program of sixty-four corvettes was being hurriedly commissioned, while the debilitating effects of bad weather and an ever-expanding war meant that the navy was literally learning on the job.

The most startling example of Canadian shortcomings in the latter half of 1941 was the disastrous passage of convoy SC 42 in September of that year. . . . But it was not the spectacular failures which left the lingering impressions. It was the day-to-day exposure of professional servicemen to these fledgling "warships." The senior officer of the escort of convoy SC 45, for example, found his Canadian escorts more trying than the U-boat threat. In his report of proceedings, he noted laconically that the Canadian corvettes were sloppy and reckless signallers (particularly at night) and concluded that their convoy discipline was "not good."[11] A memorandum submitted to Commodore L.W. Murray, RCN, the commodore commanding Newfoundland Force (CCNF), in November observed, "RCN corvettes have been given so little chance of becoming efficient that they are almost more of a liability than an asset."[12] And if they were of questionable value in a defensive role, they were of equally dubious value as a threat to the enemy. Referring to the latter quality, captain (D[estroyers]), Newfoundland, wrote in September 1941, "At present most escorts are equipped with one weapon of approximate precision—the ram."[13]

As many British officers were exposed to this trying phase of Canadian naval expansion, the RCN suffered from the RN's suspicion and doubt about its merits. John Costello and Terry Hughes, in *The Battle of the Atlantic*, adopted the Macintyre thesis in their characteristically brief passage about the RCN.[14] As in other general works, salutary remarks about the tremendous growth of the Royal Canadian Navy form the basis of their comments on the performance of the RCN which follow. Wartime expansion has been equated with inefficiency in a way which suggests that the Canadians knew little of, or cared less about, the finer points of antisubmarine warfare and trade escort.

Fortunately, Canadians can take some solace from the Americans, who, in general, tend to look more favourably on the RCN. The idea that Canadians should have submerged their identity in some form of Commonwealth navy never emerges from American literature. Although at least one American writer, Patrick Abbazia, author of *Mr. Roosevelt's Navy*, describes the RCN as ill-disciplined and rather misguided, his criticism is based on different grounds. The Canadians, Abbazia claims, were inefficient because they lacked the necessary mechanical aptitude to keep their escorts in fighting trim.[15] Though this is clearly part of the myth that the Americans were naturally more mechanically minded than the British, or, in this case, near-British, the criticism is not without foundation. Certainly United States Navy officers serving with MOEF felt this way with good reason, and it is likely that Abbazia derived his opinions from them.

Nonetheless, on the whole Americans have treated the RCN rather better than the British have. This is certainly true of writers who were themselves serving officers. Though perhaps it is not fair to let the British case rest with Macintyre's heavily subjective appreciation, the general sense of his stand is typical. Captain Stephen Roskill simply avoided the issue of operational efficiency in the RCN, as though he felt constrained by his position as the official historian of the Royal Navy.[16] No such sentiment need have inhibited his American counterpart. Perhaps the feeling that they shared a similar experience with the Canadians may have tempered American opinion. Certainly neither Admiral Samuel Morison, in his official history,[17] nor Captain J.M. Waters, in *Bloody Winter*,[18] voice strong condemnations of the Royal Canadian Navy. On the contrary, both find reason to praise the Canadians for doing a good job under very trying circumstances. Even Abbazia inadvertently suggests the link between problems of inefficiency, which were seen to be peculiarly Canadian, and those which affected American forces in the same zone of operations. In the winter of 1941–42—even before it had undergone wartime expansion—the USN found it difficult to maintain a professional service on the Newfoundland to Iceland run.[19] Even the British, Abbazia observes, were forced to neglect their professional appearance to allow more time for shore leave.[20]

The RCN had some very serious problems, more serious perhaps than the operational history would have us believe. In *50 North*, Alan Easton pointed to the weakness of the RCN's manning policy,[21] and more recently James Lamb has argued that the policy was "the biggest impediment to operational efficiency."[22] Their point is well made, for it is clear that the long-term benefits of a wide distribution of experienced personnel were achieved only at the expense of efficiency initially. The Naval Staff appreciated this problem but insisted that quantity, not quality, was the immediate goal.[23] The lack of modern ASW and navigational equipment aboard Canadian escorts also had a profound impact on operational efficiency. It was said of Canadian escorts that they lagged behind their British counterparts in the fitting of new equipment by as much as a year.[24] Not one RCN escort, for example, had been fitted with the anti-submarine mortar "Hedgehog," by the autumn of 1942, and of the Canadian ships in the MOEF only one was fitted with high-frequency direction-finding and four with modern radar. In addition, only one of the Canadian corvettes of the MOEF, HMCS *Eyebright*, was modernized. The remainder continued to operate with wet and cramped living conditions as well as with outdated bridges and navigational equipment.

While Tucker mentioned what is now known as the equipment crisis in his second volume,[25] most historians seem to have overlooked this most important piece of Canadian naval history, or at best dismissed a work on shore establishments as having no application to the study of operations at sea. Certainly there are no subsequent references to Tucker's discussion of equipment in any of the general texts. It was not until 1970, and the publication of C.P. Stacey's *Arms, Men and Governments*, that the issue of equipment and RCN operational efficiency was "resurrected" in the literature.[26] This theme was further developed by W.A.B. Douglas and B. Greenhous in *Out of the Shadows*. They suggested that the poor showing of the RCN during the crisis of 1943 was a direct result of the equipment crisis.[27]

In fact, the crisis of 1943 was more complex than Douglas and Greenhous imply. On 7 January 1943 the War Committee of the Canadian cabinet agreed to the temporary transfer of four escort groups then operating with the MOEF to the RN's commander-in-chief Western Approaches, whose area of jurisdiction encompassed the waters immediately west of the British Isles.[28] Ostensibly, this was to permit a reorganization of the Atlantic escort systems designed to facilitate the movement of oil convoys direct from the Caribbean to the United Kingdom. But this was only a half-truth. Certainly, there was an oil crisis of considerable proportions in Britain as a result of the Operation Torch landings in North Africa in November 1942. However, the real reason why the Canadians were involved in this shuffling of escort groups, and why they were now to switch their base of operations from St. John's, Newfoundland, to the eastern Atlantic, was the apparent alarming decline in the operational efficiency of the "C" groups, the Canadian formations in the MOEF, over the previous few months.[29]

In December 1942, after three years of war during which the RCN had experienced as much of the Atlantic battle as any service, a British suggestion that Canadian escorts be withdrawn from the most important theatre in the Atlantic was greeted by the Naval Staff as a breach of faith. They could blame overextended commitments in support of the USN and the RN for their difficulties in 1942. Problems had begun when the RCN committed unprepared escorts, recently commissioned from the first construction program, to the newly established Newfoundland Escort Force [NEF]. The Naval Staff's estimation of the size of the force that it could dispatch to St. John's quickly had been cautious. Nonetheless, the old axiom that any escort was better

The war meant partings for hundreds of thousands. Neither these soldiers leaving for overseas nor their friends and families had any idea when—or if—they would return. National Archives of Canada (NAC), PA 114801

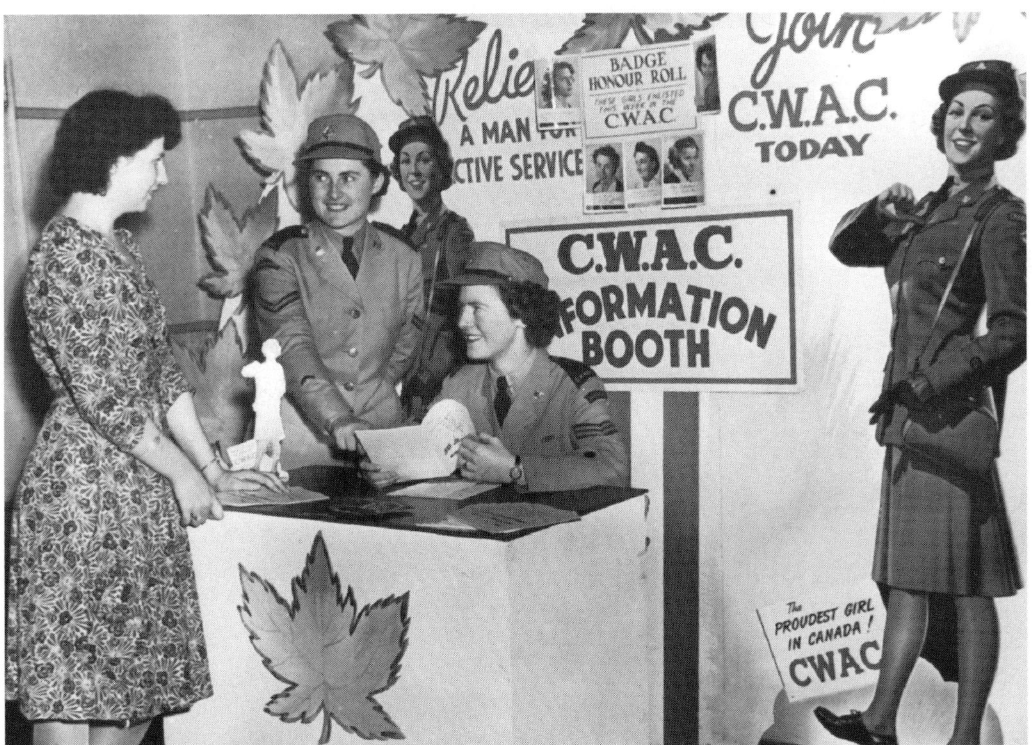

As manpower became scarce, the armed forces began to enlist women. The Canadian Women's Army Corps, here recruiting in Manitoba, enrolled more than 21 000 women, each of whom, as the poster said, relieved a man for active service. Provincial Archives of Manitoba, Canadian Army Photo Coll. 162, N10857

(left) The war at sea was vicious, with U-boats sinking everything that floated. In the cold North Atlantic, life could be limited to minutes, but these survivors from the SS *Eurymedon* were lucky that the destroyer HMCS *Ottawa* was nearby in September 1940. NAC, DND Navy N-239, PA 111512

(below) Men in combat often relied on good luck charms to keep them safe. This RCAF navigator drew comfort from his stuffed lion as one way to get through his "ops." Courtesy NAC

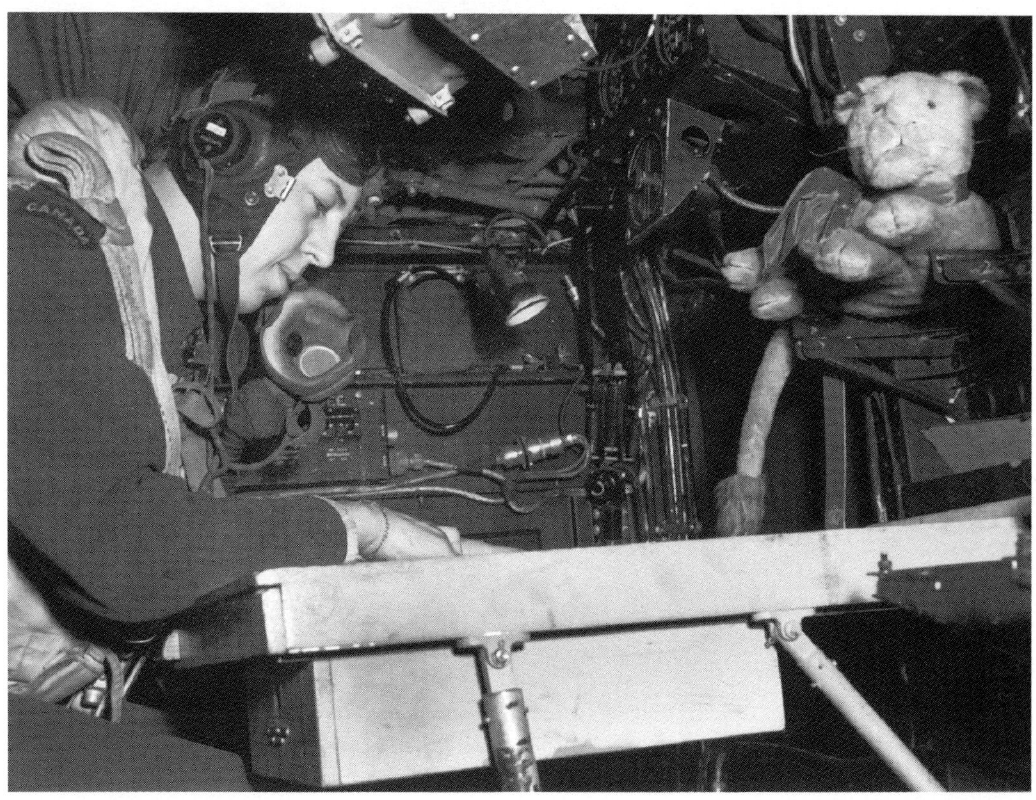

The Forestry Unit constituted one of Newfoundland's major contributions to the war effort. Here Britain's Deputy Prime Minister Clement Attlee (centre, wearing a Homburg and smoking a pipe) watches two loggers spar in their camp in Aberdeenshire, Scotland. Public Record Office, DO 35/745/N264/209

The Dieppe raid in August 1942 turned out to be a disaster for Canadians, with most of the attacking force killed, wounded, or captured. The Nazis carefully recorded the carnage to support their propaganda that Europe was unassailable. NAC, C-14160

Canadian dead were first buried where they fell. Only later were they gathered into the war cemeteries where they now lie. French civilians in 1944 care for the grave of a Canadian soldier. NAC, PA 107940

The RCN's corvettes were cramped and, on short and long voyages alike, fetid. Sailors slung hammocks wherever they could. In warm weather, that meant on deck. NAC, PA 13291

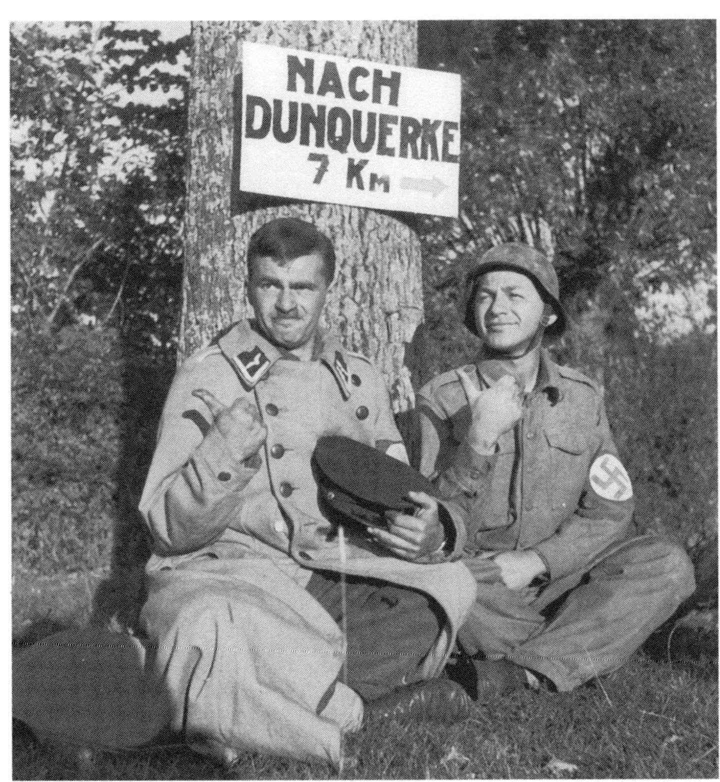

(left) Canadian troops wanted to be entertained by comedians from home. The not-yet-famous duo of Wayne and Shuster got their start in the Army and in France in 1944. NAC, PA 137316

(below) As had not been the case in the Great War, battle fatigue was recognized as a malady that could be treated. These doctors and nurses from the neuropsychiatric wing of a Canadian hospital at Bayeux, France, in August 1944 already had hundreds of patients. NAC, DND, PA 132842

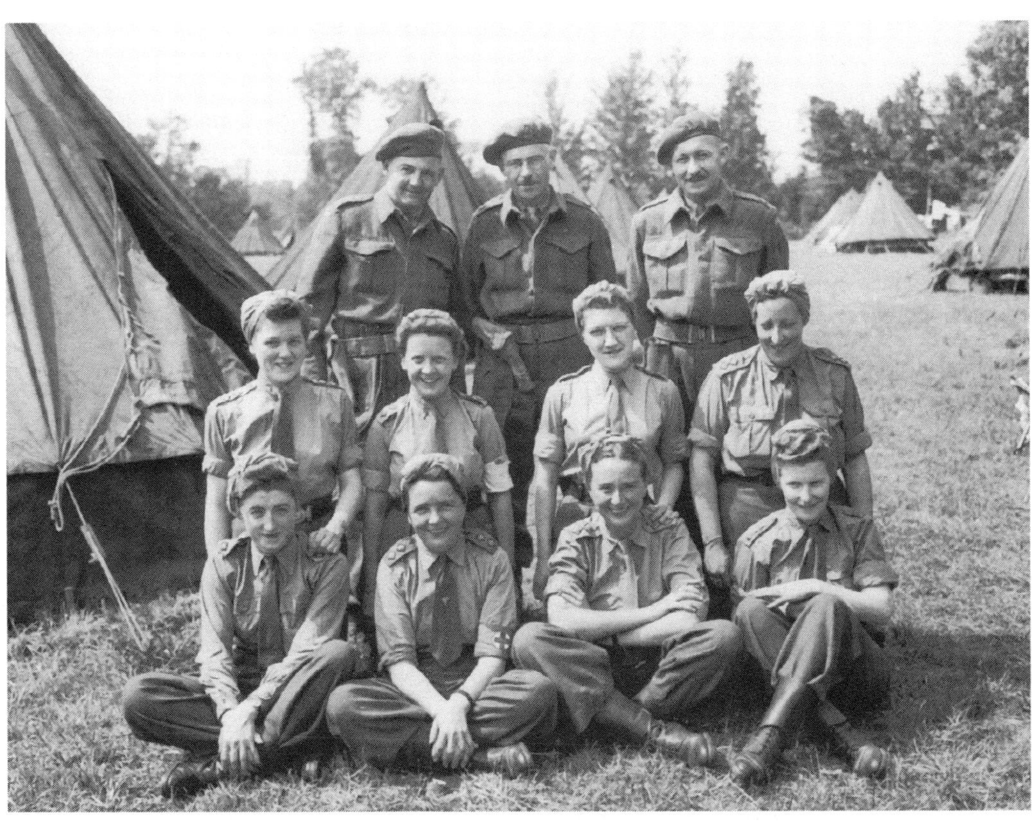

"The D-Day Dodgers," the I Canadian Corps serving with the Eighth Army in Italy, never received the recognition their efforts deserved. Here infantry cautiously proceed up an Italian street under fire. NAC, PA 114482

After VE-Day, there was time for tourism. Even though it, like Berlin itself, was largely destroyed, the Reichstag was a "must-see." NAC, DND Army 55852

than none prevailed. As one senior RCN officer wrote later, "they were only sent to sea in this condition on the urgent request of the Admiralty."[30] In any event, the NEF was intended to be simply an interim measure, designed to fill the Western Atlantic gap until the United States assumed such responsibilities.

The participation of the USN in the escort of fast convoys between Newfoundland and Iceland, which commenced in September 1941, lifted some of the burden from the NEF. Along with the continued influx of newly commissioned Canadian corvettes, this gave the NEF a measure of flexibility in terms of ship numbers which Commodore Murray, now flag officer Newfoundland Force, planned to channel into training programs in early December.[31] Unfortunately, his plans to make qualitative improvements to the Canadian escort forces came to naught. With the bombing of Pearl Harbor on 7 December 1941 and the hurried withdrawal of all but a token USN force, the RCN was left holding the proverbial bag, and Murray's plans evaporated before the increasing demands of operations.

Once RCN escorts were fully committed to operations, events passed beyond the control of the service, and mid-ocean operations became a severe impediment to orderly expansion. Not only did they rob the RCN of much-needed surplus escort time to make material improvements to the ships and upgrade the training of crews but also, aside from giving men sea experience, they denied it the opportunity to master techniques of antisubmarine warfare. The operational burden also caused the escort group system, upon which so much ultimately depended, to collapse. The British had learned, at some cost, that good teamwork, depending on the permanent group composition of escort groups, was the very basis of convoy defence. The lesson had not been lost on the RCN, and initially the NEF was organized into groups with this concern in mind. However, by December 1941, attempts to keep the same escorts together in distinctive groups had been abandoned by the NEF in the face of increasing operational demands.

The continued expansion of the war during 1942, and the extension of the convoy routes that this involved, reduced the leverage that the navy might have expected from its growing fleet. The Canadians were forced to expand operations nearer home, partly to provide escorts for shipping along the American coast which the Americans were incapable of protecting. As the year wore on, commitments grew. Canadian-based escorts operated as far south as New York, six corvettes were lent to the commander Eastern Sea Frontier, USN, and in August seventeen corvettes were made available at British request for support of the North African landings. All navies were hard-pressed during 1942, and it was only natural that the RCN should have done its utmost. However, it was the least able to absorb extended commitments and consequently suffered the greatest for its selflessness.

The effect of all this on "C" groups was devastating. Both the men and the ships of Canada's MOEF commitment were nearly exhausted by the autumn of 1942 (indeed the same can be said of the whole RCN escort fleet). Despite Admiral Murray's protests, group strength was reduced to meet the growing need elsewhere. Murray also complained that his groups were short in destroyer complements, while most of the destroyers he had were old and unreliable.[32] In addition, virtually all of the escorts in "C" groups, the RN escorts excepted, were seriously behind in the fitting of modern equipment.[33]

By November Murray's warning that heavy losses would befall convoys escorted by the much weakened "C" groups came true. Early in the month convoy SC 107, with C.4 as its escort, was severely mauled as it passed through the Greenland air gap beyond the protective range of Allied aircraft. Fifteen ships were lost in the worst RCN disaster since SC 42, fourteen months before. Moreover, it was another manifestation of the declining success rate being experienced by Canadian groups in the mid-ocean since the renewal of the German U-boat wolfpack campaign in July. The earlier battles in defence of convoys ON 113 and ON 115 went well. Losses were slight, and the enemy paid in each case with the loss of an attacker. The same could be said if SC 94 in August, when losses to the convoy were admittedly high, but two U-boats were destroyed in exchange. However, with the battle of SC 97 later in August, the RCN's ability to make the enemy pay for his successes came to an end. The tragedy of ON 127 in early September was a portent of things to come, and with the passage of SC 107 the pressure for change—or for help—was overwhelming.[34]

The British always suspected that the Canadians were long on energy and zeal but rather short on the finer points of ASW [anti-submarine warfare] and trade escort. The battle of SC 107 tended to confirm this point of view. So when the Chief of the Naval Staff, Vice-Admiral Percy W. Nelles, sought help from the RN through the "old boy" network in late November, the British were only too willing to give it—but on their terms.[35] By late 1942 the general situation in the North Atlantic was deteriorating rapidly. Mounting losses to shipping reduced imports into the United Kingdom at a time when Britain's reserves were being quickly eroded by the North African landings.[36] The war effort demanded that losses be cut, and, since quantitative improvements to the escort forces were out of the question, the one method available was to improve quality. Indeed, this had been one of the priorities of the new commander-in-chief Western Approaches, Admiral Sir Max Horton, upon assuming his command in mid-November.[37] Thus it happened that the Canadians were, by their own admission, in some difficulty at the very time the British took up a new resolve to settle the matter of the North Atlantic.

The British proposed to handle the Canadian request for help, and their own need to move oil convoys directly from the Caribbean, by a reorganization of the escort system. Four long-range RN escort groups on the United Kingdom–Gibraltar route were to be withdrawn to move oil convoys direct from the West Indies, and their place on the North African run was taken over by the four "C" groups currently operating with MOEF. British-based Canadian escorts would have a greater opportunity to use the fine training facilities available at numerous RN bases. The fairer weather of this route, and the easier cycle, would guarantee ample time during lay-overs for training to be done. Finally, the British assured the Canadians that the availability of continuous air cover would help offset the "inexperience" of the RCN groups. These proposals were transmitted to Ottawa on 17 December 1942.[38]

The British proposals were received with disbelief, a response which soon changed to anger and resentment. Not only was the RCN being asked to abandon its primary and most prestigious commitment, but the blame for the recent rash of disastrous convoy battles was laid squarely at its door. This was not the type of help the RCN had in mind, nor was it a continuation of the load-sharing which was characteristic of the Allied cause. The Naval Staff, doubtless irked by the Admiralty's allegation that the Canadian escorts were inexperienced, was not prepared to let the British proposals go unchallenged. An investigation undertaken into the reasons for recent Canadian shortcomings concluded that the poor state of equipment in RCN escorts was primarily to blame. Canadian escorts lacked sufficient modern equipment to make them "competitive" with their British counterparts. In addition, Canadian groups were chronically under strength, both in overall numbers and in the allocation of destroyers.[39] The RCN did not skirt the fact that it needed more and better training, but it argued that this alone could not account for past failings.[40] However, the installation of modern equipment, particularly on the scale required by the RCN, would take time, and there was precious little of that. Modernization of the fleet was a long term project, but what the British could offer in terms of immediate assistance they extended to the Canadians.

As the Naval Staff marshalled its case, events at sea took a turn which robbed it of all legitimacy. Between Christmas 1942 and the new year, convoy ONS 154, escorted by group C.1, sailed into infamy. While luck and poor routing had a direct effect on the outcome of the battle, the terrible handling of ONS 154's defence and the heavy losses which ensued left the RCN's challenge hopelessly undermined. The British proposals were accepted a few days after the beleaguered C.1 pulled alongside in St. John's. The four Canadian groups of the MOEF, C.1–C.4, were handed over to the British, reducing the command of the flag officer Newfoundland force (FONF) from an active strength of thirty-three escorts to two destroyers and nine corvettes, most of which were engaged in inshore duties.

It was several weeks before any of the "C" groups were actually transferred. In the meantime, steps were taken to ensure that the disasters associated with SC 107 or CON 154 were not repeated. First, there was an infusion of RN destroyers and frigates into "C" groups. These fast and powerful escorts were much needed, and the Naval Staff had been trying for some time to obtain a large number of them from the British for commissioning into the Royal Canadian Navy. The British, however, were reluctant to hand over any destroyer or frigate, assuming that they were available, because that would further dilute the RCN's limited cadre of experienced personnel.[41] Nevertheless, in the end, RN escorts were assigned to fill the gaps in the "C" groups. Infusion of British escorts brought with it a subtle, but significant, change in the command of the groups. Whereas it was accepted practice for the most senior officer present to assume command, and since in three out of four instances the RN ships carried officers of greater rank or seniority than the RCN ones present, command of the groups passed to the Royal Navy.[42] Thus, it may well be that the British lack of faith in the Canadians extended to RCN officers as well. Certainly, Admiral Horton, upon assuming his post in November, had declared that poor leadership had contributed to the losses in the autumn battles of 1942 and that resourceful leadership was to be one of the goals of his qualitative improvements.[43]

One final and equally important step was taken to lessen losses in Canadian-escorted convoys. It was the Canadian lot during 1942 to escort the bulk of the slow trade, an unfortunate continuation of a previously established pattern. However, in the first two months of 1943 "C" groups escorted as many HX convoys (the medium to fast convoys now originating out of New York) as they had the previous six. While it has been argued that this was a mere coincidence, the change suggests that care was being taken to provide "C" groups with a speedy passage through the Greenland air gap.[44]

It is not yet clear when the official transfer of the groups took place. The appearance of "C" groups under commander-in-chief Western Approaches in the 1 March 1943 edition of the Admiralty's *Pink List* suggests that this was the date of the transfer.[45] In practice, groups were turned over to Admiral Horton's command throughout January and February as they arrived in Londonderry. The first "C" group to be affected secured alongside at 'Derry on 22 January having escorted HX 222 safely across. Not surprisingly, it was C.1 of ONS 154 fame, composed of the destroyer HMCS *St. Croix* (recently assigned following refit), two British destroyers, HM Ships *Chesterfield* and *Vansittart*, which were attached for HX 222 only, and the Canadian corvettes *Battleford*, *Chilliwack*, *Kenogami*, *Napanee*, and *Shediac*. The destroyer *St. Laurent*, though still part of the group, had been diverted to Halifax with defects but later made an independent passage to the U.K. to rejoin.

Though for the next month or so the activities of individual escorts of C.1 varied considerably, the group set a pattern which the others would follow. The activities of the corvette *Kenogami*, for example, are indicative of the Canadians' experience.[46] Immediately upon arrival in

'Derry, a week's leave was granted to half the ship's company. Those remaining on board set about cleaning, scraping, painting, and doing minor repairs. *Kenogami* did not require dockyard work, but others did and were taken in hand as space allowed, with new equipment (notably modern radar and oerlikon guns) being added whenever possible. After the return of the liberty men, the crew spent the rest of the week finishing work already underway, and Sunday, 2 February, was observed as a day of rest. It was the last idle moment *Kenogami's* crew would enjoy for quite some time. Starting Monday they began a week of feverish training ashore. Depth-charge crews, lookouts, machine gun and 2-pounder crews, boarding parties, 4-inch gun crew, ASDIC and radar crews, and the bridge personnel were all exercised. Officers and men were trained alike, and every warlike function of the ship was put through its paces under the direction of RN instructors. As the week drew to a close, *Kenogami* prepared for sea. She slipped out on 11 February 1943 and proceeded to Moville, where she refuelled from the duty oiler. There she was joined by at least one member of C.1, the destroyer *St. Croix*. The following day the two escorts went to sea and conducted ASW, towing, and fleet manoeuvres in company, after which they returned to their berths alongside the duty oiler. In the early hours of 13 February, *Kenogami* and her consort, being in all respects ready for sea, slipped and shaped a course to the northeast. Gloom and doom forecasters aboard the Canadian ships doubtless took comfort in the fact that the thirteenth had fallen one day short of Friday. But any smugness they may have felt evaporated as the ships came to anchor under the watchful gaze of Commodore G.O. Stephenson, RN, the "Terror of Tobermory." Tobermory, this otherwise peaceful haven on the Isle of Mull, was the home of the RN's escort work-up base, HMS *Western Isles*. Its notorious commander spared neither man nor ship, and he made no exception for Canadians. Their stay in Stephenson's lair began with his customary visit to the ships, one which, no doubt, instilled a desire to do well. The first full day at Tobermory was spent ashore covering the same ground that had been covered in 'Derry. The rest of the time alternated between training ashore and at sea, in the latter case with a tame submarine. Group exercises were conducted (and as far as can be determined all of C.1 was present) under the supervision of RN training officers from the depot ship, or from the recently commissioned training ship HMS *Philante*. *Philante* eventually eliminated the need for sailing the other "C" groups to Scotland as similar exercises could be conducted off Lough Foyle. The training period invariably ended with a night firing exercise, followed in C.1's case by a night passage to Northern Ireland.

C.1 secured alongside at 'Derry on 21 February and began a one-week stay during which the crews attended yet more training exercises ashore while the ships were prepared for an extended period at sea. Finally, on 27 February the group sailed as escort to convoy KMS 10, bound for North Africa. The passage of this convoy was the most spectacular of the six such convoys escorted by "C" groups and provided C.1 with ample opportunity to put its recent training into practice. Though attacking U-boats managed to sink one ship and torpedo another, the escort accounted for U-87. It was the only wholly Royal Canadian Navy U-boat kill in the Atlantic during this phase of the war, and perhaps the newly acquired expertise and equipment were responsible.

In February two other "C" groups arrived in Londonderry to follow C.1's lead. Both of these, C.2 and C.4, spent roughly a month in and around 'Derry, training, repairing, painting, and fitting new equipment. C.4, made up of the British destroyer *Churchill*, carrying the senior officer of the escort, the Canadian destroyer *Restigouche*, the corvettes *Amherst*, *Brandon*, *Collingwood*, *Sherbrooke*, and the British *Celandine*, sailed on 1 March to escort KMS 10B. Two weeks later, C.2, comprising the British destroyer *Sherwood*, the British frigate *Lagan*, the British corvettes *Polyanthus* and *Primrose*, and the RCN corvettes *Drumheller* and *Morden*, departed with KMS 11.[47] Neither of these operations, or the return trips, were noteworthy.

The last group to arrive in Londonderry under the terms of the transfer was C.3: the British destroyer *Burnham*, the British frigate *Jed*, and the Canadian corvettes *Eyebright*, *La Malbaie*, *Bittersweet*, and *Mayflower*. This was the famous "Barber Pole" group, and of all the Canadian escort groups, its record was the best. Perhaps this is why its training period was much reduced from that given the others. C.3 remained out of action for only two weeks. It then returned to the North Atlantic, bolstered by the addition of three RCN corvettes returning from the North African landings, to escort ON 172—the only Canadian-escorted convoy in the mid-ocean during the crucial month of March 1943.

The break in the pattern which C.3 represents is not yet fully understood. Perhaps it was felt that the "Barber Pole" group could hold its own with the British groups provided it received some assistance. But this seems unlikely. More likely, C.3 was recalled to duty with the MOEF because the British were unable to maintain schedules with the reduced number of escort groups available to the MOEF, following the transfer. The Admiralty had hoped to manage the work of eleven groups with only nine by making them work a little harder.[48] It is conceivable that this proved to be too much. Indeed, it was the British who proposed at the Washington Conference in early March 1943 that the four "C" groups then doing coastal work be re-assigned to the MOEF, a suggestion which led to all the groups returning to duty with the MOEF by the end of the month.[49] However, the groups remained, for the time being, under commander-in-chief Western Approaches.

The situation in the mid-Atlantic by the end of March 1943 was not what it had been mere weeks before. The extension of land-based air cover from the U.K., Iceland, and later Newfoundland

and the deployment of escort support groups changed the character of the battle for all time. From then on, the close escort which for so long had fought against mounting odds could count on reinforcements in very considerable strength. Thus, as the "C" groups returned to the MOEF, the scene was greatly changed, and since only the slow convoys increased sailings in April (the reason given by the British for the needed return of the four groups), the cycle for the Canadians remained relatively slack, and the training program continued. The long weeks of intensive training were not repeated, but the lengthy layovers in 'Derry were used for training by HMS *Philante* and her officers.

Despite the fact that the Battle of the Atlantic was passing through its most important phase, the month of April was singularly unspectacular for the RCN. In large part this was a result of the cautious routing given Canadian-escorted convoys, a routing which kept them clear of the enemy.[50] Therefore, although very heavy losses were inflicted on the Germans over the next two months, few Royal Canadian Navy escorts gained sight of the enemy. Instead, the laurels went to British escort and support groups, aided by aircraft and excellent intelligence, which brought the mid-ocean campaign to an end. Only two Canadian-escorted convoys were remotely threatened in April: SC 127 and its escort C.1 were simply routed clear of danger, while HX 235, escorted by C.4, slipped unseen between two U-boat lines, screened from the nearest by a support group.[51]

With the increased sailings of fast convoys in May 1943, the tempo for the "C" groups returned to something nearer normal. However, though Canadians were now pulling their weight in the MOEF, they were merely the inner ring of a defence system which spanned the Atlantic. Nonetheless, it appears that May brought with it a renewed faith in the ability of Canadian escorts, since they were once again allowed to face the enemy. In the second week of May, C.2 with HMS *Biter*'s support group punched HX 237 through a U-boat line, the combined escort accounting for U-89. About a week later, HX 238, escorted by C.3, slipped gingerly through a pack sent to intercept it, while C.1 and the sixth support group safely escorted ON 184 through another concentration. The RCN was back in the fight, and by mid-month the "C" groups were all under RCN command, the terms of their transfer having expired.[52]

Thus, by the middle of May 1943, the RCN's effort in the Atlantic finally achieved the focus it had lacked for so long. Not only had the RCN's contribution to the MOEF been returned to Canadian command, but the reduction of support to the Allies—the return of the Operation Torch corvettes and those on loan to the UCN—gave the RCN the leverage with which it set about putting its own house in order. The Battle of the Atlantic had reached its climax and found the RCN wanting. There was no shame in that, for Canada's contribution to the Battle was crucial, nonetheless, and would not be forgotten by those who understood its significance. As Admiral Sir Percy Noble observed, "The Canadian Navy solved the problem of the Atlantic convoys."[53]

It is now clear why the Royal Canadian Navy played so small a part in the final mid-ocean battle and why it has not received mention commensurate with the scale of Canada's contribution. What is not clear is why there is no mention of the transfer or its impact on operations in early 1943 in either of the official histories. Even though, in the final analysis, the Canadian component of the MOEF was only absent from the force for a brief period, the transfer of twenty RCN escorts to a British command was an event of major significance, if for no other reason that that it reduced FONF's command to little more than care and maintenance of a few coastal vessels. Moreover, the circumstances surrounding the transfer and the consequent minor role of the navy in the final defeat of the U-boat campaign are crucial to the history of the RCN. One is left to wonder what happened to the transfer in the writing of the Canadian histories.

While the period from January to May 1943 is the accepted crisis of the Battle of the Atlantic, the crisis of Canada's Atlantic war occurred in the period immediately before. Not only were Canadian escorts heavily engaged at that time, but the whole focus of wartime expansion was shaken and redirected in the process. The tendency has been to heap the blame for all the ills of hurried growth on the Canadian Naval Staff and Naval Service Headquarters. However, the choices which faced naval planners in the early years of the war were never enviable. The war and its insatiable demands for men and materials robbed the RCN of its opportunity to make expansion work. Even the RN had problems with operational efficiency during 1942 and was quite surprised to find that its wartime fleet had not lived up to prewar expectations.[54] Operational necessity was a curse which had to be accommodated.

Aid to the British in 1941 and 1942, and to the Americans after Pearl Harbor, directly affected the operational efficiency of the RCN—a fact its critics would do well to remember. Further it is hardly surprising that Canadian historians have not focused on the defeat of the U-boats in May 1943. Whereas the British look upon the May victory as the crowning achievement of their naval war, for Canadians it was secondary to Canada's overall experience in the war. The crisis of 1943 was not an end in itself for the Royal Canadian Navy but merely one hurdle along the way to the final achievement of wartime competence.

Notes

1. See W.G.D. Lund, "The Royal Canadian Navy's Quest for Autonomy in the North West Atlantic: 1941–43," chap. 9 (138–57) of James A. Boutilier, ed., *The RCN in Retrospect, 1910–1968* (Vancouver: University of British Columbia Press, 1982). See also Gilbert N. Tucker, *The Naval Service of Canada: Its Official*

History, vol. 2, *Activities on Shore During the Second World War* (Ottawa: King's Printer, 1952), 405, where he credits the Commonwealth with having 98 percent of the escorts.

2. Tucker, *Naval Service of Canada*, and Joseph Schull, *The Far Distant Ships* (Ottawa: Queen's Printer, 1952).
3. Stephen W. Roskill, *The War at Sea*, 3 vols. (London: HMSO, 1960), 2 (appendix O): 485.
4. Tucker, *Naval Service of Canada*, 2: 457.
5. Ibid., 412.
6. Schull, *Far Distant Ships*, 161–76.
7. J. Marc Milner, "Canadian Escorts and the Mid-Atlantic 1942–1943" (M.A. thesis, University of New Brunswick, 1979), appendices 2 and 3, 172–74.
8. Donald Macintyre, *The Battle of the Atlantic* (London: B.T. Batsford, 1961); *The Naval War Against Hitler* (New York: Charles Scribner's Sons, 1974); and *U-Boat Killer* (London: Weidenfeld & Nicolson, 1956).
9. Macintyre, *U-Boat Killer*, 78–82.
10. W. Chalmers, *Max Horton and the Western Approaches* (London: Hodder and Stoughton, 1958), 157.
11. National Archives of Canada (NAC), RG 24, vol. 11, 595, MS 1-2-6. Report of proceedings, HMSC *Veteran*, SC 45, 17 Oct. 1941.
12. NAC, RG24, vol. 3892, NSS 1033-6-1. Commanding officer, HMSC *Chambly*, to captain (D[estroyers]) Newfoundland, 4 Nov. 1941.
13. Ibid., captain (D) Newfoundland to commodore commanding Newfoundland Force, 2 Sept. 1941.
14. Terry Hughes and John Costello, *The Battle of the Atlantic* (New York: Dial Press, 1977), 233.
15. Patrick Abbazia, *Mr. Roosevelt's Navy* (Annapolis, MD: United States Naval Institute Press, 1975), 262.
16. Roskill, *The War at Sea* and *White Ensign: The British Navy at War 1939–45* (Annapolis, MD: United States Naval Institute, 1960).
17. Samuel E. Morison, *History of United States Naval Operations in the Second World War*, 15 vols. (Boston: Little, Brown, 1947–62), 1: 12–13.
18. J.M. Waters, Jr., *Bloody Winter* (Princeton, NJ: Van Nostrand, 1967), 23–24.
19. See also Morison, *History of United States Naval Operations*, 1: 117. One of the reasons the eastern terminus of escorts operating from Newfoundland was switched to Londonderry was that the USN wanted access to proper training facilities.
20. Abbazia, *Mr. Roosevelt's Navy*, 426.
21. Alan Easton, *50 North* (Toronto: Ryerson, 1963). Easton's book contains perhaps the best appreciation of Canada's corvette fleet in the fall of 1941. See especially page 49.
22. James B. Lamb, *The Corvette Navy* (Toronto: Macmillan, 1979), 134–35.
23. Directorate of History (DOH), National Defence Headquarters (NDHQ), NS1033-7-2. J.O. Cossette, naval secretary to the commanding officer Atlantic Coast, commanding officer Pacific Coast, commodore commanding Newfoundland Force, and other senior RCN commands, statement on "Training and Manning Policy," 24 Dec. 1941.
24. Tucker, *Naval Service of Canada*, 2: 457.
25. Ibid., 2: 436–67.
26. C.P. Stacey, *Arms, Men and Governments* (Ottawa: Department of National Defence, 1970), 315–19.
27. W.A.B. Douglas and B. Greenhous, *Out of the Shadows* (Toronto: Oxford University Press, 1977), 59–70.
28. NAC, RG2, 7-C, C-4875, Minutes of the Cabinet War Committee, 7 Jan. 1943.
29. In the autumn of 1942 the MOEF comprised eleven escort groups: six British, B.1, B.2, B.3, B.4, B.6, and B.7; four Canadian, C.1, C.2, C.3, C.4; and one

American, A.3. The designations indicated the nationality of the groups, but in practice the groups were seldom composed of escorts from a single service. The corvettes of B.6, for example, were Norwegian, while the four "C" groups contained within their number one wholly British escort group. The lone American group contained only a token American force of destroyers or cutters, the bulk of its numbers being made up of RCN or RN corvettes.

30. DOH, NSH 1000-973, H.G. DeWolf, director of Plans, to the Chief of the Naval Staff (CNS), 29 Dec. 1942.

31. The new commissions included the corvettes that would play prominent roles in the 1942 battles, such as HMC Ships *Amherst* and *Battleford*. By early December 1941, 44 of the 57 corvettes, and 10 of the 12 RCN destroyers then in commission were assigned to the NEF — 78 percent of the RCN's ocean-going escort forces. See Milner, "Canadian Escorts and the Mid-Atlantic," 39.

32. NAC, RG24, vol. 11, 929 MS-00220-3-6, "it is essential that groups sail from St. John's at full strength if we are to avoid [a] repetition of SC 42 losses." Flag officer Newfoundland Force to Naval Service Headquarters (NSHQ), 30 May 1942.

33. Milner, "Canadian Escorts and the Mid-Atlantic," 73–93.

34. Ibid., chap. 3.

35. Nelles wrote to Vice-Admiral E.L.S. King, RN, an old friend who was just stepping down as assistant CNS (Trade). King's reply can be found in DOH, NS 8440.

36. See C.B. Behrens, *Merchant Shipping and the Demands of War* (London: HMSO, 1955), chap. 14, "The Effects of the North African Campaign and the Beginnings of the World Shipping Crisis."

37. Chalmers, *Max Horton and the Western Approaches*, 162–63.

38. Public Record Office (PRO), London, PREM 3, 331/8, A.V. Alexander to W.S. Churchill, 15 Dec. 1942.

39. In fact, destroyers were crucial to the defence of a convoy, and the RCN was in such need of these ships that Prime Minister W.L. Mackenzie King sent a personal plea to Winston Churchill in early December 1942, asking that fourteen be made available to the Canadian Navy.

40. For an account of this affair see Milner, "Canadian Escorts and the Mid-Atlantic," 107–24. The various memos that formed the RCN's case were submitted to the CNS in late December 1942, and can be found in the following DOH files: M-11, NS 8780, NS 8440-60.

41. Milner, "Canadian Escorts and the Mid-Atlantic," appendix 15. The relationship between the British position on the apparent poor showing of the RCN and the request for destroyers emerges in a letter from an official in the British prime minister's office to an Admiralty colleague. The former, who was engaged in drafting an interim reply to Mackenzie King's request, wrote: "we feel it would be difficult to send an interim reply without the risk of prejudicing the Canadian reply on the tanker escorts or explaining the relation of the two questions." Boyd-Shannon to Chapman, 22 Dec. 1942. PRO, Adm. 1, 12564.

42. The fact that Canadian groups had fallen under the command of RN officers became a bone of contention between the two navies, for Naval Service Headquarters clearly wanted "C" groups operating with RCN commanding officers. See commander-in-chief Western Approaches to NSHQ, 29 March 1943. NAC, RG24, vol. 3995, NSS 1057-1-27.

43. Chalmers, *Max Horton and the Western Approaches*, 163.

44. Milner, "Canadian Escorts and the Mid-Atlantic," appendix 15.
45. PRO Adm. 187, vol. 24, Admiralty *Pink List*, 1 March 1943.
46. This section is based on a study of all the available deck logs of HMC ships in the "C" groups, NAC, NS 7000-7999, the Admiralty's *Pink Lists*, PRO, Adm. 187, vols. 23–25, and the RCN "Daily States," DOH, NS 1650-DS.
47. Milner, "Canadian Escorts and the Mid-Atlantic," appendix 15.
48. DOH, M-11, H.G. DeWolf, to CNS, 21 Dec. 1942.
49. Tucker, *Naval Service of Canada*, 2: 412.
50. Milner, "Canadian Escorts and the Mid-Atlantic," 143.
51. J. Rohwer and G. Hümmelchen, *Chronology of the War at Sea, 1939–1945* (New York: Arco, 1972), 319–20.
52. DOH, NS 8440-60, Nelles to First Sea Lord, 7 Jan. 1943. Under the terms of the agreement the "C" groups were to remain under the commander-in-chief Western Approaches until they were deemed operationally efficient, or in any event no later than mid-May 1943.
53. Schull, *Far Distant Ships*, 122.
54. PRO, Adm. 1, 12062. The director antisubmarine warfare, RN, conceded in his "Battle of the Atlantic Summary" of May 1942: "what was not sufficiently foreseen was the enormous expansion of our A/S effort that [the] war would demand and what a decrease in killing efficiency this would entail as a result of the inevitable decrease in initial training and the curtailing of A/S practices caused by operational requirements." The British had just come through a period when their own training programs had been greatly reduced in order to man new construction quickly, and they were obviously dissatisfied with the poor level of competence of hurriedly trained crews—the price of expansion. A further indication of their stretched resources at this time is the recall, without replacement, of the RN anti-submarine warfare liaison officers at St. John's and Halifax in July. See naval historian's notes, DOH, NS 1700-193/96.

The Canadian government's decision to send two battalions of infantry and a brigade headquarters to Hong Kong in the fall of 1941 did not seem difficult when it was taken. But the fall of the Crown Colony to Japan on Christmas Day 1941, the deaths of many Canadians in action, and the brutal captivity endured by the rest made it a contentious issue ever after. This account, based on Canadian, British, and Japanese sources, briefly treats the political and military events.

The Hong Kong Disaster

Patricia E. Roy, J.L. Granatstein, Masako Iino, Hiroko Takamura

The British chiefs of staff in August 1940 had declared the Crown Colony of Hong Kong to be virtually indefensible, and they had recognized that the colony and its defenders could be neither reinforced nor relieved in the event of war with Japan. "Hong Kong," they said in a memorandum that was sent to the Canadian chiefs of staff, "is not vital and the garrison could not long withstand Japanese attack.... In the event of war, therefore, Hong Kong must be regarded as an outpost and held as long as possible." Militarily, the appreciation concluded in the unsparing style ordinarily favoured in such documents, "our position in the Far East would be stronger without this unsatisfactory commitment."[1] A few months later, the governor of the Crown Colony actually recommended removing the garrison entirely "in order to avoid the slaughter of civilians and the destruction of property which would follow a Japanese attack,"[2] but London turned down that sensible advice. Nevertheless, Churchill also rejected insistent requests from the British high command in the Far East to increase the size of the garrison, explaining early in 1941 that "If Japan goes to war with us there is not the slightest chance of holding Hong Kong or relieving it. It is most unwise to increase the loss we shall suffer there."[3] Churchill added that "we must avoid frittering away our resources on untenable positions."[4]

But the sound judgments of the chiefs and Churchill were eventually overridden, in part because the retiring British commander of troops in China, the Canadian-born Major-General A.E. Grasett, passed through Canada on his way home in August 1941. Grasett thought the Crown Colony could be defended against the Japanese army, which he, like so many British and American officers, considered to be inferior in training, equipment, and leadership to white or white-led forces. "They fought well against third-rate Chinese," Grasett argued, "but they had yet to meet first class troops such as his battalions, which would give them a bloody nose." Moreover, Grasett was convinced that Japan was bluffing and believed the bluff should be called.[5] In discussions with General H.D.G. Crerar, the chief of the Canadian general staff, Grasett had argued that "the addition of two or more battalions to the forces then at Hong Kong would render the garrison strong enough to withstand for an extensive period of siege an attack by such forces as the Japanese could bring to bear against it." When he returned to London, Grasett suggested that Canada could supply those battalions, and the British chiefs of staff, apparently now convinced, reversed their position and recommended that Churchill approach the Canadian government. "A small reinforcement of one or two battalions would increase the strength of the garrison out of all proportion to the actual numbers involved," the chiefs now argued. It would "have a very great moral effect in the whole of the Far East."

The British prime minister duly changed course and, accepting the advice of his military staff, asked Ottawa for one or two battalions. "There have been signs of a certain weakening in attitude of Japan towards United States and ourselves," the Dominions Office telegram to Canada of 19 September said.[6]

In Ottawa, London's request came before the Cabinet War Committee on 23 September and was deferred pending the advice of the army. General Crerar indicated the next day that it was possible to provide two battalions "without reducing the strength of our Coast Defence garrisons and without further mobilization." By 27 September Ottawa had made the fateful decision, and two days later London was so advised.

As C.P. Stacey, the official historian of the Canadian army in the Second World War, has noted . . . , in 1941 Canada had no intelligence organization, either military or civilian, capable of making an adequate assessment of the situation in the Far East: "Essentially, Ottawa depended upon London for such information. Nor was any military appreciation requested of or prepared by the Canadian General Staff as to the situation of Hong Kong in the event of war with Japan."[7] The decision to send troops to Hong Kong, therefore, was made in ignorance, and the history of the army's intelligence operations notes that the Canadian troops

"were not provided, as they should have been, with adequate, accurate information on their opponent."[8] Had the information to prepare a proper military appreciation been available, and had it followed the line of the British paper of August 1940, the government might have held back.

But in the political circumstances of the day in Canada, with opposition critics and important newspapers across English Canada charging that recruits for the armed forces were lacking and that conscription was necessary if Canada was to fight a "total war," rejecting a direct British request for troops could have been enormously damaging if word of it leaked out. The government of Mackenzie King was caught between a rock and a hard place and the Hong Kong decision, in the circumstances, was inevitable.

By the end of September, Crerar had decided which units to send. He wanted "efficient, well-trained battalions capable of upholding the credit of the Dominion in any circumstances," and he recommended the Royal Rifles,[9] a unit recruited from the Quebec City area, and the Winnipeg Grenadiers, an infantry battalion whose members came from the Manitoba capital and its surrounding area. Both battalions had spent their war service on garrison duty, one in Newfoundland and the other in Jamaica, and Crerar believed that "The duties which they carried out there were not in many respects unlike the task which awaits the units to be sent to Hong Kong." That was a gross misjudgment. As Crerar later told a royal commission set up to investigate the Hong Kong disaster, "Information at my disposal during the latter part of September 1941 indicated that the outbreak of hostilities with Japan was not imminent and that time would, in all probability, be available to carry out adequate and possibly extensive training of Canadian forces at Hong Kong after their arrival."[10]

The government compounded its mistake on 11 October when London asked that the Canadian commitment be expanded to include a brigade headquarters and various specialists. Ottawa agreed, and Crerar recommended that Colonel J.K. Lawson, an experienced Permanent Force officer should be given the command with the rank of brigadier.

The two battalions in fact were not quite the "well-trained" units that General Crerar had claimed—and likely believed. Their experience with their weapons was scanty, shortages of arms and ammunition had hampered their work on the rifle ranges, their field training was limited, and the Winnipeg battalion in particular had taken fifteen new officers and a substantial number of men on strength just before embarking. "The two battalions" Stacey noted, "had clearly not reached that advanced state of training which one would wish troops to attain before being sent against the enemy." Moreover, the battalions had no preparation for service in semi-tropical Hong Kong. Presumably the assumption was that the battalions would have time

in Hong Kong to become accustomed to the climate.

Nonetheless, on 27 October the battalions and the brigade headquarters boarded the *Awatea*, a British transport, and the HMCS *Prince Robert*, an armed merchant cruiser, and sailed that night. In all, ninety-six officers and 1877 men left Canada for Hong Kong. Unfortunately, none of the 212 vehicles that were to accompany the force was loaded on the *Awatea*, although there was space available for some twenty vehicles. The motor transport was put aboard an American ship on 4 November, which sailed by way of Honolulu and Manila, and did not reach the Philippine capital until 12 December, after war had begun. The Canadian vehicles were turned over to the American forces that were vainly attempting to defend the Philippines.

The Hong Kong force reached the Crown Colony on 16 November. The Canadian troops marched through the streets to their quarters at Sham Shui Po camp. The officers soon attended a briefing on the Japanese army and were told that there were only 5000 troops in the vicinity, ill-equipped, with little artillery, unused to night fighting, and supported by obsolete aircraft flown by myopic pilots incapable of dive-bombing attacks.[11] Some of the private soldiers had sounder instincts. "The minute I got off the boat in Hong Kong," one Canadian soldier recalled with a clarity that was certainly sharpened by hindsight, "I realized that if the Japanese attacked they'd wipe us out. 'We've got no air force, no navy, no place to go,' I told my pals. . . . My pals laughed. 'We won't have to worry, Wilf. It's them that will be running away.'"[12]

The Japanese army was not to run away from Hong Kong. Indeed, the Crown Colony was viewed by the Imperial Headquarters as a festering sore, the major route through which Chiang Kai-shek's Nationalist armies received the war supplies that permitted them to continue their resistance.[13] Estimates were that war *matériel* shipped through Hong Kong amounted to as much as 6000 tons a month. Chiang's government openly maintained offices in the British colony, and there was weekly air service to Chungking, the Nationalist capital.[14] The British colony was thus a natural focus of Japanese attention.

As early as the end of 1939, therefore, Imperial Headquarters in Tokyo and the staffs of the army in China began secret efforts to stir up anti-British plots among Chinese in Hong Kong. Simultaneously, a Chinese volunteer force was formed in Canton, ready to intervene in the event that anti-British riots broke out in the colony.[15] In fact, there was divided counsel on how to proceed to take Hong Kong. Some military officers insisted on using the pretext of anti-British riots as an excuse for intervention; others preferred an attack by Imperial forces, arguing that such an attack would not result in a general war with Britain.[16] Caution

won out, however, and in July 1940 Imperial Headquarters decided that Hong Kong should be seized only in the context of a general war with Britain.[17]

Orders to prepare for the attack on the Crown Colony came on 6 November 1941. The intention, to strike at the same time as Japanese forces fell upon British Malaya, was to launch an assault on Hong Kong Island immediately after the New Territories and Kowloon were seized. On that basis, the army and navy completed their planning on 30 November.[18] The plan called for air strikes on the Royal Air Force's base and an attack on the Gin Drinkers' Line, the mainland defences of Kowloon. The air force, while not bombing indiscriminately and attempting to preserve bridges and wharves to permit their later use, would strike every identifiable military position on the island. Artillery was to be positioned on the Kowloon shore, immediately it was taken, in order to soften up British defences. At the same time, efforts to stir up revolt among Chinese and Indians—and to encourage the assassination of British officials and officers—were stepped up.

Japanese intelligence on British preparations was effective. The Japanese army had learned that the British now intended to defend the colony vigorously, a reversal of the earlier policy. Estimates of the troops available to the British commander were 3000–4000 British soldiers, 3000–4000 Indian soldiers, and 1000 Chinese. In addition, one intelligence report noted, "Canadian troops had arrived in the middle of November. Their strength is 1000–2000, and these men are not excellent in character."[19]

The two Canadian infantry battalions and a brigade headquarters had indeed arrived in Hong Kong on 16 November 1941. "We climbed mountains all day long," one private of the Royal Rifles of Canada had written in his diary on 21 November, "and we are shown the many posts for which soon we shall be fighting for our own lives."[20] The men barely had time to accustom themselves to the subtropical climate before Japan's powerful armies fell upon the Crown Colony at 3:40 a.m. on 8 December 1941 Hong Kong time. The Crown Colony's garrison had no air cover (the five obsolete aircraft flown by the Royal Air Force were destroyed on the first day of fighting exactly as the Japanese attackers had planned), insufficient artillery, mortars, and ammunition, and far too few trucks. Soon there were shortages of food, water, and medicine.

The British planners who had considered the defences of Hong Kong had persuaded themselves that the Japanese army would easily be handled by good white or white-led troops. They also believed the stereotypical view that Japanese soldiers had difficulty operating at night, something almost instantly disproven when the Gin Drinkers' Line, ill-planned and scarcely completed, was largely overrun with ease. The steep hills of the New Territories, now an extraordinary forest of high-rise buildings stretch-

ing from Kowloon almost to the border with China but then only lightly populated, the indented bays, and the limited number of roads that channeled any attacking force should have enabled a commander of even limited competence to mount time-consuming blocking operations before the main defensive works were reached. But, secure in their prejudices, the British had done little and their mainland defences fell quickly. The attackers never forfeited the moral ascendency gained by this first victory, and the morale of the defenders and of the European and Chinese population of Hong Kong could not recover.

Curiously, the Japanese army had expected the colony to surrender after the debacle on the mainland, and there was some surprise at the governor's refusal to order arms to be laid down.[21] Forced to continue the battle, the Japanese army launched its amphibious assault on Hong Kong island on 18 December, rapidly establishing itself ashore in force with the aid of Chinese fifth columnists and local Japanese, who cut the wire entanglements on the beaches, sabotaged vehicles, and sniped at the defenders.[22] The Canadian battalions, dispersed and often under British command that was not always competent, soon found themselves engaged in hand-to-hand combat against heavy odds. "The officers of the new Brigade Staff," the war diary of the Royal Rifles recorded on 11 December, even before the Japanese had launched their assault on Hong Kong Island, "were in a highly nervous state and apparently very tired."[23] "The whole thing was disorganized confusion," a private of the Winnipeg Grenadiers recalled. "Nobody was prepared for it. There was no communication. We didn't have transportation. You carried everything on your back."[24] For a week, the Canadian troops took part in a succession of hopeless counter-attacks against superior forces and grim defensive actions against well-equipped and heavily supported Japanese units. On 19 December Brigadier Lawson, the Canadians' commander, was killed when his brigade headquarters defending the critical Wong Nei Chong gap in the centre of the island was overrun. Lawson had told General Maltby, the island's commander, that he was "going outside to fight it out" with a pistol in each hand. The Canadians had resisted fiercely, one Japanese account noting that "a narrow path was soon filled with a line of Japanese casualties." In all, about 600 Japanese soldiers were killed or wounded in this three-day assault on the Canadian position.[25] A Japanese colonel later said that "We wrapped up [Lawson's] body in the blanket of Lt. Okada, OC No. 9 Company, which had captured the position. I ordered the temporary burial of the officer on the battleground on which he had died so heroically."[26]

That was almost the only chivalry shown by the Japanese. When the defenders, their position completely hopeless and with no prospect of either evacuation or reinforcement, surrendered on Christmas Day, the Japanese reported the capture of 1689 Canadians, 5072 British, 3829 Indians, and 189 Chinese soldiers. Japanese casualties in all were 2096, including 683 dead.[27] Perhaps that higher than anticipated toll was responsible for the orgy of rape and brutality that preceded and followed the capitulation.

One Canadian nursing sister wrote that just before the surrender the "Japanese took the hospital," St Stephen's College at Stanley. "The two M[edical] O[fficer]s tried to stop them from entering the hospital by showing them the Red Cross and telling them there were only wounded there, but it didn't do any good. They were both killed. . . . The Japanese troops went wild—bayonetted patients in their beds. [Nursing] Sisters and 4 [female volunteer aides] were raped and then they killed three of the [volunteers].[28] Forty male captives, patients and orderlies, were locked in a storeroom at the hospital. Every half hour Japanese troops took two or three at random and killed them. Four Royal Rifles soldiers were then taken out. "The Japanese," one account of the day said, "made the four stand by while soldiers cut out one man's tongue and chopped off another man's ears." "Go to Fort Stanley and tell your officers what you have seen," the Japanese commander told the four. 'Hong Kong must surrender or else all prisoners will be killed in this manner.'"[29] The chaplain of the Royal Rifles, Captain James Barnett, was also held in this storeroom. After the war he testified before the Tokyo War Crimes trials about his experiences there, about the killing of "fifteen to twenty wounded men" in their hospital beds and the rape of nurses at the hospital.[30] At another hospital, however, or so one Hong Kong escapee reported, "the kindest and most considerate treatment was accorded by the Japanese Commander who did everything in his power to be friendly and courteous." The difference in treatment, he added, "depended entirely upon the character of the Commanding Officers in charge,"[31] something that held true for virtually all prisoners of war and civilian internees in the Far East.

Moreover, Japan had not ratified the 1929 Geneva Convention on the treatment of prisoners of war; the army and navy had opposed it, arguing that favourable treatment for POWs would weaken military discipline. Nonetheless, once Japan was advised that Britain, Canada, and other dominions intended to apply the Geneva rules to Japanese prisoners, Tokyo stated that it too would observe its provisions for both civil and military prisoners.[32] Unfortunately, the Japanese army did not formally recognize a soldier as a prisoner of war until he had reached a POW camp. In other words, as the chief delegate of the International Red Cross in the Far East noted, "From the time a man was captured to the time when he entered a *formal* prisoner of war camp there were no regulations regarding his treatment, and before 1943 there were no regulations for formal camps."[33] One Japanese academic, Junpei Shinobu, writing in 1942, observed that a "POW is not a guest," and that POWs were not entitled to favourable treatment, although the provisions of the Geneva Convention must be respected. Shinobu added that military operations could make it necessary to abandon humanitarian treatment—if, for example, there was no way to feed or intern prisoners and it was dangerous to free them, then "under the rules of belligerency it could be justifiable to kill them. . . . Favourable treatment in such a case would not be of benefit but of harm" to Japan.[34] Moreover, as the Japanese wartime prime minister, General Hideki Tojo, stated at his war crimes trial, "It is the Japanese custom for the commander of an expeditionary army in the field to be given a mission in the performance of which he is not subject to specific orders from Tokyo, but has considerable autonomy. This can mean that under the Japanese method of warfare such atrocities were expected to occur, or were at least permitted, and that the Government was not concerned to prevent them."[35] Japanese soldiers had been trained to believe that capture was worse than death—"Never live in shame as an imprisoned captive," their orders went—and they took a dark view of white soldiers who surrendered when a position could no longer be held. General Yamashita, one of the Imperial army's most successful commanders, expressed just this view when he inspected British POWs in Singapore. "Serves you right," he said. "I wish to send them to Japan to work in the coal mines, but it would waste shipping space."[36] Prisoners of war, in other words, were at the mercy of their captors.

Not only soldiers but Japanese civilians also sometimes believed that capture was shameful. One 1942 magazine article argued that the Geneva Convention "provided too favourable treatment for POWs" and to abide by it would "spoil our captives." The provisions on food and tobacco, for example, "made no difference between prisoners of war and guests." In the west, the article noted, "nothing was more honourable than capture for soldiers who had fought their utmost." That was not true in Japan: "we have been taught since childhood that we should choose to kill ourselves by biting off our own tongue rather than to be captured."[37] The Japanese newspapers added that white POWs lacked patriotism and had low morale. *Tokyo Asahi* reported that prisoners worried about their wives and children, not the fates of their own countries, and one report jeered at the words of an American POW who had asked, "When can I go home? I was reluctantly drafted into the army. My girl friend is waiting for me."[38] Japan's warrior code of *bushido* viewed such considerations as those of weaklings, not soldiers.

In such circumstances, mercy was often in short supply. A corporal of the Royal Rifles remembered being marched away after the surrender. "We went by different groups of our fellas that had been bayonetted. They were tied up in groups of six to ten and butchered."[39] A private in the Grenadiers remembered that "they were pretty rough on us. They tied our hands together with barbed wire. A lot of the boys that fell and couldn't walk because they were wounded so badly, they were cut loose and bayonetted right there. They didn't believe in taking too many prisoners," he said.[40] That seemed to be so, for Captain Barnett testified at the war crimes trials that Lieutenant Honda, the camp commandant of North Point Camp, said that "his orders were all prisoners must die."[41]

Fortunately, that order must have been countermanded. The atrocities against prisoners were horrific, but not universal. Most Canadian and British soldiers who surrendered were not physically abused, though tales of the killings at the hospital and the abuses witnessed by many of the captured terrified all the survivors. One American assessment later was that most atrocities against captured soldiers came in the first months of war "when the Japanese were drunk with triumph and thought that they had virtually won the war already."[42]

The last message from Hong Kong to reach Canada arrived in Ottawa after the surrender: "Situation critical. Canadian troops part prisoners residue engaged casualties heavy. . . . Troops have done magnificent work spirit excellent." It was all true, especially the reference to the heavy casualties. The Canadians had suffered severely in the fighting—twenty-three officers and 267 other ranks killed, twenty-eight officers and 465 other ranks wounded, a high percentage of the 1973 Canadians at Hong Kong. The brief battle was over; the long captivity was to begin.

The Canadian prisoners of war were initially held in temporary camps with others captured at Hong Kong. In late January 1942 the Japanese concentrated all the Canadian captives at North Point Camp and shifted British prisoners to Shamshuipo camp. The Canadians' camp had been built by the Hong Kong government in 1939 to house Chinese refugees. During the fighting, it had been seriously damaged, and later the Japanese army had stabled horses there. As a result, insects, lice, and flies abounded in the huge piles of manure and garbage just outside the wire.[43]

The International Red Cross visited North Point on 3 July 1942 and reported that the accommodation was crowded, especially the hospital. But the men were said to look well. "Have own bakery and well-equipped Dental Clinic. . . . Commanding Officer states that they are being well treated and that they could not complain about the food."[44]

In fact, that report was either incorrect or made while the Red Cross delegate was wearing rose-coloured spectacles. Rations were in appallingly short supply and the accommodations provided the POWs were completely inadequate, particularly in the first four months after the capture of Hong Kong. Even the Japanese admitted this.[45] During the first months of captivity, the daily food intake was less than 900 calories per soldier, totally insufficient for men averaging 170 pounds. From July to November 1942 a reduction in rations as collective punishment for an escape attempt led to semi-starvation. By the end of the war 195 Canadian POWs had died in the Hong Kong camp.[46] One report from the Canadian minister in China to Ottawa, received in July 1943 through "most secret underground channels" from Lt.-Col. J.H. Price, the commanding officer of the Royal Rifles and the senior Canadian officer surviving, noted that the men were in poor shape. But Price added, "Since last December health of men has improved due to Red Cross food which is sufficient to prevent further deterioration but not to build up. Present supplies will last to September when return to purely Japanese diet will probably cause increase of disease and death."[47] A U.S. Joint Chiefs of Staff paper a few months later noted that conditions in POW camps "could scarcely be much worse and unless conditions are improved, few American prisoners will survive."[48]

A detailed interrogation of a New Zealand naval officer who had escaped from captivity in Hong Kong in July 1944 provided more information in terms of the caloric intake prisoners received. British camp doctors had prepared a report for the Japanese camp commandants in an effort to get increased rations, and the escapee provided details. The medical officers had argued that, in October 1942, POWs received 2338 calories a day and, in November 1942, 2395, figures that seem improbably high against later estimates of 900 calories per day.[49] If those figures were correct, it is difficult to account for the diary kept by Rifleman D.L.W. Welsh of the Royal Rifles, a diary devoted entirely to food:

> April 1, 1942. Breakfast—Had rice, syrup, one bun and black tea. Dinner—Had rice patties, bread and cold water. Supper—Had rice, Chinese sauce, bread and black tea.
>
> May 1, 1942. Breakfast—Had rice, brown sugar, one bun and black tea. Dinner—Had two buns and black tea. Supper—Had rice, one egg plant and cold water.

Welsh's diary continued in this vein until 5 October 1942, when he died.[50] If those were the good conditions and the high caloric intake, a year later conditions had worsened and food value had fallen to 2032 calories a day in October 1943 and 1869 a day in November, or so calculations had it.[51]

Operating with different attitudes to standards of diet, hygiene, and the treatment of their own soldiers, the Japanese military was not impressed by complaints about the treatment and status of POWs. The POWs and their governments at home seemed to expect that the Japanese would recognize that whites were "different" and entitled to better treatment and food than the Japanese military provided for its own troops. That was not forthcoming, nor could it have been expected. What might have been provided, however, what ought to have been provided, was enough food to prevent starvation and enough medicine to allow the effective treatment of the sick. The Japanese army failed to meet this standard, something to which prisoners of war were entitled under the Geneva Convention.

In the circumstances, with food so scarce and so deficient in vitamins, the health of the Canadian POWs rapidly deteriorated. As a result, medicines were in critically short supply. Other than the stocks held in the Bowen Road hospital and the small amounts saved from the infantry battalions' stocks, there were almost none. Within weeks of the capture of Hong Kong dysentery swept the POW camps and men died, including the commanding officer of the Winnipeg Grenadiers. Beriberi, pellagra, parasitic infections, and diphtheria also developed quickly, the latter reaching epidemic proportions and killing fifty men in early 1942. Only a small quantity of anti-diphtheria serum was available on the black market and the Japanese provided little more.[52]

So grim was the medical situation by mid-1943 that secret reports received in London estimated that only 40 percent of the Canadians were now "fit for fatigues." Even that dreadful state of affairs was stated to be an improvement over the situation six months before.[53]

Since the Japanese made POWs work, the health of the prisoners ought to have concerned them. But since the POWs were supposed to be paid for their work in accordance with the Geneva Convention, it may be that money was being siphoned off. According to the Japanese army's pay regulation for POWs, the Japanese were to pay commissioned officer POWs a salary equivalent to that paid Japanese officers of equal rank, while not paying POWs of other ranks; after paying for their own food, the officers contributed most of the remainder of this money to a fund to buy food and medicines, often on the black market, for their men. Fit men who were put to work by the Japanese, initially on extending the runways at Hong Kong's Kai Tak airfield, were paid a pittance—15 yen for NCOs and .1 yen for other ranks.[54] By contrast, Japanese day labourers in 1939 received 1.97 yen per day. Captain Barnett of the Royal Rifles testified later that sick men on stretchers were also sent out on work parties. "Even though they could not work, the numbers had to be made up," he said. "The men would be called at four o'clock in the morning, and although work did not start actually until nine o'clock in the morning, the intervening hours were spent in counting out the men and getting them sorted out and transferred to the place of work."[55]

The medical, food, and labour conditions at North Point were bad enough, but the Canadian POWs also suffered from the special attention of Kanao Inouye, the "Kamloops Kid." Inouye served as an "honorary corporal" and interpreter at Shamshuipo camp and later for the *Kempeitai* in Hong Kong. Born in 1916 at Kamloops, BC, Inouye had lived in Canada until 1935, when he had returned to Japan.[56] "When I was back in Canada and going to school," Inouye told one Royal Rifles corporal, "they called me 'slant eyes' and 'yellow' and all the names you could think of. I've got you SOBS now where I want you. You're going to pay for it." And they did. Three Canadian POWs reportedly died as a direct result of the interpreter's malice; others, notably two officers of the Winnipeg Grenadiers, were subjected to "severe and brutal public beating[s]."[57] "He was a sadist, no question about it," the corporal recalled. "He was so evil against the white man, against the Canadians, particularly."

At the end of the war, the Kamloops Kid was charged as a war criminal with twenty-seven counts of overt cruelty, presumably the soundest cases from the more than 200 affidavits filed about his activities.[58] His case involved a number of difficult legal questions about jurisdiction, and for a time it seemed possible that, "having regard to the cowardly and treacherous nature of his conduct and to the feelings of the Canadians to whom he directed his attentions," as an External Affairs officer put it to his minister,[59] he might be tried in Canada for offences under the Treachery Act. The cabinet considered this question in May 1946 and decided that Inouye instead should be brought to justice at a war crimes tribunal in Hong Kong. Probably, although the records are not entirely clear, "the possible effects" on "the internal political situation here, having special regard to the deportation, etc., of persons of Japanese race" helped persuade the cabinet to minimize publicity by holding the trial in the Far East.[60] The case duly proceeded but, after Inouye's defence counsel pointed out that he was a Canadian citizen, he was retried by the civilian courts in Hong Kong for treason, found guilty, and executed on 25 August 1947.[61]

Among other war crimes to which Canadian POWs were subjected was the murder or execution of four soldiers of the Winnipeg Grenadiers, Sergeant John Payne, Lance-Corporal George Berzenski, and Privates John Adams and Percy Ellis, after a failed escape attempt on 20 August 1942. The Japanese claimed that the men had been shot and killed during the escape, but other POWs heard no firing, and rumours persisted that the men had been seen alive in Stanley Prison and tortured.[62] The officers responsible and other Japanese, most of whom were soldiers ranging in rank from private to major-general, were among the ten men prosecuted by Major G.B. Puddicombe of the Canadian army in war crimes trials also held at Hong Kong.[63] All but one were found guilty and sentenced to terms ranging from two years' imprisonment to death. Two officers, Colonel Tokunaga and Captain Saito, the commanding officer and medical officer in charge of the camps in the Hong Kong area, were held responsible for the deaths of more than a hundred Canadians and sentenced to be hanged. But the sentences were commuted by the acting general officer commanding at Hong Kong, a British officer, to life imprisonment and twenty years, respectively, a decision that angered the Canadian military authorities.[64]

For the Canadians, the viciousness that had been directed at them by the Kamloops Kid was unusual, largely because American and British POWs, not Canadians, were ordinarily singled out for especially severe treatment by the guards. "They did not dislike us, or hate us," a private of the Royal Rifles said. "If you were American you got the worst treatment. The British got the next worst."[65] Whatever their rank on the hate list, the Canadian POWs at Hong Kong paid heavily for their government's too easy acquiescence to London's request for reinforcements for the Crown Colony.

Notes

1. Department of National Defence Records (DND), National Archives of Canada (NA), vol. 772, file 349, memorandum, 13 Aug. 1940.
2. Ted Ferguson, *The Desperate Siege: The Battle of Hong Kong* (Toronto, 1980), 5.
3. W.S. Churchill, *The Second World War*, vol. 3, *The Grand Alliance* (Toronto, 1950), 177.
4. Oliver Lindsay, *The Lasting Honour* (London, 1978), 1.
5. Ibid., 3; Ferguson, *Desperate Siege*, 5–6. In those views, Grasett sounded almost exactly as did his peers. The best account is John W. Dower, *War Without Mercy: Race and Power in the Pacific War* (New York, 1986), 98ff.
6. This telegram and others between Canada and Britain are collected in Public Record Office (PRO), Dominions Office Records, DO 114/111, 66ff.
7. C.P. Stacey, *Six Years of War* (Ottawa, 1955), 441–42. This section is based on Stacey and all unreferenced quotations are from his exemplary account.
8. S.R. Elliot, *Scarlet to Green* (Toronto, 1981), 375.
9. On the Royal Rifles of Canada see *The Royal Rifles of Canada in Hong Kong: 1941–1945* (Sherbrooke, PQ, 1980), especially part 1.
10. Lindsay, *Lasting Humour*, 10.
11. Elliot, *Scarlet to Green*, 375.
12. Ferguson, *Desperate Siege*, ix.
13. Institute of Defense, *Hon Kon Chōsa Sakusen* [Hong Kong and Changsha Operations] (Tokyo, 1971), 13.
14. Ibid., 4, 13.
15. Ibid.
16. Institute of Defense, *Daihonei Rikugunbu* [Army Section, Imperial Headquarters] (Tokyo, 1967), 1, 100.
17. *Hon Kon Chōsa Sakusen*, 18.
18. Ibid., 39–40, 56–61.
19. Ibid., 48–49, 79–80.
20. Department of External Affairs Records (DEA), NA, Acc. 83-84/259, box 160, file 2670-A-40, "Extracts from the Diary of Rifleman Sydney Skelton."
21. *Hon Kon Chōsa Sakusen*, 208–11.
22. DEA, box 160, file 2670-A-40, Skelton Diary, gives ample testimony to the presence of fifth columnists.
23. *Royal Rifles*, 48.
24. Daniel Dancocks, *In Enemy Hands* (Edmonton, 1983), 223.
25. *Hon Kon Chōsa Sakusen*, 241–43.
26. Stacey, *Six Years of War*, 481.
27. *Hon Kon Chōsa Sakusen*, 320.
28. DEA, Acc. 83-84/259, box 230, file 4464-D-40, "Report by Miss Anna Mae Waters, nurse with the Canadian Forces at Hong Kong, as given on board the S.S. *Gripsholm*," Nov. 1943.
29. Ferguson, *Desperate Siege*, 211. See DEA, Acc. 83-84/259, box 160, file 2670-D-40, Canadian Postal Censorship memoranda, 10, 20, 27, 30 March 1942.
30. R.J. Pritchard and Sonia Zaide, eds., *The Tokyo War Crimes Trials* (New York, 1981), 6: 13114–17.
31. DEA, Acc. 83-84/259, box 160, file 2670-D-40, Mr. Duff's report on Hong Kong, n.d.
32. House of Commons, *Debates*, 16 March 1942.
33. DEA, vol. 2089, file AR 23/2, pt 7, "Notes on a Talk Given by Dr. Marcel Junod," 21 June 1946.
34. Junpei Shinobu, "Daitōa Sensō to Horyotoriatsukai Mondai," *Gaikō Jibō* 102 (May 1942): 3.
35. L. Friedman, ed., *The Law of War: A Documentary History* (New York, 1972), 2: 1078.

36. *Yomiuri Hochi*, 9 Nov. 1944.
37. Kazunobu Shinozaki, "Horyo 210,000" [210 000 POWs], *Jikyoku Jibo* (April 1942), cited in Yoshio Chaen, *Daitoa Senka Gaichi Horyo Shūyōjo* [Overseas Prisoners' Camps During the Greater East Asia War] (Tokyo, 1987), 97.
38. *Tokyo Asahi*, 18 March, 13 May 1942.
39. Dancocks, In *Enemy Hands*, 225.
40. Ibid., 228–29.
41. Pritchard and Zaide, eds., *Tokyo War Crimes Trials*, 6: 13122.
42. United States National Archives, Washington, RG218, Records of the Joint Chiefs of Staff, pt 1: 1942–45, The Pacific Theatre, reel 1, Elmer Davis to Adm. Leahy, 24 Dec. 1943, f A102782.
43. An account of conditions in late January 1942 is in DEA, Acc. 83-84/259, box 160, file 2670-A-40, "Report on Events . . . by Sub-Lieut. Proulx."
44. Ibid., box 175, file 2998-D-40, pt 2, "Interim Report on First Visit to Prisoners of War Camps . . . in Hong Kong."
45. Ibid., box 160, file 2670-A-40C, press release, "Conditions at Hong Kong," 12 July 1942, based on information from the British protecting power, Argentina. See the account of a Red Cross visit to a POW camp in Martin Booth's novel, *Hiroshima Joe* (London, 1986), 169–71, and PRO, Cabinet Records, Cab 66/22, W.P. (42) 82, 14 Feb. 1942, where the question of giving publicity to maltreatment of POWs was raised in Churchill's War Cabinet and with Canada. Significantly, Ottawa advised caution, the minister of national defence clearly preferring to withhold all comment. See ibid., C. Ritchie to Sir E. Machtig, 14 Feb. 1942.
46. DND, Mf C5338, file HQS 9050-17-3, War Office to Foreign Office, n.d. [late 1942].
47. DEA, Acc. 83-84/259, box 160, file 2670-A-40, minister to China to secretary of state for external affairs, 24 July 1943.
48. Records of the Joint Chiefs of Staff, pt 1, reel 1, JCS 504, "Japanese Atrocities—Reports by Escaped Prisoners," 17 Sept. 1943, ff A74066ff.
49. "Hong Kong Vets Raise an Awkward Question," *Globe and Mail* (Toronto), 15 Aug. 1987.
50. *Royal Rifles*, 172–73.
51. DEA, Acc. 83-84/259, box 160, file 2670-A-40, Interrogation Report No. SKP/5/44, 20 Oct. 1944.
52. Ibid., "Note as to the Activities of Mr Zindel—CICR Delegate in Hong Kong During the Month of March 1943."
53. Ibid., box 175, file 2998-D-40, pt 2, "Conditions in Hong Kong PW Camps," 4 July 1943.
54. Yoshio Chaen, *Dai-Nippon Teikoku Naichi Horyo Shūyōjo* [Imperial Japanese Domestic Prisoners' Camps] (Tokyo, 1986), 76.
55. Pritchard and Zaide, eds., *Tokyo War Crimes Trials*, 6: 13140.
56. DEA, Acc. 84-85/019, vol. 248, file 8767-40, F.J. Mead to E.H. Coleman, 27 Sept. 1945. The account in Roy Ito, *We Went to War* (Stittsville, ON, 1984), 269, is slightly incorrect.
57. Affidavits are in Directorate of History (DHist), National Defence Headquarters, file 163.009(D41), "Investigation of War Crimes, Jan 44/Sep 46." See also DEA, Acc. 84-85/019, vol. 248, file 8767-40, E.R. Hopkins to deputy minister, 22 March 1946.
58. DEA, Acc. 84-85/019, vol. 248, file 8767-40, Memorandum for acting secretary of state for external affairs, 15 May 1946.
59. Ibid.
60. Ibid., and extract from letter from minister of justice, 24 May 1946.
61. Ibid., L.B. Pearson to L. St. Laurent, 18 Dec. 1946; DHist, file 113.3A1013(1), "Final Report, War Crimes Investigation Section, Directorate of Administration,

Army Headquarters, 30 Aug 47." See also Ito, *We Went to War,* 269ff, which is again incorrect. Ito suggests Inouye came to Hong Kong in 1944, but there are depositions by POWs citing beatings by Inouye in 1943. DHist, file 163.009(D41), "Investigation of War Crimes."

62. DEA, Acc. 84-85/019, vol. 248, file 593(D8), "Notes of Conversations with Officers Going to Districts to Assist AJAGs in Preparation of Depositions from Repatriates," 8 Jan. 1946.

63. On Canadian war-crimes organization for Tokyo and Hong Kong trials see Maj. W.P. McClemont, "War Crimes Trials," *Canadian Army Journal* 1 (July 1947): 16ff, and *Documents on Canadian External Relations*, 12: 290ff.

64. DHist, file 593(D8), "Notes of Conversations," 8 Jan. 1946; ibid., "Final Report."

65. Dancocks, *In Enemy Hands*, 239–40.

Raymond Souster's poem about Company Sergeant Major John Osborn's battle at Hong Kong, a struggle that won Osborn a posthumous Victoria Cross, was written long after the incident. Souster's war experience was with the RCAF, but he nonetheless captures something of the hold Hong Kong still exercises on the Canadian conscience.

Pictures From a Long-Lost World: Hong Kong, 1941

Raymond Souster

"You bastards are going with me
right to the top and we'll kill
every one of those bloody Japs,"
Sergeant-Major John Robert Osborn
told his sixty-five men.

(All that was left of "B" Company,
Winnipeg Grenadiers, a regiment
"not recommended for operational training,"
on December 19, 1941.)

And thirty minutes later
with now only thirty men left,
he stormed to the very top
of Mount Butler, then stayed there
for eight and a half long hours.

(Osborn, able-seaman at Jutland,
farmer in Saskatchewan,
Manitoba railway worker —

now at forty-two
a soldier at Hong Kong.)

"Dig, you sons-of-bitches,
dig like you've never dug before,
they'll be back for us very soon,"
he told them with a grin.

(Meanwhile, three thousand miles away,
in Ottawa, Mr. Ralston,
Canadian Minister of Defence:
"The garrison's position is undoubtedly,
for the time being anyway,
a very trying and difficult one."
John Osborn, Regimental Sergeant-Major,
his bayonet caked thick with blood,
an ugly gash showing on his forearm,
would have damn well agreed with him . . . .)

And before long the Japs came back,
slinging grenades by the dozen,
and soon there were twelve,
then only six Grenadiers;
five finally as Osborn
threw himself on a grenade
he couldn't reach in time. . . .

Is there still a Mount Butler
in Hong Kong today?
If there is it should be called
John Osborn's Hill.

Home-front propaganda was highly developed in Canada. This comic book, printed in black and white like all wartime comics (due to a shortage of dyes), was widely distributed after the raid on Dieppe. It aimed to inspire young Canadians; the artists and writers, however, were likely as misled as most of the public about the raid's events

SPITFIRES, HURRICANES, AND BOSTON BOMBERS SWEEP IN BY THE HUNDRED TO ATTACK SHORE BATTERIES. AN UMBRELLA OF FIGHTERS COVERS THE INVASION FLEET.
MY BROTHER IS UP IN THAT SHOW — SORT OF A FAMILY AFFAIR, ISN'T IT?
THE LANDING BOATS CREEP INTO SHORE UNDER COVER OF SMOKE-BOMBS WITH TANKS AND MEN.
THE BEACHES ARE AN INFERNO OF ENEMY MACHINE-GUN AND MORTAR FIRE — BRITISH DESTROYERS BLAST GERMAN SHORE BATTERIES.
GIVE IT TO 'EM, LADS
WE'VE WAITED TWO YEARS FOR THIS CHANCE!
OVERHEAD, ONE OF THE WAR'S GREATEST AERIAL BATTLES DEVELOPS AS R.A.F. AND R.C.A.F. PLANES BREAK UP ENEMY BOMBER FORMATIONS.
NO PICNIC ON THE BEACH TODAY!
ENEMY BOMBERS AT GREAT COST, WRECK THE DESTROYER "BERKELEY," AND SHE HAS TO BE SUNK.

AT THE POINT OF THE BAYONET THE HAMILTON LIGHT INFANTRY SWEEP INTO THE FAMOUS CASINO AND CLEAN OUT STRONG ENEMY FORCES.
THE COMMANDOS GAIN SHELTERED POSITIONS, LOCATE TEMPORARY HEAD-QUARTERS, AND START BRINGING IN PRISONERS—
—MISERABLE SPECIMENS, SIR, BUT THE BEST WE COULD FIND—
WOUNDED MEN WERE BEING COURAGEOUSLY BROUGHT IN UNDER DEADLY ENEMY FIRE-
HE'S IN BAD SHAPE, BUT HE'S GOT A CHANCE, IF WE MAKE IT.
GERMAN SNIPERS INFEST EVERY BUILDING!
STUKA BOMBERS ATTEMPT TO ATTACK NEW LANDING FORCES ON THE BEACHES, BUT DESTROYER'S ANTI-AIRCRAFT FIRE FOUGHT THEM OFF.
MARK UP ANOTHER ONE, GUS!
BOSTON BOMBERS SWEEP IN TO DEAL WITH SECONDARY DEFENSES.

OUR TRACKS ARE SHOT AWAY, BUT WE'RE STILL BLASTING 'EM!
CALGARY TANK UNITS PULVERIZED ENEMY POSITIONS BARRICADING THE STREETS.
THEY'LL HEAR THAT IN QUÉBEC!
VOILÀ!
SOME COMMANDOS BLEW UP AMMUNITION DUMPS AND A RADIO LOCATION STATION.
HURRY IT UP— OR WE'LL BE LATE GETTING BACK FOR SUPPER!
WATCH THAT CURVE!
WINNIPEG HIGHLANDERS REACHED THREE MILES INLAND, AND DISPOSED OF ENEMY ARTILLERY BATTERIES.
FOUR OUT OF ELEVEN "FUSILLIERS DE MONTRÉAL" BATTERED THEIR WAY TO THE SUBMARINE BASE AND DAMAGED SEVERAL U-BOATS.
U16
THE BEACH WAS WRACKED WITH EXPLODING SHELLS AND BOMBS AS TROOPS EVACUATED WOUNDED FIRST.
THE COLONEL'S GOT IT BAD—TAKE IT EASY CHUMS—
BLESS THOSE NAVY BOYS— ALWAYS AROUND WHEN YOU NEED 'EM!
H60
DESTROYERS AIDED THE SMALL BOATS TO EVACUATE

ROLL OUT THE BARREL!
WHY DON'T WE DO THIS MORE OFTEN?
E17
WEARY TROOPS SANG AS THEY LANDED ON THE ENGLISH SHORE
WORKERS AND SAILORS CONGRATULATED THE MEN ON ARRIVAL HOME.
WE COULDN'T HAVE DONE MUCH WITHOUT YOU SALTIES!
GOOD SHOW, BOY!
-WORTH WAITING FOR
HOTTEST THING I'VE EVER SEEN!
WE'LL MAKE IT HOTTER NEXT TIME
BIT OF THE BEST, MEN, YOU DID A GOOD JOB! NOW MAKE THE MOST OF 48 HOURS LEAVE.
48 HOURS OF SLEEP FOR ME!
THERE WILL BE GREATER ATTACKS THAN DIEPPE!
PRIME-MINISTER MACKENZIE KING, CABLED LT.-GEN. McNAUGHTON, COMMANDER-IN-CHIEF OF THE CANADIAN ARMY OVERSEAS —
WE'RE PROUD!
CABLEGRAM
LT. GEN. McNAUGHTON -
ALL CANADIANS SHARED THE THRILLS AND SATISFACTION OF CANADIAN TROOPS IN THEIR OPPORTUNITY TO STRIKE A TELLING BLOW AT A NAZI STRONGHOLD, AND WE ARE PROUD THAT CANADIANS TOOK A FOREMOST PLACE IN THE OPERATION.
SACRIFICES OF THE TROOPS HAVE STRENGTHENED OUR DETERMINATION TO GIVE COMPLETE SUPPORT TO OUR ARMED FORCES
MACKENZIE KING.
OTTAWA
GREAT BRITAIN

Poet and writer Mona McTavish Gould was born in Saskatchewan and raised in London, Ontario. She worked both as a journalist and advertising agency writer. Her poem to commemorate her brother's death at Dieppe was widely hailed when it first appeared.

This Was My Brother

(For Lt.-Col. Howard McTavish,

killed in action at Dieppe)

Mona McTavish Gould

This was my brother
At Dieppe,
Quietly a hero
Who gave his life
Like a gift,
Withholding nothing.

His youth . . . his love . . .
His enjoyment of being alive . . .
His future, like a book
With half the pages still uncut—

This was my brother
At Dieppe—
The one who built me a doll house
When I was seven,
Complete to the last small picture frame,
Nothing forgotten.

He was awfully good at *fixing* things,
At stepping into the breach when he was needed.

That's what he did at Dieppe;
He was needed.
And even Death must have been a little shamed
At his eagerness!

Best known as an enormously successful nature writer, Farley Mowat has also written extensively about his wartime service in Italy with the Hastings and Prince Edward Regiment or, as they were generally known, the "Hasty Pees." Most notably, his war writing deals honestly with fear and its effects. "The Worm," as Mowat calls it in this excerpt from *And No Birds Sang*, eats away at the innards, sapping courage. That men in battle often overcome their fear remains astonishing.

The Worm

Farley Mowat

THE BATTLE THAT FOLLOWED began at 1400 hours on December 6 and ended on December 15, barely a mile north of where it had begun. It was a ten-day blood bath that cost the Regiment over a hundred and fifty battle casualties.

The opening attack was made in broad daylight by Charley Company under cover of the strongest artillery support Division could muster. It was a devastating barrage . . . but the enemy replied with equal violence and within minutes Charley was being pounded into the saturated valley floor under a titanic upheaval of mud and steel. Dog [Company], coming up behind, tried to avoid the worst of that holocaust and swung to the left into a smoke screen being laid by our own heavy mortars, and the entire company simply vanished from our ken. When, after nearly an hour, there was still no word from Dog, Kennedy became so distrait that he ordered me and a Battalion Headquarters runner to follow, then flung himself hell-bent down the slope.

My whole being screamed resistance. Three times we were pinned, grovelling in the mud, before we reached the river and struggled through its icy waters. On the far shore we fell into a slimy ditch with the survivors of one of Charley Company's platoons. We tried to find out from them what was happening, but nobody knew. The German counter-barrage had by then become so heavy that platoons and even sections were isolated and out of communication with one another, cowering into the muck as almost continuous explosions leapt about them.

Kennedy led us on in search of Charley Company Headquarters, and we miraculously stumbled on it in a tiny cave at the foot of a steep cliff; but the company commander was missing and a terrified sergeant could tell us nothing. Kennedy realized the situation was hopeless and that we would have to withdraw, but he had no way of issuing the necessary order until he could get to his radio. So he led us back across the valley.

My memory of that return must be akin to what a drowning man feels during the endless, agonizing moments when he is sinking slowly into the depths. My chest felt crushed and I was gasping for air by the time we reached the road which climbed the south slope. There must have been a lull in the shelling then or else Kennedy was just so anxious to reach the radio that he did not care what the enemy might do, for he led us straight up the road in full view of the Germans opposite. We had not gone fifty feet when they bracketed us with a salvo of Eighty-eights.

Something struck my right foot a numbing blow and a stunning concussion flung me face down into the mud. I heard screaming close at hand and, struggling to my knees, saw Kennedy on *his* knees in the centre of the smoking road, shaking his head slowly from side to side like an old and tired dog, but the screaming was not his. Ten feet behind him the runner, a young lad whose name I never knew, was humping jerkily away from *his* own leg which had been severed at the thigh. In the instant that I saw him, he gave one final bubbling shriek, collapsed, and mercifully was still.

I heard Kennedy's voice as from some distant mountain peak.

"Get up, Mowat! Goddamn you! *Up!*"

He was standing over me, swaying, but apparently unhurt.

"Can't," I said quite calmly. "Hit in the leg, I think."

In a moment he had me by the shoulders and hoisted me to my feet. We stumbled over the crest and fell into the cover of a gully as another salvo of Eighty-eights ploughed into the road behind us.

There was no pain in my foot and glorious euphoria was overwhelming me. *I had a Blighty!* Soon I would be on my way back down the line to a field hospital and then perhaps still farther back for a sea voyage to England or even Canada! The sound and fury . . . and the fear . . . would be behind me. But somewhere within my skull a spiteful voice poured vitriol on my joy. "Coward!" it said. "You gutless wonder!"

A couple of men from Baker Company spotted us and now they helped me to the regimental aid post which the medical officer, Capt. Charlie Krakauer, had pushed forward to the doubtful shelter of a ruined hovel on the very lip of the valley. Kennedy was in a desperate hurry to get on to BHQ [Battalion Headquarters] but he spared a moment for me.

"Good lad, Squib. You've done okay."

I gave him a lying grin but I was thinking, Thank Christ I'm getting out of here!

Someone helped me onto a stretcher in the dim-lit room and Krakauer was soon bending over my feet. I heard him grunt and felt a tug, then his face was above me, split by a lopsided grin.

"You lucky little prick! Shell cut your boot open from end to end and hardly creased the skin. Wait till we get a band aid on it and you can go right back to work!"

I did not believe him! Outraged, I rolled over and sat up . . . and shrieked as a flame of agony seared deep into my backside. Krakauer's smile faded as with one big hand he pushed me back on the stretcher and rolled me over. Again I heard him grunt as he swiftly scissored off the seat of my trousers . . . then a bellow of raucous laughter burst from him.

It must have been the last laughter heard at the regimental aid post that day and for days thereafter. It was justified. Sticking out of the right cheek of my ass, unnoticed until I sat upon it, was a wedge of steel shell casing which had penetrated to a depth of perhaps half an inch. Charlie yanked it out with his fingers and presented it to me with a flourish.

"Keep this in memory of me," he said.

I departed limping slightly, for feeling had not yet returned to my foot, and with the seat of my pants held together with a large safety pin contributed by a stretcher-bearer. I was not on my way to Blighty. My destination was rear BHQ, there to seek out a new pair of boots and a whole pair of trousers. I also had some hopes of being able to hide for awhile in the relatively shellproof gully where rear headquarters was located, but even this was not to be.

I was met by a white-faced and fluttering Jimmy Bird who told me Kennedy had been unable to contact Dog Company on the radio and had therefore decided the attack would have to be renewed in order to rescue Dog. Charley Company, whose survivors had mostly dribbled back by now, was in no shape for another round; so I was to fetch what was left of Able and lead it up to take part in a new attack in company with Baker.

There was no time to change either boots or trousers. Physically sickened by the mere thought of going back into the valley, I stumbled down the road to Able's area where I found Alex's replacement, a newly arrived captain whom I did not know, and gave him my message. He hardly seemed to hear.

Al Park was standing nearby, a strange, obdurate look on his face, and his eyes hooded. He beckoned me off to one side.

"Paddy's bought it," he said in a voice thin with grief or rage—I could not tell which. "Phosphorous grenade exploded in his face and burned him to a crisp . . . died in the ambulance on the way out. We just now heard . . . the company's down to about forty bods still able to pull a trigger. God almighty, Squib, they can't send us back in now!"

Yes, I thought dully, they can. They will. But I said nothing, and Al's gaze dropped from my face to the mud at our feet. Memory flickered and I saw Paddy kneeling beside the dead Italian officer on that dusty road in Sicily. The Irish Rover . . . gone now for good.

Al uncorked his water bottle and offered it to me. We both took choking gulps of the straight issue rum. It did not restore my failing courage but at least it helped a little to deaden the throbbing fear.

Kennedy was waiting for us near the aid post, which was now clustered about with jeep ambulances taking out the wounded from Charley Company. Moments later we were descending into the void again.

The German fire, which had slackened somewhat after Charley's withdrawal, started up anew and, so it seemed, with redoubled weight and fury. Most of the artillery of the German Corps holding the coast section, augmented by self-propelled guns and an avalanche of mortar bombs and rocket projectiles, was now concentrated in the valley. However, the very massiveness of the bombardment served to partially defeat its purpose. It would not permit us to retreat. We had no choice but to stampede forward up the enemy-held slopes, for there alone could we hope to find shelter from the annihilating blast.

I have no recollection of that second crossing until I found myself in the same little cave that had been Charley Company's Headquarters during their ill-fated attack, and being roundly cursed by the battalion signals sergeant who did not recognize me in my mud-caked state and thought I was one of his signallers. Then Kennedy appeared, wild-eyed and glaring like a maniac.

"*Jerry's on the run!*" he cried. "But the goddamn radio's gone out! Mowat! Go back and get what's left of Charley!"

Of *that* crossing of the Moro I have no memories at all. Darkness had fallen by the time I returned to Kennedy again. By that time a few men from Able and Baker had thrust forward to the edge of the northern plateau, where German tanks and a savage infantry counterattack forced them to dig in.

What followed was the kind of night men dream about in afteryears, waking in a cold sweat to a surge of gratitude that it is but a dream. It was a delirium of sustained violence. Small pockets of Germans that had been cut off throughout our bridgehead fired their automatic weapons in hysterical dismay at every shadow. The grind of enemy tanks and self-propelled guns working their way along the crest was multiplied by echoes until it sounded like an entire Panzer army. Illuminating flares flamed in darkness with a sick radiance. The snap and scream of high-velocity tank shells pierced the brutal guttural of an endless cannonade from both German and Canadian artillery. Moaning Minnie projectiles whumped down like thunderbolts, searching for our hurriedly dug foxholes. Soldiers of both sides, blundering through the vineyards, fired with panicky impartiality in all directions. And it began to rain again, a bitter, penetrating winter rain.

December 7 dawned overcast and brought black news. The engorged Sangro River had risen twenty feet in as many hours and washed away the precious pontoon bridges, leaving First and Second brigades isolated from the rest of the army. Worse still, the Germans had smashed a bridgehead which had been established across the Moro at grim cost by Second Brigade near San Leonardo, leaving us holding the sole remaining foothold on the northern bank.

As icy rain squalls swept the smoking valley, things grew worse. A troop of British tanks attempting to cross in our support became hopelessly bogged and were picked off, one by one, by German self-propelled guns. Then came word that despite our success at the mouth of the river, the divisional commander intended to persist with the bloody attempts to make a main crossing at San Leonardo. Therefore, we were not to be reinforced, and much of the artillery support which had been vitally instrumental to our survival was to be switched to the San Leonardo sector. Left on our own, our orders were to "engage the enemy closely" in order to draw his attention away from Second Brigade's assault.

This order was superfluous, for the Germans now proceeded to engage *us* as closely as they could.

During the next thirty-six hours eleven separate counterattacks were flung against us. Yet somehow we clung to our precarious salient across the Moro, and by drawing upon ourselves the German fire and reinforcements, including a fresh regiment from the First Paratroop Division, enabled our sister brigade to make a new crossing of the river at San Leonardo and consolidate a bridgehead there.

The cost had been appalling. When the firing died down on our sector, stretcher and burial parties scouring the slimy slopes and the tangles of shell-torn debris found one hundred and seventy German corpses. Our own dead and wounded amounted to a third of the four hundred or so Hasty Pees who had gone into the valley of the shadow.

For me the Moro is to be remembered as the lair of the Worm That Never Dies—and of one particular victim. He was a stretcher-bearer, an older man—he might have been all of thirty-five—who had been with the Regiment since the autumn of 1939.

By day and by night the bearers had to make their ways across the valley, crawling forward to the lead platoon positions, if necessary. Some of them must have made that agonizing passage a score of times. For them there was no rest and no surcease; no burrowing in a slit trench to escape the sound and fury. For them there was only a journey into the inferno, then the withdrawal to momentary sanctuary, and the return to hell once more.

That was the hardest thing to bear. Those who remained under sustained and unremitting fire could partially armour themselves with the apathy of the half-dead; but those who had to come and go, knowing the searing repetition of brief escape followed by a new immersion in the bath of terror—those were the ones who paid the heaviest price.

On the last night of our ordeal I was descending the north slope, numbed and passionless, drugged with fatigue, dead on my feet, when I heard someone singing! It was a rough voice, husky yet powerful. A cluster of mortar bombs came crashing down and I threw myself into the mud. When I could hear again, the first sound that came to me was the singing voice. Cautiously I raised myself just as a starshell burst overhead, and saw him coming toward me through that blasted wasteland.

Stark naked, he was striding through the cordite stench with his head held high and his arms swinging. His body shone white in the brilliant light of the flare, except for what appeared to be a glistening crimson sash that ran from one shoulder down one thigh and dripped from his lifted foot.

He was singing "Home on the Range" at the top of his lungs.

The Worm That Never Dies had taken him.

Securing the Moro bridgehead brought us no respite. Until December 19 we remained in action, first defending what we had taken, then breaking out in an attempt to drive the paratroopers back toward the ramparts of Ortona which we could now see encrusting a blunt promontory jutting into the leaden waters of the Adriatic. Ambulance jeeps were perpetually on the move, weaving their way along cratered tracks back and forth across the devastated valley through a desultory fall of shells. For the most part they were laden with men who could have served as illustrations for a macabre catalogue of the infinite varieties of mutilation; but for the first time since we had gone to war they also carried casualties who bore no visible wounds.

These were the victims of what was officially termed "battle fatigue"—"shell shock" they called it in the First World War. Both descriptions were evasive euphemisms. The military mind will not, perhaps does not dare, admit that there comes a time to every fighting man (unless death or bloody ruination of the flesh forestalls it) when the Worm—not steel and flame—becomes his nemesis.

My father had warned me of this in a letter I received just before we left Castropignano for the Adriatic sector. It was a letter so unlike his usual robust and cheerful chronicles of trivia at home that I can believe it was dictated by the Celtic prescience which he claimed as part of his inheritance.

> Keep it in mind during the days ahead that war does inexplicable things to people, and no man can guess how it is going to affect him until he has had a really stiff dose of it . . . The most unfortunate ones after any war are not those with missing limbs; they are the ones who have had their spiritual feet knocked out from under them. The beer halls and gutters are still full of such poor bastards from my war, and nobody understands or cares what happened to them . . . I remember two

> striking examples from my old Company in the 4th Battalion. Both damn fine fellows, yet both committed suicide in the Line. They did not shoot themselves—they let the Germans do it because they had reached the end of the tether. But they never knew what was the matter with them; that they had become empty husks, were spiritually depleted, were burned-out.

My own understanding of the nature of the Worm, and of the inexorable way it liquefies and then consumes the inner substance of its victims, was chillingly enlarged on the day we broke out of our bridgehead.

Baker Company led the breakout and fought its way for nearly a mile along the coastal road leading toward Ortona before being halted by flanking fire from the far lip of a ravine to the left of the road. Kennedy took me with him and went forward to assess the situation, and we got well mortared for our pains. The Germans overlooked and dominated our line of advance to such a degree that we could not push past until they were driven off. We assumed that a unit of Third Brigade, which was supposed to be advancing on our flank, would take care of this and so we dug in to await events.

We had not long to wait. Still anxious to divert attention from his main thrust out of San Leonardo and unwilling to reinforce the coastal sector, the divisional commander passed the word that we must take out the enemy position ourselves. Furthermore, we were ordered to attack immediately and in such a way that "the enemy will conclude you are the spearhead of the main assault." Once again we were to be the goat in the tiger hunt.

From an observation post my section had hurriedly established in the dubious shelter of a collapsed shed, I looked out over a sea of mud dotted here and there with the foundered hulks of shell-shattered farm buildings and strewn with flotsam of broken vineyard posts and twisted skeins of vineyard wire. It was a scene of mind-wrenching desolation, one that seemed doubly ominous beneath the lowering winter sky.

It also seemed grimly lifeless . . . except . . . something was moving near a ravaged ruin on the valley floor. I focussed my binoculars . . . stared hard . . . and wished I hadn't. Looming large in the circle of my lenses were two huge sows gorging themselves on the swollen corpse of a mule. I knew they would as greedily stuff their gravid bellies with human meat if chance afforded . . . and I knew the chance would certainly be afforded—all too soon.

The battle we were about to enter promised nothing but disaster—a frontal attack in daylight over open ground, in full view of determined paratroopers manning prepared and fortified positions and well supported by heavy weapons. Only a massive weight of accompanying armour could have given an infantry attack the ghost of a chance, and we had only a troop—three tanks—in support. Furthermore, it was obvious to all of us, tankers and infantrymen alike, that neither wheels *nor* tracks could move far through the morass of mud in the bottom of the valley.

Shortly before the attack was due to begin, Kennedy, to my belly-quivering dismay, detailed me to accompany the tanks *on foot*, in order to provide liaison between them and the infantry should radio communication fail.

Zero hour came at 1600. There was a brief outpouring of artillery shells and heavy mortar bombs from our supporting guns; and as the far side of the gulley began to be obscured by muddy geysers, flame and smoke, the men of Dog Company started down the slope.

I watched them go from behind the protection of the troop commander's tank, terrified on their behalf and on my own as well. Not more than fifty men remained to the Company, an insignificant and pathetically vulnerable handful, thinly dispersed across that funereal waste of mud and wreckage.

As was intended, the Germans did not suspect this attack was only a diversion; and since it seemed to directly threaten Ortona, the coastal anchor of their new defence line, they reacted by flinging everything they had at us. Dog Company and the valley floor itself disappeared under the smoke and fumes of the most concentrated bombardment I had yet seen.

As the enemy barrage thundered up the slope, I plastered myself against the back of the troop commander's Sherman, desperately wishing I was inside its armoured carapace. The din was so tremendous I did not even hear the roar of accelerating engines and, before I knew what was happening, all three tanks were lurching away from me.

Because the Shermans were tightly "buttoned up"—all hatches closed and dogged—the troop commander had been unable to let me know he had received an urgent call for help from Dog. The remnants of that company, having somehow succeeded in reaching the far side of the valley, had been pinned down by machine-gun fire hosing into them from several bunkers which were impervious to anything except point-blank shelling from tank guns. Fully aware of the odds against them, the tankers were gamely attempting to respond to Dog's SOS.

With their abrupt departure I was left nakedly exposed to the tempest of explosions. Wildly I looked about for shelter, but the nearest was a shattered house two hundred yards away, from which I knew Kennedy was watching the battle. I could not go there. There seemed nothing else for it but to fling myself in pursuit of the tanks, impelled by a primal need to interpose their armoured bulk between me and the apocalyptic fury of the German guns.

Reaching the bottom of the slope, the Shermans encountered a maze of drainage ditches in which one of them immediately got itself bogged while the other two, slewing helplessly in deepening slime, dared go no farther. I reached the mired tank in a lung-bursting sprint and, so consuming was my need to escape the cataclysmic bombardment, I began beating on its steel flanks with my fists while howling to be taken in.

My voice was lost even to my own ears in a bellowing drumfire of shell bursts. The Germans had spotted the tanks and were now bent on annihilating them. Bombs, shells and streams of machine-gun bullets converged on the Shermans. The sound and fury rose to a level beyond my powers of description . . . and beyond the limits of my endurance.

Reason abandoned me. I dropped to my belly and, heedless of what must have happened if the bogged tank had attempted to move, tried to burrow under it, between its tracks. But it had already sunk so deeply into the mire that I could not force my way beneath it. There was no place there to hide.

Then an armour-piercing shell struck the Sherman. I did not hear it hit but felt the massive machine jolt under the impact, and at once my lungs began to fill with raw petrol fumes.

Somewhere inside myself there was a shriek of agony, for I could already feel the searing heat that would engulf me as the tank flamed into a livid torch. It did not happen. There was no brew-up—but that I did not know, for I was already in full flight up the slope, churning through the muck like some insensate robot. A salvo of heavy stuff dropped close enough to slap me flat on my face under a living wall of mud. But the robot got to its feet and staggered on.

I did not pause at the ruins where Kennedy was sheltering. Reaching the shell-pocked road I trotted along at a steady, purposeful lope. God alone knows how far I might have run—perhaps until exhaustion felled me—had I not been intercepted by Franky Hammond, commander of our anti-tank platoon, who was trying to get forward with one of his 6-pounder guns. He caught my arm as I trotted sightlessly past his halted jeep and spun me up against the little vehicle. Then he shook me until I went limp.

"Drink this!" he ordered, and thrust the neck of his rum-filled water bottle into my mouth.

Then, "Get in the jeep! Now show me the way to BHQ."

Franky had saved me from the Worm.

When, a few minutes later, I reported to Kennedy that I had lost contact with the tanks and with Dog Company as well, he seemed too preoccupied to care. Having heard that Dog Company's commander and his entire headquarters group had been wiped out and two of the three platoon commanders had been killed or badly wounded, Kennedy had immediately radioed Brigade for permission to call off the attack. Brigade had replied that, under orders from Division, *we were to renew the battle and keep on renewing it until told to stop.*

I did not remain to witness the ensuing debacle as Able Company was put into the meat grinder. Kennedy sent me back across the Moro in Hammond's jeep on some now-forgotten errand to rear BHQ, which by then was out of range of most of the German guns. Presumably I did whatever it was I had been told to do, after which our quartermaster, George Hepburn, found me wandering aimlessly about and took me into his snug retreat in the cellar of an undamaged house where he plied me with rum until I passed out.

When I woke next morning it was to find a worried Doc Macdonald standing over me with a mug of tea in his hand.

"Jeez, boss, I figured you for a goner. You was yellin' and whoopin' like a bunch o' chimpanzees the whole damn night. You gotta take it easy with that issue hooch."

The butchery in the gully lasted for three days and ended only when units of Third Brigade, finally breaking out of the San Leonardo positions, came up on our left flank. The Regiment had done what it had been told to do.

Turvey was the quintessential Canadian soldier of the Second World War, and Earle Birney's novel about him was one of the great comic creations to emerge from the war. Birney served overseas as a personnel selection officer, in effect a psychologist—the Canadian Army was very modern in its unfailing efforts to cram the square pegs into the round holes—and this excerpt is definitely based on what he knew well.

Turvey is Psychoanalyzed

Earle Birney

THE NEXT MORNING Turvey, who had spent the fag-end of the night in Baron van Duffelputten's authentic seventeenth century coachhouse (now serving as a brig), was marched between two armed guards into the Orderly Room and plunked on a bench outside the C.O's office. The Old Man's door was shut but plyboard was scarce and the partition, like most in the German-built hutments added to the estate, stopped a yard from the ceiling. Turvey had no trouble following the loud nasal voice of his Commanding Officer and the precise tones of the adjutant.

" . . . one that raised the rumpus last night, sir."

"O God, *that* one. Woke me out of my first good sleep in a week. What's he pegged with?"

There was a pause and the rattling of papers. Turvey held his breath.

"Destruction of one greatcoat-for-the-use-of; breakage of one Sten-mark-one-star; unlawful discharge of a weapon; unlawful expenditure eighteen-rounds-ammo-nine-millimetre."

"Now who the bloody hell slapped all that on him?"

The adjutant said something about Sergeant Swingle and an Enquiry.

"Court of Enquiry my backside! We've got a bellyful of them now. And if he turns out to be a barrackroom lawyer and—" The C.O. lowered his voice and Turvey didnt quite get the next sentence; but Colonel Rawkin was not used to soft-pedalling anything, particularly his own tones, and soon Turvey and his guards and indeed the whole Orderly Room (the clerks had kindly stopped typing) were able to follow again.

". . . Love a God, Charlie, cant you stop these sergeants from throwing the book at every dimwit that steps out of line? What's wrong with this, this Tur—Turkey—?"

"Turvey, sir."

"—Turvey anyway? Trying to work his ticket?"

The adjutant's reply didnt quite carry.

"Thought his greatcoat was a par— Say, maybe he's really shell-happy." The colonel's voice rose with hope. "O God. If we could just get him boarded out!"

The adjutant murmured something.

"Listen, Charlie; if the Swami will play ball and call him Mental, we can bang him off to England on tomorrow's outdraft. And the quartermaster can bloody well write off his Sten."

Turvey's righthand guard elbowed him slyly and the one on his left whispered in admiration, "By jeez, you're gonna work it."

"But, sir, you know the psychiatrist. He wont play. Not unless there's really—"

"Dammit you cant tell me this Tur-, Turnkey isnt crazy as a coot. Hanging his greatcoat on a gate and coming right back and shooting it. Unless, of course, he's swinging the lead. And the Swami will soon put a rocket under that. That's what he's for, Charlie. And he can start right now. I wont see the bugger till the Swami sends me a report. If he says the fellow's swinging it I'll chew his bollocks off and you make sure Spo gives him the worst job on the X-14 list, shovelling coal or something,—but away from here."

"Yessir, . . . right, sir . . . different if it were one of our Permanents . . . court-martial . . . Sergeant Swingle got in a tizzy." The adjutant seemed to be climbing over on the winning side.

"Hell's bells, Charlie, you *know* the brigadier shot us down in flames last time he was here about the number of courts-martial we have. Cant make him understand it's because we're always filled to the gills with these loony transients. You bloody well tell the R.S.M. to see the sergeants dont go around putting the hooks on em or it'll be bowlers for you and me, Charlie."

"Yessir."

"After all, there wasnt anybody inside the coat and, and, well, it *might* have been a paratrooper!"

"Yessir . . . send him to the Sike at once, sir." The adjutant sounded worried. Turvey wasnt feeling too well either, despite the envious winks of his guards. If the Nut Doctor decided he was crazy, they'd send him back to England. If the Nut Doctor decided he wasnt crazy, and trying to wangle it back to England, they'd keep him in Belgium, but behind the lines. It looked bad for getting with Mac again.

"Doggone," he muttered, "just after the Board raised me to P-One and I'm all set for the front."

"Shh, there's the Old Man again," one of the guards whispered.

"Wait, Charlie, I'll get Pugs on the ticker. I'll make him put the squeeze on the Sike." There was the whirr of a field telephone. "Senior Medical Officer." Craarh, crackle . . . "Major Pugston, please . . . Pugs, about that cuckoo fired off the Sten last night . . . Yeah. Listen, I want him out of here. I'm sending him over to the Sike right away. He's a menace. Must be S-Five . . . Sure, sure, I know you have to . . . Well, S-Four anyway . . . But if Hairy dont give him an S something or other, we'll have to hold a Court of Enquiry on the Sten he bust . . . well, there you are. Court-Martial, too, maybe . . . Listen Pugsy, if there's a C. of E. and CM about this, you and your Standing Medical Board, every mother's son of you, will serve on it every day for the next two weeks . . . No . . . You'd have to hold your boards at night and sleep when the courts are damned well over . . . O.K. Then you better ring the Sike pronto and tell him he's got to slap an S on the bugger . . . Roger." The receiver banged on the cradle. "O.K., Charlie, Pugs'll make the Sike play ball. Get that Turkey over to him, but fast."

"Yessir." The adjutant shot out the door. "Guards!" Turvey and his watchdogs scrambled to attention. "Conduct the prisoner to Captain Airdale's office and wait outside. When the psychiatrist is through with him, take him back to the guard hut."

Another conversation was floating across another partition when Turvey and his guards sat down on a bench outside the psychiatrist's door. It wasnt as loud as the previous one, but two benchfuls of soldiers were already tuned to it in happy silence.

"That's Pugston, Senior M.O. He's givin Hairy the bee on you," one of Turvey's guards interpreted after a moment. "He sure hotfooted it over, after the Old Man's blast. You'll get an S all right, you lucky split. You'll be in Blighty by the week-end."

"I dont wanna S. I wanna get back to the Koot—"

"Can it; listen! Hairy's talkin now." It was a tired voice and Turvey caught only phrases:

" . . . eight ahead of him . . . back to their huts . . . half an hour just to read his file . . . "

"Well, Hairy, . . . worth it if you can justify an S. Of course . . . not attempting to influence your diagnosis, but you know how the Old Man. . . . "

"Yes, sir, . . . play it the way I see it, but . . . examine him as thoroughly as I can . . . write it up big . . . Old Man cant say I didnt try. . . . "

"That's fine, Hairy, W.A.T. I suppose?"

"T.A.T. too, if I have time." He added something else that sounded like "having a bang at a Roar Shack."

Turvey trembled at the unfamiliar prescriptions and one of the guards nudged him. "Boy, you're goin to have to sweat shit for that boat."

"I dont wanna boat, I just wanna get back to the Koot—"

"Sergeant!" A very young captain emerged from the psychiatrist's office.

"Sir!" a voice echoed and a hoarheaded NCO popped from the second cubicle down.

"W.A.T. for Private Turvey. Immediate. And send the others away, cant see them this morning."

Turvey went along, baring his arm for another inoc, but he found that W.A.T. was only a very amusing game called the Word Association Test. The sergeant sat him with a sheet of foolscap at a table in his dinky office. Then he droned off a series of words at ten-second intervals and Turvey had to scribble the very first ideas that tinkled in his head after each word. He tried hard to put down as much as he could because he figured the more he wrote the more proof the Sike would have he wasnt an S-something-or-other and was O.K. for the Kootenay Highlanders.

When it was over there was a wait. Capt. Airdale, the venerable sergeant explained, was still ploughing through Turvey's file. The sergeant filled in the time with sedate chatter about the captain, whom he rated high.

"He's really going to enjoy talking with you, Turvey. Isnt often he takes time to lay on a W.A.T., poor fellow. Generally he interviews twenty in a morning and has to write out a diagnosis and recommendations on all of them by 1500 hours so I can type them in time for the Medical Board."

"Gosh, are there that many nuts around here every day?"

"Well, of course"—the sergeant coughed good-humouredly—"we dont use such a word as 'nut.' Not in psychiatry. We have all sorts of *cases* though, you'd be surprised. Psychopaths, aggressive or inadequate," the sergeant rolled the words fondly, "suspected epileptics, schizoid personalities, manics. And scads of neurotics—compulsives, depressives. But battle fatigues mainly. Anxiety states, you know."

"What're they all in a state about?"

"O, about getting killed, mostly, though some'r more worried about their wives."

"Because they cant get home to them, you mean?"

"Or because they *have* to go home to em, or," the sergeant considered dispassionately, "because somebody else's home with em. O, you'd be surprised the things fellows worry about. We had one in here last week, depressive type, couldnt sleep because he had it doped out the Second Coming was due at dawn sometime this year, but he hadnt got the exact day taped. Another chap sent in with undiagnosed headaches. Up at his unit they thought he was a malingerer. But Captain Airdale found out he got them every time he saw wire. Had an emasculation obsession, of course."

"A what?"

"Emasculation obsession. He'd got it in his head he was bound to lose his testicles the next time he got into barbed wire. Course it's all very hard on the captain. He's very young, you know." The sergeant smiled paternally. "Had a sheltered home life, then went direct from interning into the army. Hasnt had much of a chance to develop himself as a clinician. Sent straight over here just a month ago. Now he gets enough material in one day to last him a year on Civvy Street, and no time to analyze it. Some of it really shocks him, too. He's kind of a shy type really. Has personality problems himself. All these psychiatrists have. We had one was transferred to a Base Hospital at his own request. Having trouble with sprees. Course they're all supposed to have been analyzed. But it doesnt always take."

When the sergeant finally led him into the captain's office, Turvey entered feeling that at least he wasnt as crackers as some who had been here before him. It wasnt a feeling that gave him much comfort, however, and it disappeared under the strain of explaining to the young captain a number of complicated chapters in his martial career which were hinted at in his file. Then they got on to Turvey's W.A.T. The captain was plainly fascinated by Turvey's big pencilled responses to the stimulus words. As his eyes ran down the column he would pause, scratch his curly head and wrinkle his nose.

"Why did the word *naked* make you think of a can of green peas, Turvey?" His voice was professionally colourless but high and it squeaked a little on "naked."

"Well, sir, in the cookhouse, where I was pearl-divin, sir, they got a lot of cans like that—picture of a pin-up type, without any duds on."

Captain Airdale looked disappointed. But his nose quivered again immediately, like a hound-dog's.

"What did you want to say for *Body*? 'With her head tu—' is all you have."

"Didnt have time to finish, sir. Words was comin at me awful fast. It's just the song. You know." But the captain didnt. "With her head tucked underneath her arm." The captain poised an eyebrow. "The fellows in my Iron Lung sing it sometimes. All about Henry the Eighth and the Bloody Tower."

"Of course, yes," the captain murmured, but he didnt sound at all convinced. He began reading Turvey's responses aloud, in a brooding kind of way. "'*Love*. I love animals.' Hmmm. Farm boy?" His voice held a touch of anxiety.

"Yessir, Skookum Falls, B.C."

"Ahhh . . . '*Women*. I love women too.'" The captain flashed a relieved smile. "Hmmm . . . '*Soldier*. He's not a soldier he's a—' What were you going to write there?"

"Canadian, sir."

"Ca-Canadian!?"

"It's a kinda wise-crack, sir. The limey girls say it."

"Oh." The captain's soft brow contorted. "'*Money*. I'm flat . . . *March*. Wonder where June is . . .' Hmmm. What was your mother's first name, Turvey?"

"Mary, sir."

"Ahhh . . . '*Red*. Blanket drill'?" The captain's forgetmenot eyes came up blinking.

"Oh, sorry, sir. Thought the sergeant said *Bed*." The captain still looked puzzled, and disappointed. "Blanket drill is what the fellahs call grabbin off a nap durin duty hours."

"Oh . . . '*Bang*. Petrol'???"

"Bang-water, sir. That's petrol."

"Yesss . . . '*Kiss*.' You've got S-W-A-K in capitals???"

Turvey blushed. "Sealed with a kiss, sir. 'Swhat we wrote on the back of a nenvelope, to a girl, like."

The captain cocked his head as if he were memorizing it. Then he went on. "'*Drink*. Red ink.' Have you ever, uh, had the impulse to drink ink?"

"That's just what we call that red wine, sir."

"Oh, sorry. '*Patrol*. Skirt'?"

"O, shucks, that's just skirt-patrol. You know, lookin for beetles." The captain stayed blank. "Well, just sorta moochin around lookin for girls to pick up."

"Ahhhh. Ummm . . . '*Blast*. The C.O. gave me . . . *Happy*. As a pig in . . .' Pig in what?"

Turvey tilted his head bashfully. "I didnt like to write it, sir."

The captain stared, saw light, and struggled on. "'*Medal*. Shoved my arm.' Now *how* did you come to associate those ideas?"

"Well, that *is* kinda tangled, sir. You see, a chap I was out drinkin wallop, er, beer with a few nights ago got a skinful and started foolin around and he shoved my elbow just as I was goin to take a pull, and it sloshed on my battleblouse and it's kinda on my mind because I havent got the stains out quite and the sergeant noticed it yesterday."

The captain thought this over. His nose twitched again. "But I still dont see the connection with *medals*!"

"O, canteen medals! That's what we call beer-stains on a blouse, that's all."

"Ahhh." The captain scratched his head. "'*Armour*. Crabs.' That's an unusual one. I rather like that. Streak of poetry in you, eh? Lived sometime on the Pacific, havent you? Thinking of crabs as armoured, eh?"

"Well, it's kind of a sayin, too, you know, sir. Armoured cooties, some of the fellahs call em. And," he added, warming up—he was enjoying this very much, "I've heard em called ballplayers." But again the captain seemed to be left in a daze. This time he didnt try any further but dropped his eyes to the next word, wriggling his brows.

"'*Blood*. Ketchup . . . *Steady*. Peggy.' That—that wouldnt be"—he seemed quite unsure of himself now—"your girl-friend?" His voice squeaked again, and he jiggled his pencil.

When Turvey admitted it was, the psychiatrist's face came alive like a flashlight. He made Turvey tell him all about Peggy. "Now," he said, "just three more words. *Killer.* You thought of, er, *knickers*. Er?"

"Passion-killers, sir." Turvey looked abashed again.

"? ? ?"

"What the Airforce girls wear. Kinda big and blue. And, and baggy. It's what I hear the fellahs call em."

The captain sighed. "Well, at least the next one's different. '*Sentry. Greatcoat.*' You were thinking of last night?" Turvey nodded, trapped at last. "Tell me all about it." Turvey told him. When he'd finished, the captain leaned over impressively and twitched his slender nose at him. "And now, Turvey, I want you to answer this question very carefully and truthfully. Why, when the sergeant said *father* did you write down the word 'greatcoat' again?"

Turvey was startled. "Did I?" The captain pointed a soft finger at the revealing line in the W.A.T. and twisted the paper for Turvey to see. "Gosh. I guess I was still thinkin of pottin my greatcoat. *Father's* the word right after *sentry*."

"Ah. I wonder if it was that simple. The mind doesnt make these errors without reason. Tell me about your father. He was nearly seventy-six when you were born. Did you get on well with him?"

Turvey told the captain what little he remembered of the old boy, how he'd tie one on over in Kuskanee, and come home and play his fiddle to the cows in the barn when the old lady threw him out of the house. The more he talked the more the captain nodded his head and made rapid little sniffs with his nose. "Turvey," he said finally, "honestly now, werent there times before your father died, when you were so angry with him you wished he was, well, that he would die?"

"Holy gosh, I dont think so. Maybe I might have when I'd get into some hellery and he'd give me the end of a trace, but not really for long or like I meant it or anythin. He wasnt such a bad old bird, the way I remember, but course I was only eight when he died."

"Umhmm, think carefully now, in answering this. Did your father wear an overcoat much?"

Turvey thought. "Every winter. Course everybody did. It was cold."

"Was he a big man? Tall?"

"Yeah, as I remember, he was quite a size . . . "

Later Turvey was allowed to look for things in the same comical ink-blots the psychiatrist at Great Buzzard had shown him, and then make up stories to fit some rather vague pictures the captain brought out of a drawer. He found it as interesting a morning as he had spent in the army though he couldnt help worrying whether the captain hadnt found an S somewhere in it all. He told him how much he wanted to get up to the Sharp End with Mac and the Kootenay Highlanders.

"Well Turvey," the captain said finally, sagging back in his chair as if he were really pooped out—he had been writing steadily for the last twenty minutes—"I think we can make everybody fairly happy about this. I'll give you an S all right and the C.O. can wash out the charges. But it'll be the smallest S I can find. An S-Three-*T*. That means you have a slight nervous condition which will clear up of itself, probably, once you're out of here. In thirty days another psychiatrist can examine you and pronounce you fit for the field. *And*, meantime, I'll send you up near the front, to a Special Pioneer Detachment."

"Gee, that sounds swell," said Turvey, relieved and impressed. "Thanks a lot. My mum and dad were pioneers. In the Kuskanee Valley."

"Er, not at all. best of luck, and take this chit to the sergeant on your way out with your guards."

"Very interesting," said the sergeant, gravely scanning Turvey's report. "'Temporary hysteria . . . Possible latent father-rivalry . . . Mild anxiety condition. . . .' Havent had one quite like this before. But he says you're getting over it fast. What you've got my boy is probably an Oedipus complex, though the captain wouldnt come right out with it."

"What's that?" asked Turvey anxiously. "It aint anything you get from girls, is it?"

"No, no, my boy. Father complex. Mother too. There's the dinner gong. No time to explain. Anyway he's marked you for No. 29 SPD. You'll leave tomorrow."

"Is that at the front?"

"O, couldnt answer that, Turvey. Security, you know, confidential info . . . Guards up!"

"O yeah, sorry. Anyway, I'll be a specialist till I get all right again, wont I?" Turvey had to talk over his shoulder as the guards hustled him off; they were hungry too.

"A, uh, specialist? O, yes, sure. But dont worry. Prognosis . . . very favourable."

"What's a prog nose?" Turvey asked his guards as they trotted him out into the sunlight. But neither of them knew.

How do men act under fire? Mowat's autobiographical account provides one answer, while military historian Bill McAndrew, a long-serving specialist at the Directorate of History at National Defence Headquarters, Ottawa, tries to explore others. What emerges clearly, despite his fine effort, is that battlefield behaviour remains largely unexplored.

The Soldier and the Battle

*Bill McAndrew**

> To look at old facts through new glasses, then to make use of the facts in order to gain a better understanding of those glasses—that, after all, is what makes history worthwhile.
> —Martin Van Creweld, *Command in War*

On 10 August 1944, just south of Caen in the Normandy bridgehead, a twenty-year-old Canadian infantryman shot himself in the left foot with his Bren gun. One of four soldier brothers, another of whom had been killed in Italy a few months before, he had fought well for two months. After a week's rest, his battalion was moving back into the line when it was bombed by friendly aircraft, taking about 100 casualties. Badly shaken, he moved forward where, two days later, a report on his case observed: "Two enemy tanks were bringing fire to bear on his position and had killed men in the immediate vicinity. This was too much for him and he lost his nerve and shot himself." He was hospitalized and then court-martialed, and was sentenced to two years' imprisonment with hard labour.[1]

*The author is grateful to Jack Granatstein and Desmond Morton, and to colleagues at the Canadian Forces College, including Col. Keith Eddy, SLDSH, and Lt.-Col. Michael Greene, USMC, and David Buchanan, RAF, for their stimulating advice, not all of which (possibly unwisely) found a way into the text.

This soldier's fate was unusual only in the classic structure of its catch-22. Because he was able to make a rational choice between unpalatable alternatives, presumably he was of sufficiently sound mind not to be considered a battle exhaustion casualty. Had his shaky condition been acknowledged earlier, instead of prison he could have been given a job in his unit's rear echelon. Alternatively, he might have been medically evacuated to his unit medical officer, and then, perhaps, to a field psychiatrist in No. 1 Canadian Exhaustion Unit. From there he could have been sent to Britain for further therapy or to a Special Employment Company for labouring jobs behind the front line. In this way, his record would not have been stained with a dishonourable discharge.[2]

This by no means isolated case prompts several questions about the behaviour of men in battle. How typical was this soldier's situation? Was that normal or aberrant behaviour? What alternatives were available for soldiers who succumbed to intolerably stressful conditions? What distinguished disciplinary from medical responses to noneffective soldiers? What was the relationship between actual soldierly behaviour and operational doctrine and performance? On the assumption that there is as much to learn from examining a snowflake as in scanning the universe, the Canadian Army's World War II experience may offer a useful microcosm for exploring universal questions about men in battle.

Soldiers in Battle

The first point to note is that we do not know much about how soldiers, Canadian or otherwise, actually performed. Anyone without direct experience who tries to participate vicariously in battle through a spectrum of contradictory sources will soon be bewildered. Generally there is more, or sometimes less, than meets the eye. Few Canadian historians have probed beyond romanticized notions of heroic warriors. Campaign and operational histories generally assume effective behaviour, and regimental accounts naturally exclude all but the exemplary. Fewer Canadian social scientists have displayed an interest in how their countrymen reacted to combat. If they thought about the topic at all, Canadian academics simply extrapolated from American and British research. Roger Spiller's comment that "the competition between science and military tradition to explain the human dimension of combat makes clear that knowledge, after 3500 years of recorded military history, is very crude" applies even more so in Canada.[3] A few novels and memoirs offer hints, but, however informative, their slim slices of reality are necessarily idiosyncratic. Donald Pearce, a subaltern in the North Nova Scotia Highlanders, recalled how individual battle experiences were just that. "No one else has really been in the same places as anyone else," he wrote "and I refuse to play the game of comparing experiences. The whole war seems to be a quite different war from mine, and ultimately everyone is separated from everyone by layers of privacy or egoism."[4]

The impossibility of describing endless layers of realities may account for a certain reluctance to probe further. To cite Spiller again, he remarked that "because the soldier's history of war does not readily submit to the orderly requirements of history, and because, when uncovered, it often challenges the orderly traditions by which military history has shaped our understanding of warfare, the soldier's war has been the great secret of military history."[5] Like military commanders, historians prefer tidy, not chaotic, battlefields. Most mistrust individual recollections and differ over how many it takes to form a theory. Anecdotal evidence, however, can add much to incomplete war diaries and sometimes self-serving after-action reports that are confidently cited. Perhaps their most valuable insight is to warn against easy generalizations that presume the average soldier's thoughts and moods. A certain scepticism may be in order, for example, when a corps commander writes that his exhausted troops were "keen to get into battle again," or about a historian's equally remarkable conclusion that "the reward of General Patton's efforts was the confident enthusiasm with which his soldiers willingly put their lives on the line to help him achieve his destiny."[6]

Front-line fighters are seldom as bloodthirsty as distant commanders, or theorists, but it is a curious, not to say unrealistic, fact that correct and effective soldierly behaviour is commonly taken for granted. This is especially puzzling in an age when the behavioural sciences have been mobilized to explain the diversity of human reactions to stress. Nonetheless, strategic analyses, operational accounts, and tactical narratives proceed as if soldiers who have to implement tidy map plans expose themselves more or less casually to mutilation and death. Self-sacrifice invariably prevails over self-preservation, an extraordinary proposition that is explained as the natural result of training or inherent courage. To the extent that this did occur, it likely demanded a certain suspension of belief. After all, it was hardly rational for a soldier to break cover and advance toward hostile machine guns. One platoon commander has described how his role in battle was

> essentially histrionic[,] . . . to feign a casual and cheerful optimism to create an illusion of normality and make it seem as if there was nothing in the least strange about the outrageous things one was asked to do. Only in this way could he ease the tension, quell any panic, and convince his men that everything would come out right in the end.[7]

It was not always possible to establish an illusion of normality. While most soldiers performed their unenviable tasks doggedly, and some, with exceptional courage, a significant minority found ways to avoid the stress of battle. Some straggled, ran, or hid; some became medical—and others, disciplinary—cases. There was nothing new in this, nothing unusual about individuals losing their will or self-control. The wonder is that more did not. A northerner at Antietam captured the essence of the fighting soldier's dilemma when he wrote:

> The truth is when bullets are whacking against tree trunks and solid shot are cracking skulls like egg shells, the consuming passion in the heart of the average man is to get out of the way. Between the physical fear of going forward, and the moral fear of turning back, there is a predicament of exceptional awkwardness, from which a hidden hole in the ground would be a wonderfully welcome outlet.[8]

It is impossible to know how many soldiers in any battle, in any war found "hidden holes." In his persuasive description of World War I trench life, Tony Ashworth concluded that informal agreements between opposing front-line troops to live and let live were sufficiently common to be considered normal.[9] It is reasonable to suppose that widely dispersed World War II battlefields offered more, not fewer, holes, and scattered evidence suggests that the outcome of many clashes was decided by relatively few fighters. It seems natural that soldiers would find ways to avoid stressful situations. Although records are incomplete, some, particularly those accounting for what may ironically be termed aberrant behaviour, suggest an understandably diverse range of human responses to the terrors of battle.

The first are those concerned with battle exhaustion or neuropsychiatric casualties. Like other World War II armies, Canadians at first ignored their "shell shock" experience of World War I. When finally forced to acknowledge the phenomenon once more, commanders and medical staffs reacted much as they did with venereal disease: they were never quite sure whether to call military police for a disciplinary problem or doctors for a medical one. Despite reservations, however, an army psychiatric establishment evolved during the war. A psychiatrist landed in Sicily with 1st Division, others joined him in Italy, and even more accompanied the troops to North-West Europe (NWE).[10]

These psychiatrists had an active practice that fluctuated in intensity with the course of battle. Psychiatric cases consistently tracked physical casualties at a rate of one to four, three, or even two. In Italy the two-division Canadian Corps had just over 5000 cases in nineteen months. In NWE, three divisions had a like number between D- and VE-Days. The numbers reflect only soldiers diagnosed in the medical evacuation system and exclude those looked after in their units, undetected psychosomatic cases, and dysfunctional soldiers killed after they lost their self-control.[11]

The second category of aberrant behaviour for which there is some statistical evidence is that of military crime. Self-inflicted wounds were difficult to prove, but more than 230 incidents were reported in Normandy, and the Italian rate was comparable. Courts-martial numbers were more detailed. There were 4383 Field General Courts-Martial (FGCM) in NWE in 1944–1945: 2088 in Italy in 1944 and the first quarter of 1945 before the corps moved to Holland. A large proportion heard charges of desertion, cowardice, or leaving a reinforcement draft while proceeding to the front. Disciplinary screws were tightened severely in the final winter of the war. During the last six months in Italy, FGCMs averaged between five and ten a day. With the death penalty unavailable as a deterrent, courts awarded exemplary sentences of two to five years' imprisonment with hard labour as a matter of policy. Severe sentences may have deterred some soldiers, but the possibility of losing wartime credits for postwar gratuities was probably an even more effective control on unsoldierly behaviour.[12]

Battle exhaustion and disciplinary losses together presented a serious drain on limited manpower resources. The Italian theatre offers a convenient measure of its scale and scope. When I Canadian Corps left Italy in the spring of 1945, its consultant psychiatrist, Lieutenant-Colonel Arthur Doyle, conducted a survey of Canadians in the military prison system. He found about 1600. Most were infantrymen, and many had been previously evacuated as physical or psychiatric casualties. In addition, there were at least another 1300 noneffectives reassigned from combat units to labour companies. Most, also, were infantrymen. Placing these numbers in perspective, there were seldom more than 75 fighters in an operational rifle company; that is, 300 in a battalion. The nine battalions of an 18 000-man infantry division, then, might deploy around 3000 riflemen. The total was about equivalent to the number of noneffectives.[13]

Medical and disciplinary behavioural explanations merged because, except for extremes, it was difficult to define a reasonable line between them. Especially late in the war, it became largely a matter of random circumstance whether a soldier who could no longer function effectively in combat ended up peeling potatoes in his company kitchen, loading trucks with ammunition, staying in the hospital, or doing hard time. In action a soldier might be reported as being "useless and demoralizing to other men," "shaky and weak in action. Froze to slit trench," or as "jeopardizing the lives of other men in the platoon. Stays in slit trench all the time, except during shelling, when he runs around everywhere." If he could not regain his self-control with the help of his mates or unit medical officer, the soldier would be channeled to a forward field psychiatrist. One recalled that these soldiers presented

> a rather monotonous and anything but dramatic picture—dejection, fatigue, and apathy being the outstanding features, with varying degrees of tremors,

unshaven faces, dull eyes and muddy uniforms completing the "beat up" appearance. The complaints were also stereotyped—"I just can't take it anymore; I can't stand those shells; I've had it."[14]

Unit medical officers and psychiatrists faced perplexing diagnostic challenges. Very few of their patients presented symptoms of classic mental disorders. The incidence of schizophrenia or psychosis was no greater than in a comparable civilian environment. Some were clearly dysfunctional, with physical impairment having a psychological cause—for example, paralysis, blindness, or aphonia—which required medical intervention. Were the others more properly dealt with by doctors or military policemen? The psychiatrists were in an unenviable position. Conscious of their dual responsibilities—to their individual patients who wanted out of battle and to the army who wanted them back at the front, the field psychiatrists found effective guidance for restoring broken psyches in rediscovered World War I handling principles of immediacy, proximity, and expediency. However, for their soldier patients, recovery meant returning to the milieu organized for their violent death that had caused the problem in the first place. The psychiatrists whose medical specialty in this era hovered only on the fringes of medical respectability, faced a most delicate dilemma. Surviving records reflect a most conscientious search for a pragmatic balance between toughmindedness and humane concern which is remarkable under the circumstances. They returned to their units those with the most promising prognosis, sent others to noncombat labouring jobs, and evacuated the rest for more intense treatment in base hospitals.[15]

In time the doctors detected patterns of incidence. The great majority of psychiatric as well as physical casualties were infantrymen. Soldiers who were new to battle were vulnerable. If they survived initial shocks, individuals might acquire protective battle experience, but too much fighting eventually wore out even the strongest. Virtually everyone had his breaking point. Precipitating causes might be battle stress or personal distress, which could sap will, motivation, and morale and, as British General Frank Richardson aptly remarked, the psychiatric casualty is "the last stage in the failure of a man's personal morale."[16]

Morale and motivation dictated how soldiers would behave on the battlefield, but they were beyond the control of psychiatrists. "The psychiatric problem was always in two parts: the symptoms of neurosis and the morale of the men," the official medical history observed. "In a soldier who failed the test of battle, the neurosis was first treated and then morale was considered. In short [the psychiatrists were] dealing with two distinct problems long differentiated by the vulgar but accurate terms 'nerves' and 'guts.'"[17] The psychiatrists saw the results of collapsed morale, but producing and sustaining morale was a command, not a medical, problem. As the U.S. Army's inspector-general remarked about a like problem in his army: "The majority of [battle exhaustion] cases are not psychoneurotic conditions because medical officers wish to make patients out of them but because line officers have been unable to make soldiers out of them."[18]

It is necessary, then, to probe beyond the battlefield in exploring battlefield behaviour. Explanations of soldiers' conduct connect the individual and his field unit to the entire complex process of transforming civilians into soldiers, a mob into a disciplined force. The army's manpower policies, enlistment practices, recruiting standards, training, leadership, and group cohesion all affected morale and, hence, the eventual outcome: whether or when, and in what circumstances, a soldier became psychologically ineffective. Some were in that state before joining up, others became so in training, more broke down early in combat, and yet others burned out after long exposure. All these stages offer fruitful research possibilities in neglected documentary, statistical, and anecdotal sources. A few themes suggest themselves.

Manpower Policies and Military Effectiveness

ONE THEME is the ultimate effect on the battlefield of wide oscillations in Canadian wartime manning policies between indiscriminate recruiting and excessive personnel screening. The source of many of the army's early behavioural problems arguably lay in the chaotic scramble for bodies at the beginning of the war. When 57 000 men were enrolled in 1939 to form 1st and 2nd Infantry divisions, the mere act of volunteering was assumed to be sufficient evidence of fitness for war. Medical instructions noted simply that "the recruit should have the appearance of being an intelligent and sober man and likely to become an efficient soldier."[19] That premise proved deficient. Recruit motivations were bound to vary, especially in the social and economic aftermath of the Great Depression. The president of an Edmonton medical board, himself a World War I veteran, wrote about the men he saw. While some were "promoted by patriotism and ideals, willing to do anything they can and make any necessary sacrifice in defence of the cause," he thought many others were "promoted largely by a desire to wear a uniform, with pay and allowances [and] did not intend to do any real soldiering if they could get out of it. . . . [Moreover, a large number were] obviously mentally or physically unfit for the stress of front line warfare . . . and [there were] the unemployed, making a choice between two evils without seriously considering what is in store for them."[20] This was not unusual. Recruiting standards are invariably set by supply and demand. However, the army lacked a training organization that could systematically winnow out those either unable or unwilling to soldier. Instead, they were shipped untrained to Britain, where they formed a pool of persistent behavioural problems that severely taxed training and administrative resources.

Partially in response to the difficulties these soldiers created, the social sciences were mobilized. In the early 1940s, psychologists assumed that they were able to predict an individual's potential military effectiveness by evaluating his personality. They persuaded personnel administrators, in turn, that once neurotic, psychopathic, and other personality defects were excluded, few behavioural problems would remain. Consequently, the army formed a Personnel Selection Service and the manning pendulum swung rapidly from no winnowing at all to full-scale screening.[21]

Employing screening methods derived from dubious World War I and industrial models, personnel selection officers tested and interviewed thousands of recruits to assess their intelligence, aptitudes, functional capabilities, and personality profiles. The degree to which examiners were able to rationalize the use of available manpower talent by, for instance, identifying potential officers, NCOs, and skilled tradesmen, is problematic, but they probably helped. Less successful were their efforts to screen out personality defects according to a scheme of unproven presuppositions. No one knew what personality profile made a successful soldier, let alone an effective combat infantryman. Casual selective criteria like "good nervous stability[,] . . . interested in hunting and outdoor life generally[,] . . . likes the notion of commando training," were hardly helpful.[22]

While recruits were scrutinized in Canada, the overseas army was also intensively screened. The random initial recruiting process had scattered talent indiscriminately throughout units. Too many cooks were driving trucks and too many drivers were cooking. Hastily organized teams of examiners canvassed units to find round pegs for round establishment holes. The primary selection premise was that the war would be a mechanized one fought by specialists rather than infantrymen. Consequently, the examiners identified those with useful civilian skills and trades and those who might potentially acquire them, and posted them for specialist training. Infantry battalions were thus stripped of many of their best qualified men and left with the rest.

Several unfortunate results trailed the mass screening exercise. Unit commanders became understandably disturbed when "agents of a superior body, Canadian Military Headquarters[,] . . . [arrived] to spy out and remove some of their best men." Commanders' efforts to foster unit cohesion, which provided the external supports that individual soldiers needed in battle, were not helped by the disruptive turnover. In addition, excessive numbers of specialists were trained while infantry requirements were neglected. Further, large numbers of soldiers were jarred loose from their unit homes and sent for reallocation to those dismal repositories of the unwanted, Reinforcement Units. Some, unable to successfully complete training, settled into housekeeping jobs somewhere in the system until called on as reinforcements. Still others, detached from their familiar homes and lacking direction and leadership in Reinforcement Units, ended up in the Headly Detention Barracks and the Aldershop psychiatric outpatients' clinic.[23]

As manpower resources grew scarce, manning policy swung away from rigid selection. Large numbers of recruits were being rejected while shortages loomed. Critics charged that standards were too high when army recruiters were having difficulty in filling infantry ranks from a diminishing supply of volunteers. Consequently, standards were lowered and indifferently applied across the country. Filling a recruiting quota, however, did not necessarily mean obtaining more trainable men. One medical officer at an advanced training centre that had to prepare these men for battle described his experience. Believing that

> an ounce of exclusion is worth a pound of discharges, [he] interviewed each man on his arrival . . . [and] could hardly believe the number who were obviously misfits. . . . However, we could and did pamper, bully, and encourage most of them through their training and send them overseas. I have seen them either just out of hospital following investigation and with a diagnosis of "No Appreciable Disease," or just out of detention and labelled a "bad actor," bundled off with special precautions to see that they do not escape the troop train.[24]

Overseas psychiatrists agreed that it made little sense to send unprepared men to combat. It simply passed the disposal problem overseas, where several thousand combat noneffectives had already accumulated. One extreme example was of a man going directly from ship to psychiatric ward on arrival. Colonel Fred Van Nostrand, the army's chief psychiatric consultant, protested that

> Regarding the effectiveness of the present method of screening recruits at intake and weeding out of the unfit, we are not in a position to express opinion, except to state that neither the rejection of recruits, nor the weeding during training have been too strict, since we are still getting as reinforcements a fair number of soldiers who give histories of former inadequacy or mental ill-health, and who break down under the stress of very short battle experience. The rate of psychoneurotic breakdown in both theatres of war has been higher in reinforcements than in soldiers serving with units to which they had been posted during the training period. . . . One soldier who stated that he enlisted in Canada on D-Day, was invalided from France in August with psychiatric disability. A fair number of other casualties admitted to [the psy-

> chiatric hospital] at this time had less than six months in the army.[25]

Similarly, a staff officer wrote of self-inflicted wound incidents that "in the normal case the soldier is young, 18 to 21, and in most cases has arrived in the UK from Canada in late Spring or early Summer of 1944, and is sent almost at once as a reinforcement to France."[26]

The gaps in the army's manning and training system beg to be explored further, because maintaining a dependable supply of trained and motivated men was vital to unit performance. Part of that process was ensuring that soldiers could be integrated into cohesive sections and platoons. Sustaining fighting groups was exceptionally difficult when a well-placed machine gun or an ill-timed mortar concentration could wipe out months of hard training in a few minutes. The Royal Winnipeg Rifles, for instance, lost a company on D-Day, the equivalent of two more on 8 June, and a like number a month later. A short time later the South Saskatchewan Regiment was maimed in the Forêt de la Londe, after which it "reformed four rifle companies—23 men in A Company, 21 in B Company, 9 in C Company and 12 in D Company."[27] Reinforcements sent forward as individuals to shattered battalions like these, even if well trained, too often lacked an opportunity to form the self-supporting groups that were the key to combat effectiveness. The army was unable to take full advantage of its regimental system to sustain units overtaken by casualties. By the fall of 1944 it was engaged in an unseemly scramble for bodies to fill depleted combat ranks.

Reinforcement problems struck morale, and if there is a grain of truth to the truisms about the significance of morale in battle, it would be remarkable if diminished motivation did not affect operational performance. The most evident impact at the front was through the incremental drain of burned-out leaders and reliable men who could not easily be replaced. A company commander in Italy described how, on moving forward to an attack,

> before D Company had even reached the area of the guns 4 men had deserted. During the subsequent ten days of action the men were unreliable, partly owing to lack of good NCOs. One was killed and four wounded out of D Company during the first attempt to cross the River Savio . . . because they had to go back, or expose themselves unduly so as to force their men to go with them. The company went into action 20 men under strength, and the men knew that few if any reinforcements would be coming up. . . . In mid-December, men who became lance corporals in October, were commanding platoons in action.[28]

Cumulative losses in companies meant that control, initiative, and effectiveness suffered throughout the chain of command. General Vokes described how heavy physical and psychiatric casualties at Ortona wore out his 1st Division. "It is most noticeable that the standard of minor tactics and unit tactics has deteriorated," he wrote, "and opposition which at one period would have been brushed aside in their stride, now causes untold delay and stickiness."[29] The staff of 7 Brigade in the Normandy bridgehead remarked similarly how losses slowed their capacity to react quickly. They wrote:

> For set piece attacks, higher formations and brigades must leave units more time, firstly for outline planning and recce [reconnaissance], and secondly between final orders and H hour. . . . Commanding Officers and sub unit commanders require more time for orders than formerly due to the large number of green reinforcement officers, NCO's and men. They must not only give orders in the normal way, but go into much greater detail as to the course to be followed by their officers, NCO's and men. Each time a battalion attacks is the first time in action for some officers and men, and they by no means know the correct action to be taken as a result of the approved concise verbal orders.[30]

Declining efficiency from accumulating losses was to be expected. However, by 1944 a badly flawed manning and reinforcement system that was unable to sustain infantry battalions effectively had become the army's most serious deficiency.

Neglected links between recruiting practices, training, personnel policies, unit integration, discipline, and battle exhaustion hold much research promise. Equally worthy is the interaction between morale and behaviour on the one hand and operational doctrine on the other. It seems reasonable to suppose that doctrine, or the manner in which soldiers were deployed in combat, also affected morale and, consequently, battle worthiness.

Operational Doctrine and Battle Performance

THERE IS SOME SUGGESTIVE EVIDENCE about that obscure seam in the detailed questionnaires that scores of combat officers completed on returning from Italy and Normandy.[31] One persistent thread in their responses to items concerning morale was their lack of opportunity to exercise initiative. This seems odd because the message runs counter to commonly received wisdom about Canadian soldiers. Nonetheless, their view from the bottom was of higher staffs issuing detailed, inflexible plans that they were expected to implement. When, often, battle procedures were foreshortened, they then had little time to brief their subordinates adequately. When leaders became casualties, their soldiers, knowing little of their unit's mission except to follow a moving artillery barrage toward an objective circled on a map, went to ground and forward movement stopped. A variation of this approach to battle was the curious habit of always attacking the enemy at his strongest point, with one exhausted battalion being committed after another decimated one.[32] As well as adversely affecting morale and performance, this style of war prompted scepticism of higher commanders. Morale was not enhanced when these same commanders habitually faulted their soldiers for not successfully implementing their "perfect" plans.

Was that the doctrinal chicken to the behavioural egg? There are World War I echoes in these fighters' complaints about higher commanders and their staffs. There are also doctrinal tactical links between the two wars that are worth exploring. Much has been written during the past decade about the origins of modern tactical doctrine, especially *auftragstatik* as practised by the *Wehrmacht*, which accounted for its extraordinary battlefield flexibility. In *Stormtroop Tactics*, Bruce Gudmundsson traced the roots back to the decentralized pre-World War I German Army, which produced two quite different tactical responses to the open battlefield. Some commanders chose to retain traditional close-order ranks because they were unsure how their soldiers would react if dispersed. They feared that too many would find convenient holes to avoid battle. In contrast, other commanders accepted dispersion and loose control to gain flexibility. Much of the initiative to find ways of manoeuvring on the battlefield came from below, from relatively junior officers in the trenches and, Gudmundsson remarked, "Despite the fears of some pre-war officers, battalions and companies advancing in open order did not degenerate into purposeless masses of individuals trying to avoid combat."[33] That doctrinal foundation was codified between the wars and practised after 1939. One practitioner has observed that delegated responsibility throughout the chain of command leading by mission, was made possible only because German soldiers were made full shareholders in their operations.[34]

British/Canadian tactical doctrine evolved differently, with soldiers being handled more as unconsulted employees than shareholders. Tactical stalemate produced a highly centralized planning structure whose purpose was to eliminate, not exploit, the natural chaos of the battlefield. One observer remarked that as early as 1916, "a mechanistic theory of the conduct of war was being developed which bade fair to make cyphers of the individual and the unit. The foundation of a bureaucratic means of handling operations was well and truly laid during the winter lull."[35] The artillery barrage became the arbiter of tactical planning because staffs could control massed gunfire. Movement was less easily managed.[36] Staffs could not track infantrymen spread over an open battlefield as readily as they could impose a rectangular artillery grid over it. Even well-trained soldiers might not react predictably. Hence the Somme, where thousands of troops were herded toward fixed defences in packed ranks.

There were both doctrinal and behavioural reasons for this rigidity. Faith in organization, technology, and high explosives played a part. One British commander wrote that "nothing can exist at the conclusion of the bombardment in the area covered by [the barrage] and the infantry would only have to walk over and take possession." Lack of faith in soldiers also played a part. The New Armies were thought to be insufficiently trained or trustworthy or do other than follow a barrage. Tim Travers observed: "First, there was the underlying theme that sufficient 'weight' and 'energy' would always carry a position, and secondly . . . [a] 'social' feeling that it was more important to stress control and discipline of one's own troops than worry about the enemy. . . . In fact, Fourth Army sometimes seemed more worried by their own men than by the enemy."[37] As Bill Rawlings recently pointed out, the Canadian Corps reorganized its training after the Somme to emphasize platoon-level fire and movement drills which units implemented at Vimy Ridge.[38] However, at Vimy and elsewhere, artillery still dictated the limits of manoeuvre and tactical innovation remained largely concerned with rationalizing firepower.

The Somme was just the most disastrous example of systemic weakness. Whether this staff-driven management style evolved from a distinctive British/Canadian mind-set or because of infantry inadequacies is arguable. The outcome was the same: a centralized bureaucratic structure that attempted to control the uncontrollable. That legacy, leading by command and not mission, persisted through World War II. With some notable exceptions, confining infantry movement to following a barrage remained the predictable tactical signature of Canadian operations, as the Germans frequently noted. The Canadian assaults on the Hitler Line in Italy in May 1944 or at Carpiquet airport in Normandy a month later, to cite just two of many examples, were mounted on a familiar World War I model.

The price paid for control and order in both wars was inflexibility. One German commander observed after the Somme that "the individual English soldier is well trained and shows personal bravery. The majority of the officers, however, are not sufficiently trained. They are lacking in ability to exploit a success and follow it up quickly."[39] In 1944 the British Army distributed a tactical paper that suggested a remarkable continuity. "Our own tactical methods are thorough and methodical but slow and cumbersome," it concluded. "In consequence our troops fight well in defence and our set-piece attacks are usually successful, but it is not unfair to say that through lack of enterprise in exploitation we seldom reap the full benefits of them."[40] Rather than flowing freely, battlefield movement still resembled that of a child's slinky toy, confined to lurches within the range of the artillery's 25-pounder field piece. It is ironic that an authoritarian society produced a more flexible, decentralized approach to battle than its democratic enemy, but that seems to have been the case.

Again, it is unclear whether the British/Canadian approach derived from predilections for the technological efficacy of artillery or was a pragmatic command response to uncertain soldierly behaviour and morale. The latter view surfaces in records of discussions at infantry training centres, where a proper battlefield balance between fire and movement was endlessly debated. Some thought that platoons should manoeuvre internally with their own mutually supporting sections. Most preferred the company as the smallest practicable movement unit, and then only behind an artillery shield. Brigadier Lorne Campbell, who won his Victoria Cross in North Africa, concluded that soldiers' actual battlefield behaviour dictated reliance on massive artillery support. "One of the most surprising differences between war as it is and war as one imagined it would be is the ease with which men break and run," he wrote.

> Few troops, the enemy's or our own, will wait till it comes to real hand-to-hand fighting. In face of a determined attack the defenders withdraw or, if the attackers are too close, surrender; quite often they withdraw in face of fire alone. The attack which meets a stubborn defence halts short of the objective or fades back to where it started.[41]

In order to compensate for the infantry's reluctance to close, Campbell advised using massive artillery supporting fire:

> a barrage or line of concentrations from overwhelming artillery, which starts at a fixed time, moves ahead of the attackers at a pre-determined rate from start line to objective.... All the infantry has to do then is walk steadily behind the shells, keeping as close as possible, halting for nothing and turning neither to right or left. It is the simplest way of "getting from here to there and stopping there."[42]

This was virtually the same argument cited before the Somme debacle. Unfortunately, as before, artillery fire too often moved inexorably along at its own mechanical rate, while the following infantry became machine gun targets. Failure to close that intellectual and physical gap between fire support and infantry movement in turn drove down morale and induced soldiers to avoid the stress of battle. The loop connecting doctrine and behaviour was all encompassing.

The link between doctrine and behaviour demands further exploration because one inevitably affects the other. In the meantime, a United States Marine Corps veteran of Vietnam has described the symbiotic relationship as well as anyone. "Faulty doctrine frustrates an intelligent and otherwise capable soldier and then exposes him to enemy fire," he wrote.

> The soldier then feels the lack of trust, lack of information, the betrayal of unrealistic training and the shock of fire, all competing with his desire to act with and in support of his unit. When fear wins the competition, the individual sinks into anomie and fails to participate. When courage is frustrated by

the impossible situation, there can be a nervous breakdown. Physical exhaustion hastens the process.[43]

Any exploration of soldiers' reactions to battle, or more properly to combat, in Roger Spiller's fine distinction, builds naturally on his insights, along with those of John Keegan, John Ellis, Denis Winter, and a few others who have looked at old facts through new glasses. Their imaginative projections of ordinary human beings reacting to the extraordinary strains of combat touch anyone who follows. Several possibilities hold promise for illuminating further the murky realities of battlefield behaviour. One is following the soldier's behavioural trail backward from the battlefield to look closely at how he was enlisted, trained, and motivated to withstand the extraordinary conditions of combat. A particularly important aspect of that theme concerns the handling of reinforcements. Training a formed unit beforehand is a much more straightforward matter than sustaining it effectively once it has become actively engaged in combat.

The sources of operational doctrine, and how they may have affected battlefield behaviour, also beg further exploration. Presumably an army's collective soul, its style of war, will be shaped in some fashion by its country's norms, practices, and civil institutions. In the Canadian case, military doctrine that emphasized bureaucratic centralization followed naturally the style of the country's business, commercial, and other civil institutions. Rigid hierarchical control, limiting flexibility and discouraging initiative, will dampen morale in the trenches or the workplace. The state of a soldier's morale will affect his responses when leaderless and directionless. Cross-disciplinary research may illustrate elusive continuities between civil and military experience.

Notes

1. The correspondence on this case and on self-inflicted wound handling is in National Archives of Canada (NAC), RG24, vol. 12, 726.
2. For more detailed discussion, see Terry Copp and Bill McAndrew, *Battle Exhaustion: Soldiers and Psychiatrists in the Canadian Army, 1939–1945* (Montreal: McGill-Queen's University Press, 1990).
3. Roger Spiller, "Isen's Run: Human Dimensions of Warfare in the 20th Century," *Military Review* 68 (May 1988): 31. See also Roger Spiller, "The Tenth Imperative," *Military Review* 69 (April 1989): 2–13.
4. Donald Pearce, *Journal of a War* (Toronto: Macmillan 1965), 179.
5. Roger Spiller, "Shell Shock," *American Heritage* 41 (May–June 1990): 78.
6. Lt.-Gen. Charles Foulkes to Gen. H.D.G. Crerar, 7 Dec. 1944, NAC, Crerar Papers, vol. 7; Steve E. Dietrich, "The Professional Reading of General George S. Patton, Jr.," *Journal of Military History* 53 (Oct. 1989): 418.
7. Norman Craig, *The Broken Plume* (London: Imperial War Museum, 1982), 75.

8. David L. Thompson, "With Burnside at Antietam," *Battles and Leaders of the Civil War*, vol. 2 (New York, 1887), 662.
9. Tony Ashworth, *Trench Warfare, 1914–1918: The Live and Let Live System* (New York: Macmillan, 1980).
10. Copp and McAndrew, *Battle Exhaustion.* See also A.M. Doyle, "The History and Development of Canadian Neuropsychiatric Service in the CMF," and J.C. Richardson, "Neuropsychiatry with the Canadian Army in Western Europe," NAC, RG24, vols. 12630 and 12631.
11. Copp and McAndrew, *Battle Exhaustion.*
12. On discipline, see Judge Advocate General, "Records of Trials by Court Martial during the Period 1 Sep 39 to 30 Sep 46," copy in author's possession. On Italy, see the "Stats Bible" and "Liaison Letters," in War Diary, No. 2 Echelon CMF, NAC, RG24, vol. 10410. On North-West Europe, see vols. 10734 and 10825.
13. A.M. Doyle, "Report of Survey of Canadian Soldiers under Sentence in the CMF," NAC, RG24, vol. 12631.
14. A.E. Moll, "Psychosomatic Disease Due to Battle Stress," in Eric D. Wittkower and R.A. Cleghorn, eds., *Recent Developments in Psychosomatic Medicine* (Montreal: J.B. Lippincott, 1953), 436–54; and case reports of No. 2 Canadian Exhaustion Unit, NAC, RG24, vol. 12559.
15. For example, see Captain C.D. Taylor, "Resume of 223 cases at No. 1 Canadian General Hospital," Jan. 1943, NAC, RG24, vol. 2089.
16. F.M. Richardson, *Fighting Spirit: Psychological Factors in War* (London: Leo Cooper, 1978), 4.
17. W.R. Feasby, *Official History of the Canadian Medical Services*, vol. 2 (Ottawa: Queen's Printer, 1953), 77.
18. Quoted in A.J. Glass, ed., *Neuropsychiatry in World War II*, vol. 2 (Washington, DC, 1973), 103–4.
19. Canadian Army Medical Instructions, 1939, copy in Directorate of History, National Defence Headquarters, Ottawa (DHist).
20. H.H. Hepburn to J.P.S. Cathcart, 27 Nov. 1939, NAC, RG24, vol. 19466.
21. H.S.M. Carver, "Personnel Selection in the Canadian Army," Directorate of Personnel Selection, 1945, DHist.
22. Ibid.
23. Ibid. See also H.D.G. Crerar to A.G.L. McNaughton, 24 Aug. 1943 and 25 Sept. 1943, NAC, RG24, vol. 10771; B.H. McNeel, "Report of Survey of Soldiers under Sentence at the Canadian Detention Barracks, November 1943 to April 1944," NAC, RG24, vol. 12630; C.E.G. Gould, "Observations on 1000 Referred Neuropsychiatric Cases," NAC, RG24, vol. 2089.
24. Captain R.A. Stanley, "Why Did the Psychiatrist Turn Him Down?" *Journal of the Canadian Medical Services* 1, 4 (May 1944): 334.
25. F. Van Nostrand to Brigadier W.P. Warner, 2 Nov. 1944, NAC, RG24, vol. 2089.
26. Major L.R. MacDonald, "Memo to File," 11 Nov. 1944, NAC, RG24, vol. 12726.
27. Quoted in DHist, AHQ Report No. 63, "Manpower Problems of the Canadian Army during the Second War."
28. "State of Morale in D Company" PPCLI, DHist. 145.2P7011 (D3). See also Captain T.J. Allen, "Summary of Operations," NAC, RG24, vol. 10881.
29. C. Vokes to GOC 5 Corps, 3 Jan. 1944, copy in DHist CMHQ Report No. 165.
30. "Combat Lessons, 7 Brigade," copy in author's possession.
31. The questionnaires are in NAC, RG24, vol. 10450.
32. The United States Army had similar practices and problems; see R.L. Brownlee and W. Mullen, *Changing an Army: An Oral History of General William E. Depuy*

(Washington, DC: U.S. Military History Institute and U.S. Army Center of Military History, 1988).

33. Bruce I. Gudmundsson, *Stormtroop Tactics: Innovation in the German Army, 1914–1918* (New York: Praeger, 1989).
34. Oberst Hans Von Luck to author, 18 April 1985.
35. *The War the Infantry Knew* (London: Cardinal, 1987), 177.
36. The best account of the evolution of artillery is Shelford Bidwell and Dominick Graham, *Fire-Power: British Army Weapons and Theories of War, 1904–1945* (London: George Allen & Unwin, 1982).
37. Henry Rawlinson, quoted in Michael Howard, "Men against Fire: The Doctrine of the Offensive in 1914," in Peter Paret, ed., *Makers of Modern Strategy* (Princeton, NJ: Princeton University Press, 1986). Tim Travers, *The Killing Ground: The British Army, the Western Front and the Emergence of Modern Warfare, 1900–1918* (London: Allen Unwin, 1987), 144–46.
38. William Rawling, "Tactics and Technics: Technology and the Canadian Corps, 1914–18" (Ph.D. diss., University of Toronto, 1990).
39. Quoted in Travers, *Killing Ground*, 152.
40. "Notes from Theatres of War, No. 20, Italy, 1943–44," DHist 82/ 267.
41. Minutes of Training Conferences, and Campbell, "Ideas about Battle, June 1944," DHist 171.009 (D160). General William E. Depuy, U.S.A., observed, in a similar vein: "Well, I certainly came away with a feeling that only a small percentage of the soldiers did almost all of the fighting. If you just left them alone then some 10 percent of the soldiers were the ones who actually took the initiative, moved, fired their rifles, threw hand grenades, and so on. . . . I learned that you couldn't depend on them doing things simply because there was a plan to do it, or because of some generalized order to do it, and this included the junior officers. You had to say, 'do this,' 'do that,' 'now fire there,' 'now do this,' and 'now move there.' You would always end up with a good sergeant or a good officer and three or four men doing all the work." Brownlee and Mullen, *Changing an Army*, 45.
42. Ibid. Canadian doctrine was unavoidably influenced by an uncritical acceptance of General Montgomery's approach to battle, which, Sir Michael Howard has recently observed, was "determined by his perception of the limited capacity of the troops under his command. Montgomery was concerned to keep everything simple by the greatest possible amount of preparation before the battle as he did not expect the units under his command to take any bold initiatives. . . . He was in fact a very good First World War general, and he did not regard his troops as capable of any higher performance." Richard H. Kohn, ed., "The Scholarship on World War II: Its Present Condition and Future Possibilities," *Journal of Military History* 55 (July 1991): 379. General William E. Depuy, U.S.A., has remarked that: "I really believe, based on my experience, that the combat power provided by the artillery, I'm sorry to say, probably represented 90 percent or more of the combat power actually applied against the enemy. That's why I say that getting a forward observer to a high piece of ground and protecting him was the most important function that the infantry performed in that war. That's not to degrade the infantry, it's just objective analysis." Brownlee and Mullen, *Changing an Army*, 91.
43. Lt.-Col. Michael Greene USMC, a member of the Directing Staff of the Canadian Forces Command and Staff College, to author, 16 April 1991.

Tens of thousands of women served in the Canadian Forces during the war. Hundreds of thousands more worked in war plants, many earning money for the first time. How did men react to this sudden change in female status? The leading historian of women during the war, Ruth Roach Pierson, here explores the nervousness that resulted.

Wartime Jitters Over Femininity

Ruth Roach Pierson

"THEY'RE STILL WOMEN AFTER ALL" was the title given, with an audible sigh of relief, by L.S.B. Shapiro, Canadian foreign correspondent and future novelist, to a piece he did for *Saturday Night* in September 1942. In a light, jocular vein, the article expressed one man's fears, aroused by the British wartime sight of so many women stepping into formerly male jobs, that women might cease to be women, that is "feminine individuals," synonymous terms in Shapiro's vocabulary. Although closer observation convinced Shapiro that his fears were unfounded, similar fears continued to plague many other Canadians, male and female, as they viewed women entering the munitions plants and, what in the eyes of some was even worse, joining the Armed Forces.[1]

As the primary purpose of the services is the provision of the armed might of the state, their male exclusivity had been in keeping with a deeply rooted division of labour by sex that relegated women to nurture, men to combat, women to the creation and preservation of life, men, when necessary, to its destruction. Closely connected to the sexual division between arms bearers and non-arms bearers was a gendered dichotomy of attributes that identified as masculine the military traits of hardness, toughness, action, and brute force, and as feminine the non-military traits of softness, fragility, passivity, and gentleness. Hence, the very entrance of women into the Army, Navy, and Air Force sharply challenged conventions respecting women's nature and place in Canadian society.

. . . Two specific sets of circumstances induced the Department of National Defence to admit women into the armed services: manpower shortages, felt first by the Canadian Army and the Royal Canadian Air Force, and a reserve of womanpower embodied in a Canada-wide paramilitary movement of women eager to serve. For the men in charge of Canada's military, efficient prosecution of the war was the reason for putting women in uniform and under service discipline. They had no desire to tamper with existing gender relations by altering the sexual division of labour or the male-over-female hierarchy of authority. Obviously the members of the women's volunteer corps eager to become part of Canada's official forces wanted to end the male exclusivity of the military. But even they gave no indication of a desire to erase the demarcation line between male and female spheres. There was thus a tension inherent in the admission of women to the armed services: the tension between the Canadian state's wartime need for female labour within those pre-eminently masculine institutions and Canadian society's longer-term commitment to a masculine–feminine division of traits as well as separation of tasks. This tension was also apparent, albeit to a lesser degree, in the entrance of women into non-traditional trades in war industry. In both cases, under the pressure of the war emergency, women appeared to be breaking sex barriers on an alarming scale.

Reactions to women's admission to the Forces, similar to but more pronounced than those to women's mobilization for war industry, provide a good index of the social attitudes toward women prevailing in Canada at the time of the Second World War. And the records of the Department of National Defence provide a good source for those reactions. The department had to be sensitive to the values of the larger civilian society: its dependence on women volunteers, not conscripts, made it especially so. To inform itself of those attitudes it made use of opinion surveys, and to influence public opinion it made use of the media. Also, as a part of the established order, the Department of National Defence itself incorporated and acted on widely held, unexamined notions of women's nature and capabilities. The dilemma facing the department thus brought the current social attitudes toward women into high relief: by admitting women to the services, it had violated the convention that the Armed Forces were no place for a woman; in seeking volunteers, it had to advertise its conformity with as many other received notions of proper womanhood as possible.

What were the reactions to women's entrance into the Armed Forces (as well as into non-traditional trades in war industry)? One was that the war was opening up for women a world of opportunity unrestricted by sexual inequalities. The ceremonial launching of a ship that women workers had helped to build "from the first bolts and staves to the final slap of paint and piece of polished brass" moved journalist Lotta Dempsey to suggest that the event symbolized the launching of women as well: "the great and final stage of the movement of women into industry . . . on a complete equality with men."[2] The office of the Directorate of Army Recruiting suggested in February 1943 that recruiting officers should speak of the war's having "finally brought about complete emancipation of women."[3] Evidence for this was to be found in women's admission to the forces and to an ever-increasing number of jobs within the Forces. News stories designed to promote interest in and support for the women's services often played up the achievements of individual women. And women were racking up many firsts. "First woman in the history of the R.C.A.F. to take the officers' administrative course at Trenton" read the caption of a photograph in the *Globe and Mail* of 24 December 1942; "First Class of Airwomen Graduated from RCAF Photography School" was the headline of an article in the same newspaper later that same month.[4] The 1944 article in *Saturday Night* celebrating the expanding number of trades open to CWACs [the Canadian Women's Army Corps] singled out in illustration the first "qualified girl armourer in the CWAC" and the first CWAC to operate "a Telecord recording machine."[5]

This perception of the war's having fully emancipated women and of the war's having made it possible for women to "Achieve Heights Hitherto Undreamed Of"[6] meshed with the view that women were participating in the war effort on an equal footing with men. "Shoulder to Shoulder," which was an Army motto adopted by the Canadian Women's Army Corps and made the title of their official marching song, epitomized that sense of the equality of women's and men's service. When the Corps was celebrating its second anniversary in August 1943, Headquarters of Military District No. 12 (Regina) dedicated its regular monthly bulletin to the CWAC and placed under the bulletin's title, *Shoulder to Shoulder*, an illustration of a CWAC marching shoulder to shoulder with two Army men, all three wearing steel helmets on their heads and gas mask bags on their chests (but only the men shouldering rifles).[7] This image was also used on a recruitment poster for the Corps.

Of a piece with the celebration of equality and emancipation was a kind of wartime advertisement that proclaimed the end of women's confinement to the domestic sphere. Many companies advertising in the Canadian press between 1939 and 1945, especially those trying to hold on to postwar markets, sought to give a patriotic cast to their messages. One such series of advertisements run by General Motors of Canada in the special 1943 issues of *Mayfair* on "Women at War" took as its theme women's movement into the wide open spaces of the public domain. Running for five pages, the ad was set up so that a reader would encounter in bold print on a right-hand page "Woman's place . . ." and then turn to find not "is in the home" but "is

Everywhere . . ." followed on the fourth and fifth pages by the qualifier "with Victory as Their Business" and a brief description of the many fields in which women were serving the nation at war.

Canada's mobilization of women for the war effort necessitated violation of the social ideal of the woman dedicated to home and family. Even without challenging established patterns of work and behaviour considered appropriate to each sex, war cruelly disrupted and dislocated human lives. To contain the disruptive and destructive forces of war as far as would be compatible with its efficient prosecution seems to have been a goal tacitly agreed upon by those in charge of the war effort and by many in the media. Thus, with respect to women's participation in the Armed Forces, alongside the talk of emancipation, equality, and the overcoming of tradition, recruitment propaganda and wartime advertising also sought to minimize the degree of change required and to hint at and occasionally even stress the expectation of a rapid return to normalcy once the war was over.

So, at the same time recruiting officers were led to speak to NSS officials of the war's "complete emancipation of women," they were also instructed to stress that women's employment in the Armed Forces was "an emergency measure" and that "After this war they will go back to their place in civil life; they will retake their positions in the household and in the office or anywhere else where they originally came from."[8] For *Mayfair*'s 1943 celebration of women's contribution to the war effort, Westinghouse of Canada provided a more graphic statement of the expectation that at war's end women would return to motherhood and child-rearing as their principal life's work. A large two-page ad headed "These Are Tomorrow's Yesterdays" showed the pride the future son of the female war worker would take in his mother's war service. Looking through a book on *Women At War* in the school library in 1955, the boy was surprised by a picture of his mom, taken in a war plant in 1943. Overcome with emotion, the child has sat down to write his mom to tell her how proud of her he is. The ad carried not only a tribute to Canadian women's role in Canada's struggle, but also the projection that in ten or twelve years' time the women would all be back where they belonged, taking care of the home and rearing Canada's future generation.

Recruitment propaganda, promotional newspaper stories, and patriotic advertising, then, reveal a deep ambivalence toward women's joining the Armed Forces. On the one hand was the celebration of the trailblazing and achievement of women in the services and, on the other, the assurance that joining the Forces changed nothing in women's nature and place in Canadian society. In 1943 the ambivalence intensified as more and more women were needed but recruitment met resistance and monthly enlistment figures dropped. From the first enrolments in September 1941 to July 1942, 3800 women had "stepped forward to serve" and been accepted into the

Canadian Women's Army Corps.[9] Many of these came from the women's volunteer corps.[10] By March 1943, the strength of the Canadian Women's Army Corps had risen to just over 10 000.[11] Although the CWAC's peak strength in 1945 would not exceed 14 000 (636 officers plus 13 326 other ranks, totalling 13 962, on 25 April 1945),[12] military authorities in 1943 geared up for a considerable expansion of the women's Forces on the assumption that "the Army, Navy and the Air Force urgently need 65 000 more service women to release men for combat duty."[13]

In February, National Selective Service began participating "in the recruiting of women for the Navy, the Army, and the Air Force" by providing information to interested applicants and referring them to recruiting offices.[14] In March the Defence Council concurred in the recommendation of the National Campaign Committee for an intensive tri-service campaign to recruit women for the three armed services.[15] A Combined Services Committee was established to co-ordinate joint promotional and publicity endeavours for the CWAC, the WRCNS [Women's Royal Canadian Naval Service], and the RCAF (WD) [Royal Canadian Air Force (Women's Division)]. The recruitment push coincided with the growing signs of opposition to women in the military.

The monthly enlistment figures for the women's services in late 1942 and early 1943 were disappointing.* Faced with this slowdown, the National Campaign Committee granted authorization to two opinion surveys in the first half of 1943.[16] The Combined Services Committee charged with joint recruitment endeavours for the three women's services proposed that a commercial market research agency conduct a general survey of public opinion. The firm of Elliott-Haynes Limited of Montreal and Toronto was retained to determine: (a) public awareness of the need for women in the Armed Forces; (b) factors believed to influence women in favour of joining the Forces; (c) factors believed to influence women to avoid joining the Forces. The survey, which collected the opinions of 7283 civilian adults from "56 Canadian centres and their surrounding areas," claimed to have covered "both sexes, all races, all geographical regions, all age levels, all economic levels, all occupations and all classes of conjugal condition."[17] Conducted in March and April of 1943, the results appeared under the title *Report: An Inquiry into the Attitude of the Canadian Civilian Public Towards the Women's Armed Forces.*

In April and May the Directorate of Army Recruiting carried out the second

* Comparative monthly enlistment figures for CWAC:

October 1942	843
November 1942	730
December 1942	530
January 1943	699
February (3 weeks)	570

survey: a study of CWAC opinion. Based in part on the results of the first study insofar as they pertained to the CWAC, the in-house inquiry drew primarily on the "written answers to a questionnaire prepared by NDHQ [National Defence Headquarters] in both English and French" and administered to a cross-section of 1100 CWAC other ranks from all CWAC units, 18 percent of whom were non-commissioned officers and 10 percent French-Canadian women.[18] The secret and confidential report of the second inquiry, "Canadian Women's Army Corps: Why Women Join and How They Like it," was ready for limited distribution in July.

Both surveys revealed that there was widespread disapproval of women's joining the armed forces. The public opinion survey disclosed that few Canadians in the spring of 1943 gave high priority to enlistment in the armed forces as a way for women to contribute to the prosecution of the war. In answer to the question "How can women best serve Canada's war effort?" only 7 percent replied "by joining the women's forces." Five other categories of work took precedence. "Maintaining home life" ranked first in importance for the highest proportion of Canadians (26 percent), followed by "doing war work in factories" (23 percent), "part-time voluntary relief work" (13 percent), "conserving food, rationing" (11 percent), and "buying war bonds, stamps" (8 percent).[19] The ranking remained the same when the answers from French Canada were treated separately, the main difference being that an even higher proportion of French Canadians (40 percent) thought "maintaining home life" was the most important job for women in wartime, while only 18 percent thought working in war industry was; a minuscule 3 percent thought "joining women's forces" was most important. Separating out the answers from parents and from young men did not change the ranking either. Only the answers from young women showed a different order of priority: "maintaining home life" switched places with "doing war work in factories."[20] But the young women also placed ahead of "joining the forces" the same five kinds of war service as mentioned above. Furthermore, as "part-time voluntary relief work," "conserving food, rationing," and "buying war bonds, stamps" were all compatible with "maintaining home life," the inescapable conclusion is that an overwhelming majority of Canadians in 1943 saw women's place to be in the home, wartime or not.

Furthermore, according to the public opinion survey, among friends and relatives of young eligible women disapproval of their joining the Forces ran higher than disapproval of their taking jobs in war industry. Of parents, husbands, boyfriends, and brothers, 39 percent disapproved of their daughters, wives, girlfriends, and sisters joining the Armed Forces (43 percent approved, and 18 percent didn't know), while only 27 percent disapproved of their female friends and relatives entering munitions factories (59 percent approved and 14 percent didn't know).[21] When the data for English and French Canada were segregated, the level of disapproval of women in the Forces was found to be significantly higher in French Canada.[22] If one took the "don't know" as indifference or neutrality, a more negative construction could be put on the data, as was done in the report of the CWAC survey. "When pressed," it submitted, "57 percent of the public stated that they would not give open approval to their friends and relatives enrolling in the women's forces."[23] The public opinion survey highlighted another noteworthy contrast in level of disapproval. By separating mothers and fathers from boyfriends and brothers, it revealed that a higher proportion of young men objected to their girlfriends and sisters joining the forces than parents did to their daughters doing so.[24]

Young eligible women were aware of this disapproval among relatives and friends. When asked about expected responses to their joining up, 46 percent of the women eligible for enlistment assumed their parents' attitude would be unfavourable and 51 percent expected an unfavourable response from their brothers and boyfriends.[25] The only group from which support was expected to any significant degree was that of young women friends already in the Forces: from that quarter 59 percent of the eligible women responding assumed they would receive encouragement.[26] According to the CWAC survey, even the women who had ended up joining the Canadian Women's Army Corps had "received about as much discouragement as encouragement" from the friends and relatives whose advice the women had sought.[27] The CWAC survey and the public opinion survey led to the same conclusion: "Women friends already in the forces were the only people which [sic] gave outspoken approval and encouragement."[28]

Given the extent of the disapproval, it is not surprising that 61 percent of the eligible women (56 percent in English Canada, 72 percent in French Canada) responded that they had never considered joining the Armed Forces.[29] Nor is it surprising that of the 39 percent who did consider joining, about one-half finally abandoned the idea.[30] There was a connection between the disapproval of family and friends and the reluctance of eligible women to join. Of those who entertained the idea of joining but ended up rejecting it, 33 percent gave as their reason that the family objected (24 percent of the English Canadians, 54 percent of the French Canadians).[31] Of the members of the Canadian Women's Army Corps who remembered hesitating before they joined, the largest proportion (35 percent) reported that "disapproval of family and friends" was what had given them pause.[32]

In light of that sentiment, it is no wonder that those in charge of women's recruitment for the three services saw their task as essentially one of educating the public. The big push to recruit women for the Armed Forces, initially planned for 15 March to 15 June 1943, was actually mounted between 15 June and 15 September. In late summer 1943 the Combined Services Committee was given the go-ahead to continue its operation from 1 October to 31 December. In its proposal to continue the campaign to recruit women for a second three-month period, the working committee of the Combined Services Committee observed that "overcoming established tradition and developing acceptance of a new idea is obviously a long-term educational proposition." The proposal went on to define as the primary object of the campaign and the essential task of the Committee: "overcoming the tradition that women's place is exclusively in the home . . . or at least not in military uniform."[33]

Both the inquiry into public opinion and the investigation of CWAC opinion played an important part in the educational campaign. The results of these surveys were studied and analysed and the analyses pored over by members of the working and policy committees of the Combined Services Committee and officials in the Directorate of Army Recruiting [DAR]. From the CWACs' answers to the question "How did you first learn of the CWAC?" DAR analysts concluded that recruitment advertising had been woefully inadequate. The more conspicuous "news items, feature stories and pictures about the Women's Services" in newspapers and magazines had been interesting but had not carried sufficient "sell" copy, and radio had "been used extensively and effectively only on the Prairies."[34]

The tri-service campaigns of the second half of 1943 represented a massive increase in promotion of the women's services. The Combined Services Committee paid for 1000-line recruitment advertisements to be run in all daily newspapers across Canada and for full-page ads to appear in magazines and in the rotogravure sections of the metropolitan weekend papers. It contacted newspaper editors and arranged for them to sell recruiting ads "on a sponsored basis to local advertisers," providing the ad design in mat form and suggesting the pitch to the local businessmen: "a convenient, direct way for him to help along the war effort."[35] At the committee's bidding the National Film Board produced two women's recruitment films: *Proudly She Marches* and *Canada's Women March to the Colours.* Five-minute radio spots and "flash" announcements were scheduled on the CBC national and regional networks and on local radio stations across Canada. Stores and other commercial establishments were persuaded to donate some of their window space to displays promoting women's recruitment. In co-operation with others, "special events," such as conventions held by national organizations, were used to publicize the women's services. Finally, recruitment posters and streetcar signs were displayed as widely as possible.[36] In this intensification of recruitment for the women's forces, the Combined Services Committee and the Army's Directorate of Recruiting aimed to apply the lessons learned from the results of the two surveys. They sought to play up any features that had elicited a positive response and to play down, deny, disguise, or reinterpret the sources of disapproval.

One source of disapproval was a fear, similar to that expressed in L.S.B. Shapiro's *Saturday Night* piece, that the woman who joined the Forces did so at the risk of her femininity. Although neither survey posed the question in so many words—is fear of loss of femininity a reason why their family and friends are reluctant to see them join the Forces?—other questions carried much the same meaning, such as, is the reason for objection that military life is considered unsuitable for young women? According to the Elliott-Haynes survey, 20 percent of the "young eligible women reported that they thought their parents, husbands, brothers, sisters," and male and female "friends would object to their joining the forces" on the grounds that "army life" was "unsuitable."[37]

In the hopes of dispelling that notion, speeches of recruitment officers, recruitment literature, sponsored advertising, and promotional news stories, even before but especially after the surveys, were full of assurances that membership in the CWAC—or RCAF (WD) or WRCNS—was not incompatible with femininity. "Our women in the Canadian Armed Forces are nothing if not thoroughly feminine in manner and appearance," recruiting officers instructed National Selective Service personnel being trained to help with servicewomen's recruitment in February 1943.[38] Clearly, while the Armed Forces could persuade a male potential recruit that military service would make a man of him, they felt they had to do the reverse with a female prospective volunteer, that is, convince her that military life would not make her less of a woman.

From the start Army authorities assumed women in the services would be concerned about their appearance. Opposition to wearing a uniform per se was not anticipated from the women in the volunteer service corps (as many such corps sported their own uniforms), only opposition to a poorly designed one. In general, the planners of the CWAC calculated they would have a better chance of attracting volunteers the more attractive the uniform. The basic costume "underwent a considerable evolution before it settled into" the two-piece khaki suit identifiable as the CWAC uniform of World War II.[39] After National Defence Minister Colonel Ralston, his wife, the Master-General of the Ordnance, and a Toronto dress designer had all had a hand in the design, a committee at NDHQ produced the final model: the two-piece khaki ensemble of gored, slightly flared skirt and single-breasted tunic with hip pockets and one breast pocket, brown epaulets and brown CWAC and Canada badges, khaki shirt and brown tie, khaki peaked cap, and khaki hose and brown oxfords. According to the Director-General's preliminary history of the Corps, the CWAC uniform was "voted in some American and Canadian quarters to be the smartest of all women's service uniforms on this continent."[40] CWAC recruitment literature used this reputation to sell the Corps. The 1942 brochure *Women in Khaki* boasted: "C.W.A.C. uniforms have been acknowledged by leading dress designers to be the smartest in the world."[41] Enlistment ads sought to sell the wartime fashionableness of wearing the khaki with the line: "the C.W.A.C., the best dressed women of '43."[42] In addition, the Army went to greater and greater trouble to ensure a good fit in women's uniforms, much more so than in men's. In 1944 it was observed that "The equipping of C.W.A.C. personnel is considerably more complicated than this function for male personnel." And the evidence produced was that "C.W.A.C. clothing is supplied in as many as eighteen different sizes."[43] One ex-servicewoman of Prince Rupert, BC, recalls that the colour and cut of the CWAC uniform led her to choose the Canadian Women's Army Corps over the WDs or the Wrens [WRCNs].

> Perhaps if I had had big baby blue eyes, I might have considered the blue uniforms of the R.C.A.F. or the Navy, but be that as it may, not only did the khaki match my brown eyes (used for coyly rolling and flirting in those days, besides the lesser use of just plain seeing); the trim, fitted tunic and the A-line skirt of the C.W.A.C.'s was known to be the most attractive of the three services. And the peaked cap fit nicely on the head to allow a modest fall of curls from under its back and sides.[44]

While only 5 percent of the CWACs surveyed in 1943 mentioned wearing the uniform as a reason for joining, in answer to the further question of why they had selected the CWAC rather than the RCAF (WD) or the WRCNS, the highest proportion (37 percent) gave "neat, smart uniform" as their reason.[45] On the other hand, only 13 percent of the CWACs "stating likes" cited "wearing the uniform" as a "factor contributing to satisfaction" with life in the Corps.[46]

Certainly no one would have argued that pride in uniform was exclusively or particularly feminine, for men also took pride in their uniforms. There was, however, an important difference. A long association linked males with military uniform and military uniform with the masculine traits of forcefulness, toughness, and, in the case of an officer's uniform, commanding authority. When a man donned a uniform he stood to see his masculinity enhanced. Hence the popular notion that uniforms (on men) turned women's heads. Literary evidence exists that where the war effort was strongly supported and there were large concentrations of men in uniform (such as in London, England, or Ottawa, Ontario), men of military age not in uniform felt threatened not only by the possible charge of cowardice but by the possible loss of girlfriends to the soldiers, sailors, and airmen.[47]

Just the reverse was the fear in the case of servicewomen in uniform (or, for that matter, of women war workers in overalls and bandanas). Here reassurance was needed that such garb did not diminish femininity. For the 1 January 1943 issue of *Maclean's*, Lotta Dempsey contributed an article entitled "They're Still Feminine!," the point being to convince readers that "khaki, Air Force and Navy blue, or well-worn denim and slacks" had no lasting effect "on the softer side of Womanhood."

> Clothes don't make the man
> and uniforms and overalls
> don't seem to be unmaking
> the female of the species

was set out in bold print. And accompanying the article was a cartoon showing a CWAC, a Wren, and two women war workers congratulating a WD who blushingly holds out a diamond engagement ring for the others' admiration.[48]

Uncertain of the public's attitude toward the uniforms of the women's services, the Combined Services Committee had the public opinion questionnaire pointedly ask: "Do you think the uniforms of the Armed Forces make the average woman more or less attractive?" The results were equivocal: "Overall opinion was split." Once again, when the English- and French-Canadian data were looked at separately, it turned out that a much higher proportion of the latter registered a negative attitude. Still, not even half of the English Canadians polled felt that a service uniform made the average woman more attractive.[49] Servicewomen themselves particularly disliked "certain items of apparel" that they regarded as "definitely unflattering to any woman's appearance."[50] One example was the "antiquated style of overshoes furnished members of the C.W.A.C." and known facetiously as "'glamour boots.'"[51] CWAC women also resented the dress regulations that required the uniform to be worn even during off-duty hours when out on a date or on a forty-eight-hour leave. Only on a furlough of seven days or longer (or when taking part in sports) could a CWAC appear in public in civilian clothes. Out dancing in uniform, CWACs felt on an unequal footing with civilian women. They felt particularly disadvantaged by the cotton lisle stockings on issue to all members of the women's services. They wanted to be allowed "to wear civies or at least silk stockings when out with men."[52]

A Combined Services recruitment advertisement developed in response to the opinion surveys of 1943 showed a mother before a framed photograph of her three uniformed daughters, one in the WRCNS, one in the CWAC, and one in the RCAF (WD), confidentially telling the public: "My Girls are the real Glamour Girls." With that heading plus the conventionally pretty faces of the three servicewomen, the ad was clearly trying to overcome the association of women in uniform with loss of glamour. But at the same time, in smaller print, the ad had the mother locating the glamour of her daughters not in their uniforms (or even their pretty faces) but in their service, the important job they were doing. Here the recruitment propaganda was sending out two messages: the first, loud and clear, that the glamorous women of wartime were the women in uniform and the second, more muted, that the real core of their glamour lay in their sacrifice of self to the cause. A year before a woman's magazine had taken practically the same line in promotion of the woman war worker. In September 1942, *National*

Home Monthly chose as its "Glamour Girl" for the year the first woman welder to be approved by the Canadian government for National Defence work and published a picture of her "in blue denim overalls and goggles, and wielding a welding torch." "We chose her," the editors explained, "for exactly the reasons that anyone would choose any glamour girl, for her beauty and for her importance."[53]

Military officers in public relations never lost sight of the promotional value of "sex appeal." To enhance the image of the woman in uniform, recruiting officers singled out the servicewomen with the beauty-queen or movie-star good looks of the day to advertise the women's services. One "glamour shot" of a CWAC private, complete with respirator and helmet, appeared in the *Montreal Standard* of August 1943, along with a number of other photos of the same model in a piece promoting the Canadian Women's Army Corps. The same shot was used as the basis for a CWAC recruiting poster. Assuming that a function of good-looking women was to decorate, public relations officers also used "glamour shots" to publicize events in support of the war effort. For example, to draw attention to an exhibit of armaments in Ottawa in May 1944, Army photographers took a series of shots of war equipment with which they posed a pretty CWAC corporal. The caption to one photograph in the series read:

> The huge spot-light on display with a collection of modern war material in Ottawa, has a valuable use in searching out enemy night raiders, but Cpl. Wilma Williamson, C.W.A.C. of Dundas, Ont., has found another use for it . . . it provides an excellent reflection for straightening a crooked Service tie.[54]

A lot was conveyed by that photograph plus caption: the contrast between the serious operational function of the war equipment and the ornamental function of the CWAC; and the assumption of a narcissism on the part of the servicewoman so ingrained that she would even use a piece of war equipment as a mirror.[55]

World War II was the era of the "pin-up"—photos of female models and film stars or drawings of imaginary beauties, often scantily clad in bathing suits or less, which soldiers "pinned-up" on the inside of their lockers. In this way Canadian servicemen exercised the male prerogative to feed their sexual imaginations with visual images of beautiful women. Canadian women, by the same token, were conditioned to see themselves through the eyes of their male beholders. The more beautiful, the more feminine, was the equation. The *C.W.A.C. News Letter*, started in January 1944, specifically to keep the channels of communication open to CWAC personnel overseas, and generally to keep up Corps morale, encouraged members to participate in pinup contests run by *KHAKI*, the Army bulletin and parent organ of the CWAC publication. In the September 1944 issue, *C.W.A.C. News Letter* editor Corporal Caroline Gunnarson urged her readers: "So if you're the type of gal that sends men swoonin' NEL suggests that you get busy and send in your photo." And in the Spring 1945 issue she proudly reported that Canadian Forces overrunning German dug-outs had found on the wall of one a *KHAKI* pin-up of a CWAC.

In the face of the persistent association of femininity with frills, fabrics soft to the touch, cheerful colours, and curving lines, Army authorities made concessions. The 1944 CWAC recruiting pamphlet announced that "recently silk stockings have been issued for off-duty wear."[56] In fact, they were made of rayon; nonetheless, they and their "happy neutral shade" received a warm greeting in the February 1944 issue of the *C.W.A.C. News Letter*. The April 1944 issue hailed the order allowing members of the CWAC in future to wear civilian clothes on any pass over thirty-six hours as the "happiest new ruling" governing the Corps. This "weekend permission," the *News Letter* cheered, "will mean that twice a month girls will be able to cast aside the khaki for something more feminine."

Insofar as the four-square, drab, and durable uniform resisted feminization, femininity could still find expression underneath the drill and serge. Already in the earliest draft of regulations and instructions for a women's army corps, it was arranged that the women who joined would not have to wear "issue" underclothing or lingerie. Instead each recruit would receive on enrolment (later enlistment) a dress allowance of $15 for "necessaries" and thereafter $3 every quarter for replacements and upkeep.[57] All subsequent revisions of the regulations for the Canadian Women's Army Corps preserved this arrangement for CWACs serving on this side of the Atlantic. Its intent may well have been to spare the Master-General of the Ordnance's branch the headache of providing underclothes for women in suitable styles and a sufficient range of sizes (as the task seems to have been experienced when NDHQ did take over the issuing of underclothes to CWACs stationed overseas). Its effect was to leave open what was perceived as a sphere of feminine self-expression. The 1943 CWAC recruiting film *Proudly She Marches* contains a sequence in which a female recruit trips on her way up the path to the basic training centre barracks, dropping her suitcase and spilling its frilly contents on the ground. The 1944 RCAF (WD) promotional film *Wings on Her Shoulder* contains an almost identical sequence, thus underscoring the clichéd statement that femininity consists of a penchant for lacy, diaphanous undergarments (as well as of a certain degree of flightiness).

Not all CWAC other ranks, however, could afford to buy much in the way of finery out of the clothing allowance for necessaries. Its amount was not increased from 1941 to the disbanding of the Corps in 1946, even though CWAC officers testified to its insufficiency before the Army's Dress and Clothing Committee as early as July 1943.[58] Whether they could afford to or not, servicewomen, according to the press, gave positive proof of their irrepressible femininity in the parade of multi-hued apparel to be seen any night in the living quarters of women in the forces. In the words of Lotta Dempsey:

if you were privileged to sit around a barracks in the evening at a service women's training centre, you'd note a pretty exciting transformation as you look down the long rows of bare army cots, and see the dull drab of the uniform being replaced by the most exquisite array of rainbow-colored dressing gowns and housecoats and lounging robes you could imagine outside of a Hollywood color-picture set.[59]

Even though the intent of the military was not to alter conceptions of femininity, the campaigns to promote women's uniformed service did have an effect on fashion. Hollywood, that powerful image-maker, also helped to validate women's military service and the military look for women with such movies as *Here Come the Waves* (1945), starring Betty Hutton, and *Keep Your Powder Dry* (1945), in which heiress Lana Turner joined the U.S. Women's Army Corps. The fashionable "mannish" suit for civilian women, with its severe lines and padded shoulders, could be seen as partly in imitation of servicewomen's uniforms. The clothing regulations issued in 1942 by the Wartime Prices and Trade Board also had an impact. As Thelma LeCocq observed in *Maclean's*, all frills and furbelows, ruffles and ruchings were slashed. There were to be no more five-yard skirts or voluminous bell sleeves.[60] With all excess yardage and detail shorn, fashions would be, as the *National Home Monthly* put it, "Streamlined for the Duration."[61]

It was also during the Second World War that the popularization of pants for women began. This was directly the result of women's recruitment into war industry as factory workers—in armament, munitions, and aircraft assemblage plants. Although eventually the overalls and bandana or the slacks and turban of the woman war workers became symbols of service, in the early stages government officials were concerned that disapproving or ridiculing attitudes toward women wearing trousers would keep women from applying for essential jobs. The Department of Munitions and Supply for Canada considered it necessary to issue the message PLEASE DON'T STARE AT MY PANTS in March 1942, and to illustrate it with the following picture: a middle-aged matron in hat, gloves, and furs has stopped to look disdainfully at a young woman in slacks, while a man in white collar and overcoat has a condescending smirk on his face. The fine print gives the supposed reply of the diffident object of all the attention: "Would you like to know why I wear trousers like the men when I go about the streets? Because I'm doing a man's job for my country's sake."[62] Just a year and a half later attitudes had changed enough that *National Home Monthly* could put on the cover of its September 1943 issue a humorous drawing that reversed the roles depicted in the earlier poster. Now it is the female worker, swinging her lunch pail and striding along confidently in her slacks, who wheels around to take a second rather scornful look at a passing kilt-clad member of a Highland regiment.

The extension of slacks as wearing apparel for female military personnel, however, remained slow and restricted. Only in 1944 did the Navy's traditional bell bottoms begin to be issued for wear to members of the Women's Royal Canadian Naval Service, and then only to a select number of Wrens on coastal duty. To announce the new departure, a photograph was released to newspapers across Canada in June 1944. When it appeared in the *Toronto Telegram* it carried the following caption:

> No wonder this husky sailor seems slightly puzzled. He has just spied a WREN wearing, of all things, bell-bottomed trousers! The once strictly male attire has recently been approved as official working uniform for Wrens on duty as signallers and (the Signalwoman shown here) is one of four west-coast Wrens who is entitled to wear them. She is stationed at a west coast Naval base, where she sends and receives important Navy messages in code and cypher.[63]

Similarly, in the Army, the wearing of trousers by women had to be justified by working conditions or by the task to be performed, but even then could still meet up with opposition. For instance, trousers were authorized early on as part of the winter (but not summer) uniform for CWAC drivers of trucks and jeeps, but not of staff cars.[64] Then in the summer of 1944 the Master-General of the Ordnance authorized "Trousers . . . for summer wear by C.W.A.C. drivers" but "of Trucks and Jeeps only" and went on to specify in no uncertain terms that CWAC drivers of staff cars would have to continue to wear skirts, both summer and winter.[65] In October 1944 the chief commanding officer on the Pacific Coast wrote the Women's Dress and Clothing Committee of the Army recommending the CWAC drivers of staff cars also be allowed to wear trousers for the sensible reason that "drivers may be employed on trucks part-time and then immediately have to switch over to staff car duty." But the committee ruled "that there should be no difficulty in drivers changing from trousers to skirts when it becomes necessary for them to change from truck driving to staff car duty."[66] As at least half of the committee's members were CWAC officers, it was clearly not a male-versus-female decision. Also, as the same committee one month later agreed that thirty-four CWAC personnel employed in a gun operations room should be allowed to wear trousers, the committee members' opposition to staff car drivers wearing pants had to do with something specific to driving staff cars. In contrast to plotter telephonists in a gun operations room, staff car drivers were visible to the public. But then, so were truck and jeep drivers. Driving a truck or jeep, however, was a lower-class job than driving a staff car. Thus the male and female officers at National Defence Headquarters in Ottawa, who were removed from the workaday reality of the commander in the field, might have regarded pants on the woman staff car driver as inappropriate because [they were] too closely associated with manual labour. Also, since slacks would not have been accepted at the time as proper attire for the female secretary of an important businessman, there might have been similar objection to trousers on the female chauffeur of a high-ranking officer, especially if that officer were male. Furthermore, given the public's apprehension that military life was unsuitable for women, officers, particularly female officers, were concerned with building up a genteel image for the women's services. The serious attention given to these regulations governing when servicewomen could or could not wear trousers provides one example of the wartime politics of dress, indicating the symbolic power that could be invested in attire as a regulator of gender and class relations.

In the area of makeup, the Army was prepared to make accommodation to current criteria of feminine attractiveness, as defined and limited by officers' conceptions of gentility. The 1920s had seen the introduction of artificial cosmetics as commodities to be purchased on the market. Adoption by women of the middle and upper classes had established their use as fashionable if applied with restraint. Excessive use was associated with less respectable women, especially prostitutes. By the Second World War most urban women were reliant on cosmetics for their feminine self-image. *National Home Monthly*'s "Glamour Girl of 1942" was reported as saying that "you have to work ten hours with a welding torch in a defence factory to really appreciate what soap, cream, rouge, powder and lipstick can really do to a woman's morale."[67] Beauty soap and cosmetic manufacturers played on the fear of loss of femininity by suggesting that the female factory worker would remain "womanly" only if she made sure to use their product. An advertisement for Palmolive soap, for instance, had a woman war worker proclaiming "I'm a woman in a man's world—But I'm still a woman!" because she gave herself Palmolive beauty baths and facials.[68]

From first draft to last, the regulations for the Canadian Woman's Army Corps permitted women in uniform to wear makeup, as long as it was applied lightly and in moderation. A 1944 CWAC recruiting pamphlet answered the anticipated question "May I Use Cosmetics?" by stating: "Of course the Army wants you to be attractive and feminine, so go ahead and use your lipstick, powder and rouge, but use good taste and make it inconspicuous."[69] Similar restraint was to govern the use of nail varnish: clear or lightly tinted shades were all right, but "highly coloured" polish was not.[70]

The wearing of jewelry also came under tight restrictions. For the CWAC in uniform, watch chains, bracelets, earrings, and "trinkets" were expressly forbidden, as were any other than wedding, signet, and engagement rings.[71] Later an exception was also made for identification bracelets. The only other jewelry permitted was the wrist watch. As the 1944 CWAC recruiting booklet explained: "Your shining buttons make enough glitter."[72] These regulations catered to a number of different concerns. The restrictions on jewelry, practically identical to those for men, accommodated the Army's general requirement for uniformity. The pamphlet's warning about "glitter" hints at the preoccupation with gentility. A certain ambivalence is apparent in the regulations on makeup and nail polish. While finding it prudent to allow servicewomen the means to strive to meet the current standards of female beauty, military authorities felt constrained to regulate against possible "vulgarity." On the other hand, the personal decision of the first Officer Administering the CWAC, Lieutenant-Colonel Joan B. Kennedy, to wear no makeup or jewelry was regarded as unnecessarily severe.[73] Concern lest the servicewoman acquire the image of a "painted lady" was counterbalanced by concern lest she appear manly.

Both concerns lay behind the public-spirited decision of the National Council of the YMCA to offer "beauty culture" classes at their Women's Active Service Club in Ottawa. "Seated at long tables before individual mirrors," the servicewomen were "taught the importance of good skin grooming."[74] "'Rouge should be natural looking'" was one piece of advice handed out by the "well-known beauty consultant" who acted as "volunteer instructress" of the classes.[75] Open to women of all three services, the classes were photographed by the Army to use as further proof that genteel feminine beauty and membership in the CWAC were not incompatible.[76]

All three women's services enforced regulations governing the length at which women in uniform could wear their hair: it had to be off the collar. It was anticipated that this requirement might act as a deterrent to those women whose feminine self-image depended on long tresses and elaborate hair-dos.[77] *Wings on Her Shoulder*, the 1944 recruitment film for the Women's Division of the RCAF, warned that hair had to be worn off the collar of the tunic and therefore recruits would have to sacrifice their "curls and glamour bobs." The film went on to assure the viewer that styles could still be beautiful and meet regulations. The RCAF (WD) and the Women's Royal Canadian Naval Service took the lead in providing their own hairdressers, while the Canadian Women's Army Corps initially only promised prospective recruits that "pay and allowances" would be "adequate to cover hairdos even at the better beauty parlours."[78] By 1944, however, the Army was offering training in hairdressing and manicuring to a limited number of CWACs and the beauty salon in the CWAC Basic Training Centre at Kitchener, Ontario, was doing a brisk business.[79] The Army could also show that with or without beauty salons the conviviality of barracks life included CWACs helping one another with hair sets.[80]

In April 1944, Army Public Relations did a photo series of two CWAC corporals shopping for new spring outfits. The purpose of the series was to demonstrate once again that female personnel retained their femininity even after months of military service. The proof provided this time was that donning the uniform of the CWAC in no way diminished a woman's passion for clothes. Nor did it weaken her love of the purely decorative, as represented by choosing a new spring hat.

"Off to a head start, Cpl. Wilma Williamson had only one complaint: 'So many hats and only one head.' The sympathetic salesgirl spent half an hour offering models and making suggestions." The series also got a lot of mileage out of the clichéd identification of frequent changes of mind as typical feminine behaviour. "A woman's prerogative remains—even after months of Army life" read the caption to a photo duplicating countless cartoons of the era: Cpl. Thelma Palmer sits surrounded by a pile of shoes, unable to make up her mind, while the salesman, with a look of mild exasperation on his face, rests his head on his hand.[81]

The "attractiveness" so central to the prevailing notion of femininity ultimately meant attractiveness to men. Heterosexuality was certainly one of the norms of femininity subscribed to in official publicity about the women's services. While advertisements acclaimed the good wholesome fun women could have together in the services, as in a shot of a Canadian Women's Army Corps Christmas party at Kildare Barracks in Ottawa in 1943,[82] celebrations of female camaraderie stopped far short of any suggestion of lesbianism. Under military law, after all, homosexuality could be construed as grounds for discharge.[83]

The survey of CWAC other rank opinion had revealed that, after patriotism and the urge to travel, the third strongest motive for joining the service had been the desire "to be near family, friends in the forces." While 68 percent had been influenced by having women friends in the forces, a larger proportion (77 percent) had followed men friends into the military.[84] Recruitment propaganda, capitalizing on this information, came up with the poster: "Are you the girl he left behind?" In Army photo stories on life in the CWAC, public relations made a point of including material on dances and dates and boyfriends. The first photo in a series on Kildare Barracks showed three CWAC sergeants "with plans for a big evening ahead" approaching the company sergeant-major in the orderly room "on the subject of late passes." The caption to a later photo in the same series read: "There is no place for 'shop talk' in C.W.A.C. barracks after duty hours. Girls go typically feminine." Depicted as "typically feminine" was the one CWAC sergeant writing to a boyfriend in the RCAF while the two other CWAC sergeants looked "admiringly" (if not enviously) at his framed photograph. In the series' last photo the letter-writing sergeant had paused, pen in hand, to gaze dreamily at the photograph, which shows an Air Force officer clenching a pipe between his teeth and looking, even with the trim mustache, a lot like Henry Fonda.[85]

The message of one Army photo in a series on CWACs in Washington, DC, was that members of the Canadian Women's Army Corps stationed outside Canada could find dates in the armed forces of Canada's allies. It showed two CWAC privates stepping out with a soldier and a sailor of the United States forces.[86] Attached to a similar photo in a later series on the same subject was the caption: "Carrying out the 'Good Neighbour

Policy' to a 'T', Private (X) of the U.S. Engineers shows Private (Y), C.W.A.C. of Toronto, Ontario, a few of the scenic highlights of Washington, D.C."[87]

Servicewomen were also shown as not having lost the ability to be pleasing to men. "The Quickest Way to a Man's Heart—Even a Sergeant's Heart" appeared below a photograph publicizing the parties held in honour of the fourth anniversary of the Canadian Women's Army Corps (14 August 1945). The sergeant is identified as a guest at the CWAC's birthday party at Kildare Barracks; the CWAC corporal, as the one who "is seeing that the guest is satisfied."[88]

Indeed, the concern whether life in the Armed Forces made a women more or less attractive boiled down to a concern whether enlistment made a woman more or less marriageable. The public opinion questionnaire contained the question: "Do you think the wearing of a uniform interferes with a girl's chances of marriage?" While 58 percent of those polled answered "no" (68 percent in English Canada, but only 43 percent in French Canada), a remaining 42 percent either thought the wearing of a uniform did restrict "a girl's chances of marriage" (22 percent) or were not sure (20 percent didn't know).[89] Thus, dispelling the fear that enlistment would scare away dates was not enough. Recruitment literature had to give the further assurance that membership in the women's services would not reduce one's marriageability.

The 1944 CWAC recruitment pamphlet assured the prospective volunteer that "yes" she could get married while she was in the service, provided she had her commanding officer's permission.[90] The Army's Department of Public Relations encouraged news coverage of marriages between servicemen and servicewomen. The *Globe and Mail* of 2 December 1942 reported "the first marriage of a member of the C.W.A.C. to a member of the Army" (it had taken place the day before in Halifax between a CWAC private and a corporal of the Provost Corps attached to a Highland regiment) and thereafter announcements of such military weddings became a regular feature of the women's activities columns of Canadian newspapers.[91] Official Army, Navy, and Air Force photographers took pictures of such weddings for release to the press.[92] In the *C.W.A.C. News Letter* announcements of "military alliances," as weddings of Armed Forces personnel were sometimes called, took precedence over announcements of military promotions. Early issues carried only a few mentions but by the end of 1944 whole pages were devoted to marriage news. "The Bride wore Khaki," a full-page item in the November 1944 issue, told the romantic story of a Canadian Army sergeant and a CWAC corporal exchanging vows in a bombed-out church in Italy.

One of the least examined and most unshakable notions of the time about women was that subordination and subservience to men were inherently female characteristics that dictated women's role and place in society. . . . [T]his assumption converged with the real position of CWACs in relation to Army men, for in jobs, pay and benefits, and place in the command structure of the Army, the servicewomen were in general subordinate. As reflected in mottoes and enlistment slogans, the very function of the women's services was to subserve the primary purpose of the Armed Forces: the provision of an armed and fighting force. Having been excluded/exempted from combat, the women of the Canadian Armed Forces could adopt as their motto: "We Serve That Men May Fight."[93] That general motto had been adapted from the airwomen's "We Serve that Men May Fly." Even more expressive of the secondary status and supportive role assigned to Army women was a slogan used on enlistment ads: "The C.W.A.C. Girls – The Girls behind the Boys behind the Guns."[94]

In preserving the male monopoly on armed service, the Department of National Defence was acting in harmony with social convention and conviction. The only evidence of women strongly desiring admission to jobs classified as operational came from the handful of women in Canada with pilots' licences who were eager to put their flying skill at the service of their country, and who were to be denied that opportunity. A few joined the British civilian Air Transport Auxiliary, formed to ferry aircraft from "anywhere to anywhere" and open after 1940 to women pilots.[95] The prevailing view was that men were by nature suited to dangerous, life-risking jobs, while women were naturally adapted to monotony and behind-the-scenes support work. This view was reflected in the remarks of one Air Force officer on the suitability of airwomen for the trade of parachute rigger.

> Take parachute packing. To a man it's a dull, routine job. He doesn't want to pack parachutes. He wants to be up there with one strapped to his back. But to a woman it's an exciting job. She can imagine that someday a flier's life will be saved because she packed that parachute well. Maybe it will be her own husband's life or her boy-friend's. That makes parachute packing pretty exciting for her and she does a much more efficient and speedy job than an unhappy airman would.[96]

Deeply entrenched as the assumption was that the female was the second sex, there still surfaced from time to time the fear that women who were serving with the Army would lose their deference toward men and become "bossy." Mainly, it was the prospect of female officers that seems to have aroused this fear. When Jean Knox, director of the British Army's Auxiliary Territorial Service, toured Canada in the fall of 1942, newspaper coverage showed a preoccupation with the fact that she, the first female major-general in the British Army, outranked her husband. As if looking for qualities to counterbalance her high military rank, news stories invariably described Knox as the "petite and pretty general" or "petite and completely feminine." Speaking of the women of the British Auxiliary Territorial Service and the Canadian Women's Army Corps, she herself remarked: "They're not an Army of Amazons doing men's work—

they're still women." In her view, "All women should share with men the experience of this war—but I would be violently displeased if in so doing, women lost their femininity."[97]

Similarly, when Lionel Shapiro covered Major Alice Sorby's arrival in London, England, to command the CWACs overseas, he approved of the fact that she was "pretty" and had "graciously submitted" to the press conference. But at the perception that she was also "a woman full of the barbed-wire quality of a colonel in the Indian service," Shapiro confessed, "my man's world was beginning to totter before my eyes." But a question of his that "penetrated her military facade and revealed her in all her feminine vulnerability" saved the day for Shapiro. "'Major Sorby,'" he asked, "'your husband is a lieutenant and you are a major. I assume he will have to salute you when you meet. Is that not so?'" After a moment's thought, Major Sorby replied that, yes, she supposed that would be regulations, but as she had not seen her husband for more than a year, she doubted whether they'd "'bother about salutes.'" Missing the irony of Major Sorby's retort, Shapiro was jubilant. "Moment triumphant!" he exclaimed. "My man's world returned in full flower. Major Sorby was really only Mrs. Sorby with a King's crown on her epaulettes, and Mr. Sorby, though a mere lieutenant, was still master of the Sorby household."[98]

Female other ranks also expressed uneasiness at having women in command over them. The CWAC other ranks surveyed in 1943 registered a lot of complaints against their CWAC commanding officers. The survey revealed that in general female other ranks "disliked taking orders from women" and that "some felt men administrative officers would be better."[99] However large that "some" was (unfortunately not measured by the survey), the existence of such a feeling among female other ranks in a women's corps speaks for the pervasiveness of the association of male with authority and command. One suspects that the charge of "playing soldier"[100] leveled against some female officers was a criticism that such women were putting on "masculine airs" of commanding authority. The apprehension that women serving in the forces would lose their femininity included the fear that the male-over-female hierarchy of authority might be upset.

Just as importantly, the public had to be assured that the work women in the forces were asked to perform was suitable to women. With an ambivalence typical of the promotion of the women's services, speeches or publications in one sentence applauded women's breakthrough into positions theretofore dominated by men and in the next denied that servicewomen were being asked to do anything inimical to their feminine nature. The *CWAC Digest: Facts about the C.W.A.C.*, a 1943 recruiting booklet, is a case in point. The middle pages were given over to photographs with captions of women performing tasks conventionally identified as male: one showed a CWAC fitter working on a lathe; another a class of

CWACs at a motor mechanics' school. But the inside cover contained "A Tribute to the Canadian Women's Army Corps" from the Governor General of Canada, stating: "In a modern army women are a necessity, not in order to replace men in men's jobs, but to take over from men jobs which," while previously done by men, were women's anyway. "If a woman can drive the family car, she can drive a staff car" is another example of the recruitment line that sought to reassure the public that military jobs for female personnel, although performed in new settings and under different conditions, remained essentially "women's work."[101] Thus the contradiction between the armed services' need for women in uniform and the ideology of woman's place being in the home (or in a paid job long sex-typed as female) was reconciled through the redefinition of certain military jobs as womanly.[102]

In actual fact, as we have seen, the overwhelming majority of uniformed women employed by the Army were assigned to jobs that had already become female niches in the civilian labour market or could be regarded as extensions of mothering or housework.[103] In propaganda and practice, a "woman's place" was created within the wartime armed services. Nonetheless, the very association of women with the military touched off fear of an impending breakdown of the sexual division of labour, akin to that triggered by the entrance of women on a massive scale into waged work. Under the anxiety over the changed appearance of women lay a more profound but often less articulated fear that women were invading male territory and becoming too independent. Humour of various sorts provided an outlet for these fears. In a 1942 article on "Woman Power" in *Maclean's*, for instance. Thelma LeCocq jokingly proposed a number of possibilities "that make strong men break out in a lather." What if, at war's end, she speculated, the thousands of war working women

> refuse to be stripped of the pants and deprived of the pay envelopes? What if they start looking round for some nice little chap who can cook and who'll meet them lovingly at the door with their slippers in hand? What if industry has to reorganize to give these women sabbatical years for having babies?[104]

These fears survived till the end of the war. In September 1945, despite the fact that approximately 80 000 women war workers had already been laid off by then, *Maclean's* ran a cartoon by Vic Herman that derived its humour from the preposterous yet feared possibility of a reversal of the sexual division of labour between male breadwinner and dependent female domestic. A husband wearing an apron and standing with a mop in his hand and a bucket at his feet frowns in annoyance at his overalls- and bandana-clad wife, who, home from the factory, has headed straight for the refrigerator, tracking muddy footprints across his nice, clean floor.[105]

After studying the results of the CWAC survey, the Director of Army Recruiting requested discontinuance of the recruitment pitch "You Can Free a Man to Fight." While the strongest reason CWACs had given for enlisting was "patriotism, help win the war," a significant proportion, as already noted, had cited the desire to be near family and friends, a category including fathers and brothers as well as sweethearts. To emphasize releasing men for combat, the Director of Army Recruiting argued, was thus in conflict with the real interest of the women to keep their loved ones alive, as well as contrary to his conception of the eternally feminine—woman's nurturant and preservative nature:

> In reality, women have joined up to be near, help and protect their boy friends and brothers overseas. It is woman's natural tendency to protect her loved ones from danger, not force them into the line of battle.

He inferred from the report also that too many members of the CWAC were not convinced their jobs were essential. He therefore recommended a new line of appeal that would both stress the vital importance of women's work in the forces and identify it as an essential part of the "intricate web of supporting services and pre-battle planning" whose purpose was "to protect their boy friends and brothers from unnecessary battle dangers."[106]

The *CWAC Digest* of 1943 apparently went to press before the analyses of the CWAC survey took effect, for it still stressed the non-combatant servicewoman's part in releasing servicemen for combat. "Would you deprive a fighting man of his opportunity to fight?" it asked. "Do you want some fighting man to do *your* job?. . . Don't let a man take your place if you can help it." Other new recruitment material, however, reflected the spirit of the suggestions from the Director of Army Recruiting. In one Combined Services leaflet of 1943, for instance, emphasis was taken off the need for women to release men for combat and put on the vital importance of women's work in the service per se: joining the forces was sold as "The Most Important Job Ever Offered Women."[107] And some enlistment ads designed for sponsorship by patriotic businesses took up the theme of women's respect for life. Under the heading "YOUR TALENT may save a life," one asked the prospective volunteer to reflect on "what it would mean to you in long years ahead, if you carried in your heart the knowledge that some talent of yours—great or small—had saved a life in a battlefront—perhaps even dozens of lives." Another interpreted the slogan "This is a Woman's War, too" to mean enlistment was a way of hastening the return of loved ones. "THIS IS *OUR* WAR, TOO," said the pretty CWAC in the drawing, "—our homes are upset, sons, brothers, husbands away defending us. Help bring them home sooner!"[108]

Here the military was no longer seeking only to mollify a public fearful that women in uniforms would lose their femininity. The military had turned inward and was reexamining its own policies for fear they were not attending sufficiently to important components of the feminine nature of women. This was occasioned by the knowledge of a deterrent to women's recruitment more serious than the fear that servicewomen would cease to be women: the fear/suspicion that they would become "loose" women. The preoccupation with preserving women's sexual respectability, like the preoccupation with preserving women's femininity, was triggered by war's destabilization of gender relations and both reflected and reinforced prevailing definitions of womanhood.

Notes

1. *Saturday Night*, 26 Sept. 1942, 10.
2. Lotta Dempsey, "Women Working on Ships and Aircraft," *Mayfair*, June 1943, 74.
3. Notes for the Assistance of Speakers at School for NSS [National Selective Service] Employment Office Personnel, Feb. 1943, National Archives of Canada (NAC), RG24, reel no. C-5303, file HQS 8984-2.
4. *Globe and Mail*, 24 Dec. 1942, 8; 31 Dec. 1942, 13.
5. "'Jill' Canuck Has Become CWAC of All Trades," *Saturday Night*, 4 March 1944, 4.
6. Margaret Ecker, *Globe and Mail*, 26 Dec. 1942, 8.
7. Copies in NAC, RG24, vol. 2256, file HQ 54-27-111-144, vol. 1.
8. "Suggested Notes for the Guidance of Speakers at the N.S.S. Schools," "Further Suggested Notes . . . ," Feb. 1943, NAC, RG 24, reel no. C-5303, file HQS 8984-2.
9. *Women in Khaki*, n.d., but internal evidence places publication in second half of 1942, Department of National Defence (DND), DH, 164.069 (D1).
10. According to the nationwide survey of CWAC other ranks carried out in April–May, 1943, "about 20 percent of CWAC women belonged to a volunteer women's part-time service organization prior to enrolling in the CWAC. Most of these belonged to one of the unofficial uniformed women's corps or the Red Cross." *Report of Enquiry—Canadian Women's Army Corps: Why Women Join and How They Like It* (hereafter *C.W.A.C. Report*), April–May 1943, 23, copy at DND, DH, 168.009(D91).
11. "Strength—Canadian Women's Army Corps as at 27 March 1943" was 354 officers plus 9741 other ranks, totalling 10 095. NAC, RG24, reel no. C-5303, file HQS 8984-2.
12. Weekly Strength Returns by D. Org. DND, DH, 113.3C1065 (D3) CWAC.
13. Letter of 1 Oct. 1943, to newspaper editors from Captain T.H. Johnstone, Combined Service Committee, NAC, RG24, reel no. C-5303. file HQS 8984-2. By 1 July 1943, 28 000 women had been accepted by the three services, 13 000 by the CWAC. *C.W.A.C. Report*, 11.
14. Communication of 30 Jan. 1943, to all regional superintendents, from R.G. Barclay, assistant director, Employment Service and Unemployment Insurance Branch, NAC, RG24, reel no. C-5303, file HQS 8984-2.
15. Memorandum of March 1943, to the Minister from Major-General H.F.G. Letson, NAC, RG24, reel no. C-5303, file HQS 8984-2.

16. Minutes of the 89th Meeting of the National Campaign Committee, 22 Feb. 1943, NAC, RG24, reel no. C-5303, file HQS 8984-2.
17. *Report: An Enquiry into the Attitude of the Canadian Civilian Public Towards the Women's Armed Forces* (Montreal: Elliott-Haynes Limited, 1943), 3, hereafter Elliott-Haynes, *An Enquiry*.
18 *C.W.A.C. Report*, 3–4.
19 Elliott-Haynes, *An Enquiry*, 8.
20. Ibid., 9.
21. Ibid., 12.
22. Ibid., 13.
23. *C.W.A.C. Report* 28.
24. Elliott-Haynes, *An Enquiry*, 14.
25. Ibid.
26. Ibid.
27. *C.W.A.C. Report*, 28.
28. Ibid.
29. Elliott-Haynes, *An Enquiry*, 15.
30. Ibid.
31. Ibid., 25.
32. *C.W.A.C. Report*, 26.
33. NAC, RG24. vol. 2252, file HQ 54-27-111-1, vol. 2.
34. *C.W.A.C. Report*, 12.
35. Letter of 26 July 1943, to Gentlemen from T.H. Johnstone, Captain Combined Services Committee, NAC, RG24, reel no. C-5303, file HQS 8984-2.
36. NAC, RG24, vol. 2252, file HQ 54-27-111-1, vol. 2; reel no. C-5303, file HQS 8984-2, passim.
37. Elliott-Haynes, *An Enquiry*, 24.
38. Notes for the Assistance of Speakers for NSS Employment Personnel, Feb. 1943, NAC, RG24, reel no. C-5303, file HQS 8984-2, NSS Representatives Conference, London, ON, 15–17 Feb. 1943, NAC, RG24, reel no. C-5322, file HQS 9011-11-5.
39. Director-General, CWAC, presumably Col. Margaret C. Eaton, "Preliminary Historical Narrative, History of the CWAC & Appendices" (n.d. but internal evidence suggests ca. mid-1945), 33, copy at DND, DH, 113,3CI(DI).
40. Ibid., 34.
41. *Women in Khaki*, 20.
42. Cut-sheet of suggested sponsored ads for the CWAC, summer/autumn 1943, DND, DH, 164.069 (D1).
43. Minutes of meeting to discuss CWAC depot companies, 10 Feb. 1944, in office of D. Org. (R), NAC, RG24, reel no. C-8410, file HQS 9011-11-0-2-1.
44. Bowman, *We Skirted the War!* (published by the author, 1975), 3.
45. *C.W.A.C. Report*, 24.
46. Ibid., 33–34.
47. Lionel Shapiro, *The Sixth of June* (Garden City, NY: Doubleday, 1955); Geoffrey Cotterell, *Westward the Sun* (London: Eyre & Spottiswoode, 1952).
48. *Maclean's*, 1 Jan. 1943, 7.
49. Elliott-Haynes, *An Enquiry*, 27.
50. "'Manpower' Problems of the Women's Services During the Second World War," Report No. 68, Historical Section (GS), Army Headquarters, by J.M. Hitsman, 17 June 1954, DND, DH, AHQ Rpt.(D68), 12.
51. NAC, National Photography Collection, Z-2600-8, 7/3/44, Maj.-Gen. Potts and daughter, Cpl. Edith, CWAC, at Kitchener, CWAC, #3 Basic Training Centre.
52. *C.W.A.C. Report*, 15.
53. "Glamour Girl of 1942," *National Home Monthly*, Sept. 1942, 36.
54. NAC, National Photography Collection, Z-2766-8.
55. Some World War II servicewomen remember without fondness their having been used as sex objects. One wrote that "as an RCAF (WD) I was involved in displaying my legs on a float in an advertising effort to recruit young men (so-called) still in high school. What a horrid memory." Letter to author from Shirley Goundrey, dated 17 Oct. 1977.

56. *50 Questions and Answers about CWAC* (Ottawa: King's Printer, 1944), 7.
57. Draft copy of Regulations and Instructions for the Canadian Women's (Army) Service, 23 June 1941, NAC, RG24, vol. 2252, file HQ 54-27-111-2, vol. 1.
58. The five CWAC officers, including Lt.-Col. Margaret Eaton, later Director-General, CWAC, had recommended that in lieu of the cash allowance "articles of underclothing, etc., be added to the present scale of issue of clothing for CWAC serving in Canada." Although the committee members concurred, no action was taken at higher levels. Proceedings of a Meeting of the Dress & Clothing Committee (Army), July 6, 1943, NAC, RG4, vol. 2255, file HQ 54-27-111-40, vol. 1. Lt.-Col. D.I. Royal, then senior staff officer, CWAC, reported that the cash allowance for underclothing had been inadequate in her "Report and Recommendations on the Canadian Women's Army Corps" of 29 Aug. 1946, NAC, RG24, vol. 2254, file HQ 54-27-111-2, vol. 9.
59. Lotta Dempsey, "They're Still Feminine!" *Maclean's*, 1 Jan. 1943, 7.
60. Thelma LeCocq, "War Wear," *Maclean's*, 15 Aug. 1942, 15.
61. From Marjorie Winspear's column, "Beauty & Fashions," *National Home Monthly*, Oct. 1942, 58.
62. *Maclean's*, 1 March 1942, 3.
63. RCN photo by Photographer Sheraton, RCNVR, *Telegram* Print Collection, York University Archives.
64. NAC, National Photography Collection, Z-61-2, "C.W.A.C. Winter Driving Uniform," 9 Jan. 1942.
65. Emphasis in original. Master-General of the Ordnance Letter No. 64/1944, 22 July 1944. NAC, RG24, vol. 2255, file HQ 54-27-111-33, vol. 3.
66. Proceedings of a meeting of the Women's Dress and Clothing Committee (Army), 6 Oct. 1944, NAC, RG24, vol. 2255, file HQ54-27-111-40, vol. 1. See also Army photo of a military transport driver in dress uniform of skirt and jacket, pumping up a tire of a staff car. NAC, National Photography Collection, Z-3187-1, 27 Sept. 1944.
67. "Glamour Girl of 1942," 38.
68. *Maclean's*, 15 Nov. 1942.
69. *50 Questions and Answers About CWAC*, 9.
70. Section IX, para. 120(b), "Regulations for the C.W.A.C, 1941," NAC, RG24, vol. 2252, file HQ 54-27-111-2, vol. 1; Section IX, para. 40(b), "Regulations for the C.W.A.C., 1942," HQ 54-27-111-44, DND, DH, 113-3CI(DI).
71. Section IX, para. 118(e), "Regulations for the C.W.A.C., 1941," Section IX, para. 137(e), "Regulations for the C.W.A.C., 1942."
72. *50 Questions and Answers About CWAC*, 9.
73. W. Hugh Conrod, *Athene, Goddess of War: The Canadian Women's Army Corps, Their Story* (Dartmouth, NS: Writing and Editorial Services, 1983), 55.
74. Caption to Army photo, NAC, National Photography Collection, negative Z-2337-5, 3 Dec. 1943.
75. Caption to Army photo, NAC, National Photography Collection, negative Z-2337-2, 3 Dec. 1943.
76. See also NAC, National Photography Collection, "C.W.A.C. Beauty Culture," negative Z-2431-3, 8 Jan. 1944.
77. "Army hair-do regulations of no hair below collars caused a little trouble but most CWACs were quick to the occasion, passed off glamorous tresses as a war luxury and now more and more appear with boyish and military hair cuts." James C. Anderson, "Police Women for the Army," *Saturday Night*, 24 April 1943, 26.
78. "Sergeant To Dress Airwomen's Hair: Department is Set Up as Morale

Booster," *Globe and Mail*, 8 Dec. 1942, 10; "A WREN's Life Aboard HMCS *Conestoga*," *Mayfair*, July 1943, 22; *Women in Khaki*, 24. While morale-boosting clearly was the main purpose behind the provision of hairdressing facilities within the women's services in Canada, in England, according to the one-time Director of Auxiliary Territorial Service, another purpose was served: keeping heads clear of lice. Leslie Violet Lucy Evelyn Mary Whateley, *As Thoughts Survive* (London: Hutchinson & Co., 1948).

79. NAC, National Photography Collection, caption to Army photo, Z-3082-32, 18 Aug. 1944; Army photos "C.W.A.C. Training Class, High School of Commerce," Z-3528-(1-4), 27 Jan. 1945.
80. NAC National Photography Collection, Army photo, "C.W.A.C. (C.B.) at Argyle Barracks," Z-2440-18, 11 Jan. 1944.
81. NAC, National Photography Collection, Army photos, "C.W.A.C. Buy New Spring Clothes," Z-2710-(1020), 17 April 1944. See also the cartoon drawn for *Maclean's* by Jaboo, 1 May 1939, 22.
82. NAC, National Photography Collection, Z-2405-3, 27 Dec. 1943.
83. Rosamond "Fiddy" Greer's account of life in the Women's Royal Canadian Naval Service during World War II contains this personal recollection: "When two sisters slept together in a lower bunk across from mine, the thought of lesbianism never crossed my mind. This is not at all surprising, as I had never even heard of it. The more worldly-wise than I (which was probably almost everyone) may have known about 'it,' but none spoke the unmentionable word and for some time I thought how nice it was that the girls could comfort one another when they felt homesick. However, one day I heard that they had been 'found out': shortly afterwards they disappeared from *Stadacona*; and I surmised that 'something funny' had been going on. I was learning; although not too swiftly. . . . [F]or a long time after the incident I thought lesbians were rather peculiar sisters." Rosamond "Fiddy" Greer, *The Girls of the King's Navy* (Victoria: Sono Nis Press, 1983), 83–84.
84. *C.W.A.C. Report*, 18, 24.
85. NAC, National Photography Collection, Army photos "In Barracks," negatives Z-1765-(1-9), 7 July 1943.
86. NAC, National Photography Collection, Army photo, negative Z-1885-17, 11 Aug. 1943.
87. NAC, National Photography Collection, Army photo, negatives Z-2544-23 and 24, 16 Feb. 1944.
88. NAC, National Photography Collection, Z-4037-2.
89. Elliott-Haynes, *An Enquiry*, 27.
90. *50 Questions and Answers About CWAC*, 11.
91. "Private of C.W.A.C. Weds Army Corporal," *Globe and Mail*, 2 Dec. 1942, 11.
92. NAC, National Photography Collection, Army photos "C.W.A.C. Wedding," negatives Z-2586-(1-9), 1 March 1944; "C.W.A.C.–Navy Wedding at Kildare Barracks," negatives Z-3796-(1-4), April 1945.
93. NSS Representatives Conference re Recruitment of Women for Armed Services, London, ON, 15, 16, 17 Feb. 1943, NAC, RG24, reel no. C-5303, file HQS 8984-2.
94. CWAC Recruiting Pamphlet used in Military District No. 4 in Jan.–March 1943, campaign, DND, DH 164.069(01).
95. Godfrey Winn, "Through Fair Weather and Foul, Britain's . . . Women Ferry Pilots Fly that Men May Fight," *Saturday Night*, 28 Nov. 1942, 4–5; D.K. Findlay, "Anywhere to Anywhere," *Maclean's*, 15 April 1943, 12–13, 57–61.

96. Mary Ziegler, *We Serve That Men May Fly: The Story of Women's Division Royal Canadian Air Force* (Hamilton, ON: RCAF (WD) Association, 1973), 66–67.
97. *Globe and Mail*, 9 Sept. 1942, 9; 10 Oct. 1942, 11. Discussed in Marie T. Wadden, "Newspaper Response to Female War Employment: *The Globe and Mail* and *Le Devoir* May–October 1942" (History honours essay, Memorial University of Newfoundland, May 1976), 13–14. Statement of Major-General Knox quoted in Conrod, *Athene, Goddess of War*, 96.
98. L.S.B. Shapiro, "They're Still Women After All," *Saturday Night*, 26 Sept. 1942, 10.
99. *C.W.A.C. Report*, 15.
100. Memorandum of 22 July 1943, to DAG(C) from Director of Army Recruiting, NAC, RG24, reel no. C-5303, file HQS 8984-2.
101. "Suggested Notes for the Guidance of Speakers at the National Selective Service Schools," 9 Feb. 1943, sent out from the Office of Director of Army Recruiting, NAC, RG24, reel no. C-5303, file HQS 8984-2.
102. See Ruth Milkman, "Redefining 'Women's Work': The Sexual Division of Labor in the Auto Industry During World War II," *Feminist Studies* 8, 2 (Summer 1982): 336–72, for a discussion of the flexibility of what she calls "the idiom of sex typing" as a component of "the resilience of the structure of job segregation by sex." Milkman shows how shifting composition and application of the idiom of sex typing in the U.S. auto industry both legitimated and curtailed the "redefinition of the boundaries between 'women's work' and 'men's work'" during the war and helped facilitate the return to prewar patterns of occupational segregation by sex during postwar reconversion. "[T]he reproduction of *job segregation* by sex," Milkman argues, is "a process that is always occurring." And this "job segregation," she further argues, "coincides with a *gender hierarchy* within the labor market."
103. See Ruth Roach Pierson, "*They're Still Women After All: The Second World War and Canadian Womanhood* (Toronto: McClelland & Stewart, 1986), ch. 3.
104. Thelma LeCocq, "Woman Power," *Maclean's*, 15 June 1942, 10–11, 40.
105. Drawn for *Maclean's* by Vic Herman, 15 Sept. 1945, 32.
106. Memorandum of 22 July 1943, to DAG(C) from Director of Army Recruiting, NAC, RG24, reel no. C-5303, file HQS 8984-2.
107. Copy at DND, DH 164.069 (D1).
108. Sponsored CWAC advertising, summer/autumn 1943, DND, DH, 164.069 (D1).

The Canadian air effort was enormous, astonishing even the most optimistic Canadians in 1939. The British Commonwealth Air Training Plan (BCATP) got under way in 1940 and began to produce aircrew by the thousands. This account by a bomber pilot who distinguished himself flying Lancasters over Germany recalls his training in Yorkton, Saskatchewan, one of many small towns across the country that housed BCATP bases by 1941.

Service Flying

Walter R. Thompson

THE WINTER SNOWS had arrived and settled when we reached Yorkton in East Central Saskatchewan on 8 November 1941 but clouds were absent and wisps of smoke from the town and the farms could be seen to the horizon as we approached by rail. The tracks were pencil lines of steel on the white, flat land extending for miles, as far as one could see to the light-blue sky. The snow crunched and squeaked to the walk, the tiny crystals flashing like diamonds. We were loaded into trucks at the station, our worldly possessions squeezed into a light-blue kit-bag, with a name and service number painted on the side. W.R. Thompson R-106592 was mine. The total strength of the RCAF for both air and ground crew was about 90 000 at this time. I suspected that our service numbers were started at several thousand just to confuse the enemy.

The attention of the enemy was elsewhere, however, as he paused for what was to be the final assault upon Moscow. The formidable panzer divisions, elite of the German army, had taken Kharkov and pushed into the Crimea. They were snorting in the snow, thirsty for the oil of the Caucasus. Yasnaya Polyana, Tolstoy's home, had been overrun, but a month later, on 6 December the Russians counterattacked before Moscow. The daylight air was quiet in West Europe, save for the fighter sweeps over France. Much of the Luftwaffe's strength had been removed to the east. Major Hans-Ulrich Rudel, who was to become Hitler's favourite airman, was beginning his remarkable assault on Russian tanks—in excess of 500 put out of action during the war by this one airman! Rudel flew in combat for six years, mostly in Stuka dive bombers. He was the only Luftwaffe pilot to be awarded the order known as the Knight's Cross with Golden Oak Leaves, Swords, and Diamonds.

Sergeant Fogarty was a pilot, too, but he was of that great majority of early graduates of the British Commonwealth Air Training Plan who were themselves immediately trained as instructors in order to pass on to a larger group the skills they had acquired. This seemed analogous to the division of cells so as to provide a sufficient concentration that some could be spared for a different function. Fogarty was obviously not enraptured with this role, but with his strong sense of duty and dry wit he was determined to be a competent instructor, which he was. He introduced two of us to the Cessna Crane. Frail in appearance, with its metal tubular skeleton visible behind a yellow fabric exterior, its stiltlike undercarriage legs looked exceedingly weak for the pounding it must be receiving from ham-fisted student pilots. It had, of course, not a cockpit but a cabin, not a joystick but a control column, a wheel like that of a car for control of the ailerons. This was attached to a metal stick, which went not into the floor but in and out of the dash in front of the pilot for control of the elevators. There was a second control column beside the first for use by the instructor in demonstration, or in moments of panic when forced to take control from the student. The only thing I found to admire about the machine was the appearance of the two 225-horse power Jacobs air-cooled engines protruding aggressively forward of the cabin from the main wing spar. A most unmilitary-looking aircraft it was, I rationalized, not designed for any but a training function, and in this it was faithful to its designers.

The living quarters at Yorkton were of the usual steel-hut style, but there was ample room for sleeping and studying. We were impressed with the dining hall and its food content. These were often critical factors in the lives of young men living in accommodation and consuming food similar to that in logging and mining camps; if good they were taken for granted, if bad they elicited loud complaints.

The Air Force knew enough to feed us and to house us properly. It knew something else as well; conspicuously displayed in the dining hall were four large oil paintings of four Canadians from WWI: Bishop, Collishaw, McLaren, and Barker. If this was indoctrination we approved it. Bishop with a Victoria Cross and a history of utterly fearless attack, he of whom the American Rickenbacker had said that he didn't know what fear was—and this was true of Bishop—most men swallow their fear, but Bishop seemed devoid of it—not because he was insensitive or unimaginative—(many people can push fear aside while it nevertheless persists in looking over their shoulder) but with Bishop fear would not have dared try to influence his actions. And Barker, too, a man of such valour as legends are made of, who, although grievously wounded, fought a brilliant single-handed battle with German scouts over France in October 1918 and also won the V.C. And Raymond Collishaw from the West Coast, the third highest scoring British scout pilot of WWI. Yes indeed, the Air Force knew what it was doing when it put those portraits before the eyes of young warriors. . . . [I]n November 1941 at Yorkton we admired the portraits and ate our meals. The one of Collishaw was familiar because I could see the family resemblance to his cousin, whom I knew well, and to his sister, whom I had met—the same ruddy complexion and angular-faced good looks. I thought, "Why, they were only boys!"

We were Course No. 42—Red Section, and the aircraft we flew were of "D" Flight, No. 1 Hangar. Military authorities love numbers and letters and the organization techniques of industry. They are particularly fond of organization charts that look like family trees, with the title at the top of the chart showing the office of the person who ordered the chart to be drawn up. Our first day at Yorkton required a word or two from the top of the chart.

"You will do some of your dual instruction two at a time, two pupils to the instructor; one will observe while the other is under active instruction. When Red Section is flying, Blue Section will be at Ground School. You will do 50 hours dual and 60 hours solo. Included will be six cross-country navigation flights and some night flying and formation flying. If either your flying or your ground school is substandard, or if you disobey orders, you will be washed out. Upon graduation the upper 20 percent of you will be commissioned as officers, and the remainder will become noncommissioned officers of Sergeant rank." This was the Chief Flying Instructor speaking. "Your success here and your chances for officer status upon graduation will be determined as follows: take this down, so that you won't forget it. (I took it down so I wouldn't forget it, as you can see below). Your performance will be evaluated under three main heads, Ground School, Flying, and Qualities of Leadership. We allot 750 marks to each of these for a total of 2250 marks. Flying Officer Heslop will explain to you the Ground School."

"Thank you, Sir," said Heslop. "In the Ground School you will require a 60 percent mark to pass, with a minimum of 50 percent on any one course. The subjects covered and the time of instruction will be:

Airmanship	10 hours	150 marks	
Aircraft maintenance	2 hours	50 marks	
Armaments	35 hours	200 marks	(100 of these will be oral and 100 written)
Navigation	54 hours	150 marks	
Meteorology (weather)	10 hours	50 marks	
Signals	19 hours	150 marks	(100 marks written 50 marks oral)
Totals	130 hours	750 marks	

The 54 hours spent on Navigation will be futher broken down into:

Maps and Charts	6 hours
Compasses	6 hours
Instruments	6 hours
Dead Reckoning Navigation	36 hours”

An audible sigh passed through the room. There would be much work to do.

Fogarty wasted no time in getting us flying. You have seen, no doubt, pilots making a tour around an aircraft, examining its external features and controls before getting in. Fogarty showed Woodhouse and me the points of interest on this tour. Not only did he determine that a finch had not built a nest in the air intake, or that a chipmunk had not chewed a hole in the wingtip, he established that there were in fact two propellers, each firmly attached to its drive shaft, and he exhibited that the control surfaces were not locked and had been spared from sabotage; he established that the pitot head was uncovered, was free of dirt and ice, and had not been bent. What is a pitot head? (Pronounced pea-toe.) It is a little tube sticking out from the wing or fuselage, which provides a source of outside air for the airspeed indicator, that it may register changes in speed.

Fogarty made a special point of checking the level of extension of the undercarriage oleo legs. The Crane, as I have mentioned, had long and delicate legs, which it was advisable to check periodically lest one find oneself in the nesting position prior to take-off. These things done, one entered a Crane by the side door, careful not to kick a hole in the fabric. I thought I had seen stronger looking box kites.

Most of a pilot’s concern is in getting an aircraft safely on and off the ground, and all his early training is directed to that end. What happens in between is, in many cases, not even “flying.” Once the aircraft controls are trimmed for a journey or put on automatic pilot, it is only a matter of correct navigation and steering and, where possible, avoiding inclement weather, ground obstructions, and other air traffic. This sounds simple and it is, but flying itself, even without hostile action, has a habit of eliminating both the undesirable and the unlucky. And sometimes it is difficult to tell which is which.

On 7 December, my twenty-first birthday, Japan attacked Pearl Harbor. While tactically this was a brilliant operation, strategically Japan could not have done a more stupid thing. Germany, if she had reflected, would also have regarded it as stupid. Until now it was clear that Britain alone could not have launched a counterattack in the West, whether assisted by the Commonwealth or not. But with the United States at war against Japan, Germany considered herself bound by the Axis treaty and on 11 December declared war on the U.S. She was stupid in not ensuring that the slumbering giant stayed asleep. We in Canada were keenly aware of these facts, having for years slept next to the giant. So, although shocked by Japan's attack, we were relieved as well. We knew now that we would win the war.

Meanwhile, as you might expect, the course of training was not uneventful. There was the problem that Fred Stevenson had, for example. Fred was a fine pilot, who took off one day in an easterly direction to fly a cross-country. When he returned a few hours later the wind had shifted 180° from the east and was now blowing out of the West. Fred misread the windsock and landed facing east. This was one of the things no one did, that is to land down wind, although frankly it was an error anyone could have made. But flight cadets are merciless. For a month or so Fred had to put up with "Downwind Stevenson." Or, take the worse case of another who took off on a cross-country and forgot to raise his undercarriage after take-off. He unknowingly flew for two and a half hours with undercarriage down, and upon returning to Yorkton moved the undercarriage lever to the opposite position to lower the wheels, only of course it had the reverse effect. His wheels came up and he made a surprise belly landing, surrounded by red flares with which the control tower tried to warn him.

We even learned to navigate. The student would take off and climb to the selected height, set the directional gyro to read the same as the compass, and fly over the centre of the airfield at the correct height and airspeed on the precalculated course. He would note down the exact time of departure. Good, he's on his way, patting himself on the back for efficiency. The books then told him to "maintain the course accurately until the position of the aircraft can be checked in relation to a landmark." This was Air Force language for taking a bearing, or, as we broadly interpreted it, for noting where the nearest railway line went and thence peering at the grain elevators to see if this was perhaps Springside, Foam Lake, Yellow Creek, or some other point on an aerial line to Prince Albert. Going to Saskatoon was even easier. But the books also said that one should estimate wind drift, correct the course, and calculate the ground speed. So there was a nice amount of computation and genuine effort necessary to bring back a log coherent enough to dazzle the navigation instructors. They had been there, too, and were expert at detecting fraud. There existed, however, a manually operated device called a Dalton computer, which, like a circular slide rule, would yield quick answers to such computations. After a while, Navigation became simple.

In addition, at Yorkton we did some formation flying. To a pilot who has never done formation flying it comes as something of a shock to find how much manoeuvring of throttles and controls is necessary to stay in formation with two or three other aircraft. Just as you've caught up with and taken a proper station next to the aircraft on your right, he finds it necessary to speed up in order to catch the man on his right, who meanwhile thinks he should slow down a bit, and so on. It is exhausting. One's throttle arm gets tired moving the throttles back and forth, but with practice it becomes less exhausting, until ultimately three or four can fly in a gaggle like geese.

But I was never satisfied with "V" formations, and was pleased to hear later that fighters had switched to two pairs in a "finger four" formation. This sounded a great deal freer, more sensible, and easier to fight from.

My sister Ivy bought me a diary for Christmas in 1941 and inscribed it: "To a future William L. Shirer." If I did not follow Shirer as a war correspondent, I was grateful to my sister that she thought I might have. I faithfully kept the diary for a month, after which other matters intervened and no further entries were made. It had a clasp lock for privacy and I lost the key, so it was kept locked until now, when I prised it open. I have set out here, quaint though they now seem, some excerpts as they were then written.

Jan. 3, 1942 I've been looking at pictures on my locker—two are "Petty" pictures. (Of what else? Girls!) The other is of Jean Willcock. I'm buying her a watch for her graduation from business college. Sometimes I think I'm in love with her. Yet I imagine if I really were I'd want to marry her. As it is, I want to travel the world and satisfy this infernal thirst for adventure. We started night flying last night and I managed to get in an hour solo after dual instruction by Flying Officer Patterson.

Jan. 4 My flying is coming along satisfactorily, but it's not as good as I'd like it to be. It's a marvel to me that someone else's carelessness combined with my own hasn't led to an accident. We got hell for not turning back when we met fog on the way to Weyburn today. What with night and day flying we haven't time to go down town. I'm disappointed, too—I did so want to see a certain lovely, young blonde, who makes my heart jump. Ah, me!

Jan. 5 We fly two hours every night now and it certainly is fun. The instructors insist that we depend entirely upon our flight instruments, but it's usually too well lit by moonlight to do so.

Jan. 8 My instructor is pretty grumpy these days. He just got back from a couple of weeks' leave. He sure ate my ass out all around the circuit today. And I was growling back at him and mumbling objections as I came in to land. We were both like bears with a sore hind foot.

Jan. 9 We had a fire on the station last night. The "bombing teacher" building burned down. There was an improvised aircraft on the top floor of this building and on the ground floor was a moving mosaic of a section of ground, simulated to look like a target and its surrounding country. You sit in the aircraft, the controls of which are so synchronized that the ground pattern seems to change beneath you as the aircraft responds to the controls. A bombsight and a system of lights is hooked up so that a light flashes when the bomb is gone and another shows where and when it hits the ground. We feel that the loss is deplorable but not irreparable.

Jan. 10 Nothing much of interest. We went downtown tonight. Same old routine. Movie-show, a bottle of pop or grog, and perhaps a game of pool, then sit in the local restaurant, which is the cafe society of the village. It seems that this blonde I was so ardently pursuing has gone somewhere with her girl friend. They were evidently craving something besides the monotony of their life here, so they have gone down to the States.

Jan. 11 I had my "wings" navigation test today. I passed it all right but made a couple of silly little mistakes in computation. My partner for the trip had bad luck in his test. He followed the wrong railroad and got himself completely lost. (We were not allowed to assist each other.) We were even off the map sheet that we were using. This kid is a Hollander, named Speetjens. He's only been in Canada a year and a half—left Holland when the Germans advanced. He seems quite determined to fight for the freedom of his homeland. The testing sergeant isn't very amiable, but I managed to endure him without getting angry—which fact was a great surprise.

Jan.12, 13 Exams.

Jan. 14 More exams. We write them and then hold a post mortem. It's funny to see guys kicking their ass for some silly mistake, and believe me some of them are silly—things that if they only reread their paper they would know are silly. But they don't. They write it feverishly, sign their name, and get out.

Jan. 15 Still more exams. I scratched my head over Navigation all morning. Radius of action—interception—course and airspeed, track and groundspeed. I poured the whole works onto the paper.

Jan.16 & 17 Just flying now. They're getting the exams corrected. I was first in Armaments—oral and written.

Jan. 18 Had a wonderful time last night. I was in the local cafe with the best looking girl in town. She really is lovely—she drinks a little, but then what girl doesn't these days? She treats most of us with a great deal of justified suspicion.

Jan. 19 More exam marks. I only got 50 percent in meteorology, but everyone got low marks. Question: "What effect have convection currents upon the smoke conditions in Central England?" Now how the hell do we know what happens to smoke in Central England? Of course I put a lot of bullshit down, but I'll bet I lost some marks on that one.

Jan. 20 "Signals" marks are out now. I got 48 out of 50 on the written exam and 95 out of 100 on Morse sending and receiving. My mark in Navigation was 129 out of 150. It was a comprehensive exam, quite characteristic of Flying Officer Heslop. He's a thoroughly intelligent, clear-thinking man. He used to be a mining engineer, and I'll bet he was a good one.

Jan. 21 Now all we need to know are our Airmanship and Maintenance marks. There were four repetitious questions on the Airmanship exam. If we did badly on one, the same will be true on the other three. They all dealt with the loss of an engine. Of course we gave them the story of "Full throttle, fine pitch, hold straight with rudder, maintain height, and trim the machine for single engine flight." Same old stuff all the way, but it must be right—it's what they've been pounding into us, day after day in the air.

Jan. 22 I got 139 out of 200 on Airmanship and Maintenance. That isn't very much worse. That gave me a total of 615 out of 750 and an average of 82%, which seems to be pretty good so far. I'll know tomorrow where I stand in relation to the rest of the class.

Jan. 23 What do you know? I finished second in the class on the examinations. Second out of sixty-four. I can hardly believe it.

Jan. 24, 25, 26 & 27 Haven't been flying much lately. A low-pressure area has moved in and brought with it the usual bad weather, low ceiling, fog, and snow. We just sit around the crew room when we can't sneak out. Using the parachutes for pillows, it's a good opportunity to catch up on our reading—I've read two books in the last two days. "The Stray Lamb" by Thorne Smith and "The Jungle" by Upton Sinclair. I also read the gospel according to St. Matthew. I've always wanted to read the teachings of Christ but hitherto scorned Christianity because I judged the religion by its exponents in the pulpit.

Jan. 28 More bad weather—no flying—I'm enjoying it no end. The rest of the fellows have just come from the show. They're all extolling the amorous advantages of a posting to the Bahamas. The movie was "Bahama Passage." They say that the hero didn't want to play Adam to her Eve and they doubt if any sane man really has that much self-control.

Jan. 29 It's snowing like hell. The aerodrome is unserviceable, but there is one ray of sunshine. We're going to get four days' leave. I guess I'll try to stall off some of my urgent creditors so that I can go to Winnipeg. We're certainly going to rip that town apart.

And so ends the diary. I think we actually got two days in Winnipeg. I remember the snow blowing in my eyes and against my greatcoat at the corner of Portage and Main. The city must have withstood our onslaught.

On 28 February 1942 we graduated from SFTS. The sun shone. We shined our shoes, polished our buttons, cleaned up the barracks, pressed our uniforms, and had a hair trim. Clean-shaven and full of good will, we formed up to march according to flights, in columns of three, past the station headquarters to one of the hangers where the instructors and station staff had been mustered to act as audience while the Station Commander pinned a cloth badge, four inches long and shaped like wings, to the left chest of each of us. We were officially pilots in the RCAF. We were made sergeants and sent to our homes on leave, equipped with rail vouchers, some money, and, in the case of 20 percent of us, with a warrant to buy an officer's uniform. We were also issued with rail vouchers to Halifax and instructions to report there on 14 March. With two days' travel to the West Coast and five days by train from there to Halifax, this meant a week at home. No one of course travelled by air. The Rocky Mountains had been crossed in late 1939 by Trans-Canada Airlines, but the service was limited and expensive.

In the late 1930s, the United Kingdom and Newfoundland built an airfield on the plateau north of Gander Lake, Newfoundland, to facilitate experimental fights aimed at the introduction of regularly scheduled transatlantic air service. When the war began, the Newfoundland airport became an indispensable stopover point for aircraft being ferried from North American production centres to the United Kingdom. In June 1940, Canada took over the operation of the airport for the duration of the war. The account that follows is taken from the war diary of the Royal Air Force Ferry Command unit stationed at Gander.

Diary of the Royal Air Force Ferry Command, Gander, 8–23 December 1942

Tuesday 8th. December 1942 . . .

WEATHER: Varying overcast and visibility, mainly moderate until dusk when a heavy snowstorm caused zero zero conditions for several hours.

The brakes gave out on *Boston BZ 295* (Capt. Schaffer) when landing here from Dorval at 1447 local time, but the machine was kept under control until taxying down the slope from the Administration Building to Ferry Command hangars when it ran into a ditch at the end of the taxying area, severely damaging the undercarriage and losing the belly tank, besides serious damage to airscrews, wing, fuselage.

Boston BZ 222 crashed near Martlesham Heath, Suffolk, after flight of 13 hrs 31 mins. Crew baled out safely.

Boston BZ 247 missing on flight to Prestwick. . . .

Bostons BZ 248 and *304* returned due [to] engine trouble.

Bostons BZ 294 and *319* circled over Gander for considerable period due [to] snowstorm after flight from Dorval. *BZ 319* eventually landed at Stephenville. *BZ 294* reported force landed near Benton, 8 miles east of Gander, at approximately 2015 local time. At 2115 local time the following party set out by rail to Benton to search: The Commanding Officer, F[light]/L[ieutenant] Wilson RCAF (doctor), Corbett, Kerr and Blandford arriving at midnight and proceeding on foot. Capt. Williams, the C[ommanding] O[fficer], and R[adio]/O[fficer] Jarvis accompanied the party to Benton to obtain local information, returning by rail with object of searching from the air next morning. . . .

Wednesday 9th. December 1942 . . .

Weather: C.A.V.U. [ceiling and visibility unlimited] until afternoon when there was a little broken cloud. Thin coating of powdered snow on runways.

The ground search party under Mr. Corbett returned at 1600 hours local time, having spent 14 hours in the bush without finding any trace of the missing *Boston BZ 294*. Five other Bostons, two Hudsons and several RCAF aircraft also searched all day without finding any trace. The previous night, from 0130 hours until about 0600 hours, an RCAF Canso, having located a fire close to where the aircraft was reported to have crashed, had patrolled between the fire and the ground party which he located by their torch signals. Unfortunately the pilot completely failed to realise the importance of getting the search party to the fire, so dropped no messages nor descended below 900 feet. On his return to camp, the pilot made out no written report and went to bed without realising the implications of what he had seen. On his return to camp, Mr. Corbett reported what had occurred to the CO, who immediately called a conference in the Canadian Op[eration]s. Room, to which the Canso pilot was summoned. It became apparent that further aerial search must be made immediately. Mr. Corbett and Mr. Kerr went as observers in a Canadian Canso and soon located a torchlight being flashed from the bush. By the time they landed back, the CO had food and supplies ready which he dropped by parachute but as the light was only displayed momentarily at infrequent intervals, accuracy was impossible. It was subsequently discovered that the supplies dropped half a mile from the man, but owing to the thickness of the undergrowth, he was unable to reach them. On return from this flight, the CO organised further search by RCAF planes at dawn. . . .

Thursday 10th. December 1942 . . .

Weather: C.A.V.U. still slight snow on runways. Short but severe snowstorm just before midnight until approximately 0100 11/12.

Boston BZ 294 Soon after dawn, a RCAF Harvard located a man in the bush about three miles South East of the Radio Range station. The man spelled out in the snow the word "EAT." Shortly afterwards, a small packet of food wrapped in a blanket was dropped from a Harvard, then a larger parcel by parachute from a Norseman. At the same time, a ground party was being organised by Mr. Corbett to bring him into camp. A Taylor Cub which the Americans, at the request of the CO, had flown up from

Argentia could not, unfortunately, be used for guiding the ground party, as it was required to pick up the missing Hurricane pilot who had been in the bush without food or fire for six days. He was rescued by Captain Treher, USAAC [United States Army Air Corps], who put up an extremely good show, landing and taking off from very rough muskeg. The pilot of the Hurricane appeared little the worse for his experience. While the ground party were walking a compass course to the man from the Boston, a RCAF Sergeant Pilot started diving and firing lights near them. This misled the search party into thinking the man was in the direction in which the Harvard was firing lights. They, therefore, went off in that direction but neither saw nor heard anything of the man and eventually returned to camp after a fruitless search. . . .

Friday 11th. December 1942 . . .

Weather: C.A.V.U. except for occasional light cloud. Still some snow on runways.

Boston BZ 294 Mr. Corbett's search party set out once more soon after daylight, but this time with the CO directing them from the air in the USAAC Taylor Cub which had been the means of rescuing the RCAF Hurricane pilot the previous day. First a message was dropped on the man "What is your name?" He spelt out in the snow "COATES," the name of the radio operator of *BZ* 294. A message was then dropped asking if there were any other survivors, and he spelt out "NO. ONE KILLED. ONE DIED." The CO then flew back to camp and dropped a message asking S[quadron]/L[eader] Dundee to pass this message on to Dorval. From then until the ground party reached Coates, the Taylor Cub patrolled the intervening distance ready to indicate short cuts and prevent straying off course. The ground party made very good time keeping to a frozen brook which fortunately ran from close to the Range Station to where Coates was sheltering in a clump of trees on its bank. They found him in good general condition and soon had him back in camp where he was admitted into hospital suffering from nothing worse than minor bruises and reaction. . . .

Saturday 12th. December 1942 . . .

Weather: Overcast with poor visibility early then C.A.V.U. except occasional patches light cloud. Light coating of snow on runways. The story Coates had to tell of the crash of *Boston BZ 294* was that they were coming in to land and could see the lights of the airport when suddenly he felt a series of ever increasing shocks culminating in a terrific crash. The pilot subsequently told him that the altimeter was reading over 1000 feet when they hit. Coates had great difficulty in pulling himself together and forcing his muscles to work enough to get him out of the machine. Once out, he saw that the aircraft was already beginning to burn. He shouted out and heard groans coming from the pilot's cockpit. He has not very much recollection of how he got the pilot, F/Lt D.G. Chown, RCAF, out, but shortly afterwards one or more tanks exploded. Coates fears that the navigator, P[ilot]/O[fficer] K.H. Wells, RCAF, who was beside him at the time of the crash, must have been killed, though he saw nothing of his body afterwards in the wreckage. He also searched back over the hundred yard scar made as the aircraft plunged through the trees. The pilot's legs were broken in at least two places, and he complained of internal injuries. Coates lit a fire and tried to keep him warm with his own body. When he saw the Canso coming over, he flashed his torch sending morse signals, which, however, were not acknowledged and, it transpires, were not recognised by the Canso as being morse signals. He realised that the aircraft had seen his signals because parachute flares were dropped right overhead; it also blinked its landing lights. When nobody came to his rescue, he decided to try and walk for help but very shortly found he was back on his own tracks in the snow. He, therefore, returned to the pilot and stayed with him until he died at 1100 hrs in the morning. It is tragic to think that there was a doctor and rescue party within a mile of them from about 0100 hours onwards. After the pilot died, Coates started walking in what he thought was the direction of Gander but found he had little strength, and although there were aircraft overhead all day, none of them saw him or his signals. As soon as night fell, he climbed a tree and saw the lights on the Radio Range Station towards which he started walking. Next time he climbed a tree, he found that he had gone round in a circle, and was walking away from it. This happened altogether six times, but while he was walking the Canso was overhead and he periodically flashed signals to it. When the Commanding Officer dropped the supplies by parachute, although he could not reach them, he felt very confident that he had been located and would be seen next day. He, therefore, stayed by the brook in the shelter of some trees, from where he was finally collected at about 1400 hours, 11th. December. . . .

Wednesday 23rd. December 1942 . . .

Weather: Closed in early with snow falling, clearing from midday on to good visibility and unlimited ceiling except for slight broken cloud.

The funeral of F/Lt Chown and P/O Wells who were killed in the crash of Boston BZ 294 on 8th. December took place in the RCAF Drill Shed at 1430 hours local time. Present were S/L Turnbull representing the A[ir] O[fficer] C[ommanding-in-Chief], Ferry Com-mand and G[roup]/C[aptain] Wray, RCAF, Commanding Officer, Gander, and two RCAF WD [Women's Division] officers. The RCAF provided the band, firing party, escort and bearers and the Protestant and Roman Catholic padres together conducted the service. The bodies were afterwards interred in the Gander cemetery.

Arguably the best known poem of the Second World War, and certainly the one that captures the mystic beauty of flying, "High Flight" was written by John Magee, Jr. An eighteen-year-old American at Yale University, Magee crossed the border to join the RCAF in 1940. In December 1941, he died when his Spitfire was destroyed in action. The poem for which he will be remembered had been sent to his mother a few months earlier.

High Flight

John Gillespie Magee, Jr.

Oh, I have slipped the surly bonds of earth,
And danced the skies on laughter-silvered wings;
Sunward I've climbed and joined the tumbling mirth
Of sun-split clouds—and done a hundred things
You have not dreamed of—wheeled and soared and swung
High in the sunlit silence. Hov'ring there,
I've chased the shouting wind along and flung
My eager craft through footless halls of air.
Up, up the long delirious, burning blue
I've topped the wind-swept heights with easy grace,
Where never lark, or even eagle, flew;
And, while with silent, lifting mind I've trod
The high untrespassed sanctity of space,
Put out my hand, and touched the face of God.

One of the greatest autobiographies of the Second World War was written by Winnipeg lawyer and jurist Murray Peden. His account of his RCAF training in Canada and service overseas as a bomber pilot remains a superbly moving story of courage. Published by a small press, Peden's book unfortunately remains largely unknown. This excerpt, recounting a raid against a German town, may help expose Peden's fine book to a wider audience.

Gelsenkirchen

Murray Peden

ON 21 JUNE I learned in the morning that there was to be a war on that night, and that Peden's crew were on the battle order in F Fox. We went out and did our air test immediately. It was on this occasion, as I recall, that we were standing waiting for the crew bus, when it pulled up at the dispersal next to ours and we saw Johnny Corke and his crew disembarking to climb aboard their aircraft. Johnny's engineer was a chap named Barber, and he was known to the ground crew to be meticulous in his requirements. One of the erks obviously thought him too damned meticulous. As he saw Barber alight from the rear step of the crew bus, I heard him call in a low voice to one of his mates: "Oi . . . 'ere comes Ali Barber and the 40 snags."

At 4:30 that afternoon we sat in the briefing room and watched in the usual strained silence as the curtains swished noisily open to reveal route tapes running to Gelsenkirchen, in the heart of the Ruhr. Someone in the crew muttered: "Christ, Happy Valley." I responded with supreme confidence, "Piece of cake." Our target was the Nordstern oil plant in Gelsenkirchen.

I really did not feel the confidence I had expressed as I looked at the big target map in front of us. Heavy flak areas on that map were marked with red circles. The Ruhr was one solid turnip-shaped blotch of red, many inches wide and a foot long on our map; and it had a deep belt of searchlights all round it, denoted by a continuous broad blue border framing the whole blob. Ruhr trips had one good quality: they were short. That was their only redeeming feature. Happy Valley was probably the most heavily defended industrial area in Europe. Apart from the hundreds of flak batteries and the dense concentrations of searchlights, it was well protected by swarms of night fighters, and it was extremely difficult on such a short trip to mislead them by routing as to the intended target area. When I said "piece of cake" it was just so much whistling past the graveyard; but I was to be reminded of it later.

We had skirted the fringes of the Ruhr's defences on more than one occasion, had seen that seemingly impenetrable palisade of searchlights, and knew only too well that to run through the heaviest belt of those defences—Gelsenkirchen was like another suburb of Essen—was going to be no picnic. Main Force was actually going to split as it approached our target area and attack the oil plants at nearby Wesseling and Scholven-Buer as well.[1] All these attacks, and those delivered by the RAF in the days immediately preceding, were part of the co-ordinated Allied bombing campaign against German oil plants initiated some weeks earlier, with gratifying success, by the Americans. These strikes were hurting the Germans, and their fighters were reacting accordingly.

Takeoff was late these summer nights. It was just after 11:00 p.m. when the Aldis lamp's green flash sent F Fox roaring down the flarepath. We crossed the coast outbound near Cromer, and climbed steadily to 22 000 feet in the clear night air.

Once we hit the enemy coast, the ever-present strain mounted rapidly to the higher level that was the concomitant of being in the enemy's ball park, blindfolded by night. I always waited tensely for the first burst of flak to stab at us, hoping it would not be too close. Once that first burst came up, and I recovered from the violent start that the sudden flash in the darkness always caused, I breathed a little easier and began the game that every pilot had to play, changing altitude, course, and speed, to throw off the next burst; counting the seconds carefully and watching to see where that next burst came; then varying the course again, being careful not to "balance" the pattern with a nice symmetrical correction to the other side. The German predictors were quick to average symmetrical evasions and fire a burst at the appropriate moment along the mean track.

The human system is incredibly adaptive, and what constantly surprised me, when I thought about it in safety on the ground, was how matter of factly we could play this deadly game, and even derive a certain nervous satisfaction from it, watching shells burst two or three hundred yards away, at the very spot you would have been had you not changed course as the gunners were launching their speeding projectiles on their way.

We thrust inland, threading our way through the welcoming flak, and Stan soon began reporting contacts on Monica, the radar set which he monitored in his cabin. It became apparent that Sam had positioned us well toward the middle of the bomber stream, and that the concentration of Lancasters was dense. In a way I hated these frequent radar contacts, for we always had to assume that they might be night fighters, and everyone strained unconsciously until one of the gunners came on intercom with something like "Ah, I've got him, Skipper, it's a Lanc. He's three or four hundred yards dead astern and down just a little bit." On black nights they could not be seen at anything like that range. This night they could be spotted while they were well away from us. We had a second concern, however, even after the gunners identified the contact as a Lanc. The question uppermost in our minds then was: has he seen and identified us? The Fortress, of course, had a prominent single fin. Most of the aircraft with a single fin and rudder flying the night skies were German, and we wanted no "friendly" machine gun bullets put into us by mistake. If the friendly aircraft was slightly above you, the waiting period until you parted company was extremely tense, since it was easier for you to spot him than vice versa.

At a point about 20 minutes from the target we began to approach an outlying belt of searchlights which stood before us on either side of our intended track in two great cones. I feared and hated those baleful blinding lights more than anything else the Germans used against us. While in themselves they seldom caused death—although there were reported cases of pilots, particularly at low level, apparently becoming completely disoriented by their glaring beams and diving into the earth—they were all too often the harbinger of death. A pilot trapped in a large cone had little chance of escape. For long seconds on end the dazzling glare would render him helpless, spotlighting him as the target and making it almost impossible for him to see his instruments and maintain any sense of equilibrium. Meanwhile the searchlights' accomplices, the heavy guns, would hurl up shells in streams, and all too frequently the aircraft would explode or begin a crazy, smoking dive to the ground.

As I watched these two cones warily, I noticed that they were remaining stationary for 30 seconds or so at a time, leaving a corridor between them, then abruptly moving together and establishing one giant cone right in the middle of what had been the safe passage. Twice I saw them do this, and twice when they came together in the centre they trapped a Lancaster attempting to slip by. Each time the Lancaster was destroyed. It was an unnerving spectacle to watch, particularly when your turn to run the gauntlet was fast approaching. It was Hobson's choice with a vengeance. You could not fly straight into either cone while they were standing separate; that was committing suicide; and detouring all the way around the outside would have involved a major departure from the prescribed track and thrown out the aircraft's time over target by several minutes. You had no practicable alternative but to take the black void between the two cones, knowing that the lights would swing inward and illuminate some part of the safe passage every few seconds. You headed for the open spot and prayed that you would get through. I chose a spot slightly right of centre and sweated. We were lucky.

Hardly had we cleared this hurdle than Stan came on the intercom again to report another contact, a close one. This time we were not left long in doubt. In less than a minute our rear gunner, Johnny Walker, spotted an aircraft directly astern at a range of about 300 yards. This was approximately where Stan had predicted the contact would be found, but it was another 30 seconds or more before Johnny Walker and Bert Lester confirmed that it was a Lancaster. Then, for a minute or two, we seemed to be holding the same relative positions. I was reluctant to weave away if I could avoid it, since Sam's navigation thus far had kept us dead on track, and I preferred not to mar his handiwork. However, after another minute, Johnny Walker reported that the Lanc had closed further and was now just about 200 yards astern.

"If he comes any closer, any closer at all," I said, "let me know, and I'll weave off to the side a bit."

It was at that precise moment that Fate dealt us a card off the bottom of the deck.

The Lancaster abruptly stood on its wingtip and dived away. Directly behind it, and now directly behind us and in perfect firing position, was a Messerschmitt 410 which had been stalking the Lancaster.

As Johnny Walker shouted a warning and began firing himself, the air around us was instantly filled with white flaming shells that flashed past our windows with horrifying speed, and F Fox shuddered heavily to the pounding of a hail of close range cannon fire. Through the back of my seat I felt a rapid series of staccato blows that jarred us like the strokes of a wild triphammer.

I had instinctively thrust the control column forward and twisted the ailerons to dive into a violent corkscrew; but in the second it took to initiate the manoeuvre, F Fox absorbed heavy punishment from the torrent of shells the Messerschmitt's cannons poured into us. Before I had 15 degrees of bank on, the starboard inner engine burst into great leaping flames and the intercom went dead.

As we rolled into the dive to starboard, the heavy vibration of a long burst fired from our mid-upper turret shook the instrument panel in front of me into a great blur; it was as though the instruments were mounted on the sounding strings of some giant lyre. With remarkable presence of mind, Bill ignored the tracers flying around his head, and moved to feather number three at the same time as he activated its fire extinguisher. I was dimly aware of his actions, and of the frightening flames that gushed out of the engine and were snatched back across the cowling as I rolled to begin my climb to port.

The firing ceased as suddenly as it had started—on both sides. With some difficulty I levelled up, after a fashion, and tried to take stock of the situation. F Fox was sickeningly sluggish and unresponsive; but for the next two minutes that problem paled into insignificance as I struggled to stop her swift descent, and watched Bill fight to get number three feathered so that we could get the fire under control. We had been told frequently that a fuel-fed fire, blown against the interior of the wing by the slipstream, could eat right through the main spar in as little as two minutes. If the main spar went, our chances of getting out of the aircraft as it cartwheeled earthward would be remote. Bill was unable to coax the recalcitrant propeller to feather properly, although the blades did rotate to the point where the propeller was turning over at a low speed.

Meantime J. B. had clambered back to find out what had happened in the rear of the aircraft. For all we knew, the four crew members behind the mid-upper might have abandoned the plane—or been killed.

F Fox continued to lose height, and without warning number three began to wind up. In moments it was up past its safe maximum and was overspeeding with a terrifying banshee wail. As it screamed itself into hysteria, the fire, which had been dying down, flared up in all its fury again.

Scared half out of my wits by the flames, and the knowledge that they were only inches away from enough gasoline to blow us into eternity, I tried vainly to remember what one did with an overspeeding propeller. In a moment Bill suggested throttling back the other three, and I strained to pull F Fox's nose up at the same time so that the overspeeding propeller would be carrying a substantial load.

It worked. Like a screaming circular saw suddenly deprived of power the propeller began to slow down, its terrifying note gradually subsiding like some manic thing being quieted. As it sank back below normal speed, we shifted the load onto the other three engines, staring appraisingly at number three and trying to gauge whether that fire would kill us with an explosion. Although it was not extinguished, it had subsided again with the propeller, so I turned my attention momentarily to the task of coaxing F Fox to hold height.

As though cursed with a devilish spirit of its own, number three began to overspeed again. I knew this nerve-wracking phenomenon, with its continually rising crescendo of shrieking sound was a condition which could not long endure. The propeller shaft would let go in a short time, and when that happened, in a Fortress, the propeller from number three would fly into, or perhaps through, the nose or cockpit. Despite the fact that the manoeuvre resulted in a partial stall which then lost us more precious altitude, I had no alternative but to throttle back again, haul the nose up, and try to force some load onto number three. As I did so, the flames were flaring above the cowling once more. The technique worked again, soothing the maddened outcry of the propeller and coaxing its speed back within a range the engine could tolerate. Again F Fox mushed down in a weary stall, the inevitable product of the unnaturally nose-high position coupled with the loss of power. Bill and I bent once more to the task of restoring the power very gradually, so as not to precipitate another runaway, and nursing the weary aircraft into a normal attitude.

As we levelled up, the air around us was suddenly filled with a hail of tracers again, and once again I threw F Fox into a corkscrew. But this time we could only manage a travesty of the prescribed manoeuvre, and we would have died then and there but for the good shooting of Johnny Walker. A JU 88, drawn by the irresistible sight of fire aboard a wounded prey, had stalked us and closed to finish us off. But the German pilot had reckoned without Johnny Walker. Hollering into the dead intercom in a fruitless attempt to warn me, Johnny drew a careful bead on the German and, in the face of the fighter's overpowering weight of fire, traded lead so accurately that the German was shortly forced to break off.

F Fox had absorbed more punishment in this second combat, although nothing like what she had taken the first time. She had lost even more of her characteristic responsiveness, and her struggle to fend off the clutch of gravity was palpably less successful. Another result of the second attack, however, was that it forced us to dive again, and this in turn had immediately started number three winding up. Once more the fire flared wickedly, ugly tongues of flame visible from a great distance at night, and again we went through our scary exercise, stalling the sluggish aeroplane to get the screaming propeller back under control. The second attack, therefore, inflicted additional structural damage upon us, rekindled the fire in number three, and cost us altitude we could not afford to give away. It did one other thing: it convinced me that it would be foolhardy to try to make our way through the main flak and searchlight defences over the target in the condition we were in. Night fighters too were clearly in the stream in force. The JU 88 had picked us up within minutes of the first attack, and I felt it would be simply asking for it to count on escaping from a third attack in our present condition. Although we were now no more than ten minutes away from the target, I coaxed F Fox into a gentle turn and reversed our course.

Bill went forward to get me a proper course from Sam, and again I surveyed the situation with what few crumbs of equanimity I could muster. Our most worrisome problem, apart from the smouldering fire which kept threatening to flare and spread, was the generally precarious performance of the aircraft. Flying on three engines with the fourth propeller properly feathered is one thing. It is quite another doing it with an engine which is windmilling and refuses to feather, and in an aeroplane which has been torn open and battered to the point where its aerodynamic efficiency has been seriously compromised. Pulling an aeroplane through the sky with an engine windmilling is much the same as pushing a stalled car while leaving it in gear. The drag is tremendous, and the net effect is to subtract and waste a substantial amount of your remaining power. When I turned F Fox about, we were down to 15 000 feet, having lost close to 7000 feet in the two combats and the ensuing struggle with the burning engine. We were still losing height at about 500–700 feet per minute, were still without intercom, and were seriously limited as to manoeuvrability.

As Bill and I were setting the remaining three engines to the most power we felt we could call upon them to deliver for a protracted period, and trying to trim the aircraft into the best attitude for its sorry condition, I felt a tap on my shoulder and looked round to see Hembrow, the German-speaking special wireless operator, standing just behind my seat. He looked dishevelled and more than slightly shaken. (In fact he had been slightly wounded, with a cannon splinter in the back of the shoulder.) His terse message registered indelibly on my brain as he raised his voice and called above the noise: "The wireless operator's been hit . . . And I've been hit . . . And we all want to go home."

This trusting message, implying that I could somehow wash out the balance of the exercise, and ordain safe delivery to Blickling Hall despite fire, battle damage, and anything else that might follow, made me feel rather fatherly. I reached back and clapped him lightly on the shoulder and told him everything was okay, that we were heading for home.

Then the first piece of good luck to come our way since takeoff manifested itself—the intercom came back on, although it remained intermittent and undependable. Actually it was not luck as it turned out, but good work by Stan, assisted by J. B. In a few minutes I had some knowledge of what had happened. Stan had been badly wounded, including at least two splinter wounds in the head which caused him to lose a lot of blood and subjected him to a great deal of pain. J. B. had promptly decided that Stan should be given an injection of morphine, and prepared to administer it; but Stan had insisted on struggling to repair the intercom before submitting to the injection. I hoped within the next few minutes to be able to make up my mind as to whether we would be likely to make it back across the North Sea or whether we should bail out and take our chances while we were over land.

It was not to be an easy decision. Time seemed almost to stand still, measured only by the intervals that elapsed between the repeated overspeedings of number three engine, which I came to loathe and fear. Time after time it went through its hellish performance, causing the flames to spring up fiercely again, and forcing us to lose precious height in each stall. I aged ten years, worrying about how long the starboard wing would stay on, and at one point ordered everyone to prepare to abandon the aircraft, so that they would at least have their chest packs on if F Fox came apart in the air. (It was at this juncture that Bill discovered that my chute had disappeared in the jinking.) However, as we neared the coast, I could not defer the decision any longer. I had to make up my mind whether we would try to make it across the North Sea or whether it would be better to have the crew abandon the aircraft, bailing out while we were over land. We had fallen from 22 000 to 6000 feet by this time, but in the denser air F Fox was now finding her strength again, and had almost ceased losing altitude. I decided the whole crew should try to make it to England, and got Sam to work out a course for Woodbridge, on the coast in Suffolk, one of our three big crash dromes.

Over the water I told Bert to get the proper colours of the period ready for the Very pistol, thinking of our troublesome intercom and radio. Bill and I now felt justified in making a very slight reduction in power to ease the strain on the three good engines, which had laboured nobly but were showing the effort in their cylinder head temperatures After a further tense wait the English coast appeared ahead, and in a short time we were approaching Woodbridge. Sam had brought us to it as straight as a homing pigeon, and my biggest remaining worry, or so I thought, was that at any moment the main spar on the starboard side might let go.

I called the tower repeatedly as we approached, and although our reception of their response was extremely disjointed, I gathered that we were cleared to land. To make doubly sure, I told Bert to fire the colours of the period several times and follow with a signal indicating that we had wounded aboard. I flashed the appropriate letters on our recognition light, then began to concentrate on the all-important task of getting F Fox safely on the ground.

I kept remembering that the main spar behind number three had been subjected to the effects of what amounted to a giant blow torch playing on it intermittently for an hour and three-quarters, and as I pictured its possible condition in my mind's eye, I was at pains to avoid increasing the wing loading with any steep turns in the circuit, much as I wanted to get on the ground and far away from the 2000 gallons of gasoline and that seemingly unquenchable fire smouldering a foot or two in front of it. I offered up a silent prayer that the undercarriage would come down when I pressed the selector. F Fox had absorbed a lot of cannon shells—I had felt them striking home—and there was a distinct possibility that the electric motors or cables which activated the undercarriage mechanism had been damaged. I had not dared try it earlier, seeking to avoid both the additional drag and the vibration it produced swinging into place.

Now was the time to find out. Bert fired another signal from the Very pistol, and after ordering the rest of the crew, with the exception of Bill, to take Stan and get into their crash positions, I turned gently toward the flarepath and flipped the undercarriage selector switch. Immediately I could hear the whine and then feel the reassuring drag effect indicating that the wheels were dropping out of their nacelles; the undercarriage motors seemed to be okay. In a few moments the green light on the instrument panel glowed: undercarriage down and locked. I stole a glance away from the flare path and peered into the gloom below the inboard engine nacelle on my side. The port wheel looked all right. Bill was having a more difficult time on his side. The smoke and intermittent showers of sparks made it difficult to see anything in the darkness. But in a few moments he straightened up in his seat and gave me a thumbs-up. I prepared to make the best landing I could.

We touched down very lightly, and for a few brief seconds I began to relax. But our troubles were not over. One of the German fighters had shot our right tire into useless pulp. F Fox vibrated roughly and began sinking lower and lower on her wounded side. I had a terrible vision of the starboard wingtip catching and the aircraft cartwheeling into one final detonation. In a second or two we were down to the hub on the right wheel, and beginning to veer to that side as the hub dragged more and more heavily. I tried to correct the swing with a touch of brake, only to discover that we had no brakes—our hydraulics had been shot out. Immediately I applied a burst of throttle from the starboard outer to see if I could straighten our course that way, but F Fox was beyond responding; she hurtled on, continuing to veer to the right. I sat clutching the control column with both hands and practically bending the rudder bar with my foot as I tried vainly to check the swing with maximum left rudder.

Out of the darkness 50 yards in front of us, the silhouette of a Lancaster suddenly loomed up directly in our path. As I threw my left arm over my face we collided with the other aircraft at 75 miles an hour, severing it completely a few feet to the rear of its mid-upper turret with our right wing. F Fox spun around violently for two or three seconds and shuddered to a halt a short distance further on. Bill and I both snatched at the master switch to cut everything off, then snapped our belts free and turned speedily to open the side windows to escape.

My window jammed. I gripped it fiercely and tugged twice more. It stuck fast. Bill had wrenched his window open and was disappearing through it, so I flung myself to the right side of the cockpit to follow him out. His foot slipped as he thrashed clear, and his heavy flying boot came back into my face like the kick of a Clydesdale. I never even felt it, but twisted through the window like a limbo dancer and sprang rearward from the battered starboard wing like an Olympic athlete.

Fast as Bill and I were, the others had had a few seconds head start and had been covering ground. They had boosted Stan out the rear door and were many yards ahead of us, running for all they were worth. When Bill and I had sprinted 60 or 70 yards I turned for a moment to look at F Fox, and remember thinking that the person who had warned us about the vulnerability of main spars had clearly had no idea of how rugged the Fortress's was. True, the outer 25 feet of F Fox's wing had been splayed open in the violent collision with the Lancaster; but the centre section was still in place and still intact.

I turned to join the other members of the crew, who were now 30 or 40 yards further on. As I panted up to them, I called out to J.B.: "Where's Stan?"

He motioned behind him to a dark bundle lying on the ground. I hurried over and took a look. Stan seemed to me to be unconscious although his eyes were half open. Even in the semi-darkness I could see that his face was as white as parchment and his hair ominously matted.

"Oh the poor bastard . . . he's had it," I said.

This was not an example of my best bedside manner, of course; had I not been labouring under a considerable strain myself I should not have been so tactless. My sympathy and concern were genuine. (Although rather heavily drugged, Stan was still aware of what was going on, and heard my pessimistic prognosis. It made him mad, he told me later; but not as mad as he got a short time afterward in the station hospital, when a chap wandered in beside him by mistake, saw Stan, and immediately began to throw up.)

Off to the side another Lancaster, apparently in dire straits, was emulating our performance, firing Very lights as it swung toward the funnel. After our own experience, we kept a wary eye on the Lanc which also proceeded to swing out of control on landing and head in the general direction of F Fox and the Lancaster we had clobbered.

As the ambulance came hunting for us, the last card of the hand was turned over: the Tannoy gave vent to a strident announcement warning all ground crew to keep clear of the Lancaster we had just cut in half, advising in stentorian tones that it had a 12 000 pound high explosive bomb aboard.

I peered across to where the truncated Lancaster squatted, now pointing skyward at an unnaturally sharp angle, and guessed thankfully that we must have missed the bomb by about two feet as we slashed through the aircraft. The third aircraft had meanwhile piled in a short distance from ours. Shaken, I climbed into the second van and we were speedily borne to sick quarters to see the MO.

If you were involved in a crash, even if you walked—or ran—away from it, the rule was that you had to be given a medical inspection by the MO. In fact, the inspection varied considerably in scope and thoroughness, depending on what had happened and how busy the doctor was. We had to wait some time while they began looking after Stan. When it was my turn, the doctor called me in, looked at me, and said: "Were you hurt?"

"No, not a scratch," I said.

"You may not have a scratch, but you look as though you could use this," he rejoined, pouring what looked like about four ounces of service rum into a graduated beaker. "Toss that off," he said.

I took the medication as directed, and was unable to get any breath for approximately two minutes. But he was a better doctor than this rough-and-ready sounding treatment suggested. In half an hour my incipient case of the shakes—which he had doubtless spotted—was gone.

After everyone had been thus inspected, we went over to the mess hall for our customary reward of bacon and eggs. As I walked toward the steam table, a pilot standing with a small group ahead of us detached himself and came rather uncertainly toward me.

"You the pilot of that Fortress?" he asked.

"Yes, I am," I said, "who are you?"

"I'm the pilot of the Lancaster you chopped in half," he said with a little laugh, sticking out his hand. "We were standing underneath the kite when you swung and came heading for us. We had a 12 000 pounder sitting in the bomb bay over our heads. I'll bet we raced out of there faster than you flew in."

While we waited to pick up our food, he told me that they had been attacked by a fighter just before they reached the target. In the course of the combat the fighter had shot out the Lanc's hydraulics, effectively preventing him from opening his bomb doors and getting rid of his load. His crew had been on the ground only a few minutes when they saw our Very lights and watched F Fox come in to land. Like us, they had thought everything was all right when we touched down safely; but in a moment they had realized the peril they were in. I could imagine the thoughts that went through their minds as they saw the lights of F Fox curving through the night toward their huge bomb. I suppose that for ten seconds they were more intensely frightened than I was—difficult as that is to visualize.[2]

After we had eaten, we were directed to an empty Nissen hut not too far away. For an hour I lay on a cot vainly trying to relax and get some sleep; but my mind was too full of the night's events. I kept reliving the fire, the fighter attacks, and the crash. Eventually I decided to get up and go for a walk. I rose quietly, taking care not to disturb the others, and tiptoed out the door. Outside, I could see that we were only a few hundred yards from the field, and all at once I felt the urge to go back and see F Fox. I had walked no more than 50 yards, when I heard a slight sound and turned to see the rest of the crew strung out behind me in Indian file.

We found F Fox without any trouble. Now she sat peacefully in the grey dawn light, the tumult of her final hours—for one glance told us she would never fly again—all too easy to recapture from her dreadful appearance. Under her wing I sank onto my knees and thanked God for bringing us home alive. No one offered any comment on the Skipper's unusual reverence.

Notes

1. See Sir Charles Webster and Noble Frankland, *The Strategic Air Offensive Against Germany, 1939–45* (London: Her Majesty's Stationery Office, n.d.), 3: 161.
2. The pilot was PO "Butch" Passant, the Aussie skipper of Lancaster JB351 of No. 61 Squadron. The whole crew, with one exception, were killed a fortnight later on another target. Dennis Copson, the rear gunner, was wounded in the attack on Gelsenkirchen and was convalescing when his crew went on their last op. The author tracked down both Dennis Copson and Mr. W.G. Francis in 1977, the latter the NCO in charge of the crash crew at the scene when F Fox cut Lancaster JB351 in half.

What the Germans did in their extermination camps remains a blot on humankind. Neo-Nazis have recently argued that the Holocaust was a postwar propaganda exercise, but René Lévesque, the leader of the Parti Québécois from its founding until the mid-1980s, knew better. Lévesque had served as a war correspondent with the American army, and he went to Dachau, not at all the worst of the camps, at war's end.

Dachau

René Lévesque

THE SIN AGAINST PROPERTY was nothing, absolutely nothing, compared to the hell on earth we were to get our first sight of the next day or the day after. In the outskirts, at Dachau, we knew there were mysterious places called "concentration" camps. Rumours had already reached us, first from Poland, where the Russians were telling incredible stories that we took with a grain of salt, and more recently from French units over by the Black Forest, who had also been speaking of things to make our hair stand on end. Now it was our turn to see what it was all about.

We passed neat rows of pretty little Bavarian houses each with a niche over the door with a statute or image of a patron saint in it. In their shady gardens stood pleasant-looking old people who at a sign from us would come timidly over and very politely show us the way.

"*Konzentrazions Lager? Ja, ja,* over there. Five minutes at the most. *Danke. Bitte.*"

Our first sight of the camp was freight trains on a siding, two lines of boxcars with some cadavers hanging out the open doors, and more scattered on the embankment. A torrid sun shone down and the smell was atrocious. We quickly entered the town, for that's what it seemed to be: behind low walls interspersed with watchtowers there was some kind of industrial complex with small factory buildings and repair shops. But this first impression was dissipated at sight of the indescribable crowd that rushed toward us. Riddled with questions in a dozen languages, pulled here and there by hands of frightening thinness attached to translucent wrists, we stood there stunned, staring at these phantoms in striped pyjamas who were staggering out of the huts where they had been hiding until we had arrived on the scene with some of the members of the first health services. In fact, the last traces of the German garrison had taken to their heels less than a quarter of an hour before.

A man who was still young but who was nothing but skin and bones told me in excellent French that he had lived some time in Montreal and, like everyone else, asked for a cigarette. I felt in my pocket; the package had disappeared. I discovered that all the pockets of my jacket had fared likewise. The depths of misery and hunger sometimes bring out the hero and the saint, at least that's what they say, but more often they debase and bring out the bird of prey.

This was illustrated by the following spectacle. Holding each other by the hand as though in some kind of children's game, a group of prisoners, surrounded by others watching them avidly, came toward us. Suddenly, savage cries of joy broke out when, from the middle of the circle, a young fellow was cast forth. He had plenty of meat on him, for he was a "Kapo," one of the prison guards who hadn't been able to escape and who had been lying low waiting for the right moment. They forced him to kneel down, held his head up straight, and a big Slav with a toothless leer came up with a stick and methodically, chuckling with pleasure, smashed the lower part of his face and jaw until it was nothing but a mass of bone and bleeding flesh.

One couldn't do a thing. We wouldn't have known what to do anyway. And wouldn't have wanted to do anything when we learned it had been literally a case of an eye for an eye and a tooth for a tooth. Before putting their prisoners to work the Germans always stripped them of all their possessions, including their gold teeth. Then they worked them to death, especially the last year when rations were becoming scarce. At the end of the road they were sent to the "baths" (*Baden*), shabby-looking sheds linked to a reservoir by a couple of pipes. When the baths were full to the seams they opened the gas, and then, when the last groans had ceased, the bodies were taken to the ovens next door.

When news of this reached Quebec, and for some time after, people refused to believe. Heavy scepticism greeted such stories, which surpassed understanding. And even today, so many years later, it's sometimes worse. People who have the gall to proclaim themselves neo-Nazis, knowing that memory is a faculty capable of forgetting, go so far as to maintain that none of this really happened.

I can assure you that it was real, all right, that the gas chamber was real in its nightmarish unreality. The loaders had gone, trying to save their skins, leaving behind their last load of corpses, naked as worms in their muddy pallor. Near me was a cameraman whom I had promised a few words of commentary; he had to come out twice before he could film his ten seconds. On seeing it, the American Brigadier who had turned up on the scene took his revolver out of its holster and strode around with haggard eyes, muttering that he had to kill some of those bastards. His men had all they could do to calm him down.

Deloused and covered from head to foot in DDT, we retraced our steps to our billet in the harmonious-sounding village of Rosenheim. On the way, passing through the quiet suburb with its kindly old people, we asked each other with our eyes, "Did they know? How could they not have? What was behind those good, old, pious-looking faces?" But what was the use questioning? We were beginning to wish we hadn't seen anything ourselves.

III

War Art

Joan Murray, a leading historian of Canadian war art, is director of the Robert McLaughlin Gallery in Oshawa, Ontario. Her essay provides an introduction to Canadian art of the Second World War by the country's official war artists. Some of their work is reproduced in the pages that follow.

You'll Get Used to It

Joan Murray

You'll get used to it; You'll get used to it,
The first year is the worst year;
Then you'll get used to it.

. . .

You'll get to like it more and more and more,
You got-ta get used to it,
And when you're used to it,
You'll be twice as happy as you were before. . . .

When T.R. MacDonald painted *You'll Get Used to It*, John Pratt, the star of Canada's *The Navy Show*, wasn't portrayed singing the song he popularized. MacDonald painted a charming, nonchalant actress. But the song,[1] a hit in London's West End, is an apt comment on the Canadian artists who became Official War Artists in the Second World War.

MacDonald never did get used to it. "I was never asked to be a war artist," he later said.[2] (MacDonald's *Night Travellers* is reproduced as plate 1 in the colour insert that follows this page.) Even though he recognized the ancient place of war in art history, he hated the war. But most of Canada's Official War Artists thrived on the mixture of crisis and boredom that is wartime. Usually they were commissioned from the ranks of the three services—an advantage, because they had a greater understanding of the services and could interpret them more effectively. From 1943 on, Army war artists received the rank of lieutenant or its equivalent in the RCAF or the Navy, and if they remained in the program six months to a year they were promoted. Will Ogilvie and

Plate 1

Night Travellers, c. 1945
T.R. MacDonald

CWM 13177

National Gallery of Canada, Ottawa
Lent by the Canadian War Museum
Reproduced by permisson of the Estate of T.R. MacDonald

Plate 2

Entry into Assoro
Will Ogilvie

CN 13341

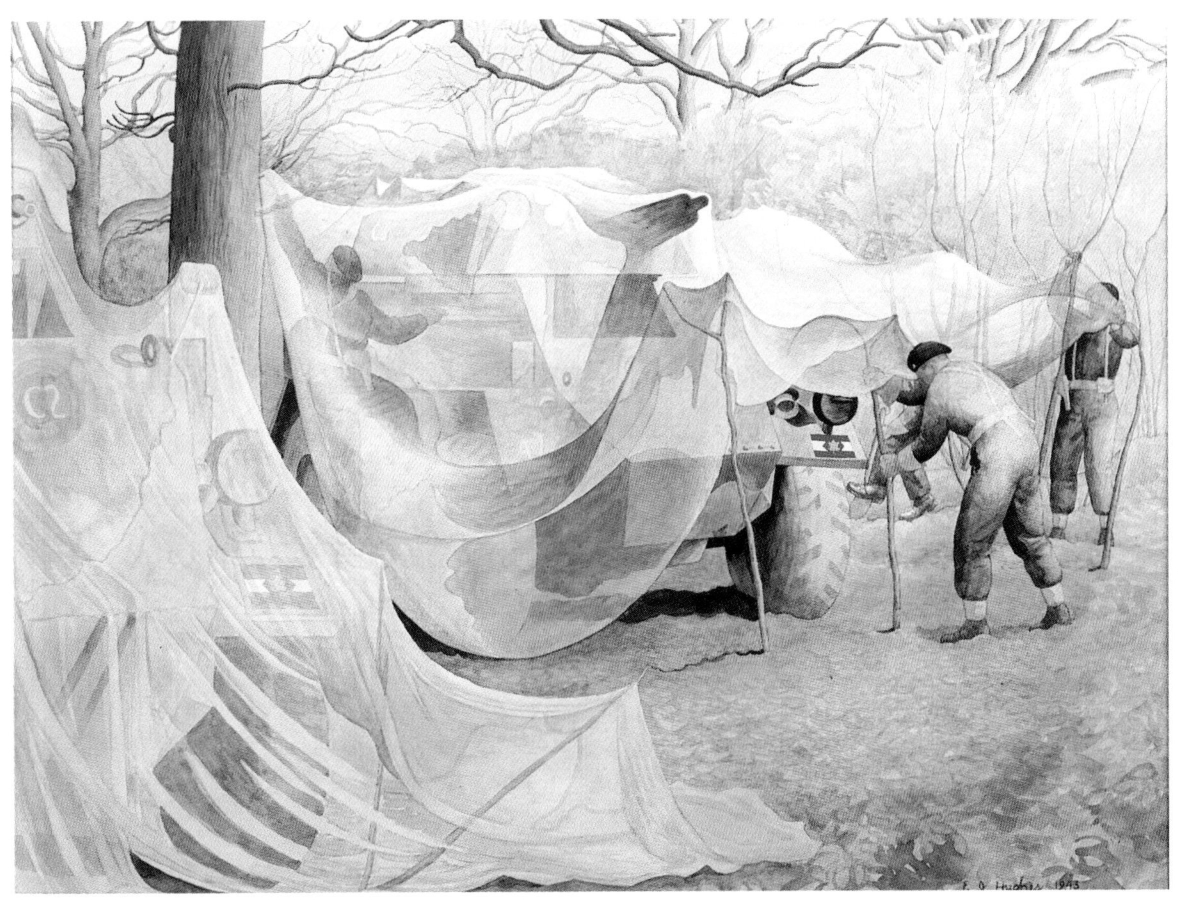

Plate 3

Camouflaging an Armoured Car with Nets, 1943
E.J. Hughes

CN 12785

Plate 6

A Tragic Landscape, 1945
Alex Colville

CN 12219

Plate 7

Dead German on the Hitler Line
Charles Comfort

CN 12272

Plate 8

Morning Parade
Pegi Nicol MacLeod

CN 14193

Charles Comfort both became majors. Orville Fisher and E.J. Hughes were initially staff artists for the Army and Paul Goranson for the Air Force. However, they later became "Official," as did Ogilvie and Lawren Harris. The Air Force found artists like P.G. Cowley-Brown, Aba Bayefsky, and Moses Reinblatt in an open juried RCAF exhibition held in April 1944 at the National Gallery of Canada. An art competition in the Army discovered Bruno Bobak and Molly Lamb Bobak. Some artists, like Miller Brittain and George Broomfield, would not leave active duty. Robert Pilot preferred to remain a camouflage officer.

Most Canadian war artists were grateful for being selected—the war artist scheme offered them full-time employment. It offered Leonard Brooks the first chance to paint day and night "with no other thought in mind."[3] Donald Mackay felt it was a unique opportunity for young artists. Before the war, artists had supported themselves as portrait painters, teachers, illustrators, and commercial artists.[4] During it, they were given the opportunity to work as full-time artists and achieved professional status immediately.[5] For Molly Lamb Bobak, the war art program was "one of those wonderful things for a young person, either sex, as you were given all your paints and asked to paint."[6] Above all, it was a job. Some, like Tom Wood, hadn't had jobs for a long time.[7]

The war offered subjects and a stylistic approach that stayed with artists the rest of their lives. Bayefsky, among others, had been raised in the landscape tradition of Canada's Group of Seven. The war reinforced his interest in drawing the figure, and he continued to do so.[8] Alex Colville found the roots of his representational, literal style during the war. As Molly Lamb Bobak has said of Colville: "There's an extension of his whole philosophy from then till now. He just developed in a single continuous way."[9] Bobak herself painted streets and crowds, which are among the subjects that interest her.[10]

A generation earlier, Canada had been first in establishing a program to record the war in art. However, during the Second World War it was late in starting. In September 1939, shortly after the outbreak of hostilities, the British government began an art record under the direction of Sir Kenneth Clark, director of the National Gallery. British war art was already being circulated by 1941: an exhibition was shown at the National Gallery of Canada and toured this country. It set an example for Canada, like other nations, to follow. Some Canadian artists even slightly echoed the British in style. Will Ogilvie's crisp, deft use of pen in *Entrance to Vizzini, Sicily*, recalls Edward Ardizzone's similar approach, particularly the works he did in 1940 in the Low Countries.

Vincent Massey, Canadian high commissioner in London, was the mainspring of the program. An enthusiastic patron of Canadian art and a long-time friend of Sir Kenneth Clark, he had considerable stature—and the necessary prestige to set the scheme into motion. Massey encouraged artists and helped them escape red tape. In organizing the program, he was warmly supported by H.O. McCurry, director of the

National Gallery of Canada, and by that gallery's board of trustees. The heads of various Canadian art societies, such as Caven Atkins, the president of the Canadian Society of Graphic Art, and Charles Goldhamer of the Canadian Society of Painters in Watercolour, together with Charles Comfort, A.Y. Jackson, Arthur Lismer, Rowley Murphy, and Frederick B. Taylor, were some of the many who wrote in support of the war art program in the recently founded magazine *Maritime Art* (later to become *Canadian Art*). Fearful of wasting public money, the Department of National Defence showed reluctance. It was not until the autumn of 1942 that the program was authorized by an Order-in-Council, and not till January 1943 that the three services and the National Gallery of Canada reached final agreement with cabinet approval on the comprehensive plan. In London, Massey became chairman of the war art committee and was responsible for the activities of artists in the various theatres of operations, along with senior officers of the Army, Navy, and Air Force. In Ottawa, McCurry managed the selection of the artists, with the aid of the historical officers of the three branches—Group Captain K.B. Conn of the Air Force (a travel agent), Col. A.F. Duguid of the Army, and Dr. G.N. Tucker of the Navy, a historian who remained a civilian. As advisors, there were eminent artists such as Edwin Holgate, A.Y. Jackson (a member of the Group of Seven and president of the Royal Canadian Academy), and Charles Comfort. When Comfort and Holgate were on active duty, André Biéler and A.J. Casson replaced them. Massey, in his concern for the necessity of compiling war records, arranged with General Montague, the Senior Officer of Canadian Military Headquarters, to transfer Will Ogilvie to "special duties." Because Ogilvie was at work as an artist from 1941, there are records of the early war years. Massey planned to give employment to the English artists Henry Lamb, a British war artist who held the rank of captain, and Wyndham Lewis (then living in Canada)—Lamb painted a number of portraits of Canadian troops, and other pictures of Canadian activities.

Jackson's notes to McCurry about suitable war artist material were blunt. Holgate, he said, "can if he will." Jack Humphrey drew well and needed the chance, but "he's difficult." He said of Leonard Brooks, who served in the Navy, he "might respond—he can stand cold weather. Good out-door guy."[11] There was a distinct prejudice against women—because as artists they were to be at the scene of combat. (Massey attempted to change this prejudice and indeed suggested Lilias Torrance Newton.) Modern artists such as J.W.G. (Jock) Macdonald and Alfred Pellan were considered but not sent.

There were some curious judgments. After going over Colville's work with Charles Comfort in 1943, Jackson was not impressed.[12] He felt Colville wasn't as good as Fred Brigden.[13] McCurry told Holgate that he had been quite worried by the dilution of the committee's suggestions by the nominees of the historical sections. He wondered if the Army had switched the recommendations and appointed the worst ones from the bottom of the list, such as Lawren P. Harris, T.R. MacDonald, and Colville. He found them "not an inspiring lot."[14] Among the artists selected, there was continual praise only of Will Ogilvie (see Ogilvie's *Entry in Assoro, Sicily*, plate 2) and Charles Comfort: the rest were subject to review. Sometimes the committee was not happy with the work—as with Beament, who, it was felt, needed "a good talking to."[15] Nor did they always like the work of Eric Aldwinckle, Orville Fisher, and E.J. Hughes.[16] If an artist like Peter Whyte didn't measure up, another—in this case, Bayefsky—could be appointed[17] and the artist returned to active service. Sometimes the decision to resign came from the artist. Holgate, who felt that his superior, Conn, had not the slightest interest in his work, seems to have suffered a nervous breakdown.[18]

At its fullest, the program had over thirty artists. Certain areas of the war zone were never recorded, like Canadian action in the Far East. Historical officers within the five Army divisions helped as best they could, encouraging artists to do certain subjects and providing transportation—a real problem in wartime.[19] Often the officer travelled with the artist in order to tell him what was happening. Ideally, each artist was to be supplied with a driver and a jeep or a van. Senior established artists were also given work outside the active war zone. Pegi Nicol MacLeod painted the women's forces. Caven Atkins and Alma Duncan, among others, worked in Canadian munitions plants.[20] Sydney Watson recorded the home front.

Canadian art of the Second World War forms a remarkably authoritative, accurate, and often magnificent record. The war artists took their duty to posterity seriously: it was their main concern. As Campbell Tinning recalls, "a lot of us painted as though there weren't any cameras."[21] (On the other hand, glamorous propaganda like the kind found in *Life* magazine was "out."[22]) The works were often covert journals, as is clear from *verso* inscriptions that record the place and date, whether it was painted or drawn from life or memory, frequently with small details about the scene. Aldwinckle describes what is in the foreground of *Maintenance Hanger for Sunderland*: hosepiping drying in the sun, a work trestle, and night lamp. Molly Lamb Bobak's *Canteen Near Doorn* was, she says, where 3rd Division personnel came for "Coke, cakes, and a game of snooker." "As I made the drawing the number of bodies increased," Colville writes on his drawing of *Dead Women, Belsen*. On *Dead German on the Hitler Line*, Comfort wrote, "I am not given to painting lugubrious subjects of this kind." (The most avid recorder, he also cites what he used in his reconstructions like *Dieppe Raid*—reports, official photos, maps, etc.)

Scrupulous attention to detail was no doubt encouraged by the presence of private soldiers looking over the artists' shoulders.[23] At the same time, as Harold Beament[24] and Donald Mackay have agreed, being in the services inhibited the artist by encumbering him with excessively detailed knowledge and associations. "You thought more slowly instead of working spontaneously."[25]

Above all, the philistines in Ottawa like Colonel Duguid, a man of little imagination, wanted the art to look "real." Some of the artists received a mimeographed directive, drafted by him and approved by the Ottawa committee in March 1943, which charged them with the "portrayal of significant events, phases and episodes of the war, especially those which could not be adequately rendered in any other way" (e.g., photographed).[26] It told them to record and interpret "vividly and veraciously" the spirit and the character, the appearance and the attitude of servicemen and women as individuals or groups. "Any instruments, machines, equipment, weapons, or clothing which appeared in the work had to be authentic." ("The machines should *work*," as Jack Shadbolt puts it.[27]) Signs and other aspects of the environment surrounding the men had to be correct (note the carefully painted 1st Corps insignia in E.J. Hughes's *Camouflaging an Armoured Car with Nets* (see plate 3). To achieve authenticity, artists had to be involved in active operations. (Sometimes this meant being shot at, Carl Schaefer recalled.[28]) Ogilvie was the first to see action, while Beament, Fisher, Law, Nichols, and Wood were in the D-Day assault. The English war artist Eric Ravilious lost his life while on active duty in 1942. Carl Schaefer suspected that the Army had seven artists, more than the Navy or Air Force, because some of their men would be killed.[29]

All the work produced by the artists during their appointment was to be the property of the Government of Canada. Thus, for a few dollars a day (the artists were paid according to their rank as officers), a large art collection was amassed. (In 1946, when the National Gallery of Canada was given custody of the collection, it included 5000 works.)

During a six-month period, the artist was expected to produce two oil paintings 40 by 48 inches, two 24 by 30 inches, ten watercolours 22 by 30 and fifteen 11 by 15, not counting field sketches. This demand turned out to be too high, leaving no time for finding and studying significant subject matter, or for bad weather or bureaucratic red tape. As with the First World War program, subjects were to include studies done "in action, from eye witness accounts and reconstructions." Certain personalities were to be recorded and Robert Hyndman, Charles Comfort, Lawren P. Harris, and T.R. MacDonald painted a number of portraits. Works were restricted to "exhibition" size—there was no desire to reproduce the colossal dimensions of some of the First World War art. At all times, accuracy was the main aim. There was not much place for cubism or surrealism. Lawren P. Harris's tanks (see, for example, *Tank Advance*, plate 4) seem like magical apparitions in a sea of dust—earlier he had been fascinated by Dali's famous *Persistence of Memory* in Toronto's Canadian National Exhibition.[30] Some abstraction does occur in Michael Forster's work—he wrote McCurry that he did not want to draw like Paul Goranson (see Goranson's *Flight Engineer*, plate 5). However, in general the treatment was subdued. A strong background in commercial art and particularly design helped—as in the case of Aldwinckle, who recognized that war is "very abstract."[31] But realism was not enough, as the British modern art critic Herbert Read recognized. It "does not change anything, but only administers to the appetite for vicarious experience," he said. "Only the tragic in art can change us."[32]

Despite the severe strictures the Ottawa committee laid down for artists, there was no recognition that such regulations could be an impediment. "I have not interfered with their technical methods but have tried to direct them so their product will be of the highest historical value in the future," Colonel Duguid wrote to Major C.P. Stacey, the Army's Historical Officer at Canadian Military Headquarters. His letter, which concerned E.J. Hughes and Orville Fisher, continued: "Thus on sending them for a week to cover a camp or station, such as Petawawa or Lansdowne, I have given them a list of a dozen military activities, as a general but not specific guide, and have called on them to produce a dozen sets of sketches illustrative of these or other activities with colour and other notes, and supplemented by still photographs, sufficient to enable them to make a coloured cartoon, about 10 inches by 15 inches . . . all sketches and notes for each picture should be dated when made, and should be fastened together and docketed."[33] By contrast, Stacey's letters to artists were characterized by a maturely sympathetic tone. He sought to make army life easier for the artists, dealing with accommodation, travel claims, hotel bills, and even dentists. He was always ready with advice and recommendations but refrained from hampering them with detailed instructions. Most important, he tried to provide freedom of movement—as did the Navy historical officers. Such support made a difference.

Curiously, many of the artists felt they lacked guidance. "I never really knew what I was supposed to do," MacDonald complained.[34] For him, this was a loss. Donald Anderson remembered sketching and seeing strafing in a wood—the battlefront he found later.[35] Campbell Tinning expressed the lost feeling of working "inside the storm"; it was all "just happening to you."[36]

Sketching, usually in watercolour (a favourite medium because it dried quickly, except when it rained),[37] pastel, or pencil in the field did not always lead to accurate results. These sketches were developed into canvases back in London headquarters at Fairfax House or in Canada in the Ottawa studios in the Militia Stores Building or Toronto's Eglinton Hunt Club. Conditions in the field generally did not lend themselves to lengthy communion with the subject. Today, the finished canvases painted in the studio seem, for all their drama and style, to be less candid than the vigorous works done on the spot. Sketches, at least, give a sense of direct contact.

The most important subject developed by the war was something art schools never taught—how to portray death. Artists like George Broomfield would not paint it. There were too many bodies lying around, stacked like cordwood, "being buried with two feet sticking out of the blanket—or . . . cut in half because they were caught between tracer bullets."[38] Others explored this new subject; Alex Colville in *Tragic Landscape* (plate 6), Charles Comfort in his *Dead German on the Hitler Line* (plate 7), and Jack Nichols in *Drowning Sailor*. Lawren P. Harris contrasted the dead and the living in his macabre *Section of the Hitler Line,* portraying dead bodies lying in a field while peasants reap the harvest. Animals died, too, and Ogilvie as well as Bruno Bobak drew them. Three artists—Donald Anderson, Bayefsky, and Colville—drew Belsen. Colville was sent there officially. Charles Goldhamer studied the wounded, particularly the burned.

The Second World War revealed a new kind of conflict: the modern battlefield was bleak and empty, as unreal as a stage set. There was action, but not the kind that produced subjects for dramatic paintings. Concealment was paramount in the Second World War—"darkness, camouflage, dispersal, smoke, deception, surprise."[39] But nothing could convey the gigantic and preposterous sound of modern war. As Comfort pointed out, the burst of a seventeen centimetre shell is like the "soul-shaking crack of doom . . . it jars the brain with unmerciful violence and then reverberates and echoes in the darkness in grotesque and terrifying spirals of dissonance."[40]

In quieter times, artists shared in the boring inactivity of war, as in Miller Brittain's *Sam Wakes Us Up*, card-playing in Goranson's *Via Boxcar to Algiers*, or Wood's *Mess Deck, No. 1 on a Landing Craft Infantry,* or writing letters home in Anderson's *Nissen Hut, Interior.* The characters of the men were accurately captured by Holgate. For some it was the first chance to depict machines and equipment with understanding.[41] Harris and Hughes studied and painted tanks with moving eloquence. Eric Aldwinckle was fascinated by the delicate instrument panel of a plane—the plane as the pilot sees it. Comfort writes glowingly of the imagery of a gunsite, which he called "a strange fusion of machined surfaces, kinetic routines, and the delicate transparent tracery of the nets."[42] (His fascination is evident in the dramatic way he handles the dark shape of the gun in *Destroyed Panzerturm*, *Hitler Line.*) Broomfield drew camouflaged aircraft; Bruno Bobak showed destroyed equipment, or landscape, as did Tinning in *Tomba di Pesaro, Gothic Line*, *Italy*, and Pepper in *Drowned Land, Holland.* Shadbolt drew London's Canadian Military Headquarters decorated for VE-Day. Happier moments occur in the work of Molly Lamb Bobak, as in her colourful *Wedding Reception at the Kit-Cat Club* with its huge tableful of food—or in the lighthearted *Morning Parade* by Pegi Nicol MacLeod (plate 8), where the Canadian Women's Army Corps is depicted.

In many cases the works had a personal reference; Miller Brittain included his own image, Goranson painted himself among the survivors in *Torpedoed*, *North Atlantic*, an incident that involved him, and Alex Colville portrayed his hands in the first soldier in *The Nijmegen Bridge* and drew for the face his father as a young man.[43]

During the nineteenth century, Canadian artists like William Blair Bruce had glorified the turning of a wheel in his *The Smiths* (1894, National Gallery of Canada, Ottawa). Now "Industry is Terrific!" said and painted Frederick B. Taylor.[44] Artists like Alma Duncan echoed the black Conté with which Van Gogh drew miners. Often, as in Atkin's *Arc Welders by Night*, workers are seen as powerful figures in a primitive world.

For some artists, like Orville Fisher, the kind of work, as well as the contact with more senior artists, helped to develop a broader style. Charles Goldhamer recalls: "I had to work faster because of the conditions there. I was more nervous."[45]

Artists had a variety of experience. Aldwinckle sat on the cliffs at Normandy and watched the landing craft—the boats with wheels came right up the cliffs. There was urgency, the feeling of being a target. As Winston Churchill recalled, "There is nothing so exhilarating as being shot at without effect." There was also awe. "An experience I couldn't buy," as Aldwinckle remembered.[46] Goldhamer felt it made him richer.[47] He met people, saw things that he'd never seen before. Others, like Schaefer, felt drained. Their usual painting subjects were neutralized.[48]

After the war, it was difficult to get back to regular work. It might take some five or six years. "I was filled with memories of death," recalled Schaefer,[49] whose brother was killed on active service with the RCAF in France in 1942. Because he had to work at night during the war, he was obsessed with light when he got out.[50]

"I lived two lives. I put my uniform on, went to sea, and was part of the discipline and life of a ship. Then I would return to London, to take off my uniform, tuck myself away, and try to put together some of the paintings which I did as an artist alone in my room." This contrast made Leonard Brooks seek to justify his special role.[51] He was constructive, like a doctor or priest, he felt. But was he simply a mascot? Aldwinckle said *he* was.[52]

Before the war art program existed, A.Y. Jackson had already warned against tying it like an albatross around the national cultural neck—another collection without a museum. No government had been persuaded to provide a building for the Canadian War Memorials.[53] After the war, Jackson felt more optimistic, describing the work as honest and sincere. Its real value, he felt, was that through their experiences, artists would have a fresher vision to stir up the "rather sluggish stream of Canadian art."[54] While the war was being fought, it was hoped that the art would make an immediate contribution to the experience of Canadians through an appeal to their pride,[55] perhaps even maintain public morale.[56] It might have other, more spiritual, returns. Possibly it would help in forming the Canadian identity.

After the war, the program was criticized. There were too many illustrators, and few large works.[57] Sir Kenneth Clark and others said of the Canadians that the Army made the best showing, the RCAF the weakest.[58] Writers attributed the weakness of the RCAF section to the fact that the RCAF prevented artists from flying on operations and ruled that they "wear the regular brass when working—no battle dress and no sweaters." To this criticism Schaefer replied: "They might take time to look at more of my pictures and after a long time come to realize something of that great mystery of uncharted space, intangible drama and the feeling of such a new form of warfare."[59]

But no one could put a finger on the real problem: modern art in its more advanced form was eliminated by the guidelines. Accuracy was a deterrent, as Harris recalls.[60] (He often wondered why war photographers couldn't do the job.[61]) Thus war art stands as a monument to a certain kind of thought, and as a bastion of the old guard.

Jackson's initial fears were soon realized. The artists spent six months working up their rough sketches into finished canvases to produce the paintings that were necessary to give the collection as a whole "weight and dignity and scale," as Massey put it.[62] In 1946, the best of the work was exhibited at the National Gallery of Canada in a show opened by Earl Alexander, the new governor general of Canada. After the exhibition, most of the work was buried, to emerge only at gradually lengthening intervals in the National Gallery of Canada. After a few years of permanent hanging, fewer works saw light. People did not seem to want to see them, perhaps because they put the war as much out of their mind as possible. As Jackson had warned: "A world weary and sick of war, aware of all the stupidity, selfishness and incompetence which plunged it into such misery a second time, will likely be indifferent to monuments and battle pictures with all the difficulties of reconstruction, debt, and disillusionment to worry about."[63] In 1971, most of the First and Second World War material was transferred to the Canadian War Museum, where it remains today. There it is more visible than ever before, but restricted space means that only ten percent is on view.

Because the works created in the war were drawn from an experience common to all, they have the immediate appeal of popular art. They form a bridge between "Art" and the part of the public that never comes to a gallery. But whether as records or as high art, the works provide—as Leonard Brooks puts it—a "legacy of truthful seeing and feeling," and have caught for posterity, "some of the deep and terrible days of courageous despair and brave hopes for a better future."[64] War is history through which many generations have had to live. The fact that art can be made during it signifies another, happier, condition.

Through the war program, artists became accustomed to making art with a purpose. After the war, many of them found the same feeling in careers as disparate as the design of stage sets (Paul Goranson) and textiles (George Broomfield). Jobs, of course, were scarce. For many, the applied arts or teaching were the answer. Only a few remained artists pure and simple. The rule seems to have been that those who felt they would be artists became so in the end. Serving as war artists got them used to it.

Official Canadian War Artists*

Royal Canadian Navy

Commander Harold Beament	(Montreal)
Sub-Lieut. Leonard Brooks	(Toronto)
Sub-Lieut. Michael Forster	(Toronto)

*This list is from *Canadian Art* 2 (April–May 1945): 149, with corrections from *Canadian Art* 2 (Summer 1945): 226.

Lieut. Donald Cameron Mackay	(Halifax)
Lieut. Rowley Murphy	(Toronto)
Lieut. Jack Nichols	(Toronto)
Lieut. Tom Wood	(Ottawa)
C. Anthony Law	(Ottawa and Quebec)

The Canadian Army

Lieut. Bruno Bobak	(Toronto)
Major Charles Comfort	(Toronto)
Lieut. D.A. Colville	(Amherst, NS)
Captain Orville Fisher	(Vancouver)
Captain Lawren Harris, Jr.	(Toronto)
Captain Edward J. Hughes	(Vancouver)
Lieut. T.R. MacDonald	(Montreal)
Captain William A. Ogilvie	(Montreal)
Captain George Pepper	(Toronto)
Captain Campbell Tinning	(Saskatoon)
Lieut. Molly Lamb, CWAC	(Vancouver)

Royal Canadian Air Force

F/L Eric Aldwinckle	(Toronto)
F/O Donald Anderson	(Toronto)
F/O Aba Bayefsky	(Toronto)
P/O Miller Brittain	(Saint John, NB)
F/O Albert Cloutier	(Montreal)
F/O P.G. Cowley-Brown	(Vancouver)
F/O Charles Goldhamer	(Toronto)
F/L Paul A. Goranson	(Vancouver)
F/O Edwin H. Holgate	(Montreal)
F/L Robert Hyndman	(Ottawa)
F/O Moses Reinblatt	(Montreal)
F/O Goodridge Roberts	(Montreal)
F/L Carl Schaefer	(Toronto)
Sgt. Peter Whyte	(Banff)

Notes

1. Freddy Grant, a German national and a music writer for the English songstress and movie star Gracie Fields, wrote "You'll Get Used to It" in 1940 at a wartime internment camp in Quebec. When he was released in 1942, he teamed up with Victor Gordon (Toronto songwriter and music publisher Gordon V. Thompson) to create a new version of the song. He wrote the music, Gordon the words.
2. Interview with T.R. MacDonald, Hamilton, 30 Sept. 1977, the Robert McLaughlin Gallery archives, Oshawa (hereafter McLaughlin archives).
3. Interview with Leonard Brooks, Toronto, 25 Oct. 1977, McLaughlin archives.
4. Interview with Donald C. Mackay, Halifax, 31 Aug. 1978, McLaughlin archives.
5. Interview with Bruno Bobak, Fredericton, 28 Sept. 1979, McLaughlin archives.
6. Interview with Molly Lamb Bobak, Oshawa, 5 Sept. 1977, McLaughlin archives, published as "Molly Lamb Bobak," *Canadian Collector* 13 (Sept./Oct. 1978): 40–43.
7. Interview with Tom Wood, 2 May 1979, McLaughlin archives.
8. Conversation with Aba Bayefsky, Toronto, 27 April 1979, McLaughlin archives.
9. Molly Lamb Bobak interview.
10. Ibid.
11. Letter from A.Y. Jackson to H.O. McCurry, 27 Jan. 1943, National Gallery of Canada archives, Ottawa (hereafter NGC archives).
12. Letter from A.Y. Jackson to H.O. McCurry, 2 Feb. 1943, NGC archives.
13. Letter from A.Y. Jackson to H.O. McCurry, 4 May 1944, NGC archives.
14. Letter from H.O. McCurry to Edwin Holgate, 8 June 1944, NGC archives.
15. Letter from H.O. McCurry to Vincent Massey, 17 January 1944, NGC archives. Massey replied that he applied the stimulus, 21 Jan. 1944.
16. Letter from H.O. McCurry to A.Y. Jackson, 12 May 1944, NGC archives.
17. Note from Vincent Massey to H.O. McCurry, 9 Aug. 1944, NGC archives.
18. Letter from A.Y. Jackson to H.O. McCurry, 19 June 1944. Three days later, McCurry replied, "They think he is slow and perhaps he is a little." Both letters are in NGC archives.
19. Conversation with Charles Stacey, 10 Aug. 1981, McLaughlin archives.
20. F.B. Taylor, Fred Brigden, Nicholas Hornyanski, and Cloutier, Holgate, and Schaefer before they went overseas also worked in Canadian Munitions Plants. For a complete list of those who were there, see the list approving the work, 12 Dec. 1942, NGC archives.
21. Interview with Campbell Tinning, Montreal, 16 May 1979, McLaughlin archives.
22. Brooks interview.
23. Stacey conversation. Ogilvie also mentions that the men themselves were always interested—and critical. Conversation with Will Ogilvie, 18 Aug. 1980.
24. Interview with Harold Beament, Montreal, 15 May 1979, McLaughlin archives.
25. Mackay interview.
26. The draft of "Instructions for War Artists" was prepared by Colonel A. Fortesque Duguid, director of the Army Historical Section, with suggestions from the Navy and Air Force. A copy of it is in the

Department of National Defence Archives, Ottawa. The instructions were signed by McCurry on behalf of the War Artists' Committee, 2 March 1943 (a copy is in NGC archives). Carl Schaefer still has his copy (interview with Carl Schaefer, Toronto, 28 March 1979, McLaughlin archives). Jack Shadbolt remembers that the artists received the letter and says that E.J. Hughes remembers his copy. Conversation, 13 July 1981. There is no evidence that it was distributed to artists appointed overseas.

27. Shadbolt interview.
28. Schaefer interview.
29. Ibid.
30. Interview with Lawren P. Harris, Ottawa, 29 June 1979, McLaughlin archives.
31. Interview with Eric Aldwinckle, Toronto, 20 April 1979, McLaughlin archives.
32. Herbert Read, *The Listener*, 4 July 1940, cited in a memo, "The Visual Aspects of War Information Services" to H.O. McCurry, 21 Sept. 1940, NGC archives.
33. Letter from A. Fortesque Duguid to C.P. Stacey, 23 Feb. 1942, Public Archives of Canada, Ottawa.
34. MacDonald interview.
35. Interview with Donald Anderson, Oshawa, 23 June 1981, McLaughlin archives.
36. Tinning interview.
37. Rowley Murphy complains of the difficulty in making watercolours in the rain in a letter to H.O. McCurry, 28 Oct. 1943, NGC archives.
38. Interview with George Broomfield, Mississauga, 5 July 1981, McLaughlin archives.
39. Charles Comfort, *Artist at War* (Toronto: Ryerson Press, 1956), 135.
40. Ibid., 70.
41. Aldwinckle interview.
42. Comfort, *Artist at War*, 92.
43. Conversation with Alex Colville, 20 Aug. 1981.
44. See F.B. Taylor, "Industry is Terrific!" *Canadian Art* 3 (Oct.–Nov. 1945): 30 ff.
45. Interview with Charles Goldhamer, Toronto, 28 March 1979.
46. Aldwinckle interview.
47. Goldhamer interview.
48. Paul Duval, "War Artist Carl Schaefer's Life is No Dilettante's Existence," *Saturday Night* 60 (3 March 1945): 17.
49. Carl Schaefer, "Personal Reminiscences." *Carl Schaefer Retrospective Exhibition, Paintings from 1926 to 1969* (catalogue) (Montreal: Sir George Williams University, 1969), 71.
50. Ibid.
51. Brooks interview.
52. Aldwinckle interview.
53. A.Y. Jackson, [War Records], *Maritime Art* 2 (Feb.–March 1942): 89.
54. A.Y. Jackson, "A Record of Total War," *Canadian Art* 3 (July 1946): 152.
55. W. Abell, "Editorial Comments— Canada at War," *Maritime Art* 2 (Feb.–March 1942): 75.
56. R.S. Lambert, "Art in Wartime," *Maritime Art* 3 (Oct.–Nov. 1942): 10.
57. D. Buchanan, "Exhibition of Canadian War Art," *Canadian Art* 2 (April–May 1945): 142.
58. G.P. "Work of Ottawa Artists Outstanding in War Exhibit," *Ottawa Journal*, 14 Feb. 1945.
59. Letter from Carl Schaefer to H.O. McCurry, 10 Nov. 1946, NGC archives.
60. Harris interview.
61. Ibid.
62. Letter from Vincent Massey to H.O. McCurry, 29 Aug. 1944, NGC archives.
63. Jackson, *Maritime Art*, 89.
64. Brooks interview.

IV

The Home Front

Diary

King was fortunate in the timing of the 1940 election. It was held in the period of the "phoney war"—the lull between the Nazi conquest of Poland and the blitzkrieg against the Low Countries and France that was launched in May 1940. During this period, King's policy of "limited liability" was easy to defend.

Mackenzie King's Diary, 26–27 March 1940

Thursday, 26 March 1940

I SLEPT only fairly well throughout the night. Was quite wakeful and got up at 7.30. First thought of dressing and going at once to the polls but decided that would be a little spectacular. Also better to have further rest, so went back to bed and had dozed off when Nicol[1] came to wake me. Nicol brought me the paper and a cup of tea. When I had finished the latter and given him the cup to take away, he suddenly brought it back and drew my attention to the leaves, saying: "Like a March hare." When I looked at the cup I said: "It is like one of the sphinx on my table upstairs. Do you notice the figure standing at the top of it? A man with a plume floating over his head, the feathers of which rise above the rim of the cup." It was clearly a symbol of triumph and victory. . . .

When I had finished my prayers, I felt my first duty was to go and record my vote. Little Pat[2] went with me to the polls in 1925, 1926, 1930 and 1935. I thanked God that his little life has been spared to go with me today. MacLeod[3] remarked that the last time we had both walked. This time, however, the walk would have been too far for him. The day too was pretty cold so we went by the car and I wore my beaver coat and mink cap. As we went out of the front door of Laurier House,[4] the *Toronto Star* photographer was waiting to take pictures and Green of the *Star*[5] was with him. We stopped on the steps for the photographers. When we reached the polling booth the photographers were also there. Then a man walked in behind me into the booth and was at my side when I marked and later deposited my ballot. Something says to me, as I dictate: Note the significance of the X on the step of Laurier House in the photograph of Pat and myself at the front door. That is no mere chance. The Returning Officer, the scrutineers and others were all very pleasant. Another photograph was taken in the booth itself and on the steps as we came out. Small boys with helmet caps were waiting with little slips of paper to be autographed. They were all very polite. . . . Pat seemed much to enjoy his little drive. He was determined both going and coming to sit on the seat beside me. He seemed fully conscious that a little event of real significance was taking place. . . .

I did not get a chance to work out any address for tonight. I felt a great mental weariness after luncheon so did not try to prepare anything. Then went to bed and had a rest of a couple of hours. I[t] was a quarter past three when I went down. Was called at a quarter past five and got up at 5.30. Again to work over something, using the draft Brockington[6] had prepared on lines I had suggested to him as a basis. . . . Curiously enough I had quite forgotten that the returns might be coming in from the Maritimes almost immediately after the close of the polls here. I had forgotten they were an hour ahead in the East. . . .

I had arranged earlier in the day to have it understood that I did not wish photographs taken of myself receiving the returns as the *Star* had wished to arrange for. That I would be agreeable to having a picture taken at the time of broadcasting this evening. Also that I would be prepared, either before or after the news, when sufficient returns would be in, to be sure of the results. . . . MacLeod, at a quarter to 6, came to the Library and told me that a flash had come over the radio that Liberals were leading in Nova Scotia. Five minutes later J.[7] phoned to say that the Liberals were leading in the Maritimes, that the results as she had heard them were 14 Liberals, 4 Conservatives, the latter in N.B. That Ilsley[8] was elected. . . .

By 8.47 the Canadian Press had conceded the election of the Liberals. The figures at that time stood at 97 to 12. . . .

I had to give up keeping track of the results to complete the broadcast which it had been decided I would make at 11.30. I kept working on it while the returns were coming in. Brockington, J. and Pickersgill[9] all had a hand in the pot at the last minute. They did their best to persuade me to say nothing about the methods employed in the campaign itself. I had intended to refer to the Nazi mentality making its evil pleasure felt and the necessity of "scotching" this viper at once to save the example of our public life and of our institutions. I agreed to modify the language but insisted in bringing out that this was one of the factors which had contributed in no uncertain way to the result. However I was receiving help from others as I kept working on the broadcast. Earlier in the day I had almost despaired of being able to get it to my liking in time. As it was, I had the typing completed at 10.15 only. Had to rush to the Chateau[10] and there had time to read the pages over once before broadcasting to the nation.

They gave me a room on the 7th floor as Manion[11] had gone up to the studio and was following me immediately. I suppose they thought it would avoid embarrassment to each of us. As it was when I came out of the room he was just going downstairs. When he and his secretary saw me they did not wait but continued going on downstairs. I was just as pleased. When you lose respect for a man, it is difficult to show him the sympathy you might wish in an hour of defeat. The boys at the Chateau were all very pleased and those looking after the broadcast most helpful. I enjoyed speaking to the country particularly in the terms and the tones of the message I had prepared. It was a great opportunity to say the right thing. Nothing could have been so appropriate as the paragraphs from Lincoln's speeches which I quoted: how the victory of our party in time of war will always stand at the side of his own at the time of the Civil War, though his was an infinitely more difficult situation. No victory for democracy however could have been greater than the one we won at the polls today. After being photographed at the microphone I came back to L.H.,[12] accompanied by Turnbull.[13] Learned about results all coming our way. . . .

I was anxious to hear from Prince Albert[14] so left my guests and came to the library. Phoned Sanderson.[15] He told me that a thousand of a majority had already come in and would be increased by outlying polls. He said the fight had been a desperate one in the last couple of weeks. It was clear that every effort was being made to defeat me. Much money must have been used to influence the foreigners and others. This I had been warned about as certain to go from Hepburn's[16] crowd in Toronto. Sanderson said they had played much on the fact that I had not been in the riding during the last parliament. All circumstances considered, it is really miraculous I should have been returned. I felt very badly to think I had not sent a message yesterday to the committee or some communication to the people on the eve of the elections. Thinking of other matters I had forgotten completely about my own constituency. This, properly handled, would have made, I am sure, a considerable difference in the results. I spent sometime, later in the evening, after the others had gone, in drafting a message sent in care of Sanderson to be published in the *Prince Albert Herald*. . . . We really cleaned up the province of Quebec and I thought often of what Sir Wilfrid[17] said to me in this very house when I told him of my intention to stand by him in North York against conscription—that I would have the province of Quebec for the rest of my life. . . .

My guests left a little after midnight. . . .

I was glad to be pretty much alone for an hour or two before going to bed. Got off my message to Prince Albert last thing. Pat and I had our little supper together. It was exactly 2 a.m. when I turned out the lights. My mind and heart were much at rest at last. I was so glad because I know that the right has triumphed. . . .

Wednesday, March 27, 1940

Slept fairly well, though a little wakeful. At 8.00 Nicol brought in the morning paper and extended his congratulations. The *Citizen*[18] headline was: "Liberals Sweep Dominion"—"Victory Comparable to Smashing Win of 1935."—"McIlraith and Pinard Victors in Ottawa District." The photograph by Karsh, in the centre of the page, with the title: "Prime Minister Mackenzie King," and headed: "Canada Puts Its Trust in Him." It was a great bringing together of all things—a complete fulfilment of the covenant. I had no feelings of elation, but of profound satisfaction and peace and quiet inner joy. I thought much of the added responsibilities and how much more easily they would be discharged with this verdict and the voice of the people to support and sustain me. I think what I felt most was the relief of having the elections out of the way, so as to be able to concentrate on our war effort and the duties of Government. Even the prospect of a session did not seem to bring any sense of burden with it. I can see the way now through it all. . . .

I kept reading 'till 9.00, feeling the rest advisable. Gave Pat his roll-over (he, by the way, is appearing in print). Just before going to breakfast, MacLeod was in the Library and I pointed to my grandfather's photograph on the table, which he had been admiring. I said that Scotland had produced no finer man. MacLeod replied: "Canada has produced no finer man than his grandson," which was very nice coming from one who has been many years in one's own service.

Notes

1. Member of his household staff.
2. His dog.
3. Member of his household staff.
4. His Ottawa residence.
5. *Toronto Daily Star*.
6. Leonard W. Brockington, special assistant to King, 1940–41.
7. His friend Joan Patteson.
8. James L. Ilsley, them minister of National Revenue. He was elected in Annapolis–King's, Nova Scotia.
9. John Whitney Pickersgill of the Department of External Affairs.
10. The Château Laurier hotel.
11. Robert Manion, the Conservative leader.
12. Laurier House.
13. Walter J. Turnbull of the Prime Minister's Office.
14. King had been the member of Parliament for Prince Albert, Saskatchewan, since 1926.
15. Liberal Party official in Prince Albert.
16. Mitchell F. Hepburn, Liberal premier of Ontario and King hater.
17. Sir Wilfrid Laurier, leader of the Liberal Party, 1887–1919, and prime minister of Canada, 1896–1911.
18. Ottawa newspaper.

The 1940 General Election

One of the casualties of the 1940 election was Dr. Robert Manion, the leader of the Conservative Party, who was defeated in Fort William, Ontario. King was returned for Prince Albert, Saskatchewan, which he had represented since 1926. At the time of the emergency session of Parliament in September 1939, King had promised Manion that the House of Commons elected in 1935 would meet again before an election was called. It did—but only on the afternoon of 25 January 1940, when Governor General Lord Tweedsmuir announced in the speech from the throne that the government had decided to go to the people. Parliament had been called together only to be told that it was being dissolved. Manion felt betrayed by King, but in reality he had been outfoxed. He was not alone.

Result of the General Election of 26 March 1940

	Conservative (National Government)	Liberal	Co-operative Commonwealth Federation	Social Credit (New Democracy)	Other*
Nova Scotia	1	10	1	–	–
New Brunswick	5	5	–	–	–
Prince Edward Island	–	4	–	–	–
Quebec	1	61	–	–	3
Ontario	25	57	–	–	–
Manitoba	1	15	1	–	–
Saskatchewan	2	12	5	–	2
Alberta	–	7	–	10	–
British Columbia	4	10	1	–	1
Yukon	–	–	–	–	–
Total	40	181	8	10	6

*In Quebec, three Independent Liberals were elected. In Saskatchewan, one Unity member and one United Reform member were elected. In British Columbia, one Independent was elected.

Popular Vote: Liberal, 51.5%; Conservative (National Government), 30.7%; Co–operative Commonwealth Federation, 8.5%; Social Credit, 2.7%; other, 6.6%.

Total seats: 245.

The announcement that a plebiscite would be held was made on 22 January 1942 in the speech from the throne opening a new session of Parliament. "My advisers," the governor general (now the Earl of Athlone) intoned, "believe that the magnitude and balanced nature of Canada's war effort is being obscured and impaired by controversy concerning commitments with respect to the methods of raising men for military service which were made prior to the spread of the war to all parts of the world." Hence the need for the vote, which, it was hoped, would give the government "complete freedom to act in accordance with its judgment of the needs of the situation" as they arose.

Mackenzie King's Diary, 27–28 April 1942

Monday, 27 April 1942

MY OWN GUESS as to the result of the plebiscite is that the affirmative vote should be about 70 percent over the Dominion as a whole. If it is that, it will be good indeed. That will mean it would run up to 80 percent and more in some of the provinces. It might be between 75 and 80 percent in all the provinces outside of Quebec. Quebec, I feel, might give 30 percent for the affirmative. It might even reach 35. That the vote will amply justify the taking of the plebiscite, in that it will make quite clear the wish of the people as a whole to have a free hand and no longer be bound by past pledges or promises in the nature of restrictions, I feel quite sure. Some of the Tories will immediately be after declaration of conscription for overseas. My belief is that we shall never have to resort to conscription for overseas. We will repeal the clause in the National Resources Mobilization Act, which limits the government's power to the confines of Canada. I will announce that we intend to extend the application of the provisions of the N.R.M.A.[1] to cover the coasts of Canada possibly going the length of using Canadians anywhere in the northern half of this hemisphere. I doubt if we shall ever have to go beyond that, as our people will become increasingly concerned about keeping men within Canada itself. All we shall have to be sure of is reinforcements of the army at present in Britain. If there is any pressure on the part of our men to enforce conscription, just for the sake of conscription, I will fight that position to the end. Quebec and the country will see that I have kept my promise about not being a member of the government which sends men overseas under conscription. The only exception I will make in that will be that our men need additional numbers which could not be obtained voluntarily, but I do not think this will be the case. I am particularly pleased that there has been no need for conscription thus far, which could not have been applied, as we had not the power, but no need to use it if we had had the power. . . .

Around 9.30 I began to get the returns from different constituencies. I got particulars of several polls from the Maritimes, all showing an affirmative vote. First Quebec polls—three gave NO vote, and one gave YES. By 10.30, many returns, including some from Manitoba. Returns from Quebec were quite depressing. I found it difficult to shape up anything for the press that would help to save the feelings of the Quebec people. Pickersgill[2] was quite depressed, and I found it more than usually difficult to discover suitable words for the occasion. As it got on towards midnight, I thought once of leaving everything over until tomorrow, but concluded it would be best to make at least a tentative statement, as the B.C. returns began coming in.

By midnight, I had begun to make the different revises and shortly after got a copy to the Press Gallery of what, I thought, seemed on the whole, a pretty satisfactory statement. It made clear that the plebiscite had given the government and parliament a free hand, and that the will of the people would now prevail. I cannot say I felt any real elation over the result, though an amazingly large affirmative vote made clear the people had trust in myself and the government to see that their rights would be wholly protected. A table showing the returns by constituencies made it perfectly apparent to me that the governing factor was the racial and, possibly, race and religion combined, the French Catholic minority feeling it would be at the mercy of English Protestant majority. I felt very strongly that to keep Canada united, we would have to do all in our power from reaching the point where necessity for conscription for overseas would arise. As I looked at the returns, I thought of Durham's report on the state of Quebec when he arrived there after the rebellion 1837–38, and said he found two nations warring in the bosom of a single state. That would be the case in Canada, as applied to Canada as a whole, unless the whole question of conscription from now on is approached with the utmost care. The returns show clearly the wisdom of not attempting any conscription through coercion and in violation of pledges. Whatever is done now will be done with the will of the majority, expressed in advance, and which, if proceedings are taken in the right way, will be gradually acquiesced in by those in the minority. The returns show clearly the deplorable lack of an educational campaign in the parts of Quebec other than the Montreal district. There, the vote was surprisingly evenly balanced. . . . It is a great relief to have this vote over before anything happened to interfere with it or to render necessary, up to the moment, any extreme action on the part of the government. . . .

Tuesday, 28 April 1942

. . . Then attended Cabinet. As I took my seat, I said to the Ministers that the govt. appeared to be safe. That while we were not claiming the results as a vote of confidence in the administration, there could be no doubt that the vote was such in large part. I thanked the Ministers for the part they had taken in the campaign. Mentioned that all had made a fine effort and then said we should be careful not to interpret the vote as a vote for conscription. That as I read it, all who had voted NO were against conscription. Of those that had voted YES, a very considerable number had done so having faith in myself and other members of the administration to see that conscription would not be imposed for overseas particularly for the sake of compulsion, but only where it might be necessary. I said the vote was to give us a free hand in deciding what was necessary but that if we were to keep the country united, I felt we should do our utmost to prevent to make the result a means of introducing conscription beyond the point necessary.

I made the reference to Durham's statement which I had thought of last night, and said that the parallel situation was one which men governing the country would have to meet with the utmost caution and care. I spoke about the first step being to extend the application of conscription to islands about Canada but seeking to continue by voluntary method to raise the men necessary for overseas.

Notes

1. National Resources Mobilization Act.
2. John Whitney Pickersgill of the Department of External Affairs. Seconded to the Prime Minister's Office.

The No campaign in Quebec was run by La Ligue pour la défense du Canada (League for the Defence of Canada), which was hastily organized for this purpose. André Laurendeau, a young journalist, was one of its principals. In effect, the Ligue's message was banned from the stations of the Canadian Broadcasting Corporation (CBC), when the national broadcaster took the position that only those speaking on behalf of parties represented in Parliament could be heard over its airwaves. Since all the national parties (albeit for quite different reasons) were supporting a Yes vote, this was the only point of view presented on the CBC. The Ligue had access, however, to private stations that would transmit its arguments. Its campaign was a triumph for Quebec's nationalist intellectuals, who for once enjoyed mass support.

The Plebiscite

André Laurendeau

ON 22 JANUARY the speech from the throne announced that a plebiscite would soon be held on conscription.

"Treason!" cried [Conservative leader] Meighen, who was then in the midst of his election campaign and wanted immediate conscription.

"Cowardice," accused Premier Hepburn [of Ontario].

"I am opposed to conscription, which would be a crime in the present circumstances," declared Premier Godbout [of Quebec] at a stormy meeting of Young Liberals.

What was it all about?

King continued to finesse. He had bound himself never to impose conscription, but he now wished his government to regain its liberty. He intended, he said, to ask the Canadian people to free him from his promises. But this would not mean conscription, at least not necessarily. According to the happy formula he discovered later: "Conscription if necessary, but not necessarily conscription." The military situation remained favourable; there were more than enough volunteers, and for the moment there was no question of change. All his government wanted, he repeated, was to be given a free hand. He wasn't holding a referendum in which the people would make the decision; he was organizing a plebiscite to learn the views of the electorate. After that, it would be for Parliament to decide. For that matter, the text of the question Canadians would be asked in the plebiscite was not made public until mid-March. Here it is in all its elegance and limpidity:

> Are you in favour of releasing the government from any obligation arising out of any past commitments restricting the methods of raising men for military service?

But these commitments were made with the consent of the French-Canadian people, and King himself recalled this when he explained to the proconscriptionists the reasons that had determined his acceptance of these commitments in the first place:

> Every honorable member of this house knows that, except for the assurance that, in the event of a European war, there would be no conscription for service overseas, this parliament would never have decided, in the immediate and unanimous manner in which it did, to stand at the side of Britain. . . .
>
> Honourable members are also aware that if, at the time when Canada's participation in the war was challenged in an election in the Province of Quebec by a government professing a different political faith, a like assurance with respect to service overseas had not been given in the name of the present government . . . the verdict of the people of that province might have been wholly different.

In short, the anticonscription promise had had its little hour of utility; it had facilitated Canada's entry into the war and the conduct of the country's war effort, since it had preserved Canadian unity. The government had committed itself to French Canadians; that is, to the minority. Why now was it asking the country as a whole to "free" it from its obligations?

This was the question that the nationalists were to repeat time and time again. Maxime Raymond formulated it first in the Commons on 5 February, and stated it with particular clarity. He referred to Ernest Lapointe's explanation of the compromise accepted at the beginning of the war. This compromise had become a "contract" between the two nations, a pact of honour ratified by the general election of March 1940. French Canadians had accepted participation in the war; English Canadians had consented never to resort to conscription.

"Now with this plebiscite," the nationalist MP told the Commons, "what is being sought is not the complete setting aside of the pact of September 1939, ratified by the people in March 1940—this being impossible, since one of the parties thereto has already fulfilled its obligation and the parties can no longer be replaced in their previous state—but the setting aside of the obligation of one of the parties, the sole condition which the abstentionists set to their participation, namely, that there should be no conscription for service overseas."

Raymond pressed his case with apparent coolness, using legal terminology, but you can sense the undercurrent of revolt that runs through his words. "Now," he continued, hammering his point home, "now, as I say, that one party has fulfilled its pledge, the other party to the contract, the conscriptionist group, would like to repudiate their sole obligation, which was to abstain from demanding conscription for overseas service."

Directly addressing "all sincere advocates of conscription in this house," the member for Beauharnois repeated to them:

> On September 9, 1939, a compromise was made whereby you agreed not to demand conscription for overseas service, provided those who opposed participation in the war, especially in the Province of Quebec, consented to participate in that war. On the strength of that agreement, the important part of our population which opposes war has consented to participate in it. Were you sincere at that time? I dare not question your sincerity. Did you wish to obtain that consent through false representations? I dare not believe it. Now that those who opposed war have liberally and generously fulfilled their pledge—and God knows how much fervour and devotion M. Lapointe brought into the fulfilment of his pledge—will you refuse to fulfil yours?

Raymond had a weak voice. He was no crowd mover, but he was logical and tenacious and was stirred by indignation to the depths of his being. He kept pressing his adversary with questions: "Since when is a debtor left free to decide himself whether he will pay his debt or not?" Since when do democracies at war with Hitler accept the principle that the stronger party can tear up a contract if it doesn't suit them any more?

The member for Beauharnois was a confirmed Bourassist. He believed in Confederation, in the union of races, and in the independence of a bi-ethnic Canada. So how could he conclude a speech like this? "We are not advocating separatism," this moderate-minded man was led to say:

> but we should not be driven to it. We are willing to live in the same house as long as it is comfortable for all. We are advocates of national unity on certain fair terms and once our conditions, laid down in advance, are accepted, we demand that they be adhered to.
>
> I greatly fear that the Toronto Committee of Two Hundred who are leading the struggle in favour of conscription for overseas service, in direct violation of the

> agreement of September 1939, are forging the weapons that will slay national unity and possibly Confederation as well.

In short, the French-Canadian nationalists were opposed to the very principle of the plebiscite. They refused to let the government ask the majority to wipe out a promise made to the minority. In advance, they denied the validity of the response Canadians would make.

The contract involved was a moral one. Judicially, Parliament could impose conscription. What the French-Canadian minority demanded of the majority was that it should refuse to act on a thing that it had the political power to enact.

Is this not an absurd position in a democracy? No. Public life in a complex state must be based on fundamental postulates of this sort or else the state becomes an open persecutor. For if strength of numbers alone regulates relationships between an ethnic majority and the minority, then life in common becomes impossible, and all that remains is to separate. The minority must quit the house that has become uninhabitable.[1]

To demand the execution of a moral pact when one hasn't the strength to enforce it is to put a great deal of faith in mankind. The men whom Raymond was addressing were carried away by quite different preoccupations: they had the war to win, the Empire to save, and what, in their eyes, in such circumstances, could be the worth of a promise made by a few crafty politicians to several million French Canadians?

Here, for example is the response of the *Winnipeg Free Press* to the nationalist attitude. The *Free Press* was Liberal and enjoyed great prestige on the Prairies.

> Those who, in 1942, continue to insist on the maintenance of any kind of limit [on the war effort] will do themselves and their fellow citizens of the same race and religion the most grievous and lasting damage.

The supreme law once laid down—". . . the majority must prevail . . ."—then came the threat:

> Is Quebec going to share in the terrible corruption which besmirched the name of France herself and covered it with shame? We do not think so. But time is running out when virtue could speak effectively.

The *Globe and Mail*, the Conservative paper in Toronto, shared the views of the *Free Press* and the tone soon became injurious. A little later the *Ottawa Citizen* denounced "the aggressive drive to make Quebec the leader of this country"; which is to say that, in demanding that a promise be respected, the minority was taking itself for the majority.

Take this line of thought, push it to the limit, stir in the idea of the congenital cowardice of French Canadians, and you have this pregnant little piece taken from Toronto's *Saturday Night*: "The desire to influence the population ratio by incurring less than the proportional risks in active service against the enemies of Canada will be deeply resented."

In the same journal, the Reverend M. Silcox explained us to his compatriots. He did so with a great effort of good will, since our medieval shortcomings, as he saw them, as well as our poverty, were attributable to the church, and not to the fact that we were simply French. However, French Canadians, he opined, "have reached the critical point in the history of their survival." On 27 April (the date of the plebiscite) they themselves would provide the answer to the problem of their continued existence. Let them beware, he said, "of destroying the faith we have in them. . . . For if they do so they will find themselves a despised and helpless minority of some 3 million people on a continent of 140 million English-speaking people." The seventy-fifth anniversary of Confederation might well be the last, he concluded, for its dissolution might be the only wise step, "with whatever transfer of minority elements of the population may be necessary." Ship them all off to the reservations! This time the separatist thesis came from Toronto.

T.S. Ewart, son of the famous jurist, tried in vain to defend the principle of the contract on radio CFCF in Montreal. In vain, too, other voices were raised in attempts at appeasement—for example that of J.T. Thorson, minister of National Selective Service. According to him it was unjust to assert that opposition to conscription was restricted to Quebec. "I myself could name twenty-five Ontario ridings," he declared in April, "and some of them exclusively of British extraction, where opposition to conscription runs strong. And I could do the same for other regions in Canada."

Who had the ready answer for Thorson? Another of King's cabinet ministers, Colin Gibson, minister of National Revenue, who had it printed in a government advertisement.

> As I see it—Hitler would vote "No," Quisling would not vote, and Canadians will vote "YES."

It was only the enemy or the traitor then, a Quisling, a turncoat, or a filthy collaborator, only types who in the eyes of official propaganda deserved to be cast into outer darkness, who would dare vote anything but Yes.

It would be easy to cite many more examples of statements of this kind, all drawn from respectable newspapers or made by men in positions of authority. For incomprehension had reached gargantuan proportions and on both sides people indulged the worst elements of themselves. And yet I find the most basic explanation of one type of Anglo-Canadian reaction elsewhere—in the words of a political figure who didn't really have the soul of a politician and who spoke for widespread popular feeling. Not that everyone shared his thought to the same degree, but it coloured, I think, the most diverse attitudes, and those who did not accept it in its most absolute form still felt its reality in their hearts.

It was the same day or the day after Maxime Raymond's speech. The finance minister, J.L. Ilsley, one of King's principal aides, rose in the Commons and said:

> I represent people whose ancestors for the most part left the British Isles centuries ago, people whose loyalty to the British empire, whose belief in the British empire and its institutions, are deep-seated, and for that matter taken for granted. They call it the British empire and not the British commonwealth of nations. They do not think too much about home defence. . . . The distinction between serving in Canada and serving overseas is a distinction which for them has no meaning whatever. They would consider it their duty to defend what they call the British empire, and what I call the British empire, in any part of the world in which the continued existence of the empire was in peril.

Compared with the sharp squeals I quoted earlier, can't one decipher here the booming tones of the great organ? A religious note is struck and the weighty words and resonant phrases bespeak total deep-seated conviction. Ilsley is one of the true believers anchored in a faith, in a rite even, for he does not deign to speak of the "Commonwealth," a mere desecrated version of the old British cult. He prefers the good old word "Empire." In the circumstances he was the incarnation of English Canada, just as Maxime Raymond was the symbol of French Canada—that is to say, beyond the norm, though in direct line with it, well out in front of the pack, though not cut off from it, having the courage to indulge to the full feelings that were everywhere dominant but that most people were afraid to admit to themselves. Certainly Frank Scott didn't belong in this company; but can one be sure that Ilsley's credo didn't awaken a sympathetic echo in King or even in Coldwell [leader of the Co-operative Commonwealth Federation]?

If we had been a little more cool-headed we simply should have said: "Here is the adversary, the honest and implacable adversary who must be defied and who deserves our respect. For he knows the name of the thing he is fighting for and even if his ideals seem old-fashioned to us, they do have a human dimension, they are based on a system of values and they represent a certain mode of existence."

And he had warned us himself: we weren't to mistake him for some recent British emigrant. His ancestors had left the isles centuries ago. In his own way he was a Canadian. Perhaps he was a descendant of those Loyalists who, in Scott Symons's definition, had accepted "the great upheaval" of coming north in order to be able to live a life in conformity with the truth symbolized by the British Crown.

Ilsley had old English-Canadian roots, roots that are often denied nowadays. He represented in every detail the English Canada that we could not tolerate, for it stood for our own disappearance, our downfall, our servitude. Naturally, he had drawn certain advantages from his situation, which he clung to, but having a sense of responsibility, he was ready, in the present crisis, to accept some sacrifices along with the advantages.

What were we to him? A thorn in his side. He went on: "These are the people . . . whose view-point, which is my view-point, I reflect in the cabinet. . . . These people believe and I believe that this government, without too much regard for remotely distant consequences, should adopt the most efficient and effective methods now of carrying on the war."

Needless to say, the anticonscription promises were a tether he could no longer abide. He told Canadians to vote Yes. "I need hardly say that I will do my utmost to obtain this result. And when we have full liberty to act, we will act in the best interests of this country and of its war effort."

So the landscape was coming into focus. In one solid block English Canada leaned toward Yes. Of course there was debate. Conservatives and socialists denounced the Machiavellian ways of Mackenzie King. But the prime minister had set up the problem in such a way that, like it or not, everyone had to pull with him. The federal parties—Conservatives, Liberals, CCF, and Social Credit—asked their members to vote Yes. They pulled Quebec officialdom in after them. Cardinal Villeneuve did not take a stand on the question that was so patently political, but he was known to favour the central government and the war effort. The ministers in Ottawa kept rank with their colleagues. The Godbout government leaned the same way.

Notes

1. In 1917 in the Quebec legislature, Liberal member J.-N. Francoeur had proposed a motion in favour of separation. Five years later, Abbé Groulx's *Action française* proceeded to make its inquiry into *Our Political Future* and concluded that in certain circumstances separation was the solution.

On 28 April 1942, the day after the plebiscite was held, the *Free Press* of London, Ontario, editorialized as follows:

> It is now up to the Government to give the fullest expression in action to this decisive challenge. There can be no pussyfooting. The result is clear-cut. The people have no cause to reproach themselves. But it will go ill with any Government which fails to give full and immediate effect to this verdict. . . . In a democracy such an overwhelming verdict cannot be overlooked or explained away. If the people of Quebec are to regard themselves as good Canadians they must submit gracefully to the wishes of the majority of their compatriots realizing that this is no imperial war, but a struggle which the vast majority of Canadians regard as their own. It is up to responsible leaders in Quebec, a province where leadership of one kind or another has played a dominant part, to see that the idea of co-operation with the rest of Canada is carried out to the full.

These sentiments typified much of English-Canadian opinion. But the notion that there could be no "pussyfooting" showed how little the editors of this paper understood Mackenzie King. In expecting Quebec to "submit gracefully" the *Free Press* misread another Canadian reality.

Result of the Plebiscite of 27 April 1942

Are you in favour of releasing the Government from any obligations arising out of any past commitments respecting the methods of raising men for military service?

	Number of votes cast in the affirmative	% of total	Number of votes cast in the negative	% of total	Total votes*	% voting
General Population						
Nova Scotia	120 382	77.85	33 043	21.37	154 624	45.46
New Brunswick	105 602	69.12	45 940	30.07	152 786	62.92
Prince Edward Island	23 660	82.36	4 841	16.85	28 728	57.22

	Number of votes cast in the affirmative	% of total	Number of votes cast in the negative	% of total	Total votes*	% voting
General Population, *continued*						
Quebec	376 188	27.09	993 663	71.57	1 388 469	75.71
Ontario	1 217 604	82.97	235 350	16.04	1 467 489	63.94
Manitoba	221 198	79.05	55 735	19.92	279 810	67.17
Saskatchewan	188 116	71.13	74 371	28.12	264 469	59.42
Alberta	186 172	70.44	75 427	28.54	264 289	64.86
British Columbia	254 301	79.08	63 314	19.69	321 569	68.68
Yukon**	1 173	72.18	437	26.89	1 625	60.91
Total	2 694 396	62.31	1 582 121	36.59	4 323 858	66.50
Service Vote						
United Kingdom, Jamaica, NF	60 474	70.97	23 707	27.82	85 205	
NS, NB, PEI	41 720	87.56	5 821	12.22	47 649	
Ontario, Quebec	93 203	81.10	20 341	17.70	114 917	
MB, SK, AB, BC, Yukon	55 721	82.90	11 016	16.39	67 218	
Total service vote	251 118	79.72	60 885	19.33	314 989	
TOTAL VOTE	2 945 514	63.50	1 643 006	35.42	4 638 847	

Source: *Canada Gazette*, 27 June 1942, 5456–61.

* Includes rejected ballots.

** Includes Yukon Territory and Yellowknife Administrative District. In the Territory, 860 voted in the affirmative, 317 in the negative, and there were 12 rejected ballots. The equivalent figures for the Yellowknife Administrative District were 313, 120, and 3.

The Electoral Districts in Quebec that voted in the affirmative were: Cartier, Jacques-Cartier, Laurier, Mount Royal, Outremont, St. Ann (Sainte-Anne), St. Antoine-Westmount, St. Lawrence–St. George (Saint-Laurent–Saint-Georges), and Verdun.

The Electoral Districts outside Quebec that voted in the negative were: Prescott, Russell (Ontario); Provencher (Manitoba); Gloucester, Restigouche-Madawaska, Kent (New Brunswick); Rosthern (Saskatchewan); and Vegreville (Alberta).

The highest percentage affirmative vote (95.19) was in Eglinton (Toronto, ON). The highest percentage negative vote (96.77) was in Beauce, PQ.

The Montrealer Frank Scott was a prominent constitutional lawyer, civil libertarian, academic, and littérateur. He was a strong supporter of the CCF and in 1943 was co-author (with David Lewis) of the influential *Make This Your Canada: A Review of CCF History and Policy*. His perspective on the outcome in Quebec of the plebiscite was that of the English-Canadian intellectual left. He hankered for national unity based on pan-Canadian symbols and a new social and economic order. Many of the reforms he favoured eventually came into effect, but the nationhood he dreamed of remained illusory.

What Did "No" Mean?

F.R. Scott

THE IMPORTANT THING for Canadians to understand about the plebiscite of April 27th is not what the "yes" vote meant, but what the "no" vote meant.

The "yes" vote itself is obscure enough to satisfy even the prime minister. It was not a vote for conscription, since the question was never asked whether or not Canadians wanted conscription for overseas. That simple question would have been altogether too straightforward to suit our political tradition. The question was whether or not the government was to be free to use Canadian manpower as it saw fit for the future. But there can be no doubt that many who voted "yes" meant that they wanted conscription, and wanted it now. Many others who voted "yes" did so because Mr. King made it appear that a negative vote would have indicated a want of confidence in himself; he thus neatly converted the Conservative and CCF parties, which had urged a "yes" vote, into Liberal election machines. Though at the last minute this intention was denied, the impression was not eradicated, as any glance at the newspapers will show. So people voted "yes" for many different and even contradictory reasons.

Nevertheless this does not confront the country with any great difficulty or danger. The yes-men will for the most part approve of a more resolute war policy. It is the "no" votes which should be studied and weighed, because a misunderstanding of this vote, and action by the government based on that misunderstanding, could easily result in grave peril to our country. No man in his senses, even if he is willing to sacrifice the whole future of Canada as a nation in order to increase her present war effort, could wish to take a step which would immediately divide our forces and so weaken the national will. It would be about as sensible as if the English Tories were to start a major drive on Trades-unions in order to speed up war production, or Chiang Kai-shek were to revive his former attacks upon the Communist armies now fighting in his ranks. Aggravating internal dissensions is a curious sort of loyalty to the United Nations.

Yet that is what certain groups in Canada have already done by their treatment of the conscription issue, and what these same groups are still doing by their misreading of the plebiscite vote. And though French Canada is not without her own groups who play politics with these vital matters, nevertheless the major responsibility for the difficulty lies with English Canada. It is English-speaking Canadians who have been in charge of the major domestic decisions in this as in past wars in which Canada has engaged. Seldom has an effort been made to get to the roots of what appears to be a peculiar reluctance on the part of Quebec to see things as Anglo-Saxons see them. Seldom has a sympathetic analysis been made of the currents of thought in French Canada. Every English-speaking Canadian knows that though Mr. Meighen and Tim Buck [Communist Party of Canada General Secretary] both urged a "yes" vote in the plebiscite, they did so from very different reasons. Yet how many people can distinguish between those French-speaking Canadians who voted "no" because they like isolation, and those who voted "no" because they like Canada?

British people everywhere would do well to reflect on one fact that this war has brought strikingly to light, namely, that the non-British peoples who are supposed to "enjoy" the blessings of the British Empire do not seem to appreciate those blessings as much as we have been taught that they did. The Irish underwent British rule for 800 years, and in this crisis prefer not to fight with Britain at all. The Boer leader, Hertzog, advocated neutrality for South Africa in 1939, and though Smuts found enough support to defeat him there is still a dangerous antiwar element in that Dominion. The great Indian leader Nehru was in jail a long time because he refused to fight for India on British terms, and recently rejected [Sir Stafford] Cripps' offer of Dominion status as inadequate. The Burmese, after 100 years within the Empire, seem actually to have fought for the Japanese invaders. And now Quebec votes "no" on the plebiscite. No doubt the Colonel Blimps will say that this all goes to prove the superiority of the Anglo-Saxon over the "native." But people possessed of any intelligence and any concern for the cause of human freedom will be profoundly disturbed by these danger signals, and will take time off for a little self-criticism. There obviously have been serious mistakes in policy. It may not be too late to rectify some of these mistakes.

Now there is one common factor that has been present in all these situations, and which may go a long way toward explaining them. It is the factor of British rule *over* these other races. These curious non-British people seem to like freedom so much that they want to be free even from British rule. Where this freedom has been most conceded, there is less difficulty, and where it has been least conceded, there is more difficulty. There would never have been a General Smuts in South Africa if there had not been a grant of Dominion status to his country. Perhaps if Premier U Saw of Burma had been granted the new status he was seeking conditions might have been different there. The Irish do not yet feel they are really free, since Ulster is still under British rule; and though Mr. de Valera [prime minister of Eire] does not grant bases to the Allies, he nevertheless suppresses the Irish Republican Army. In other words, it is generally true to say that the unwillingness of certain parts of the British Empire to fall in line with a British idea of "total war" is at bottom due to a love of liberty. They want democracy at home before they begin dying for it abroad. This attitude can be pressed too far, no doubt, when the enemy is at the gate; nevertheless it is a very human attitude and at bottom a very proper attitude.

How does all this relate to Quebec and the plebiscite? It is very closely related. The large "no" vote was a protest, not against the war, but against the idea of imperialism.

The people of Quebec have long memories. Is not the motto of the province "Je me souviens"? They look at each new political event from the point of view of their own special experience. No political issue in Canada is so surrounded by imperialist associations as conscription for overseas service. A country called Canada with European connections has existed for over four hundred years. When was the first expeditionary force of Canadians sent by a Canadian government to serve in an overseas war? Not till forty years ago, in the Boer War. Then Canadians went to assist the Empire in imposing its rule upon a small nation against its will. That evil act has been dearly paid for in this country. Even those who may still think it was justifiable will recognize that it started an association of ideas that has never yet been eradicated—the idea that Canadian armies go abroad only in the interests of British imperialism. And if any reader thinks this is opening up an old sore, let him remember that the Boer War produced Henri Bourassa, the founder of *Le Devoir*, and that both of these avowed enemies of imperialism are very much alive and active in this war.

The First World War added another complication in Quebec to the idea of imperialist expeditionary forces. It introduced the idea of compulsory overseas service for French Canadians at the insistence of the British majority in Canada. And mixed up with the conscription campaign of 1917 was a degree of political corruption and financial scheming (a Union government was needed as much to save railway investments as to impose conscription) enough to obscure even the highest motives. During the interval between the two world wars much of English-speaking Canada came to the view, that conscription for overseas service was a bad mistake which ought not to be repeated. That was the official view of every political party.

Then came World War II. From the point of view of Quebec, what had changed? At the outset, very little. The conflict started as a European war: England and France against Germany. The Tories were running England. Should Canadians be conscripted for that? Not another country in this hemisphere considered the issue a life and death struggle between democracy and tyranny. Quebec accepted the factual situation, and certainly cannot be blamed if she was not immediately caught up with the idea of a great crusade. And for all the talk there has been about our free entry into the war, the fact remains that from Quebec's point of view we had no right to neutrality—had not Mr. Lapointe said so?—and therefore there was no choice in the matter. In the same way the sending of the expeditionary force to England was accepted as inevitable, even though there was no vote in the Canadian Parliament on the question. But when Quebec saw the conscription issued being raised once again by a group of Toronto imperialists and a small clique in the Conservative party, and being used once more as a weapon with which to defeat a Liberal premier and the Liberal party, then Quebec closed its ranks. This was something they knew all about; this was what Mayor Houde [of Montreal] had predicted when he marched off to the concentration camp. And no new factors in the world situation, such as Pearl Harbor, the United States entry into the war, or the sweeping Japanese victories, even when added to the fall of France, had altered the internal appearance of the conscription issue in Quebec. Along both shores of the St. Lawrence it still looked like conscription imposed by imperialists, run by imperialists and utilized by imperialists. The ill-considered Canadian expedition sent to Hong Kong at British request did not improve matters. Besides, were not Canadian troops really needed now at home, and had not Australia, South Africa and Northern Ireland refused conscription? So history repeated itself. Quebec voted on 27 April not on the question as to whether the government's hands should be freed, but on the question as to whether Canadians should be forced to defend England and the British Empire. It emerged surprised and strengthened by its own unanimity.

Surely all English-speaking Canadians, and people outside Canada, can understand such a result even if they regret it? Surely, if one grants the premises from which Quebec's thinking started, there was no other vote that could have been given by any self-respecting people. There did not seem to be any need for Canada to have any more conscription for her own defense. And surely for all Canadians the remedy is fairly clear. As Mr. Leslie Roberts has so well expressed it, Canada has to make up her mind whether she is fighting this war as a British colony or as one of the United Nations. It is the continuing element of colonialism in Canada's war effort, real or apparent, that is causing so much trouble. We have not made up our minds to be an independent nation in world affairs, thinking out our own policy and making whatever contribution that policy requires, and consequently everything we do looks as though it were done for somebody else and not for ourselves. We have failed even to provide ourselves with the symbols of nationhood. Our war posters and publicity are filled with suggestions that we are just a little lion alongside a Big Lion. We pretend that the bravery of Londoners is greater than that of the people in Chungking or Leningrad. We have been guilty of forms of racial pride that are naturally obstacles to co-operation with other races. There is a close parallel between certain difficulties in Canada and certain others in India.

The French Canadians mean what they say when they say they will do everything necessary for the defence of Canada. They have already accepted conscription of manpower for this purpose, and they do not mind whether this means going to Alaska, Greenland or Panama. It is a good deal farther from Quebec City to Alaska than from Quebec City to London. Why the difference in attitude toward compulsory service in the two places? Solely because service across the Atlantic represents the imperialist tie, and looks like defence of the British Empire rather than defence of Canada or Canadian interests. Who will decide the use of Canadian troops overseas? Who really decides when they are to go and where they are to go? These questions touch the realities of the problem in Quebec. The more Canada insists on having a voice of her own in the joint Allied councils, the more she gets away from the old military tradition that her part is just to "offer" troops for Britain to use where Britain wants them, the easier it will be to bridge the gulf between Quebec and the other provinces. This is not a new issue in Canada; it dates from 1763. All that Quebec means by the "no" vote is that she does not wish her children to die for any country other than their own. This is nothing very startling.

A fair assessment of the whole situation, of course, must include the small vocal element in Quebec that is trying to capitalize on the present discontent in order to gain power and prestige, and that has leanings toward a clerical-fascism of a Spanish or Italian type. There are such people, but they are not more Quebec than Mr. Meighen is Canada. There are, shall we say, impure democrats in all parts of Canada, but the ones in Quebec are much less powerful than those outside in Quebec, and less misleading because they do not beat the patriotic drum so loudly. The same people who voted "no" so overwhelmingly in Mr. St. Laurent's constituency, only a short time ago preferred [Minister of Justice] St. Laurent to a nationalist candidate who posed as the "De Valera of Canada." A war effort planned by Canadians for Canadians, in conjunction with all our Allies, respecting minority points of view and deeply concerned for the common man in office, field and factory, will receive all the support that is needed from Quebec no matter where the battlefields may be. But it must be a war effort free from the restricting concepts of race and empire, free from control by vested interests at home, and devoted in deeds as well as in words to the great principles of human liberty and human brotherhood which it professes to be serving.

Roch Carrier is arguably the Quebec francophone writer with the biggest following in the rest of Canada. *La Guerre, Yes Sir!* (1968) is a definitive statement of the response of ordinary Québécois to the events of the war. Roch Carrier has served as principal of Le Collège Militaire Royal de Saint-Jean, and in 1994 became head of the Canada Council.

Corriveau's Return Home

Roch Carrier

THE DOOR WAS NARROW. It wasn't easy to bring the coffin into the house. The soldiers were very embarrassed not to be able to keep the symmetry of their movements. The door of the Corriveaus' little house had not been built to accommodate a coffin. The bearers put it down in the snow, calculated at what angle it could pass, studied how they should arrange themselves around it, argued. Finally the sergeant gave an order; they picked up the heavy coffin again, inclined it, placed it almost on edge, made themselves as narrow as possible, and finally succeeded in entering, out of breath and exhausted.

"Leave it now," grumbled old man Corriveau. "It's enough that he's dead, you don't have to swing him around like that."

The door opened into the kitchen. In the middle was a big wooden table.

"Put him there," said Mother Corriveau, "on the table. And put his head here, at this end. It's his place. Like that he'll feel more at home."

The English soldiers didn't understand the language the old people were speaking. They knew it was French, but they had rarely heard it.

"On the table!" repeated Mr. Corriveau.

The carriers put the coffin back on their shoulders and looked around for a place to put it.

"On the table!" ordered Mother Corriveau.

The Anglais shrugged their shoulders to show that they did not understand. Mr. Corriveau was getting angry. He said, very loud, "On the table! We want him on the table!"

The sergeant smiled. He had understood. He gave a command. The obedient soldiers turned towards the door: they were going to take the coffin outside.

Mr. Corriveau ran to the door and spread his arms to block their passage. *"Vieux pape de Christ!* They come and take him by force, they get him killed without asking our permission, and now we're going to have to use our fists to get him back from them." The old man, red with anger, threatened the sergeant with his fist; the latter wondered why everyone didn't speak English like he did.

"Vieux pape de Christ!"

"Put it on the table," said Molly in English. She had come in after carefully shaking the snow from her dress.

"What's she come here for, that one?" asked Mother Corriveau. "He's our dead."

When she saw the soldiers obey Molly, Mother Corriveau accepted her presence, and asked her, with an air of recognition on her face, "Tell them to take away the cover; our little boy is going to be too hot in there."

Molly translated. The soldiers gave Mother Corriveau a withering look. How dare she refer to the British flag as a "cover"! The old lady had no idea she had offended England; she would have been astounded if someone had told her that this "cover" was the flag her son had died for. If she had been told that, she would have kissed the flag as she kissed the relics of the tunic of the twenty-three-year-old Jesus Christ every night.

The sergeant decided to ignore the insult. The soldiers folded the flag, the sergeant blew on his bugle a plaint that made the windowpanes shudder and the villagers, already assembled around Corriveau, weep. The sound of the bugle stunned Anthyme Corriveau, who nervously dropped his pipe. He cursed his rotten teeth that couldn't hold a pipe any more. At twenty, Anthyme had had hard teeth that could crumble a glass, chew it. Now his rotten teeth were a sign that all his bones were going rotten too. He was so old, Anthyme, his sons were beginning to die. "When your sons begin to leave you, it won't be long before you go to join them."

"Anthyme," said his wife, "go find your screwdriver. I want to see if our boy's face has been all mashed up or if he knew enough to protect it like I told him. In all my letters I used to tell him, 'My child, think first of all of your face. A one-legged man, or even a man with no legs at all, is less frightening for a woman than a man with only one eye or no nose.' When he wrote back the dear child always said, 'I'm taking good care to protect my face.' Anthyme! I asked you for your screwdriver. I want that coffin opened."

Molly, in practising her trade, had learned several words of French. The French Canadians in Newfoundland liked Molly a lot. She explained, according to what she had understood, the Corriveaus' wish. The sergeant said, "No! No! No! No!"

His men shook their heads to say "No" too. Mother Corriveau took the sergeant's hand and squeezed it with all her might: she would have liked to squash it like an egg.

The sergeant, with a courteous strength, freed himself. His face was pale, but he smiled.

The sergeant felt sorry for these ignorant French Canadians who did not even recognize their country's flag.

"Anthyme Corriveau, you're going to take your shotgun and get these *maudits* Anglais out of my house. They take my son from me, they let him get killed for me, and now they won't let me see him. Anthyme Corriveau, take out your shotgun and shoot them right between the buttocks, if they've got any."

Crushed by the heaviest despair, old man Corriveau relit his pipe. At this moment there was nothing more important than managing to light his pipe.

"Anthyme!" shouted his wife. "If you don't want to use your shotgun, give them a kick. And get busy! After that you're going to look for your screwdriver."

"*Vieille pipe de Christ!* You can ask me for my screwdriver as often as you want. I can't remember where I put it last time I . . ."

"Anthyme! Get these *maudits* Anglais out of this house!"

The old man put out his match; the flame was burning his fingers. He spoke after several puffs. "Mother, we can't do a thing. Whether you see him or not, our boy is gone."

Mother Corriveau said simply, "We're going to pray."

Her husband had reminded her of the most obvious fact: "We can't do anything," Anthyme had said. An entire life-time had taught them that they could do nothing. Mother Corriveau was no longer angry. It was with a gentle voice that she had said, "We're going to pray."

She knelt, her husband did the same, then the villagers who had come, then Molly. . . . The old woman started the prayer, the prayer she had learned from the lips of her mother, who had learned it from hers: "Our Lady of the faithful dead: may he rest in peace among the saints of the Lord."

The seven soldiers knelt: the old lady was so astonished that she could not remember the rest of the formula.

"Anthyme," she muttered, "instead of getting all distracted while your son is burning in the fires of purgatory it might be a good thing if you'd pray for him. Your prayers will shorten his suffering. But then when I think of how you brought him up, I don't know if he's in purgatory or already in hell. Maybe he's in hell. In hell . . ."

She was choked by sobs. Anthyme started again, with the words of a man who has had to pray every time his wife threatens him with hell: *"Que le Seigneur des fidèles défont les lunes en paix dans la lumière du paradis."*

Everyone replied, "Amen."

"Je vous salue Marie, pleine et grasse, le Seigneur avez-vous et Bénedict et toutes les femmes et le fruit de vos entailles, Albanie."

"Amen."

The incantation was taken up several times. Then, Anthyme Corriveau was praying alone. No one was replying to his invocations any more. What was going on? He continued to pray, but he opened his eyes. Everyone was looking at his wife, who was lost in a happy dream. She was smiling.

The Blessed Virgin had given her mother's heart to understand that her son was in heaven. All of his sins, his oaths, his blasphemies, the caresses he had given the girls of the village, and especially the girls in the old country where he had gone to war, his drunken evenings when he used to go walking in the village throwing his clothes in the snow, the evenings when bare-chested and drunk her son would raise his fist to Heaven and shout, "God, the proof that you don't exist is that you aren't striking me down right now," all these sins of Corriveau had been pardoned; the Blessed Virgin had breathed it to his mother.

If the hand of God had not struck down Corriveau on those nights it had weighed on the roofs of the houses. People in the village would not forget those alcoholic evenings, even if God had forgiven Corriveau for them. His mother felt in her soul the peace that must now be her child's. Her son had been pardoned because he had died in the war. The old lady felt in her heart that God was obliged to pardon soldiers who had died in the war.

Her son had been reclothed in the immaculate gown of the elect. He was beautiful. He had changed a little since he had gone off to war. A mother gets used to seeing her children look more and more like strangers. Dying transforms a face too. Mother Corriveau saw her son among the angels. She would have liked him to lower his eyes towards her, but he was completely absorbed in the prayer that he was murmuring, smiling. The old lady wept, but she wept for joy. She rose.

"Take my son out of the kitchen and put him in the living room. We're going to eat. I've made twenty-one *tourtières*. Anthyme, go dig up five or six bottles of cider."

Ralph Allen grew up in Oxbow, Saskatchewan. He wrote for the *Globe and Mail* during the war, and was one of the country's most celebrated war correspondents. In this passage, he explores the relations that existed between volunteers and conscripts, the two solitudes of the Armed Forces. As the war progressed, R-men or "zombies" found themselves under more and more pressure to "go active," that is to say, switch over to voluntary service and go overseas. Like Forsee in this story, "zombies" were often made to feel like outcasts, even though they were serving in a manner the government of their country deemed appropriate.

Going Active

Ralph Allen

THE MAJOR walked with a permanent list. He stood with a list, his whole left side adroop under the weight and prestige of his old campaign ribbons. His sharp sallow face seemed to list beneath the scraggly gray counterbalances of a moustache which he allowed to grow too long because it would not grow thick enough. His speech listed; he began his longer sentences strongly and confidently, but they trailed off and fell away in threshing shadows Some of the individual words listed. He pronounced "ing" like "een."

The major was smiling and his yellowing teeth listed humorlessly beneath the smile. "Well men," he said, "I have good news for you. At least I think it will be good news for you. You've been traineen hard and workeen hard and I know you've found companionship and in spite of the hardships you have experienced, I know you have profited by the experience of the ah experience."

The major paused. "And now," he said, "you will soon be goeen away. I shouldn't tell you when you will be goeen, but you have been such good soldiers here that I was just sayeen to Mr. Johnson I don't believe there has been a finer platoon in camp than Number Nine and I have been watcheen men come and go ever since."

Kennebec, lounging in the rear file, scratched his ear ostentatiously and whispered out of the side of his mouth: "Good old Wylie!"

"You will be goeen on to your advanced traineen centres in five days from today," the major said. He waited indulgently for the ragged cheer to subside.

"Some of us," with a great effort the major adjusted the list of his body—"Some of us will have to stay. We envy you. I think all of you know a bit about my record and when I think of the humble part I have been able to play as a soldier of the British Empire I can't help thinkeen of the humble part and envyeen, yes envyeen."

"A heart as big as all outdoors," Kennebec whispered.

"But you don't want to hear a speech," the major said. "There's just one thing I want to say. You will be goeen on to other camps where you will find that they are not as generous in giveen you leaves as we have tried to be here. And before you go, as a reward for your fine performance here, I want you all to have a leave with your families because you may not for a long time. I have put it up to the colonel."

Under cover of another cheer, Kennebec said aloud: "When they made old Wylie, they threw the mould away. And none too soon."

"The colonel consented," the major said, "on one simple little condition. It's a fair condition. It applies to all the other platoons in the camp and they will be getteen leaves too if they meet."

The major's voice grew sentimental. "We are proud of the record of this camp," he said. "When we can send out a draft that is one hundred percent active, we are proud and we know that you are proud too, because in the final analysis. Today is, let's see, Monday. You'll have to be back here Friday to join your drafts to your new traineen centres. So that leaves two days. If good old Number Nine platoon can show a one hundred percent active service roster by Wednesday morneen, the whole platoon will leave on forty-eight hour passes at noon and I'm confident. It just means all pulleen together and talkeen it over among yourselves. I know that some of you, perhaps for what seem to you like good personal reasons, haven't been as fast as the rest to decide about goeen active, but I know that no man in Number Nine would want to deprive his entire platoon of the last leave they'll be getteen for a long time and I know even if they did. So talk it over among yourselves and pull together among yourselves, and that's the British way, the way that means so much to all of us."

The major smiled affably and listed to attention. "That's all, Mr. Johnson," he said.

Before the subaltern called them to attention, Mike glanced down the length of the platoon's rear rank. Most of the men looked the same; their eyes were bright with excitement, their lips were parted above their teeth, and their breathing had become a silent steady panting. It was not the same with the three R men he could see at the end of the rank. Sumner had dropped to the parade ground on one knee and was conspicuously absorbed in adjusting a gaiter. Drayton had taken off his dark-rimmed glasses and was polishing them jerkily with a dirty handkerchief. Forsee was staring straight ahead and his pale eyes were dull and without feeling.

Kennebec turned to Mike.

"God bless our happy home," he said.

"God damn our happy home!" Mike said savagely. . . .

The hut was nearly empty. The beds were silhouetted flat and naked in the sludgy bath of starlight from the windows. There was no sound but the complacent crackling of the stoves, and now and then a muffled cough. The room smelled empty; it was warm, but much fresher than usual. The washroom door was closed but a slab of yellow light fell through its crack across the middle of the floor.

Mike put one hand on the floor and pivoted his body halfway out of bed into the slab of light from the door, holding his head and his free hand close together in the light. His wrist watch said a quarter to one. He swung his head back to the bunk and half sat up, searching the other bunks in the semi-opaque gloom.

They were all there. That was Sumner on the third bed down, across the room. And Drayton two more beds away. He could hear Forsee breathing in the bunk above and see the light bulge of his body through the mattress. They didn't even have guts enough to go loose. They were just lying there, pretending to be asleep, and listening to the minutes drag by.

Maybe they knew going loose would be no use either. Maybe they knew they could either take it or give up, and there was no third alternative. They knew how far Miczawicz got. Miczawicz knew his rights. He went running to the major with his black eye and his two loose teeth, and the major threw him out. And Miczawicz walked back into the cubicle and said: "All right, I'll go active." Barton, Judson, Crowther and Denman—they knew when they were licked too. . . . "Eight little R Boys, scared as they could be. One got his kisser smacked, then there were three." . . . That Lister was a riot.

It would be worse tonight. Last night the corporal was in, and they had to be quiet enough that the corporal could pretend he didn't hear. But the corporal wouldn't be in at all tonight. He'd made a point of telling them. There was no bed check and no roll call tonight. The sentry was still on the gate, but they all knew the way over the fence anyway. They should be coming any time. And they'd be drunk tonight. Some of them anyway. That was the idea. That was what the corporal meant. Or the lieutenant. Or the sergeant. Or the major. All of them, probably. Kennebec knew what he was talking about after all. They'd played it the same way right from the first day, now that you looked back.

He wanted to say something to Forsee, but what could he say? He couldn't say he was sorry for what he'd said the other night, because he wasn't sorry for saying it at all. The only thing he was sorry about was that Forsee happened to be what he was.

No, not that exactly either. He was sorry that the others were what they were and that he himself was what he was, and that what they all were, the others and himself and Forsee, would have to be exposed and proclaimed for all of them to see. He knew what they were going to do. They had told him, and asked him to help. He had said he wouldn't help, nor would he hinder them. And perhaps that made him worse than any of them. It was all right deciding there was no use, but if it was wrong you still had to try and stop it. But was it wrong?

There was nothing he could say to Forsee. But he could ask Forsee for a match, and perhaps asking him for a match would tell Forsee something that he could not tell him in any other way. It might tell him, at least, that the matter which was about to begin would not really be a matter of personalities, however much it must seem to be. It might tell him that the matter had been ordained by forces far beyond the control of anyone in the hut, and that it would be as ridiculous to take it as a personal matter as to take the war itself as personal.

He slapped his hand softly against the mattress above his head. "You got a light, Forsee?" he said.

The clothing hanging behind the bed rustled and a grey arm sheathed in a woollen undershirt reached down over the sill.

"Thanks."

"If you're short of cigarettes, you'll find some in my half of the kit box," Forsee said.

Mike stopped in the act of striking a match. . . . They were coming now. . . .

Their feet were scuffling in the frozen gravel outside the hut. The door creaked open and their boots rang hollowly through the vestibule. They wouldn't all come in together. Three or four or half-a-dozen at a time.

"Not so much noise!" the voice at the end of the room was thick and sententious.

It was answered by a high giggle, and then two tearful voices were singing low from the black corner bunk beside the vestibule:

"If I had my way, dear,
"You'd never grow old—
"A garden—"

A shadow lurched down the hut, threw open the door into the washroom as the doors shuttered back on the sudden flare of light. The bed creaked thinly as Mike felt Forsee's body relax against the upper bunk.

A babel of noisy whispers broke out at the far end of the hut, and a bottle rang a hollow High C against the iron rail of a bedstead. The whispering stopped, and a swaying file of shadows moved down the hut through the slab of light from the wash-room door, past the glowing stove, and merged in an uncertain knot near the middle of the corridor between the beds. Mike swung his legs to the floor and padded on his bare feet to the fringe of the knot. He recognized the bulky form of Lister at its centre.

The knot dissolved away from him and he followed it. A bed creaked heavily in the darkness ahead. Mike looked down at the bed. There were three men sitting on each side of it, hunched together in the darkness like merging black mounds. The covers between them stirred blackly and then were still.

A glaring beam of light stabbed through the darkness, played whitely on the white corner of a pillow for a moment and then moved across the pillow and focused on a face. The eyes in the face were a single slash of copper, like the eyes of a cat caught in headlights at night. The face was white and flabby.

"Wake up, Sumner!" The words shivered roughly through the silence.

"Shut up, Davis! I'll handle this." Mike could make out Lister's heavy features now, thrust close behind a flashlight, close to the white face of Sumner on the pillow.

"It's me, Lew. Al Lister."

"Hello, Al." Sumner's eyes were closed tight now against the light. His voice tried to duplicate the casual warmth of the other. It failed; it sounded scared.

"Good old Lew." Lister leaned forward with the torch. His own body and the other bodies on the bed pressed hard against each other, wedging tightly into the shapeless contours of the blankets. Lister's free hand reached down and patted the right cheek of the face on the pillow. And then, lightly but sharply, it slapped each cheek three times. There was no sound of protest.

"Like a drink, Lew?"

"No thanks, Al."

"Sure he does. Give him a drink. Who's got the jug of goof?"

Another hand thrust the neck of a bottle into the beam of the torch. It glinted purple in the light as it probed for the lips of the man imprisoned under the blankets and the wine spilled over the lips and rolled down Sumner's flabby chin in a red smear. Sumner tried to rub it off with his shoulder, but the six men holding him in the vise of their bodies leaned forward again, pinioning him closer than before. Lister curled a loose fringe of blanket into his free hand and swabbed the chin dry with delicate, over-solicitous stabs.

"All right, Lew?"

"All right, Al."

"That's not the first drink we've had, Al." Lister turned his head away from Sumner, but still held the flashlight close to Sumner's face. "Me and Lew used to kick around a lot when we first come here," he said. "Me and Lew are pals. Ain't we, Lew?"

"Ain't we, Lew?"

"Ain't we what?" For the first time Sumner spoke with a hint of spirit.

"Pals."

"Sure."

"Sure what, Lew?"

"Pals."

"Pals, who?"

"What do you mean, Al?" Sumner no longer spoke with spirit.

"That's what I mean. Al. Al. Just Al. You remember my name, Lew. You just said it. It's Al. Tell them what we are, Lew. Tell the boys right."

"We're pals, Al."

Lister patted one of the cheeks again and then slapped the two cheeks again, three times on each side, as he had done before.

"Well, Lew," Lister said, "I guess you know what the boys have been saying." He moved the flashlight closer, so close it was almost touching Sumner's nose.

"The boys have been saying you're yellow, Lew," Lister said. "That hurt. The boys say you're not only yellow, but you don't wanta play ball with the rest of us. The boys say you don't care if we get our leave tomorrow or not. The boys say you'd do us out of it."

"I don't like that kind of talk, Lew," Lister said. "And that's not all, Lew. The boys were real mad at you. They wanted to toss your stuff outside in the snow. And then they wanted to throw you in the shower. I said you can't do that fellahs. You can't throw a man in the showers at this time of night. It's too cold. The water's just like ice. You can't do that to my pal Lew. That's what I said to the boys, Lew."

Lister said: "And that's not all, Lew. The boys said if that wasn't enough, they'd get rough. Real rough, Lew. I said they couldn't do that either. I said it was all right to have a little fun between friends, but rough stuff don't go. I said it was all right to do like this."

Lister's foot scraped against the floor as he bent his body forward on the bed. He removed the flashlight a little way from Sumner's face and drew his free hand back to the level of his shoulder and then slapped Sumner hard across the mouth, twenty times or more. Each slap made its own sick crash.

"That's all right, Lew," Lister said when he was done. "That's between pals. I told the boys you wouldn't mind that."

The man pinioned in the bed tried to twist his face toward the pillow. His tongue ferreted across his swollen lips but there was no moisture on it.

"I told the boys you'd go active in a minute, Lew," Lister said. "I told the boys if we'd put it up to you man to man there wouldn't be any argument. And there wouldn't either. Would there, Lew?"

Sumner tried to open his eyes, but the harsh light from the torch ground them shut again.

"Would there, Lew?"

Lister waited for a minute. They all waited. Their waiting ceased to be an abstract thing. It was physical and it possessed the whole room; you could hear it and you could smell it. The six soldiers sitting on the bed leaned forward to look at Sumner's face and the springs of the bed drew together under their shifting weight with a constricted, half-throttled twang. The sound was like an unfinished sigh. A man standing behind the bed coughed primly. The only breathing that could be heard was Sumner's; it was heavy but even, like the breathing of a man taking ether. The unheard breathing of the others soaked and deadened the air with the stale sick fumes of cheap wine. The men were sweating, and the sweet musty smell of their sweat mingled with the smell of the wine, drenching the room with the heavy odor of climax.

Under the flashlight, Sumner's loose face was relaxed and bland, like a weathered marble statue seen by moonlight. The harsh light cleansed his face of all line and expression. He had ceased screwing his eyebrows toward the little jowls of fat beneath his eyes to shut out the glare of the torch, and his closed eyelids were smooth and round. You could not have told by any of the conventional yardsticks whether he was afraid or not, and yet every inch of his face spoke of fear. If you could hear the waiting in his breathing and smell the waiting in the air, you could see it still more clearly in Sumner's face.

"Lew!" Lister said at last, "the boys are tired of waiting."

"All right," Sumner said lifelessly. "All right. I'll do it. I'll go."

The torch snapped out and the room was black again. There was a congestion of bumping shadows and the smothered ring of clothed bodies lurching against metal bed frames.

A new voice said: How do we know he'll go through with it? How do we know he won't wording double-cross us?"

"He won't. Because if he wording double-crosses us, we don't get our leave. And we'll all be here together for three more nice long days."

Drayton was sitting erect in his upper bunk, waiting for them. When Lister sprayed the torch on him, he looked for all the world like a juvenile and highly Nordic Gandhi, sitting cross-legged under his blankets with his absurdly large issue undershirt billowing away from his skinny neck to lose his skinny chest under its glazed white folds, and his short-sighted eyes blinking nakedly in the bleached sacs of flesh that had been pinched out under them by a lifetime of wearing glasses.

"Go ahead," Drayton said, shrilling out the words in a fractured parody of resolution and defiance. "Do whatever you want. It doesn't matter what you do. I still won't."

"All right," Lister commanded, "let's have a look at his stuff."

Drayton watched immovably while they dumped his kit bags on the floor, swept the clothing behind the bed into a bundle and rolled it into a pile on the floor with their feet and methodically dumped the contents of his brushes box into a smaller pile beside the bed.

Davis rummaged through the debris but found nothing that seemed of interest. Dubiously, he held a white envelope up to the beam of the flashlight.

"Let's have that," Lister said.

"Give it back!" Drayton said fiercely. "You can't take that." He squirmed free of the blankets and made a grab at the letter across the edge of the bed, but another man threw him back on the bed and three others ringed themselves around him, pinning his skinny body against the mattress with their arms. Drayton kicked for a while and then lay still, panting malevolently.

"*Dear Ernest*," Lister read. And then he repeated prissily: "*Dear Ernest.*"

The others chorused: "Dear Ernest."

"*We received your letters sixty-four and sixty-five today. It hardly seems like sixty-five days, even though we have seen you since, but in some ways it seems longer.*"

A high sniggering voice interrupted, with mock-approbation: "Ernest writes every day!"

"*I am glad you are not finding the life too hard*," Lister read, "*or at least that you think you are not finding it too hard. But you were always inclined to take things too robustly.*"

Another interruption: "Just look at that robust ole hunk man!"

"Lister!" Drayton panted desperately, "Stop! Please stop, Lister!"

"*I am sending another bottle of milk of magnesia along with the cod liver oil, the cake and the woollen scarf. I know it will do you good and if the other boys tease you about taking it, all I have to say is they ought to be ashamed of themselves.*"

A sharp smack interrupted Lister again as one man hidden in the darkness slapped another's wrist and squealed: "There! That will teach you not to tease Ernest again."

Drayton was crying. "For God's sake, Lister, don't. Please Lister. It's from my mother."

"*I think it's wonderful about you passing all your T.O.E.T.'s. They sound terribly hard and complicated. How did the other boys make out with them? I'll bet not many of them finished ahead of you.*"

"Ernest finished ahead of everybody," a man behind Lister said triumphantly, "That is, if you read from the bottom up."

"*It's nice that you get along with the other boys so well*," Lister read. "*I know that somewhere deep down in your secret self you have always considered yourself a little bit backward, especially in sports. But there are other things besides sports and I'm sure that when the other boys get to know you better, you'll be still more popular with them.*"

"Boy, is Ernest popular!" the man behind Lister said. "We're going to make him Queen of the May."

"Jesus!" Drayton was crying softly and hopelessly. "Oh Jesus!"

"*Your last letter worried me just a little*," Lister read. "*Now, I know most of the other boys are going overseas, Ernest, and I can understand why you want to go with them. I don't want to hold you to your promise against your will, but I know it's for the best. You're not as strong as the others. I shudder to think what might happen if you ever got over to England, in all that damp, and eating that terrible food, not to mention the other things.*"

"Ernest might get hurted, Ernest might get hurted," the man behind Lister chanted.

"*There are plenty of important jobs to be done right here in Canada*," Lister read, "*and goodness knows, if everybody was needed over there we'd have had conscription long ago*."

The man behind Lister beat time with his hand on the end of the bed and uttered a nasal, "Ta-ra-ra-ra ra-ra-ra-ra", apeing the playing of a fanfare by a band.

Lister read on: "*Dr. Purvis was out today with a specialist from Toronto to see your father. The pain has become worse in the last few days, and I think your father knows now too, although he will give no hint of it. It is no worse and no better than Dr. Purvis feared. At the most your father still has six months left. We must still try to pretend—*" Lister's voice died away emptily.

The man behind him tittered nervously but afterwards, for a while, nothing could be heard but the naked sobbing of the boy on the bed. Lister's hand dropped to his side and the letter slipped out of his fingers to the floor. You could not see his face, but pale hint of light reflected back on it from the wall, from the flashlight, and it was enough to show the sudden sagging droop of his mouth, a dead sag and yet as live as pain. The light was not enough to show his eyes, but it was enough to show the shamed narrowing at their corners; his whole face was a silhouette of shame. The light could not have been crueller to Lister if it had been turned away from the wall and focused full on him.

"Let go of him," Lister said.

"Let go of him," he said.

The men standing beside the bed obeyed and Lister said to Drayton: "We'll leave you alone now. You don't have to do it."

Drayton's sobbing had stopped. He sat up in the bed again and held his arm over his face like a garment thrown across his unclothed hurt.

Drayton said: "It's too late. I want to do it now."

Lister said doggedly: "No. Forget it. It doesn't matter."

"I'm going to," Drayton said. "Whether anybody wants me to or not. I thought nobody could make me, and now nobody can stop me."

"No," Lister said, "Forget it."

"It's no use telling you what you've done," Drayton said. "You wouldn't understand. But you've done what you set out to do. I'm going active. We don't have to talk about it any more."

Lister turned and shuffled stupidly away from the bed, into the dark aisle of the hut. The others followed him. They knew he would not stop at Forsee's bed now, and the wish to stop there had drained out of them as it had drained out of Lister. But two of them, Davis and another, paused uncertainly.

"There's only Forsee left," Davis whispered. "It's all wasted if we let him go."

Forsee heard them, and they heard Forsee drawing his body in on the bed, and the uneasy dregs of ferment that were left in them by the dispersing mob began to stir again. Davis and the other man moved close to the bed and two more men came up and stood close beside them.

Mike found himself still on the outskirts of these uncertain figures, standing barefooted in the middle of the floor, almost exactly where he had been when he first stopped beside Sumner's bed. For the first time, he felt thoughts taking shape in his head again. He wondered what had rooted him like this so long, rooted not only his body but the workings of his mind, and more acutely still, he wondered what he would really have thought of the things he had heard and seen if his mind had been less deadened by them. The answer would not come, but he found a part of it. This was the way he had felt, one night years before, when he left a stag party with some other men and went to a house where they featured something called an "Exhibition." The mechanical, a-thousand-times-rehearsed eroticism of the exhibition had left him horrified and physically sick. Yet, while the grisly burlesque was on, he had been unable to tear his eyes away from it. He had sat through it all, fascinated and sick, and then gone outside and spilled the contents of his stomach.

This night was much the same. Standing barefooted in the middle of the floor, he wondered abstractly, without putting his wonder in words, whether there was such a thing as having carnal knowledge of a man's soul. He wondered if it was less right that men should look with too much detail at women's bodies than that they should look with too much detail at the hearts of men. The shame and revulsion of the night struck and engulfed him in one swift overpowering wave; his body trembled with it.

For the first time since the others had come into the hut, he spoke aloud. His voice was tired, but it rang out loudly through the black room.

"That's enough!" Mike said.

He walked back to his bed and shoved his way through the gathering knot of men to the top of the bed. He felt in the darkness for Forsee's shoulder and when be found it, he sank his fingers into it and dragged it up from the pillow until Forsee's face was close to his.

"We've all had enough, Forsee," he said. "We're not going to have any more arguments and we're not going to have any more trouble. You're the only R man left in this whole hut and you're going active in the morning. There's no use talking about it, Forsee. That's what you're going to do."

Forsee's body tautened and tried to pull away from him. But Forsee said: "You don't have to do anything Tully. I'm going active. I was going anyway."

The platoon went on leave at noon. In the officers' mess, the colonel stood the company commander a double whiskey and the company commander stood the platoon commander a beer. A few days later a tiny set of fresh statistics passed across a chain of desks at Ottawa and the owners of the desks observed that the recruiting policy was continuing to work very well.

By 1939 many Canadians must have forgotten about the existence of the War Measures Act, just as another generation would forget between the end of the Second World War and the October Crisis of 1970. The Defence of Canada Regulations revealed anew just how powerful an instrument of executive authority the government of Canada had in its statutory arsenal.

National Security

William Kaplan

CANADA was hoping for peace, but well before the German invasion of Poland it began to prepare for war. A committee on emergency legislation was struck, and its preparations established the framework for preserving national security in Canada throughout the Second World War. The proclamation of the War Measures Act and the passage of the Defence of Canada Regulations affected all Canadians' liberty by imposing restrictions on where they could go, what they could read, and what they could say. And it was these regulations that gave to the police and to the state wide general powers to maintain national security during the war. Not only could men and women be arrested and interned without trial, but organizations, including such religious groups as the Jehovah's Witnesses, that had previously been lawful could be declared unlawful by a stroke of the federal cabinet's pen. Canada was not a police state; far from it. But the powers assumed by the executive were enormous, and they were exercised without any real opportunity for review. Significantly, the drafting and passage of these emergency powers took place behind closed doors.

Well before the war began, the RCMP began to prepare for it. The Mounties compiled long lists of enemy aliens, Nazis, Communists, and suspected spies. "Orders to arrest these people," Stuart T. Wood, a career officer and the commissioner of the force, reported to the minister of justice, "could be put into effect at a moment's notice."[1] The RCMP did not want to take any chances, so it also proposed that, in the event of war, the government outlaw and seize the property of all the German and Italian consulates, even though Italy was still neutral. The undersecretary of state for external affairs, Oscar Douglas Skelton, was somewhat alarmed by these proposals.

Skelton, a liberal democrat and former dean of arts at Queen's University, was, until his death in January 1941, the preeminent Canadian civil servant and the prime minister's most senior advisor on both foreign and domestic policy. After considering the RCMP recommendations, he wrote the prime minister to advise that not only were such repressive measures unnecessary, but that King consider issuing a statement when war came, calling for vigilance but also reminding the public that there was no reason for it to be stampeded into hysterical or "unwarranted persecution of Canadian citizens who happen to be of the race or language of our opponents."[2] This was an enlightened and thoughtful suggestion, and it deserved consideration. But when war came, Skelton's advice was not followed.[3] Rather, the recommendations of the Committee on Emergency Legislation were implemented.

That committee, an interdepartmental one, drawing in senior civil servants from most government departments, was established in March 1938 to review existing emergency legislation.[4] At the time of the Munich crisis, the committee had not yet completed that review, but the appeasement policies of British prime minister Neville Chamberlain postponed the inevitable, thereby giving the committee more time to go about its work. The committee eventually concluded that the War Measures Act, an omnibus act, passed during the First World War, that gave the cabinet wide regulation-making authority, continued to provide the government with sufficient power to meet any emergency, and that special legislation would be required only for the vastly increased financial expenditures certain to be demanded by another world war.[5] By invoking the War Measures Act, the government would have all the powers it needed, save possibly some financial ones, to fight the war overseas and to protect national security at home. The interdepartmental committee drafted a set of emergency security regulations, the Defence of Canada Regulations, which were submitted to cabinet in July 1939.[6]

There is no evidence that the federal cabinet ever considered the draft regulations,[7] and the fact that the recommended regulations were adopted without any amendment suggests that they were accepted without debate. On 3 September 1939 an order-in-council was passed, invoking the Defence of Canada Regulations.[8] The regulations were announced during the September 1939 special war session, but as Parliament was not required to review them, and as other business was judged more important, discussion of the regulations was postponed until Parliament returned, which satisfied almost everyone.[9] There were a few exceptions, of course. The attorney general of Ontario, Gordon D. Conant, wrote Justice Minister Lapointe, recommending that section 98 be reenacted. An editorial in the *Globe and Mail* endorsed this recommendation, but, for the moment, the regulations were not changed.[10] Sixty-four regulations, in six parts, set out how national security was to be preserved while the country was at war.

In general, the regulations were sensible and acceptable in scope and in object; they were intended to prevent espionage and sabotage by fifth-columnists at home and by enemy agents sent from abroad. To achieve these aims, designated ministers of the Crown were given broad order-making powers, such as the power of the minister of transport to control radio transmissions. Similarly, the secretary of state was given censorship authority,[11] while the minister of national defence was empowered to order blackouts and curfews. Initially, only a few of these regulations provided for judicial or other review of ministerial orders, but it was to be the policy of the government that the regulations be interpreted so as to interfere as little as possible with "the ordinary avocations of life and the enjoyment of property."[12] It was almost four years before another order-in-council was passed, providing for appeal to the courts for actions taken under these and other wartime regulations.[13] A few of the Defence of Canada Regulations were just silly, and two stood apart from the rest: Regulation no. 21, which authorized internment, and Regulation no. 39, which imposed severe restrictions on what Canadians could say. Neither regulation could be justified as a limited but essential restriction on the rights of citizens occasioned by the circumstances of war.

Regulation no. 21 was, in fact, the only one not unanimously approved by the Committee on Emergency Legislation. In brief, the regulation provided that the minister of justice, in order to prevent a person from engaging in activities prejudicial to the public safety or the safety of the state, could make an order directing the detention and internment of that person.[14] The regulation further provided that a person who was subject to detention and internment under Regulation no. 21 was deemed to be in legal custody. The power to arrest and detain was unlimited, but it was subject to modified review. Regulation no. 22 provided for the establishment of one or more advisory committees to hear appeals from any ministerial detention order. The advisory committee could not order anyone's release; all it could do was make recommendations to the minister of justice, who was under no obligation to follow them. Indeed, the criteria to be considered by the minister of justice in making an internment order, the powers of the advisory committee, and the standards of review were all very vague. The only definite obligation was the duty of the minister of justice to ensure that every person detained under Regulation no. 21 was advised of the "right of appeal."[15]

The Committee on Emergency Legislation divided over the recommendation of this regulation. Some members of the committee believed a mechanism was necessary, should war come, for the immediate internment of individuals of "internationalist affiliation" likely to attempt to undermine the war effort. Other members were unwilling to recommend the regulation, believing it to be an unnecessary interference with individual liberty. The committee, in its report to the governor-in-council, attempted to draw the attention of cabinet to the division in its ranks over the propriety of this regulation by marking it with a black line in the margin. Cabinet could then "consider whether such a wide power should be assumed by the executive and also whether it is expedient to introduce this regulation at the outset of an emergency or whether its introduction should be postponed until it is known how the situation will develop."[16] Cabinet, if it considered the matter at all, decided to let the recommendation stand as it was.

Regulation no. 39 made it an offence to spread reports "by word of mouth" or make statements, false or otherwise, intended or likely to cause disaffection to His Majesty or to interfere with the war effort or to prejudice relations with foreign powers. It was also an offence under this regulation to spread reports or make statements, again false or otherwise, intended or likely to prejudice the recruiting, training, discipline, or administration of the Armed Forces. A rather blunt piece of regulatory drafting, this particular regulation made no provision for criticism of the government in good faith. Nor did it provide for the defence of the truth. As with Regulation no. 21, enforcement of Regulation no. 39 presented ample opportunity for, and the possibility of, executive abuse. Not everyone, of course, saw it this way. In an editorial praising the first conviction under this regulation, the *Globe and Mail* declared: "Freedom of speech must be curtailed when the nation is at war." What use was there, the editorial asked, of fighting enemies overseas if enemies here at home were given a free hand?[17]

Three of the enforcement provisions of the Defence of Canada Regulations added to these particular concerns. The first, Regulation no. 58(2), granted to any "senior police officer," or any person authorized by the minister of justice, the authority to conduct a search without a warrant obtained from a justice of the peace.[18] All a constable or designated person had to do was prepare a written search order in his own hand. This regulation provided for the possibility of virtually unfettered and unreviewed police access to every Canadian home. The second, Regulation no. 62(2), allowed for the prosecution to request a closed trial.[19] While the application for the closed trial had to be made on the grounds that publication of any evidence would assist the enemy or jeopardize public safety or the efficient prosecution of the war, the scope of these three criteria was left undefined. The potential impact of this regulation was modified, however, by a requirement that sentencing take place, in every case, in public. This eliminated any possibility of secret trials, with the accused disappearing into the night, although with Regulation no. 21 on the books there was, needless to say, no need for any secret trials. The third of these questionable enforcement provisions, Regulation no. 63, made breach of the Defence of Canada Regulations a hybrid offence, meaning that the Crown had the choice to proceed summarily, with a lesser maximum fine and prison sentence, or by indictment, with the possibility of more serious penalties.[20] However, unless the Crown proceeded by indictment, the accused would be denied the option of a jury trial. There was a reasonable likelihood that some accused charged with breaching Regulation no. 39, for example, would want his conduct judged by a jury of their peers, not by a provincial magistrate or police-court judge.[21]

The other sections of the Defence of Canada Regulations that deserve mention are nos. 24, 25, and 26, which provided for the registration of enemy aliens, for their internment in specified circumstances, and for their appeal from internment orders. While Regulation no. 24 proclaimed that enemy aliens in Canada, "so long as they peacefully pursue their ordinary avocations, shall be accorded the respect and consideration due to peaceful and law abiding citizens," there was, in fact, significant scope under what amounted to a miniature criminal code for interference with their ordinary activities.[22]

Who were the enemy aliens? They were the nationals of countries with which Canada was at war. In September 1939 this meant German and Austrian citizens. Nationals from other countries would, from time to time, be added to this list, and these men and women were required to register with the registrar of enemy aliens. Approximately 100 000 people had to register and report, usually to their local postmaster. Following registration, more than 20 000 enemy aliens of unquestionable loyalty were exempted from the regulations. The remainder were required to report monthly to one of 3000 reporting offices for endorsement of their parole certificates. While the authorities had broad powers to intern enemy aliens, by and large this power was not widely used. There was an initial round-up at the start of the war and another dragnet nine months later. However, relative to the overall number of designated enemy aliens in the country, few were actually interned, and their numbers decreased steadily throughout the war.[23]

Neither those Defence of Canada Regulations providing for the registration and possible internment of enemy aliens nor any of the other regulations were debated during the special war session of Parliament. Significantly, some of these regulations were amended soon after the start of the war, and, one way or another, almost all of them underwent some modification during the six war years.[24]

One of the first amendments to the regulations was a positive one. It replaced the two civil servants on the Regulation no. 21 advisory committees with a judge or former judge. If the committees were to exercise a quasi-judicial function, however limited, it was appropriate that they be headed by members of the judiciary, or, at the very least, not by civil servants appointed for that purpose by the minister of justice. The problem this amendment did not eliminate was that in practice these "committees" were committees of one—a judge, perhaps, but still someone appointed to the job by the minister of justice. A much less positive amendment was the change to Regulation no. 39 made on 27 September 1939, the first of several amendments the section would undergo. A new subsection was added to it, with the effect of broadening the provision by making it an offence to spread reports or to make statements "intended or likely" to be prejudicial to the safety of the state or the prosecution of the war.[25] It was not at all clear what reports or statements were intended to be caught by this amendment: its wording was ambiguous enough to result in its application to a wide variety of criticisms of the war, and it made no provision for the defence of truth. An almost identical, and equally deficient, regulation was soon added, making it an offence to do any of the prohibited things in Regulation no. 39(a), (b), and (c) by publication, in contrast to speech.[26] One immediate result of this amendment was closure of the Quebec French Communist newspaper, *Clarté*, in early October.

It is a general principle of the common law that for an accused to be found guilty of a criminal offence, he or she must not only commit the act in question, but must have the mental intent to commit that act. Persons found not guilty by reason of insanity, for example, are so found because, being insane, they do not have the mental intent to commit a crime. The Ontario Court of Appeal, however, ruled that it was not necessary, in a prosecution under Regulation no. 39, to prove any guilty intent. The case that came before the court, *Rex v. Stewart*, concerned the business manager of the English Communist Party newspaper, *The Clarion*, which was also closed. Douglas Stewart was charged with an offence under the regulations, namely with publishing materials likely to cause disaffection to His Majesty. At trial he argued that, as business manager, he knew nothing about the content of the newspaper, and so could not be guilty of an offence. In support of this argument, he pointed naturally enough to the language of the regulations, which described the offence as saying or publishing something "intended or likely" to cause disaffection. The regulation itself, Stewart argued, required the accused to have intended to do what he was charged with having done. Both the trial judge and the court of appeal disagreed. Commission of the act itself was sufficient for a conviction to properly result.[27] What this ruling meant, in effect, was that not only could one be charged and convicted for breaching this regulation quite inadvertently, but one could be convicted even if what one had said or published was true. These amendments, along with all the other regulations were, however, positively liberal compared with the proposed changes Justice Minister Lapointe recommended to the cabinet in mid-November.

Lapointe had become concerned that the regulations did not give him any power to deal with subversive groups. An analysis of the provisions makes it clear that they applied to individuals, and while hundreds of Canadian Nazis had been taken away to internment camps at the beginning of the war, their associations remained and activities continued. Initially, this lacuna in the regulations only caused limited concern. Domestic fascists were keeping to themselves, and for the first two months of the war the Communist Party was floundering, in part as the result of the breakdown in international communications and the consequent lack of instructions from the Soviet Union on what position to take on the world war. By early November this position had been clarified, and Communist associations became increasingly active in denouncing the "imperialist war," calling on the government to make peace, and, as Lapointe apparently told Prime Minister King, distributing anti-government literature.[28]

What the justice minister proposed, in a draft order-in-council that he submitted to the cabinet, can only be described as the recommended reenactment of the worst features of both section 98 of the Criminal Code and the Padlock Act in Quebec. As a memorandum prepared for O.D. Skelton put it, "if the purpose of the new Regulation is to facilitate a Nazi or Fascist revolution in this country, it is well designed.[29] This assessment could not have been more correct. The additional regulations Lapointe recommended were, simply put, dangerous, unnecessary, and extreme.

First the minister of justice suggested a procedure for outlawing groups and associations. Any association, organization, society, or corporation that suggested, advocated, encouraged, advised, or defended: 1) any governmental or industrial or economic change in Canada by any means that would or might be prejudicial to the safety of the state or the efficient prosecution of the war; 2) the establishment by unlawful means of a form or system of government not authorized by the British North America Act [BNA Act]; or 3) the principles of the German Communist Party, the Communist Party of Canada, the Communist International, or any other similar group, was, under this draft regulation, an unlawful association.

Clause 1 was far too broad. As drafted, it could apply to almost any activity the executive wished to suppress, such as a trade union threatening to strike and demanding profit-sharing, or it could apply to the policies of a legitimate political party, such as the Social Credit Party. Clause 2 was equally problematic. Communism may not be Canadians' preferred political ideology, but there is nothing in the BNA Act that forbids the establishment by democratic means of a communist government. Clause 3 might have carried more force if it had also banned the various domestic fascist groups. In the form submitted by Lapointe, it led to the inescapable conclusion that the government was pursuing a hard line on domestic communists, but going soft on fascists.

The draft regulation directed that the property of these unlawful associations, or of persons belonging to them, was to be forfeited to the Crown, without any warrant and with only the most limited provision for judicial review. It was an offence under Lapointe's proposal to be either a member or an officer of an unlawful association. Indeed, even a donation made on the street to a proscribed association was an offence under this regulation. Just as under section 98, it was an offence to attend a meeting of an unlawful association, with the burden of proving that one had not attended falling upon the accused rather than the Crown. And just like the Padlock Act, the draft regulation provided that it was also an offence to let premises to unlawful associations. The proposed regulation made only a minor change to the already broad search powers, with the effect of widening them even further. Instead of requiring a warrant for all searches, albeit one prepared by the police themselves, the new regulation granted the right of a warrantless search in cases where the police officer in question believed an offence was about to be committed.

Enactment of these draft regulations was, of course, a matter for cabinet to decide. Prime Minister King approved generally of the suppression of subversive activities and believed the communists, in particular, to be "our real enemies," but he also thought that Lapointe, in describing the dimensions of the problem, had gone too far and had, in fact, been won over by the RCMP, which reported directly to him. On 16 November 1939, Lapointe, who expected the regulations to obtain immediate council approval, learned that a decision on his proposal was to be delayed until the following cabinet meeting.[30]

In that meeting, held on 21 November 1939, there was considerable discussion about the new draft regulations. Lapointe argued adamantly in favour of the cabinet passing the regulations. King did not like the proposed regulations at all, but he liked even less the dissension the matter was causing within the cabinet and the increased isolation from his colleagues of Ernest Lapointe. One report after another analysing the recommended regulations confirmed King's own view that they were excessive. One government memorandum reported quite accurately that repression was not an effective means of dealing with the threat from either the left or the right.[31]

According to the memorandum, the regulations were "not consistent with the principles of the Canadian government, the traditions of the Canadian people, or the aims for which we are fighting in this war."[32] Moreover, the memorandum added, while dressed up as anti-communist in inspiration, the proposed regulations had plenty of scope for use against any group unfortunate enough to attract the wrath of the executive. "Already free discussion in Canada is blanketed and discouraged by fear of censorship, by colonialism, by the docility of our people."[33] There was no demonstrated need for the changes, and the regulations went far beyond the comparable provisions in Great Britain, a country so much closer to the front line of the war. Instead of a bill of rights, the memorandum concluded, "we are to have a string of 'verbotens.'"[34] The point the anonymous author of the memorandum was making could not have been more clear: the draft recommendations had no place in a free and democratic society in war or in peace.

Yet Lapointe persisted. "At Council, this afternoon," King again confided to his diary, following another meeting on the subject of the proposed regulations on 23 November 1939, "I saved an unpleasant situation by suggesting that we should wait until Parliament met before giving to the police more in the way of power to search on mere suspicion or without the warrant."[35] King did, however, agree to meet and discuss the matter further with Lapointe and the commissioner of the RCMP, S.T. Wood.

At this meeting Wood showed King some papers illustrating what had become, by this point in the war, the well-evidenced intention of the Communist Party to create disaffection for the war effort among Canadians. The papers also alleged plans by fascist organizations to sabotage strategic transportation facilities at Windsor and Welland, along the St. Lawrence River system, and at the Montreal airport. The evidence was apparently compelling to King, but he did not agree that a case for Lapointe's draft regulations had been made, and he told the two men as much. The prime minister agreed in principle to an amendment to the regulations with the effect of providing that an organization could be found guilty for any of the offences that then applied to individuals, but this was as far as he would go. Wood conceded that such an amendment would be sufficient, and Lapointe promised to consider the matter. One matter, however, that the justice minister was not disposed to consider was having a committee of the House of Commons study the regulations when Parliament returned. Lapointe was against the idea, to King's surprise. The minister of justice had, King later wrote, become quite "reactionary." This, King added, was the result of "nerve strain" and the justice minister's apparent inability to resist the demands of his officials.[36]...

His first attempt to bolster the regulations having failed, Lapointe decided to try again, and he wrote the prime minister toward the end of December 1939 to say that he had taken heed of the criticisms of the earlier draft regulations and had made some important changes.[37] Cabinet met to consider a new proposal in early January 1940.[38]

Regulation no. 58 was amended to prohibit warrantless searches. Henceforth all searches were to be authorized by a justice of the peace. The Censorship Regulations were revoked. Censorship would now be under the authority of the Defence of Canada Regulations, with the secretary of state continuing in his general supervisory role.[39] As the naming of particular groups and associations in Lapointe's first draft recommendations elicited some cabinet criticism, the minister of justice redrafted the regulations to allow him to achieve this same result less directly. The regulations now provided that when an officer of an association was convicted, on indictment, of breach of one of the regulations, it was within the discretion of the court to declare the association illegal. Why Lapointe thought that this change, which placed the responsibility for declaring groups and associations illegal in the hands of the court rather than those of the executive, was an improvement over the previous proposal is far from clear. While the War Measures Act gave the governor-in-council virtually unfettered power to protect national security while Canada was at war, the cabinet remained, at some level, accountable to Parliament and to the people. The same could not and cannot be said about appointed judges. But by this amendment Lapointe, and cabinet, had given them the power to declare associations of Canadian men and women illegal. Requiring judicial approval of searches is one thing; giving judges the power to declare formerly lawful organizations unlawful is quite another. The former seeks to restrict the exercise of state power in the name of individual freedom; the latter poses a direct threat to that freedom. The fact that the regulations provided for the appeal of any such declaration fell far short of removing this fatal flaw, for appeal—naturally—was to another appointed judge.

Lapointe was able to impose his unpopular views on the majority of his colleagues because King, out of personal regard for his justice minister, agreed. When [Postmaster-General] Chubby Power, who had not been able to attend the meeting at which the new regulations were actually passed, heard about it, he was enraged and went to see King, threatening to resign and protesting strongly the failure of council to refer the whole question of the Defence of Canada Regulations to the cabinet Committee on Legislation, which he chaired. King's view of Power was mixed. He admired his organizational and other political abilities, but deplored his drinking, which Power often allowed to interfere with his work. King did not, however, wish to lose the valuable Quebec City MP, and convinced him to stay on, taking responsibility for the matter having been dealt with while Power was away. He also told Power that while he privately agreed with Power's civil-liberties views, he could not oppose Lapointe, "who had been his right hand man ever since he became prime minister."[40] All of this seemed to satisfy the minister and King, as he happily wrote in his diary that night, was ultimately able to put Power in a good mood before sending him away.[41] A possible cabinet crisis had been averted, but at what cost? Only time would tell.

There were other amendments to the Defence of Canada Regulations during this period that passed without any controversy. In November 1939, Regulation no. 39B was enacted, providing that the consent of the attorney general of Canada, who is always the minister of justice, or the attorney general of one of the provinces, was a prerequisite to a prosecution under the Defence of Canada Regulations.[42] Passage of this particular amendment undoubtedly reduced administrative demands on the Department of Justice in Ottawa, as henceforth the provincial attorneys general, who were normally responsible for law enforcement in the provinces, could authorize prosecutions. But this very advantage could easily become a disadvantage and source of unfairness if, as a result, the regulations were unevenly enforced. One provincial attorney general might, for example, exercise greater vigilance than another. More seriously, this new regulation offered much room for abuse. If an attorney general, instead of the police, had the discretionary authority to lay or not lay a charge, what was to stop him from prosecuting some offenders but not others?

One amendment to the regulations that received almost universal support was order-in-council PC 146 passed on 17 January 1940. It provided that criticism in good faith of any government in Canada would constitute a legitimate defence in prosecutions under regulations 39 and 39A. The amendment came too late for prominent trade-unionist and First World War hero Charlie Millard, who was charged in early December 1939 with breach of Regulation no. 39. Millard had said that he expected a lot of men would join the Army because that was the only way they could be sure of eating properly. Millard magnified this crime by adding that "we should have democracy here in Canada before we go to Europe to defend it."[43] The amendment, however, failed to clarify whether guilty intent was necessary for a conviction under the regulation. And even as amended, this regulation still provided, by implication, that good-faith criticism of the war effort, if likely to cause disaffection, was a crime. Nevertheless, the amendment was a welcome one and it came just in time for the 1940 general election.

Notes

1. National Archives of Canada (NAC), MG 27, III, B10, Ernest Lapointe Papers, vol. 41, file 41, S.T. Wood to E. Lapointe, 25 Aug. 1939.
2. See NAC, MG26, J4, Mackenzie King Papers, vol. 230, file 2218, O.D. Skelton to W.L.M. King, 28 Aug. 1939. See also RCMP Report to Skelton of same date.
3. For a review, and scathing critique, of the government's policy of internment as applied to German Canadians, see Robert H. Keyserlingk, "'Agents within the Gates': The Search for Nazi Subversives in Canada during World War II," *Canadian Historical Review* 66 (June 1985): 211–39.
4. The single best collection of records relating to the work of the committee is to be found in NAC, Department of Finance Records, RG19 vol. 3535, file, Committee on Emergency Legislation.
5. The War Measures Act, *Revised Statutes of Canada*, 1927, c. 206. For a history of this act see F. Murray Greenwood, "The Drafting and Passage of the War Measures Act in 1914 and 1927: Object Lessons in the Need for Vigilance" (unpublished paper, June 1987).
6. *First Report*, Committee on Emergency Legislation, July 1939 (Ottawa: King's Printer, 1939).
7. Cabinet minutes were not taken until February 1944. The Cabinet War Committee took minutes (although it did not begin to meet regularly until May 1940), but there is no evidence, from this period, indicating any discussion of the Defence of Canada Regulations. See King Papers, vol. 424, Minutes of the Cabinet War Committee, Aug. and Sept. 1939.
8. Order-in-council PC 2483.

9. For one of the few early protests against the Canadian regulations see Canadian Civil Liberties Union, Montreal Branch, "The War and Civil Liberty" (Montreal, n.d. [c. Oct. 1939]). Similarly, in Britain, although there was opportunity for debate, the comparable regulations passed without dissent. Even the arrival of a lawyer from the National Council for Civil Liberties with amendments in hand failed to arouse many members of Parliament or attract their support. See Ronald Kidd, *British Liberty in Danger* (London: Lawrence & Wishart Ltd., 1940), 194. For information about wartime emergency legislation in the United Kingdom see also *Annual Survey of English Law, 1939* (London: Sweet & Marshall Ltd., 1940).
10. *Globe and Mail*, 9 Sept. 1939 and 21 Sept. 1939. Section 98 was a draconian part of the Criminal Code and was dropped in 1936.
11. Specific censorship regulations were passed on 1 September 1939, also pursuant to the War Measures Act. These regulations were revoked on 22 January 1940 by PC 254 and from that point forward the regulatory basis for censorship was Defence of Canada Regulations, no. 15. The secretary of state, however, continued to exercise control over censorship. See King Papers, vol. 42, file, World War II, Chronology Internal Security, 1039–44.
12. *Defence of Canada Regulations*, 1939, Regulation no. 1 (Ottawa: King's Printer, 1939).
13. PC 4600, 7 June 1943.
14. Separate provision was made for enemy aliens in Regulation no. 24.
15. Regulation no. 22, Defence of Canada Regulations, Consolidation 1939.
16. *First Report*, Committee on Emergency Legislation, July 1939 (Ottawa: King's Printer, 1939), 7.
17. *Globe and Mail*, 23 Sept. 1939.
18. Regulation no. 58(2), Defence of Canada Regulations, Consolidation 1939.
19. Regulation no. 62(2), ibid.
20. Regulation no. 63(2), ibid.
21. See King Papers, vol. 290, file 1940, Lab to Lawrson, J.W.P. to W.L.M. King, 27 Jan. 1940, re W.P.M. Kennedy.
22. Regulation no. 24(2), Defence of Canada Regulations, Consolidation 1939.
23. It is noteworthy that following the start of the war, applications for naturalization tripled from 700 or 800 a month to more than 2000. See "Topical Chronology of War Effort—Internal Security and Pubic Welfare" in King Papers, vol. 42, file PCO, Emergency Council and War Committee Minutes, 1939–40. It is also noteworthy that the number of enemy aliens who were actually required to register and report amounted to only a small percentage of the people who technically fit within the class of enemy aliens. By various orders-in-council, for example, PC 3623 of 14 November 1940, provision was made to reduce the number of enemy aliens registering and reporting. Furthermore, the reporting requirements were in almost all cases merely procedural. See House of Commons, *Debates*, 11 June 1940, 676. While the regulations did not provide that the person appointed to hear enemy-alien appeals had to be a judge, in practice this was the case, and the advisory committees that came into being appear to have had their release recommendations accepted and executed.

In most respects Canadian internal-security measures during the war were far more severe than those in Great Britain. The treatment of enemy aliens is the single exception. At the outbreak of war, for instance, the United Kingdom immediately interned some 600 enemy aliens, including some Jewish refugees. Canada interned fewer than 300 enemy aliens, although that number later increased. The critical difference, of course, was that the United Kingdom was literally swamped with German and other European refugees. Some of the enemy aliens interned in Britain were later sent to Canada. For one account of this see Eric Koch, *Deemed Suspect* (Toronto: Methuen, 1980). For an account of the Ukrainian experience see Thomas M. Prymak, *Maple Leaf and Trident: Ukrainian Canadians during the Second World War* (Toronto: Multicultural History Society of Ontario, 1988). See also Lester H. Phillips, "Canada's Internal Security," *Canadian Journal of Economics and Political Science* 12 (1946): 18–29, at 22, 27.

24. Reconstructing the amendments is much easier said than done. While consolidations of the regulations were published in 1939, 1940, 1941, and 1942, these consolidations were not published on a specific and consistent annual date; nor can one determine from direct examination of them when exactly a particular amendment was passed. To determine that, it is necessary to examine all the orders-in-council during this period. A multi-volume listing of all orders-in-council creating, amending, and deleting orders-in-council does exist, but it is not complete.
25. Regulation no. 22 was also amended. See House of Commons, *Debates*, 11 June 1940, 667.
26. Regulation no. 39A was passed by PC 2891 on 27 Sept. 1939.
27. *Rex v. Stewart*, [1940] *Ontario Weekly Notes*, 95. His sentence was, however, reduced on appeal. See *R. v. Stewart*, [1940] 1 Dominion Law Reports 689 (CA); *Canadian Forum* (April 1940), 20. See also House of Commons, *Debates*, 2 July 1942, 3890.

    In England the equivalent regulation not only required intent but also falsity in the statement made by the accused. In Canada the prosecutions under this regulation made it look more than a little ridiculous. Countless persons were sentenced to jail for drunken statements prejudicial to the war effort, a handful were remanded for mental examinations, and most were acquitted with a tongue-lashing from the magistrate hearing the case. For a partial list, see NAC, Special Committee on the Defence of Canada Regulations, RG14, acc. 84-5/384, box 2, file 53. See also *R. v. Bronny*, [1940] 3 *Western Weekly Reports* 423 (BC Court of Appeal).
28. King Papers, King Diary, 16 Nov. 1939.
29. "Memorandum for the Secretary of State," 20 Nov. 1939, King Papers, vol. 156, file 1381, Communism.
30. King Diary, 16 Nov. 1939.
31. "Proposed New Defence of Canada Regulations," 23 Nov. 1939, King Papers, vol. 155.
32. Ibid.
33. Ibid.
34. Ibid.
35. King Diary, 23 Nov. 1939.
36. Ibid., 24 Nov. 1939.
37. See Lapointe Papers, vol. 16, E. Lapointe to W.L.M. King, 20 Dec. 1939.
38. Following the meeting, amendments to the regulations were passed by PC 37, 4 Jan. 1940.
39. King Papers, vol. 42, file World War II, Chronology Internal Security, 1939–44.
40. Norman Ward, ed., *A Party Politician: The Memoirs of Chubby Power* (Toronto: Macmillan, 1966), 375.
41. King Diary, 4 Jan. 1940.
42. PC 3139, 11 Nov. 1939.
43. Ramsay Cook, "Canadian Liberalism in Wartime: A Study of the Defence of

Canada Regulations and Some Canadian Attitudes to Civil Liberties in Wartime, 1939–1945" (MA thesis, Queen's University, 1955), 179. The amendment to the regulation regarding good-faith criticism did not necessarily mean that free speech was restored. See *R. v. Coffin,* [1940] 2 *Western Weekly Reports* 592 (Alta. Police Ct.).

On amendments to the Censorship Regulations see King Papers, vol. 352, file 3794, World War Two Censorship; PC 254 on 22 Jan. 1940; Phillips, "Canada's Internal Security," 23.

The rhetoric of war emphasized equality of sacrifice and collective effort for the common good. Not all Canadians, however, were willing to join the crusade, as the existence of a flourishing black market clearly showed.

One for All or All for One: Black Marketing in Canada, 1939–1947*

Jeff Keshen

If there was, as the American oral historian Studs Terkel wrote, a "good war,"[1] certainly it was the battle against Nazism. The popular images still reverberate: the "V" for victory sign, those wonderful swing bands, and, of course, the idea that everyone pulled together to defeat an unquestionable evil. When thoughts turn to Canada's home front, similar memories dominate; undoubtedly stories of gouging and black marketing are not the first to be recalled. Indeed, since people here had to endure relatively few privations, it should have been easy for citizens to maintain loyal conduct. In Britain, where civilians managed with three ounces of beef per week, and where new clothes were practically unknown, the "spiv" who hung around docks and diverted goods to the underground economy was a more understandable occurrence.[2] Therefore, one cannot help but be struck when opening up the pages of Canada's wartime daily papers. For there, beside all the patriotic pledges, appear countless stories of the thousands unwilling to make small sacrifices and of those who exploited circumstances in the most mercenary manner to garner hefty, tax-free returns.

With the end of the "phoney war," Canada's military expenditures grew tremendously: from $60 million in 1939 to $2.5 billion three years later. Unemployment evaporated, and total

* The author would like to thank professors Douglas Owram, Paul Voisey, David Mills, and especially J.L. Granatstein for their critical commentary. Financial support for this research was provided by a Killam postdoctoral fellowship.

wages nearly doubled between 1938 and 1942. The combination of increased demand and the diversion of supplies from civilian to military requirements threatened to engender profiteering and destructive inflation. Indeed, from late August 1939 to October 1941, the Consumer Price Index (CPI) rose by 17.8 percent.[3]

A Wartime Prices and Trade Board (WPTB) had been created on 3 September 1939 to control such trends. By mid-1940, it set maximum rates for basic commodities such as wheat, and had established a division to control rent. In August 1941, its direction passed from the Department of Labour to Finance, and called in to replace the low-key Hector Mackinnon as chairman was Donald Gordon, an outspoken and rather charismatic mandarin from the Bank of Canada. That November, he implemented a comprehensive freeze. Prices were not to exceed the highest level charged during a four-week base period between 15 September and 11 October, while wages were pegged at levels prevailing on 15 November. A cost of living bonus amounting to 1 percent of wages, with a maximum of twenty-five cents per week for each one-point rise in the CPI, could be granted by the National War Labour Board. On a purely statistical level, the program was successful for the next four years; total inflation amounted to 2.8 percent.[4]

Dollar-a-year men from the business community were recruited to run WPTB departments. The rationale was that such people could plan most effectively, and garner compliance from fellow capitalists. Citizens also helped; having remembered or heard of high inflation during the Great War, all were eager to display their patriotism. There were, for example, 2000 women who volunteered with the Consumer's Branch to "list prices paid in the base period," and to point out any rise in costs or deterioration in quality.[5]

The WPTB maintained scrutiny over public opinion. "The head office of the [Information] Branch," wrote a former employee, "subscribed to 38 dailies and 21 weeklies."[6] Surveys by the Canadian Institute of Public Opinion were carefully studied, and the WPTB also commissioned some of its own polls. An advertising budget of $750 000 (1943) permitted the distribution of millions of pamphlets, posters, and other propagandistic paraphernalia. Assistance also came from the National Film Board (NFB) and War Information Board (WIB). So far as the WPTB was concerned, one of the WIB's more useful initiatives was the Rumour Clinic, which uncovered and then disputed potentially damaging scuttlebutt that was circulating on the streets.[7]

Such efforts no doubt played an important role in maintaining support for control programs throughout the war, and throughout the peacetime reconversion process. On the other hand, surveys also revealed that enthusiasm waned as the war lengthened. In December 1941, only one-quarter of Canadians thought the country was sacrificing enough for the war effort; by February 1943, when some, but not all ration orders had been introduced, only 45 percent supported the implementation of more restrictions.[8] With successful Royal Air Force attacks upon Germany, the failure of the Nazis to take Stalingrad, and the defeat of Rommel in North Africa, many Canadians, from their sheltered vantage point, envisaged victory around the corner, and concluded that extra suffering on their part would not alter the war's outcome. An October 1943 sampling of 309 Torontonians revealed that 84 percent believed that war with Japan would end within one year, while the figure for Germany was 57 percent.[9]

Some people were outspoken in their criticism of controls. When announcing the wage freeze, Prime Minister King dutifully praised organized labour for its co-operative attitude. While most workers did slog away as hard as ever, the wage ceiling, charged Trades and Labour Congress leader Tom Moore, represented "the longest step yet taken by any democracy toward the establishment of a totalitarian state."[10] Besides fuming over lack of representation on the WPTB, unions denounced the so-called static CPI. The forty-six items the CPI covered were supposedly incomplete, and increased taxation and the tendency of firms to eliminate sales were not reflected in official statistics.[11]

Taxation policy caused resentment in all classes, and convinced many Canadians that they were already sacrificing enough. During the Great War, Ottawa obtained 87 percent of revenue through nontaxable sources, but the greater mobilization of resources during this more mechanized conflict required unprecedented expenditures.[12] In 1940, the Rowell–Sirois Commission (a body created three years earlier to deal with Ottawa's inadequacy in combatting the effects of the Great Depression) recommended, among other things, that the federal government take over the collection of income and corporate taxes. While much of the commission's report was ignored, this idea was adopted in 1942, over the objection of several premiers. To finance the war, Ottawa used its new powers boldly.

Obviously, the wealthy were not happy with the tax structure, but those of more modest means were also not celebrating. Rather than focusing upon progressive tax policies, what caught the middle class's attention was the novelty of shelling out to Ottawa. Taxes were deducted from the pay cheques of those who earned at least $660 annual income for a single person, and $1200 for couples. As well, compulsory savings were applied, repayable after the war, consisting of 8 percent of taxable income for the unmarried and 10 percent for couples. Polls confirmed the average person's exasperation. Asked in 1943 why they sometimes stayed away from work, 39 percent of labourers gave as their reason the burden of taxes, which, they said, claimed too large a chunk out of each extra dollar earned.[13] Such people dismissed the fact that, in the aggregate, Canadians still had, even after taxes, more money than ever to spend. But after years of deprivation during the Depression, many desired a little enjoyment from their labours, and feared the finance department would deny them that opportunity. To sell goods on the sly for cash was, in part, an expression of protest against a tax system that had become, in the minds of many, something of an out-of-control monster.

Aware of such attitudes, Gordon adopted a rather cautious approach. He knew that many thought the board to be overbearing, with its numerous short decrees, and he tried not to heighten people's resentment. Even so, Gordon's image was affected, for he obtained the nickname of "price czar." While most Canadians appreciated his skilful administration, a number said he was power hungry. On more than one occasion, the chairman felt it necessary to remind citizens that ultimately both he and his department were "under the jurisdiction and control of a responsible Minister of the Crown, subject at all times to the people's will."[14]

The WPTB's approach was to indict black marketeers and tax evaders only when the offence was serious, and where conviction was practically guaranteed, so as to avoid charges of public harassment. Although it never became official policy, Gordon felt that "it might be a rule that persons over 75 years of age should never be prosecuted," because the public backlash would more than outweigh any benefits achieved. Moreover, he understood that people would balk at the creation of an elaborate Enforcement Branch, because its costs would likely exceed funds collected from fines. Conservative backbench MP John Diefenbaker even went so far as to suggest that the WPTB fire its thirty-five lawyers and 300 investigators, and use officials already paid by federal and provincial justice departments, as well as local constabularies.[15]

With such a paltry force, the WPTB was often compelled to ignore lesser offences. Between 1 September 1939 and 28 February 1946, a total of 23 416 people were convicted of breaking its many rules, of whom 253 were given jail terms. No doubt the figures could have been much higher. Not until 1943 did the WPTB enforce regulations with any vigour. Gordon felt it was wise to give people time to get accustomed to the provisions. That policy, a growing array of restrictions, along with war weariness, increased convictions from thirty-one between September 1939 and December 1941, to 1201 in 1942, 3663 in 1943, 4170 in 1944, and 4481 the following year—all inconsiderable figures when one notes that WPTB offices received approximately 35 000 complaints per month.[16] Of those convicted, most received relatively light penalties, considering that a $5000 fine and/or five years in prison were possible. For example, in May 1943, there were 433 successful prosecutions. Of these, 147 received fines of $25 or less, 170 were tagged with a penalty of $25–$100, 81 had to pay more than $100, and the rest served short jail terms.[17]

So long as the majority generally followed WPTB regulations, Gordon stuck by the cautious approach. Perhaps he was correct, especially since it was impossible to catch all perpetrators without creating something akin to a Gestapo. But his critics also had a point, because there were more than a few Canadians who, perhaps as a protest against taxation, or perhaps out of sheer greed, seized upon opportunities to make illegal profits.

The first problem faced by the WPTB, and one that bedeviled it throughout the war and postwar periods, involved rents. As more people flowed into cities for war-related jobs, the number of available living places decreased at an alarming rate.

Ottawa's response to the situation was drawn up by the deputy minister of finance, W.C. Clark, a man whose private-market philosophy guided Canada's housing policies well into the 1960s. The solution, argued Clark, lay not in a government takeover of the housing sector, which he predicted would discourage investment and capital formation; instead, the challenge was to create conditions to spur private-sector growth. Such an approach was articulated in the 1935 and 1938 National Housing Acts (NHA), which had the federal government co-operate with the Dominion Mortgage Insurance Association to reduce down-payment requirements and subsidize interest rates. However, during the Depression, few could afford to take advantage of the program, especially since mortgages were amortized over no more than ten years. By 1939, the number of government-assisted loans had not even hit the 5000 mark.[18]

Needless to say, the war made a bad situation worse. Between 1940 and 1943, about 300 000 Canadians moved from the countryside to urban centres and decent accommodation soon became rare. At a 1940 meeting of Canadian mayors held in Ottawa, the situation was already described as an "emergency," and a request was made for Ottawa to provide at least $30 million for the immediate construction of low-cost housing. Besides quantitative deficiencies, the quality of accommodation available promised nothing but disappointment to those searching for housing. For example, in 1941, 27 percent of homes in Montreal were described as "substandard."[19] Yet, to produce military supplies, the National Selective Service continued to arrange for the relocation of thousands to major manufacturing centres. These people, especially after gasoline rationing was introduced, were crammed into downtown cores so that they might make use of their public transportation systems.

Private developers were incapable of improving the situation. Given shortages of building supplies for civilian needs, house construction by 1943 hit an all-time low of 24 900 units. Assuming the average lifespan of a house was fifty years, a figure then accepted by Ottawa, it was necessary to construct 45 000 dwellings per annum just to maintain the prevailing inadequate stock.[20] To make matters worse, several home owners, especially in established neighbourhoods, refused to rent to newcomers, claiming that overcrowding produced disease, crime, and decreased property values. Others excluded children from their premises, considering them noisy and destructive. Sometimes, parents were forced to place their offspring in foster homes while they searched for accommodation.[21]

Severe congestion convinced people to accept pitiful living conditions. In Ottawa, 8000 extra civil servants, a good portion of whom were single women recruited for low-paying government secretarial jobs, enlarged the population that had been only 168 000. "The landladies knew the girls were green, and desperate to get settled" read an account that revealed how eight women were herded into one bedroom. As well, people throughout the BC interior and the Prairies were attracted to the Vancouver shipyards. Here, municipally sponsored surveys exposed cases such as that of a house with five bedrooms, two bathrooms, two toilet rooms, and forty-four residents.[22] The influx of Air Force personnel (and in many instances their families) into Calgary created a supply crisis by 1940. "We hear of one house," reported the Local Council of Women, "which sheltered 52 people—and provided only one bathroom for them." A 1943 investigation in Montreal discovered, as did inquiries elsewhere, people living in warehouses, garages, huts, factories, sheds, and five-foot high cellars.[23]

What was the federal government doing to alleviate this crisis? On 24 February 1941 it created Wartime Housing Incorporated, a Crown company whose task was to build prefabricated temporary structures for servicemen's families and war workers who relocated. Under the program, municipal governments supplied serviced lots to Ottawa for $1 each. With Deputy Minister of Finance Clark playing a key role in the direction of this enterprise, however, it fell far short of national needs. Private realty interests, he insisted, would be unable to play their critical role in the eventual postwar recovery if government-assisted housing emerged as a major competitor.[24] By the time hostilities had ceased, Wartime Housing had completed only 18 300 structures, all of which were intended as temporary. Although some city officials were loath to give up lots so cheaply, most still clamoured for far more government housing than they received.[25]

The WPTB responded to the housing crisis by setting up registries in more than thirty congested cities to match newcomers with accommodation. They managed to place 77 318 people by 1944, but during the same period over 300 000 new families were formed. In 1943, the number seeking housing on the Vancouver registry compared with rooms listed stood at 2371 to 15![26]

Obviously, conditions were ripe for those wanting to make a substantial amount of cash. People who did not need to be in the city could sell their homes for huge profits. During the first three years of the war, Toronto prices increased by approximately 50 percent, and following the influx of Americans into Edmonton to build the Alaska highway, talk circulated about 300 percent profits.[27]

Most, however, had jobs in the city and replacement accommodation was difficult to find. But home owners needed only to glance at the classified pages to see their other golden opportunity—renting. "Naval officer, wife, baby, urgently require small apt." and other such advertisements beckoned from newspapers. Many offered a "reward for information leading to an . . . apartment."[28] The more enterprising checked obituary columns or bribed undertakers for tips. In Saint John, New Brunswick, "veteran home seekers don't miss an angle," reported *Maclean's*. "A doctor or nurse attending a citizen who, according to the househunter's grapevine, is seriously ill, are amazed at the number of calls they get enquiring about the patient's condition."[29]

The WPTB tried to make clear its determination to prevent landlords from exploiting the situation. In January 1940, rents were frozen in Halifax, Kingston, and Calgary, all places that experienced an "invasion" of service personnel.[30] By September 1940, fifteen more communities were placed under rent control, and the next year, the system became nationwide, with rent rates of 2 January 1940 used as a limit. Rooms were to be registered with the board, and a description of their amenities and rent rate were provided. Accommodation let for the first time after the freeze had its rent set by a WPTB investigator hired from the real-estate sector.

There was, as might be expected, considerable opposition among landlords. Setting returns at levels prevailing in early 1940 was terribly unfair, they asserted, because it still reflected Depression-type conditions. Wages and prices, it was pointed out, had been permitted to rise for another twenty-two months. While government studies showed that only half of Canadian households could comfortably afford more than $25 a month in rent, many landlords continued to believe that "tenants [were] making large wages in war plants" and could certainly afford to pay more.[31]

Convinced that they had legitimate grievances, and with tax-free money in the offing, many took matters into their own hands. During the war, just over 2000 landlords were charged with breaking rent-control rules, a figure that would have risen much higher if Enforcement Branch personnel had been more plentiful and aggressive. Too harsh an approach from the outset, it was feared, would drive many landlords out of the rental business, thus exacerbating an already grave situation. Even if lessors were found guilty of misconduct, a typical fine ran to $50, an amount that had limited effect as a deterrent. As well, low arrest figures, explained a WPTB official, were attributable to the fact that "tenants were conscious of the shortage of shelter and were more anxious to retain possession of the space they occupied than to argue the rate." Many worried that if they refused to pay extra, they might end up like the Frickens, a family of six who, reported the *Toronto Star*, after losing their apartment, spent nights crammed into an automobile.[32] The WPTB promised it would protect those who lodged complaints, but many tenants were not so trusting. Some figured that the board's investigators, being former real-estate men, would side with landlords. In some cases they had a point. In May 1942, one official wrote with exasperation to the finance department about displaced tenants who aroused "false sympathy" because they had "nowhere to go."[33]

By citing government statistics, the WPTB congratulated itself on doing a marvellous job with rents. Whereas the CPI showed rates up 5.7 percent between August 1940 and September 1941, the figure for the next year was zero. Of course, the weakness of such numbers related to the many unrecorded transactions. "Landlords with the connivance of bureaucrats are calmly flouting all leases and ordinances," charged a tenant from Montreal, a city where over 80 percent of householders rented. "They do not seem to care one iota for the public who are suffering."[34]

To restrain such behaviour, the WPTB stepped up efforts to control rents and evictions. In December 1942, legislation was introduced stipulating that a landlord "could no longer evict . . . on the grounds that he needed the house . . . for a relative"—the exceptions being parents and children. If the eviction was accepted by authorities, not only was the family member required to sign a statement saying that he or she alone would use the premises, but under no circumstances could the landlord obtain monetary remuneration for the room for one year. The following October, the WPTB increased the period from notification to actual eviction from three to six months, and specified that the termination date fall between 30 September and 30 April. Key money, forced purchase of furniture, and any other forms of tribute to the landlord or a third party were outlawed.[35]

Those with accommodation enjoyed a little more security, but aggressive landlords still found ways to extort money. Eviction between May and October remained legal, and there were too few Enforcement Branch personnel to ensure that rooms vacated for a member of the landlord's immediate family did not generate income. Home owners could also evict for reasons of personality differences. In Edmonton, one couple who paid $35 monthly for half a house complained to the WPTB after twelve other tenants were admitted. Although the couple received a rent reduction of $2.50 a month upon the arrival of the new tenants, it must have hardly seemed worthwhile, since their protest against the overcrowding caused the landlord to cut off the hot water, have his children shout insults, and go to the police "complaining of unbearable noises."[36]

Tenants were not only defrauded out of rent, but sometimes they were forced to purchase decrepit furniture at inflated prices. Perhaps some renters derived consolation from the fact that many others were likewise cheated in this, as well as in a host of other ways. With the Department of Munitions and Supply requisitioning metals, wood, and many other basic materials for war purposes, a number of civilian goods became scarce. Between 1940 and 1943, furniture production dropped by 50 percent. During the same period, output of household refrigerators plunged from 53 161 to 358, while the number of washing machines being manufactured decreased from 117 512 to 13 200. To obtain new appliances, one needed a permit from the Controller of Supplies proving the old unit was unrepairable.[37]

Sometimes people coped with the situation by becoming experts in home repair. Neighbours were also known to co-operate when it came to washing or cooking a special meal. On the other hand, there were those who realized that, in addition to appliances, much of their old junk had become "tax-free gold." "Baby carriages, breakfast sets, kitchen cupboards, day beds and travelling bags are among the many articles wanted by *Star* readers," reported the paper to drum up business for its classified pages. "These things were advertised recently . . . with the results that the baby carriage was sold by half past two, the breakfast set, kitchen cupboard and day bed by quarter to three, and the travelling bag by 8 o'clock." Interestingly, most ads for such merchandise did not quote a price. This gouging became so bad, and so threatened the legitimacy of the price ceiling, that in 1943 the WPTB issued orders specifying a schedule of prices based upon the condition and age of the item.[38] But given the cumbersome nature of the regulation, along with a dearth of personnel to ensure its effective application, many continued to extract more than the legal maximum.

Of the myriad consumer durables sold under the table, the exchange of automobiles generated the most controversy. Civilian car production stood at 102 664 in 1940, but over the next three years only 11 966 automobiles rolled off assembly lines, almost half of which were reserved for physicians, police, and firefighters.[39] In setting prices for used cars, the WPTB stipulated 25 percent depreciation during the first year and 10 percent per annum thereafter. Needless to say, many ignored such guidelines and sold to fellow citizens for up to twice the official price. The real killing, so to speak, was made by auto dealerships. "Cash for your car, highest price paid" promised signs above huts in used-car lots.[40] The full price allowed, and usually a little more, was offered. Some people preferred selling at a dealership rather than taking out an ad to find someone to gouge. Dealers also obtained stock by sending agents out to the countryside. The agents bought from those whose potential market was not so strong. Besides the trick of reselling these cars for cash at above the ceiling price, other ploys included charging the legal price, but throwing in an $800 automobile rug. Off the record, some dealers explained that it was imperative they be compensated for the loss of the new-car market; however, many did much better than that, making up to $40 000 extra cash per month above declared profits.[41]

A black market in automobiles inevitably led to fraud in the tire market. Canada obtained much of its rubber from the Far East, and the declaration of war on Japan meant an end to this supply and the beginning of severe shortages.

Between 1941 and 1942, domestic tire output dropped from 3.8 to 2.9 million, but most of those produced were designated for the military. In May 1942, three civilian classifications were established for the acquisition of tires; most people needed a permit just to obtain used tires and inner tubes.[42]

With new tires fetching up to $70 each, and good used ones $40 on the black market, illegal private sales reached an estimated $40 000 in Toronto during the first eight months of 1943. There was also a notable increase in tire thefts. In Vancouver, the number of recorded thefts in May 1942 was 27, but by September the number had risen to 115.[43] Police in Montreal and Quebec City reported that gangs were swiping tires from parked cars; in this way, thieves even disabled several official automobiles at the Second Quebec Conference![44]

When gasoline rationing was instituted, people found more ways to cheat the system. In June 1940, Ottawa appointed an Oil Controller to encourage production and direct distribution. That August, additional gas pumps and storage tanks for retail purposes were prohibited. The following July, hours of sale at gas stations were restricted from 7 a.m. to 7 p.m., Monday through Saturday. Despite these measures and lowered speed limits, mounting war requirements made rationing necessary by 1 April 1942. Gas was sold in five-gallon units, and at each fill-up, the coupon book, in which the car owner's licence plate number was written, had to be presented to the attendant. Once again, people were divided into classes. The majority fell into category A, those whose cars were considered non-essential for their jobs. They received 120 gallons a year, enough to drive about 2000 miles.[45]

Many Canadians made the necessary lifestyle adjustments. "When the car goes out now the great thing is to make the trip count," wrote a Toronto wife to her husband overseas, the day after rationing was introduced. "So I visited the hair dresser, the grocery store, shoe repair shop, Heliconian Club [a woman's organization] . . . and mother's."[46]

There was more than enough bitterness to counterbalance such positive responses. Numerous citizens were not prepared to give up the convenience of their car. The supply situation could not be that serious, they figured, if tour guides were still allotted 120 gallons. Although there were no polls conducted in Canada about gas rationing, a December 1942 U.S. survey showed that among car owners, only 60 percent believed that rationing was necessary.[47]

Given limited support among the driving public, and outright hostility from many whose occupation required heavy use of petrol, cheating flourished. Charges were levied against farmers for selling extra "coloured" gas they received to run their equipment. Arrests mounted against people for siphoning fuel. One soldier recalled that at Camp Borden, near Barrie, Ontario, extra night picquets were established to thwart what was either civilian gasoline thieves or soldiers secretly selling petroleum.[48] As well, more newspaper stories appeared about gas stations being robbed not only of cash, but also ration coupons.[49]

Such thefts indicated that many service stations were accepting used, loose, and outdated ducats, especially if the patron offered a cash bonus. While not admitting their own guilt, a few station owners claimed that reduced hours of operation and the drop in demand due to rationing brought profits to dangerously low levels. "I find my business cut down to almost half," wrote one proprietor to Edmonton's mayor John Fry in a fruitless effort to get his licence fee for operating pumps reduced from $60.[50] Some station owners may well have turned to the black market just to get by, but the sheer volume of illegal sales made it clear that for others, unadulterated greed dominated. The Oil Controller estimated that gasoline rationing had reduced overall consumption by 5 percent in 1942, but it was also admitted that about 300 million gallons, or one-third of total deliveries to filling stations, escaped through black market sales.[51]

With numerous gas stations accepting loose coupons, counterfeiters appeared on the scene. Many business people viewed counterfeiters as saviours. For example, one freight-company owner on the verge of bankruptcy told his poker buddies about his woes. Then "Half an hour later there's a knock, and I let this fellow in, and his friend with him, and they've got a suitcase," he recalled. "He put it on the bed and opens it and there it is, full, with [what was believed to be forged] gasoline ration books. I guess you could say my eyes bugged out, and my brother [who was a business partner] ... let out a war whoop like he'd found the lost goldmine." One such operation in Montreal that was broken up during the summer of 1944 netted 320 000 coupons. Twelve more arrests that season recovered forged ducats capable of purchasing 7 million gallons![52]

Gasoline was not the only fuel that attracted such illegal practices. During the war, demand for coal increased about 10 percent per annum. Canada was in a relatively vulnerable position because prior to 1939 "considerable quantities of anthracite" were obtained from Great Britain, Belgium, Germany, the Netherlands, Indo-China, Russia, and Morocco. Military recruiters compounded matters by continuing to recruit volunteers from the pits until 1943, leaving 3800 vacancies in the coal industry.[53] As well, that year, opposition to wage ceilings produced mine strikes in Alberta and British Columbia. As the winter of 1943–44 approached, shortages affected several cities, and some rural schools closed temporarily due to an inability to heat classrooms.

Coal was not rationed by coupons since demand remained manageable except in colder months. Still, starting in October 1939, Ottawa appointed a Coal Administrator to ensure that military, industrial, and civilian needs were met—a task sometimes complicated by rapid population shifts. To minimize waste, people were instructed to clean furnaces regularly, seal windows, close off unused rooms, and not heat garages. For many, however, hoarding provided the answer to temporary shortages. "Many persons had extra bins built and now have them crammed," declared Toronto's Labour-Progressive alderman J.B. Salsberg. "I am not going to let them wallow in luxury while other families freeze."[54]

Coal companies, contended Salsberg, could reveal the names of hoarders, but as he and some others on council intimated, they, too, contributed to the problem. It became an unwritten rule in several cities that those who wanted coal had to pay extra either at the office, when ordering, or to the delivery man. "Many complaints have been made that drivers . . . have been gouging customers for extra charges which run as high as $1.25 a load," said *Saturday Night*. "Some are quite ready to dispense their fuel at the wrong house if back swish comes their way." Delivery men, who in some cases undoubtedly provided kickbacks to head office, were said to make "up to $200 a month from these extortions."[55]

Prospects for extra cash also flourished in the clothing trade. Shipping problems reduced supplies of cotton from Britain and of wool from Australia and New Zealand. The shortage was made critical by the need to produce new uniforms, bedding, and other such items for one million military personnel. Civilian consignments were closely monitored by both the War Industries Control Board and the WPTB. Manufacturers were told to emphasize work clothes, winter underwear, and children's apparel. To save material and obtain maximum output, styles were simplified. The production of bloomers, cloth-on-cloth designs, cuffs, double-breasted suits, and most fancy items were prohibited.[56]

Some citizens charged that businesses used standardization to make extra money. The elimination of frills, they claimed, should have lowered unit costs, but it seemed that all goods, no matter what their quality, were priced at the maximum ceiling. A Standards Branch was created in 1943 to stop this process, but the WPTB admitted that "it was very difficult to make a determination of a fair relationship between price and quality."[57] Complaints mounted, leading some to conclude that they might as well use any excess cash to obtain desired fashions via the black market, since Ottawa was unprepared to adequately police manufacturers. Queues that stretched for blocks outside department stores when goods such as silk stockings were received testified to the demand for stylish articles. People also believed that it was imperative to act fast to obtain as much decent clothing as possible, because soon the unassigned coupons at the back of ration books would be used to limit purchases, as in England.[58]

While some hoarded clothing, others made private arrangements with tailors who obtained illegal supplies of material. "Investigations revealed," read an RCMP report, "that an organization existed in the Halifax area which acted as receivers of cloth stolen by longshoremen." Items made on the sly invariably had cuffs, pleats, and other details. A number of buyers rationalized that such purchases might ultimately save cloth, since one would not be returning every few months to replace shoddy "standardized" apparel.[59]

No doubt the WPTB had reason for concern as the prospect of food rationing grew nearer. A poll released in November 1941 showed that 18 percent of the population laid away goods to protect themselves from anticipated shortages. When asked about the actions of others, 42.5 percent said that they knew of a "few people" who hoarded, while 56.5 percent said they were aware of "quite a few." Some merchants acted in advance of legis-lation by limiting consumer purchases, while others sold goods in short supply over the counter rather than by self-serve, not only to control hoarding, but also theft.[60] Formalized rationing promised to ensure that everyone would receive a fair share at the official ceiling price. That, at least, was the theory.

The Medicine Hat *News* assured readers that the vast majority of Canadians would "not resent the tightening of the belt another notch or two." The Calgary *Herald* took a different tack, arguing that "death and wounds are a sacrifice . . . rationing is just a pinprick," about which no citizen had the right to complain.[61]

While such sentiments were heartening, Ottawa remained cognizant of hoarders, whose activities increased as rumours of legislated quotas spread. In January 1942, voluntary rationing was applied to coffee, tea, and sugar: imported items in short supply due to the Nazi U-boat menace, and Japan's occupation of Java and the Philippines. It did not take long for people to grow apathetic about cutting back. Therefore, between 1 April and 21 December 1942, those items, plus butter and alcohol, had legal allotments established. On 27 May 1943, beef joined the list, and in September, preserves.

The rules governing rationing were printed on the inside cover of coupon books. Coupons had to be detached in front of storekeepers, whose job it was to ensure that the coupons had not expired and that they were the property of the bearer. Despite regulations and patriotic proclamations, countless people bent the rules to lessen their hardships. One of the most common activities that citizens regarded as harmless was trading coupons or rationed goods. Since the total quota was not surpassed, most viewed this as acceptable conduct. To little avail, the WPTB stressed that such trading broke the spirit of the regulations (and the law if coupons were exchanged) because people still exceeded their allotment of goods and, more important, pushed total demand for each commodity to the absolute maximum, thus making it more difficult to supply needs overseas.[62]

At the retail level, some grocers paid people for unused ration coupons, and then proceeded to sell those products to others above the regulated price. Such transactions were usually conducted with a well-known clientele that would not betray the grocers or undermine their ability to sell coupons and/or buy extra commodities. "I believe," wrote one discouraged

WPTB Enforcement Branch official, "that nearly every merchant is making a black market . . . with regular customers."[63]

Obviously, racketeers flourished because of the public's proclivity to cheat. A number of cases were uncovered, usually by the local postman or undertaker, of ration-book applications being filled in for dead family members.[64] Polls showed that about 20 percent admitted some "tolerance" for the black market. Their reasons were many. Complaints emanated from western Canada and the Maritimes that shortages were artificial, caused by WPTB administrators who procured for Ontario and Quebec far more goods than they required. Some justified their illegal purchases by citing rumours about military waste of so-called scarce resources. In major Quebec papers, the WIB's Rumour Clinic found it necessary to plant stories assuring people that "at army camps, quantities of food are not being tossed in garbage cans."[65] Then there were those who simply remained incredulous that in this country food shortages could exist. "Everyone has known for generations that food in Canada is abundant," said *Maclean's*. "The opinion persists unconsciously, and no mild and commonplace statements can change it." A January 1944 poll showed that only 39 percent believed it necessary to ration the things on which Ottawa had applied quotas.[66] If shortages did exist, many people maintained it was not due to excess demand, but to a price ceiling set so low that it discouraged output. Such people convinced themselves that they were actually helping to solve deficiencies by paying higher prices on the black market, and thus stimulating production. And finally, since rationing was imposed during a period when war news became more hopeful, cheating engendered less guilt because citizens concluded that their sacrifices would not change the war's outcome.

What foods were most prevalent on the black market? Cheating involving coffee and tea actually subsided by 1944 when shipping conditions improved. That year, individual rations were hiked 40 percent, and restaurants were permitted to serve unlimited quantities.[67] Black marketing of these commodities, and of sugar and preserves, paled in comparison to illegal transactions involving meat.

Those who raised cattle resented Ottawa's call that they produce more with less help. In addition, they viewed the price ceiling set for meat as unreasonable. Ranchers argued that during the Depression their returns had dipped to record lows, and that prices had not been given a chance to rise again before the freeze went into effect. Ottawa disagreed, noting that up to 30 June 1942, 60 percent of food-price increases were attributable to meat. As well, throughout much of 1942 the United States did not impose a price ceiling on beef, and when one was created, it was higher than in Canada. Therefore, record shipments of cattle went south, forcing Ottawa to impose an export embargo to secure Canadian and British supplies. Ranchers flooded the federal government with protests, demanding that either the domestic price be raised or the embargo lifted, and predicted black markets if neither transpired.[68]

While some ranchers held back stock, others, rather than absorbing extra costs, tried to smuggle steers and hogs to the United States. As well, a number slaughtered animals themselves, and distributed the meat (at illegal prices) to anyone passing by. Since gas rationing curtailed trips to the farms by city dwellers, far more ranchers sold livestock to black-market dealers, who resold the untagged meat to slaughterhouses. One report submitted to Parliament revealed that "the number of cattle shipped from western to eastern Canada increased in 1942; yet the number of inspected killings fell by 5.9 percent." There were "no records of uninspected killings," but estimates placed "the increase . . . at 100 percent."[69] Eventually, such beef ended up at butcher shops, where customers paid for all the illegal mark-ups, including that applied at the retail level.

By early 1943, black marketing of beef, either at the farm or at the wholesale, packing-house, or delivery levels, had become so widespread that many shops and restaurants reported an inability to obtain supplies unless extra was paid. "It seems no legitimate business man can carry on without [dealing on] the black market," complained a Montreal butcher to Donald Gordon. The A & P grocery chain, which refused to deal with meat racketeers, had to close five Ontario stores temporarily.[70]

With demand, both at home and abroad, continuing to rise, and with some ranchers holding back supplies, Ottawa responded with meat rationing on 27 May 1943. Coupons allowed the purchase of two pounds per week made up of various cuts, and this quantity could be supplemented by unlimited amounts of brains, heart, tongue, liver, tripe, sweetbreads, and pieces containing more than 50 percent bone.[71]

Countless Canadians responded to the moral imperative of feeding the less fortunate overseas and accepted the government's claim that their nutritional needs would be satisfied. Yet Prime Minister King realized that a battle still lay ahead. Asked in mid-1943 what product they found most difficult to cut back, most citizens named meat. A number of people who performed physically taxing jobs insisted that the allowed amounts of beef failed to provide enough energy. For the most part, Canadians bought to the ration limit for each family member, a trend that actually produced higher overall consumption levels than in the previous year.[72] Record amounts of fish and chicken were also purchased. In the case of the latter, surveys taken at restaurants showed demand up 25 percent, producing temporary shortages and black marketing in some parts of the country. And except on Tuesdays and Thursdays, the days meat-selling was illegal, thousands utilized their extra earnings and dined out as a way to squeeze more beef into their diet. Between 1942 and 1945, total expenditures at Canadian restaurants climbed from $157 million to $211 million.[73]

In March 1944, meat rationing was suspended due to a shipping bottleneck in Canada and to shortages of storage space overseas. When rescinding the ration order, Ottawa tried to impress its temporary nature upon the population. At the cessation of hostilities, it was emphasized, refugees would unquestionably require masses of food. Instead, to many, the halt confirmed that the war was winding down and that things would soon return to normal. In 1944, Canadians ate more beef than ever. Weekly per person consumption reached just over 3 pounds—approximately 40 percent higher than the 1935–39 average.[74] To Ottawa, such behaviour made clear that the implementation of postwar meat rationing would, at the very least, be problematic.

Black markets also existed for goods that helped relieve the stress of war, whether this stress resulted from anxiety over friends and family in khaki, or from longer hours at the factory. Between 1939 and 1944, cigarette consumption in Canada grew from 6.9 to 11.4 billion. Although some of this increase was due to stress and more ready money in civilian pockets, much of it was attributable to soldiers who, even during training, turned to smoking as a way to alleviate the extremes of tension and boredom associated with military life. Canteens provided cigarettes to those in uniform at a bargain price. Few begrudged soldiers this perk; indeed, families and charitable organizations ordered cartons at special rates for those overseas. But some controversy revolved around the use of labour to produce massive numbers of cigarettes for the civilian population. Ottawa attempted to reduce consumption by raising taxes to $10.50 per thousand by 1944. The tax was $4 per thousand before the war.[75] Thus revenue increased, but with demand refusing to subside, opportunity for unlawful transactions emerged.

Since cigarettes cost less in the United States, smuggling increased. A 1945 RCMP report revealed that "Customs and Excise Acts charges [for illegally importing cigarettes] reached the highest total since 1934 with 3226 seizures." Citizens were told that their complicity as buyers ultimately diverted supplies from Allied soldiers. It is safe to conclude, however, that such tactics had a limited impact, considering that the other chief source of illegal cigarettes was servicemen. At military bases across Canada, regimental orders told soldiers that "the sale of cigarettes at the special rate is for troops only and disciplinary action will be taken if the privilege is abused."[76] Still, many peddled this product as a way to fund their leave time. Moreover, on both of Canada's coasts, naval personnel sold supplies obtained in Newfoundland and in several American cities. There, canteens made up to 40 000 cigarettes available to each man at about 20 percent of the price civilians paid![77]

For alcohol, it became necessary to move beyond higher taxation to outright rationing, a decision the prime minister approached with trepidation. As a religious man, King abhorred excessive consumption, but he understood that beer, for example, was important to workers, especially in wartime, when long, hard shifts became the norm. Since organized labour was already upset over wage controls and the absence (until 1944) of federal legislation guaranteeing union recognition, King balked at undertaking another measure that might expedite their migration to the increasingly popular Co-operative Commonwealth Federation (CCF).

Nevertheless, certain facts had to be faced. Between 1939 and 1942, spirit consumption in Canada rose from 3 433 064 to 4 348 440 gallons. Beer consumption soared from 63 302 752 to 89 505 475 gallons. At first, just as with cigarettes, the government raised taxes. By 1942, a $3.50 bottle of rye netted Ottawa $2.70.[78]

It soon became apparent that increased taxation had failed to quench the population's thirst. Pressure on King to copy Canada's 1917 prohibition order and to requisition alcohol for the production of explosives increased. Liquor, it was also argued, fostered absenteeism at a time when maximum output was required. As one might expect, temperance associations and church groups were most vocal in this campaign. For instance, Dr. Ernest Marshall of Winnipeg's Westminster United Church reminded King "that France which collapsed in 1940 had the highest per capita consumption in the world."[79]

Ottawa's decision in mid-1942 to ration sugar convinced more people that the diversion of 11 million pounds to distilleries was immoral. King proposed alcohol restrictions to caucus that August, but still found "little enthusiasm." This was especially true among Quebec MPs, who realized that newspapers in the province received much of their advertising revenue from liquor companies. They, and other Liberal Party members, argued for yet higher taxation, a plan rejected by King, not only due to its previous ineffectiveness, but also because it might produce large-scale bootlegging.[80] However, the prime minister's course became clear that November when Washington appropriated most U.S. alcohol production to make munitions. King was not prepared to permit Canada to become, as it was during the 1920s, a base for rum-running operations. Nevertheless, before making any announcement, the politically coy prime minister waited until by-elections were completed in Winnipeg and Montreal. He was aware of surveys conducted in late 1942 showing that only 37 percent of Canadians supported prohibition, something a rationing scheme might soon engender.[81]

On 16 December Ottawa's plan was finally presented. Typical of King, it was one of compromise. In describing his strategy to an aide, he said that "an intelligent approach . . . would take cognizance . . . of drinking habits since the war began." Therefore, 1942 rather than an earlier year was used as a base for determining quotas. The goal was to reduce spirit consumption by 30 percent, wine by 20 percent, and that most savoured of all beverages, beer, by just 10 percent. Each month, Canadians twenty-one years and older were permitted to purchase one case of beer, forty ounces of spirits, and four bottles of wine. Frequently, however, such quantities were unavailable. At one point during the war, only twelve ounces of spirits could be procured per month by each Ontarian, through legal channels.[82]

Provincial liquor stores, hotels, and other places where alcohol was available were asked to open no more than eight hours daily. Following a six-week adjustment period, liquor advertising was outlawed, a move that King had hesitated to make. However, because most English-speaking provinces had already imposed such a measure, and in light of his "soft" stand on conscription, the prime minister knew that it was politically untenable that he be perceived as giving Quebec more special treatment.[83]

The result was widespread anger. The Montreal *Gazette*, one of many Quebec dailies that lost advertising revenue, claimed that liquor companies provided a key source of tax revenue. The Hotel and Club Employees Union denounced the restrictions, especially against beer, as class-based legislation likely to cause job losses.[84] Some sources expressed doubt about the order being successful. "The bootleggers will be back among us like swarming flies," predicted the Calgary *Herald*. If the American experience was anything to go by, Ottawa could expect problems. Within two weeks of Washington's directive confiscating alcohol supplies, reports came in about liquor trucks being held up along highways and of bathtub gin making a strong comeback.[85]

At liquor outlets across Canada, lineups stretched for blocks as everyone seemed determined to get their promised allotment—especially since establishments often ran short. A 1945 poll showed that during the previous two years, the number of Canadians who "used alcohol" jumped from 59 to 64 percent. On Vancouver's Pender Street, several merchants complained that customers could not get near their stores due to the crowds outside places nearby selling liquor. There, and in other cities, police stood by not only to keep people orderly, but also to prevent the robbery of those leaving with their allowance of intoxicants.[86]

For teetotallers and those not prepared to battle queues, there was the option of scalping coupons for about $3 each. One report issued by the Vancouver police claimed that so-called rings were acquiring up to 1500 bottles of spirits monthly through such purchases, a haul worth about $15 000–$20 000 on the black market.[87]

In frustration, some people sought out black-market booze, for which they paid as much as five times the legal price. Some supplies were maintained by the increase in thefts from trucks and warehouses. Between 1939 and 1944, alcohol-related convictions (excluding drunkenness) grew by approximately 30 percent to just over 12 000. Many of those charged made moonshine, which was sold in massive quantities since its price was lower than legal liquor's, and its potency was higher. Buying such stock, however, carried risks. Some confiscated liquor was discovered to contain shaving cream and shoe polish, the taste of which was camouflaged by ingredients like lemon extract.[88]

Antagonism from organized labour groups to liquor rationing refused to abate. In March 1943, signs mysteriously appeared in Vancouver shipyards warning "No Beer, No [Victory] Bonds." That May, *Maclean's* reported that "some Members [of Parliament] were loathe to go home at Easter recess without more beer for thirsty warworkers."[89]

The need for explosives prevented King from reversing the policy, but the shrewd Liberal leader believed that it was possible to compromise. In 1944, he announced a number of social welfare programs to undermine labour support for the CCF; perhaps his decision on 13 March to end the 10 percent cutback in beer output and to allow the provinces to decide whether or not to ration the product was in the same vein. Black marketing of spirits remained a part of wartime Canada, but after Ottawa relented on beer rations, criticism, particularly from labour, declined substantially.

By the end of 1945, liquor supplies approached normal levels, although rationing still remained in effect for a few more months. As the first postwar Christmas approached, 30 000 people poured through Toronto's liquor stores daily, and police were also called out to manage crowds in Winnipeg, Montreal, and Vancouver. However, everyone remained orderly and perhaps even cheerful because they obtained promised quotas. Thus ended this type of black market activity.[90]

While the liquor situation improved relatively quickly after the war, stabilization took longer for other commodities. Ottawa was aware that this could pose problems. A 1944 sampling disclosed that with $6.5 billion in citizens' total savings, 21 percent of people planned to buy a new car, 13 percent a new home, and 22 percent a major appliance at their first opportunity following the cessation of hostilities.[91]

A major propaganda initiative, which was started in 1944 and carried on after the war, tried to convince Canadians to demonstrate patience, warning that they might win the war only to lose the peace. People were reminded that following the November 1918 armistice, the lack of government controls released a buying frenzy, which in turn produced a cycle of rapid inflation, followed by overproduction, deflation, and high unemployment.[92]

Public pronouncements and polls provided some encouragement to authorities. "If with the peace we imagine that the price ceiling . . . can [be] cast aside, we shall be tragically mistaken," wrote the Ottawa *Journal*. It was pointed out that under the WPTB's guidance, Canada's wartime inflation rate remained lower than that of the other Allies. Surveys in early 1946 showed that about three-quarters of those polled still believed that "some price controls" were a "good thing."[93] Such an opinion was probably buoyed by figures from the U.S. There the Office of Price Administration removed ceilings faster, producing an 18.6 percent rise in the CPI during the twelve months following Japan's surrender. A more cautious Canadian approach generated a figure of 5.4 percent.[94]

Still, the federal government realized that it was imperative to wind up controls over consumer goods expeditiously. Canadians wanted to avoid high postwar inflation, but businesses were clamouring for greater profits, labour for better wages, and all walks of life were loath to wait too long before enjoying the fruits of victory. WIB officials predicted that within ninety days of Germany's surrender, "C-Day—Complacency Day" would arrive.[95]

To shorten the reconversion process, starting in 1943 the Department of Munitions and Supply directed that some industries that had been placed on a war footing switch a few production lines back to nonmilitary manufacture. As victories overseas mounted, this procedure intensified. Under the guidance of C.D. Howe, who was appointed reconstruction minister by war's end, low-interest loans were extended to businesses for the purchase of new machinery that could be written off faster as a result of Ottawa's new policy allowing accelerated depreciation.[96]

Following the war, the WPTB, operating under the National Emergency Transition Powers Act, decontrolled items as soon as it believed that supplies had reached levels at which the removal of the ceiling would not create significant inflation. By February 1946, about 300 products, such as firearms, jewelery, and a variety of services were decontrolled.[97] However, not until 1947 did many big-ticket items that Canadians craved join the list. The delay was produced in part by major strikes of the previous summer, like the steel-sector strike.

Since it proved difficult to convince everyone to stop cheating during wartime, obviously compliance was less than perfect after the conflict. Illegal transactions in used appliances, cars, and furniture continued to flourish. Perhaps what now made gouging especially odious was that veterans were often the victims. Many citizens viewed ex-servicemen as fair game, especially since the government provided them with generous gratuities. A private returning home after three years overseas was given $720, a Rehabilitation Grant of one month's pay, and a Re-establishment Credit amounting to about $200.

Before repatriation, troops received lectures on civilian scams, and the NFB supplied a five-minute movie entitled *Goodbye Mr. Gyp,* which was a "warning in humorous cartoons of some of the ways in which the veteran may be swindled by unscrupulous people." By February 1946, the *Toronto Telegram* claimed that 750 schemes had been recorded by police.[98] For instance, used tables, worth perhaps fifty cents before the war, were sold to ex-servicemen for $10. In 1946, one junk dealer, who did most of his business with veterans, made $26 000.[99]

Another challenge lay in convincing Canadians to accept postwar food rationing. "Bombs and shells have ceased," went one WPTB appeal, but Europeans were still "stalked by death from hunger." There were costs, citizens were warned, for refusing to respond. "If we expect to get a fair share of those products in which Canada is in short supply," explained the deputy minister of agriculture, "then we must be prepared to make a contribution of those foods which we have in abundance." As well, aiding the political and social stability of postwar Europe by continued sacrifice was presented as being in Canadians' interest. From a desperate population might well come another Hitler or Mussolini. Moreover, as a trading nation, Canada would benefit tremendously from revitalized European markets.[100]

The first postwar tests were made with butter and sugar, both of which in mid-1945 had their civilian quotas cut by 20 percent. In Quebec, the newspapers *La Tribune* and *L'Action Catholique* supported cutbacks in the amount of butter allowed to civilians, since some of the surplus could help to feed the starving. On the other hand, the Quebec City municipal council went on record as expressing opposition, especially since Ottawa, fearful about angering rural Canada even more, balked at legalizing the sale of margarine.[101] Black marketing was reported not only in Quebec, but also in Toronto, where one grocer informed the WPTB about "a truckload" of butter brought to the city each Monday from the countryside that was sold for well above the ceiling price. From Saint John in late 1945 came rumours of corruption involving the distribution of sugar. These illegalities, however, faded in comparison to those in Montreal, where counterfeiters were discovered poised to sell 800 000 sugar coupons.[102]

Still, the greatest headache for the WPTB involved illegal dealings in the beef market. In February 1945, Norman Robertson, the undersecretary of state for external affairs, informed the prime minister that the Allies' Combined Food Board predicted "a global shortage of approximately 3 600 000 000 pounds of meat . . . and that extraordinary measures on the part of supplying countries may be required." Canada's ability to resist calls for cutbacks were tenuous. Despite having increased beef and pork exports during the conflict, its per capita meat consumption rose substantively between 1939 and 1944, and even under rationing, each Canadian ate more beef than civilians in other Allied nations. Nonetheless, King dawdled, aware of surveys released in early 1945 showing that only half of Quebeckers supported postwar rationing of beef. There, many interpreted such a plan as yet another example of English Canada kowtowing to Britain.[103] "The general tenor," read a WPTB report, "was that the United Kingdom was not buying meat in the Argentine because she could get it 'for nothing' in Canada." The WIB's Rumour Clinic rebutted that, while Britain did indeed purchase much of its Canadian beef on credit, the price charged was actually higher than in South America. Elsewhere, support was better, but not overwhelming. Many English Canadians were not prepared to accept that some beef might end up in Germany.[104] Given such views, King agreed with advice tendered by the ninety-nine-year-old William Mulock, the former postmaster general in the Laurier government. "If rationing [of meat] is introduced now," he said that spring, "we might as well 'write off' chances of winning the election."[105]

Only after having secured another parliamentary majority that June was King ready to act. In August, meatless Tuesdays and Fridays (to satisfy Catholics, who said the previous order stipulating Tuesdays and Thursdays was discriminatory) were introduced. A temporary shortage of cold-storage space and the need to prepare coupons delayed the general ration order for another month. Once again, each Canadian was allowed two pounds of meat per week, an allotment, they were told, that exceeded the allowance in France by twenty times.[106]

Of all black market activities, the most enduring involved rental rates. Ottawa's antipathy to socially assisted accommodation meant that Wartime Housing played a minor role in solving the postwar supply crisis. The 8902 units it completed between 1944 and 1946 were simply not sufficient for the 620 000 veterans who were demobilized by June 1946, 40 000 of whom had married overseas. In Edmonton, "fortunate" servicemen and their families settled in abandoned American army barracks disassembled and transported by Wartime Housing from Dawson Creek.[107]

It was impossible, though, for the federal government to ignore the dilemma. A 1944 subcommittee set up under C.A. Curtis recommended a nationally administered public housing program to construct, during the first postwar decade, 750 000 dwellings. The response from politicians, however, adhered to patterns established in 1935. The 1944 NHA once again had Ottawa co-operate with private lenders to make mortgages more affordable. Prospective buyers could get a home costing up to $4000 for 10 percent down, and a twenty-year term fixed at 4.5 percent interest, thus producing monthly payments of $22.61.[108] The next year, a Central (later renamed Canada) Mortgage and Housing Corporation (CMHC) was created to administer funds supplied by Ottawa. Criticisms were registered: Winnipeg's municipal council contended that few homes could be constructed for $4000. In lieu of public housing, it demanded forty-year mortgages at 3.5 percent.[109]

Only time would reveal the wisdom or folly of Ottawa's approach. For the short term, however, pressing matters had to be addressed. In 1944, the WPTB set up Emergency Shelter Administrations in several cities. They co-ordinated with churches and community groups to find temporary accommodation, and designated some public buildings as living quarters. As well, a permit system was introduced to prevent civilians from migrating to designated cities unless they already had a formal job offer. Although the threat was practically unenforceable, it was believed that full-page newspaper advertisements warning people to stay away from Halifax, Vancouver, New Westminster, Victoria, Toronto, Ottawa, Hull, Hamilton, and Winnipeg might ease the worst crises.[110]

The most significant initiative was eviction control. As 1 May 1944 approached, over 5000 termination notices were pending in Montreal. Local newspapers predicted widespread homelessness, and a newly formed and quickly growing citywide tenants' association threatened a series of massive demonstrations. With a provincial election in the near future, King hesitated to further upset the political feeling in Quebec. The result was a one-year moratorium on evictions in cities identified as congested.

The moratorium scared some potential landlords out of the rental business, but for those who remained, the growing gap between supply and demand provided considerable leverage. They could still evict on the charge of tenant unruliness. Many renters were unwilling to take the chance of being thus evicted, so they made supplementary payments. Obviously, the situation was worse for those still searching for a place to live, such as the 50 percent of soldiers who, military surveys revealed, had no shelter arranged upon their return. A number of civilians tried to help, not only by opening up their own homes, but by establishing veterans' registries in several communities.

Such efforts, while commendable, hardly made a dent in the number who still needed housing. In Ottawa, for example, a two-day publicity campaign produced just six rooms. While this result was partly attributable to a bona fide scarcity of space, it was also true that numerous civilians had decided to seize the moment, just as they had with sales of unused furniture to veterans. Inquiries in Montreal and Halifax revealed dingy, tiny flats garnering $70 a month from soldiers.[111] In Edmonton, one ex-serviceman joked that landladies must have "attended night school classes to learn how to be mean." And, as a Winnipeg veteran recalled, there were other civilians who managed to hitch a ride on this gravy train.

> I'd go down to the *Free Press* building and when the edition came off, I'd grab one from the kid who was selling them at the door. . . . There was always fifteen or more . . . [taxis] swarming around. . . . There they'd be, lined up like a bunch of vultures. They didn't use the meter. . . . They drove you to where you were looking . . . and then they'd ask for four dollars. . . . They were gouging the troops . . . but you had to fork over. . . .[112]

If the new Department of Veterans Affairs had not provided generous benefits, resentment among soldiers over housing may well have precipitated a serious threat to social order. Signs of this were evident in Vancouver. Probably because of its mild climate and aesthetic appeal, thousands of troops who had passed through the city during the conflict decided to resettle there after the war. But in April 1945, Vancouver, with its population of 309 000, had "reasonable" accommodation for 225 000. Faced with a near-impossible search for decent shelter, in January 1946, 300 veterans occupied the Hotel Vancouver, which was slated for demolition. Heading up their list of demands to Ottawa was the approval of construction of 250 000 public-housing units.[113] Although condemned by some as Communists, overall the veterans received considerable public sympathy. Within a month, the crisis ended. The federal and municipal governments agreed to turn the premises, at least temporarily, into a hostel. This arrangement lasted until 1948, when it was decided that the housing situation had improved to the point where most could find shelter.[114] By the late 1940s, Ottawa eliminated federal rent controls, arguing, somewhat contradictorily, that not only had the accommodation crisis eased, but that it was imperative that prices rise to stimulate further construction.

For citizens who were asked to make relatively few sacrifices, the amount of cheating in wartime Canada was certainly noteworthy. Perhaps the explanation for this lies in the distant nature of most war horrors. More than a few soldiers returning home observed that the war appeared to exert little impact upon the daily lives of civilians. Certainly they read of battles and suffering overseas, but it was quite another thing to witness first-hand its magnitude. Relative isolation allowed Canadians the luxury to dwell upon and complain about wage ceilings, taxes, and compulsory savings, and explains why it took only a few victories in 1943 to convince so many that hostilities would soon end. Canadians were not inherently selfish (at least not more or less than others), but to many, war remained a far-off event. With little concrete evidence to make them understand the need to cut back, more than a few felt little compunction about eating that extra steak or obtaining a double-breasted suit.

To keep people in line, Donald Gordon was probably correct in relying more upon propaganda than tough enforcement. Citizens were not prepared to accept a "police state," and it was, the WPTB chief knew, practically impossible to track down and prosecute every petty criminal. Unfortunately, there was no shortage of businesses and private citizens willing to take advantage of lax enforcement. Landlords and ranchers justified their actions by citing what they believed were legitimate grievances, but for others, like counterfeiters and various scam artists, barefaced avarice served as the sole motivation.

Canadians are rightfully proud of their nation's record of service in the Second World War. The story is told through images of tragic heroism at Dieppe, and of the bloody triumphs at Ortona, Juno Beach, and the Scheldt. The home-front picture shows everyone pitching in to back the attack. Perhaps a little ration-coupon trading *was* admitted, but never anything akin to disloyalty. There is much truth to this idealized characterization; to varying degrees, most citizens sacrificed their lifestyles, and sometimes a son or spouse, to help win the war. But buried deeper in the collective memory are images of those tens of thousands who, rather than uniting with fellow Canadians in common cause, chose to serve themselves.

Canada's crusade against fascism in the Second World War brought cleavages to the nation just as did the First World War. Much has already been written about the French–English divide, and of the rise of unionism and working-class protest.[115] Perhaps what needs more recognition is the tension and conflict that arose in the civilian population. Despite all the patriotic pronouncements (and despite the so-called collectivist nature of Canadian society that some political theorists write of),[116] citizens here proved just as susceptible as those anywhere else to greedy, individualistic, and survivalist conduct. Clearly it was fortunate that in wartime this country remained a fireproof house whose civilian inhabitants were, on the whole, not severely tested.

Notes

1. Studs Terkel, *"The Good War": An Oral History of World War Two* (New York: Ballantine Books, 1984).
2. Raynes Minns, *Bombers and Mash: The Domestic Front, 1939–45* (London: Vigaro Ltd., 1980), 110.
3. J.L. Granatstein and Desmond Morton, *A Nation Forged in Fire: Canadians and the Second World War, 1939–1945* (Toronto: Lester & Orpen Dennys, 1989), 36; National Archives of Canada (NAC), Charlotte Whitton Papers, MG30 E256, vol. 31, file "Typescript, 1943–4," Assistance to the Unemployed.
4. Pauline Jewett, "The Wartime Prices and Trade Board: A Case Study in Canadian Public Administration" (PhD diss., Harvard University, 1950), 30; Ernest J. Spence, "Canada's Wartime Prices and Trade Board, 1941 to 1947" (PhD diss., Northwestern University, 1947), 24.
5. Joseph Schull, *The Great Scot: A Biography of Donald Gordon* (Montreal: McGill-Queen's University Press, 1979), 66–67.
6. Jewett, "Wartime Prices and Trade Board," 271.
7. NAC, Wartime Prices and Trade Board records, (WPTB), vol. 1566, Government of Canada—Cost of Living, n.d.; NAC, Boards, Offices and Commissions, (BOC), RG36, series 31, vol. 10, file 4-22, Publicity Coordinating Committee, Departmental Advertising Plan, n.d.
8. *Public Opinion Quarterly* (1942), 165; BOC, series 31, vol. 8, file 2-6.
9. National Defence Headquarters, Directorate of History (DHist), 113.3R 4003, VI (D1).
10. NAC, Canadian Labour Congress Papers, MG28 I 103, file "Trades and Labour Congress, 1941."
11. *Canada Year Book* (1946), 762; Spence, "Canada's Wartime Prices and Trade Board," 243–44.
12. *Canadian Forum*, June 1940, 72.
13. *Saturday Night*, 19 Sept. 1942, 40; *Public Opinion Quarterly* (1944), 143.
14. Schull, *Great Scot*, 62; *Canadian Affairs*, 15 May 1943, 8.
15. NAC, WPTB, vol. 1386, Memo from J.A. Corry, 9 July 1942; ibid., Extract from House of Commons, *Debates* (April 1943), 1807.

16. Ibid., vol. 888, file 1-20-1, "The Black Market Situation," 26 April 1946; ibid., vol. 1388, "Enforcement Administration —Prosecutions," 31 Jan. 1946; WPTB, *Annual Report* (1945), 55.
17. NAC, WPTB, vol. 1386, Memo from F. MacGregor, 23 June 1943.
18. For discussions of early housing legislation see John Bacher, *Keeping to the Marketplace: The Evolution of Canadian Housing Policy* (Montreal: McGill-Queen's Univeristy Press, 1993), 87; J. David Hulchanski, "The 1935 Dominion Housing Act: Setting the Stage for a Permanent Federal Presence in Canada's Housing Sector," *Urban History Review* 15, 1 (June 1986): 34.
19. City of Vancouver Archives (VA), Department of Social Service records (DSS), RG27 E1, file 10, Building, Civic Planning, and Parks Committee Minutes, 6 May 1940; Jill Wade, "Wartime Housing Limited, 1941–1947: Canadian Housing Policy at the Crossroads," *Urban History Review* 15, 1 (June 1986): 43.
20. Bacher, *Keeping to the Marketplace*, 163; *Saturday Night*, 6 Sept. 1941, 26.
21. NAC, Canadian Council on Social Development Papers (CCSD), MG28 I 10, vol. 54, file 1942-46, undated excerpt from Montreal *Herald*.
22. *Chatelaine*, Aug. 1942, 12; VA, SSD, file "Housing 1940," A Report of Housing Conditions in Certain Sections of the City, 14 June 1940.
23. Glenbow Institute, M5841, file 21, Local Council of Women, *1941 Year Book*, 54–55; *Canadian Welfare*, Oct. 1945, 11.
24. VA, City Clerk records (CC), RG28 A1, file 52, Memorandum, 21 July 1944; Bacher, *Keeping to the Marketplace*, 136.
25. NAC, BOC, series 31, vol. 17, file 9-6-2-5, Post-War Planning Information, 15 Sept. 1945.
26. *Canadian Welfare*, April 1944, 7; Montreal *Star*, 2 Sept. 1943, 27.
27. City of Edmonton Archives (CE), City Clerk records (CC), RG11, class 210, file 35, M. Mills to Mayor Fry, 26 May 1944.
28. *Canadian Affairs*, 15 Jan. 1944, 1; NAC, William Lyon Mackenzie King Papers (WLMK), MG26 J2, vol. 372, file W-130-1, Woodery to King, 16 Jan. 1943.
29. *Maclean's*, 15 Nov. 1943, 57.
30. DHist, 77/636, *Foothill Fliers*, Dec. 1941, 7.
31. *Canadian Affairs*, 15 Jan. 1944, 2; NAC, BOC, series 31, vol. 17, file 9-6-2-5, Income Levels and Low Rental Hosing, n.d.
32. NAC, WPTB, vol. 29, Canadian Rental and Eviction Control, n.d.; *Toronto Star*, 2 Oct. 1943, 3.
33. Bacher, *Keeping to the Marketplace*, 158.
34. NAC, WLMK, vol. 372, file W-310, Albert Urquart to King, 28 Jan. 1944.
35. NAC, WPTB, vol. 29, Canadian Rental and Eviction Control, n.d.
36. CE, CC, RG11, class 213, file 12, A.M. Arnold to Mayor Fry, 22 Feb. 1943.
37. *Canada Year Book* (1943–44), 522; NAC, BOC, series 31, vol. 16, file 9-5-9-0, Report on Consumer Income and Consumer Purchases, n.d.
38. Toronto *Star*, 2 Oct. 1943, 25; WPTB, *Annual Report* (1943), 40.
39. M.C. Urquhart and K.A.H. Buckley, *Historical Statistics of Canada* (Toronto: Macmillan, 1965), 484; *Canada Year Book* (1943–44), 522.
40. Barry Broadfoot, *Six War Years, 1939–45* (Toronto: Doubleday, 1974), 192; Ottawa *Evening Citizen*, 5 July 1944, 15.
41. NAC, WLMK, vol. 372, file W-10, Ross Slute to King, 6 March 1945.
42. Urquhart and Buckley, *Historical Statistics*, 483; Mary Jane Lennon, *On the Homefront: A Scrapbook of Canadian World War Two Memorabilia* (Toronto: Boston Mills Press, 1981), 46–47.

43. *Maclean's*, 15 Sept. 1943, 15; VA, Police Commission records (PC), RG74 D7, Statistical Clerk to D. Mackay, 10 Nov. 1942.
44. *Toronto Telegram*, 26 Sept. 1944, 2.
45. *Canada Year Book* (1942), 282; *Canadian Business*, March 1942, 7, 9.
46. Private collection, Grace Morris Craig Letters, G. Craig to J. Craig, 2 April 1942.
47. NAC, BOC, series 31, vol. 13, file 8-5-2, Current Rumour Clinic, 15 July 1943; *Public Opinion Quarterly* (1943), 162.
48. NAC, WPTB, vol. 690, file 23-30, G. Young to D. Gordon, 2 Aug. 1943; York University Archives, (YUA), Jack Lawrence Granatstein Papers (JLG), box 8, file 115, Robert Thomas, *Fortunes of War* (Unpublished MS), 93.
49. See for example NAC, WPTB, vol. 690, file 23-30, Excerpt from Ottawa *Evening Citizen*, 17 April 1944.
50. CE, CC, RG11, class 66, file 56, F. Orton to Mayor Fry, 11 Feb. 1943.
51. *Canadian Business*, Sept. 1943, 67.
52. Broadfoot, *Six War Years*, 195; Ottawa *Journal*, 30 Aug. 1944, 4.
53. *Canada Year Book* (1942), 281; *Canadian Business*, Sept. 1943, 67.
54. *Toronto Star*, 7 Oct. 1943, 10, 6 Oct. 1943, 2.
55. *Saturday Night*, 2 Jan. 1943, 28.
56. NAC, WPTB, vol. 1537, "March of Time," 13 Sept. 1944; Granatstein and Morton, *Nation Forged in Fire*, 40.
57. WPTB, *Annual Report* (1943), 48.
58. Lennon, *On the Homefront*, 42; WPTB, *Annual Report* (1944), 17.
59. Royal Canadian Mounted Police (RCMP), *Annual Report* (1946), 34; Canadian Forum, Jan. 1945, 232.
60. *Public Opinion Quarterly* (1942), 147; *Canadian Business*, May 1943, 60.
61. Medicine Hat *Weekly News*, 15 April 1941, 2; YUA, JLG, box 6, file 47, Excerpt from Calgary *Herald*, n.d.
62. *Canadian Business*, Jan. 1943, 18.
63. NAC, WPTB, vol. 690, file 23-30, L. Plamondon to D. Gordon, 30 July 1943.
64. Toronto *Globe and Mail*, 9 Dec. 1943, 2.
65. *Maclean's*, 15 May 1943, 15; NAC, BOC, series 31, vol. 82, file 1944, Report of the Committee on Morale, Research on Rumours, n.d.
66. *Maclean's*, 5 June 1943, 3; *Public Opinion Quarterly* (1944), 159.
67. *Canada Year Book* (1945), 569.
68. Spence, "Canada's Wartime Prices and Trade Board," 215; NAC, WLMK, vol. 372, Undated resolution of Kent County Council; ibid., C.G. Rutter to King, 8 Jan. 1943.
69. NAC, WPTB, vol. 690, file 23-30, K. Lyons to H. Brown, 18 Sept. 1943; House of Commons, *Debates* (18 Feb. 1943), 547.
70. NAC, WPTB, vol. 690, file 23-30, Owner of Morantz Beef to Gordon, 17 Feb. 1943; ibid., W. Lackey to F. MacGregor, 14 Aug. 1943.
71. Ibid., vol. 1547, Memo to Local Ration Boards, 27 April 1943.
72. *Public Opinion Quarterly* (1943), 312; WPTB, *Annual Report* (1943), 18.
73. NAC, WPTB, vol. 1194, file 19-6-1, F. Gridsale to J. Driscoll, 31 May 1943; Spence, "Canada's Wartime Prices and Trade Board," 290.
74. Christopher Waddell, "Wartime Prices and Trade Board: Price Control in Canada during World War II" (PhD diss., 1981), 477; WPTB, *Annual Report* (1943), 18.
75. *Canada Year Book* (1945), 936; *Canadian Affairs*, 15 Jan. 1944, 12.
76. RCMP, *Annual Report* (1945), 32–33; Lord Strathcona Regimental Archives, Regimental Orders, 10 Oct. 1940.
77. YUA, JLG, Thunder Bay Naval Interviews, 1984–86, box 8, file 117.
78. *Canada Year Book* (1943–44), 552–53.
79. NAC, WLMK, vol. 244, file "Liquor Control—1942," Rev. E. Marshall to King, 24 May 1942.

80. Ibid., vol. 226, file 1942, J. Jones to King, 3 June 1942; ibid., MG26 J5, vol. 72, Liquor File, Memo entitled "What Government Can do to Promote Temperance," n.d.
81. J.W. Pickersgill, *The Mackenzie King Record*, vol. 1 (Toronto: University of Toronto Press, 1980), 460; John English, "Politics and the War: Aspects of the Canadian National Experience," in *The Second World War as a National Experience*, ed. Sidney Aster (Ottawa: Canadian Committee for the History of the Second World War, 1981), 56.
82. NAC, WLMK, vol. 72, Liquor File, King to Pickersgill, 14 Nov. 1942; Granatstein and Morton, *A Nation Forged in Fire*, 182.
83. NAC, WLMK, vol. 72, Liquor File, Copy of Radio Broadcast, 16 Dec. 1942.
84. Ibid., MG26 J2, vol. 365, file W-303-5, Excerpt from Montreal *Gazette*, 14 July 1943; Ibid., file W-303-2, H. Kramer to King, 18 Feb. 1943.
85. Ibid., MG26 J5, vol. 72, Liquor File, Excerpt from Calgary *Herald*, 18 Dec. 1942; *Star Weekly*, 15 Jan. 1944, 5.
86. *Public Opinion Quarterly* (1945), 526; 16 VA, PC, Secretary of Police Board to Chair of Liquor Control Board, 10 April 1943; Broadfoot, *Six War Years*, 315.
87. CV, PC, Inspector i/c Liquor Detail to Chief Constable, 6 July 1945.
88. NAC, WLMK, MG26 J2, vol. 244, file N-305-38, Deaths Increase Under Government Control of Liquor, n.d.; DHist, 112.3 M3009 (D 138), Morale Report, May 1943.
89. NAC, WLMK, MG26 J2, vol. 365, file W-303-2, Excerpt from Vancouver *News-Herald*, 29 March 1943; *Maclean's*, 15 May 1943, 59.
90. NAC, Clive Cardinal Papers, MG30 E368, vol. 3, file 31, *Maple Leaf*, 24 Dec. 1945, 3.
91. *Public Opinion Quarterly* (1944), 139; Schull, *Great Scot*, 94.
92. NAC, WPTB, vol. 1566, Government of Canada—Cost of Living, n.d.
93. Ottawa *Journal*, 28 Aug. 1944, 8; WPTB, *Annual Report* (1945), 61; *Public Opinion Quarterly* (1946), 279.
94. WPTB, *Annual Report*, 1946, 55.
95. Waddell, "Wartime Prices and Trade Board," 574.
96. Robert Bothwell, "War into Peace: C.D. Howe as Minister of Reconstruction," *Proceedings of the Canadian Committee for the History of the Second World War*, (1977), 12.
97. NAC, WLMK, MG26 J4, vol. 377, 260, 942.
98. NAC, Young Men's Christian Association Papers, MG28 195, vol. 272, file 8, "Rehabilitation: Learn About It," 1945; NAC, Department of National Defence records, RG24, vol. 12,278, file 27-1, Press Survey on Rehabilitation, Feb. 1946.
99. Barry Broadfoot, *The Veterans' Years* (Vancouver: Douglas and McIntyre, 1989), 70–73.
100. NAC, WPTB, vol. 1194, file 19-6, Press Release, n.d.; Irene Kahn Atkins, "Seeds of Destiny: A Case History," *Film And History* (1981), 27–30; Ottawa *Journal*, 1 Oct. 1945, 8.
101. WPTB, *Annual Report* (1946), 6; NAC, WPTB, vol. 1566, Weekly Prices and Trade Bulletin, 18–23 Feb. 1946.
102. Ibid., vol. 888, file 1-20-1, Memorandum, 18 April 1946; ibid., Mayor James D. McKenna to H. Hobbins, 7 Nov. 1945; Waddell, "Wartime Prices and Trade Board," 533.
103. NAC, WLMK, MG26 J4, vol. 274, 188, 647-79.
104. NAC, WPTB, vol. 1194, file 19-6, K. Taylor to J. Close, 12 Oct. 1945; ibid., vol. 1566, Weekly Prices and Trade Bulletin, 26 Nov.–1 Dec. 1945.
105. NAC, WLMK, MG26 J4, vol. 377, 260, 923.

106. NAC, WPTB, vol. 1547, Meat Rationing Guide, Sept. 1945.
107. Jill Wade, "Wartime Housing," 47; *Canadian Welfare*, June 1946, 33–34.
108. John T. Saywell, *Housing Canadians: Essays on the History of Residential Construction in Canada* (Ottawa: Economic Council of Canada, 1975), 188; NAC, BOC, series 31, vol. 17, file 9-6-2-5, Post-War Planning Information, 15 Sept. 1945.
109. CE, CC, RG11, class 210, file 55, Resolution on the Housing Shortage Adopted at a Public Meeting Held in Winnipeg, 25 April 1946.
110. CV, 80-22, shelf 19, box 4.
111. NAC, Department of Labour records (DL), RG27, vol. 2349, file 22-5-17, I. Mackenzie to H. Mitchell, 1 Oct. 1945; NAC, Montreal Soldiers' Wives League Papers, MG28 I 311, vol. 2, file 33, Unidentified newspaper article entitled "Rent Inquiry Promised Here."
112. Broadfoot, *Veterans' Years*, 64–66, 142.
113. NAC, DL, RG27, vol. 2344, file 22-3-30, Citizens' Rehabilitation Council of Greater Vancouver, Minutes, 25 April 1945; NAC, Ian Mackenzie Papers, MG27, III B5, vol. 21, file 41-110, pt. 2, Excerpt from *Vancouver Sun*, 8 March 1946.
114. Jill Wade, "A Place for the Public: Housing Reform and the 1946 Occupation of the Old Hotel Vancouver," *B.C. Studies* 69–70, (Spring–Summer 1986): 308–10.
115. See, for example, J.L. Granatstein, *Canada's War: The Politics of the Mackenzie King Government, 1939–1945* (Toronto: Oxford University Press, 1975).
116. See Gad Horowitz, *Canadian Labour and Politics* (Toronto: University of Toronto Press, 1968), chap. 1.

In "The Voice of Business," a special section of the 7 January 1943 issue of the Toronto *Globe and Mail*, one government official wrote as follows: "A Canadian factory that once made dome fasteners is now turning out ammunition. A plant that once made refrigerators is now making tank turrets. The former street-car factory is now making parts for bombers. Of all the hundreds of Canadian industrial plants now making munitions and supplies of war, only two were turning out exactly the same products three years ago." In "an amazing feat of expansion, adaptation and improvisation" the country had leaped forward economically by literally beating "her plowshares into machine guns." Minister of Munitions and Supply C.D. Howe was thought by many to have personified this transformation.

Visible Hand: The Years of C.D. Howe

Michael Bliss

It is obvious that in Canadian business history the years "Before C.D." were not totally dark. Canada's basic industrial plant was in place when war began in 1939. The steel mills and power stations, aluminum and chemical plants, textile mills and foundries, and auto and implement factories that provided the bulk of the nation's war production had been created in a long developmental process extending over eight decades. They did not spring full-grown from the desks of bureaucrats in Munitions and Supply. Nor did the leading bureaucrats themselves, Howe's dollar-a-year men, leap from kindergarten to industrial statesmanship under his tutelage. Most were seasoned industrial veterans, already at or near the top of the executive ladder, whose careers would probably have been much the same if the war had never occurred. The idea that most of these men got their start or learned their skills in C.D.'s Ottawa is almost exactly wrong. It was C.D. Howe and Ottawa who learned from them.

The war effort is often exaggerated in Canadian memory because it was such a radical change from the Great Depression. The war seemed to end the Depression, with its grey, aching unemployment, its insecurity, and its national drift. War brought full employment, fat pay cheques, busy-ness everywhere, a sense of national purpose—and for Canadian industry a huge surge of capital investment. And there was no depression after the war, only growth, growth, and more growth. So the war was the turning point, the birth of a new age for Canada. All the past could fade into memory as prologue, the dark years Before C.D. took everything in hand and the real boom began.

In fact the Depression was gradually ending anyway. If Canadians had not had to make shells, tanks, and fighter planes in the early 1940s, many of them would have prospered making electric irons and washing machines, television sets, automobiles, and airplanes for civil aviation. The recovery would have been slower, and full employment much less likely. But war work for all was a long way from economic utopia. Canada's wartime "full employment" included the stationing of more than a million men and women in low-paying, numbingly tedious, and tragically hazardous jobs in the Armed Forces. To sustain the war economy and divert resources to war, extremely heavy taxes were levied and elaborate controls limited civilian purchasing power. More pay went in taxes and forced loans to the government than ever before; the remainder could not be spent on luxury goods because they were not available. The corollary of jobs for all in a war economy was sacrifice by all. Many more Canadians worked during the war than in the 1930s, and they worked longer and harder. But because so much of their production was used for battle, consumers' total disposable income did not rise from Depression levels. In the mid-1930s Windsor did not make many automobiles because so few could afford new ones. In the mid-years of the war it did not make *any* automobiles because it was directed to make troop-carriers instead. In either case the civilian did without a new car. In the war he could not get new tires or unrationed gasoline either.

The raw success of the wartime economic effort is undeniable. Canada's gross national product increased from $5.6 billion in 1939 to $11.9 billion in 1945. The production of war materials totalled almost $10 billion. Among the Allied countries, Canada was the fourth most important supplier. Its automobile factories turned out more than 800 000 transport vehicles, more than 50 000 armoured fighting vehicles. The most spectacular growth was in aircraft manufacture. In 1939 Canada's eight small aircraft plants employed 4000 and produced about 40 airplanes a year in 500 000 square feet of factory space. In 1944 there were 116 000 employees in Canada's aircraft industry, which assembled more than 4000 airplanes in 15 million square feet of plant. By the end of 1945, Canada had delivered 16 418 military aircraft. Statistics like these caused the Munitions and Supply people themselves to believe the myth of wartime industrialization. Howe wrote in the foreword to the department's *History* that these had been "the years during which the country emerged from its position as a producer of basic supplies to that of a highly industrialized state."

A much larger percentage of GNP was devoted to making war in 1939–45 than in 1914–18, but with less damaging results on the home front. Inflation, the scourge of the Great War and its aftermath, was held to a minimum by a combination of high taxes and, after 1941, tight wage and price controls. During six years of war the consumer price index increased by a total of only 20.6 percent, with most of the increase coming before the controllers got tough. Other government policies minimized inequalities, kept labour unrest to a minimum, and paved the way for a smooth transition to peacetime. Altogether a job well done by the Government of Canada. Historians have traditionally applauded the Mackenzie King administration of the war years for having operated at an unusually high level of managerial competence.

The gross figures and the apparent magnitude and ease of the achievement were misleading. A country that was building tanks and destroyers and bombers and radar and advanced optics, that had created an important synthetic rubber plant, that had special Crown corporations devoted to advanced research, and was refining uranium and pondering the development of nuclear energy, seemed to have made great strides toward industrial self-sufficiency. Canada had leaped onto the frontier of advanced technology. "Never again," Howe himself boasted in 1943, "will there be any doubt that Canada can manufacture anything that can be manufactured elsewhere."

This was not true. Canada's war effort caused the economy to surge forward along fairly traditional lines. It was primarily a raw materials producer (particularly a supplier of foodstuffs), and a manufacturer of small ships, ammunition, and small arms to British and American specifications. The main vehicular production was the assembly of motorized transport in the Canadian branches of General Motors, Ford, and Chrysler. Capacity existed in these plants because Canada was actually doing so little in the way of tank manufacture. The air-frame factories were gigantic by prewar Canadian standards, ordinary by British or American (fifteen million square feet was not a huge amount of factory space), and there were many disappointing production delays, few of which were discussed in Parliament or described in official histories. After the foreign-designed Mosquitos and Lancasters and Hell Divers and M-4 tanks were assembled (and the Canadian-designed Ram tank, which was not deemed acceptable for combat), their imported engines were installed.

Great strides in engineering and technological sophistication did occur in Canadian industry as a result of the intensity of the effort, the willingness of government to help, and the pace of wartime technological change. These were matched in all other countries producing war goods. By learning how to run very quickly—a feat that astonished many Canadians, and often caused those who did it to sweat blood in the attempt and then feel justifiably proud of their achievement—Canada managed almost to keep up with Great Britain and the United States. It was true that by 1945 Canadian manufacturers had gained significant medium-term competitive advantage over formerly advanced producers in countries like Germany and Japan, whose factories had been bombed to rubble.

Wartime conditions could not be easily or desirably duplicated in peacetime. Most of the government's control programs were temporary, patchwork arrangements held together only by the glues of patriotism and the War Measures Act, adhesives that would both dissolve with the peace. Price control, administered by the Wartime Prices and Trade Board, was particularly fragile. The basic device was an attempt to freeze prices for the duration of the war at levels in effect in September and October 1941. It was soon realized that there were too many prices (hundreds of thousands in an economy that, by today's standards, was still fairly simple), too many levels, too many buyers and sellers, for the freeze to hold without all kinds of shaving and trimming and exhortation and exceptions. Manufacturers who were caught with raw material price increases they could not pass on simply cut back on quality, sometimes literally degrading their products. Retailers in the same boat cut back on service (no more home delivery, much more self-service, less credit). Primary producers whose 1941 prices were uneconomically low insisted on and got increases, sometimes through subsidies. Workers used strike threats to get wage increases.

For four years the WPTB, headed by a former banker, Donald Gordon, fought a complex and gradually losing holding action, offering subsidies here, rationing schemes there, exemptions somewhere else, hiring bureaucrats by the hundred to help plug leaks, running massive propaganda campaigns to increase compliance. Price control succeeded, more or less, because most citizens, including businessmen, voluntarily accepted the controls and because the war ended. Had it not ended in 1945, the sweeping control structure could not have been maintained much longer. Donald Gordon liked to settle down at night with his bottle of scotch, his accordion, and what he called the price-board hymn: "It's me, it's me, O Lord, standin' in the need of prayer." Talk of making wartime price control a permanent fixture in peace horrified most of the controllers, let alone the controlled.

Many workers in the United States had come to enjoy the benefits of collective bargaining under law through the National Labor Relations Act (Wagner-Connery Act) of 1935, one of the achievements of the New Deal. Canadian workers won equivalent rights in the crucible of war.

The Formation of the Canadian Industrial Relations System During World War II

Laurel Sefton MacDowell

THE WAR YEARS were a period of antagonistic labour–government relations and serious industrial unrest, which labour attributed to wage controls, the failure of the government to consult on policies which directly affected employees, and the inadequacy of the existing collective bargaining legislation. As a result, trade unions organized aggressively in the new war industries, struck with increasing frequency, and eventually became involved in direct political activity. At the centre of this conflict was the demand for collective bargaining. Collective bargaining was not just a means of raising wages and improving working conditions. It was a demand by organized workers for a new status, and the right to participate in decision-making both in industry and government. Thus, it became an issue not only on the shop floor, where employers and unions met directly, but also in the political arena.[1] Eventually this demand for a new status in society was met by the introduction of a new legislative framework for collective bargaining, which has been modified only slightly since that time. Yet in order to appreciate the evolution of this policy, it is insufficient to consider simply the political debate or the crises which precipitated the change. Even the important strikes which crystallized labour's discontent and prompted specific concessions took place within the special context of the war economy and a general realignment of industrial and political forces. Over a period of years, the economic tensions associated with the war generated pressures for reform which could not be contained.

The most dramatic change in these years was the growth of the labour movement itself. At the outbreak of the war, there were only 359 000 organized workers. During the war, union membership more than doubled, so that by 1946 there were 832 000 organized employees engaged in collective bargaining.[2] In 1939 there were still 900 000 registered unemployed in a work force of approximately 3.9 million, but this labour surplus was quickly absorbed, and soon there was a labour shortage.[3] These conditions were very favourable for trade union organizing.

The new industrial unions expanded with the industries from which they drew their support. The labour market conditions also produced higher wages, rising expectations, and demands for better working conditions. Wartime wages were high by Depression standards, although in 1941 most industrial workers were still not earning an adequate wage, as defined by welfare agencies of the day.[4] Paradoxically, those industries with the highest and most rapidly increasing wage rates were also the industries being unionized most quickly. Wages were rising but apparently not as quickly as the expectations of workers, who were reacting, to the tight labour market, the rising cost of living, and their experiences during, the Depression. They were determined not to return to their situation in the 1930s. Some of the older workers remembered the extent to which real wages were undermined during World War I.[5] These insecurities prompted workers to join unions, even at a time when wages were strictly controlled, so that there was no guarantee of any immediate economic benefit. After the proclamation of the wage control policy in 1941, most wartime wage increases were not increases in the basic wage rates but in cost-of-living bonuses. Workers feared that even these wage gains would be rescinded at the end of the war.

This increased organizational activity met with considerable employer resistance and resulted in unprecedented levels of industrial conflict. Until the government passed legislation supporting collective bargaining in 1944 there was a continual increase in the number of strikes, workers involved, and man-days lost. The peak of industrial unrest was reached in 1943. In 1943, one out of every three trade union members was involved in strike activity, a level of membership involvement exceeded only in 1919 and then only marginally. Indeed, to the extent that membership involvement in industrial conflict is a measure of employee disaffection, 1919 is the only year with which 1943 can be compared.[6]

The growth of trade unionism during the war involved structural changes in the movement itself which had both organizational and political ramifications. Traditionally, the most effective unions had been organized on a craft basis. These craft skills could not be easily acquired, so that by controlling the supply of labour and eliminating competition between tradesmen, the trade union could enhance its bargaining power and guarantee both employer recognition and collective bargaining. Its effectiveness depended upon its ability to define and protect their "job territory" against the encroachments of other craftsmen, mechanical innovations, or less skilled employees who were hired in order to reduce labour costs (and who subsequently provided the organizational base for the industrial unions). The principles of craft exclusivity within carefully defined work jurisdictions had been the basis for the successful early organization and expansion of trade unionism, and had ensured the survival of craft unions when broader based industrial organizations had failed.[7] Moreover, the jurisdiction of each union was defined by the trade unions themselves, and jurisdictional disputes were resolved by their central organization, the American Federation of Labor (AFL) and the Trades and Labour Congress of Canada (TLC).

In contrast, the industrial unions proposed organization on an industrywide basis, without regard to an employee's skills. Bargaining power was based on numbers, not on a monopoly of available skills. This fundamental difference in outlook made interunion rivalry inevitable, and made the craft unions cautious about the legislative changes which the new unions proposed. Legislation such as the American Wagner Act, which gave a government agency the authority to define the jurisdiction in which unions could organize, was as great a challenge as industrial unionism itself. It implied that an unskilled majority might "swamp" the less numerous craft employees. This conflict ultimately resulted in the expulsion from the TLC of the industrial unions affiliated to the American CIO [Congress of Industrial Organizations],[8] but it was also evident in the legislative program of the TLC in the years immediately prior to the war.

By 1939 there were 22 000 members in the TLC who belonged to the CIO international industrial unions.[9] The industrial unions pressured the TLC to support legislation patterned after the American Wagner Act. The TLC responded by drafting a "model bill" in 1937 and presenting it to provincial governments. This bill was sharply criticized at two successive TLC conventions[10] because it did not compel employers to bargain with unions with majority support, did not prohibit "company unions," and did not include machinery to determine the exclusive bargaining agent when jurisdictional disputes arose between unions. The new unions, which lacked the economic strength to establish collective bargaining relationships, required government intervention to protect their organizations. The craft unions, which were strong and entrenched, did not need government intervention to gain recognition from employers, and were wary of the increased role of government implicit in the Wagner principles. Later in the war, craft unions would unite with industrial unions in support of this legislative demand, but not until the craft unions had embarked on a more dynamic organizing policy and had begun to broaden their own organizational base.[11]

The conversion of the economy to a war footing required unprecedented government intervention and regulation of economic life. New policies administered through the National Selective Service (NSS) restricted workers' freedom in the labour market, since a worker could be frozen in his job, transferred, or placed in a military training plan.[12] This system was intended to distribute manpower more efficiently and increase production, but the essence of all these policies was to regard labour as a factor in production which could be regulated by legislative and administrative fiat.[13]

The regulation of wages and working conditions by the political authority inevitably brought trade unions into politics, and increased labour's criticism of the lack of labour representation on government policy-making bodies. Labour resented the antilabour attitudes of many of the "new men" drawn from business into C.D. Howe's Department of Munitions and Supply. Labour developed a deep distrust of the personnel entrusted with administering government policy, since unionists remained outside the formal power structure. Business influence in the government and society was much greater, and that influence was reflected in the government's wartime labour policy.

The common effort industrial workers were making to wage war, their common insecurity with regard to wages and the status of their unions, their common resentment about their lack of influence on the government, and the inequities of the wage-control policy led to trade union organization, industrial unrest, and ultimately political opposition. Labour's increasing resentment of the government's wage and collective bargaining policies caused the "labour problem" to escalate during 1941 and 1942, and to reach explosive proportions by 1943. In Canada, all were being asked to make a contribution and sacrifice as equals in a war effort for democracy, but this only heightened the dissatisfaction with "industrial autocracy." As "equal" participants in the war effort, industrial workers wanted equal rights on the job, in the economy, and in the councils of the nation. Strong unions were their vehicle to acquire those rights.

In 1939, when the War Measures Act made the federal government preeminent in labour matters, the government had no positive collective bargaining policy. At a time when thousands of employees were joining unions, there was no legislative support for their endeavour, nor protection should their employer take reprisals. Section 502A of the Criminal Code made it an indictable offence for an employer to refuse to employ or dismiss or intimidate any person for "the sole reason" that he was a member of a union; however, the wording of the section and the burden of proof made it virtually impossible to secure a conviction. Even if an employer were found guilty, he could be penalized, but there was no remedy (such as reinstatement) for the employee.

The Industrial Disputes Investigation Act (IDI Act) was extended by a 1939 order-in-council to cover 85 percent of all industrial activity; but it did not contain any provisions for union recognition, and was primarily concerned with avoiding strikes through the process of compulsory conciliation, which was a necessary precondition for a lawful strike. Conciliation implied a built-in compulsory delay that was particularly troublesome in recognition disputes where time was of the essence. Timing of strike activity was crucial, and delay could interrupt the union's organizational momentum, as well as give the employer the opportunity to relocate production, recruit strike breakers, and promote management-controlled "employees' committees" to compete for the loyalty of the workforce and to hinder the development of independent unions. The application of the IDI Act therefore handicapped trade union organization. Moreover, the IDI Act took no account of the different types of industrial dispute. Disputes concerning union recognition and collective bargaining required different treatment from those primarily about wages and working conditions. The act proved "unsuited to deal with disputes arising out of the refusal of the employer to recognize and deal with trade unions."[14] Such disputes increased throughout the war, but because they involved the very existence of the union, and the legitimacy of its activities, they were not amenable to mediation and compromise. The very existence of one of the parties was not an issue for which there was a "middle ground." The result was that the IDI Act merely contributed to delay, and this inevitably benefited management, and undermined trade union activity.[15]

Despite its expressed concern about delay, the government created two further mechanisms which exacerbated the problem: the Industrial Disputes Inquiry Commission and compulsory strike votes. The former was supposed to provide a speedy preconciliation fact-finding procedure, while the latter was apparently based on the belief that the union leadership was fomenting discontent, and that if the rank and file were permitted to express their views they would exercise restraint.[16] In fact, neither mechanism was successful and such restrictions merely contributed to labour discontent.

In order to deal directly with the increasing number of disputes where employers refused to bargain collectively, the government could have enacted legislation similar to that which was in force in the United States. Between 1937 and 1939, the provinces had enacted legislation providing for some recognition for trade unions and collective bargaining, but such laws were unenforced and therefore ineffective.[17] At the beginning of the war, however, the federal government had no intention of enacting a Canadian Wagner Act. Instead, in June 1940, the government was persuaded to proclaim order-in-council PC 2685: a declaration of principles which the government hoped labour and management would adopt. The government wanted to prevent industrial unrest which might prejudice the war effort. The order was an effort to furnish a voluntary formula for the resolution of recognition disputes. It encouraged employers to voluntarily recognize unions, negotiate in good faith, and resolve disputes by means of the conciliation machinery. The government sought to maintain a position on collective bargaining which it alleged to be "neutral." By its statutory silence it implied that the contest between labour and management was essentially a private matter. It ignored the fact that a legal system under which the government played a "neutral" role had the effect of tipping the balance of bargaining power in favour of employers.[18] As J.L. Cohen, a prominent labour lawyer of the day, wrote:

> It [PC 2685] ignores the essential fact that in the main, employees are not free either to organize or to negotiate and that no legislative protection, whether the right to organize or to negotiate is furnished by the order in council, by Section 502A of the Criminal Code or by any of the provisions of the IDI Act.[19]

This unenforced "declaration of principles" became the focus of much bitter debate and contributed to labour's disaffection. In contrast to the wage-control policy (PC 7440, issued in December 1940), which was widely publicized and firmly enforced, these labour-relations principles were ignored by employers and never followed by the government itself in industries under its own control. While the government was prepared to impose compulsory wage controls, compulsory conciliation, compulsory strike votes, and compulsory reallocation of labour, it continued to maintain that its opposition to "compulsion" precluded the introduction of collective bargaining legislation.[20]

Unions were particularly dissatisfied with the wage-control policies. Early in the war, the labour movement had tentatively supported wage controls. After watching their application in specific situations, this support changed to opposition. In their view, the program was inequitable in its effect on industrial wages as compared to salaries, did not properly account for low-wage industries, and was detrimental to collective bargaining. Despite the price controls, it appeared that business was being subsidized for its capital expenditures and was allowed to maintain a comfortable profit. Profits were not strictly controlled. Business had refused to accept a 5 percent ceiling on profits, and the government did not impose one.[21] To many workers there appeared to be a marked discrepancy between the sacrifices which labour and business were asked to make.[22]

Closely related to these criticisms was the general concern that labour remained unrepresented in the policy-making apparatus of government, although workers were profoundly affected by these policies. Unlike the business community, which was virtually running the war production effort and reaping considerable benefits, the labour movement remained unrepresented and unheard, except when, through the exercise of industrial strength, a government economic objective was jeopardized. Because labour was excluded from the formal decision-making process, its opposition to the government was expressed only on the industrial scene. In order to understand the basis for this opposition, it is necessary to examine the government role in several key strikes. Each involved an important element of the government's labour policy, and each contributed to labour's alienation. Eventually this alienation prompted the two major labour federations to adopt common legislative goals, to forge new political alliances, and to engage in overt political opposition.

The National Steel Car (NASCO) plant in Hamilton was originally organized in late 1940 by the Steelworkers' Organizing Committee (SWOC). When the company refused to meet, the union applied for a conciliation board, which was eventually established after a delay of five weeks. The conciliation board, recommended that a plant-wide, government-supervised representation vote be conducted, and if the union won, the employer should begin negotiations. The union accepted the report but heard nothing further for a month. On 29 April 1941 the membership unanimously voted to strike. Immediately the government became concerned about the possible disruption of war production, since it appeared that the steelworkers in Sault Ste. Marie and Trenton might strike in sympathy with the Hamilton workers, Its response was immediate. Within two days, the government appointed Ernest Brunning controller of the plant, and assured the union that the conciliation board report would be implemented. The representation vote was taken and the union won, but the controller refused to meet. Significantly, he advised the conciliation board that he was pursuing this course of action in accordance with instructions that he had received from the government.[23] The absurdity of this situation was noted by the labour nominee on the conciliation board who wrote to the government:

> There appears to me to be something incongruous in the suggestion that a government appointed Board should be required to inform a government appointed Controller that the principles and policy of an order-in-council (PC 2685) enacted at the behest of the government appointing both the Board and the Controller should be observed and lived up to.[24]

When the conciliation board reconvened in June, Brunning advised that, "The matter of union recognition cannot be dealt with at the present time in view of the fact the plant is being operated by a controller appointed by the government."[25] He then called upon the employees to appoint "a representative committee" to meet with him and consider his proposals regarding hours and wages. These proposals were implemented a week later. This procedure was contrary to the principles of collective bargaining embodied in PC 2685, but it was obvious that the government was not going to enforce its own order. In July, the union called a second strike. After mediation activities by officials of the departments of Labour and Munitions and Supply, the strikers returned to work on the understanding that negotiations would finally begin. No negotiations took place, but the controller announced that the workers would be "free" to join any union or employees' association of their choice. He obviously preferred to deal with the association which he himself had established and encouraged in the summer of 1941. Shortly thereafter, the impasse was resolved by the appointment of a new controller, who eventually negotiated collective agreements with both the union and the employee association. Despite the representation vote, the union had not achieved official recognition or the status of exclusive bargaining agent. The two organizations in the plant vied with each other until the United Steelworkers of America was finally certified in September 1945. The conduct of the government and its appointee created considerable disillusionment within the trade union movement. Not only was the government unprepared to support union recognition or the principles of PC 2685, it also had condoned the establishment of an employer-dominated committee which had been used to undermine the existing union.

Concurrent with the NASCO dispute, the first major dispute concerning the application of the government's wage-control policy arose at the Peck Rolling Mills plant in Montreal. Peck Rolling Mills was a wholly owned subsidiary of Dominion Steel and Coal Company (DOSCO). The Steelworkers' Organizing Committee had organized 93 percent of the workforce and was granted recognition by the company on the recommendation of a conciliation board. The conciliation board also found that 50 percent of the workers received less than 30.7 cents an hour. In addition to poor wages, the Peck employees worked long hours (50 to 80 hours) in substandard working conditions. The parties fundamentally disagreed on both the level of wages and the proper interpretation of PC 7440, the wage-control order. The minority and majority reports of the conciliation board reflected this disagreement.

The employer took a narrow view of the effect of the order. The adequacy of wage rates under the wage order was to be determined in relation to a "norm," which was either the average wage in the 1926–29 period or such higher rate as might have been attained after 1926. The employer submitted that since Peck wages in 1941 were above the 1926–29 average, they were therefore "fair and reasonable." This was not an exceptional case of depressed or subnormal wage rates. The Peck wages were comparable to other industrial rates in the Montreal area. The majority of the board concurred with this view, and decided that the most recent wage order freezing wages[26] precluded it from recommending a raise, even though it was recognized that the wages were inadequate. Accordingly, the board recommended a continuance of the basic wage rate of 30.7 cents an hour and no cost of living bonus, except the 15 cents per day which had been paid from September 1940.[27] No national wage level had been established in the steel industry; wage scales were determined locally. Since the Peck rates were not "depressed" by Montreal standards, there was no justification under the order to raise them.[28]

The union supported a broader interpretation of the order and argued that the Peck employees' wages should be compared to wages of other workers across the country engaged in similar work. Since workers in the steel industry were heavily engaged in the national production effort, they should be paid equally for work of equal value. In its view, the Peck wage rate was obviously "depressed and subnormal" and could be adjusted in accordance with the provisions of the order. The Minority Report adopted this argument and contended that the government's wage policy was aimed solely at preventing wages which were already reasonable from rising unduly; wages which were unreasonably low could still be raised. The order was not intended to freeze inadequate wages. There was nothing in the cost of living in Montreal or in the company's ability to pay which justified abnormally low wages in comparison with those paid to other workers in the same industry, especially since the majority interpretation would condemn workers to a low-wage condition for the duration of the wage policy.[29] The minority recommended an increase of the basic rate to 40 cents an hour. The positions of the parties and the proceedings of the board were closely monitored, for labour believed that the management interpretation was in conflict with government assurances which had been given to organized labour at the time the wage order was proclaimed.[30] Labour feared that the Peck case would become a precedent for other conciliation boards handling wage disputes, as indeed it did. In addition, SWOC was beginning to formulate its demands for a general basic-wage increase throughout the steel industry across the country.

In April 1941, after the publication of the two reports and in spite of the wage controls, the Peck workers struck for 40 cents an hour. The government sought to persuade them to return to work without giving in to union demands.[31] Ultimately, the Peck employees received an increase in their basic wage rate when the federal government, avoiding any direct reference to the dispute, increased the minimum wage for men to 35 cents an hour and for women to 25 cents an hour.[32] The employees returned to work and the dispute ended with the temporary collapse of the SWOC local.[33]

The inequities of the wage policy, the rigidity with which it was applied in the Peck dispute and the inconsistencies with which it was applied elsewhere,[34] increased labour alienation. To labour, it appeared that "its only real effect was to provide employers who wished to resist wage demands with an elaborate rationale."[35] Labour dissatisfaction with the wage policy mounted, as did its hostility to the government, which again appeared to be supporting the interests of employers. But it was the defeat of the Kirkland Lake miners in the winter of 1942 which crystallized labour's discontent, unified the movement, and moved the CCL [Canadian Congress of Labour] unions into a position of outright opposition to the government.

In Kirkland Lake the issues were very clear. Local 240 of the International Union of Mine Mill and Smelter Workers was seeking recognition from the gold-mining operators. When recognition was refused, the union applied for a conciliation board. In Kirkland Lake, the government decided early not to appoint a controller. It was no more prepared to establish a collective bargaining relationship between a controller and the union than it had been at NASCO, but it was equally reluctant to risk the embarrassment which the NASCO dispute had involved. Instead, the government appointed the Industrial Disputes Inquiry Commission (IDIC), chaired by Humphrey Mitchell (soon to be the new minister of labour), to investigate the dispute before granting a conciliation board. The IDIC was intended only to be a "fact-finding body" and was not supposed to make proposals for settlement. Nevertheless it proposed "the Kirkland Lake Formula" as the basis for a settlement. This formula suggested that the miners should elect "employee" committees in lieu of a "union" committee to negotiate with the mining companies. Management agreed to negotiate with such "internal" bodies while at the same time opposing "unalterably"[36] the recognition of the Mine Mill local. The proposal for new employee committees was a challenge to the legitimacy of the existing union and was bitterly resented. Indeed, the proposal was reminiscent of that of Controller Brunning in the NASCO dispute, except now, it came directly from a senior government official.

The conciliation board was finally appointed and unanimously recommended recognition of the union. Its recommendations were ignored by management. Before it could legally strike, the union was obliged by PC 7307 to apply for a government supervised strike vote. Delay followed upon delay, until the strike was fought in the middle of a northern winter, and eventually lost. The union and the CCL recognized that the strike could be won only if the federal government intervened in support of the conciliation board report. The only intervention that took place was by police constables, who were ordered by the provincial government to assist the mining companies to operate with strike breakers.[37] The federal government refused to intervene despite strenuous efforts on the part of CCL unions and some TLC locals, including public conferences in Kirkland Lake and Ottawa, and the establishment of a network of strike committees across the country. This position was not mere procrastination but a conscious policy adopted by the prime minister and his minister of labour.[38] The government was unwilling to endorse the principle of compulsory recognition, even where the trade union enjoyed the support of a majority of the employees, and a conciliation board unanimously recommended recognition as the only way to avoid a strike. Although the government was exercising compulsion every day in order to meet its wartime economic objectives, it continued to oppose compulsory recognition and maintained its belief in the efficacy of employees' committees as an alternative to independent trade unions. In the circumstances, it is difficult to avoid the conclusion that it was not "compulsion" which the government opposed, but rather, collective bargaining itself. Apparently, the government accepted the management view that collective bargaining legislation would encourage union growth and result in more unrest.

Unlike the "New Deal" labour policy of the 1930s, which sought to redress the imbalance of bargaining power and encourage collective bargaining, the Canadian labour policy throughout the war was concerned only with eliminating industrial unrest. The government continued to believe that legislative recognition of collective bargaining would only promote an "adversary relationship," but since there were real differences of interest between labour and management, an adversary relationship and some degree of conflict was inevitable. Labour stressed that the recognition of its status in industry and the introduction of collective bargaining would eliminate recognition strikes, develop negotiating relationships, and thereby improve labour–management relations. The government in 1942 did not agree. For political reasons, the government felt it necessary to conciliate business, its wartime ally in developing the war economy. It was therefore unprepared to establish collective bargaining as a "right," or grant labour an important role in running the war.[39] It was even unprepared to take the lead and set an example as a "good employer" by recognizing existing unions in its own war industries. Although it had a close working relationship with the business community, the government had no close relations with the industrial union movement. When the new union leaders openly questioned the government's good faith and asserted their members' rights even in the critical war situation, King dubbed them "irresponsible." King preferred the leaders of the TLC, with whom he had more influence.

Refusal of the government to intervene resulted in the loss of the Kirkland Lake strike. The effects of the strike were several. The local union was temporarily decimated, but in the long run, the labour movement may have benefited. Many younger miners, experienced in trade union organizing, but blacklisted across the north, left to find work in southern Ontario. They invariably became active trade unionists in their new jobs and promoted trade union organization in the expanding war industries. Several rose to leadership positions in the industrial union movement.[40]

H.A. Logan has suggested that the "Kirkland Lake strike marked the low point in industrial relations in the war. But from it began the march toward PC 1003."[41] The strike unified the divided labour movement in a common political endeavour. In 1942 the briefs to the government of both the TLC and the CCL favoured positive collective bargaining legislation.[42] The CCL convention soundly condemned Humphrey Mitchell, the new labour minister, and demanded his removal from office. Both conventions demanded immediate enforcement of PC 2685, particularly in the Crown corporations. King was shaken by his meetings with the delegations from the two Congresses[43] and by the level of opposition at TLC and CCL conventions. In response to labour pressure, he personally intervened[44] to proclaim PC 10802. This order authorized Crown companies to bargain collectively with their employees. While it did not clearly make collective bargaining compulsory,[45] it made eventual legislative support of collective bargaining inevitable.[46] However, the delay in its implementation angered organized labour and contributed to its continuing opposition to government policies during 1943.[47] Any hope of accommodation was shattered by the government's handling of the 1943 steel strike.

The steel industry was crucial to war production. It was nationally mobilized and closely controlled, and as such it was an appropriate place to test the government's flexibility in the application of its wage policy. Steelworkers initially proposed wage increases to the Regional War Labour Boards, which bore the primary responsibility for implementing the policy. Both the Ontario and the Nova Scotia Regional Boards refused any increase and, as a result, the workers voted overwhelmingly to strike. The threat of a strike by employees of DOSCO and Algoma Steel in the late summer and fall of 1942 represented "the most serious threat to the government's wage policy since its inception,"[48] but the dispute was temporarily postponed by the appointment of a three-man commission of investigation. In January 1943, the Barlow Commission reported. The positions of its members were similar to those taken by the conciliation board in the Peck Rolling Mills dispute. The Majority Report interpreted the most recent wage order narrowly. In its view, further adjustment in the basic wage rates was unjustified since there had recently been a cost-of-living bonus and the prevailing rates for unskilled employees were not "substandard." Despite the application of the "national" wage policy, the board rejected the recommendation that the steel industry be classified a national industry as the union had requested. The Minority Report recommended that the steel industry should be given a special exemption from the wage policy because of the "peculiar arduousness" of the work, and the "inhumanly long hours." At Algoma more than 40 percent of the steelworkers received less than 55 cents an hour and in Sydney the proportion in this category was closer to 60 percent. "Testimony . . . told a story of hardship and privation, of overcrowding, of financial worry, of acute distress occasioned by illness against which there was no financial protection."[49] Such families did not receive the bare subsistence income set by the Department of Labour, the Dominion Bureau of Statistics, the Toronto Welfare Council, and other welfare agencies. The Majority and Minority Reports also differed on the interpretation of the Commission's terms of reference. The Majority believed its jurisdiction was limited to interpreting and applying the wage order. The Minority member believed the Commission had been appointed because of an acute crisis in the steel industry, and its job was not to duplicate the functions of the Wage Labour Board but rather to provide the government with a solution to the crisis. He therefore sought to interpret the wage order in light of the situation in the steel industry, the war production effort, the government's labour policy, and the public interest.

Following the release of the commission's report, 9000 employees went on strike. Some 2700 Trenton steelworkers struck in sympathy. Immediately the government called a conference of the interested parties to Ottawa. Negotiations took place directly with the government and senior members of the Cabinet (including King, Howe, and Mitchell) were involved. Despite considerable disagreements in the Cabinet, the union secured a number of concessions and a prolonged strike was avoided. In a "Memorandum of Agreement," the government agreed to some recommendations of the Majority Report; but steel was to be designated a national industry; the union could present a new case to the National War Labour Board (NWLB); and the steelworkers would be paid a new basic rate of 55 cents an hour.[50]

The strike had a significant impact on the form of future labour legislation, for under pressure, the prime minister developed a new policy.[51] During the conference the prime minister proposed that the union take its case before a reconstituted "independent" National War Labour Board. His unpopular labour minister, Humphrey Mitchell, would resign as chairman of the NWLB and be replaced by Justice McTague. In this way Mitchell's influence would be limited, but his position as minister of labour would not be compromised. King "was optimistic that McTague could do what Mitchell failed to do: enforce the government's wage policy without alienating the labour movement completely and without mishandling disputes which would result in national crises and Cabinet intervention."[52] In fact, the NWLB did not succeed in lessening labour opposition. When it reviewed the steel wage case, it lowered the basic wage rate agreed upon in the "Memorandum of Understanding" and withdrew the designation of steel as a national industry. The union had understood that the board would not be able to change the terms of the Memorandum except to improve on them. Since the board was now "independent of politics" the cabinet would not intervene to guarantee its own commitment. There followed a total disillusionment about the worth of any understanding with the government.

By early 1943 the labour movement and the government were completely at odds over the related issues of collective bargaining and wage controls. The government was asking labour to sacrifice wages as part of the war effort, and labour believed that in return there should be a guarantee of collective bargaining rights to protect workers from arbitrary employer action. The lack of collective bargaining legislation and the rigid enforcement of wage controls effectively undermined collective bargaining, and thereby threatened the labour movement itself.

In 1942, the labour movement's bitter experiences caused it to engage in more militant industrial action and also active political support for the CCF, whose labour platform accorded with their own. Throughout 1942, the CCF was attracting members, supporters and revenue, and was becoming a credible alternative to the two old parties, particularly in the province of Ontario. "The greatest new source from which the CCF was deriving members and revenue was Ontario's mushrooming trade union movement."[53] Three days before the Kirkland Local ended its strike, Joe Noseworthy, the CCF candidate, defeated Arthur Meighen in York South. This campaign, which was actively assisted by organized labour, provided further impetus to CCF organizing. The CCL moved toward a more formal relationship with the CCF, and the CCF–Trade Union Committee in Ontario worked toward this end. Its activities eventually culminated in a labour conference sponsored by the CCF which formally endorsed the party as the "political arm of labour." Only eight months after the CCF victory in York South, the 1942 CCL convention recommended that its constituent unions study the CCF program.[54]

These events did not pass unnoticed. The level of industrial unrest and the surge of support for the CCF motivated Hepburn's previously anti-labour government to do an about-face. At the 1942 CCL convention, Ontario Labour Minister Peter Heenan announced that his government was planning to introduce an Ontario collective bargaining act.[55] This announcement was premature, as the Ontario Collective Bargaining Act was not enacted until April 1943, but, against the background of Kirkland Lake and the federal government's continued opposition to collective bargaining, its effect was electrifying. Labour's increasing support of the CCF also influenced the Ontario Conservatives, who adopted a Twenty-Two Point Program for the 1943 campaign, which included "comprehensive collective bargaining legislation." The federal Conservatives chose progressive premier John Bracken of Manitoba as their new leader and drafted a new program designed to combat the CCF. At the end of 1942, King himself expressed "some concern" with the marked rise in CCF support and its developing alliance with organized labour; his man concern was not yet with the CCF.[56] As has already been noted, he responded to labour dissatisfaction directly during the steel strike by reconstituting the NWLB, which became a tripartite body which included J.L. Cohen as the labour representative. The new board was more independent of the Labour Department. It was to meet in public and function as an "industrial court" which would develop a specialized "labour jurisprudence,"[57] and was empowered to inquire and report to the minister of labour on labour matters. Thus it would have an indirect role in policy making.

In April 1943, following a public inquiry by a committee of the Ontario legislature, the Collective Bargaining Act was passed. This legislation represented "the first attempt in Canada to enforce on employers in positive terms a duty to bargain collectively."[58] Like PC 10802, it increased the pressure for a comprehensive federal code. The Ontario Liberals had enacted the statute in order to indicate their concern with the state of labour–management relations,[59] but it did not take effect until June, and its passage was too late to prevent the defeat of the Liberals in August. Nevertheless, it was an important influence on the federal government and its provisions were later substantially reproduced in the federal order-in-council PC 1003. In addition, the public hearings preceding the bill provided a public forum which labour used to mobilize support for its position.

At the hearings there was only token opposition from business. The committee canvassed the issue of compulsory collective bargaining, the legal status of trade unions, the principle of majority rule in determining support for a union, and the status of "company unions."[60] Labour, of course, supported compulsory collective bargaining and proposed an exclusive bargaining agency for the majority union, legally binding agreements enforceable through arbitration procedures, and the proscription of employer dominated "company unions." Business only tentatively opposed compulsory collective bargaining since it realized that its legislation was now inevitable. However, business groups sought the registration and incorporation of unions so they could be sued for damages, and favoured proportional representation in situations where there existed a union and employee association. Employers proposed that employee committees which were not "unduly influenced" by the employer should be eligible for certification and sought a legislative guarantee of the employer's "right" to state his position on the question of unionization.[61]

The Ontario legislation was a compromise between these two positions. The principle of compulsory collective bargaining was recognized, as was the concept of majority rule and the exclusive bargaining agency. Unions were not incorporated, but they did have to file their officers' names and a financial statement with the registrar of the Labour Court. The wording of the act was vague about "company unions," but presumably if they were reasonably independent, they could be certified. Labour had advocated a tripartite administrative tribunal to enforce the act, and stressed the importance of industrial relations experience if the act was to be effectively administered. Business did not express much concern about enforcement. The Ontario Collective Bargaining Act, while modelled in general on the American Wagner Act, established a Labour Court, rather than a labour relations board, to administer the statute. The Labour Court was part of the High Court of Ontario and was granted exclusive jurisdiction to handle all questions arising under the act. Judges rotated and sat for two-week periods in the Labour Court. The court was empowered to determine the unit of employees appropriate for collective bargaining, and certify the trade union which represented the majority of them. It could also order the "decertification" of a union which lost majority support and could refuse to certify an employer-dominated organization. In addition, it had broad remedial powers to deal with violations of the act, and could, for example, order the reinstatement of employees unlawfully discharged. The Labour Court mechanism was criticized by labour for its "legalism" and formality, but organized labour generally supported the act. Despite its imperfections, it was serving a need. It effectively ended the need for recognition strikes. In its first six months of operation, the Labour Court was primarily preoccupied with certification proceedings, and received 130 applications affecting approximately 80 000 persons. While employees' associations continued to be certified as well as unions, certification of unions predominated.[62]

The Labour Court experiment influenced later federal legislation, for, after considering the problems faced by the court, the federal government rejected this device in favour of a quasi-judicial administrative tribunal. The Labour Court mechanism had been rather cumbersome. The judges had no specific labour relations expertise, and, since they sat in rotation for short periods of time, they did not have the opportunity to develop such expertise. Formal court procedures and rules of evidence were inappropriate and unnecessary. For example, the industrial relations criteria necessary for a sound determination of the appropriate bargaining unit were not necessarily amenable to legal proof.[63] Interestingly, the court proved less sympathetic to craft unions than the U.S. National Labour Relations Board, and in administering representation votes tended to emphasize the majority principle, and give relatively less weight to the demands for independent status made by small groups of skilled craftsmen. In this respect, the early reservations of the TLC craft unions concerning the desirability of the Wagner principles turned out to be entirely justified.

In April 1943 the federal government had announced that the NWLB would conduct its own public inquiry into the causes of labour unrest (which in 1943 involved almost a quarter of a million workers and resulted in over a million man-days lost).[64] In February, when the NWLB was reconstituted, the government had had no intention of introducing a national labour code or of using the board for this purpose. The change in its attitude was a response to the high level of industrial unrest, and the increasing popularity of the CCF, which was now strongly supported by organized labour.[65] The public hearings of the NWLB gave labour a national platform from which to air its grievances. As in Ontario, there was not a great deal of opposition from business. CCL president A.R. Mosher characterized labour policy to that date as "trying to crowd out the effect rather than eliminate the cause of much of the discontent that prevails among the working people of this country."[66] The UAW [United Auto Workers] brief asserted that in a period of industrial growth, it was unreasonable of the government to attempt to curtail the organizing and bargaining activities of unions,[67] which were intended to modify the old system of managerial paternalism. The labour movement demanded a permanent national labour code which recognized the right of labour to organize, enforced recognition of the majority union, outlawed "company" unions, and established a board to effectively administer the act.

In August 1943 the stunning result of the Ontario election brought the defeat of Harry Nixon's Liberals and the election of George Drew, but more significantly, the election of the CCF as Official Opposition. The CCF caucus consisted of 34 members, of whom 19 were trade unionists, (ten TLC and nine CCL) including Charlie Millard, head of the Steelworkers, and Bob Carlin, head of the Mine, Mill, and Smelter Workers.[68] The results of this election finally induced the federal government to alter its labour policy. King recognized that the "CCF had made a telling run in all industrial constituencies, particularly where there had been labour unrest, making clear the combination of the industrial C.I.O. with the political C.C.F."[69] When the federal Liberals lost four by-elections—two to the CCF—shortly after the Ontario results, King feared that it might even be "the beginning of the end of the Liberal Party federally."[70] He attributed his party's setback to "bad handling of labour policies," and poor party organization. J.W. Pickersgill confirmed that at this point in time King "felt the loss of labour's support was the greatest threat to the chances of the Liberal Party winning the next election."[71]

King immediately acted to forestall "this calamity." In August he made a surprise visit to the TLC convention. At that convention, the TLC finally established a political action committee, although it maintained its policy of nonaffiliation to any political party. In September, the CCL convention endorsed the CCF as the political arm of labour. In September, in a speech to the National Liberal Federation, King presented a new platform, which attacked the CCF and appealed to the labour vote. King was, above all, an astute politician. As Daniel Coates has observed:

> The party forming the government between 1935 and 1944 did not accept labour union demands for a change in national labour policy until labour achieved sufficient strength during a war emergency period to join with the CCF party and appear to threaten the survival of the Liberal Party and the government.[72]

In August 1943 both the Majority and the Minority Reports of the NWLB Inquiry were presented to the minister of labour. Both recommended a new labour code which would include the principle of compulsory collective bargaining. The government was now committed to legislation, although the board's reports were not released until January 1944 so that the government could consider its position on both collective bargaining and wage controls. Both issues had played a part in the recent labour unrest. In the interim, the government dismissed J.L. Cohen, the labour representative, from the board (in part for his public discussion of the reports prior to their release). The government finally decided to maintain its system of wage controls despite their unpopularity. In these circumstances, legislation on the collective bargaining issue became a political necessity. The political consensus which King was always seeking to preserve had crumbled during the war, as organized workers sought a new status in industry and government.

PC 1003 was issued in February 1944. It has been viewed as a turning point in the development of our industrial relations system since it became a model for postwar legislation. It adopted the major points of both NWLB reports. It guaranteed the right to organize and bargain collectively, established a procedure for the certification and compulsory recognition of trade unions with majority support, recognized the exclusive bargaining agency principle, defined unfair labour practices, provided for remedies, and outlawed company unions. It established an administrative tribunal (rather than a court) to enforce the order. It incorporated the basic principles of the American Wagner Act but also continued the distinctly Canadian policy of compulsory conciliation prior to a legal strike. Unlike the American legislation, it contained no preamble or policy statement indicating that collective bargaining was in the public interest or a desirable method of conducting employer–employee relations.[73] Again, in contrast to the American legislation, the parties were not entitled to strike or lockout during the term of the agreement. The collective agreement itself, however, was now legally enforceable. The government's primary concern had been, and continued to be, the elimination of industrial conflict, and the concessions to labour contained in the new order were primarily designed to accomplish that purpose. Nevertheless, the order was welcomed by labour, since both trade union organizing and collective bargaining were accorded protection and a clear legal status. Recognition strikes were no longer necessary in order to initiate bargaining. The aspirations of employees were sanctioned by law, and could no longer be regarded as illegitimate. Employer opposition to trade unionism was not eliminated, but many of its manifestations became illegal.

The immediate political impact of the order was to undercut labour's opposition to the government, but because it was implemented in the form of an order-in-council, it would be in effect for the duration of the war only. When it was introduced, the government was responding to an immediate political situation. It was not meant to be a permanent measure. This fact and the increased uncertainty which unions felt at the end of the war concerning the permanence of their organizational and legislative gains, resulted in a new wave of industrial unrest. The emerging issue in this strike wave was union security. These strikes and the decisions taken at a federal–provincial conference immediately following the war, ultimately ensured that the wartime advances would be maintained in the postwar era, albeit in a more decentralized industrial relations system than the one developed during the war emergency. In 1948 the Industrial Relations Investigation Act (IRI Act) replaced PC 1003 and the IDI Act at the federal level. The provinces either opted into this legislation or adopted similar acts of their own.

The war years were crucial for the development of the Canadian labour movement. Union membership grew tremendously. Large industrial unions proved to be permanent. Labour achieved legislative protection as a result of pressure on both the industrial and political fronts. The change in wartime labour relations consisted of a process whereby bargaining relationships were facilitated and thereby stabilized. At the beginning of the war, the government's labour policy had been "noninterventionist," but despite its alleged "neutrality" it had in practice been restrictive. The old industrial relations system based on little government intervention except through the imposition of conciliation proved inadequate to deal with conflicts over the issue of collective bargaining. The NASCO dispute pointed out these legislative inadequacies. The loss of the Kirkland Lake recognition strike was such a threat to the future of organized labour that thereafter the TLC and the CCL, despite their organizational rivalries, united to demand legislative remedies. The government's refusal to implement collective bargaining legislation and labour's opposition to wage controls impelled the labour movement to take political action.

The year 1943 was a watershed in the development of wartime labour policy as labour's strike activity and political action reached a peak. Such action did not end wage controls, but did result in positive legislation in a new system which recognized trade unions, institutionalized collective bargaining, defined unfair labour practices and provided remedies, and legitimized trade union activity through legally binding collective agreements. To regulate industrial relations, the government introduced a new independent mechanism, the specialized administrative tribunal. Henceforth the "rules of the game" would be determined, in part, by a body representative of the parties bound by those rules, and the roles of the judges and courts would be reduced. This mechanism, (which was originally merely an extension of wartime political control of the economy) became a permanent part of the policy-making apparatus following the war.

Labour did not gain significant representation in government, but it did win a limited role on the new tripartite tribunal. These legislative and administrative reforms were not achieved within the context of a socialist society as some labour leaders had hoped. Consequently, the conservative administration of labour legislation would inevitably create tensions between labour, business, and government. Because of their wartime experiences, the CCL industrial unions formed a relatively permanent political alliance with the CCF. This factor probably decreased labour's influence as an interest group. The labour movement would never achieve the degree of participation in government which it had sought during the war years.[74]

The impact of trade unionism during the war on the position of employees was significant. Trade union pressure helped to initiate improvements on the job and preserved them at the end of the war. The seniority principle, for example, introduced a new measure of job security. The trade union became a permanent part of the labour relations process at every organized plant, and acted to ensure that the agreement was properly interpreted and administered. The grievance procedure provided a practical method for resolving disputes if an employee believed that he was being treated in an arbitrary or discriminatory manner or had been discharged or disciplined "without just cause." This was perhaps the most important achievement of the period. Mackenzie King could incorporate social welfare measures into the Liberal platform in order to undermine the political gains of the CCF (though not its alliance with labour) to ensure his reelection in 1945. But the restrictions on the previously unfettered authority of management and the resulting changes in the status of employees on the shop floor were permanent. To that extent a degree of democracy in industry was achieved.

Notes

1. Selig Perlman quoted in E.W. Bakke, C. Kerr, and C. Anrod, eds., *Unions, Management and the Public* (New York, 1967), 47.
2. *Labour Organizations in Canada* (Ottawa, 1949), 15.
3. Ruth Pierson, "Women's Emancipation and the Recruitment of Women into the Labour Force in World War II," in *The Neglected Majority*, ed. S.M. Trofimenkoff and A. Prentice (Toronto, 1977), 126.
4. Charles Lipton, *The Trade Union Movement in Canada 1827–1959* (Montreal, 1968), 267.
5. This was a factor among older workers in the Kirkland Lake strike; *Sudbury Star*, 3 March 1942.
6. In 1946, which is often considered a peak year of industrial unrest in Canada, only one trade union member in six was involved in strike activity. The most recent comparable example of membership participation in strike activity was in 1976 on account of the political "National Day of Protest" against wage controls. See *Strikes and Lockouts in Canada* (Ottawa, 1977).
7. For example, the Knights of Labor and the One Big Union.
8. Canadian labour historians have emphasized AFL pressure on the TLC expulsion. Certainly this was a factor, but the fundamental disagreements within the TLC prior to 1939 were important. Note Charles Lipton, *Trade Union Movement*, 261–64, and Irving Abella, *Nationalism, Communism and Canadian Labour* (Toronto, 1973), chap. 2.
9. William Arnold Martin, "A Study of Legislation Designed to Foster Industrial

Peace in the Common Law Jurisdiction of Canada" (PhD diss., University of Toronto, 1954), 291.

10. Ibid., 299–302.
11. *TLC Convention Proceedings* (Ottawa, 1942).
12. *Labour Gazette* (Ottawa, 1943), 1613.
13. "The pressures of taxation, controls and restrictions were beginning to get ordinary men and women down. . . . In 1941 for the first time the war began to hit home" in J.L. Granatstein, *Canada's War* (Toronto, 1975), 159.
14. J.L. Cohen, *Collective Bargaining in Canada* (Toronto, 1941), 26.
15. The Kirkland Lake strike was an example of a union whose bargaining position was undermined by prolonged delays prior to the walkout.
16. There was a close similarity between management and government views of "irresponsible" union leaders, by whom they usually meant CCL trade unionists.
17. William Arnold Martin, "Industrial Peace," 292.
18. Irving Bernstein, *The Turbulent Years* (Boston, 1971), 78.
19. J.L. Cohen, *Collective Bargaining in Canada* (Toronto, 1941), 34.
20. This position was clearly stated by the minister of labour, Norman McLarty, in a speech on 7 November 1941. See *Ottawa Morning Journal*, 7 Nov. 1941.
21. J.L. Cohen, *Collective Bargaining in Canada*, 47. See also Granatstein, *Canada's War*, 185–86.
22. *Canadian Unionist* (Montreal), Sept. 1941, 87.
23. Public Archives of Canada (PAC), CLC Papers, vol. 38, Memo to Prime Minister from SWOC, Local 2352, 3 July 1941.
24. Ibid., J.L. Cohen to Norman McLarty, 18 May 1941.
25. Memo to Prime Minister from SWOC Local 2352, 3 July 1941.
26. PC 7440 was interpreted publicly in a narrow way by the minister of labour in his "Wartime Wages Policy" speech of 31 March 1941.
27. PAC, CLC Papers, vol. 38, Conciliation Board Report.
28. Ibid.
29. Ibid., Minority Report.
30. The government's assurances were to the effect that the wage-control policy would be administered flexibly to take account of factors in individual cases. Daniel Coates, "Organized Labor and Politics in Canada: The Development of a National Labor Code" (PhD diss., Cornell University, 1973), 84.
31. PAC, King Papers, vol. 310, William Lyon Mackenzie King Memoranda, Memo on Peck Rolling Mills, 21 May 1941.
32. Ibid.
33. PAC, CLC Papers, vol. 38, Minority Report.
34. T. Copp, "The Impact of Wage and Price Controls on Workers in Montreal 1939–47" (unpublished paper delivered at CHA Meetings, 1976), 5.
35. Ibid., 6.
36. Conciliation Board Report, in *Canadian Unionist*, Oct. 1941, 108–109.
37. Archives of Ontario, Hepburn Papers, 1942 Strikes—Kirkland Lake, Private Correspondence.
38. PAC, King Primary Correspondence, vol. 310, Memo, Norman McLarty to William Lyon Mackenzie King, 3 Dec. 1941.
39. Ibid.
40. Jim Russel, Joe Rankin, Jock Brodie, and Bill Sefton became international representatives on Staff of the United Steelworkers of America (USWA). Eamon Park, who worked on publicity during the strike, became an international representative and subsequently assistant to the national director in Canada of the USWA. Larry Sefton, the young recording secretary of Local 240, went on staff as an interna-

tional representative of the Steelworkers and in 1953 was elected as director of district 6 of that union. He later became a member of the International Executive Board of the Steelworkers' union and a vice president of the Canadian Labour Congress. Bob Carlin, Local 240's financial secretary became the Canadian representative for district 8 on the International Board of the International Union of Mine Mill and Smelter Workers (IUMMSW) in 1942. In 1943, he was elected to the Ontario legislature as the CCF member from Sudbury. William Simpson, president, Local 240, became a staff representative for the IUMMSW.

41. H.A. Logan, *Trade Unions in Canada* (Toronto, 1948), 547.
42. Daniel Coates, "Organized Labour," 102–106.
43. Ibid., 106.
44. Ibid., 105.
45. Bora Laskin, "Recent Labour Legislation in Canada," *Canadian Bar Review* 22 (Nov. 1944): 776–92.
46. W.A. Martin, "Industrial Peace," 346.
47. Daniel Coates, "Organized Labour," 105.
48. Ibid., 108.
49. *Labour Gazette* (Ottawa, 1943), 61–68.
50. Ibid., 193.
51. Daniel Coates, "Organized Labour," 126.
52. Ibid., 128.
53. G. Caplan, *The Dilemma of Canadian Socialism* (Toronto, 1973), 95.
54. Ibid.
55. *CCL Convention Proceedings* (Ottawa, 1942).
56. Daniel Coates, "Organized Labour," 138.
57. *Labour Gazette* (Ottawa, 1943), 167.
58. Bora Laskin, "Collective Bargaining in Ontario: A New Legislative Approach," *Canadian Bar Review* 21 (Nov. 1943): 684.
59. Daniel Coates, "Organized Labour."
60. Ontario, *Proceedings of Select Committee Re Bargaining between Employers and Employees* (1943), Legislative Library, Toronto.
61. Ibid.
62. Archives of Ontario, Ontario Department of Labour Papers, Ontario Labour Court, "Summary of Activities of the Labour Court, June 14, 1943, to December 31, 1943."
63. Bora Laskin, "Collective Bargaining in Ontario," 693.
64. *Strikes and Lockouts in Canada* (Ottawa, 1977).
65. Daniel Coates, "Organized Labour," 137.
66. Stephen Purdy, "Another Look at Order-In-Council PC 1003" (unpublished graduate paper, York University, 1976), 8.
67. Ibid., 10.
68. Gad Horowitz, *Canadian Labour In Politics* (Toronto, 1968), 77.
69. Daniel Coates, "Organized Labour," 138.
70. Ibid., 139.
71. Ibid., 140.
72. Ibid., 225.
73. Such a provision became part of the Ontario legislation in 1970, and the federal legislation in 1972.
74. In its recent opposition to the present wage controls, the CLC requested greater consultation in government. When it did not get it, it embarked on its "National Day of Protest." *CLC Manifesto* (Ottawa, 1976).

One of the toughest wartime strikes was fought by gold miners at Kirkland Lake, Ontario, November 1941 to February 1942. Events there became part of Canadian labour and left-wing political legend.

Kirkland Lake 1943

James Wreford

Under the dark industrial sky
we wonder why we have to die
who living, were valued at a wage
that starved our youth and murdered age.
Or why engage for tyrants here
to end the tyranny of fear,
whose quarrel is with all of those
the heavens of our desire that close?
For justice undertake a cause
that has no justice in its laws,
but claims for unity the right
forbids the citizen unite.
For thirty dollars shall we sell
our happiness to mend their hell,
to save their cuckoos, clear our nest,
redeem by our unrest their rest
and fight for freedom who are not free?
Let freemen die, but why should we
who toil to set the rich on high
three shifts beneath the smoking sky?
Let those who call on us to keep
their freedom safe and safe their sleep

account and pledge us higher for
the wealth and peace our griefs ensure:
a week-end fit for play like theirs
and futures guaranteed from cares,
evenings when not too tired a man
his leisures takes and pleasure can,
a chance for more than daily bread—
their daughters for our sons to wed,
so working and in wanting we
may equal them and be as free.
But till that day let them not cry
upon our loyal sons to die,
who with our usual logic see
they die for freedom that are free.

Mackenzie King believed that the scheme for family allowances would be remembered as one of his most enlightened achievements in Canadian politics. Some diehard Tories were convinced that the scheme was really a bribe to Quebec, where *la revanche du berceau* would work to the province's advantage. Naturally, the Liberals emphasized the benefits the payments would bring to all Canadian children. In the end, the scheme proved irresistible, and the Tories supported it to demonstrate that they now really were Progressive Conservatives. In the boom period that followed World War II, welfare-state issues were front and centre in Canadian politics.

Mackenzie King and the Genesis of Family Allowances in Canada, 1939–1944

Raymond B. Blake

In July 1945, the Canadian government introduced a system of universal family allowances providing monthly cash payments to all families with children under the age of sixteen. This was one of the most important events in Canada's evolving social security system. However, Canadian academics who have studied family allowances have rarely treated them primarily as a social security measure, perhaps because of the scepticism with which they view the enigmatic prime minister Mackenzie King, who introduced the measure. Whatever the reason, King's family allowances have been portrayed as a policy to appease labour and maintain the wartime price- and wage-stabilization program, as a political weapon to beat the surging socialist hordes in the Co-operative Commonwealth Federation, and as the triumph of macroeconomic management and Keynesian economics.[1] In other words, Mackenzie King believed Canada should have family allowances if necessary, but not necessarily because of social security. This is only part of the story, however.

The Mackenzie King government adopted family allowances as part of its postwar social security program, but it realized that there were other benefits too. Mackenzie King had a lifelong commitment to the ideals of social security. Academics have often commented derisively that he loved to point out that he had outlined the need for social security and many other things in 1918, when he wrote *Industry and Humanity: A Study in the Principles Underlying Industrial Construction*. There is also general agreement that King was a cautious politician and acted only when he was convinced that policies would serve the interests of his country, his party, and his leadership. King believed that the conditions were right for the introduction of family allowances in 1945, as they had been in 1940 for his unemployment insurance scheme. Moreover, King was influenced by international discussions on social security and family allowances, and he believed that action on his part would re-establish his claim to be a pioneer in the field, a claim he made often to other allied leaders. Finally, King and many others in Canada recognized the importance of social security, together with increased government intervention to maintain full employment, as a way of preserving the liberal democratic state.

Mackenzie King and other world leaders were obviously worried about the postwar period. The memories of the turmoil and uncertainty in the aftermath of the First World War were fresh in their minds. So, too, was the prolonged economic crisis of the 1930s. Governments everywhere realized that the transition from war to peace had to be made without a return to the problem of unemployment and want that had characterized the prewar period. "When the war is won, there will be an immense task to repair the great physical destruction caused by the war," King told the American Federation of Labor at its 1942 convention in Toronto. "These tasks alone will provide work for millions of men and women for many years. But the work of repairing and restoring the ravages of war will not be enough," he warned. Governments everywhere had to work to eliminate the fear of unemployment and the sense of insecurity that workers faced when their capacity to meet the needs of their families was threatened. "Until these fears have been eliminated," he told labour leaders, "the war for freedom will not be won. The era of freedom will be achieved only as social security and human welfare become the main concern of men and nations." The specifics of social welfare, he admitted, would have to be spelled out in due course, but the "new order" he envisioned for Canada would include, as a "national minimum," full employment, adequate nutrition and housing, health insurance, and social security. "Men who have fought in this war, and others who have borne its privations and sufferings, will never be satisfied with a return to the conditions which prevailed before 1939," he acknowledged in closing. "The broader and deeper conception of victory will be found only in a new world order."[2]

Mackenzie King was not alone in recognizing the need for greater social security. Earlier, in January 1941, President

Franklin D. Roosevelt had told the American Congress that international security rested upon four essential human freedoms. One of these was freedom from want. Only when each nation could provide an acceptable standard of living for its people would there truly be freedom. Anthony Eden, the British foreign secretary, had told his compatriots on 29 May 1941 that one of the postwar aims of the British government was to establish "social security abroad as well as at home, through co-ordinated efforts of Britain, the Dominions, the United States and South America to stabilize currencies, feed starving peoples, [and] avert fluctuations of employment, prices and markets."[3] Roosevelt and British prime minister Winston Churchill reiterated these principles in the Atlantic Charter on 14 August 1941: "[We] desire to bring about the fullest collaboration between all nations in the economic field with the object of securing, for all, improved labour standards, economic adjustment and social security." At a conference on social security in Chile in September 1942, over twenty countries from North and South America agreed that they should adopt policies promoting greater social security. The conference co-ordinator, Nelson Rockefeller, captured the outlook of the participants when he stated that "This is a war about social security; it is a war for social security."[4]

King's minister most interested in social security agreed. Ian Mackenzie, the minister of pensions and national health, epitomized fears for the postwar period when he told an audience in June 1941 that "if old dogmas and old doctrines—old philosophies of government—cannot solve that problem—then we must look to newer remedies and new faiths and newer solutions."[5] Speaking in September 1942, he said, "I want the working man in the factory, the soldier on the battle front, the young mother caring for her overseas husband's little children to know that the Government in whom they have reposed their confidence not only shares their aspirations for a brighter tomorrow, but is, in a direct and positive way, planning to that end."[6]

Reconstruction planning in Canada was a major concern almost from the onset of hostilities. Shortly after Canada declared war on Germany, the King cabinet started to think about the postwar period and created a Cabinet Committee on Demobilization and Re-establishment on 8 December 1939, chaired by Ian Mackenzie. Initially, the committee was only interested in the demobilization and reintegration of the Armed Forces into civilian society. In 1941, Mackenzie convinced the cabinet to create a Committee on Reconstruction "to examine and discuss the general question of post-war reconstruction, and to make recommendations as to what Government facilities should be established to deal with the question."[7] The committee was chaired by Dr. Cyril James, principal of McGill University; Leonard C. Marsh was appointed research director.

In its first memorandum, prepared in May 1941, it suggested that the major aim of reconstruction policies must be to have adequate employment for veterans and displaced workers who had been engaged in war production. Like many other Canadians, members of the James Committee were worried about the preservation of democratic institutions. "If, for any reason, reconstruction should not proceed smoothly, during the postwar recession the country would inevitably be confronted by rapidly mounting unemployment and widespread dissatisfaction."[8] Later, when the James Committee produced a series of recommendations, calling for, among other things, a minister of economic planning to administer the planning for the postwar period, it raised the ire of the Economic Advisory Committee (EAC), a group of senior bureaucrats in Ottawa who were managing the war effort and who, perhaps, saw James as a threat. In an attempt to control postwar reconstruction themselves, they persuaded the cabinet that the James Committee be made responsible to the Privy Council Office—to which the EAC ultimately reported. In January 1943, this was done, and the James Committee was renamed the Advisory Cmmittee on Reconstruction.[9] The EAC also created its own committee on reconstruction. The decision to have the James Committee's recommendations overseen by the Advisory Committee on Economic Policy, whose mandate had been broadened to include postwar economic policy, has been interpreted as a failure of the James Committee and an attempt by the government to weaken its recommendations. Too much should not be read into the bureaucratic in-fighting, however. No one should have really expected the government and its senior bureaucrats to have surrendered their authority over postwar planning to a committee of outsiders. What is clear is that there was considerable public interest in, and pressure for, increased social security as part of the postwar reconstruction process, and the bureaucracy was determined not to let the agenda be established by outsiders, no matter how well-intentioned these private citizens might have been.[10] Meanwhile, the House of Commons had established its own Special Committee on Reconstruction and Re-establishment in March 1942 and the Senate later followed with its own committee.

Prime Minister Mackenzie King considered social security an important aspect of the new world order he envisioned after the war, and he spoke of the great need for it early in the war. When he joined Roosevelt at the White House for dinner on 5 December 1942, he and the president discussed the British report on reconstruction, *Social Insurance and Allied Services*—popularly known as the Beveridge Report after its author, Sir William Beveridge—released a few days earlier in London. King was impressed when Roosevelt said that they should "work together on the lines of social reform in which we had always been deeply interested." Of course, King pointed out that much of the program Beveridge recommended could be found in his *Industry and Humanity*.[11] More important, King was relieved that he and Roosevelt could now turn to matters other than the war, and he thought that it was time for him to think more of reconstruction, as the war seemed to be turning in the Allies' favour. "I would have something to say in that matter," he told his diary the next day.[12]

Over the coming weeks, King would continue to contemplate the issue of social security. When Ian Mackenzie accompanied him to a funeral in Brockville, Ontario, in January 1943, they discussed the need for social security, of which Mackenzie was already an advocate.[13] When Cyril James had presented him with a draft memorandum from the Committee on Reconstruction late in 1942, Mackenzie had told him that he was disappointed that there was no specific mention of social security, which "today, more than anything else, is occupying the attention of the peoples of the world."[14] In January, King also received a memorandum from Vincent Massey, the high commissioner in London, summarizing the Beveridge Report and a speech that Beveridge made after its release in which he credited prime ministers Lloyd George and Churchill for their creative social security measures earlier in their careers. King was determined not to be outdone, and he confided to his diary that "I should be happy indeed if I could round out my career with legislation in the nature of social security."[15]

King acted immediately. At a meeting of the cabinet on 12 January, he pointed out the need to discuss social security during the upcoming session. He found a number of his powerful cabinet colleagues, including the minister of finance, J.L. Ilsley, the minister of munitions and supply, C.D. Howe, and the minister of mines and resources, T.A. Crerar, opposed to the idea of greater social security. Such resistance prompted King to write, "The mind of the Cabinet, at any rate, does not grasp the significance of [the] Beveridge report."[16] He had encountered similar opposition in 1940 when he began discussions on the unemployment insurance bill, but he pressed forward and enacted legislation over the wishes of some of his ministers.[17] Again, despite the opposition of senior and influential ministers, King pushed ahead and outlined in the 1943 speech from the throne his government's objective to pursue a policy of social security.

Discussing his plans for social security seemed to rejuvenate the prime minister. In fact, King chose to write—with the aid of *Industry and Humanity*, of course—the sections on social security for the speech from the throne. He discussed those sections with both the cabinet and the caucus so that "there could be no word said later that all was not fully understood."[18] In the speech from the throne on 28 January 1943, the governor general announced the government's commitment to social security and stated that a "comprehensive national scheme of social insurance should be worked out at once which will constitute a charter of social security for the whole of Canada." King did make it clear that the first and immediate objective of his government was to win the war. Only with victory within its grasp could the government concern itself with other matters. Moreover, he told his caucus that he would never allow an election on the matter of social security during the war, as this might be interpreted as a bribe from the public treasury. He said that his government was committed first to a policy of full employment and "it was wrong to think of increased outlays on anything that could be avoided until victory was won. Important, however, to keep everything in readiness for peace."[19] On 3 March 1943, King moved in the House of Commons the appointment of a special committee on national social insurance to study the matter further. King would later be criticized for not rushing forward to enact his plans for social security, but the British and the Americans, after showing considerable enthusiasm for the Beveridge Report and the report of the National Resources Planning Board, respectively, decided to do little.[20] In the end, King would go much further with social security than either his American or British counterparts.

Shortly after the speech from the throne, Leonard Marsh released his *Report on Social Security for Canada*. The decision to have Marsh make his report came two weeks after the release of the Beveridge Report in England. Marsh presented his recommendations to the House of Commons Special Committee on Reconstruction in March 1943. It proposed a "comprehensive and integrated social security system for Canada, set out priorities for implementation of the different proposals, [and] dealt with decisions respecting administration and constitutional jurisdiction, and with financial considerations."[21] It was a plan for freedom from want for every Canadian from the cradle to the grave. He proposed maternity benefits and children's allowances to cover children until they could earn for themselves. For most of a person's adult life there would be unemployment insurance and unemployment assistance, sickness benefits, free medical insurance, and pensions for permanent disability and for widows. For old age, Marsh proposed old-age pensions and, finally, funeral benefits.

Interestingly, King seems to have largely ignored the report. Nonetheless, he continued to discuss and think about many of the issues that Marsh raised, and he must certainly have been aware of the interest that Marsh had generated in social security across the country. The Canadian Association of Social Workers, for instance, had written King that it gave the Marsh Report its approval. He was certainly aware that both Britain and the United States had produced similar reports. Yet King might have believed that he really had no need for Marsh: King himself was the expert on social security and had seen years earlier the need for much of what Marsh and Beveridge were only now recommending. He did not record discussing the Marsh Report with either Anthony Eden or Beveridge when the two visited Ottawa late in March 1943.

Although the *Report on Social Security for Canada* was merely a position paper put forth by the James Committee on Reconstruction, and was not official government policy, it was clear to most, inside and outside Ottawa, that the King government was committed to the policy of social security. When R.B. Bryce, secretary of the EAC, produced a memorandum for W.C. Clark, the deputy minister of finance, suggesting items to be included in a statement of postwar economic policy, he reminded him that "the government will endeavour to develop and broaden the social security system of Canada."[22]

One proposal under consideration for broadening social security was family allowances. Indeed, when Ian Mackenzie appeared before the House of Commons Special Select Committee on Social Security on 16 March 1943 to discuss the government's health insurance plan, he talked briefly about the importance of family allowances.[23] Not long after, the bureaucracy started to discuss the possibility of family allowances as an alternative to wage increases. Norman Robertson, undersecretary of state for external affairs, wrote King on 8 June 1943 that he had attended a small meeting with Judge C.P. McTague, who was investigating labour conditions in Canada. It was agreed that wages rates had to increase or some alternative be found to achieve the same end. Robertson thought that family allowances might meet the needs of workers. Moreover, he told King, family allowances were inevitable in the long run, and they would go a long way to meeting the demand for social justice.[24] Graham Towers, governor of the Bank of Canada, made a similar suggestion to W.C. Clark on 13 June 1943, that children's allowances be introduced to maintain the government's wage-stabilization policy that had been implemented early in the war to control inflation. Towers noted that the government was determined to introduce a "reasonable minimum of [social] security after the war" and he would prefer to see family allowances introdued at that point. Yet family allowances would meet the "legitimate needs" of labour by placing more money in the hands of workers while allowing the government to keep the rate of inflation under control. The principle of children's allowances was not new, he reminded Clark: the government was already paying an allowance for each child in the form of an income tax credit to wage earners who made more than $1200 per year. Family allowances, he added, deserved a higher priority than old age pensions, for example, because "children are even more helpless than old people, and money spent to ensure children's minimum health and education needs are [sic] more likely to be a productive national investment." He also suggested that the introduction of family allowances would enhance Canada's prestige internationally as well as safeguard its economy. Canadian wartime controls had become an example to those in the United States who wanted to control inflation, and children's allowances "would be striking proof that Canada intended to push ahead with progressive policies after the war. It might have appreciable influence in strengthening the hand of like-minded administrations in other countries," Towers concluded.[25]

The EAC adopted Towers' suggestion in mid-July when it realized that it would

Justice Minister Ernest Lapointe (left), Defence Minister Norman Rogers (centre), and Prime Minister Mackenzie King (right) in March 1940. Only Mackenzie King would survive the war: Lapointe died of cancer and Rogers was killed in an air crash. City of Toronto Archives, G&M 64673

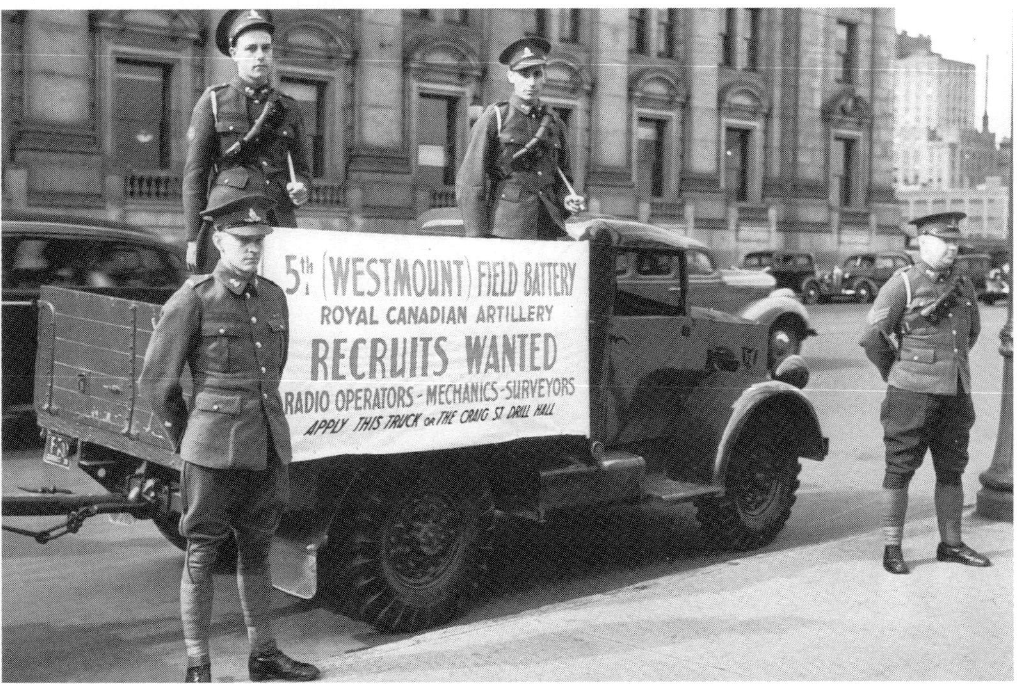

When the war began in 1939, the Canadian Army still had equipment from the Great War. This Montreal recruiting team was well turned-out in tunics, puttees, and forage caps. Its artillery pieces were similarly of 1918 vintage. NAC, PA 129601

The fall of France and the fear that Britain might be invaded galvanized the Canadian war effort. Money and goods poured forth to help Britain, not least the tinned food collected by Toronto's Boy Scouts. City of Toronto Archives, G&M 67237

Canadians opened their hearts and homes to thousands of children evacuated from the British cities that were being blitzed by the Luftwaffe. These two schoolboys, their now unnecessary gas masks at the ready, found safety in the Dominion after 1940. City of Toronto Archives, G&M 69562

After Japan entered the war in December 1941, Canadian Japanese living in British Columbia fell under suspicion. In early 1942, Ottawa ordered all 22 000 moved from the coast to town sites in the interior. NAC, C-46350, Tak Toyota

Wartime exhortations were everywhere. This gas station simultaneously sold gas, rationed to 120 gallons a year, collected war salvage, and urged conservation on its customers. City of Toronto Archives, SC 488

(left) Although the enemy had scarcely any capacity to launch air strikes at Canadian soil, Ottawa decreed that blackouts be imposed. Families had to fit their windows with blackout curtains while air raid wardens roamed the streets enforcing the orders. NAC, PA 112885

(below) Scarce foods such as meat, butter, and sugar were rationed. Butchers had to consult their chart to ensure that they did not violate Wartime Prices and Trade Board regulations. City of Toronto Archives, G&M 98887

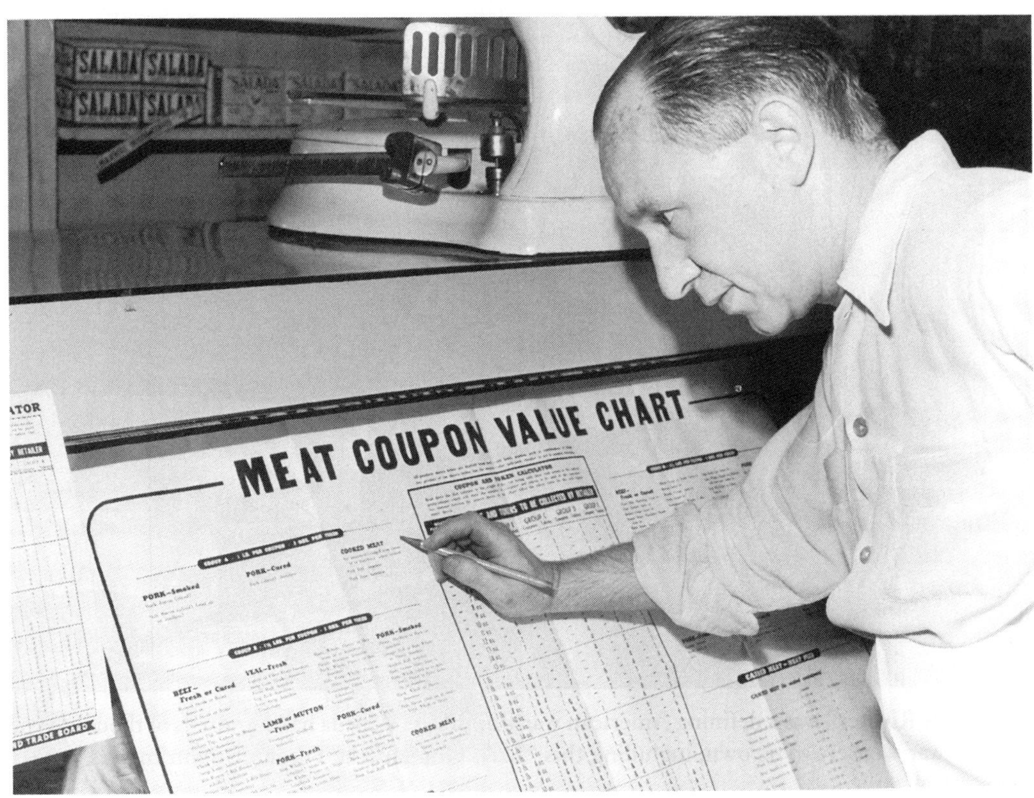

Maclean's Magazine, June 1, 1945

OPPORTUNITIES *for* ALL

YOUR Liberal Government under Mackenzie King has taken practical steps to see that every Canadian after the war shall have a wide-open chance to make a real success of his life. It can be done by giving everybody the opportunity to get ahead faster and go further.

That includes returned men, farmers and fishermen, factory workers and people in business and children—every Canadian!

Isn't that what you want—a chance to make your own way IN your own way?

Here are definite, practical steps which the Liberal Government has taken (not just talked about, but *taken*) to make this Canada a better place to work in and bring up your children.

You will have to decide whether you want the men who devised these measures to carry them through, or whether you wish to entrust your own and your family's future to others.

Every one of the following 12 steps affects your job—no matter what it is—after the war!

1 Reconstruction

Liberal aim: Jobs for 900,000 more workers than in 1939; and 60,000 more each year as the population grows. Every kind of enterprise will be encouraged. The Liberal Government has already set up the machinery: the Department of Reconstruction. The Liberal Government has the man—the Hon. C. D. Howe—under whose direction Canadians have done a great job in the war, **and are ready to do it in peace.**

2 Foreign Trade

Liberal objective: Sixty percent (60%) increase in value over Canada's pre-war export trade. This means thousands of jobs, and is based on the number of jobs created by Canada's normal export trade. Preparations are under way now: expansion of trade commissioner service; negotiations with United States and United Kingdom and other countries. **Liberal policies and trade mean full employment.**

3 Credit for Enterprise

Liberal belief: Money must serve the needs of humanity. The people of Canada shall have economic freedom. We are a great people—we are going to continue to do big things after the war. Therefore the Liberal Government set up the *Industrial Development Bank* to provide money at low interest for long terms. **Another step towards creating full employment.**

4 Exports Encouraged

War-torn countries will want to buy tremendous quantities of Canadian goods. But can they pay for them right away? Manufacturers can't pay their help unless they can get money for their goods. To overcome this obstacle to employment, the Liberal Government has set up the *Export Credit Insurance Act.* This does two things: (1) it insures Canadian exporters against loss, and (2) makes loans to foreign governments under contract to Canadian exporters.

5 Farm Improvement Loans

Your Liberal Government has made *low interest loans* available to farmers to finance their work and make improvements.

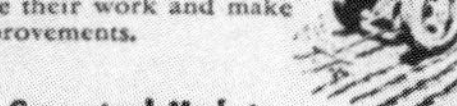

6 Guaranteed Markets

To provide farmers with a better income under wartime conditions, the Liberal Government made contracts for definite quantities of important products at agreed prices—notably bacon, eggs, cheese and beef. These contracts have worked out so well the Liberal Government extended many of the agreements for longer periods (in the above cases to the end of 1946). It has provided for guaranteed markets and income for Canadian farmers. This increased trade has brought prosperity to farmers everywhere in Canada. Liberal legislation (*the Agricultural Prices Support Act*) guarantees future prosperity.

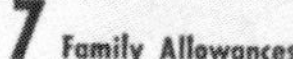

7 Family Allowances

From July next, Family Allowances are to be paid every month to parents for healthier, better clothed, better housed, better educated young Canadians. $250,000,000 a year direct spending power in the hands of people who need it most. Liberal monthly payments until age 16 (maximum total per child $1,224) will give all children a better chance to become vigorous happy citizens.

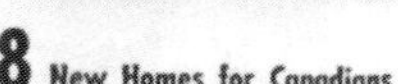

8 New Homes for Canadians

The Liberal Government's new $400,000,000 *National Housing Act* enables hundreds of thousands of Canadians to own their own homes. In the first year after Germany's defeat, at least 50,000 dwellings will be built. Low rental housing schemes are included. This means hundreds of thousands of jobs for the building trades and allied industries—**many thousands more for people who make furnishings and home equipment.**

9 Returning Veterans

Canada's generous plans for enabling returned men to take their place in civil life are now well known. Gratuities, benefits and grants of $750,000,000 will enable men and women of the Armed Services to apply their energies in **building the prosperous Canada for which your Liberal Government has been planning.**

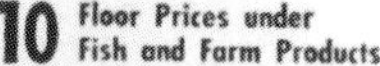

10 Floor Prices under Fish and Farm Products

Success in farming and fishing depends upon the maintenance of fair prices. To protect farmers and fishermen, the Liberal Government has provided floor prices under these products. **Prosperous farmers and fishermen make a prosperous Canada.**

11 Better Labour Conditions

In co-operation with organized Labour, the Liberal Government has confirmed collective bargaining, provided unemployment insurance, organized labour-management committees, approved labour representatives on government boards. More than 600,000 workers, because of the Liberal Government's attitude towards Labour and the labour movement, **now get annual vacations with pay.**

12 Reduction in Taxation

The Liberal Government will gradually reduce taxation now the European war is over. Taxes will come down to free spending power and to give Canadians every opportunity for prosperity, employment and freedom.

What you have done in war—you can do in peace. You can do your part by supporting the Liberal Candidate in your constituency.

BUILD A *NEW SOCIAL ORDER*

VOTE LIBERAL

PUBLISHED BY THE NATIONAL LIBERAL COMMITTEE

The Liberal campaign in the 1945 election talked of the future and of legislation in place for reconstruction, social welfare, veterans' benefits, and prosperity. This tack was much more effective than the CCF's promises and the Tories' harping on conscription for the Pacific. Courtesy *Maclean's,* 1 June 1945

Home at last. Courtesy *Maclean's*, 15 April 1945

be impossible to reconcile the wage-stabilization program with the demands of labour. It saw the introduction of children's allowances as a suitable alternative that would be popular with the general populace and with farmers and labour and, at the same time, would be an "important and well-timed step forward in social security." Hence, the EAC proposed in a draft memorandum on 16 July 1943 that a nation-wide system of family allowances be established to come into effect in January 1944. R.B. Bryce, who penned the EAC memorandum, noted that children's allowances were "widely recognized as an important element in modern systems of social security; they are in effect already in Australia and New Zealand and they have been recommended for Britain." Trying to convince the prime minister of the merits of family allowances, Bryce said that the introduction of such a policy as a wartime measure "would be the most convincing possible evidence of the government's intention to proceed with progressive measures." However, some EAC members argued that family allowances should be introduced only as a part of a postwar social security program.[26]

Throughout the summer, cabinet was concerned with developing new labour policy and was discussing the issue of wages rates and cost of living. There was considerable debate on whether wage controls could be maintained by paying allowances to families, thus avoiding the need to raise wages. King took the opportunity to cast family allowances as a social security matter, not tied to wage rates: "I found the sentiment of Cabinet swinging towards that course [subsidies to large families], on which I think a real policy may be founded for dealing with social security measures."[27] Academics have often made a connection between family allowances and the retention of wage controls,[28] but one cannot simply ignore the fact that when King announced his labour policy of continuing wage controls in December 1943, the implementation of family allowances was still a full nineteen months away.[29] Indeed, the cabinet had not even reached agreement on family allowances. Thus, such allowances could do little in the short term to make continued wage controls palatable to workers. Instead, to appease labour, the government promised to enact compulsory collective bargaining, to adjust wages where injustices and inequalities existed, to include cost-of-living bonuses into the basic wage rates, and to keep inflation under control.[30]

Meanwhile, Mackenzie King and the Liberal Party were obviously worried about the growing popularity of the opposition parties. Both seemed to be attracting popular support, and both threatened to outflank the Liberals with their emphasis on social security. This was especially true of the Co-operative Commonwealth Federation, which had slipped past the Liberals in 1943 public opinion polls and had won a number of federal by-elections. To reassert the progressive nature of King liberalism and to garner lost support, the National Liberal Federation convened in late September 1943 to outline its platform for the postwar period. It promised

Canadians social security, noting that social security and national prosperity were indivisible. The party recommended children's allowances as one of the major planks in its social security program because they would contribute to "a healthy nation with good family life and adequate support of the raising of children."[31] In November 1943, King asked his ministers to make suggestions for postwar reconstruction. Of those who responded by the end of the year, only C.D. Howe wrote that he opposed family allowances, but Howe would garner considerable support from some of his colleagues. All the others who responded to King's query suggested that family allowances be pursued by the government, and Louis St. Laurent, rapidly becoming one of King's favourites, told the prime minister that family allowances were the most important of all social security measures.[32]

Early in January 1944, the King government prepared its legislative agenda for the upcoming parliamentary session. One of the most important matters for King was the issue of family allowances, even though it created "great diversity" within the cabinet.[33] Although in the previous year King had noted in his diary that to give family allowances to everyone was "sheer folly" that might create much resentment toward him and his party,[34] he remained committed to a program of social security and continued to believe that family allowances for larger families went "to the very root of social security in relation to the new order of things which places a responsibility on the State for conditions which the State itself is responsible for creating."[35]

In the Department of Finance, senior officials were preparing the final memorandum on family allowances for J.L. Ilsley. Even though King had divorced family allowances from the wage-stabilization plan, the department still hoped that he would introduce family allowances early in 1944 to ensure support among the general population for the government's economic policy. The bureaucrats agreed with the politicians that the "fundamental basis" for family allowances was that the wage system took no account of family size. Frequently workers with many children were not earning enough to support the whole family. Allowances paid to all children represented "the simplest, wisest, and cheapest way of providing the supplementary family income." Family allowances would also end discrimination against families in the lowest income groups who did not receive tax credits for dependent children. Moreover, allowances might help alleviate the problem many families were having with housing and help to improve the level of education in Canada. A program such as family allowances would bring the government of Canada closer to the people, help children live healthier and more productive lives, and might "allow even one Canadian Milton, Pasteur or Edison to realize possibilities that might otherwise have been frustrated by the accident of his father's income." Finally, the department argued that, although family allowances might be radical for Canada, they had been tried in over thirty-five countries. The memorandum also outlined possible criticisms of family allowances, but it was clear from the document that, no matter what views the bureaucrats had, family allowances were to be presented to the prime minister and his cabinet as a social security measure.[36]

Interestingly, W.C. Clark made the presentation on family allowances for Ilsley to the cabinet. King noted in his diary that Clark "touched upon the necessity of this measure [family allowances] if wage stabilization and price ceiling were to be maintained." King agreed with Clark that family allowances would serve an economic purpose, but he argued strenuously in the cabinet that family allowances were an important social security measure that would create greater opportunity for all Canadian children. The Department of Finance wanted family allowances introduced immediately, but King refused to do so as victory in the war effort remained his most pressing concern. He stressed to cabinet that modern society had changed and that "the present war was all a part of the struggle of the masses to get a chance to live their own lives." He also pointed out that social security measures, such as family allowances, might be the one thing necessary to save liberal democracies such as Canada.[37] Later, while alone at Laurier House, King thought he might have been too aggressive at the end of the discussion, and called Clark to apologize. Clark reassured him that in "dealing with this measure we had given real evidence of our zeal for social security and there could be no questioning of motives or sincerity of the government in its endeavour to do something practical in this way."[38] The cabinet agreed to push ahead with family allowances despite the continued opposition from some of the most influential members. A few days later King told journalist Grant Dexter that he "was the only radical in the Cabinet. Some of his colleagues still think they can go out and shoot a bison for breakfast."[39] Later, in Toronto, Joseph Atkinson of the *Star* reassured King that the introduction of family allowances was a "very absolutely necessary and right measure."[40]

King turned to drafting the section on social welfare policy and family allowances for the speech from the throne. This was an unusual role for the prime minister, although he had done the same a year earlier when he had drafted the section on social security. Again, he struggled to find the right words with which to introduce family allowances. He found some of them in his *Industry and Humanity*. Later, when he read the speech to the Cabinet, he was discouraged that several of his ministers, particularly Ilsley, Crerar, Gardiner, and Howe, persisted in their opposition to family allowances. However, King would have none of it, and reminded them that the cabinet had already agreed upon family allowances.[41] The matter was no longer open for debate. Later, as the governor general read the speech from the throne, King was pleased that he had used the phrase "the equality of opportunity in the battle of life" as the rationale for the introduction of family allowances, words he had written in 1918. When King stood in the House of Commons in June 1944 to introduce the legislation making family allowances law, he repeated much of the rationale for their introduction. He emphasized that while the "primary justification" for family allowances was on humanitarian and social grounds, the scheme was also a great economic measure to stimulate the economy by increasing the purchasing power of the public; in other words, family allowances legislation was a wonderful piece of liberal ingenuity that would benefit the interest of all the people of Canada.[42] With the passage of the legislation a few weeks later, providing for family allowances to begin in July 1945, Prime Minister King was pleased that his government, which had earlier introduced old age pensions and unemployment insurance, had once again demonstrated to Canadians that it was the champion of social security.

Notes

1. See Brigitte Kitchen, "Wartime Social Reform: The Introduction of Family Allowances," *Canadian Journal of Social Work* 7, 1 (1981); J.L. Granatstein, *Canada's War: The Politics of the Mackenzie King Government* (Toronto, 1975); Dennis Guest, *Emergence of Social Welfare in Canada* (Vancouver, 1986); and Doug Owram, *The Government Generation: Canadian Intellectuals and the State, 1900–1950* (Toronto, 1985).
2. National Archives of Canada (hereafter NAC), Ian A. Mackenzie Papers, vol. 41, file G-25-15, "The Rt. Hon. W.L. Mackenzie King, Prime Minister of Canada, Address to the American Federation of Labor 1942 Convention," 9 Oct. 1942.
3. Ibid., "Watchman—What of the Night," address delivered by Ian Mackenzie to the Canadian Club, Quebec City, 20 June 1941.
4. Ibid., vol. 4, file G-25-9, "Social Security Legislation of other Countries," prepared by W.S. Woods, associate deputy minister in the department of pensions and national health, 18 Dec. 1942.
5. Ibid., "Watchman—What of the Night," address by Ian Mackenzie to the Canadian Club, Quebec, 20 June 1941.
6. Ibid., "Target for Tomorrow," address by Ian Mackenzie to the Canadian Club, London, ON, 16 Sept. 1942.
7. Order-in-council PC 1218, 17 Feb. 1941.
8. Granatstein, *Canada's War*, 257.
9. Ibid., 257.
10. Ibid., 275.
11. NAC, Mackenzie King Papers, King Diary, 5 Dec. 1942.
12. Ibid., 6 Dec. 1942.
13. Ibid., 5 Jan. and 7 Jan. 1943.
14. NAC, Mackenzie Papers, vol. 62, file 527-64 (6), Mackenzie to James, 9 Dec. 1942.
15. King Diaries, 10 Jan. 1943.
16. Ibid., 12 Jan. 1943.
17. See Granatstein, *Canada's War*, 253.
18. King Diary, 24 Jan., 26 Jan., 17 Feb. 1943.
19. Ibid., 24 March 1943. In this, King was pretty much following what was happening elsewhere. When he met Churchill in Quebec on 11 August 1943, the British prime minister told him that he had outlined his commitment to social security

but "it was necessary to devote everything to winning the war first, postponing social programmes till later." See King Diary, 11 Aug. 1943.

20. NAC, Canadian Council on Social Development Papers, vol. 70, file 518, Davidson to Cassidy, 12 March 1943.
21. See Leonard Marsh, *Report on Social Security for Canada* (Ottawa, 1943).
22. NAC, Dept. of Finance, vol. 3976, file E-3-0, Bryce to Clark, 21 March 1943.
23. NAC, Mackenzie Papers, vol. 41, file G-25D, "Statement by the Honourable Ian Mackenzie, Minister of Pensions and National Health, before the Special Select Committee of the House of Commons on Social Security, March, 1943."
24. NAC, King Papers, C187885, Robertson to King, 8 June 1943.
25. NAC, Dept. of Finance, vol. 304, file 101-53-114, vol. 1, Towers to Clark, 13 June 1943, and the enclosed memorandum, "The Case for Children's Allowances."
26. Ibid., vol. 498, file 121-0-7, "Draft Report of the Economic Advisory Committee on the Price and Wage Stabilization Program," 16 July 1943.
27. King Diary, 14 Sept. 1943.
28. See particularly, Kitchen, "Wartime Social Reform," 37–45.
29. Ibid.
30. J.W. Pickersgill, *The Mackenzie King Record* (Toronto, 1960), 599–601.
31. NAC, Dept. of Finance, vol. 3402, file 06301 to 06400, "Resolutions approved by Advisory Council," National Liberal Federation, 27–28 Sept. 1943.
32. NAC, King Papers, J4, vol. 371, file F3906, Pickersgill to King, 27 Dec. 1943 and file F3906, St. Laurent to King, 18 Nov. 1943.
33. King Diary, 6 Jan. 1944.
34. Ibid., 1 Oct. 1943.
35. Ibid., 13 Jan. 1944.
36. NAC, Dept. of Finance, vol. 304, file 101-53-114, vol. 1, "Children's Allowance," memorandum prepared for Ilsley, 12 Jan. 1944.
37. King Diary, 13 Jan. 1944.
38. Ibid.
39. See Granatstein, *Canada's War*, 283.
40. King Diary, 19 Jan. 1944.
41. Ibid., 24 Jan. 1944.
42. NAC, Dept. of National Health and Welfare, vol. 1934, file R233-100-2, "Mr. Mackenzie King—July 25, 1944."

V

The Return

VE-Day (8 May 1945), the celebration of the victory in Europe, found Mackenzie King in San Francisco attending the conference that led to the founding of the United Nations. On 11 June, to his immense satisfaction, his party won its third straight majority election victory. On 6 August, King was presiding over the first session of the Dominion–Provincial Conference on Reconstruction when he heard the news of the first use of the atomic bomb against Japan. His cold-blooded response to this event bespoke a racism that was inherent in many Canadians of his generation. On 15 August, King joined the celebration on Parliament Hill in Ottawa to mark the victory over Japan.

Mackenzie King's Diary, 7–8 May, 11 June, 6 August, and 15 August 1945

Monday, 7 May 1945 (San Francisco)

I SLEPT on the whole fairly well last night. At 7 o'clock precisely, Nicol[1] came into my bedroom and asked if I were awake. He said Mr. Robertson[2] was going to call me at 4 but did not like to ring the telephone in my room at that hour. He had an important message to give to me. It was that the war in Europe was over. I said to Nicol: that is good news, Thank God. I then turned on my side and uttered a prayer of thanksgiving and of rededication to the service of my fellow-men. . . .

My reading for today in the Bible was the 10th Chapter of Corinthians. It is not without significance that I have marked in the margin: Berlin, Germany—27.VI.37. My visit to Berlin was to persuade Hitler that he should pursue the path of peace. I have felt from the start it would be interesting to see who would come out best in the end. Hitler with his might or myself in relation to my mother and the circumstances of her birth. Today has shown. . . .

This has been a good day—a happy day, in some respects of work, but one in which the burden has been greatly lightened from the knowledge that Nazi militarism has, at last, been destroyed. What a tragic catastrophic close!—especially for those who have brought the war on. How just the retribution which has overtaken the followers of Hitler and Mussolini; it is sad beyond words that the innocent have had to suffer so terribly. That the multitudes of innocent people have had to suffer so terribly for the guilt and the folly, vainglorious ambition of a handful of gangsters. Nothing like it has been known in the whole of history. It is, however, the story of the Cross told this time on a world scale; instead of the Founder of Christendom being crucified, Christendom itself has been crucified by the same forces, but Right has triumphed over Might. God's mercy over man's folly and wrong. The law of peace, work and health begins now to triumph over the law of blood and of death. . . .

Tuesday, 8 May 1945 (VE-Day, San Francisco)

Was particularly impressed by the little verse for today: "This is the day which the Lord hath made; we will rejoice and be glad in it." Could anything be quite as appropriate for V-E day! . . .

I went on the air at about 17 past 12. Was followed by St. Laurent.[3] We each spoke with a good deal of vigour. I am told the broadcast had the largest coverage of any the C.B.C.[4] has thus far given to anyone. It included the entire Canadian network, U.S. national network and shortwave to Britain, also to sailors and soldiers. It was supposed to have gone to all the battlefronts.

From the political point of view, I believe a broadcast of the kind is worth more than two weeks' campaigning on Party matters. . . .

A wonderful message came from Churchill[5] on Canada's contribution to victory. I have read nothing equal to it. I am sure Churchill had in mind not only feelings of gratitude which he entertains but, in this way, lending a hand in the present campaign. As a matter of fact, Canada should be receiving from all countries that have been liberated, an expression of the kind. I am surprised that the Queen of Holland, Dutch govt., etc. have not sent very strong messages. As a matter of fact, many of these countries expect us to congratulate them on obtaining their freedom without thinking of sending any word of gratitude for the Canadian lives that have been sacrificed toward that end.

I received a message from the King—acknowledging my loyal message on behalf of the govt., about as little as could be said. I am becoming increasingly dubious about the institution of monarchy, save as a framework to help to hold society together. It, however, develops a social caste in the nation.

In concluding his speech, Churchill talked about Great Britain's Empire and Commonwealth in a positive way. No reference to the Dominions as such. Both Evatt[6] and I told Eden[7] we thought this was a real mistake. He also brought in *Rule Britannia* and *God Save the King*. Englishmen find it difficult to go beyond John Bull and his island. To say much that does not centre pretty exclusively on John Bull. . . .

The most noticeable thing about San Francisco today has been what one might claim to be the entire absence of any demonstration of any kind in the streets or in the hotels. No larger crowds—indeed, if anything, there seemed to be less life about the streets. I am told that the saloons have been closed yesterday and today. Sale of liquor in stores and restaurants, forbidden. A very sensible arrangement.

Tonight's press despatch indicates serious rowdy riots at Halifax. Much damage has been done to shops, stores, etc. A really disgraceful business; without question, all the result of drink. It is curious that when the last war ended, I was at Brown's Hotel at Denver. I shall never forget the demonstration there, dancing in the rotunda, etc. Here there has been nothing to suggest anything in the nature of a victory. It is interesting, however, to have been attending at the time of the defeat of Germany, the conference to bring into being the new world security organization and to be participating therein. It is a sort of a bridge between an era of conflict that has past or is passing, and an era, I pray, of peace.

To bed at 5 to 11 p.m.

Monday, 11 June 1945

[W]ent . . . to the polling booth on Charlotte Street. On the way in, on turning the corner of Hull where one gets a glimpse of the main tower immediately opposite, I looked at the clock in my car and both hands were exactly together at 12. I said to myself: this is high noon and it spells victory for today. I felt strongly that it was an evidence of the presence of an Unseen Power. That caused me to look at that moment at both the tower and the clock. When little Pat[8] and I arrived at the booth, there were many photographers about, newsreel, etc. Took some snapshots, both outside and in the booth, and when we came out, little boys in uniform asked for autographs which I wrote on the shoulders of the boys. The experience was a pleasant one. Little Pat was animated by the whole of it. . . .

J. and G.[9] arrived as planned at 6 and the *Star*[10] photographers were also at the front door at that hour. About 5 past 6, I was photographed on the front steps with little Pat. . . . At 11. left L.H.[11] to go to speak over the radio at 10 past. Here again were photographers taking pictures.

As I came out of the studio, quite unexpectedly I ran into Bracken,[12] who had come in the door and was going to speak. He put out his hand to shake hands and extended his congratulations. I thanked him but said nothing more. He then said to me "we shall be seeing more of each other soon." I said in a quiet way I hoped it may be so. The words had slipped through politeness more than aught else, but were the truth, as I would rather see him in the H. of C.[13] than anyone else. We have got him now where we want him. He is like a fly having buzzed around outside and caught with the glitter at the end into the spider's web. I am sure as I can be that it will not be too long before the Tory party will get rid of him as a leader and substitute someone else. He had a very strong grip. His hand was like that of some woodsman in its rough strength and his features were all contracted. His face is a mass of lines. He was anything but happy. I cannot forget how the fellow has sold himself to silver. He has the effrontery of a woman of the street. The kind of thing he has lent himself to and said and done from the day he was elected leader of his party. It is necessary for me to forget the past, and I am only happy to forgive it, but I feel I do not need to sacrifice my self-respect by immediately treating the whole political scene as if it were part of some circus. The photographers took a snap of the two of us shaking hands. Asked if I would repeat shaking hands with Bracken. I did this reluctantly, but resisted very strongly the effort of the C.B.C. of having me come in to the studio with Bracken and have a movietone made. I told Turnbull[14] I would not submit to anything of the kind. . . .

It was one o'clock when J. and G. left and also members of the staff. I went immediately to bed.

I had a little talk with Pat before turning in, and thanked God for having carried me safely through the campaign, also for all the guidance I have had. I prayed for renewed consecration of my life to public affairs and service of my fellowmen.

Monday, 6 August 1945

Just about noon . . . I received a note from Howe[15] saying a bomb had been dropped and that he was giving a report to the press. . . . [I]t was the atom bomb in Japan. . . . We now see what might have come to the British race had German scientists won the race. It is fortunate that the use of the bomb should have been upon the Japanese rather than upon the white races of Europe. I am a little concerned about how Russia may feel, not having been told anything of this invention or of what the British and the U.S. were doing in the way of exploring and perfecting the process. . . .

Wednesday, 15 August 1945

On reaching Parliament Hill, large numbers were gathered together there. I went to the East Block where I had asked Nicol to bring some fresh collars, etc. from L.H. As I walked over to the Parlt. Bldgs.,[16] I was given a nice reception by the people assembled on the Hill. The G.G.[17] arrived sharp on time. We reciprocated congratulations as H.E.[18] and H.R.H.[19] got out of the car in front of the main tower. All then took up position as indicated. It was a good thing to have had the platform taken down which Public Works had been constructing and having something really very beautiful and appropriate as a background for pictures. The grouping was a proper one with H.E. taking the salute, Princess Alice standing further to the right and a little behind the two, myself as P.M.[20] and on the opposite, General McNaughton[21] as Minister of Defence. Chiefs of Staff and Ministers in the background all under the archway of the entrance to the Houses of Parlt. . . .

After the Governor left, as the crowd kept expecting something more, I said a few words of thanks again to the people of Canada for all they had done in the war and particularly the armed services. Spoke of the dark epoch having closed and a new era opening up and expressed the hope for better and happier days for all.

I then joined with other colleagues in the Speaker's apartments to listen to the King's speech. I thought it was better delivered than any the King has made thus far. I did not, however, like the use of the term "my" people, etc. The feeling the speech left was that it did not tune in; that those associated with the King in its preparation have not yet come to understand the real underlying movement of today which places the emphasis on the dignity and worth of the individual man. The rights of the people; not a question of privilege, position, etc. Then I did not like the references to the Dominions, the Colonies, etc. All this is a looming up of Empire structure which will go to pieces if it continues the emphasis under centralization under the Union Jack with the monarchy at the centre of the picture. It was a great satisfaction today to have the Red Ensign flying from the tower of the Parlt. Bldgs. marking the day's ceremonies. . . .

Mr. St. Laurent today congratulated me very warmly on the end of the war. He is the only one of the Ministers who has come forward in that way. It has been a little disappointing to see how little the Ministers themselves realize what they owe to the part I have played in the last 6 years in keeping the govt. together and helping to get it returned and . . . what obviously the present hours mean to me.

I debated a little in my mind whether I would stay in the city for dinner to witness something of the evening's jubilation in the city; to have that picture in mind and to share with the people the moment of their rejoicing. I felt, however, that if I stayed up late, having had no rest, it might throw me behind in work tomorrow. Also my mood was not so much one of celebration as one of quiet gratitude to God for bringing to a close this terrible war and sparing me through it all. I decided a quiet rest at Kingsmere would be preferable so came out between 7 and 8. It was a lovely, peaceful, quiet night here at Kingsmere.[22] J. came over and sat with me while I had dinner. Shared a grapefruit from a basket. . . . It was our little celebration of the hours of victory.

Notes

1. Member of his household staff.
2. Norman A. Robertson of the Department of External Affairs.
3. Louis S. St. Laurent, the minister of justice.
4. Canadian Broadcasting Corporation.
5. Winston S. Churchill, the British prime minister.
6. Herbert V. Evatt, the Australian minister of external affairs.
7. Anthony Eden, the British foreign secretary.
8. His dog.
9. Joan and Godfroy Patteson.
10. *Toronto Daily Sta*r
11. Laurier House, his Ottawa residence.
12. John Bracken, the Progressive Conservative leader.
13. House of Commons.

14. Walter J. Turnbull, his principal secretary.
15. Clarence Decatur Howe, minister of munitions and supply.
16. Parliament Buildings.
17. Governor General (Earl of Athlone).
18. His Excellency.
19. Her Royal Highness (Princess Alice, wife of the Governor General and granddaughter of Queen Victoria).
20. Prime minister.
21. Andrew G.L. McNaughton.
22. His country residence.

C.P. Stacey, the dean of Canadian military historians, could be scathing about Mackenzie King, the man. Nonetheless, he acknowledged King's achievements as a political leader. In 1967, he offered this striking assessment of a prime minister whose career he knew intimately:

> Mackenzie King died on July 22, 1950. Very few people, it would seem, had loved him; not many had even liked him; some had entertained an almost psychopathic hatred of him; but vast numbers had voted for him. He had some unpleasant characteristics; we know more about them now than we did when he was living. As a political strategist and tactician, however, he has perhaps no equal in Canadian annals. His greatest political achievement was doubtless the creation and maintenance of a genuinely national party. There were Canadians—probably a good many of them—who were not partial to King but who nevertheless voted for him and his party simply because it *was* a national party and the only one in the field.
>
> As a statesman, King left his mark on his country and his times, and for better or for worse the mark was deep. His zeal for national unity—a thing good in itself, but in the circumstances of the day particularly good for the Liberals and for King—may not have rendered the country more genuinely united than it had been before, but at least it helped to prevent an explosion that would have made things much worse. Above all, he had left Canada a more independent community than he had found her.

In wartime Canada there was indeed much to be said for "ingenuity, ambiguity, inactivity, and political longevity."

W.L.M.K.

F.R. Scott

How shall we speak of Canada,
Mackenzie King dead?
The Mother's boy in the lonely room
With his dog, his medium and his ruins?

He blunted us.

We had no shape
Because he never took sides,
And no sides
Because he never allowed them to take shape.

He skilfully avoided what was wrong
Without saying what was right,
And never let his on the one hand
Know what his on the other hand was doing.

The height of his ambition
Was to pile a Parliamentary Committee on a Royal Commission.
The have "conscription if necessary
But not necessarily conscription,"
To let Parliament decide—
Later.

Postpone, postpone, abstain.

Only one thread was certain:
After World War I
Business as usual,
After World War II
Orderly decontrol.
Always he led us back to where we were before.

He seemed to be in the centre
Because we had no centre,
No vision
To pierce the smoke-screen of his politics.

Truly he will be remembered
Wherever men honour ingenuity,
Ambiguity, inactivity, and political longevity.

Let us raise up a temple
To the cult of mediocrity,
Do nothing by halves
Which can be done by quarters.

At the end of the war in Europe, Halifax erupted in a sudden orgy of looting and violence. Sailors and other servicemen, frequently joined by civilians, ran wild. The damage was extensive—so extensive that the federal government appointed a royal commission to sort through the wreckage and determine the causes.

Report on the Halifax Disorders

Justice R.L. Kellock

Events of May 7 and Early Morning of May 8

THE DISTRICT, within which the major portion of the disturbances in Halifax took place, is in the downtown part of the City; running from Bishop Street on the south to Buckingham Street on the north, and from the Harbour on the east to Barrington Street on the west, although there were wee disturbances outside that area on Gottingen Street, and elsewhere. In addition, the Agricola Street Liquor Store and Oland's Brewery were both attacked and they lie far beyond the downtown area.

In the downtown district mentioned, the main streets running north and south, proceeding from east to west, are Water Street, Hollis Street, Granville Street and Barrington Street. The east and west streets in the same area, commencing at the south, are Bishop Street, Salter Street, Sackville Street, Front Street, Blower Street, Duke Street and Buckingham Street.

At approximately 10:30 a.m. on May 7 the whistles in Halifax began to blow and shortly thereafter news of the surrender was broadcast by radio. People began to leave their places of employment and flow into the streets, and the day became a holiday so far as the civilian population [was] concerned.

At approximately 11:00 a.m. the policing plan went into effect and the liaison police officers of the three armed services arrived at the City Hall. At the same time two out of the three platoons of the Halifax city police came on duty, representing a total of approximately 40 men. The remaining platoon came on duty at 4:00 p.m.

The Citizens' Committee met at various times throughout the day and, under its direction, the plan designed for V-E Day was accelerated. Public address systems were set up to furnish dance music for street dancing and to make announcements, and these were in operation by 3:30 p.m.

It was not until approximately 5:30 p.m. that news was received of the official declaration of May 8 and V-E day. When this was received sound trucks were employed by the Committee to make this announcement public in the streets and to notify the people of the program for the following day.

The Committee decided also to have the fireworks in the harbour that evening and this was done between the hours of 9:00 and 10:30, while community singing on Citadel Hill was carried out during the same time, and these events were enjoyed by from 12,000 to 15,000 people.

The Wet Canteen at *Stadacona* closed at 9:00 p.m. About that time Lieutenant Commander Wood, who was then in his office at the *Stadacona* barracks in the north end of the city on Barrington St., roughly three-quarters of a mile from Buckingham St., observed a street car on Barrington St. outside *Stadacona* surrounded by a large number of naval ratings. He took thirty Shore Patrolmen he had with him there and proceeded to the spot, but before he arrived the street car moved off. He found a great deal of glass on the street and it was quite evident that the ratings, whom Lieutenant Commander Wood judged to number about one hundred, had smashed the windows in the street car. According to Lieutenant Commander Wood, "there was no way to tell who had done the damage and the crowd were quite cheerful, there was nothing nasty about them, and we got them to move off out of that vicinity," He also said:—

Q. Do I gather that the crowd of navy personnel dispersed on your arrival?—A. Maybe a matter of ten minutes.

Q. You said you got them to move off?—A. Yes.

Q. Did you persuade them to?—A. Yes.

This is the initial instance of the application of the policy laid down in Exhibit 72. In my opinion, the course followed by Lieutenant Commander Wood was unfortunate. I do not agree that what Lieutenant Commander Wood did was the "only thing" he could have done. I think that the whole group might well have been returned to their barracks at once, at the least. Instead of that, they were allowed to believe that that kind of conduct would not be discouraged and were left free for further events of the same kind. It was not long before further events of the same kind were being enacted further south in the main business section of Barrington St. These events, which coincided with the expiration of sufficient time to enable this group to reach the downtown area, rapidly assumed more serious proportions.

About half an hour later, Lieutenant Commander Wood received a call from his liaison officer, Warrant Officer Barbour, at the City Hall, advising him that a large crowd were gathering on Barrington St. in the vicinity of the City Hall and were tearing down the flags which had been placed on the electric light poles to decorate the street. It had previously been reported to the Chief of Police that sailors were occupying Barrington St. to its full width and tearing down the flags. He had sent out his own police and some shore patrol but it was found that there were too many people engaged, both sailors and civilians, to handle and the men he had sent out could do nothing. No arrests were attempted. Lieutenant Commander Wood, on proceeding to the City Hall in response to the information received from Warrant Officer Barbour, said that on his arrival at the police station he saw a number of large Victory Loan flags being taken down by naval ratings and by civilians, that he discussed the matter with the Chief of Police and that, while the latter told him he was concerned about the flags being torn down, he felt it was impossible to stop it, and that no further action was being taken by him.

Lieutenant Commander Wood remained only a few minutes at the City Hall and then drove southerly down Barrington St. where he found the same practice going on all the way down the street.

In the neighbourhood of 10:00 p.m. naval ratings had begun to interfere with the operation of street cars on Barrington St., in the southerly part of the main business section, by pulling the trolleys off the wires. City Police and shore patrol were despatched and, ultimately, all the street cars, with some damage to glass windows, got off Barrington St., with the exception of one, which was attacked by ratings in force. One soldier also was observed taking part. All the windows in the street car and the seats were smashed, and the rating then endeavoured to upset it. Finding this too much for them, they set fire to it. On the report of this reaching police headquarters, a number of city police and shore patrol were despatched to the scene, as well as a city police patrol waggon. It was by this time about 11:30 p.m. On the arrival of this vehicle, the ratings overturned it and set it on fire. The fire reels were sent for, but, when the firemen connected their hose with a hydrant and turned on the water, it was disconnected by naval personnel. It was again connected, whereupon naval men took the axes off the fire reels and cut the hose to pieces. The hose itself was also again disconnected from the hydrant and the water shut off. The Deputy Fire Chief in charge asked that he be allowed to put the fire out, but he was refused and threats were made that if he did not take the hose away, the equipment would be upset. As the equipment was very expensive, he decided that discretion was the course to follow and the fire reels went away. The ratings later righted the patrol waggon and pushed it down one of the streets leading to the harbour where it ultimately finished up on one of the docks, completely wrecked.

A city police constable, who had been on duty on Barrington St. throughout the evening and who had assisted in getting the street cars away, said that the interference with the cars was by navy men and that a mixed crowd of service people and civilians were spectators. He observed that until about 9:30 the crowd was in good humour, but after that time it was riotous. He said several street cars had their windows smashed by sailors using their fists on them while passengers were still on board. These riotous proceedings on Barrington St. went on until shortly before midnight. The police were dispersed in a number of places and such as were on Barrington St. were helpless in the face of the crowd.

News of these events were communicated by Warrant Officer Barbour to Lieutenant Commander Wood who had, in the meantime, returned to his office at *Stadacona*. Wood returned to the City Hall, where Barbour strongly advised him not to attempt to drive further as the crowd was very large and they might get into trouble with their car. Barbour reported to Wood that he had sent two trucks with thirty shore patrolmen to the scene and that these trucks had been attacked and an attempt had been made to set one of them on fire by throwing burning paper or rags on the canvas top. Wood and a subordinate, Lieutenant MacKenzie, proceeded to the scene and found a crowd which he estimated at from three to four thousand completely blocking Barrington St. Wood saw fifteen of his patrolmen and six city police there, but they were quite helpless. The situation was completely out of hand. He observed naval ratings inside the car and others outside trying to turn it over. He says that there were about 150 ratings occupied in and about the street car. A city police sergeant estimated that there was a crowd of 500 immediately around the street, the majority being ratings, with some civilians and some air force and soldiers.

Wood says he had hardly been at that point for five minutes when word reached him that the Sackville St. Liquor Store had been broken into. This store is at the south-west corner of Sackville and Granville Streets, one block east of Barrington St. The attack on this store was made by a different group from that engaged on Barrington St., as the latter were still occupied there when word came to Wood and he left for the scene of this latest disturbance.

While these events were taking place the Chief of Police spoke to Warrant Officer Barbour and asked for more shore patrol. Barbour's reply was that he would do his best, but that the odds were against him and that the shore patrol could do nothing as they had only their bare hands.

The Chief of Police then endeavoured to get Admiral Murray on the telephone. Owing to some mistake in telephone numbers on his part, or on the part of his Secretary, he did not reach Admiral Murray, but spoke to the Officer of the Watch at the Naval Dockyard and told him of what was taking place. According to the Chief, he asked that officer to reach someone in authority to send help as naval personnel were committing considerable damage and he was short of men and the shore patrol had reported that they were powerless. The officer answered "Very well, he would see what he could do," but nothing was heard from this call. The Officer of the Watch to whom he spoke was Lieutenant Tunney, who was not at Naval Headquarters at all. This officer said that the Chief of Police had told him that there were about 50 naval ratings breaking into or trying to break into one of the liquor stores. He thinks it was the Sackville St. Store and that Conrad asked him if he could do anything about it. He said to Chief Conrad that he would see what he could do. What he did, in fact, was to telephone the shore patrol officer at *Stadacona*, where he gave the message to whoever was on duty and was advised that they had already heard about it and that everything would be taken care of. Admiral Murray says that he was at his home all evening but no one reported to him that night what was going on.

Sackville St. Liquor Store

About 11:35 p.m. the watchman in these premises observed three individuals, whom he took to be merchant navy men, approaching the premises, and one of them was seen to thrust a flag pole through one of the windows. When they saw the watchman, however, they fled. He immediately telephoned police headquarters for assistance and shortly after some six city police arrived and were admitted.

At about 11:45 p.m. a number of naval ratings and one solider approached the store. They were in turn followed by larger crowd of sailors and civilians which soon filled the street in front of the store. Missiles were thrown and the plate glass windows were smashed. At this point, one of the city police inspectors went out and stood in front of the store. The soldier, already mentioned, told him that they did not wish to injure the police but that they had been denied liquor to celebrate V-Day and they intended to get it. The inspector said the liquor was not his to give. With that the soldier shouted "Come on boys" and he and the naval ratings, followed by a mixed crowd, stormed into the premises, some 24 or 30 gaining entrance. Looting immediately began as many of these broke through the police. One of the inspectors meantime had telephoned for more help and a sergeant and 15 shore patrol were sent. Wood and McKenzie joined these.

They proceeded to the store and found, according to Wood, a crowd of about 300 persons, composed of equal numbers of sailors and civilians. These were all active and he observed ratings and civilians coming out of the store carrying cases and bottles. Wood's party pushed their way along until they formed a cordon in front of the store. He himself entered the store and found the city police inside had by that time cleared out the raiders. Wood then left his patrolmen there with the city police and went to the City Hall. 30 R.C.M.P. constables arrived shortly and 5 remained till 5:00 a.m.

There was no more trouble at this store for the remainder of the night.

Hollis Street Retail and Mail Order Stores

About midnight the watchman at the retail liquor store heard a crowd coming down Sackville St. on to Hollis St. He immediately telephoned police headquarters and was told that the police would be sent as soon as possible. For some reason the city police did not call upon the army provost corps whose men were on call at the time.

In the meantime this crowd, composed of ratings, civilians and merchant seamen, had gathered at the store and a naval rating with a short piece of flag pole smashed one of the windows. Other windows were broken with similar weapons and naval ratings entered the store, followed by civilians and merchant seamen. Looting of the contents of the store commenced at once. The watchman estimates that the mob was composed of about 500 persons.

Major Crowell had observed this crowd approaching the liquor store on Hollis Street; the head of the crowd was largely naval personnel. He heard the glass breaking in the store and saw the first man, a sailor, entering. He immediately telephoned the City Hall, asking for from 30 to 50 shore patrol, stating that if they were sent immediately he felt that they could nip the trouble in the bud. He was advised that the shore patrol were on duty on Barrington St., but that they would endeavour to have other shore patrol sent. In the meantime the crowd were looting the liquor store, but the crowd did not increase and were moving away with their loot. He estimates the crowd at from 150 to 200, including the onlookers who were at the other side of the street. He says that the crowds were still around the street car on Barrington St. and the Sackville St. Liquor Store at the time this third crowd was attacking the Hollis St. Liquor Store. As late as 12:30 a.m. the street car was burning on Barrington St. and the crowd was still around it. In time, some city police arrived and were able to clear the store.

About 12:30, R.C.M.P Constable Duncan and Staff Sergeant Beale arrived at the store and found it clear, but there was a large crowd outside the store which Duncan estimated at 400 or 500 people, mostly navy and civilians, with a very small percentage of army. This crowd was about to break into the store again and shortly after they came in and the looting re-commenced. The situation was beyond the control of the police. Duncan remained for about an hour, during which the looting continued.

In the meantime the mail order store on Hollis St. alongside the retail store, was attacked and entered. Hollis St. was by this time seething with a crowd estimated, by a reliable observer, to number about two thousand, eighty-five per cent of which being made up of equal numbers of ratings and civilians, fifteen per cent soldiers and a sprinkling of airmen. They were vaulting in and out of the store with much shouting, and going along the street carrying boxes and bottles and drinking. Two trucks of about 10 shore patrol each were seen by a citizen to arrive after the second attack, and about sixty-five army provost. On the arrival of the provost it was not long before the crowd was dispersed. The provost set up a guard at the corner of Salter St. and Hollis St. and prevented the crowd again coming up Hollis St.

The 20 shore patrol and 6 city police had been sent to Hollis St. by Wood, who, at this time, was at the Buckingham St. Store where he had received word by radio of the attack on the Hollis St. Stores. Shortly after they were sent, Wood himself and McKenzie went to Hollis St. At this time the crowd had been removed. There were a few people about and it was evident to Wood that a considerable amount of liquor had been taken. He found cartons strewed over the street, as well as broken boxes and cases.

Buckingham St. Liquor Store

A few minutes after midnight Redmond, the watchman at the Buckingham St. Store, observed a crowd gathering in the neighbourhood and he immediately telephoned police headquarters. He was told they could do nothing at that time. A short time later the situation appeared more serious and he again telephoned police headquarters and was again told that all available men were down at the other stores. On both these occasions army provost men were on call but were not called upon by the city police until the store had been broken into. About 12:30 the glass in the store began to break and the crowd entered. In the lead were navy men and the majority of the crowd was composed of navy men but there were also some civilians. Looting immediately commenced and proceeded for about ten minutes. Lieutenant Commander Wood learned of this attack at the City Hall and proceeded to Buckingham St. with 20 shore patrol. About 8 or 9 city police arrived about the same time and an officer and 30 provost. Wood found a scene of great confusion, with people jumping in and out of the windows carrying out cases under their arms. The police were able to stop the looting and clear the store. After the store was cleared a large truck containing about 30 shore patrol arrived. At 2:15 Assistant Commissioner Eames of the R.C.M.P found the store strongly held by army provost.

Agricola St. Liquor Store

When the Buckingham St. Store was cleared, Wood heard someone in the crowd remark that the Agricola St. Store would be next. He left 15 of his shore patrolmen at Buckingham St. and proceeded to the Agricola St. Store with the other 35. He found everything quiet at the Agricola St. Store and posted his entire force there. At 12:10 a.m., on request of a city detective, Col. Clarke sent one officer and ten provost to this store. A few minutes later another thirty men were sent. Shortly after Wood arrived 12 city police and 12 more shore patrol arrived. While here word came to Wood of what had happened at Hollis St. He took 20 shore patrolmen and 6 city police and proceeded there, leaving the remainder of the force at the Agricola St. Store. Thereafter, any shore patrol who were not employed guarding the liquor stores were used to round up naval personnel on the streets and return them to barracks. . . .

Other Suggested Causes for Riots

DURING THE COURSE of the Inquiry, Counsel endeavoured to ascertain from various witnesses whether there was discontent with Halifax conditions, on the part of service personnel, sufficient to establish that the damage done on May 7th was premeditated and in the nature of a *quid pro quo.* A few witnesses did depose to having heard complaints by service personnel, and one or two witnesses deposed to having heard remarks from naval ratings and civilians to the effect that Halifax would have a rough time on V-E Day. There was nothing in what was said at the time which caused those witnesses to report what they had heard, or treat the remarks as anything more than discontent of the particular individuals caused by some unspecified experience. On the other hand, the Intelligence Officers of the R.C.M.P. in Halifax knew nothing of any spirit of discontent on the part of service personnel. None of the naval officers who gave evidence had any knowledge of such a condition. Colonel Clarke, the Deputy Assistant Provost Marshal of the Military District, said that, if there had been any rumours of discontent among army personnel, he would have known of it, and he had no such knowledge.

Admiral Murray did say that there was not sufficient accommodation in barracks for naval personnel and for that reason there had to be billets found in the city by the men who could not be put into barracks. (1,178 in the case of *Stadacona*; 400 in the case of *Peregrine*, and about 2,700 in the case of *Scotian.*) He thought there was no dissatisfaction to the extent of the unrest at this condition and that any dissatisfaction was not because of the way the men themselves had to live, but because of conditions under which their wives and families were forced to live. Admiral Murray also said that sufficient provision had not been made for playing fields for the ratings, but he did not think that these matters had any connection with the occurrences of May 7th and 8th. Evidence was tendered as to what had been done in Halifax in the way of entertainment, recreation and welfare of service personnel stationed in the City, mainly by voluntary work, which reached very large proportions. As no satisfactory evidence of the existence of any state of discontent or resentment on the part of service personnel toward the citizens of Halifax had been given, I did not consider it necessary to hear the proffered evidence. It would merely go one step further in establishing lack of basis for discontent. I have no doubt that individuals have had trying experiences in crowded Halifax as other people have experienced discomfort during the war in other crowded centres of population. If there were in fact any underlying discontent or feeling of resentment on the part of service personnel in Halifax on May 7th or 8th, the evidence failed to establish it, or that it had anything to do with the outbreaks. . . .

Material Loss and Damage and Personnel Charged With Offences

As a result of the two days' disorders, 6,987 cases of beer, 1,225 cases of wine, 2 cases of alcohol and 55,392 quarts of spirits were looted from the establishments of the Liquor Commission in Halifax, and 30,516 quarts of beer from Keith's Brewery, of which 1,140 quarts of spirits, 10 cases of wine and 81 cases of beer were subsequently recovered by the Commission. None was recovered by the Brewery.

In Dartmouth 5,256 quarts of beer, 1,692 quarts of wine and 9,816 quarts of liquor were looted from the Commission, of which 550 bottles were recovered.

I have already indicated the area and nature of the damage to business premises in a general way. I did not understand that I was to investigate the damage in detail. The smashing of glass windows and wanton damage to furniture and fixtures was not limited to premises of merchants. Financial houses and offices on Hollis St. in Halifax were also the object of attacks. In that City 564 firms suffered damage. 2,624 pieces of plate and other glass in these premises were broken and 207 of these firms suffered from looting in some degree. The particulars are set forth in Exhibit 52.

According to the evidence of Wing Commander McCallum, Assistant Provost Marshal for the Eastern Air Command, the number of airmen against whom charges were brought arising out of the disorders was 19 in Halifax and Dartmouth. Of the army, 41 soldiers were charged with various offences from being found in possession of loot to drunkenness and being absent without leave. In three cases the charges were dismissed, four were remanded for further evidence which later it was found could not be adduced. According to Exhibit 51, there were 34 naval ratings arrested on various charges, apart from drunkenness, and 117 civilians. In addition, 152 persons were arrested on May 8th and 9th on charges of drunkenness. The evidence does not establish particulars of the personnel so arrested. In addition, the navy had used its nine trucks on May 8th to pick up intoxicated sailors. Apparently the policy laid in Ex. 72 that no charge was to be laid for drunkenness on V-E Day was not departed from by the navy until the Admiral's signal of May 9th which provided that thereafter drunkenness was to constitute an aggravated offence.

The 1945 General Election

Despite wartime controversies, Mackenzie King's Liberals won re-election in June 1945. The prime minister, however, lost his own seat of Prince Albert, Saskatchewan, thanks to the military vote, and had to go to the bother of a by-election in August, which he easily won.

Result of the General Election of 11 June 1945

	Progressive Conservative	Liberal	Co-operative Commonwealth Federation	Social Credit	Other*
Nova Scotia	2	9	1	–	–
New Brunswick	3	7	–	–	–
Prince Edward Island	1	3	–	–	–
Quebec	2	53	–	–	10
Ontario	48	34	–	–	–
Manitoba	2	10	5	–	–
Saskatchewan	1	2	18	–	–
Alberta	2	2	–	13	–
British Columbia	5	5	4	–	2
Yukon	1	–	–	–	–
Total	67	125	28	13	12

* In Quebec the Bloc Populaire elected two members and obtained 181 784 votes. This was 12.85% of the popular vote in the province and 3.47% of the national total. Independents in Quebec obtained 260 253 votes (18.40% of the provincial and 4.96% of the national totals) and six Indepedents were elected. Quebec also elected one Independent Liberal member and one Labour Progressive (Communist) member. In British Columbia, one Independent member and one Independent Co-operative Commonwealth Federation member were elected.

Popular Vote: Liberal, 40.9 %; Progressive Conservative, 27.4 %; CCF 15.6 % Social Credit, 4.1 %; other, 12.1 %

Total seats: 245.

As leader of the Liberal party, Mackenzie King was careful to have at his side a strong French-speaking Quebec lieutenant, who was in effect deputy prime minister. For decades this role had been played by Ernest Lapointe, who was to King what George-Étienne Cartier had been to John A. Macdonald. When Lapointe died on 26 November 1941, King found a successor in the Quebec City corporation lawyer Louis Stephen St. Laurent. St. Laurent became minister of justice and attorney general on 10 December 1941, and his reputation thereafter was that of a King loyalist. He had not been in politics when the Liberals promised that there would be no conscription for overseas service, and he was not the prisoner of that promise. Once recruited by King, he supported the prime minister's every move on the divisive manpower issue. On 4 September 1946, St. Laurent became secretary of state for external affairs, and on 7 August 1948, he was chosen leader of the Liberal Party. He became prime minister of Canada on 15 November 1948.

Quebec Saves Our King

Gordon O. Rothney

IN NO OTHER PROVINCE has Mackenzie King been so bitterly denounced as in Quebec. Only last August, because of its connection with him, the Godbout Liberal government was driven from office in a provincial election. On March 1 this year Quebec's legislative assembly resolved, by a vote of 67 to 5, that it "ardently protests against the imposition of conscription in Canada for overseas service, and extremely regrets that Mr. King has broken his most sacred pledges." Again, on March 7, it resolved by 82 to 0 to "invite the Federal Government to revise the electoral map before the elections so as to render justice to the Province of Quebec"—an invitation which went unheeded. Yet, on June 11 the *bloc solide libéral* survived almost unshaken. Outside of Quebec the Liberals are in a definite minority. Quebec, in spite of everything, has therefore saved Mackenzie King.

One explanation is force of habit. The province has gone Liberal in every federal election since Laurier first led the party in 1891. Two generations have grown up watching their elders always voting *rouge au fédéral.* This year, as usual, Mr. King's unbroken record of loyalty to Laurier Liberalism was effectively played up. No other party with aspirations at Ottawa is sufficiently Canadianized to make it conceivable that a representative French Canadian could become its leader. So no other party is likely to have many French-Canadian followers.

This fact becomes particularly obvious when the United Kingdom is at war. In 1935, the Liberals took 60 Quebec seats to 5 for the Conservatives, but only after a hard fight. In 1940, however, with the war on and Dr. Manion campaigning for "National Government," the Conservative party collapsed in the French province. The Liberals took 63 seats, the other two going to Liguori Lacombe (Ind. Lib.) and Sasseville Roy (Ind. Cons.). Quebec was strewn with lost deposits. Like the southern States she had become a one party area, more confirmed than ever in her habit of voting Liberal.

The character of the National Union is another reason for Mr. King's success. In 1945, for the first time since 1896, the Liberals entered a federal election with an unfriendly government at Quebec. The rise of Maurice Duplessis had broken the Liberal domination in provincial politics, and reaction to the National Resources Mobilization Act had made him premier in 1944. But the central theory of the National Union is that Quebec's autonomy can be properly defended only by a party which keeps out of the federal arena. Aspirations at Ottawa, it holds, lead to bargains in which, because of party discipline, the province's interests are sacrificed to political expediency. This was reemphasized by Premier Duplessis in the legislature on June 1:

> We are independent of all federal political leaders. We consider that at present the political leaders at Ottawa, Mr. King, Mr. Bracken, Mr. Coldwell and Mr. Blackmore, do not have a program which satisfies the just aspirations of the Province of Quebec.

Nevertheless, two factors are involved in winning elections: attractive policy and efficient organization. Was the efficient machine, which had once served the Conservatives and which had carried the National Union to victory only last August, to lie idle this year simply because of Mr. Duplessis's political philosophy? Plans for putting it at the disposal of a National Front to be led by Mr. Cardin fell through. But in many cases it was used locally by Independents.

Sasseville Roy had repudiated all Conservative connections and declared himself an Independent in 1941, and Frédéric Dorion had won the Charlevoix-Saguenay by-election in 1942 under the same label. Many Independents appeared this spring and on June 8 the National Union organ, *Le Temps*, speaking of Quebec's problem, said, "One solution remains possible: . . . to send members to Ottawa independent of the national political groups, to revive for generations to come the glorious and profitable experience of Lafontaine. Collaboration, yes; submission, no."

But the trouble with this theory is that it offers no possibility of cabinet representation. In general, the Quebec voter had to choose between Liberals, Independents (many obviously Duplessis-backed), Social Credit, and the two-year-old Canadian Popular Bloc. Of these, only the Liberals had any chance of forming the government of Canada. "Only King can give us French-Canadian ministers," the voter was continually reminded. The recent defeat of a Liberal government in Quebec by a party without federal aspirations, therefore, did not have the same significance in terms of federal politics as did the defeat, for example, of the Ontario Liberal ministry by ambitious Progressive Conservatives who hoped, also, to get into power at Ottawa.

1945, unlike 1940, produced once more a real battle in Quebec. But, notwithstanding the election of a few non-Liberals, the confusion of parties, policies, principles, and personalities was great, and from it no strong second party has emerged to replace the old Conservatives. The Liberals had the support of practically the entire press of the province, including the most widely read journal in each language, *La Presse* and the *Montreal Daily Star*. Their funds were ample and were skilfully used. And they did not have to contend with any Canada-wide party through which Quebec could express her discontent, for no such party existed.

The obvious reason why the Progressive Conservatives are unacceptable was symbolized by the fact that, whereas when Mackenzie King came to Montreal the only flag decorating the Forum was the Canadian red ensign, by way of contrast when Mr. Bracken arrived it was the Union Jack which was displayed in all its glory. Even his basic patriotism is not the same as that of French Canadians. Consequently, in Quebec Mr. King's chief asset was Mr. Bracken. The continuous Liberal refrain was, "a vote against a Liberal is a vote for Bracken" and "*le torysme, voilà l'ennemi*."

As for the CCF [Co-operative Commonwealth Federation], it failed even to save a single deposit in the province. Last August it actually won one provincial seat, Rouyn-Noranda, but since then, in spite of so much previous talk about not conscripting men without conscripting wealth, the CCF has approved the ordering of 16,000 men to the battle front in Europe at a time when there was no conceivable danger of our losing the war. Even David Côté, the CCF's provincial member, approved this action, though it was denounced by most of the Liberals in the province.

In its rare references to the CCF, the Liberal party in Quebec argued along the lines of the following advertisement, inserted in the French press on June 9, 1945, by *Le Comité Central Libéral Montréal*: "The true picture of the CCF is state socialism, the dictatorship of bureaucracy and the death of individual liberty. It is the direct route to the totalitarianism killed in Germany and in Italy."

More important, however, is the attitude reflected by Georges Pelletier, director of *Le Devoir*, on June 2, 1945:

> Compared with Mr. King who wishes to repeat his costly comedy of 1939 and with Mr. Bracken who wishes to match Mr. King and outbids him with ill-considered promises, Mr. Coldwell wishes still better, or worse. He calls for conscription of men, of industry and of money at the same time, as if we have not had the three together since 1940, either openly or disguised. Mr. Woodsworth, who as a matter of fact was the real founder of the CCF, gave the very first place to the interests of Canada; again at the beginning of September, 1939, he reaffirmed this. Unfortunately illness struck him down and, as soon as he disappeared from the House, Mr. Coldwell and his friends hastened to trace the program of their party from that of the Labour Party of the United Kingdom. Since then our CCF has become the image of the British labour movement which throughout the length of the war gave its complete adhesion to the acts of the coalition. At the present time, Mr. Coldwell and his people are engaged in English socialism and Canada no longer exists for them except as a function of the British Empire.

This is a widespread opinion.

The result of the election has emphasized the importance of Quebec in Canadian politics. A party can obtain power at Ottawa only by acquiring a majority in either Ontario or Quebec, and also in some other important section. If French Canada feels a grievance she will support *en bloc* whichever party leader seems to her least objectionable in that connection. Such a party leader at once has a tremendous advantage over his rivals. He needs to win only a comparatively small number of seats in the rest of the country.

Grievances always seem far more important to the suffering minority than to the majority. To be successful, any federal party must realize that if French Canadians *think* a grievance is important, then politically it is important, no matter how much it may seem, from other points of view, to be irrelevant. If a party does not wish such an issue to be decisive in Quebec, then it must not allow such an issue to arise between itself and any other party. This means that the party must be fully aware of the French-Canadian fact, accept it as permanent and of major importance, and consequently adopt an attitude of the utmost generosity. Then, if a minority grievance should become an issue, your party will have a great advantage. And should no such issue arise, your party, particularly if in opposition, will be able to fight the election in Quebec on grounds of its own choosing. This result can be accomplished in no other way.

The Progressive Conservative and CCF parties sometimes listen to a French-Canadian attitude with which they disagree, but only in order to point out how wrong it is, rather than with any intention of allowing for it by modifying their own programs. Naturally neither of these groups are factors in the politics of Quebec. It is both false and futile to explain this in terms of French Canadian "ignorance" or religion. To say that the Roman Catholic Church is the Liberal party at mass would be like describing the United Church and the Church of England as the Progressive and Conservative wings of "the Tory party at prayer,"—an over-simplification to say the least.

If an apparently irreconcilable difference arises between Quebec and the rest of Canada, such as the conscription issue, it is fatal to let it become a party issue unless, like Borden, you are sure you can carry all of English-speaking Canada and are prepared to divide the country along racial lines. If the leadership is forced to take a stand on such a question it must be at least not less favourable to the minority than that of the leaders of other groups. Above all, it should not be made a matter of party discipline. This is a great secret of Liberal success. In a country like Canada you simply cannot force party discipline on too many issues and expect to get anywhere.

No greater mistake could be made than to imagine that in voting Liberal Quebec has approved of Mr. King's mobilization policy. Liguori Lacombe, the Liberal who moved the amendment against participation in September, 1939, is re-elected as an Independent; but his seconder of 1939, the no less violently anti-war Wilfrid LaCroix, is re-elected with official Liberal backing. So is Jean-François Pouliot, who in 1942 campaigned against the government in Charlevoix-Saguenay, and in 1944 crossed the floor of the House. Most of these Quebec Liberals, upon whose support Mackenzie King now depends, are men who fought his conscription policy to the extent of voting "no confidence" in 1942 and 1944. They differ from the Bloc in that they are still willing to participate in the party caucus, and, if fortunate, in the cabinet. They are more willing to compromise. But the Bloc deliberately refrained from opposing some of them, such as Maurice Bourget, François Pouliot, Wilfrid LaCroix, and Charles Parent. Another, Dr. Gauthier, was actually a Bloc candidate and regional organizer in the provincial elections. But the Liberal party holds no grudge against these men. The sin of expressing the viewpoint of their people a bit too vigorously has been quickly forgiven. The mobilization question for them is not a matter of party program or discipline, as it is with the Progressive Conservatives and the CCF. Mr. Godbout, unlike the CCF's David Côté, was able to vote against those Liberals who represent pro-conscription electoral divisions, and to condemn Mr. King's conscription order-in-council as vigorously as he pleased. It did neither Mr. Godbout, nor the party, nor the country any harm.

The Liberals were able to hold seats in all parts of Quebec, from French-Canadian agricultural Beauce, ultra-nationalist, anti-war and anti-conscription, on the one hand, to Montreal's English-speaking, plutocratic St. Antoine-Westmount, ultra-imperialist, pro-war and pro-conscription, on the other. And every French Canadian elected outside of Quebec is a Liberal. They could not be Progressive Conservative or CCF without approving military conscription. At the same time the Liberals carried the Maritimes; and Manitoba, as usual, is also on the winning side. Mackenzie King has succeeded in holding his party together because, from the point of view of minorities, it really is more liberal than its principal rivals. In Canada, minorities are politically important. That is the main reason why the Liberals rule Canada.

The war gave the Dominion government an authority and standing it had never known before. The August 1945 Dominion–Provincial Conference on Reconstruction, however, marked a reassertion of provincial rights. King sat down at the conference table with some strong-willed premiers who had scores to settle and who were determined to alter the balance of power in the Canadian federal system in their favour. Quebec was represented by the arch-autonomist Maurice Duplessis, and Ontario by the imperious George Drew. Drew had led the Progressive Conservatives to power in Ontario in 1943, but with a minority government. On 4 June 1945, a week before the Dominion election, he won a majority election victory. He came to the reconstruction conference with a strong hand and proved to be a tough negotiator. The war had transformed much in Canada, but not, it turned out, the contest for power between Ottawa and the provinces.

The Dominion–Provincial Conference on Reconstruction: The Limits of Success

Doug Owram

THOUGH IT MIGHT have seemed that Ottawa had assumed a great deal of power during the war, there were those who were sceptical of what it all meant. Frank Scott described the concern in a 1942 issue of the *Canadian Forum*. "Mr King," he charged, "by balancing a pyramid of war controls upon the pinpoint of the War Measures Act, and by his extensive use of temporary dollar-a-year men in key positions, has carefully arranged for an immediate collapse of government intervention at the end of the war."[1] Though Scott's accusations as to King's intentions were probably unfair, his charge that Dominion power rested on a pinpoint base was accurate.

Keenly aware of this were those members of the civil service who sought to employ the reconstruction period to transform the role of the state in Canada. Ever since the failure of the Dominion–provincial conference of

1941, the haunting thought had existed that the great opportunity for social change that currently existed would come to little if, with the lapsing of emergency powers, the provinces were successful in asserting their traditional jurisdictional claims upon the Dominion. Reform and economic management would then have to operate within the confines of a constitution that, as one social scientist pointed out, did not even include the concept of public administration. This was especially important in two key areas. First, the provincial hold on social welfare programs under the BNA [British North America] Act threatened to make effective co-ordination of any recovery program impossible. Second, even if the Dominion government were able, through generous grants-in-aid, to convince the provinces to allow federal intrusion into social services, without a rearrangement of fiscal powers Ottawa would not have sufficient financial resources to meet the new demands. As early as June 1943, officials warned of the "serious obstacles which [the Economic Advisory Committee (EAC)] believes the present arrangements between the Dominion and the Provinces offer to the preparation of any adequate post-war measures."[2]

Of all the civil servants, however, the man most sensitive to the issue was the one who had had so much to do with the Rowell–Sirois Report, Alex Skelton. Skelton, it is fair to say, had never had much sympathy with the provinces, and like so many others saw the defence of provincial jurisdictions as a major obstacle to the implementation of the necessary rational management of the economy within a positive nationalist state. In memo after memo he argued that "the Dominion must play all its cards and use its vast war-time powers, the present national unity of purpose and the great public anxiety for the future, to secure effective action." At all costs the Dominion should not be forced to return to ad hoc policies of the Depression years. A new system had to be found to ensure "adequate Dominion powers to regulate and assist private business" and "to initiate and administer social insurance and other social security programs."[3]

There was also growing concern among the provincial premiers about the implications of Dominion reconstruction planning for the postwar world. As federal policies unfolded in late 1943 and early 1944 it became increasingly apparent that the Dominion intended to maintain a presence in key areas of social and economic planning after the war. In January 1944 the new Conservative premier of Ontario, George Drew, wrote to King to warn him of what appeared to be an intrusion into areas of provincial jurisdiction under the protection of temporary wartime controls. The provinces, Drew realized, could do nothing about this for the moment, but his letter served notice that any continuation of such activities into the postwar era would face resistance.[4]

By early 1944, if not before, the government responded to these concerns by planning for a Dominion–provincial conference at the end of the war. Of course there had been conferences before, and little had come of them. This time, however, there was hope that the half-hearted efforts of 1941 would not be repeated. From 1943 on, reconstruction had been a subject of lively interest. Indeed, the federal government could claim, by the time the conference met, that it had won a mandate from the Canadian public on the issue of social reform and that this mandate could be implemented only if the provinces agreed to changes. All these factors led to the hope, as Mackintosh put it, that "political opinion is now ripe for a real tackling of the problems involved."[5]

When the delegations assembled in the Chamber of the House of Commons in August 1945 the social scientific experts within the Dominion civil service had a high profile. It was, after all, their meeting to a large degree. Alex Skelton was secretary to the conference and John Deutsch was his assistant. These two thus picked up where they had left off with the conclusion of the Rowell–Sirois discussion in 1941. There had been changes, however. The "advisors" that the Dominion brought to the conference reflected the tremendous growth of the economic community within the civil service through the war years. W.A. Mackintosh, Graham Towers, R.B. Bryce, and Arnold Heeney were all present, as were Bank of Canada officials like J.E. Coyne, J.R. Beattie, and W.E. Scott. The new Department of Reconstruction sent, aside from Mackintosh, H.C. Goldenberg and O.J. Firestone. Background papers were written by people like James Coyne and M.C. Urquhart. It was an impressive array, including some of the best social scientific minds of the nation. The fact that they were all in the employment of the Dominion reveals a great deal about the evolving role of the expert in Canada. The growing influence of the intellectual community at the political level was also apparent by the time of the 1945 conference. Brooke Claxton had moved up from his parliamentary secretary's position to assume the new portfolio of National Health and Welfare, while Paul Martin had become secretary of state. Mackenzie King, for his part, had gained renewed faith in reconstruction with the convincing Liberal victory in the previous election. Not since Norman Rogers' death had the intellectual community had such strong support within the cabinet.[6]

The high profile of the intelligentsia at the conference table was paralleled by the careful preparation of the government. It was one of the best documented Dominion–provincial conferences to date. Detailed background studies were prepared on each measure by the experts within the government, and a dazzling array of statistics, charts, tables, and graphs was brought to the aid of the Dominion's case. At the opening sessions of the conference itself, lengthy briefs were presented by relevant ministers in support of the various parts of what the federal civil servants involved saw as the comprehensive package necessary to develop a successful reconstruction program. Given the decision to read aloud the extended papers on these complex and often convoluted proposals, one has to admire the ability of those present to stay awake as pages of figures flowed around them.

For those who did manage to stay awake and alert during the long speeches, it became apparent that there were actually two agendas for the conference. The first was designed to try to find a means that would permit the ongoing development of the positive state in Canada under federal direction. Numerous proposals emanating from the discussions of the Marsh Report, the EAC, parliamentary committees, and other bodies were presented. In particular, health insurance, old-age pension, and unemployment assistance proposals were laid out in some detail by the federal planners. If the provinces agreed to develop such plans along Dominion guidelines they would be subsidized from the federal treasury to amounts of 60 percent, 50 percent, and 85 percent, respectively.[7]

Though the specifics of some of the Dominion proposals were new, the general arguments presented were not. Rather, the conference takes on significance for the fact that the Dominion position represented the culmination of a long process of policy formation dating back to the National Employment Commission, the New Deal, and the Rowell–Sirois Report. The personnel arguing the case for the government, in turn, represented the group that had been most actively involved in many of these earlier discussions and that were the most committed to the implementation of this new role for the state. By 1945, however, these proposals were also clearly set within the context of macroeconomic planning as it had developed in the latter half of the war. As Claxton argued to the assembly, "a significant volume of social security payments, flowing into the consumer spending stream, will stabilize the economy of the country as a whole and work against a fall in income."[8] Employment policy was thus closely related to the proposed social security measures.

The second agenda was fiscal and demanded immediate attention. The Dominion government had, under wartime tax agreements, monopolized the key fields of direct taxation. Now that the war was over, those fields could be invaded by the provinces. The Dominion, however, was unwilling to cede such valuable sources of funds. Items like income tax, which had been a relatively small part of government revenue in the 1930s, were, by 1945, the source of about 40 percent of Dominion government revenue.[9] Both Dominion and provincial governments feared the chaos that might result from uncontrolled double taxation in areas like income and corporate taxation.

The two agendas were closely related, and the hope of the Dominion planners was that they would be solved as one. For though taxation issues might be resolved independently of economic planning and social security proposals, the converse was not the case. If the Dominion were to assume the responsibility for whole new social programs it was, as Minister of Justice Louis St. Laurent stated at the opening of the conference, "essential that the federal treasury be in a position to carry these burdens."[10] A taxation agreement might be possible without an agreement on all the proposals of the Dominion for social intervention, but the proposals for social intervention would be impossible if the provinces did not agree to leave the Dominion sufficient powers of taxation to ensure dominance of the national fiscal scene.

The conference documents leave a contradictory set of impressions as to the nature of what occurred. There is, on the one hand, no doubt that both the politicians and the civil service presented a sincere case, and that the discussions around the table were thorough. The Dominion–provincial conference itself would drag on, with long intermissions, from August 1945 through May 1946. The formal record of the plenary discussions constitute more than 600 pages, and there were, in addition, a series of "off the record" talks that probably equalled the plenary sessions for verbiage. The Dominion government, for its part, stated that it was flexible and willing to listen to the legitimate concerns of the provinces. Indeed, there were a number of changes made in the Dominion position as the conference proceeded. Add to this all the thorough background documents, and the impression is given of a real effort by men of good intention to bring about the necessary changes in Canadian social and economic institutions.

On the other hand, a close reading of the proceedings soon reveals a significant degree of repetitiveness and rhetoric. Much of what needed to be said had been said within the first few sessions. More than that, it could be seen from the opening day that the intentions of the federal politicians and civil servants for sweeping alteration of federal–provincial relationships were doomed to failure. George Drew, the premier of Ontario, and Maurice Duplessis of Quebec effectively laid the conference to rest in their opening statements. Six hundred pages of talk would not sway them from their basic position. This made all the rational analysis ineffective, for the point remained that the two largest provinces in Canada stood resolutely opposed to the plans of the Dominion. "Centralization," concluded the premier of Quebec, "always leads to Hitlerism." George Drew, for his part, had as one of his purposes at the conference "the bringing of some of the 'Brains Trust' back to reality."[11] When, after numerous meetings, the conference adjourned *sine die* without any agreement in May 1946, it is unlikely that anyone was surprised.

Of course Drew and especially Duplessis were viewed with something akin to contempt by the intellectual commune in Ottawa, and the civil servants around the table must have been tempted to blame them for the failure that became inevitable from that opening day. Both were seen as the sort of reactionary, patronage-oriented politician whose attitudes proved just how necessary it was to wrest a degree of fiscal and social control from the provinces. Brooke Claxton, whose contempt for these premiers was never far below the surface, tangled with Drew on more than one occasion. The feeling was mutual, Drew at one point referring to Claxton as a "bubbling spring of misinformation." Such clashes were to a large degree the stuff of partisan politics. Drew, King charged, was interested only in the degree to which such a conference might help depose the Liberals in Ottawa. As for Maurice Duplessis, he had a good many reasons to wish to hurt the federal Liberal Party. Other premiers, even if less rancorous or designing in their motives, saw such conferences as an opportunity to restate broad grievances concerning the economic and political structure of the nation. Obstructionism was thus, to a degree, at fault. Yet it is an insufficient explanation of what occurred.[12]

If obstructionism and partisanship were not sufficient, then a further explanation is provided by ideological differences. CCF premier T.C. Douglas of Saskatchewan argued that the vision of the positive state held by the Ottawa planners was too restricted to meet the demands of the new age. Only an acceptance of the necessity of broadly based state ownership would, he believed, resolve the problems Canada faced. At the opposite end of the scale, Maurice Duplessis of Quebec took a straightforward line of opposition to the interventionist direction of the Dominion. "The issues of the conference," he argued, "are not racial issues; they are national issues; it is bureaucracy against democracy; parliamentary institutions and prerogatives against bureaucrats." The presence of a significant coterie of French-Canadian civil servants within the central ranks of reconstruction planning would not have changed Duplessis's position, but their absence was made all the more noticeable by Quebec's hostility to the emergence of the new bureaucratic and technocratic state. Duplessis was not alone in his attitude, though he was the most ideologically explicit in his resistance. Drew was far from enthusiastic about the move toward planning, and Manning of Alberta had earlier protested the tendencies of Ottawa toward centralization and planning. "The manner in which the whole situation is being developed," he warned Charlotte Whitton, "has for its purpose the rapid introduction of the Socialist State."[13]

Yet even the addition of ideological disagreements to partisan ones cannot fully explain the failure of the reconstruction conference. For at the basis of the collapse of the conference was an insurmountable difference in perspective between Dominion and provincial jurisdictions that rested not on a clash of ideologies but on a consensus. Even where partisan and ideological differences were minimal, it was impossible for the provinces simply to hand over their responsibilities to the Dominion. This position was most clearly revealed in the position taken by Manitoba. Stuart Garson, the premier, was sympathetic to the aims of reconstruction planning and seems to have held no partisan or ideological grudges against the Dominion planners. Indeed, during the war he had corresponded regularly with W.A. Mackintosh, who, in spite of his position as a Dominion official, acted as an unofficial advisor to the Manitoba premier.

Moreover, as he commented a few months before the conference began, the difficulties of reconstruction were such that "partisanship therefore is and will be a luxury which we should abandon during this critical period."[14]

However sympathetic Garson might be, he could not accept any Dominion scheme that threatened his own government's capability to meet what were, after all, demands that the public was directing at the provinces as well as at the federal government. The very logic of the positive government acted as a stumbling block to Dominion policies. "The present level of income and employment," Garson reminded the conference, "is the result of wartime spending. To maintain the total of peacetime spending by governments, businesses and citizens" was thus essential to the maintenance of high employment. Manitoba understood the implications of Keynes as well as Ottawa, and for those reasons had difficulty with the federal proposals:

> In the field of government a very substantial part of this increase must come under provincial jurisdiction, namely in education, health and public welfare, natural resources development, road building, provincial public works. An increase in the standard of these services is therefore dependent in large measure upon the financial ability of the provinces to take care of these matters which fall under provincial jurisdiction. If the provinces lack financial capacity these provincial matters will not be handled adequately, and to this important extent the Canadian standard of living will not rise sufficiently, the national income will not be maintained, and there will be greater difficulty in maintaining adequate employment.[15]

The Dominion confirmed the point raised by Garson when it was asked by the provinces whether it would assume "full fiscal responsibility for unemployment." That, said King, was impossible. There were too many areas of jurisdiction beyond the federal system that no degree of economic management could control. The provinces would thus have to undertake a share of the responsibility. Given that inescapable fact, it was difficult to deny the argument that the provinces had to have sufficient fiscal and constitutional resources to meet the responsibilities that would be placed upon them. In the end, in spite of the extremely generous Dominion subsidies proffered in the name of health insurance, old-age pensions, and other matters, the only agreement to flow immediately from the conference was a series of agreements to allow the Dominion to "rent" income taxes in order to avoid double taxation.[16]

The Dominion–provincial conference of 1945–46 reveals both the degree to which the positive state had become accepted in Canada and the limits to the influence of the intelligentsia. On the one hand, the conference revealed that practically all Canadian governments had accepted the importance of social services and the necessity of using modern techniques of economic management to reduce the impact of downturns in the business cycle. Equally important, there was widespread acceptance that in the effort to prevent unemployment it was impossible to draw hard and fast lines between the public and private sectors. Provincial governments as much as the federal government were willing to use public investment as a means of ensuring economic prosperity and, not incidentally, ensuring their own political survival. Over the previous twenty years the dominant view as to the role of government had changed drastically, and what had seemed extreme now seemed commonplace.

On the other hand, if there was a new acceptance of the positive state, though sometimes reluctant and occasionally resisted, the mandarins' view that the Dominion government should direct that planning was rejected. It was, as it turned out, the Ottawa civil servants and their academic colleagues who were isolated when it came to constitutional matters. For in spite of the prestige they had acquired and in spite of their attempt to promote a planned and centralist view of Canada, the positive state would emerge not by means of a rational. efficient, and bureaucratically dominated Dominion government, but as a series of compromises between the demands of industrial society and the public on one hand and the realities of a federal constitution and regional divergence on the other. Harold Innis, who was as suspicious as ever of the designs of his social scientific colleagues, summed it up in 1946. Across the land, he said, the social scientist "can be seen carrying the fuel to Ottawa to make the flames of Nationalism burn more brightly. Or he is constantly devising schemes throughout the Provinces to thwart the human spirit and to fasten the chains more tightly." In such a context the long-standing Canadian lament of disunity became a guarantor of freedom. "Fortunately," Innis concluded, "we are sufficiently divided in regions, races and religion to resist his demand for centralization."[17] Whatever one might think about his view of the social sciences, the results of the 1945–46 conference reveal that Innis was correct in his estimate of the nature of Canada. The social scientist had become a major force in the new managerial state that he had done so much to develop. At the same time the effects of the positive state would always be limited by the absence of a single overriding sense of priority, purpose, or authority to translate that interventionism into action.

Notes

1. Frank Scott, "Confederation: An Assessment," *Canadian Forum* 22 (July 1942): 105–6.
2. J.R. Mallory, "Changing Techniques of Canadian Government," *Public Affairs* 7, 2 (Winter 1944): 112. National Archives of Canada (NAC), Records of the Department of Finance, 3976, file E-3-0, Mackintosh to Heeney, 8 June 1943.
3. Bank of Canada Archives, Ottawa, Research Department file, 3b-172 Memorandum "Dominion Post-War

Policy," 3 April 1943. NAC, Records of the Department of Finance, 3542, Alex Skelton, "Approach to Post-War Planning II," 10 June 1943. See also 3447, Minutes of the EAC of 24 March 1943.

4. Drew to King, 6 Jan. 1944; cited in Canada, *Dominion–Provincial Conference on Reconstruction*, Session of 2 May 1946, 431. For the details of Drew's position at the conference see Marc J. Gotlieb, "George Drew and the Dominion–Provincial Conference on Reconstruction of 1945-6," *Canadian Historical Review* 66 (March 1985): 27–47.
5. Records of the Department of Finance, 4660, file 187 EAC-I, Mackintosh to Corry, 28 March 1944.
6. *Dominion–Provincial Conference*, 6–10 Aug. 1945, vii–viii.
7. *Dominion–Provincial Conference*, Session of 25 April 1946, 386–87.
8. *Dominion–Provincial Conference*, 6 Aug. 1945, Plenary Session, 85.
9. *Canada Year Book* (1946), 886.
10. *Dominion–Provincial Conference*, 6 Aug. 1945, 57.
11. *Dominion–Provincial Conference*, First Plenary Session, 6 Aug. 1945. Gotlieb, "George Drew and the *Dominion–Provincial Conference*," 42.
12. *Dominion–Provincial Conference*, Plenary Session of 30 April 1946, 431. NAC, William Lyon Mackenzie King Diary, 22 July 1944.
13. *Dominion–Provincial Conference*, Session of 8 Jan. 1946, 257. Ibid., Session of 30 April 1946, 530. Gotlieb, "George Drew and the Dominion–Provincial Conference," 34. NAC, Charlotte Whitton Papers, vol. 4, Manning to Whitton, 10 March 1945. See also Provincial Archives of Alberta, Premiers' Papers, file 1200, Manning to Patullo, 16 July 1945.
14. Records of the Department of Finance, 3563, file G-00A contains the Mackintosh–Garson correspondence. Whitton Papers, vol. 4, Garson to Whitton, 29 March 1945.
15. *Dominion–Provincial Conference*, Plenary Session of 26 January 1946, 324–25.
16. Ibid., Session of 5 April 1946, 338. The rental agreements came out of the Dominion's June 1946 budget, and the steps leading to the negotiations are contained in ibid., appendix C3.
17. Harold Innis, *Political Economy in the Modern State* (Toronto, 1946), preface, xii.

The return home of the Canadian forces that had fought overseas in the Great War had been fraught with difficulty, delay, and even violence. Veterans, moreover, had been an unpredictable element in the explosive social and economic situation of the immediate postwar period. The plans Ottawa made for demobilization at the end of World War II were designed to produce a very different outcome.

Canadian Military Demobilization in World War II*

Dean F. Oliver

MILITARY DEMOBILIZATION was among the largest and most complex problems that faced the Canadian government during the war years. Neglect or ill-treatment of those who had donned the uniform to beat back the Fascist foe was a risk that no government, certainly not Mackenzie King's, dared take lightly, for a variety of reasons. In accepting its responsiblity, the government was proving itself no less susceptible than the general population to the sincere desire to make Canada "a land fit for heroes"; it was also responding to the rather more political need to handle several hundred thousand voters and their families fairly and effectively.

Although demobilization planning was therefore essential for any "total war" effort, at least eventually, its origins lie surprisingly early in the war years, long before either the European or Asiatic conflicts had ended, and even before it was certain which side would ultimately prevail. Ian Mackenzie, minister of pensions and national health at the outbreak of the war,[1] got the ball rolling officially on 30 October 1939 in a note to Prime Minister King. "We should," he wrote, "in the very near future, direct our attention to the questions and problems that will arise consequent upon the cessation of hostilities," and he proposed the establishment of a cabinet committee to gather information and make policy recommendations.

*The author wishes to thank the Social Sciences and Humanities Research Council of Canada and the Centre for International and Strategic Studies at York University for their financial support of the research for this essay.

King's response was favourable. "I wholly agree," he wrote on 1 November, "that this problem requires very full and thorough consideration before a definite policy is decided upon and that we cannot begin upon it too soon." He promised Mackenzie that the issue would be brought before council "at the first opportune moment,"[2] and proved as good as his word.[3]

Mackenzie's concerns had already been presaged by a wide range of more public developments, including submissions to his own office. The most important of these undoubtedly came from H.F. McDonald, chairman of the Canadian Pension Commission, who urged Mackenzie on 13 October 1939 to give early consideration to demobilization and reestablishment questions.[4] A separate background memorandum, prepared for Mackenzie by his staff, surveyed Canada's experiences during the First World War, and stated the issue quite boldly: "no country has ever successfully demobilized a large army and reabsorbed the personnel into normal civilian life." Further, its author declared, Canada's efforts in this regard during the First World War had been "slipshod and inappropriate."[5] Careful planning to avoid similar problems was a necessity, and could not be initiated too soon.

Across the country, organizations and individuals were lining up to deliver or to demand promises of job security and beneficent treatment to those who volunteered for military service. The city council of Hamilton, Ontario, for example, was quick off the mark in seeking to ensure job security for those who enlisted in the war effort, setting an excellent precedent, one scribe suggested, "by making it clear that shirkers will not entrench themselves in soft jobs while decent men fight their battles."[6] The *Globe and Mail* demanded that the homes and property of enlistees be protected during their period of service, and commended those businesses that, it said, had already moved to preserve the jobs of Canadian volunteers.[7] Veterans' organizations weighed in with demands for aid to soldiers and their families, and echoed the opposition parties and labour unions in requesting the full-scale mobilization of industry and wealth for the war effort.[8]

Such pressure buttressed Mackenzie's case and was indicative of widespread concern for the treatment of Canada's veterans. Generous veterans' legislation would be a test of Canadian resolve and Canadian gratitude, many commentators argued, a test indeed of how deserving the country was of the sacrifices soon to be made in its name. For Robert England, adult-education specialist and later veterans' affairs planner, it would become "at bottom a test of Canadian society and of its orientation towards the welfare state."[9] The latter sentiment, however, carried some very particular connotations in 1940s Canada, and King's assertion in the House of Commons on 25 January 1940 that postwar planning would begin immediately[10] left many of his parliamentary colleagues unimpressed

Attacking the government for its alleged failure to provide for veterans and for postwar security would soon become a parliamentary pastime, and the record is sprinkled with clashes over vocational training, the rights of volunteers, housing, war-service grants, and demobilization priorities. Particularly virulent were critics on the left, who envisaged veterans' benefits as the springboard for a more comprehensive network of social programs. For them, as the war progressed and the government's plans gradually unfolded, King's approach smacked of, at best, ineffective incrementalism, and at worst, calculated social control. The Co-operative Commonwealth Federation, for example, committed as it was to general economic planning for the "cultural and material welfare" of all Canadians,[11] viewed any program for returning veterans to their prewar jobs as incomplete without a general commitment to full employment and "the planned utilization of all our resources."[12] In a typical outburst comparing Ottawa's impressive First World War memorial with the sorry state of the war's often destitute veterans, the New Democracy's Dorise W. Nielson expressed her desire "to bring some of these men here [to Ottawa], in all their rags and tatters, and stand them around your great monument, to form a living testimony to the ingratitude of Canada."[13] Such critics would prove difficult to appease, but their views added urgency to Ottawa's planning efforts, particularly in the case of the CCF, whose troublesome popularity bedeviled King's Liberals throughout the war.

Yet there was no doubt, partisanship aside, that federal demobilization and rehabilitation planning had begun at a remarkably early stage, and neither of the factors outlined previously quite explains why. The final influencing factor, and perhaps the most decisive, in accounting for Ottawa's receptivity was also the most obvious. Canada's demobilization after November 1918, by far its largest up to that time, had not gone altogether smoothly, and servicemen at Canadian repatriation camps had seethed with discontent at what many perceived as unwarranted delays in their return home. The result was a series of riots and violent incidents that had left several camps and villages in southern England in various stages of smouldering ruin.[14] Once back in Canada, the Great War veterans suffered from Ottawa's lack of adequate preparation for their return,[15] and from postwar economic problems that sucked unemployed ex-soldiers into the vortex of violent labour disputes, It was not an atmosphere conducive to the uneventful discharge of several hundred thousand military personnel, and the lesson was not lost on Canada's military and political planners the second time around. Veterans' welfare, the cynics might argue with some justification, was for Ottawa as much self-preservation as humanitarian concern. "Unless something is done," pleaded Douglas G. Ross, the Conservative MP for St. Paul's, "we are going to make reds of these fellows," and when he warned that some of these "agitators" had already appeared in his own riding, the parallels with 1919's "Bloody Saturday" were all too clear to miss.

Short-term solutions simply would not do. The six months' discharge pay allotted to veterans in 1919 had been squandered on "a good time," in the opinion of one of Mackenzie's staffers, after which all too many veterans became "a charge on the public." Only "a large scale economic plan" could avoid a similar outcome following the present war. The social and political consequences of inaction were daunting. "You will remember vividly," Mackenzie was reminded, "the soup kitchen disturbance in Vancouver around 1920 and 1921."[16]

This combination of public pressure and historical experience made a convincing case, and Mackenzie's efforts paid off with the establishment on 8 December 1939[17] of the Cabinet Committee on Demobilization and Re-establishment (CCDR). The committee was required to assess the problems arising from the demobilization, discharge, and rehabilitation of Canadian military personnel during and after the war,[18] and was to consist of some of the government's most powerful cabinet ministers, including those from National Defence, Labour, Finance, and Agriculture. The CCDR quickly authorized a General Advisory Committee (Interdepartmental) on Demobilization and Rehabilitation (GACDR) to handle the day-to-day fulfilment of its mandate. Operating on the deputy ministerial level, this committee would in short order become the central clearing house for the government's demobilization and rehabilitation efforts.[19] Great care was taken in its staffing, and its members would ultimately include an impressive array of civil service, military, and private sector talent. The importance accorded civil servants and government appointees in its operation however, was not lost on the members of the opposition, whose criticism[20] resulted in the formation of a House of Commons Committee on Reconstruction and Re-establishment in the spring of 1942, despite the fears of some that it would merely provide a conduit of information for its more powerful cabinet cousin.[21] In any event, the House committee proved more interested in the first part of its mandate, reconstruction, and left to the bureaucrats—albeit grudgingly—the bulk of reestablishment planning.

The GACDR began exploratory meetings in early 1940, though military demobilization was not yet the central issue absorbing the government's, or the public's, attention. Its early focus was on more immediate problems, including the discharge of medically unfit personnel, allowances for military dependants, disability pensions, and benefits for personnel returned to civilian life before war's end. Such programs concentrated on veterans' rehabilitation or reestablishment, not on military demobilization per se, but the practical and theoretical linkages between the two were very close. Effective demobilization required an existing, ongoing system of veterans' welfare to which soldiers could return; effective rehabilitation necessitated an unhurried, orderly demobilization that deposited a well-briefed, suitably disposed veteran into the arms of the reestablishment machine.

Demobilization and rehabilitation, therefore, were two sides of the same coin, though the differences between the two are worth noting. Military demobilization represented "the organization of efficient machinery to carry out the routine of discharge according to agreed upon and understood principles," while rehabilitation would enable military personnel "to re-establish themselves socially and in some measure economically" in Canadian society.[22] The former was the responsibility of the military services, acting in conjunction with their political overseers: the latter was to be handled by the departments of Pensions and National Health (later National Health and Welfare and Veterans Affairs) and Labour. Military demobilization also included, and in some ways was synonymous with, repatriation, the return of personnel to their place of discharge, and disbandment, the abolition of military units and the disposal, sale, or storage of their equipment. Rehabilitation likewise encompassed economic reestablishment, "the creation of conditions in Canada making for a high level of employment,"[23] and to some extent postwar reconstruction. Obviously, the dividing lines between military demobilization and rehabilitation were often blurred, and the rigidity of departmental responsibilities more apparent than real. In the case of educational and vocational training, for example, the government, the military, and organizations like the Canadian Legion shared responsibility.

The attention directed to veterans' rehabilitation and reestablishment soon resulted in both an extensive list of federal programs and a large and growing bureaucracy.[24] These programs included: job protection and employment preferences for civil servants in the Forces; clothing allowances and war-service gratuities; vocational and training benefits; access to unemployment benefits; university education; a revamped Veterans' Land Act; and dependants' benefits. The web of organizations to implement and monitor these programs spanned almost all federal and provincial government departments and most major municipalities, not to mention nongovernmental agencies. In addition to the CCDR, the GACDR, and the new departments of Veterans Affairs and Reconstruction, the federal government alone harboured an Advisory Committee on Economic Policy dealing mainly with postwar problems, the aforementioned special Commons committee on Reconstruction and Re-establishment, a Senate committee on Economic Re-establishment and Social Security, a cabinet committee on Reconstruction, a committee on the Priority and Seniority of Veterans, and the impressively titled Interdepartmental Committee to Co-ordinate the Information Activities of Government Departments Connected with Demobilization, Rehabilitation, Readjustment, and Related Matters.[25] Not without justification did Robert England refer to the "paper blizzard" besieging contemporary Ottawa.[26]

Despite its more immediate preoccupations, government had also taken up the business of ultimate demobilization priorities, and a subcommittee of the GACDR dealing with priorities and means had prepared a detailed report for cabinet by late 1943.[27] The subcommittee's mandate included surveying existing enlistment procedures, developing demobilization priorities in co-ordination with rehabilitation facilities and procedures, and suggesting methods to maintain the morale and confidence of the Forces in the crucial period between the war's end and actual discharge. The subcommittee's final report, submitted 18 June 1943 and revised 3 December,[28] reflected the need for close interaction with the other civilian and military planning bodies, and the desire to co-ordinate rehabilitation and demobilization procedures. It stressed the need for adequate provision of information to explain the process at every stage, especially to service personnel.[29] They were to be divided into groups according to whether or not they had a job or business to go to upon discharge, had accepted vocational or university-level training, or were returning to farm work. The remainder were to be categorized simply as skilled or unskilled, and were referred to local employment offices for job placement.

In this report, the links between demobilization and rehabilitation, particularly in terms of the availability of jobs, is quite striking, but in a draft report prepared in January 1943 the subcommittee had been even more explicit. Taking its cue from the minister, who suggested to the Special Parliamentary Committee on the Pension Act in April 1941 that "perhaps some deliberate retardation may have to be established to govern the demobilization machinery,"[30] the subcommittee felt it was crucial that the needs of civil reestablishment govern all arrangements and policies, consequent on the cessation of hostilities. In this regard, it differentiated between repatriation, or the return of units to Canada, which would be "subject to the exigencies of the situation and entirely based on criteria of a military character," and demobilization,[31] wherein political and economic considerations were of paramount importance.[32] While carefully delineating the boundaries between these spheres, however, the subcommittee felt the economy "would profit by the earlier return of technical personnel who are key men in industry and also instructors (particularly in technical subjects)," though they stopped short of making this a requirement.[33] They did feel that "retarded demobilization should, however, be applied to unskilled, untrainable labour in areas where labour demand is weak."[34]

Deliberately gearing demobilization to Canadian society's economic absorptive capacity was not without precedent or purpose. Why should personnel be released in large numbers regardless of their employment prospects? What would that do to the economy and to the men and women themselves? Would it not be better to ease into the postwar world gradually, releasing first only those who could find work and initiating training for those who could not? Even the Canadian Legion, self-appointed defender of veterans' rights, had, in a carefully worded brief to the House committee on Reconstruction, suggested just such a course in preference to the allegedly chaotic exodus of World War

I,[35] but the practical ramifications of such a plan remained murky, and the track record far from convincing. The attempted imposition of a system for the release of "key men" from the British army in 1918–1919 had resulted in widespread mutinies and disciplinary infractions. The system had been jettisoned by Britain's new war minister, Winston Churchill, in January 1919, and replaced by one relying on length of service, age, and war wounds.[36]

Choosing between long-service personnel and employable personnel offered equally unacceptable options, but the GACDR's subcommittee felt it had at least part of the answer in the ameliorating circumstances provided by the carefully crafted safety net of veterans' legislation—the other pillar of demobilization planning—already well along in its creation. It might indeed be possible to have the best of both worlds: a slow, deliberate demobilization schedule and a quiescent, contented army of dischargees, provided, of course, that the legislation could be drafted, passed, and communicated to the troops before the day of reckoning arrived.

The prime minister and the cabinet were aware of the need to co-ordinate these two potentially contradictory processes, and proved more or less in tune with the tenor of both the subcommittee report and that of its parent body, delivered to Mackenzie on 25 September 1943.[37] By the following fall, most of the GACDR's recommendations had been acted upon by cabinet, and more—including the establishment of the Department of Veterans Affairs—would soon follow.[38] The careful attention accorded the GACDR's program by officials in the United States and Britain is ample testimony to the thoroughness of its efforts,[39] and Canadians themselves seemed no less pleased with their government's exertions. In October 1944, the Wartime Information Board reported a growing need for public information on the government's demobilization and rehabilitation plans,[40] but by 30 April 1945 it showed considerable popular approval of Ottawa's proposals. Fifty-five percent of respondents felt that measures undertaken thus far for returned personnel were "about right" (versus 31 percent who said "not enough"), while 56 percent said returned personnel had no cause for complaint (versus 23 percent who said they did).[41] The soldiers, airmen, and sailors likewise appeared contented, and on 10 January 1945 a survey of 1700 overseas personnel reported that except for fears of excessive "red tape," the troops were "fairly well satisfied" with the government's efforts. "With the possible exception of New Zealand," the survey noted, "Canada appears to have gone much further than any other Allied country in its preparations for rehabilitation."[42]

Such approval ratings did not come easily, however, and the final decisions regarding overall demobilization priorities and procedures were hammered out after much debate and not a little recrimination. The issue came to a head in the Cabinet War Committee in September 1944, when King informed his colleagues that expansion of the national income and industrial reconversion were the only acceptable ways to guarantee "full and profitable employment for demobilized ex-Servicemen."[43] Therefore, he suggested, while every effort would be made to get the troops home as quickly as possible, delays were inevitable. Furthermore, because the rapid reconversion of industry was essential to the continued prosperity of the country and, by implication, that of its ex-soldiers, release of surplus military personnel in Canada for civilian work should be contemplated, if only on a temporary basis.

This was also the view of C.D. Howe, minister of munitions and supply. In the discussions on 20, 22, and 23 September, the influential Howe argued vehemently that the manpower needs of industry required immediate attention if the government's promise of a smooth transition to a peacetime footing were to be accomplished. Howe agreed "emphatically" with King that Canadian contributions to the Pacific war should be kept to a minimum,[44] and again on 22 September locked horns with the minister of national defence, J.L. Ralston, over the need for the rapid release of military personnel to industry.[45]

Ralston's point was equally relevant, however: any proposal that contemplated the early release of personnel already in Canada could, and most likely would, include men serving under the National Resources Mobilization Act (NRMA). The catch-22 in the government's proposal was therefore obvious. Reconversion was a political and economic problem demanding manpower that might only be obtained readily from troops already in Canada; effective demobilization, however, required that the men and women overseas perceive a reasonable possibility of a speedy return and postwar employment. Neither would be certain if all "the good jobs" were being snapped up by "zombies."

The indignation aroused by such "shirkers" was palpable. Ralston's spirited defence of the rights of general service enlistees may have left him virtually alone at the cabinet table by 23 September,[46] but outside cabinet the issue remained in considerable doubt. Similar advice regarding demobilization priorities had been pouring in from a variety of sources, much of it in sympathy with the embattled defence minister, and even his cabinet opponents were reluctant to lean too far toward rewarding the zombies. The reinforcement crisis demanded that as many men as possible volunteer for overseas service, but promising employment opportunities, however impermanent, to those serving in Canada was not an effective recruiting tool. Thus, while debate raged over demobilization priorities for both general service and NRMA personnel, the latter were threatened with being released last if they refused to sign up for overseas duty.[47]

Ralston's distress arose from his belief that principle—fairness especially—was being sacrificed on the basis of political and economic expediency. He believed in "first in–first out," meaning that length of service (even if slightly modified by, for example, compassionate cases) should be the ultimate criterion for speed of release. Essentially, this view was shared by the military services,[48] each of which had been developing plans since at least 1940, and—not surprisingly—by the men and women in uniform. It was also a view, as the cabinet well knew, so popular with both the public and opposition politicians that the King government could hardly fail to incorporate it into any and all of its transitional plans.

The solution, not unexpectedly, was a compromise. Discharge priorities would be established as follows: overseas personnel, other general service personnel, and NRMA personnel. As the situation permitted and the economy demanded, however, NRMA personnel could be given leave to perform essential civilian duties, pending discharge and the noninterference of such arrangements with the rights and just deserts of general service enlistees.[49] In this way, the Canadian economy could be guaranteed an early and steady supply of skilled workers, while, presumably, the rights of long-service overseas volunteers would not be unduly prejudiced.

This qualified "first in–first out" principle became the basis for cabinet policy adopted on 19 April 1945,[50] with one significant modification: since the terms of service for NRMA personnel had, in the interim, been extended beyond the Western Hemisphere, it was proposed to treat those who had proceeded overseas in a similar fashion to other overseas personnel, leaving NRMA men with only home service alone at the bottom rung of the demobilization ladder.[51] The compromise was reflected in the demobilization plans of each of the services.[52] The Army's repatriation scheme, for example, submitted by General A.G.L. McNaughton for cabinet consideration in early February 1945, saw the "first in–first out" principle qualified by preferences for several other factors, including overseas service, married personnel, compassionate cases, military exigencies, and—most importantly—"the satisfaction of critical manpower requirements in industry and the professions."[53] Likewise, the Air Force's plan, as summarized for the House of Commons by the minister of national defence for air, C.W.G. Gibson, on 4 October 1945, adhered to the "first in–first out" principle, but attached a significant list of qualifications, more than a dozen in total. Second only to overseas service was "the release of key personnel to provide for the expeditious and effective reconversion of industry from wartime to peacetime production and the maintenance of maximum employment."[54]

Thus, while military personnel were being promised an early return to home and family based mainly on length of service, they were also being told simultaneously (if somewhat less vocally) that political and economic considerations would naturally affect the process.[55] This was an eminently practical and flexible, if ultimately political, approach. The adoption of such a hybrid scheme, however, certainly opened the door for more widespread evasion of the policy's intent, and represented a clear defeat for Ralston and his conscriptionist backers. That such compromises and qualifications could reach almost comic proportions is indicated by the RCAF's priority list cited earlier; the confusion created in the public mind as a result would inevitably be voiced, and criticism of the policy ranged from the well-intentioned to the absurd. Contrary to the promise of an early release based mainly on length of service overseas, wrote one group calling itself "Those who believe in fair Play," "Jewish personal [sic] are the one's [sic] with 18 months and 2 yrs service [who] are getting discharges, and they say on compassionate grounds (baloney) but I could voucher [sic] that not true, that others have circumstances just as good and don't get out in a week or so, but who are we only a bunch with nothing behind us and no one looking after us. If this is fair play we don't think so."[56]

McNaughton's memorandum was also ample evidence that the Armed Forces, like Mackenzie's planners and King's ministers, had never been oblivious to the relationship between demobilization and domestic considerations. In the case of the Army, its Historical Section had, in the fall of 1940, appreciated that "procedure on General Demobilization will also be affected by the rate at which veterans can be absorbed into civil life, which is a matter for the Department of Pensions and National Health and the Department of Labour."[57] In this respect, at least, the military working alone had preempted by four years the conclusions of a small army of government bureaucrats. Gilbert Tucker noted, in fact, that the cabinet's somewhat tardy announcement of overall demobilization priorities prohibited the Navy from establishing a priorities board prior to 1944,[58] and that in any case until well into the fall of that year the most pressing manpower problem was reallocating forces for the war against Japan, not releasing surplus personnel. Ultimately, the Navy's priorities would mirror those of the other services, though in the event that too many men and women preferred to remain with the colours it was prepared to adopt a "last in–first out" policy on the grounds that "partly trained individuals were the least valuable to the navy."[59]

The Army's scheme of demobilization priorities based on length and location of service, and buttressed by marital status was circulated in pamphlet form within days of the German collapse. Like the government's overall policy, it was far less unequivocal than some purists might have liked, granting priority status to the occupation forces and to those destined for the Pacific war, and to compassionate and special–leave cases. Soldiers "with special qualifications who will be needed for civilian industries, or professions, in the period of reconstruction" might also be considered for preferential release.[60]

Notwithstanding the published priorities, of course, the government, the military, and commanding officers were besieged with requests from groups and individuals who felt their particular circumstances deserved special treatment. Sometimes such requests reflected simple misunderstanding or impatience, as in the case of Carl Eayrs, whose nineteen-year-old signalman son had been informed of a six- to eighteen-month delay in obtaining a discharge. The boy's high school education had been interrupted by the war, his father wrote King, and he could not wait too long to resume his studies.[61] Less easily handled was the demand by the Canadian Lumbermen's Association for the immediate demobilization of the entire Canadian Forestry Corps, and special leave arrangements for all military personnel with lumbering experience; failure to do so, the association argued in an attempt to hit the government at its most vulnerable point, would surely jeopardize Ottawa's postwar plans.[62]

A further complication was outlined by H.D.G. Crerar, General Officer Commanding-in-Chief (GOC-in-C), First Canadian Army, who noted in the foreword to the Army's demobilization pamphlet that '"time, by itself, is not necessarily an absolute or convincing argument for priority in the matter of repatriation." Of equal significance, he argued, would be merit and the return of units intact to their home districts; nothing less would allow the maintenance of morale and military efficiency in the delicate transition period.[63] Like the dispute over length of service versus employability and economic need as a basis for release, Crerar's argument represented another fundamentally different approach to the demobilization process that had been compromised in the final document. Moreover, his concerns were certainly valid. Many of the personnel with the highest point scores would be administrative, command, and logistical troops whose functions were essential to the continued operation of the overseas military establishment. They could not be sent home in one fell swoop, however unfair it might seem. Such "key men" would be required to run the repatriation machine itself, for example, and to co-ordinate the transfer of troops and equipment between Europe, North America, and the Far East. Furthermore, the fact that noncombatants in the quiescent, enemy-free rear areas and in England tended to live longer inflated their point scores to often stratospheric levels; sending them back en masse would create friction with the combat troops with lower point scores, who felt, rightly, that their additional risk taking should be rewarded.

It is difficult to determine with precision how far Crerar's views on this matter were shared by other military planners. His own opinion on the subject had not been formed quickly, but was based on his belief in the territorial reinforcement of active units as a "morale building" exercise, a policy he felt should be continued during the transition period. The demobilization of territorially composed units would be an "administrative dream," he argued, "a tidy show from start to finish. Everything under control and everybody happy."[64] Certainly he believed this view was widespread, and in the summer of 1945 telegraphed McNaughton that the formation of so-called divisional groups was a procedure "generally accepted by all ranks."[65] He also charged that the prevailing system had more detrimental results, namely the Aldershot disturbances, in which soldiers awaiting repatriation had rioted, due largely, he suggested, "to [the] situation inherent in home drafts who do not know one another before being brought together in transit and who have nothing in common but a similar period overseas or that individually each has volunteered for CAPF [Canadian Army Pacific Force]."[66]

When presented in their initial pamphlet form, however, these views were subordinated to the priorities outlined above, as agreed to by cabinet on 19 April. In other words, a dual repatriation procedure was adopted incorporating drafts of high-point-earning personnel and, later, the return of intact units.[67] After the initial return of long-service personnel in early 1945, many of whom had been overseas for more than five years, demobilization during the summer shifted to a combination of unit and individual repatriation, with the "first in–first out" principle now applied to entire military formations based on their time of arrival overseas. Furthermore, in an effort to keep units as geographically organized as possible, while simultaneously eliminating complaints about fairness, a considerable amount of personnel shuffling occurred as commanders concentrated troops with similar point levels in units with close territorial affiliations. If individual needs were to be compromised by political imperatives, it seemed no less logical to subordinate them to military demands as well.

But the change was not accomplished smoothly, and some commentators have implied—erroneously—that a wholesale change of policy occurred. In July 1945, as Crerar was ordering the formation of his divisional groups and maintaining that demobilization by "disintegration" had reached its practicable limit,[68] Ian Mackenzie was visiting the Canadian Forces overseas. It came as something of a surprise to learn that, as he saw it, Crerar was usurping the government's authority and rearranging demobilization to suit himself, much to the chagrin of those soldiers Mackenzie had interviewed personally. For Crerar, this was the natural evolution of the government's plan (with the details left appropriately in his hands), as laid down by cabinet and communicated to the troops in the pamphlet *After Victory in Europe*, which he supposed the meddlesome minister had not read.[69] For Mackenzie, it was an embarrassing twist that he had to answer for, first in confrontations with the troops and later in the press at home. He communicated this view to Crerar directly on 19 July, noting that the general's position had created a "profound discontent" in the Army. The government's pledge of "first in–first out," he said, was "a debt of honour that must be fulfilled" and "[I] am not prepared to be responsible for concurrence in its abandonment."[70]

Crerar, however, was undoubtedly correct. The points system was extremely difficult to implement, and had already returned large numbers of officers and senior NCOs badly needed to maintain a functioning military structure, not to mention the logistical nightmare of repatriation. As well, the use of divisional groups or some similar device had been contemplated in both the government's and the Army's plans. Mackenzie, however, also had a point: clearly, the emphasis in official pronouncements since the previous fall had been on "first in–first out." There were qualifying statements, he admitted, "but it was evident to me that the men attached great importance to the points system and regarded departures from it as a breach of faith."[71]

This was, in fact, something of an understatement. Civilian press reports, the Wartime Information Board, and military newspaper editorials all displayed considerable sympathy for Mackenzie's view, partially uninformed though it was. And—as Crerar well knew—perceived impediments to a speedy repatriation could be risky.[72] Not without a flurry of press releases and the muzzling of the minister of veterans affairs was the flare-up controlled. Demobilization by a combination of point scores and divisional groups continued through the end of the war, but the element of risk encountered, and avoided, was substantial, as the American experience graphically revealed.[73] The firing of the editor of the *Maple Leaf* by Lieutenant-General G.G. Simonds, General Officer Commanding (GOC), Canadian Forces in the Nether-lands, for expressing misgivings about the Army's demobilization machinery[74] is further proof, if more were needed, that equilibrium during the repatriation process was precariously maintained. In the final analysis, as the cabinet had made plain, "first in–first out" "must be a policy and not a rigid rule, since there are other considerations of which account must necessarily be taken" in the interest of fairness to the men themselves.[75]

Still, the average s[illegible] man awaiting repatri[illegible] could be forgiven s[illegible] Everyone had a story to [illegible] arrived zombie who had [illegible] or of the five-year man po[illegible] retarial staff of a Repat[illegible] Unit. Anecdotal criticism was by no means conclusive, but Mackenzie was on to something in his comments, as letters to the *Maple Leaf* indicate. "'Why,'" one wit wrote, "can't the Lord High Points Potentate of CMHQ [Canadian Military Headquarters Overseas] give you a definite statement for publication and then, daily, give some indication of progress; thus letting us know, say, within twenty days of when our points will start paying in the way of transatlantic movement." In the meantime, he chided, "many of us [are] becoming bow-legged from packing more points than the combined totals of the 'Frisco Conference, the Tablets of Moses, the Atlantic Charter and the late President Wilson."[76]

Guy Simonds, upon assuming command of Canadian Forces Netherlands, felt compelled to modify Crerar's priorities slightly in both August and September 1945, in belated recognition of Mackenzie's point, by returning higher point personnel faster. According to Simonds, he had advocated this position in the fall of 1944 and fought Crerar throughout the spring of 1945 on the policy to be adopted. Crerar "was quite adamant in his opinion that repatriation should in the main be by Divisions and units in the priority in which they had originally come Overseas."[77] Simonds compromised only because it looked as though repatriation would be completed by Christmas, but when shipping difficulties disrupted the movement schedule in the summer of 1945, he felt compelled to revamp Crerar's scheme.

There were other difficulties encountered in implementing so vast an operation, not the least of which was locating adequate shipping. Through a series of wartime agreements, Canada had consented to the joint control of Allied shipping, a satisfactory enough wartime expedient, but the prospects of multilateral control over the return of Canadian personnel from overseas were somewhat less encouraging. The main problem here was that Canadian Forces had, of course, been in Europe long before their American counterparts and, the Canadian government felt, any repatriation deals should reflect that reality. In other words, on a strict application of the principle "first over–first back," Canadians would get initial priority over Americans for repatriation shipping. The numbers involved were large, at least 100 000 in the case of the Canadian Army alone,[78] but the prime minister felt that he had reached agreement with President Roosevelt in March 1945 on a "strict chronological priority."[79]

It came as something of a shock, therefore, when the secretary of state for Dominion affairs informed Ottawa that in the first six months after VE-Day only 132 200, including all three services and ex-prisoners of war, could be returned.[80] What followed over the next several weeks was a curt and nasty exchange of cables and memos between Ottawa, London, and Washington regarding Canada's demand for at least 150 000 in the first six months, and the strict application of "first over–first back." As the summer wore on, the urgency of Canada's demands was compounded by several factors, including the Aldershot incident, newspaper reports that Canadian troops would be home by Christmas, and widespread concerns that military morale might not withstand indefinite waiting. On 4 July, Hume Wrong informed the prime minister that based on discussions with General McNaughton the military felt that at least 30 000 repatriations a month were needed. "While the Canadian troops had so far behaved very well," Wrong noted in relaying the service chiefs' view, "there was a serious danger of discontent unless the rate of repatriation could be expedited."[81]

The Canadian government, through its high commissioner to the U.K., Vincent Massey, pressed for and received modest increases in its shipping allotment, and by 7 July Massey at least was satisfied "that United Kingdom authorities, in extremely difficult situation, have done all they could to meet Canadian position and that further representations would not be successful."[82] In any case this mini-crisis was overcome by events. Extra shipping had become available in June, and the collapse of Japan in August eliminated the need for massive American redeployments to the Pacific. It would not, however, be an uneventful ride from this point, for shipping bottlenecks in the fall would create overcrowding and prolonged delays in repatriation depots in the United Kingdom, which in turn slowed the movement of personnel from North-West Europe. Nonetheless, by the following winter D.C. Abbott could inform the Canadian Club of Ottawa that the goal of 30 000 repatriations per month had been met, and even slightly exceeded.[83] By October 1946, when the Canadian armed services officially reverted to a peacetime basis, 343 000 military personnel and 45 000 dependants had been repatriated from overseas, and 713 000 military personnel had been discharged into civilian life and the waiting arms of an unparalleled network of support programs.[84]

The speed of this process created problems of its own. Railroads in Canada, for example, were hard-pressed to handle the returning men, and discharge depots in both Canada and the U.K. were forced to expand their facilities to accommodate the waiting troops. Recreational and educational programs were implemented both for morale purposes (i.e., to keep the troops out of trouble) and to prepare them for the civilian life that lay ahead. Most such snags were minor and gradually surmounted, but the Halifax riot indicated that the potential for large-scale unrest was all too real. And the hasty exit from the services became, for many veterans, a source of considerable bitterness in later life when they realized how overworked medical discharge boards had failed to identify injuries incurred during their service years—injuries that required official documentation in order to be pensionable.[85]

Preparing to return to Canada was, for units and individuals, a somewhat convoluted process that depended in part on the location and type of unit, its time spent overseas, and such variables as available shipping and the progress of the Pacific war. It could also depend on the technical and educational qualifications of the individual, and whether or not his or her services were deemed necessary to effect the demobilization of others. Once an individual was declared "essential" and assigned to the repatriation infrastructure, it could take an inordinately long time to escape. Frank Curry, for example, received his discharge papers from the Royal Canadian Navy early in August 1945, but found himself "master window-repairman" and "master baggage-controller" on HMCS *Niobe-Scotland* until October, when he was finally shipped home.[86] For many, the official estimate of 25.3 days' waiting time in the United Kingdom after arrival from Europe was a far cry from reality;[87] for others, even 25 days was inordinately long.

In general, to take Army practice as an example, units on the continent coalesced into divisional groups at bases in the Netherlands for movement to the U.K. and, later, to Canada. So-called Canada drafts, or those with high individual point scores, were combined into ad hoc units and shipped together on the basis of their point cohort, after also waiting for some time in Repatriation Depots. Notwithstanding this, however, volunteers for the Pacific war, compassionate cases, POWs and other special groups received priority, which made for considerable turnover in the staging camps, often to the great annoyance of their longer term residents.

Returned to Canada by freighter, warship, and in many cases converted luxury liner, Canadians in all three services were processed by the demobilization machine in approximately the same fashion.[88] Assuming that most of their "papers" had been processed overseas or on board ship, upon arrival in Canada they were dispatched to a "dispersal point" or "discharge depot" and, usually, given leave to travel home, at government expense, for up to thirty days. Final release was effected at the discharge centre nearest their home (or wherever else it was they wanted to be released), and most major cities contained one for each service. The Air Force had eight such centres, the Navy nineteen, and the Army twelve, At this point they were given medical and dental examinations, personal counselling on job prospects and the traumas of "civvy street," and their final discharge papers, certificates, war-service buttons, and transportation fare home. Usually a final pay parade was held, and words of encouragement were spoken by local dignataries and commanding officers. Then, they went home, presumably to resume their normal lives. As one veteran recalled, "when I come to getting out of the army I just felt that I had done my job and I was looking forward to just getting back to my wife and child. . . . I got out. That was all I was interested in."[89]

By May 1945 the Canadian military and the federal government had reached agreement on basic demobilization and rehabilitation priorities, and had established an extensive legal and bureaucratic infrastructure to handle the massive outpouring of military personnel that began soon afterward. It would be neither a quick nor an easy process. Problems along the way would necessitate adaptations and reevaluations, and in the summer of 1945 both civilian and military planners feared a general breakdown in morale if repatriation and discharge were long delayed. The Aldershot case was taken as a possible portent of things to come. That the storm did not break was as much due to luck as anything else (the early end of the Pacific war in particular), but the months of planning and preparation had, nonetheless, paid handsome dividends, and the process was ultimately carried out more or less quietly and efficiently.[90] "A cynic might remark," said C.P. Stacey, "that in this war the government began planning for demobilization even before it had made provision for a really effective war effort."[91] The foresight had been worth it.

Notes

1. Norman Rogers succeeded Mackenzie at Defence, but after Rogers's death in June 1940, and a brief caretakership by Charles G. Power, J.L. Ralston assumed the portfolio. Mackenzie remained in Pensions and National Health until the department's dissolution in Oct. 1944, upon which he was moved to the new Department of

Veterans Affairs. Brooke Claxton was then given the revamped Department of National Health and Welfare. These changes are summarized in tabular form in J.W. Pickersgill, *The Mackenzie King Record*, vol. 1, *1939–1944* (Toronto: University of Toronto Press, 1960), 697–98, and Pickersgill and D.F. Forster, *The Mackenzie King Record*, vol. 2, *1944–1945* (Toronto: University of Toronto Press, 1968), 473–75.

2. NAC, King Papers, MG26 J1, vol. 272, ff 230466–230724, Ian Mackenzie to Prime Minister, 30 Oct. 1939, and King to Mackenzie, 1 Nov. 1939.
3. Despite agreeing to the necessity for early planning, King's personal interest remained marginal at this time. A.D.P. Heeney handled most of the correspondence with Mackenzie, and on 1 December he informed the latter that the prime minister still had not personally scrutinized Mackenzie's committee proposal. NAC, Ian Mackenzie Papers, vol. 56, file 527-10(1), Heeney to Mackenzie, Dec. 1939.
4. NAC, Ian Mackenzie Papers, vol. 56, file 527-10(1), extracts from memo, McDonald to Mackenzie, 13 Oct. 1939.
5. NAC, Ian Mackenzie Papers, MG27, IIIB5, vol. 56, file 527-10 (1), "Memorandum for the Minister," 15 Oct. 1939, 8.
6. *Globe and Mail*, Toronto, 13 Oct. 1939, 4.
7. *Globe and Mail*, Toronto, 24 Oct. 1939, 6.
8. See, for example, the *Toronto Daily Star*, 20 Sept. 1939, 19 and 34.
9. Robert England, *Living, Learning, Remembering: Memoirs of Robert England* (Vancouver: Centre for Continuing Education, University of British Columbia, 1980), 115.
10. Canada, House of Commons, *Debates* (hereinafter cited as CHC *Debates*), 25 Jan. 1940, 7.
11. See Walter D. Young, *The Anatomy of a Party: The National CCF, 1932–61* (Toronto: University of Toronto Press, 1969), 102–36.
12. "CCF Federal Election Manifesto, 1944," in M.J. Coldwell, *Left Turn, Canada* (New York: Duell, Sloan, and Pearce, 1945), 225.
13. CHC *Debates*, 20 May 1940, 60
14. See Desmond Morton, "'Kicking and Complaining': Demobilization Riots in the Canadian Expeditionary Force, 1918–19," *Canadian Historical Review* 61, 3 (Sept. 1980): 334–60.
15. The government did not begin to plan in earnest for the return of the troops until Dec. 1916. Ibid., 31.
16. NAC, Ian Mackenzie Papers, MG 27, IIIB5, vol. 56, file 52710 (1), "Memorandum for the Minister," 15 Oct. 1939, 9.
17. By most accounts Mackenzie, himself a First World War veteran, was the driving force behind demobilization planning at this stage. His personal involvement in appeals cases and the minutiae of planning would later result in an almost unprecedented series of tributes from opposition politicians, especially in parliamentary debate. All admitted, for example, that Mackenzie had never failed to resolve a case in which he had become personally involved, and these were not an inconsiderable number.
18. PC 4063 1/2 is reproduced in Appendix D of Robert England's *Discharged: A Commentary on Civil Re-establishment of Veterans in Canad*a (Toronto: Macmillan, 1943), 393–94.
19. Formed in early 1940, official sanction was delayed until the fall by the deteriorating military situation and the demands of fabricating a war economy. The committee and several of its subcommittees met prior to that time, however. The GACDR was formalized by PC 5421 of Oct. 8, 1940. Robert England, *Discharged*, 72–74. See also NAC, Records of the Privy Council Office, RG2, series 18, vol. 8, file R-70, "Memorandum for Mr. Robertson," 21 July 1941.

20. CHC *Debates*, 19 Nov. 1940, 236.
21. CHC *Debates*, 24 March 1942, 1573.
22. NA, RG2/18, vol. 33, file D-19-R, pt. 1. Undated memo by A. Davidson Dunton, probably 8 Feb. 1945.
23. Ibid.
24. See the *Handbook on Rehabilitation*, 1st ed. (May 1945), NAC, RG2/18, vol. 18, file R-70.
25. See *Dominion and Provincial Agencies on Demobilization and Rehabilitation* (Ottawa: Wartime Information Board, Rehabilitation Information Committee, May 1945), and *Research and Postwar Planning Survey of Agencies*, vol. 14, *Canada* (New York: United Nations Information Office, Section for Information on Postwar Reconstruction, April 1944).
26. England, *Living*, 113.
27. NAC, Robert England Papers, MG30, C181, vol. 2, file 9. GACDR and Advisory Committee on Economic Policy joint meeting, 3 Dec. 1943.
28. Minutes of the June 13 meeting are in NAC, King Papers, MG26, J1, vol. 345; the 3 Dec. minutes are in MG26, J4, vol. 356, file 3816.
29. In *The Men Who Came Back*, Walter S. Woods recalls the Army's reluctance to distract its warriors from the business at hand by preaching to them about the postwar period. A visit to the GOC-in-C, A.G.L. McNaughton, was required to resolve an impasse that had left eleven tons of literature sitting on a Halifax dock. Woods, *The Men Who Came Back* (Toronto: Ryerson Press, 1956), 134–35.
30. NAC, England Papers, MG30, C181, vol. 2, file 9, cited in "Report of Sub-Committee on Demobilization (Priorities and Methods)," Draft, 22 Jan. 1943, 2. Most of the information in this paragraph also comes from this source.
31. This definition differs from that given previously in two respects: first, it equates repatriation solely with the military's sphere of responsibility (while absolving government of a role in prioritization of returns); and it expands the meaning of demobilization to encompass rehabilitation.
32. NAC, England Papers, MG30, C181, vol. 2, file 9.
33. Ibid., 4.
34. Ibid., 8. Shipping delays, which all planners took as a given, would be a blessing in disguise for this residual group under the circumstances outlined by the subcommittee, by allowing time for the economy to absorb the first waves of returnees.
35. York University Archives, Canadian Pamphlet Collection, CPC 1943 082, "Rehabilitation of Canada's Fighting Men," A Brief Submitted on 2 July 1943 to the House of Commons Committee on Post-War Reconstruction and Re-establishment by the Canadian Legion, passim.
36. See Winston S. Churchill, *The World Crisis, 1918–1928: The Aftermath* (New York: Charles Scribner's Sons, 1929), 40–59. A more detailed discussion can be found in Stephen Richards Graubard, "Military Demobilization in Great Britain Following the First World War," *Journal of Modern History* 19, 4 (Dec. 1947): 297–311.
37. A copy of the report is in NAC, England Papers, MG30, C181, vol. 2, file 10.
38. The GACDR was not the only breeding ground for such study. The Department of Pensions and National Health, for example, built on the 1930s Veterans' Assistance Commission to form the Veterans' Welfare Division in Nov. 1940, while National Defence eased the transition to civilian life by providing rehabilitation grants and dependants' allowances. A list of other committees established to deal with veterans' issues is in Woods, *Rehabilitation: A Combined Operation* (Ottawa: Edmond Cloutier, 1953), 19–21.
39. England, *Living*, 126.
40. NAC, King Papers, MG26, J1, vol. 359, W.I.B. memo to Cabinet, 16 Oct. 1944.

41. NAC, RG2/18, vol. 12, file W-34-10, W.I.B. memo to cabinet, 30 April 1945, 2.
42. NAC, RG2/18, vol. 99, file R-70-10 (vol. 2, 1945), Minutes of the Demobilization and Rehabilitation Information Committee, 10 Jan. 1945.
43. Cabinet War Committee Minutes, 23 Sept. 1944, 1. RG2/7C, vol. 16. See also the minutes for 20 and 22 Sept. on which the rest of this paragraph is based.
44. *The Mackenzie King Diaries, 1932–1949* (Toronto: University of Toronto Press, 1980), 20 Sept. 1944, 2.
45. *King Diaries*, 23 Sept. 1944, 3. Howe's disputes with Ralston over manpower were one of the least well-kept secrets of the war. See Robert Bothwell and William Kilbourn, *C.D. Howe: A Biography* (Toronto: McClelland and Stewart, 1979), 167–73.
46. *King Diaries*, 23 Sept. 1944, 5.
47. A.D.P. Heeney to C.D. Howe, 25 Sept. 1944, cited in J.L. Granatstein and J.M. Hitsman, *Broken Promises: A History of Conscription in Canada* (Toronto: Oxford University Press, 1977), 225.
48. There were important exceptions to this. See Crerar's comments on the Army demobilization plan cited below.
49. Queen's University Archives, C.G. Power Papers, vol. 65, file D-1093, Memo to Minister, 4 Oct. 1944, "Repatriation and Demobilization: Armed Services." All arrangements, of course, were also dependent upon operational circumstances.
50. Directorate of History, Department of National Defence, file 114.1, Document 71, Memo for the Cabinet War Committee by A.D.P. Heeney, 19 April 1945.
51. Ibid., 6.
52. It should be noted that in several areas, demobilization had already begun, as in the downsizing of Canada's home-defence forces, and the withdrawal of troops from Newfoundland. Of even greater significance was the transfer or release of surplus Air Force personnel, which became the cause of considerable unrest, both civilian and military, from 1944 onward.
53. McNaughton's memo, A.D.P. Heeney's response and summary for the cabinet and the results of the 23 Sept. 1944 War Committee meeting are in the King Papers, NAC, MG26, J1, vol. 387.
54. CHC *Debates*, 4 Oct. 1945, 763–64.
55. By way of comparison, the American army's demobilization point scheme was based on length and location of service, combat awards, and number of children. The U.S. Navy's plan was similar, giving points for age, length and type of service, and dependency. See Bert Marvin Sharp, "'Bring the Boys Home': Demobilization of the United States Armed Forces After World War II" (PhD diss., Michigan State University, 1976), chap. 3.
56. NAC, RG24, Accession 83–84/049, vol. 1805, file 390–l, part l, "From those who believe in fair Play" to RCAF Headquarters, 8 Dec. 1944.
57. NAC, RG24, vol. 2839, file HQC-8350-4, vol. 2, memo to the Adjutant-General, 29 Nov. 1940.
58. Gilbert Norman Tucker, *The Naval Service of Canada: Its Official History*, vol. 2, *Activities on Shore during the Second World War* (Ottawa, 1952), 476.
59. Ibid., 478.
60. NAC, Ian Mackenzie Papers, MG27, IIIB5, vol. 43, file G156A, *After Victory in Europe* (Canadian Military Headquarters, Great Britain, May 1945), 10.
61. NAC, King Papers, MG26, J1, vol. 381, Carl Eayrs to King, 25 Aug. 1945, 1–2. Volume 378 of the King Papers has further correspondence by J.W. Pickersgill and Doris L. Bentley on this case, dated 29 and 30 Aug. 1945.
62. NAC, King Papers, MG26, J1, vol. 385, W.J. LeClair to King, July 1945, folio 345479. King referred the matter to Howe, without extensive comment, twice.

63. Ibid., 2–3.
64. NAC, H.D.G. Crerar Papers, MG30, E 157, vol. 4, file 5-5-1, Crerar to all Commanders and Commanding Officers, 6 June 1944 (reissued 25 Nov. 1944).
65. NAC, King Papers, MG26, J1, vol. 387, Crerar to McNaughton, 18 July 1945, 1–2.
66. Ibid., 1.
67. This was not unusual. The United States Navy's demobilization plan also started with a point system, but switched to quotas in July 1946. Sharp, "'Bring the Boys Home,'" 63.
68. Cited in Stacey, *The Victory Campaign*, 619.
69. NAC, King Papers, MG26, J1, vol. 387, Crerar to McNaughton, 18 July 1945, 1.
70. NAC, King Papers, MG26, J1, vol. 386, copy, Mackenzie to Crerar, 19 July 1945.
71. NAC, King Papers, MG26, J1, vol. 386, Mackenzie to King, Aug. 1945, 2.
72. On 8 July 1945, for example, Lt.-Gen. P.J. Montague (Chief of Staff, Canadian Military Headquarters) cabled Crerar that the "slow pace of repatriation having detrimental effect upon morale generally." NAC, Crerar Papers, MG30, E 157, vol. 4, file 5-0-3.
73. See Sharp, "'Bring the Boys Home,'" chap. 9.
74. Lt.-Gen. G.G. Simonds to Lt.-Gen. J.C. Murchie, 21 Sept. 1945, Christopher Vokes Papers (in possession of F. Vokes, Ottawa).
75. NAC, King Papers, MG 26, J2, vol. 486, file R-72, R.G. Robertson to Commander William V. Hearyberd, 30 Aug. 1945.
76. NAC, RG24, vol. 12, 835, file 391–18, Lorne Haire to the Editor, *Maple Leaf*, 11 July 1945.
77. G.G. Simonds Papers, GOC Canadian Forces in Netherlands box, "Report on Repatriation," 30 Sept. 1945, 3.
78. NAC, King Papers, MG26, J1, vol. 387, copy of memo, Vincent Massey to Lord Leathers, Secretary of State for Dominion Affairs, 10 May 1945, 1.
79. Ibid., 1.
80. NAC, King Papers, MG26, J1, vol. 392, Secretary of State for Dominion Affairs to King, 10 May 1945.
81. NAC, King Papers, MG26, J4, vol. 356, file 3816, memo from Wrong to Prime Minister, 4 July 1945, 1.
82. NAC, King Papers, MG26, J1, vol. 387, Massey to King, 7 July 1945.
83. Some 280 000 had been returned by 31 Jan. 1946. NAC, Abbott Papers, vol. 15, file 4, address to the Canadian Club of Ottawa, 26 Feb. 1946, 3.
84. Ibid., MG 32, B6, vol. 15, file 20, address by Abbott to the Canadian Club of Winnipeg, 21 Oct. 1946, 1.
85. Author's interviews and correspondence with veterans.
86. Curry, *War at Sea: A Canadian Seaman on the North Atlantic* (Toronto: Lugus Productions, 1990), 140–42.
87. NAC, RG24, vol. 12 836, file 391–26, E.G. Weeks to J.F.A. Lister, 20 July 1945.
88. The following summary comes from DHist, file 110.009 (D20), "The Machinery of Re-Establishment." Flow charts in this file cover all three services.
89. Letters from William G. Spring, Toronto, 21 Nov. 1992 and Jan. 1993.
90. This conclusion is attested to by interviews and correspondence with veterans whose recollections of their repatriation and demobilization experiences are overwhelmingly favourable.
91. C.P. Stacey, *Arms, Men and Governments: The War Policies of Canada 1939–1945* (Ottawa, 1970), 63.

Public officials heaped praise on women during the war for their fine military and economic contributions. But how would they be treated by government once the victory was won? Inevitably, this question figured prominently in planning for veterans' benefits. Through enlistment and service on the same terms as men, women had acquired a claim on the Canadian state that could not be ignored.

The Veterans Charter and Canadian Women Veterans of World War II*

Peter Neary and Shaun Brown

LITERATURE about Canada's deep involvement in World War II has, to date, dealt mainly with military matters, diplomacy, the problem of national unity, and the mobilizing of the resources of the country for the war effort. Two books on the history of the period stand out: C.P. Stacey, *Arms, Men and Governments: The War Policies of Canada 1939–1945* and J.L. Granatstein, *Canada's War: The Policies of the Mackenzie King Government, 1939–1945*.[1] These masterly surveys cover a broad range of topics, but clearly much work remains to be done on the social history of the country during the war. Robert Bothwell, Marjorie Cohen, Terry Copp, Ruth Roach Pierson, and others have made notable contributions in this regard. Part of that social history concerns the planning for demobilization that went on between 1939 and 1945 and the carrying out of the plans that were made. This complex topic manifestly invites further research. Of necessity, mobilization and demobilization were simultaneous concerns of Ottawa throughout the war. The relative importance of each, however, obviously changed as the conflict progressed. Soldiers were accidentally injured on the first day Canada entered the war, and

*The authors acknowledge, with thanks, the assistance of Veterans Affairs Canada, especially Joyce Gaudet and Greg Kasycz. We thank A.P. Bates for editorial advice.

soon afterward a soldier was killed. And so, even as the Armed Forces were being mobilized to defend the country and serve overseas, the first members of a new generation of veterans were appearing. How the Dominion government responded to them and how it planned for the reestablishment in civil society of the thousands upon thousands of Canadians who were demobilized after the war form a major chapter in the social history of Canada in the twentieth century. The record of the country in relation to women veterans is embedded in this larger story, and can be understood only with respect to the scheme of benefits devised by Ottawa for the veteran population as a whole. It is with this general scheme, therefore, that this discussion must start.

After a tumultuous beginning, the administration of veterans' affairs in Canada was by 1939 settled into well-established routines.[2] The benefit rules were well known, the bureaucracy administering programs was firmly entrenched, and the lobbyists who sought to represent the veterans' point of view were well integrated into a system that had become a familiar and established part of Canada's institutional framework. The administration of benefits for veterans was the responsibility of the Department of Pensions and National Health, and the main organization lobbying for veterans was the Canadian Legion. The administration of pensions was the responsibility of the Canadian Pension Commission.[3] Unemployable and destitute veterans with service in a "theatre of war" could be awarded the veteran's allowance, which was administered by the War Veterans' Allowance Board.[4] This allowance was popularly known as the "Burnt-Out Pension."[5]

The first actions of the government for veterans of World War II were taken under the War Measures Act, and began with extending to them the benefits of the Pension Act.[6] On 8 December 1939, order-in-council PC 4068 created a cabinet committee to consider and report upon the problems that would be posed by demobilizing and discharging members of the Forces and by rehabilitating them to civilian life, both during and after the war.[7] This committee in turn appointed a General Advisory Committee that, over time, established fourteen subcommittees. Basically, the General Advisory Committee and its subcommittees addressed the question of what the state owed "to those whose lives were interrupted by their service to their Country."[8]

The answer given to this question involved the acceptance of sixteen principles. These constituted "the minimum the State should do for the veterans of World War II" and added up to a fundamentally different approach from the one the country had followed after the 1914–18 war.[9] Whereas rehabilitation benefits for veterans of World War I had been limited to those who had been disabled, the General Advisory Committee recommended that they be offered to every veteran of World War II. On 1 October 1941, acting on this and other advice from its demobilization planners, the government issued PC 7633, one of the major social documents of the war period, and therefore of modern Canadian history.[10] Entitled "The Post-Discharge Re-establishment Order," it set the agenda for subsequent policy and planning for demobilization. It promised veterans financial support while they were unemployed, pursuing vocational training or higher education, temporarily incapacitated, or awaiting returns from farming or other private enterprise. PC 7633 also laid down that service in the Armed Forces would count as insurable employment under the terms of the Unemployment Insurance Act of June 1940.

To meet the commitments made in and the promise of PC 7633 was a major bureaucratic and legislative task in Ottawa for the rest of the war, and a steady stream of related orders-in-council, regulations, and statutes followed. Ultimately, the program Ottawa devised for veterans became known as "The Veterans Charter." This was the title of a Canadian government publication of 1946 that brought together in one volume all the legislation and regulations in the government's plan of action. The benefits awaiting members of the Armed Forces on demobilization were explained to them, in layman's language, in the pamphlet *Back to Civil Life*.

In 1944 the Department of Pensions and National Health was dissolved and two new departments created in its stead: the Department of Veterans Affairs (DVA) and the Department of National Health and Welfare. Ian Mackenzie became the first minister of veterans affairs and Walter S. Woods the first deputy minister. This continued their mutually beneficial partnership, which had begun at Pensions and National Health, and gave full scope to the planning and administrative talents of the highly creative and experienced Woods, who was very much a mandarin's mandarin.

Sainsbury-Woods, as he was originally called, was born at Frome in Somerset and came to Canada from England in 1905 at the age of twenty-one, apparently attracted by a "gaudily colored" railway poster that advertised "the virginal sparsely-populated land of the Canadian West."[11] In Canada he became plain Walter Woods because Canadians "didn't have hyphenated names." His first job in the Dominion was on an Ontario farm in harvest season. In the spring of 1906 he went to Manitoba, and in 1914 he went overseas with the first Canadian contingent. He arrived in France in February 1915, and was subsequently wounded. In 1919 he served as president of the Calgary branch of the Great War Veterans' Association, and from 1919 to 1930 worked for the Soldier Settlement Board, which administered the Dominion government's land settlement program for veterans of the Great War. In 1930, Woods became chairman of the newly created War Veterans' Allowance Board, and in April 1941 was appointed associate deputy minister of the Department of Pensions and National Health, with responsibility for administering the rehabilitation program for the country's veterans that was now being developed. As associate deputy minister, he set up shop in the Daly Building in Ottawa, which thereby became the nerve centre for the massive undertaking he would soon shape and direct.[12]

Woods took pride in being a self-made man and an official who could relate to the needs and aspirations of the rank and file of the Armed Forces because he had once been one of them himself. In October 1944 the *Canadian Veteran* described Woods as "one of those many 'Other Ranks' who, without pull and by sheer merit" had "risen to the top."[13] Woods, this sketch continued, was knowledgeable, experienced, and a man of broad "commonsense." He had an "outstanding" administrative record, was known for his "all-embracing" humanity and was "in every sense a good citizen and a good comrade." That was very much how Woods saw himself and how he liked to be seen, and in this he exemplified the tradition of remembrance, comradeship, and mutual aid that defined the veteran ideal.

His approach to veterans' benefits was straightforward and easily understood. The minority who could not look after themselves—the sick, the disabled, and the dependants of those who had died or been incapacitated—must be provided with the best care and service Canada could afford. Decency and honour required nothing less. To able-bodied veterans the country had a quite different responsibility: they were entitled to the means to reestablish themselves in civil life with gainful and rewarding jobs. Veterans did not want handouts or to become long-term dependants of the state. What a veteran needed was a helping hand on the road to sturdy independence, and a recognition of the services given, the opportunities lost, and the vicissitudes of interrupted life. Given a fresh start, veterans would be leaders in promoting the well-being and development of the country. Hence, more than personal entitlement was at stake: veterans' benefits were an investment not only in individual happiness but in Canada's collective future prosperity and success. It followed from all of this that the most successful rehabilitation program was one that would have a limited lifespan. If Canada planned well, the government's role would be reduced, not long after the war was over, to looking after those who could not look after themselves. The able-bodied, having benefited from the rehabilitation program, would be back to work in short order, paying taxes, raising families, and generally building up through their own initiative the country they had so ably defended. To Woods it was a "basic truth . . . that the great majority of veterans would much rather work than receive relief in any form from the State."[14] The purpose of veterans' benefits, therefore, should be to provide "OPPORTUNITY WITH SECURITY."[15] This was what the country had to be ready to deliver en masse at the end of the war, and by 1944 Woods believed that the government had the situation well under control. In September of that year he told his minister that Canada had ready "the most comprehensive programme in the world for rehabilitation of her service men," and that they only wanted "one thing," namely, "a job and security."[16]

The scheme of benefits that Woods and his associates had devised by 1945 to meet this expectation was complex, and it involved choice on the part of the individual veteran.[17] And, in keeping with Woods' philosophy of veterans' benefits, it made a clear distinction between an immediate postwar period of rehabilitation and the long-term future. Needless to say, all benefits were available only to honourably discharged individuals. On leaving the Forces, the World War II veteran became eligible for a clothing allowance and transportation either to the place of enlistment or, provided no more than equivalent cost was involved, to an alternative destination in the country. Veterans with six months' service were also automatically eligible for a cash rehabilitation grant. Beyond this, entitlement became more conditional.

Under the terms of the War Service Grants Act of 1944 a gratuity was payable, but only to general service volunteers and to those men conscripted under the terms of the National Resources Mobilization Act (NRMA) of 1940 who had served overseas. The basic gratuity amounted to $7.50 for each thirty-day period served in the Western Hemisphere, and $15 for each thirty-day period served overseas. A supplementary gratuity was payable for each six months of service overseas. Those eligible for the gratuity were also eligible for a reestablishment credit. This was equal in amount to the basic gratuity, and was an alternative to training under the Veterans Rehabilitation Act (1945) or to land settlement under the Veterans' Land Act (1942). As its name indicated, the reestablishment credit, which expired on 15 January 1955 or at ten years from discharge, whichever came later, was a sum of money against which multiple claims could be made, rather than a direct cash payment. As finally developed, the credit could be used for various housing and furniture expenses, for obtaining tools or purchasing a business, for paying premiums on government insurance, or for the purchase of a government annuity. An individual veteran could make more than one application until the amount of the credit was used up.

Unlike the amounts payable under the War Service Grants Act, the benefits of the Veterans Rehabilitation Act were theoretically available to all veterans, and monthly allowances were payable to those who were actually accepted for vocational training or university education. These were paid on a graduated scale according to marital status and number of dependants. Under this same legislation, a veteran who went into business or took up farming could qualify for an "awaiting returns" allowance. Allowances were also payable to veterans who found themselves temporarily incapacitated or unemployed and ineligible for unemployment insurance benefits. By the terms of the Veterans' Business and Professional Loans Act of 1946, veterans who had qualified for the gratuity issued under the War Service Grants Act were given an additional advantage. Other opportunities offered veterans, based on various criteria, included the right to reinstatement in previous employment, first claim on jobs listed with the National Employment Service, and, for those with service in a theatre of war, preference in civil service appointments. The insurance scheme run by DVA offered coverage on preferential terms. Subject to a means test, all veterans were eligible for free medical treatment for a year after discharge, and payment of an allowance while receiving such treatment. Disabled pensioners and those needing medical care at time of discharge constituted special categories for treatment and were recognized accordingly. Then, of course, there were the benefits of the Pension Act and the War Veterans' Allowance Act. These applied to veterans of both world wars, and offered eligible individuals long-term income support.

The whole interlocking scheme of benefits involved co-ordinating the efforts of several departments of government and getting co-operation from many outside groups. Hence Woods' description of the process by which the promise of the Veterans Charter was realized as "a combined operation."[18] Gratuities were administered by the Department of National Defence; loans were made under the Veterans' Business and Professional Loans Act by the Department of Finance; civil-service preference was given by the Civil Service Commission; and the right of veterans to reinstatement in former employment was enforced by the National Employment Service of the Department of Labour, which also certified veterans to DVA for out-of-work benefits. The Department of Labour, moreover, was responsible for the Canadian Vocational Training scheme, to which veterans were referred by DVA for vocational training. To facilitate the post-secondary education of veterans, DVA formed, in 1945, an advisory committee that brought together departmental officials and leading university administrators.

As originally organized, DVA itself had separate units for treatment, prosthetic and rehabilitation services, and veterans insurance, as well as a Veterans' Bureau that included the office of Chief Pension Advocate. Pension advocates had to help veterans prepare and present appeal cases to the Canadian Pension Commission. That agency and the War Veterans' Allowance Board were administered separately, as was the Veterans' Land Act. Within DVA a strong emphasis was given to counselling, on which, it was believed, the success of the rehabilitation program for demobilization would hinge. Veterans did not have an automatic right to training and further education. They had the right to be considered for such benefits and, if appropriate, to be recommended for them by a counsellor. The veteran had to be received with dignity, patience, and understanding and then to be fully informed and intelligently directed.

To cope with the growing numbers in need of its services, DVA hired rapidly in its first years. The upper ranks of the department consisted entirely of men who were themselves veterans, and the belief was deeply ingrained that veterans could best administer veterans' benefits. Every effort was made to place veterans in the jobs that were opening up in the department's expanding network of offices, and to this end and in fairness to those serving out of the country, Woods made a recruiting trip overseas in 1945.[19] He found thirty-four men for senior executive positions in the department, and they returned to Ottawa forthwith to begin their new jobs. By February 1947, at the height of the rehabilitation activity, the staff of DVA had risen to 22 000, but it declined thereafter to a March 1951 total of approximately 15 500.[20] These figures reflected the progress of demobilization itself. Some 250 000 of the approximately 1 082 000 Canadians who served in the Armed Forces in World War II had been discharged by VE-Day (8 May 1945), and tens of thousands more soon followed.[21] For 1945 and 1946, the peak years of demobilization, the discharge figures were 395 013 and 381 031 respectively. By such numbers the mettle of the Veterans Charter was tested. That charter, the product of a prodigious bureaucratic effort, met the requirements of rational planning, while giving careful attention to the deep divisions that arose out of the conduct of the war. It made a clear distinction between service overseas and service in the Western Hemisphere. And it took into account the differences among general service volunteers, the NRMA conscripts who had remained in Canada, and those who, beginning in 1944, had been sent overseas. Those differences were deeply felt in the Armed Forces and also among veterans. They had their roots in the divisive recruiting experience in the Great War. But the Veterans Charter also addressed matters that were quite new in Canadian life. Of these, the question of fairness to female veterans, in relation to their male counterparts, was prominent.

Women had entered the paid labour force in large numbers during the Great War to support the military effort, and 2854 women served with the Canadian Army Medical Corps as nursing sisters.[22] However, the role of Canadian women in wartime took on an entirely different meaning during World War II, when the women's auxiliary forces were formed. The first to be authorized, by PC 4798 of 2 July 1941,[23] was the Canadian Women's Auxiliary Air Force. On 13 August 1941, PC 6289 authorized the formation of the Canadian Women's Army Corps (CWAC), and on 31 July 1942, the Women's Royal Canadian Navy Service (WRCNS) was launched by PC 56-6775. From February 1942, the women's branch of the Air Force was known as the Royal Canadian Air Force Women's Division, to which the acronym RCAF (WD) was given. Enlistments during World War II by women, including some 5000 nursing sisters, were as follows: Army, 26 063; Air Force, 17 467; and Navy, 7126, for a total of 50 656.[24] Service overseas by women began in November 1942, and women served in a variety of noncombat roles in the United Kingdom, Italy, and North-West Europe.[25] The thinking behind the formation of the auxiliary forces was to free men from work that women could do, and so make them available for heavier tasks.[26] Women would free men to fight.

The Pension Act had no provision for covering women on military service, so on 1 October 1941, the government acted to remedy this situation. By PC 4/7635, members of the women's forces became eligible for pensions for disabilities incurred while in the services.[27] These were payable according to the percentage disability and at rates that were roughly two-thirds of those payable to men. No pension was payable to a dependant due to disablement or death of a member of the women's forces while in service. The two-thirds pension scale was justified on the grounds that it accorded with the existing pay difference between men and women.[28] Subsequently, other postdischarge benefits then available to men were also extended to women,[29] but the eligibility of CWAC members for the benefits of the key Post-Discharge Re-establishment Order ran into a snag. The difficulty lay in the terms of their enlistment. While members of the Auxiliary Air Force were being enlisted "on the same basis as airmen," members of CWAC were not being signed up on the same basis as soldiers.[30] Although it was true that the CWAC was organized on "a military basis" and was "under military control and supervision," it specifically did not "form part of the Military Forces of Canada."[31] Accordingly, a discharged member of the Corps did not qualify as a "discharged person" under PC 7633, and was therefore ineligible for the benefits authorized by that order-in-council.[32]

On the initiative of the Department of National Defence, a subcommittee of the General Advisory Committee on Demobilization and Rehabilitation was formed in late 1941 to consider how to proceed, given this difference between the conditions of service of the two women's units formed to date.[33] It recommended that for benefit purposes, members of CWAC should be treated as members of the Armed Forces, even though they were not. This would ensure that "there would be no question in the public mind as to any implied discrimination."[34] To put its recommendation into effect, the subcommittee proposed a list of executive actions, one of which would amend the definition of "discharged person" in PC 7633 so as to make specific reference to members of the CWAC and the Canadian Women's Auxiliary Air Force. PC 7633 would also have to be amended so as to set the out-of-work benefit for women at two-thirds the amount payable to men and to exempt "a married woman wholly or mainly dependent upon her husband."[35]

The recommendation of the subcommittee was opposed by Woods on the grounds that granting the benefits of PC 7633 to persons who did not belong to the Armed Forces, the CWAC uniform notwithstanding, might lead to claims from "many other uniformed bodies," which might then be "hard to resist."[36] To proceed as the subcommittee recommended would set an awkward precedent, and might require more general changes to be made in veterans' legislation. In the end, Woods' cautionary advice to limit the meaning of "discharged person" to former members of the Armed Forces was heeded. On 1 April 1942, PC 7633 was amended as the subcommittee had recommended, but before this was done, another order-in-council, PC 1965, was issued on 13 March. This constituted the CWAC "as a Corps of the Active Militia on Active Service."[37] The procedure that was followed put the two women's auxiliary units on the same footing of service, while maintaining a strict definition of exactly who was eligible for veterans' benefits. All ex-servicewomen qualified as veterans, but Woods won his bureaucratic point: that is to say, he kept the definition of veteran within established limits. In accordance with all this, when the formation of WRCNS was authorized in July 1942, it, too, was designated as an "active service."[38] These developments gave Canadian servicewomen a clear advantage over their U.S. counterparts in the Women's Army Auxiliary Corps (WAAC) and the Women's Air Force Service Pilots (WASP).[39] WAAC was "attached" to the United States Army but was not "part" of it.[40] By the same token, WASP "was supposed to be militarized during the war, but never actually was."[41] Accordingly, members of WAAC and WASP "were not considered veterans for the purpose of receiving benefits administered by the V[eterans] A[dministration], even though they thought they were part of the military forces."[42] These particular American ex-servicewomen had to fight a long postwar battle to achieve the status that was put beyond question for Canadian servicewomen by 1942.

In October 1943, Woods was asked by the national secretary of the Imperial Order Daughters of the Empire for an explanation of the postdischarge benefits available to servicewomen. He wrote in reply that women were "discharged from the Service under the same conditions as men."[43] They were as eligible as men for the benefits of the Pension Act, and for medical care under the treatment regulations of the Department of Pensions and National Health. Women, however, were paid "special rates of pension" and "special rates of hospital allowances." In both instances the rates paid were lower than those paid to men, because women were paid less than men while serving in the Forces. It was also the case, Woods noted, that the out-of-work benefit payable to a woman under PC 7633 could "not exceed the rate of pay of the discharged person at the date of discharge." But all the other benefits of this order were available to women "on exactly the same basis as that applying to men." Woods did not mention in this letter that since 1 July 1943 women in the Armed Forces had been paid at a basic rate that was four-fifths of the amount paid to men of the same rank instead of the previous two-thirds.[44] At the same time that this change had been made, it was announced that women would now be given the same trades and professional pay as men, and that the allowance paid to the dependants of women in the services, husbands and children excepted, would henceforth be the same as those paid to the dependants of men. This covered "dependent parents and other close relatives." A servicewoman married to a serviceman would be able in future to receive a dependant's allowance from her husband to a maximum income of $2100. In 1944, women members of the

Forces made another gain when it was decided to make the out-of-work benefit payable under PC 7633 the same for women and men. In recommending this change, Woods noted that it had not been pushed previously lest it create a demand among women in the services for more pay.[45] Given the recent increase in women's pay, however, this problem no longer existed, and the change could be made without adverse effect on the Armed Forces.

This made good tactical sense, but it involved Woods in a testy exchange of letters with A.W. Neill, the Independent member of Parliament for Comox-Alberni.[46] If women, Neill sarcastically asked, were worth the same as men when they were idle, should they not be paid the same when they were both working?[47] This was certainly an intriguing question, and indicated the extent to which fundamental questions were being raised by the war.

In practice, nothing came of Neill's intervention, but the episode highlighted just how much the rhetoric of equality of opportunity between men and women had taken hold at DVA. In its pursuit of this goal DVA built on the work of yet another subcommittee of the General Advisory Committee on Demobilization and Rehabilitation. This was the Subcommittee on the Special Problems of Discharged Women. The formation of such a subcommittee, composed of women, was first recommended by Woods in January 1942.[48] A follow-up recommendation was next made by the Subcommittee on Post-Discharge Benefits and then accepted by the General Advisory Committee.[49] The job of the new subcommittee was "to consider and report to the General Advisory Committee on the special problems of civil re-establishment of women, as such, discharged from the Canadian Armed Forces."[50] The first meeting of the subcommittee was held at the Daly Building on 19 June 1942. Present were representatives of the women's branches of the Armed Forces and the nursing service, along with two civilian appointees, Laura Holland and Charlotte Whitton. On 23 June, the subcommittee approved an interim report that listed the major problems it had identified in its initial *tour d'horizon*.[51] The first of these concerned "problems of social care arising from or related to discharge for reasons of conduct." The second major category of concern for the subcommittee was employment. How would women fare in vocational training, professional education, and in the establishment of individual enterprises and agriculture? And how would the demand for women workers in Canada be co-ordinated with postdischarge benefits and the training available to and the work being done by women while in the Forces? The subcommittee saw a need to concern itself also with pension provisions for women, with the effect of their rates of pay and lack of dependants' allowances (these had not yet been granted) on their ability to save for their reestablishment, and with the responsibilities for them of the Rehabilitation Branch of the Department of Pensions and National Health.

As only 239 members of CWAC had been discharged by 31 May 1942, and only 61 members of the RCAF (WD) by 24 June 1942, the subcommittee understandably gave priority to the problems of care it had identified. Moreover, its work on employment issues emphasized the collection of data. This was done under three headings: the occupational histories of women in the Forces, their future training needs, and their likely job prospects once the war was over. The key assumption of the subcommittee was that most women in the Armed Forces would not need any retraining or employment assistance at all, because they would get married and become homemakers.

The most detailed attempt to predict what was in store for ex-servicewomen in the postwar job market was made by G.M. Weir in his 1943 "Survey of Rehabilitation (Interim Report)."[52] Weir had been provincial secretary and minister of education in the Liberal government of Duff Pattullo in British Columbia, and in 1943 was acting director of training in the Rehabilitation Branch of the Department of Pensions and National Health. His report included chapters on "Post-War Employment Opportunities for Women" and "Courses of Training for Discharged Men and Women." Based on survey research, Weir predicted that after the war, women workers would be most in demand in services, a category that included nurses, teachers, dentists, doctors and other professionals. The next highest general categories of projected demand were "vocational" (which had more than a dozen subclasses) and "clerical." The category "labourers," which included charwomen, cleaners, and other unskilled workers, was rated eighth of nine.[53] Weir also reported on a survey that he had done in October 1943 about the educational and occupational preferences of women in the Armed Forces.[54] In all three services the leading occupational choice turned out to be stenography. In the Army and Air Force this was followed by "home-maker" and "nurse" and in the Navy by "teacher" and "clerk." Weir found the number choosing stenography to be "disconcerting" and urged that women be encouraged to study nursing, social work, and household economics, other careers for which there promised to be a big demand in the postwar world.[55] In keeping with the occupational preferences he recorded, he also found that the largest number of his respondents favoured business education. This was followed in order by university, technical, high school, and normal school education. The occupational course most favoured in all three services was stenography. The other leading choices, though the rankings varied from service to service, were bookkeeping and accounting, home nursing, photography, arts and crafts, and hairdressing.

In January 1945, a new chapter in the government's program for ex-servicewomen opened. In anticipation of the big rush of demobilization, DVA appointed a female executive assistant to S.N.F. Chant, the director general of rehabilitation. The proposal for such an appointment had come from the subcommittee, and Woods was sympathetic to the view that the women's side of the rehabilitation program should be presided over by women, and that female veterans should be advised by female counsellors.[56] The person chosen for the position was Olive Ruth Russell, who thereafter played a pivotal role in the affairs of Canada's women veterans.

Russell was born in Delta (Leeds County), Ontario, in 1897. She was originally a teacher by profession, and served as principal of the continuation school in her home town.[57] In 1928 she left this position and enrolled at the University of Toronto, where she obtained an honours BA in psychology. She next obtained a doctorate in psychology from the University of Edinburgh. Her education also included summer courses in Vienna in educational and vocational guidance, and in counselling and personnel work at Columbia University in New York. But with all these qualifications, Russell found herself earning less than she had before she had gone to university. She later attributed this in part to the effect of the Great Depression, but she also considered herself a victim "of the fact that Canada lagged so far behind in developing Psychology and Guidance."[58] For some time after completing her graduate studies, Russell was a research assistant at the Ontario College of Education. Her next job was at Moulton College, Toronto, where she was head of mathematics and director of educational and vocational guidance. She enlisted in the CWAC in 1942, and after basic training was selected for the officers training course. She was thereafter one of the first two women appointed to the Personnel Selection Branch, where she worked as a counsellor. Commenting on a draft article about her career and work, she told the women's editor of *Saturday Night* in July 1945 that she did not want to leave the impression with the magazine's readers that she was a "feminist." "It is true," she wrote, "I try to be very on my toes all the time to protect and advance women's right to freedom of choice as an adult citizen in a democracy, and do all I can to see that the equality of opportunity and benefits provided by the legislation for ex-servicewomen may become a reality in practice, but I do try to be gracious about it all and try to avoid the antagonisms that so easily arise, especially in regard to the question of the married woman working."[59] This was revealing, but there can be no doubt about the strength of Russell's convictions as an advocate of equal rights for women in Canadian society.

In March 1944 she explained her views on the effect of the war on Canadian women in an address to the University Women's Club of Dalhousie University.[60] Women, she observed, were "participating in the war effort to an extent that few would have dreamed possible even a decade ago." In Canada the number of women at work in industry had grown from 600 000 at the beginning of the war to 1 200 000, of whom approximately 27 percent were married women.

At the end of the war, about half of the latter group would return to domestic duties. This would leave about 500 000 women for whom jobs would have to be found when war-related work was no longer available. This situation made imperative the undertaking of research to determine the future work intentions of married women. "I have come across . . . married women," Russell commented, "who tell me they can scarcely remember what their husbands look like. They married in haste shortly before their husbands went overseas and they say they feel they do not know them and have little idea what their reaction will be if and when they meet again."

Another influence on the postwar work situation was the fact that in every field of employment they had entered, women had proved their competence and adaptability. Servicewomen were showing great versatility, like "Rosie the Riveter" and "Winnie the Welder," their counterparts in industry, who had abandoned their "pretty frocks and bridge teas" for "overalls, lunch pails and production charts." The result of their efforts was a growing trend in Canadian society toward greater equality among men and women. Evidence of this was to be found in the increase in pay to women in the Forces from two-thirds to four-fifths of what men of the same rank were paid. Servicewomen were now being given the same trades pay as men, and, though initially ineligible for dependants' allowances, they were now given them. Among civilian workers, pay differentials between men and women had in many instances likewise been eroded. Women had found a "financial freedom" in wartime that men would henceforth ignore at their peril. While it was true that many women would get married and leave the labour market at the end of the war, it was also the case that many who had taken jobs since 1939 would want to go on working. Hence it was crucial "to avoid having women looked upon as competing with men for jobs":

> Some people are already beginning to discuss the demobilization of women as though the object were to take women out of employment regardless of their need to earn their living. Since woman's full right to work has been taken for granted in the war emergency and she has been able to prove her efficiency, is it not natural to assume that in the employment market after the war her claim to the right of employment should be based on her merits rather than her sex?
>
> The war has broken down much of the traditional prejudice of employers against hiring women for many kinds of work and it seems highly desirable that in future we prevent the return of such prejudices. This must not mean that women are to prevent men from overseas and others from obtaining suitable employment, and it is hoped moreover that women will not become unfair competitors for jobs through the return of lower wage rates for women. The best way to prevent pre-war barriers to women regarding employment is to keep the demand for

> labour high enough so that every worker's help is needed somewhere. This can be done; and many of our Nation's statesmen have assured us that it will be done.

The right of women to work should be based on "merit," and there should be no "discrimination on sex grounds." But it would also have to be recognized that women were "vitally important as homemakers and rearers of the Nation's children" and that many workers would be needed for "household duties." Survey data showed that women who had left housework and farm work were reluctant to return to those jobs, and that married women who had gone out to work exhibited a range of opinion about becoming full-time homemakers again. This situation posed "a special challenge": to transform housework and related jobs into "attractive and desirable occupations." The key to doing this was to introduce training and apprenticeship, and to enforce pay and hours of work standards for domestic work.

Once established at DVA, Russell began working out plans with the newly created Department of National Health and Welfare and the National Film Board for a film project on home and family life. The aim of the project was to educate ex-service men and women in successful homemaking.[61] Involving both men and women was appropriate because homemaking was "a partnership for which both husband and wife must be prepared to share responsibility." Films would be produced in English and French, and eventually Canadian Vocational Training would introduce a short course for ex-servicewomen about to become homemakers.

If education for home life was a pet project, Russell's main concern at DVA was, of necessity, how counselling of women should proceed. She explained her position on this in a lengthy statement she prepared for a counsellors' training course held on 19 February 1945.[62] To the end of January 1945, she noted, more than 43 000 women had enlisted in the Canadian Armed Forces, of whom more than 3000 were now serving overseas. Added to these were approximately 4000 nurses and 58 women doctors, of whom more than 2000 were serving overseas. Altogether about 47 000 women had entered the Forces, of whom about 5000 were still overseas. About 10 000 had already been discharged, which left about 34 000 in the women's forces plus the doctors and nurses. Of these, about 5900 were in the Navy, 14 400 in the Army, and 13 700 in the Air Force. Women who had already left the Forces had for the most part been well counselled at DVA by men. Looking to the future, however, though the department would not be setting up a separate women's division, it would be appointing women counsellors.

The government's information booklet *Back to Civil Life,* Russell continued, stated explicitly that the rehabilitation program for veterans applied "equally to ex-service men and women." The single exception to this was the provision that a married woman could not draw out-of-work benefits if her husband could support her and was legally obligated to do so. In practice, however, it was "unlikely" that women would pursue "some of the training open to men." On this critical point Russell quoted approvingly from a report to the Training Branch of the Department of Labour by Mrs. Edgar Hardy, president of the Canadian National Council of Women: "Open all courses equally to men and women and you will find only very few women will enter what might be classed as courses typical for men." While she was still working out behind the scenes her proposal for films and the Canadian Vocational Training course, Russell told the counsellors that training for successful homemaking was also being considered. It was not possible to predict accurately how many ex-servicewomen would want to undertake training courses, but the experience of the Armed Forces and war industry suggested that demand would be substantial. DVA had to be ready for all eventualities, and it had to be acknowledged that counselling was both an "art and a science" and required both "objective measures" and "subjective appraisals." From the requirements of counselling, Russell moved on to employment prospects for women, reiterating much of what she had said in her 1944 Halifax speech, but adding a few refinements. The "special responsibility for family life" of women was undeniable, but the "hard fact" was that for many this way of life would no longer be possible. After the war there would "be a much higher proportion of unmarried women." In truth, "thousands of Canadian women" would have to "accept the permanent function of breadwinner because of the loss of husbands and prospective husbands in the war." Added to these were the many other women who would not want to give up a "hard-won economic independence" and many married women who would now want to combine wage work with home management. Unfortunately, "some people" were "already beginning to discuss the demobilization of women as though the object were to take women out of employment regardless of their skills and their need to earn a living." Kathleen Kent had summed this up in *Maclean's* when she had written: "Well girls, it looks as though the old game of employment by sex, rather than merit, is on the books again." This attitude had to be fought at every turn and DVA could lead by example:

> I trust you will not think I am a feminist thinking only of advantages for women if I discuss further the matter of sex discrimination in employment. I am assuming that I am speaking to friends who share the generous and fair attitudes towards women characteristic of the Department, and also that you, as veterans, *are eager to see that ex-service women, as well as men from the services will have just treatment after their war service is over.* . . . The war has broken down much of the traditional prejudices of employers against hiring women, but there is danger of it returning. . . . After the war is over, can we justify saying to ex-service

> women (or to those civilian women who have worked so faithfully and efficiently and who wish, or need, to go on working) that we can no longer use their services? Can we look on them merely as competitors for jobs and accept policies and practices which would drive them out of employment after having worked so well in wartime? Most would agree that this is wrong; nevertheless, there is danger of it happening unless the matter is faced squarely now and employers count women in on their post-war employment plans.
>
> It does seem as though the position of women in regard to employment may need all possible support after the war. Is it not our responsibility to help create public opinion and machinery that will make it possible to *put into effect the principle adopted by the Department of granting to women opportunities and pay according to abilities and services, regardless of sex?*

"Fair play" required that women be treated equally. So, too, did the common good; women had skills that should and must be used in the national interest. No woman wanted to feel that because she had a job, a man was denied work, and this need not be the case. The answer was to provide "suitable employment opportunities for all" and with the same determination that characterized the war effort, this could be done. With this objective in view, Russell appended to her printed remarks wide-ranging lists of vocations for women and a bibliography of books and pamphlets relating to the rehabilitation of women.

Russell's "running mate" at DVA in 1945 was Mary Salter, another former CWAC officer.[63] As part of the gearing up of the department, she was appointed superintendent of women's rehabilitation. As promised, DVA also recruited women staff members to act as counsellors, interviewers, and clerks in its rehabilitation centres across the country. In September 1945, the department issued a manual of instructions on women's rehabilitation, and in February and March 1946, with demobilization in full swing, it held training conferences on women's rehabilitation in Ottawa (18–21 February), Saskatoon (27 February–1 March) and Vancouver (13–16 March).[64] A detailed record was kept of the proceedings of these conferences, and a summary of what was said was issued jointly by the superintendent of women's rehabilitation and the director of staff training. Discussion at the conference on "Occupational trends and training opportunities for women"[65] flowed along familiar lines, but the emphasis differed somewhat from that to be found in the analyses of Olive Russell. At the Ottawa conference, for example, Margaret Grier, associate director of National Selective Service, Department of Labour, pointed out that "the disorganization of women's normal occupations and pursuits during the war" had not been "as severe nor as wide-spread" as it superficially appeared.[66] The first wave of wartime women workers had been drawn from the ranks of the approximately "half a million girls and women" who normally lived at home, mainly in rural areas and small towns, because there were no jobs for them.[67] When this pool of labour had been exhausted, about 125 000 to 150 000 married women had been recruited. They had come "mainly from household service" or been drawn from the ranks of "young married women whose husbands were in the Services."[68] But married women had not been employed to the same extent in Canada as in other countries. The current expectation, Grier reported, was that "only 2 or 3 out of every 10" married women would want to remain in jobs outside the home, and that three-quarters of the single women who had gone to work during the war would eventually get married and "leave gainful employment."[69]

At the Saskatoon conference, Moira O'Neil, assistant to the supervisor of placement operations–veterans, Unemployment Insurance Commission, argued that though the war had "opened employment opportunities for women . . . [in] occupations previously considered male," the fact had to be faced that when men were "available as garage mechanics, truck drivers and such, most employers . . . [would] prefer them."[70] Some ex-servicewomen might "enter unusual occupations," but the majority could be expected to "go into the kind of work their sisters did before them."[71] Indeed, the experience of service life may have increased "the tendency to 'run with the pack.'"[72] It was true that "scientific changes" were creating new employment opportunities for women, but DVA counsellors would be "well advised to concentrate on the types of employment" in which women were "normally employed."[73] The Vancouver conference heard a similar message from Fraudena Eaton, associate director of National Selective Service, Department of Labour. In her remarks, she traced the history of the employment of women and noted that the entry of so many into the work force during the war had from its inception produced fear that there would not be enough jobs for all at the end of the conflict. This view in turn was feeding prejudice in relation to the employment of women.[74] But in fact this fear was unjustified, because many of the married women who had gone to work had made "an easy transition back to their homes or to domestic employment at the lower wage level they had left."[75] Nevertheless, economic considerations would ensure that there would be more married women in the work force after the war than before. Given the prejudice against them, married women "would be well advised to consider opportunities for self-found employment—in agriculture, owning small manufacturing establishments, crafts and trades . . . or service occupations such as hairdressing." This would prevent them from "being at the mercy of the prejudice of an employer." Eaton also recommended caution in the counselling of ex-servicewomen:

> She advised the counsellors to advise ex-service women generally to go into work accepted as women's work. She felt that although during the war

> many women performed jobs previously done by men relatively few will remain in those jobs. She felt that many jobs fell naturally into a division of men's work and women's work in terms of physical strength, attitudes, and aptitudes. She stated that the fields ordinarily accepted as women's fields offered interesting and satisfactory work and the reason that women have reached out to jobs usually done by men was not so much because of lack of satisfaction with women's work, but because of the more favourable wage rate usually given to a man's job. She felt that if equitable wage rates could be arrived at there would still tend to be a natural division in the work most suitable to the two sexes, although there would obviously be considerable overlapping.

This was sobering, but as the DVA program unfolded Olive Russell was optimistic that the goals she had in mind were being realized, and that the glad day of the postwar world she had envisaged was indeed dawning. Throughout 1946 she maintained a busy travel and public-speaking schedule and, beginning in November 1945, she contributed four articles to a series on the rehabilitation of women that appeared in *Veterans Affairs*, the official publication of DVA.[76] In a 25 March 1946 interview on the CBC in Vancouver, Russell was asked to react to the statement that because women did not "have to think quite as realistically as men in considering their re-establishment problems" some of them "were asking for unusual training courses—that is, courses a bit off the beaten track."[77] Russell shot back that she was glad to hear that this was happening. Those who thought that the only training available to women was for "hair-dressing and clerical work" were "entirely mistaken." All training opportunities applied equally to men and women. Any veteran wanting a particular course of training could have it, provided he or she met the requisite qualifying and eligibility criteria, applied within the entitlement time limit, and was setting out to do something appropriate to his or her rehabilitation. Women were already in training for over eighty-five occupations. These ranged from "the highly skilled and professional occupations" requiring several years of training such as law, architecture, medicine, pharmacy, and social work, to "those occupations requiring shorter periods of training such as Book Binding, Linotype Operating, Photography, Egg Grading and even frog farming." This diversity was to be welcomed and did not conflict with the maintenance of good family life:

> Don't make the mistake of thinking that all unusual training requested by women is necessarily unrealistic. On the whole I think it very encouraging to find that so many women are showing initiative in pursuing and preparing for occupations, which . . . are a bit off the beaten track. For instance, some women are in training as Watch and Clock makers and one is in training for an Embalmer. Could you suggest any occupations that are less likely to go

> out of business than these, or any reason why they are not suitable occupations for women? Lest you think I am forgetting the importance of Homemaking as a career for women, I wish to state that in several centres in Canada a special course of training in Homemaking and family living has been arranged for ex-service women. This course has been designed to meet the needs of those young women who will be establishing homes of their own and who recognize the importance of having training for that complex and important task. In this course, which is of at least four months duration, special emphasis is being put on both the practical household duties and general home management; budgeting, nutrition, child care and training, and the psychological aspects of family life. I am glad to be able to announce that in some centres evening classes in this subject are also being provided for those men who recognize that they too need training if they are to be successful partners in this responsible job of making happy homes.

Women had shown "their ability to perform all sorts of tasks hitherto not open to them" and "opportunities for them to use their talents to the full" should never be denied them again.

In July 1946, Russell told Betty Styran on radio station CKCO, Kitchener, Ontario, that when she had taken up her duties at DVA she had thought her main job would be to select and train counsellors. In practice, she had had to spend much of her time reminding "employers, Citizens' Committees and all who were planning to welcome veterans and assist them with their re-establishment that there were ex-servicewomen as well as ex-servicemen to be rehabilitated."[78] This effort had paid off, and the rehabilitation of women veterans was "proceeding much more smoothly that might have been anticipated." In the same vein, Russell wrote in the summer 1946 issue of *Echoes*, the magazine of the Imperial Order Daughters of the Empire, that whereas a year before there had been "danger of employers forgetting that there would be women veterans as well as men," this problem had now been overcome.[79] Thanks to "the same adaptability, efficiency and dependability" they had shown in uniform, ex-servicewomen were now receiving high marks from employers.

Russell and her female colleagues in the rehabilitation branch of DVA could also take comfort in the department's attitude toward the employment of married women in the civil service. In 1944 the Civil Service Commission decided to drop five to seven thousand married women, many of whom had entered government service through wartime expansion.[80] Henceforth, moreover, the regulation would also be strictly enforced that required an unmarried female civil servant to resign her position when she got married. In a 5 December 1945 memorandum to Woods, General E.L.M. Burns, S.N.F. Chant's successor as director general of rehabilitation, argued that instead of joining in the renewal of "policies of discrimination against married women" DVA should call for the end of such discrimination.[81] Canada had agreed in the charter of the United Nations to "the realization of human rights and fundamental freedoms for all without distinction as to race, sex, language or religion" and to bar married women from civil service jobs would violate that pledge. In support of his case, Burns cited an April 1945 report of the Woman's Advisory Committee of the United States War Manpower Commission. This report had concluded that discrimination against married women in jobs was an injustice, an unwise limitation on the availability of workers with skills that were in demand, and a breeding ground for "practices of subterfuge and deception." The Government of Canada, Burns reminded Woods, was committed to full employment covering all who were "able and willing to work," and for the civil service to act otherwise would contradict that basic policy. It was also the case that married women who had served overseas were entitled to civil-service preference as veterans. Furthermore, many male veterans with overseas service were counting on financial assistance from their wives while they were in rehabilitation training or reestablishing themselves in jobs and homes. If the civil service set a bad example in relation to married women, the government could scarcely blame other employers for following suit. To make "economic necessity" rather than "suitability for the job" the test of civil service hiring would be to promote "a dangerous practice" that, logically, "would involve men as well as women." The simple truth was that "the fact of marriage should not be the basis for denying a woman the freedom of choice granted to all other citizens in a democracy." The question of whether or not a woman should take a paying job was a private matter, to be decided by her and her husband, and there was no need for legislation on the subject.

The general reform advocated by Burns was not in fact introduced into the Canadian civil service until 1955, but married women veterans with husbands in training were apparently treated as single persons immediately after the war.[82] DVA, moreover, resisted the application of the civil service resignation rule to single female members of its own staff who got married.[83] In the same spirit, a thirty-dollar deduction formerly made from the allowance paid to married women veterans in training was cancelled on 1 January 1947.[84] Thereafter, married and single veterans were treated equally with respect to training allowances. In April 1947, Helen Hunt, Mary Salter's successor as superintendent of women's rehabilitation, recommended that a deduction of the same amount being made from the awaiting returns allowances of married women veterans who had gone into farming or business should likewise be cancelled.[85]

The progress being made in the women's rehabilitation program was monitored at DVA headquarters in Ottawa by monthly reports from women counsellors. The operation and record of the program was also analysed in two lengthy reports by the superintendent of women's rehabilitation. The first, submitted by Mary Salter on 12 July 1946, covered the events of the previous year and the second, submitted by Helen Hunt on 25 November 1947, covered developments from August 1946 to November 1947. Salter noted that women's rehabilitation was "proceeding most effectively" where it was "most separate."[86] The ideal arrangement kept the counselling of male and female veterans separate at the local level, but within the same overall administrative framework. When she had come to DVA, Salter commented, no supervisor of women's training had yet been appointed at Canadian Vocational Training and not much had been done to provide special training courses for women. Once Marion Graham had been appointed, however, matters had sped along and steps had been taken to offer training in practical nursing in all provinces but Saskatchewan. The courses in progress were almost all filled to capacity. But this was not true of homemaking courses, which had been established in Alberta, Saskatchewan, Ontario, and Quebec. These courses had been started too late, and plans to introduce them in British Columbia and the Maritimes had been dropped because there were too few applicants. The courses most in demand were for commercial training, hairdressing and dressmaking. Ex-servicewomen were doing well in finding jobs across the country, but there was "a growing discrimination on the part of employers against all married women."

In the report she submitted more than a year later, Helen Hunt showed that the basic trends Mary Salter had observed had continued through 1947.[87] Encouraging ex-servicewomen to take training in practical nursing had been a priority in counselling, while demand for homemaking courses had remained low. Only in Saskatoon was there still such a course in operation. The training courses most favoured by women had continued to be "prematriculation, commercial, hairdressing and dressmaking." Hunt ascribed this "disappointing" result and the failure of many women to branch out "into new lines" to their prewar experience. Having lived through the Great Depression, women had given priority to "security" (that is to say, to training for traditional women's occupations) when planning their future careers. The employment situation of ex-servicewomen had also remained satisfactory; the greatest difficulty was experienced in Nova Scotia and British Columbia. But the problems experienced in these provinces were minor blemishes on an otherwise rosy picture:

> Immediately following VJ day it was evident that employers, many of whom had also had service experience, were very ready to accept ex-servicewomen in their organization. This satisfactory condition has continued, even though at the present time the employer is requesting more often an employee with some experience following training. It has been very evident right across the country in conversations with representatives of the National Employment Service that

> placement of women veterans never became the problem that was anticipated. Nearly all state that they had expected some time would occur in which some of their offices would be flooded with ex-servicewomen seeking employment which was not readily available.

Happily, the expected crunch never came, and the transition to peacetime conditions was smooth. This analysis, of course, ignored the large-scale return by women to domestic life, which DVA, through the reestablishment credit scheme, was clearly promoting.

Hunt included in her report detailed statistics on what had happened to women so far under the provisions of the Veterans Charter. To 30 September 1947, 11 507 had taken training. Of these, 9083 had taken vocational training and 2424 had gone to university. The 11 507 figure represented 23 percent of the total enlistment and was higher than the equivalent figure for male veterans. To 31 October 1947, 264 women had received awaiting-returns allowances, and to the end of September, 200 had received temporary-incapacity allowances. To 30 September also, 2930 women had received out-of-work allowances. This was 5.8 percent of the total enlistment and "considerably lower" than the equivalent percentage for male veterans. To 31 October, 131 women had received benefits under the Veterans' Land Act, of whom 87 were established on small holdings and 44 in full-time farming. Also to October, women had received $3 804 488.70 in reestablishment credits. In order of expenditure, this money had been used for furniture and other household goods, home buying, working capital, premiums on Dominion government insurance, and home repairs and modernization. This pattern of use was similar to that of male veterans.

A 1949 update of these figures showed that from the inception of the rehabilitation program to 31 December 1948, 11 488 women had taken vocational courses and 3320 had gone to university.[88] The vocational course trainees were subdivided into thirty specific and one "miscellaneous" occupational categories. The largest group, numbering 3059, had trained themselves to be "Stenographers & Typists." After that came "Barbers and Beauticians," numbering 1451; "Dressmakers and Tailors," numbering 1021; and "Secretaries," numbering 964. Together these four groups constituted 56.7 percent of the total. Of the group that had gone to university, 915 were said to have done postgraduate studies, of whom the largest group, numbering 377, had studied nursing. Of the 2405 who had registered for undergraduate courses, the largest group by far, some 1179, had opted for "Arts and Science." Among undergraduates the next five leading choices were health nursing (190), social science (130), education (97), business administration, commerce and finance (79), and physiotherapy (68).

Despite the evident conservatism of the training choices being made by ex-servicewomen, Olive Russell left DVA in August 1947 pleased with her own accomplishments, and convinced of the success of the rehabilitation program. Her own reestablishment was as an assistant professor of psychology at Winthrop College, "the South Carolina College for Women," at Rock Hill, South Carolina. From there she wrote to Woods on 6 November 1947, expressing her appreciation of his "attitude towards individual human welfare, and the national interest" and his "courteous, optimistic manner."[89] These qualities, she wrote, had been an inspiration to her. So had Woods' attitude toward Canadian womanhood: "I especially appreciate the fair mindedness you showed in matters pertaining to the status of women. Even though reactionary forces seem to be at work in many Government Departments and elsewhere, and many unjustifiable discriminations still exist, you set an example in regard to status generally that is bound in the long run to benefit Canadian women." These sentiments indicate a harmonious parting of the ways between these two makers of postwar Canada, but in truth, Russell's dealings with DVA and the Dominion government generally were not always easy. In 1947 she was turned down by her superiors when she suggested visits first to Australia and then to England.[90] There is also evidence that Russell aspired to some other job with the government of Canada that she did not get. Following a conversation on 23 July 1947 with Arthur MacNamara, the deputy minister of labour, she wrote to him that "the amount I quoted as 'the price of a meal ticket' was considerably less than the salary I am justified in expecting. The kind of position in which I am really interested in the government," she continued, "is one in which I would have a voice in policy making, and such a position would naturally be at a salary at least equal to my present one, if not greater."[91]

Evidently the job or the salary or both were not forthcoming; hence her decision to go to the United States. Olive Russell and her female colleagues at DVA also failed in another regard. In report after report she, Mary Salter, and Helen Hunt all recommended that a female voice should be maintained in the policy-making upper ranks of the department, as well as in its general administration when DVA moved beyond the immediate postwar rehabilitation period and settled into its long-term role of caring for those who could not care for themselves.[92] This did not happen. When Olive Russell left, she was not replaced and when Helen Hunt departed, the position of superintendent of women's rehabilitation was downgraded as part of a general scaling-down of DVA activities. By the 1950s, with its glory days of demobilization behind it, DVA had become a male-veteran bastion, though a portion of its clientele was, *ipso facto*, female.

The entry of so many women into the labour force during World War II and the formation of the women's branches of the Armed Forces constitute an extraordinary chapter in the social history of Canada in the twentieth century. An important part of that story of necessity concerns the rights of ex-servicewomen under the Veterans Charter, one of the building blocks of the Canadian welfare state. Participation in war-related work and service in the Armed Forces gave women a claim they had not had before. And given the wartime rhetoric of solidarity and sacrifice leading to a better tomorrow, this claim was hard to deny. Rosie the Riveter and her sister, Jill Canuck, were new players on the Canadian political stage who could not be ignored. Understandably, Olive Russell liked to play up her credentials as a veteran and play down the label of "feminist," but in reality the first role served the purposes of the second. Having advanced toward pay equity and made other gains while in the services, Canada's women veterans, unlike some ex-servicewomen in the United States, were equally eligible with men for almost all the benefits of the Veterans Charter and DVA prided itself that this was so. There had never been such a social program before in Canada and it produced impressive results. Above all, it helped to avoid a social and economic catastrophe of the sort that had overtaken the country at the end of the Great War. It is easy, however, to exaggerate the gains made by women under the Veterans Charter and to confuse the equality of opportunity proclaimed in *Back to Civil Life* with what actually happened under the charter's provisions. Women constituted only about 4.6 percent of Canada's Armed Forces in World War II and the Veterans Charter was designed primarily with men, the other 95.4 percent, in mind.[93] Women were equally eligible for benefits, but within the framework of a program that first and foremost sought to meet the needs of men. As volunteers, women were eligible for gratuities and, by extension, for reestablishment credits or training (including postsecondary education). As a much smaller proportion (one in seven) of Armed Forces women had gone overseas compared with men, a correspondingly smaller proportion therefore qualified for the gratuity paid for overseas service. The veterans' preference in the civil service was likewise of limited advantage to women as it was given for service in a theatre of war, which ruled out most women. To remedy this defect, Mary Salter called in 1945 within DVA for a secondary preference. This was also being advocated publicly by the Canadian Legion. It would apply to all volunteers with a year or more of service, and therefore to most women who had served. Because of contemporary societal expectations and norms, another benefit under the charter that held little promise for women was the Veterans' Land Act. Woods understood this, and in fact few women qualified under the act. In June 1944 he told Colonel G.W. Beecroft, overseas rehabilitation officer in London, England, that while under PC 7633 it was technically true that men and women were "entitled to the same benefits," in practice the order would "be administered in a common sense way and in the case of a married woman, with entire regard to the rehabilitation of the family."[94] Women, in other words, would not necessarily be considered for all benefits simply as individuals. Woods' comment said much about the underlying philosophy of the Veterans Charter, which emphasized eligibility criteria and equality of opportunity rather than equality of condition. If the charter promoted greater equality between women and men, this would be incidental to its main business, which was to promote property owning and sturdy self-reliance.

The training program, too, had its limitations for women. Given a choice between training and reestablishment credits, most women, like most men, opted for the latter. The emphasis in the reestablishment credit scheme on household formation facilitated the return to domesticity that Ruth Roach Pierson has characterized in *"They're Still Women After All": The Second World War and Canadian Womanhood*[95] as the leitmotif of the history of Canadian women in the immediate postwar period. In effect, the state provided tens of thousands of Canadians, men and women, with the means to settle down, and Walter Woods may well qualify for the title of father of the baby boom, the term used to describe the great increase in the birth rate that followed the war. Those who opted for training, of course, had to work within the confines of available choice. Olive Russell wanted women to go where their talents led them, but even she was concerned about preserving the role of women as homemakers, although to be fair this was in the context of a new cooperation and sharing of duties between spouses. In practice, DVA counsellors, who had the final say on who would be trained for what, stressed courses like practical nursing and only a minority of trainees found their way "off the beaten track" in the way favoured by Olive Russell. As Ruth Roach Pierson and Marjorie Cohen point out, "in February, 1946, Canadian Vocational Training was offering training in over 100 types of trades in vocational schools and over 300 types under training-on-the-job schemes, yet women were to be found in only thirty-five types of trades in vocational schools and in only ninety-two under training-on-the-job schemes."[96] Olive Russell nevertheless left DVA convinced that the rehabilitation program for women had been a great success. Conversely, she, Mary Salter, and Helen Hunt, for all their professionalism and hard work, failed to leave a strong female presence behind them at DVA.

Yet it must also be acknowledged that the Veterans Charter constituted an important step forward toward full legal, social, and economic equality for Canadian women. More than eleven thousand ex-servicewomen took vocational training, and in addition more than three thousand went to university. These were substantial totals, and the subsequent contributions of these women to Canadian life cannot be gainsaid. Those who reaped the benefits of the Veterans Charter in all likelihood helped prepare the ground for the bigger gains women would make in the future. Within DVA, moreover, there was strong support for equality of opportunity in employment for married women. And thanks in part to DVA's efforts, those ex-servicewomen who swam against the returning tide of domesticity also apparently did well in the job market immediately after the war. In 1946, 1947, and 1948, work, albeit gender-divided, was seemingly readily available for almost all who wanted it. It was also widely recognized in government circles that the entry of women, married and single, into the labour market was permanent, and that there would be no absolute return to prewar conditions. Finally, war and demobilization opened debates about pay equity and the appropriateness of employment by sex, that the children and grandchildren of those who had answered their country's call to service between 1939 and 1945 would not soon resolve.

Notes

1. C.P. Stacey, *Arms, Men and Governments: The War Policies of Canada 1939–1945* (Ottawa, 1970). J.L. Granatstein, *Canada's War: The Policies of the Mackenzie King Government, 1939–1945* (Toronto, 1975).
2. For the history of Canada's World War I veterans, see Desmond Morton and Glenn Wright, *Winning the Second Battle: Canadian Veterans and the Return to Civilian Life 1915–1930* (Toronto, 1987).
3. Ibid., 212.
4. Walter S. Woods, *Rehabilitation (A Combined Operation)* (Ottawa, 1953), 386.
5. Ibid.
6. Ibid., 17.
7. Ibid., 463.
8. Ibid., 13.
9. Ibid.
10. For the text of this order-in-council and its amendments see ibid., 465–76.
11. This account of his life is based on the "Man of the Week" article in the 4 Nov. 1944 edition of the Montreal *Standard*. There is a copy of this article in file 32-3-2, vol. 2 of the records of the Department of Veterans Affairs (hereafter DVA), Veterans Affairs Canada, Charlottetown, Prince Edward Island.
12. DVA, file 65-8, Woods to Wodehouse, 13 March 1941.
13. Quoted in "Man of the Week" article in Montreal *Standard*, 4 Nov. 1944.
14. Woods, *Rehabilitation*, 5.
15. Ibid., 16.
16. DVA, file 32-3-3, Woods to Minister, 8 Sept. 1944.
17. The scheme is summarized in Woods, *Rehabilitation*, 23–30.
18. See ibid.
19. Ibid., 43.
20. Ibid., 42.
21. Ibid., 462.
22. See ibid., Appendix A, 461.
23. Carolyn Gossage, *Greatcoats and Glamour Boots: Canadian Women at War (1939–1945)* (Toronto, 1991).
24. Figures from Directorate of History, Department of National Defence.
25. Woods, *Rehabilitation*, 255.
26. PC 56/6755 of 31 July 1942, which authorized the formation of the Women's Royal Canadian Naval Service, began by citing a report to Treasury Board from the minister of national defence. According to this report there were "a number of duties now being performed by men" that were "capable of being performed by women." If women could be so employed, "the men in question would be available for duties of a heavier nature." There is a copy of PC 56/6755 in DVA, file 5431-03-4, vol. 1.

27. There is a copy of PC 4/7635 in DVA, file 5431-03-4, vol. 1.
28. See DVA, file 5431-03-4, vol. 1, Wright to Woods, 27 Oct. 1941.
29. See, for example, PC 49/8817 of 11 Nov. 1941 dealing with reinstatement in civil employment and PC 8880 of 18 Nov. 1941 dealing with the payment of rehabilitation grants. There are copies of these orders in DVA, file 5431-03-4, vol. 1.
30. DVA, file 5431-03-4, vol. 1, England to Wright, 24 Oct. 1941.
31. See PC 1965. There is a copy of this order-in-council in DVA, file 5431-03-4, vol. 1.
32. Under PC 7633 "discharged person" was defined as follows: "any person who, having been in receipt of either active service rates of pay or of Permanent Force rates of pay while serving in the Naval, Military or Air Forces of Canada during the present war, subsequent to July 1, 1941, is discharged or retired from, or ceases to serve on active service in, the said forces."
33. DVA, file 5431-03-4, vol. 1, McDonald to Woods, 26 Nov. 1941.
34. DVA, file 5431-03-4, General Advisory Committee on Demobilization and Rehabilitation, Subcommittee on Post-Discharge Benefits for Members of the Canadian Women's Army Corps and the Canadian Women's Auxiliary Air Force, minutes of meeting of 29 Dec. 1941.
35. Ibid.
36. DVA, file 5431-03-4, vol. 1, Woods to McDonald, 3 Jan. 1942.
37. Ibid., memorandum to minister of pensions and national health, 25 March 1942, from chairman, Subcommittee on Post-Discharge Benefits for Members of the Canadian Women's Army Corps and the Canadian Women's Auxiliary Air Force. There is a copy of PC 1965 in this file. The revised definition of "discharged person" in the amended PC 7633 was as follows: "any person who, subsequent to July 1st, 1941, has been discharged or retired from, or has ceased to serve on active service in any of the following Forces or Corps; (i) the Naval, Military or Air Forces of Canada, provided in respect to this class, that such person was in receipt of either active service rates of pay or of Permanent Force rates of pay while serving in the said Forces during the present war, or (ii) the Canadian Women's Army Corps, established by Order in Council, P.C. 6289, dated the 13th day of August, 1941, or (iii) the Royal Canadian Air Force (Women's Division), established by Order in Council, P.C. 790, dated the 3rd day of February, 1942, or (iv) the Military, Naval or Air Forces of His Majesty other than His Majesty's Canadian Forces, provided in respect to this class, that such person was domiciled in Canada at the time of his enlistment therein in the present war." See Woods, *Rehabilitation*, 467.
38. By PC 56/6755. There is a copy of this order-in-council in DVA, file 5431-03-4, vol. 1.
39. For the history of women's units in the United States during World War II see chapter 1 of D'Ann Campbell, *Women at War with America: Private Lives in a Patriotic Era* (Cambridge, MA, 1984).
40. June A. Willenz, *Women Veterans: America's Forgotten Heroines* (New York, 1983), 168. The formation of the WAAC was authorized by Congress in 1942. In June 1943 it became the Women's Army Corps (WAC). The WASP was formed in 1943 out of the Women's Auxiliary Flying Squadron (WAFS) and the Women's Flying Training Detachment (WFTD).
41. Ibid.
42. Ibid.
43. DVA, file 5431-03-4, vol. 2, Woods to National Secretary, Imperial [Order] Daughters of the Empire, 27 Oct. 1943.
44. House of Commons, *Debates*, 24 July 1943, 5357–58.

45. DVA, 5431-03-4, vol. 3, Woods to Dixon, 13 Sept. 1944.
46. Ibid., Neill to Reid, 29 Nov. 1944; Woods to Neill, 1 Dec. 1944.
47. Ibid., Neill to Woods, 6 Dec. 1944.
48. Ibid., vol. 1, Woods to McDonald, 24 Jan. 1942.
49. Ibid., minutes of the meeting of the Subcommittee on Post-Discharge Benefits for members of the Canadian Women's Army Corps and the Royal Canadian Air Force (Women's Division), 24 March 1942.
50. Veterans Affairs Canada, Canadian Pension Commission Records, list 8167, box 80, bin 99, minutes of the Subcommittee on the Special Problems of Discharged Women, 19 June 1942.
51. The interim report is in the same box and is attached to the minutes of the meeting of 23 June 1942.
52. There is a copy of this survey in the library of Veterans Affairs Canada.
53. Ibid., 157.
54. Ibid., 212–26.
55. Ibid., 215.
56. Canadian Pension Commission Records, list 8167, box 80, bin 99, Subcommittee on the Special Problems of Discharged Women, minutes of the meeting of 23 June 1942; and Interim Report of the Subcommittee on the Special Problems of Discharged Women, 2–3.
57. The account of her career that follows is based on "Dr. Olive Ruth Russell Occupies Important Post," Ottawa *Evening Citizen*, 15 Aug. 1946 copy in National Archives of Canada (NAC), MG31 K13, Olive Ruth Russell Papers, vol. 1, file 1); "Dr. Russell—Rehabilitation," draft article for *Saturday Night* by F.E. Whyard (ibid., vol. 2, file 14); T.J. Rutherford letter, "To Whom It May Concern," 30 April 1947 (ibid., vol. 1, file 4).
58. Ibid., vol. 2, file 15, Russell to Whyard, 19 June 1946.
59. Ibid., vol. 2, file 15, Russell to Coffey, 24 July 1945.
60. Ibid., vol. 1, file 11, "Women To-Morrow: An address by Captain Olive Ruth Russell given at the University Women's Club, Dalhousie University, Halifax, N.S., 15 March 1944."
61. Ibid., Olive Ruth Russell report, "Proposed Film, Project and Training in Homemaking and Family Living," 1. This report is attached to Russell to Burns, 25 Sept. 1945.
62. Ibid., vol. 2, file 14, "Rehabilitation of Women of the Armed Forces."
63. Ibid., Salter to Russell, 28 Nov. 1944.
64. There is a copy of the 15 Sept. 1945 "Manual of Instructions Women's Rehabilitation" in DVA, file 65-45, vol. 1.
65. Ibid., "Proceedings Training Conferences on Women's Rehabilitation," 1.
66. Ibid., 47.
67. Ibid.
68. Ibid., 48.
69. Ibid.
70. Ibid., 49.
71. Ibid.
72. Ibid.
73. Ibid.
74. Ibid.
75. Ibid., 50.
76. These and related items were collected in "Rehabilitation of Women Veterans in Canada," Ottawa, Aug. 1946. There is a copy in NAC, MG31 K13, vol. 1, file 9.
77. There is a transcript of this interview in ibid., vol. 1, file 1.
78. There is a transcript of this interview in ibid.
79. Russell's article is entitled "Women Veterans and Their Rehabilitation."
80. J.E. Hodgetts, William McCloskey, Reginald Whitaker and V. Seymour Wilson, *The Biography of an Institution: The Civil Service of Canada, 1908–1967* (Toronto, 1972), 487.

81. NAC, MG31 K13, vol. 2, file 14, Burns to Woods, 5 Dec. 1945.
82. See DVA, file 65-45-WI, memorandum "Re: Report of Visit of Superintendent of Women's Rehabilitation to Vancouver District, 11–13 February 1947."
83. See ibid., Russell to Rumball, 3 April 1946; DVA, file 65-45-CA, Salter to Sutton, 23 April 1946.
84. DVA, file 65-45, vol. 2, Rutherford to Woods, 4 Jan. 1947 and Rehabilitation Branch Instruction, 15 Jan. 1947.
85. Ibid., Hunt to Rutherford, 26 Aug. 1947.
86. DVA, file 65-45-CA, Salter to Burns, 12 July 1946.
87. Ibid., memorandum "Re: Report of Superintendent of Women's Rehabilitation—August, 1946 to November, 1947," Hunt to Wright, 25 Nov. 1947.
88. Ibid., "Women's Rehabilitation as of December 31, 1948," Rider to Mann, 31 Jan. 1949.
89. Ibid., Russell to Woods, 6 Nov. 1947.
90. Ibid., Woods to minister, 27 July 1946 and Woods to Russell, 30 Nov. 1946.
91. NAC, MG31 K13, vol. 1, file 4, Russell to MacNamara, 23 July 1947.
92. See DVA, file 65-45, vol. 2, memorandum "Re: Final Report of Supt. of Women's Rehabilitation," Salter to Burns, 12 July 1946; Hunt to Rutherford, 23 Dec. 1946; Russell to Elliott, 14 April 1947; memorandum, "Re: Report of Superintendent of Women's Rehabilitation—August, 1946 to November, 1947," Hunt to Wright, 25 Nov. 1947.
93. Calculated from Woods, *Rehabilitation*, Appendix A, 461.
94. DVA, file 5431-07-4, vol. 3, Woods to Beecroft, 29 June 1944.
95. Ruth Roach Pierson, *"They're Still Women After All": The Second World War and Canadian Womanhood* (Toronto, 1986).
96. Ibid., 92.

At war's end, Canada's newspapers and magazines were full of helpful advice to service personnel about to be discharged and those waiting to receive them back home. For many children, demobilization meant an especially challenging adjustment: the end of the single-parent family. This advice from *Maclean's* came from a well-known psychologist.

Home Won't Be Heaven, Soldier

J.D. Ketchum

THEY OUGHT TO *TELL* US," said the First Division sergeant, looking straight at his Army counsellor. "They ought to tell us how to expect things in Canada when we get home. And they ought to tell people that we've changed too. You can't be away for five years and come back to things just as you left them." He was dead serious, for he'd just had 30 days' experience of it himself—of coming home, full of happy excitement, to find things rather different from the way he'd pictured them, to find small but unexpected barriers between him and his family and friends.

Well, this article is an attempt to tell them, soldier and civilians alike, of some of the minor difficulties that may crop up when men come home, and also of how readily most of them can be overcome. I don't mean big problems like deciding on a job or mending a broken home—they don't belong here—but the little everyday adjustments that have to be made on both sides if home-coming is to be the happy experience it ought to be. We've heard enough by now from returning men and their families to know what many of these problems are likely to be, and a little understanding of them in advance can help both the serviceman and all the rest of us.

One of the most unexpected and upsetting things about coming home is that there's nearly always something of a letdown after the first excitement is over. Many boys have felt much like this one:

> You ask, what am I doing? Just bumming around, Mac, bumming around. Going to church with Mum, getting shown off to her friends, answering dumb questions about what it's like "at the front," tagging along with Dad on the same old Saturday walk, driving the old crate around if there's any gas. Pretty smalltime stuff—guess I don't enjoy things the way I used to or something. Oh, yes, there

> was a church supper and I had to make a speech. That's the highlight so far. Maybe things will be better in the summer.

Why should there be any letdown when a man comes home? Well, why shouldn't there? It's natural enough. The main reason is that when you think of home, over there in France or Italy—still more if you're a prisoner of war in Germany—you idealize it, you dream it up into a picture so brightly colored that heaven would look dull in comparison. The place is perfect, the people are perfect, everything's perfect. Home isn't like that, of course—never was like that—but you forget all the little things you didn't enjoy when you were there and remember only the good times. How can you help it when your thinking is done in the mud and icy water of Holland or in a barbed-wire enclosure in Germany? Here's part of a letter from a Canadian prisoner of war:

> We spend a lot of time talking about home, each one telling the good times he's had and the ones he's going to have when he gets back, fishing, skiing, canoe trips, and, of course, the wonderful eats. Especially now, with spring coming, I'm always thinking I'm back at the lake with you all, swimming off the dock, lying in the sun, going on picnics to Birch Point or Echo Lake. It sure makes my mouth water. If I only get back this fall in time to get a couple of ducks.

In combat areas there's less time for this sort of daydreaming, but it starts with a bang the moment a man is picked for repatriation, and during the weeks of waiting for transportation it's almost an obsession. As a First Division sapper put it, "I was so glad, it was like a dream. I didn't know what I could do afterward, but I didn't care." Home begins to look like paradise itself, and when he gets there and bumps up against humdrum reality there's bound to be some letdown.

Sometimes this upsets a chap; he wonders what's the matter with him that he doesn't feel happier. Some men find themselves getting snappy and irritable, and then their impulse is to crawl into a mental foxhole for a while. Quite a number of families have had this sort of experience:

> At the moment he doesn't seem to want to do anything or see anyone, just sits around the house, smoking and listening to the radio, or lies on his bed reading magazines. He doesn't talk, either; we've hardly got a word out of him since the first few days. I wish I knew what's the matter with him, but if you ask him he flares up like anything.

Serious? Not a bit of it. He's been switched suddenly from one world to a totally different one and hasn't quite got his bearings yet. He'll snap out of it soon, particularly when he gets something definite to do, and in the meantime, patience, affection and understanding are all that's needed. This is how an RCAF pilot described it after several months at home:

> It's quite strange at first, I didn't know what to do with myself, felt all at sea. It's like when you first join up, only in reverse. I was restless and I guess I worried the folks more than somewhat, but they were swell about it and we didn't have any real rows. I still think everyone's in a kind of a rut here, but since I got started back at school I've got something ahead of me, and things don't get on my nerves the way they did.

One thing that takes a lot of the joy out of coming home is finding changes he hadn't heard about. Even apparently trivial ones can be disturbing, because they don't fit in with the picture he's carried so long in his mind. Here's an example—rather an exceptional one, but it illustrates the point:

> Do you know what's upset Harry most since he's been back? It's Selden's being closed. Of course he used to drop in there almost every night when he was at high school and have a Coke with the gang, but I never thought it meant so much to him. Almost the first night he was back he said, "Well, guess I'll hop down to Selden's and see what's doing," and when I told him it was gone I was almost scared, he was so upset. He's still mad about it, and he won't go near that new place where the kids hang out now.

Well, of course Harry will get over that—but how easy it would have been to mention it in a letter to him. They just never thought about it, but it's exactly the kind of news that lots of the boys are interested in. A Canadian prisoner wrote this from Germany last October: "I was thinking of home today and of how much the town must have changed since I saw it, and I wondered that neither you nor anybody else has written to me about any changes. Now I wish you would, please, and also if you could send me some snaps to show the changes."

Those "Cheerful" Letters

PART OF THE BLAME for the shocks men get from unexpected changes belongs to the well-meaning people who told servicemen's relatives to write only "cheerful" letters. Sure, cheerful letters are what he wants, but that doesn't mean that you don't tell him you've had to move into a smaller flat, or that Junior wasn't promoted this year, or that the doctor wants you to have an operation. Keeping these things back is only laying up trouble. What he wants to know is that you are still cheerful, in spite of any difficulties, not to have the difficulties hidden from him. This wife's mistake is far too common:

> I don't know what to make of Jim, I'm sure. I've tried to be a good wife to him and keep things going here at home, but now he's back you'd think I'd done everything wrong. Of course it was a shock to him finding us in a place like this—I never let on in my letters, you know, just told him we'd moved. I knew it would worry him. Well, that's all right now and we're moving to a better place next month. But the way he carried on when he saw little Gloria wearing glasses—you'd think it was my fault she has to have them. She's worn them six months now and we're all used to it, but to hear Jim talk she would never have needed them if he'd been here to look after things.

Then there was the man who'd told all his buddies that he'd saved almost $1000 in Victory Bonds, and then came home to find that his wife had had to spend most of it on illness and other emergencies and hadn't dared to tell him. When it came out, and it soon did, it caused an explosion that almost broke up that family. The same story turns up in many forms—about health, war jobs, relatives, purchases—but it nearly always goes back to the fact that the man's been kept in the dark about things.

A married man's life is not a circle drawn around a single point. It's a more complex figure with two centres—himself and his wife—and the relationship between them is the key to most of the problems that may come up. If there's always a frank and open flow of thought between them, with neither trying to hide things or brooding about them alone, most difficulties melt away quickly. The story of an officer's wife is revealing:

> Mrs. S. was so determined that everything had to be perfect when her husband came home that she found herself unconsciously acting a part with him—wearing a forced smile all the time, never being ruffled by anything, never admitting the slightest difficulty. It was quite an unnatural role, but she was terrified that some little thing might upset him and spoil his home-coming. As it turned out, it was not only a strain on her but also a worry to him, making him feel that he no longer knew his wife. In the end she broke down and cried about something, and was astonished and vastly relieved to have him say that he much preferred her to be her ordinary self, and had never expected things to run perfectly from the start. Since then they talk over any little difficulties together and everything has gone happily.

"Be natural" is a first-rate prescription, especially in view of some of the nonsense that has been written about returned men, much of it leaving the impression that they must be handled as gingerly as high explosives. There's nothing peculiar about the average veteran; he's a perfectly normal person—but he's reacting to an abnormal situation. How abnormal was simply expressed by a corporal in the First Division: "I have a darn good wife and haven't suffered from any infidelity business, but I must say I almost lost her because of such a long absence. We have to learn to know each other all over again."

Three years, four years, five years. A book could be written about the delicate readjustments that may have to be made when a man and his wife start to reestablish their life together. But I'm not trying to deal with such problems here, except to repeat this: that if husband and wife feel solid enough with each other to talk frankly about any difficulties they feel, these difficulties won't last long.

In thousands of battle-dress pockets there's a well-worn snap of a 10-year-old or a four-year-old or a baby that the father has never seen. And letters from home are full of the doings of these young Canadians—baby is crawling now, Diane is learning to read, Buster is playing midget hockey. At long range there is nothing that warms the heart like the thought of one's own children, but let's be honest—at short range, though they are often adorable, they can also be pests, nuisances and worries, especially when you're cooped up with them in a small space. Here's a case that is typical of quite a number:

> Before Frank came home I was worried sick for fear he wouldn't care about me in the same way, but I never thought of him not taking to the kids. He was always writing about them, you know. But now that he's back it's just the other way round. We were a bit strange like with each other at first, but we soon got over that. It's the children that he can't seem to get on with. They're noisy and naughty sometimes, of course, and when they get a bit out of hand it upsets him dreadfully. Really, I'm glad sometimes when he's out of the house so he won't notice them. He says they haven't been brought up right, and, of course, he blames that on me, and when they do anything out of turn he's down on them like a ton of bricks. I don't know what he expected, I'm sure; they're not angels, but I will say they're a lot less trouble than some I could name. But Frank, he seems disappointed in them somehow, and it's making things hard, because, of course, they notice it.

Well, there aren't any children in the Army and the picture he's built up of his own is apt to be too rosy a one. But it's nothing to worry about; he'll soon get interested in them and these first awkward weeks will be forgotten. Sometimes it's the children who are in for a letdown, as in this case of an officer home for a course:

> I was a terrible disappointment to young Peter when I first came back, and it's taken us a couple of months to get on a decent basis. He's practically said his

> prayers to my picture for two years, of course, and everything had always been, "Wait till Daddy gets home," until he was expecting a kind of a god. The first few days he wore his toy uniform all the time and hung around me every minute, and naturally I got a kick out of it and played up to him. Then, of course, I got sick of doing route marches around the house and letting him drill me 20 times a day, and when he kept pestering I was pretty short with him once or twice. Poor little kid went crying to his mother and asked her if I didn't like him any more. Now we're getting on fine again, and I think he's a grand kid, but it took time.

As a private of the Second Division put it, "It's hard to get back to smooth home relations with children to whom you're almost a stranger." But time and good sense always achieve it in the end.

The bugbear of responsibility—and it is a bugbear—can cause more difficulty in readjusting to civil life than almost anything else. In the services most men's responsibility is strictly limited to what they're ordered to do; they seldom have to make the decisions themselves, and as long as they're doing their job they don't have to worry about others. After a longish dose of that it's often hard to take on the burden of planning and deciding things too suddenly. Many a man has echoed this soldier's complaint:

> Here I get home, hoping to relax a bit, and the very first day Mary starts asking me to decide all sorts of things. "Now that you're back," she says, "we'd better decide whether to give notice here and try to find something nicer," or, "I wish you'd make your mind up about David going to camp this summer, we've got to tell them soon." I don't know why it is, but I just can't put my mind to that sort of thing, and when she starts her "Now that you're back" stuff I generally walk out and go down to the beverage room.

Well, it won't be hard to tell when he's got his breath, as it were, and is ready to tackle things again. In the meantime a wise wife will go on settling as much as she can herself and just let the rest slide. It won't be fatal.

On the other hand some men feel a little hurt for an exactly opposite reason—they find that the wife has become pretty competent at looking after everything, don't quite like to ask her to hand over, and yet don't enjoy the sense that they're not as necessary as they used to be. Tact and understanding are needed again here, but if their own relationship is sound the problem will soon be settled in a way that's satisfactory to both.

A particularly trying responsibility to face, after doing what he's told for so long, is that of deciding what his future career is to be. And everyone, soldier or civilian, hates to be nagged about a question before he's made up his own mind. This letter gives the picture clearly enough:

> You ask what John's going to do now. My dear, I only wish I knew. He doesn't seem to know himself yet, and he's so touchy about it that I never dare mention it. I soon found that out, but the trouble is that other people keep saying, "What are you going to do now you're out of the Army?" and it makes him so mad. He was quite rude to Uncle George about it the other day.

This is another case where it's best to let things ride. Nothing needs to be said, really; the matter's in the back of his mind all the time, and the Government has set up a very complete scheme to help him. But some men find it hard to make such far-reaching decisions just at first, and the rest of us can help most by not trying to hurry them.

No matter how much a man hates war—and most fighting men hate it with all their souls—there is generally one thing that he loves about life in the services, and that's the comradeship he finds there. In the tremendous experiences that men in the same platoon—or bomber crew, or ship—live through together, each one learns that he can count on the others to the very limit. That is something that peacetime associations seldom provide, and it's treasured long after the cruelties of war have been forgotten. The ties formed on service remain strong, and when a man comes home he is often unconsciously lonely—actually homesick for his unit.

> Flying Officer X, discharged on medical grounds, had been glum and depressed for several weeks, showing little interest in his work or home. His wife was worried and asked what was wrong, but he maintained everything was all right. Then one of his old comrades turned up unexpectedly. Mr. X kept him to dinner and supper, tried to make him stay the night, and talked and laughed a blue streak all the time. His wife says that he has been much more cheerful ever since.

This particular problem is much more trying now, when the war is still on and his pals are still fighting, than it will be later when all the men come home. There won't be the same loneliness then, but there may be other sources of friction. Listen to this:

> I can't get Tim to take any interest in the friends I've made here; he disappears if anyone comes to the house, and he actually walked out on a little party I'd arranged for him, said he wasn't wasting an evening on a lot of "flannelmouths." That's an experience I won't forget in a hurry. I had to pretend he'd been called away on business. He was really over in Centreville with a couple of chaps he knows there, discharged men, too, and pretty crude specimens in my opinion. He had them at the house once, but I told him flat I wasn't entertaining that type of fellow. So now he spends half his time in Centreville, comes home half-tight at nights and won't have anything to do with decent people who could help him along. I only hope he gets over it soon.

Well, someone should tell this wife that she's asking for trouble, that it's no use trying to separate a man from his buddies. If their backgrounds and interests are entirely different from his, he'll see less of them as time goes on—but he'll do it on his own, not because they don't come up to her standards. And remember—there's a bond between him and them that's based on a lot more than smooth manners or educated speech. If civilian life can't provide comradeship as real as this, so much the worse for it, and we'd better start trying to improve it.

Those Strange Civilians

ONE REASON returned men tend to stick together is because they often find it hard to stomach us civilians. Canada can be quite a shock to a man back from overseas—we are so free from the dangers and deprivations that he's seen in Europe, we seem so untouched by the war that has meant so much to him. This is what an RCAF boy said in his first couple of weeks here.

> The people in this country just don't know there's a war on, that's all. Look at all those shiny cars in the streets, look at the fancy clothes people wear, the food in the shops and everything. As far as I can make out, all nobody's thinking about is how he can make more dough—and are they ever making it, too! A few bombs would do this town a whole lot of good, and I'm not kidding, either.

An emotional reaction, perhaps, but a very understandable one, and who's to say there's not a lot of truth in it? We haven't been hurt the way others have been, and we ought to be deeply thankful for it. But to him, thinking of his comrades on operations and his friends in Britain, our normal life looks like nothing but cold indifference. He'll come to realize that much of it's only on the surface—that thousands of Canadians are worrying every moment about their men overseas. But in the meantime we should accept his criticisms thoughtfully, even if they sometimes seem undeserved. A discharged officer's wife raised another aspect of the problem:

> Charlie's settled down pretty well at his work but he still gripes a lot at "civilians," as he calls them—though he's really one himself now. He says they're so cold, so wrapped up in their own affairs, so uninterested in the war. They'll ask him where he's been and he'll tell them, and they'll say, "Oh, you must have had quite an experience all right," and then change the subject. That's what he says, anyway. I think myself that he frightens them off, they just don't know what to say to him, with him losing an eye and everything.

She's quite right; civilians are often just afraid to strike up a real conversation with a fighting man back home. Here's what a middle-aged man in the Civil Service says about it:

> No one can say I'm not interested in the war. I read everything I can lay my hands on and I'm always thinking about it. But I must admit I find it hard to talk to the few returned men I've run into. We've been living in such totally different worlds, and I know so little about the details of Army life that the questions I ask always sound terribly stupid. I didn't even know till the other day that men from overseas don't have GS on their sleeves—the Army ought to tell us about that, and about what the various ribbons and insignia mean. And then the boys use so much Army lingo—you know, everything seems to be initials or abbreviations or nicknames—that half the time I don't know what they're talking about. So I'm afraid I tend to shut up when I'm with them. I hate doing it, because it looks as if I weren't interested, but there it is.

A Welcome From All

These little difficulties with civilians help to remind us that man has to live in a wider world than his home, that a loving welcome from the family isn't all he needs. Neither are government rehabilitation plans enough, no matter how generous. Both need to be supplemented by a warm, friendly determination on the part of businessmen, organizations and the whole community to make the returning men really feel at home. This airman's gripe was a small one, but it should have been headed off in advance:

> We got a grand reception at the station, and it's marvellous being back with Helen and the kids. But it didn't seem as if anyone else paid any attention to me after the first day or so; guess I've got a hero complex or something. They're probably waiting for me to make the first move, but the one time I did it—about getting my old job back—it left kind of a taste in my mouth. I got the job all right and more pay, too, but I do think they could handle these things better. I went down to the plant and into the front office, and some girl there looks at me as if I was something the cat brought in, writes down my name and says, "Wait here, Mr. Andrews, and I'll see if there's anyone here who remembers about you." I don't know what you think, but I thought that was a terrible greeting. It was all right afterward, mind you; old Field took me into his own office and was very nice, but that darned girl—well, I almost walked out of there for good when she delivered her load of ice.

Little things like that would never happen if every industry, every organization, would think and plan now: "What can we do to make each detail of coming back home just as enjoyable as it can possibly be?" There are citizens' committees in many centres already, working out ways to help the returning men, but there should be one in every community and it should be meeting constantly. There's no end to the ideas that come when people really put their imaginations to work. The next "quotation" is not a quotation at all; so far I've seen no reports quite like it. But with all the gratitude that Canadians are feeling for the men overseas, I expect to see plenty soon. Here's what *might* be said:

> I've certainly had a wonderful reception here, far more than I deserve, if it comes to that. I didn't stop with the welcome at the station, either. Hardly a day goes by without someone coming to the house to say they're glad I'm back and can they help me in any way. People I'd never seen before, from organizations and so on. Why, the mayor came himself with an invitation to sit in with the postwar planning committee—not that I know anything about postwar plans, but it makes you feel like somebody. Then a fellow from the Junior Chamber of Commerce comes and asks me to be an honorary member for six months, and another club sends its secretary to tell me to use the clubrooms all I like, no fee or anything. The Scouts staged a parade to the house on Friday and asked me to a wiener roast, the movie manager brought along two passes to the show, good for a month, and the rink manager did the same. And lots of people come just to say they appreciate what I've done and wish me luck. It's all organized, of course—it has to be—but it sure makes you feel good.

Home may not be heaven to the returning man—but he doesn't pretend to be an angel, either. Some of the little problems I've mentioned may come up, but if they do, don't worry about them, don't make a life-and-death matter out of them. Talk them out if you get the chance, and let time and affection do the rest. Changes there will be, of course; there must be something wrong with a person who doesn't change in four or five years of war. But the vast majority of changes will be for the *better*; soldier and civilian alike will have learned, grown and developed in these exciting years. If we embark confidently and cheerfully on the adventure of getting to know one another again life may be much richer and more interesting than it would have been without the long separation. Home will be whatever we determine to make it—and that can mean the best that this world has to offer.

What happened to the veterans after they had returned? How did they adjust to civilian life? After the Vietnam War, there was much public concern in the United States about the effects wartime stress had on veterans; there was much less public concern in Allied countries after 1945. Mordecai Richler's little-known short story demonstrates that peace could destroy many.

Benny, the War in Europe, and Myerson's Daughter Bella

Mordecai Richler

When Benny was sent overseas in the autumn of 1941 his father, Garber, decided that if he had to yield one son to the army it might just as well be Benny, who was a dummy and wouldn't push where he shouldn't; Mrs Garber thought, he'll take care, my Benny will watch out; and Benny's brother Abe proclaimed, "When he comes back, I'll have a garage of my own, you bet, and I'll be able to give him a job." Benny wrote every week, and every week the Garbers sent him parcels full of good things a St Urbain Street boy should always have, like salami and pickled herring and *shtrudel.* The food parcels never varied and the letters—coming from Camp Borden and Aldershot and Normandy and Holland—were always the same too. They began—"I hope you are all well and good"—and ended—"don't worry, all the best to everybody, thank you for the parcel."

When Benny came home from the war in Europe, the Garbers didn't make an inordinate fuss, like the Shapiros did when their first-born son returned. They met him at the station, of course, and they had a small dinner for him.

Abe was overjoyed to see Benny again. "Atta boy," was what he kept saying all evening, "Atta boy, Benny."

"You shouldn't go back to the factory," Mr Garber said. "You don't need the old job. You can be a help to your brother Abe in his garage."

"Yes," Benny said.

"Let him be, let him rest," Mrs Garber said. "What'll happen if he doesn't work for two weeks?"

"Hey, when Artie Segal came back," Abe said, "he told me that in Italy there was nothing that a guy couldn't get for a couple of Sweet Caps. Was he shooting me the bull or what?"

Benny had been discharged and sent home not because the war was over, but because of the shrapnel in his leg. He didn't limp too badly and he wouldn't talk about his wound or the war, so at first nobody noticed that he had changed. Nobody, that is, except Myerson's daughter, Bella.

Myerson was the proprietor of Pop's Cigar & Soda, on St Urbain, and any day of the week you could find him there seated on a worn, peeling kitchen chair playing poker with the men of the neighbourhood. He had a glass eye, and when a player hesitated on a bet he would take it out and polish it, a gesture that never failed to intimidate. His daughter, Bella, worked behind the counter. She had a clubfoot and mousey brown hair and some more hair on her face, and although she was only twenty-six it was generally agreed that she would end up an old maid. Anyway she was the one—the first one—to notice that Benny had changed. The very first time he appeared in Pop's Cigar & Soda after his homecoming, she said to him, "What's wrong, Benny?"

"I'm all right," he said.

Benny was short and skinny with a long narrow face, a pulpy mouth that was somewhat crooked, and soft black eyes. He had big, conspicuous hands which he preferred to keep out of sight in his pockets. In fact he seemed to want to keep out of sight altogether, and whenever possible he stood behind a chair or in a dim light so that the others wouldn't notice him. When he had failed the ninth grade at FFHS, Benny's class master, a Mr Perkins, had sent him home with a note saying: "Benjamin is not a student, but he has all the makings of a good citizen. He is honest and attentive in class and a hard worker. I recommend that he learn a trade."

When Mr Garber had read what his son's teacher had written, he had shaken his head and crumped up the bit of paper and said—"A trade?"—he had looked at his boy and shaken his head and said—"A trade?"

Mrs Garber had said stoutly, "Haven't you got a trade?"

"Shapiro's boy will be a doctor," Mr Garber had said.

"Shapiro's boy," Mrs Garber had said.

Afterwards, Benny had retrieved the note and smoothed out the creases and put it in his pocket, where it had remained.

The day after his return to Montreal, Benny showed up at Abe's garage having decided that he didn't want two weeks off. That pleased Abe a lot. "I can see that you've matured since you've been away," Abe said. "That's good. That counts for you in this world."

Abe worked extremely hard, he worked night and day, and he believed that having Benny with him would give his business an added kick. "That's my kid brother

Benny," Abe used to tell the taxi drivers. "Four years in the infantry, two of them up front. A tough *hombre*, let me tell you."

For the first few weeks Abe was pleased with Benny. "He's slow," he reported to their father, "no genius of a mechanic, but the customers like him and he'll learn." Then Abe began to notice things. When business was slow, Benny, instead of taking advantage of the lull to clean up the shop, used to sit shivering in a dim corner, with his hands folded tight on his lap. The first time Abe noticed his brother behaving like that, he said, "What's wrong? You got a chill?"

"No. I'm all right."

"You want to go home or something?"

"No."

Whenever it rained, and it rained often that spring, Benny was not to be found around the garage, and that put Abe in a foul temper. Until one day during a thunder shower, Abe tried the toilet door and discovered that it was locked. "Benny," he yelled, "you come out, I know you're in there."

Benny didn't answer, so Abe fetched the key. He found Benny huddled in a corner with his head buried in his knees, trembling, with sweat running down his face in spite of the cold.

"It's raining," Benny said.

"Benny, get up. What's wrong?"

"Go away. It's raining."

"I'll get a doctor, Benny."

"No. Go away. Please, Abe."

"But Benny . . ."

Benny began to shake violently, just as if an inner whip had been cracked. Then, after it had passed, he looked up at Abe dumbly, his mouth hanging open. "It's raining," he said.

The next morning Abe went to see Mr Garber. "I don't know what to do with him," he said.

"The war left him with a bad taste," Mrs Garber said.

"Other boys went to the war," Abe said.

"Shapiro's boy," Mr Garber said, "was an officer."

"Shapiro's boy," Mrs Garber said. "You give him a vacation, Abe. You insist. He's a good boy. From the best."

Benny didn't know what to do with his vacation, so he slept in late, and began to hang around Pop's Cigar & Soda.

"I don't like it, Bella," Myerson said. "I need him here like I need a cancer."

"Something's wrong with him psychologically," one of the card players ventured.

But obviously Bella enjoyed having Benny around and after a while Myerson stopped complaining. "Maybe the boy is serious," he confessed, "and with her club foot and all that stuff on her face, I can't start picking and choosing. Besides, it's not as if he was a crook. Like Huberman's boy."

"You take that back. Huberman's boy was a victim of circumstances. He was taking care of the suitcase for a stranger, a complete stranger, when the cops had to mix in."

Bella and Benny did not talk much when they were together. She used to knit, he used to smoke. He would watch silently as she limped about the store, silently, with longing, and consternation. The letter from Mr Perkins was in his pocket. Occasionally, Bella would look up from her knitting. "You feel like a cup coffee?"

"I wouldn't say no."

Around five in the afternoon he would get up, Bella would come round the counter to give him a stack of magazines to take home, and at night he would read them all from cover to cover and the next morning bring them back as clean as new. Then he would sit with her in the store again, looking down at the floor or at his hands.

One day instead of going home around five in the afternoon, Benny went upstairs with Bella. Myerson, who was watching, smiled. He turned to Shub and said: "If I had a boy of my own, I couldn't wish for a better one than Benny."

"Look who's counting chickens," Shub replied.

Benny's vacation dragged on for several weeks and every morning he sat down at the counter in Pop's Cigar & Soda and every evening he went upstairs with Bella, pretending not to hear the wise-cracks made by the card players as they passed. Until one afternoon Bella summoned Myerson upstairs in the middle of a deal. "We have decided to get married," she said.

"In that case," Myerson said, "you have my permission."

"Aren't you even going to say luck or something?" Bella asked.

"It's your life," Myerson said.

They had a very simple wedding without speeches in a small synagogue and after the ceremony was over Abe whacked his younger brother on the back and said, "Atta boy, Benny. Atta boy."

"Can I come back to work?"

"Sure you can. You're the old Benny again. I can see that."

But his father, Benny noticed, was not too pleased with the match. Each time one of Garber's cronies congratulated him, he shrugged his shoulders and said, "Shapiro's boy married into the Segals."

"Shapiro's boy," Mrs Garber said.

Benny went back to the garage, but this time he settled down to work hard and that pleased Abe enormously. "That's my kid brother Benny," Abe took to telling the taxi drivers, "married six weeks and he's already got one in the oven. A quick worker, I'll tell you."

Benny not only settled down to work hard, but he even laughed a little, and, with Bella's help, began to plan for the future. But every now and then, usually when there was a slack period at the garage, Benny would shut up tight and sit in a chair in a dark corner. He had only been back at work for three, maybe four, months when Bella went to speak to Abe. She returned to their flat on St Urbain her face flushed and triumphant. "I've got news for you," she said to Benny. "Abe is going to open another garage on Mount Royal and you're going to manage it."

"But I don't want to, I wouldn't know how."

"We're going to be partners in the new garage."

"I'd rather stay with Abe."

Bella explained that they had to plan for their child's future. Their son, she swore, would not be brought up over a cigar & soda, without so much as a shower in the flat. She wanted a fridge. If they saved, they could afford a car. Next year, she said, after the baby was born, she hoped there would be sufficient money saved so that she could go to a clinic in the United States to have an operation on her foot. "I was to Dr Shapiro yesterday and he assured me there is a clinic in Boston where they perform miracles daily."

"He examined you?" Benny asked.

"He was very, very nice. Not a snob, if you know what I mean."

"Did he remember that he was at school with me?"

"No," Bella said.

Bella woke at three in the morning to find Benny huddled on the floor in a dark corner with his head buried in his knees, trembling. "It's raining," he said. "There's thunder."

"A man who fought in the war can't be scared of a little rain."

"Oh, Bella, Bella, Bella."

She attempted to stroke his head but he drew sharply away from her.

"Should I send for a doctor?"

"Shapiro's boy maybe?" he asked giggling.

"Why not?"

"Bella," he said. "Bella, Bella."

"I'm going next door to the Idelsohns to phone for the doctor. Don't move. Relax."

But when she returned to the bedroom he had gone.

Myerson came round at eight in the morning. Mr and Mrs Garber were with him.

"Is he dead?" Bella asked.

"Shapiro's boy, the doctor, said it was quick."

"Shapiro's boy," Mrs Garber said.

"It wasn't the driver's fault," Myerson said.

"I know," Bella said.

World War II, perhaps like all wars, left many questions unanswered. Some of them were intensely personal and very poignant.

Canada's Children of Love and War

Carl Honoré

PETER LANGSTONE was born a misfit. In early 1945, in the village of Middleton St. George in Durham, northern England, his mother fell for a French-Canadian soldier while her British husband was away at the front. Peter, her fourth child, was the result. After the war, the wartime lover returned to Canada and the senior Langstones tried to wipe away the memories of the wife's indiscretion. They had another child, and never spoke of the circumstances of Peter's birth. But a sourness persisted.

Forty-six years later, Peter Langstone, now living in nearby Darlington, talks of the past in measured tones: "They tried to pick up the pieces, but it never really worked. Nobody forgot what happened. It was very painful."

Until 1950, parcels arrived every few months from a mysterious Uncle Paul in Quebec. By the age of eight, Mr. Langstone was putting two and two together: "It was clear that I was different from my brothers and sisters. I had a bad childhood. My English father made life very difficult for me and my mum, although nine times out of ten she took the hiding to protect me."

Today, Mr. Langstone and "war babies" from all over the country are gathered at the Savoy Hotel in Blackpool for a conference organized by War Babes, a group set up in 1987 by the British offspring of American GIs. By sheer weight of demand, a Canadian division was formed in September 1990. War Babes founder, Glen Graham, reckons that during the Second World War Canadian servicemen and British women produced some 40 000 babies outside wedlock. Her interest came after she helped her husband, the son of an errant U.S. soldier, trace his father.

Preferring to forget that foreign servicemen sired thousands of illegitimate offspring during the Second World War, postwar Britain raised its Canadian war children on lies, half-truths, and silence. War Babes, based in Walsall near Birmingham, helps people trace biological fathers in North America. After a lifetime in the dark, people like Mr. Langstone want to find their natural fathers. And, says Mr. Langstone: "It makes such a difference to know that there are so many other people in the same boat."

Actually, a fleet of ships is the more apt metaphor.

And it was not always servicemen. In September 1945, a female clerk with an Edmonton regiment entered the hospital of a Royal Canadian Air Force base in Hampshire to give birth to a daughter. Raised by adoptive parents in Durham, her child, Catherine Atkinson, now lives in Wakefield, West Yorkshire. She holds no grudge: "I don't feel deprived in any way. In fact, I'm grateful for the life she handed me. I love my husband and I have three wonderful children and a career."

Mrs. Atkinson, who is a university lecturer, also has no idea who her father was. For all she knows he also may be Canadian. She decided to go to Blackpool to get advice on how to trace her Canadian mother. She has always been curious, but five years ago, when one of her children died of cancer, her desire to find her mother became profound. "When my son died, I understood what my mother must have felt when she gave me up. No woman loses a baby lightly. I know it must have been the right thing to do at the time and that she must still be suffering deeply. I want to tell her that everything turned out for the best."

Other Canadian servicewomen had children in Britain, but Canadian males were the real demographic time bomb. A half-million Canadians—mostly young, single men—were stationed in Britain for long periods between 1939 and 1946. That relationships were struck up with local women, married and unmarried, was only natural.

With Hitler's bombers humming overhead, life was far more precarious than it had ever been during the First World War. Fear gnawed at soldiers and civilians alike. Says Mrs. Graham: "People clung together for comfort. They didn't know what was coming next, so they lived very much for the moment."

With so many young British men fighting abroad, foreign servicemen poured in to shore up Allied defences in Britain. Small towns that had never before seen a foreigner were suddenly invaded by scores of young uniformed men with strange accents and money to spend.

Canadian military authorities were keen to avoid the complications of war marriages. Restrictions were quickly instituted and chaplains and commanding officers urged to dissuade their charges from walking down the aisle. It didn't work. The first marriage between a Canadian soldier and a British bride was recorded on 29 January 1940, little more than a month after the first Canadian divisions disembarked. By the end of 1946, 44 886 Canadian service personnel had set British wedding bells ringing and produced 21 358 legitimate children. Most returned to set up homes in Canada.

John Boorman's 1987 film, *Hope and Glory*, is built around one such love affair. A starry-eyed English teenager, Dawn, falls for a dashing Canadian corporal, Bruce.

Eventually, Bruce is posted to another base in the south of England. Dawn is left pregnant and distraught. At the end of the film, the quixotic Bruce deserts, and returns and marries his English rose.

In real life, however, fairy-tale endings were hardly the norm. Peter Bates was born in Bournemouth, Dorset, in 1943. When his mother was eight months pregnant with his brother in 1946, her Canadian husband vanished. Mrs. Bates never breathed his name again until she lay on her deathbed sixteen years ago. Now living in Ashvales, Hampshire, Mr. Bates has been haunted by the silence since childhood.

"My mother just wouldn't talk about it all. No one in the family would," he says. "For my peace of mind, I need to find him, to know what happened and why. That's the reason I contacted War Babes."

That silence is familiar to nearly every war baby. According to Mrs. Graham, the progeny of Canadian (and indeed all foreign) soldiers bore a double stigma. "They were not only illegitimate at a time when illegitimacy was taboo," she says, "they were the children of foreign soldiers, who were deeply resented in a lot of ways."

Though Canadian soldiers were, broadly speaking, more popular in Britain than their American counterparts, the "over-paid, over-sexed and over here" catchphrase for GIs sheds some light on the climate in which illegitimate war babies were born.

Moral codes suspended in the crucible of war were quickly resurrected after the Allied victory and the departure of foreign servicemen. The thousands of women left holding Canadian babies were too numerous to be punished. Instead, there were whispers and nods, but no one said anything.

Certainly nothing was said to Keith Biley, not even by his wife. Born in London in 1945, he was adopted locally soon after his mother was abandoned by her Canadian fiancé, who returned home to Medicine Hat. It was only after he tracked down his mother's relatives that he learned of his Canadian background. As it happens, he was the last to know: "Everyone in the local area, including my wife, knew I was the baby of a Canadian soldier, but they never said anything to me. I couldn't believe it. It was devastating. I just didn't know how to react."

The silence—and stigma of his illegitimacy—was more invidious in the case of young Peter Langstone, whose mother had the affair with the French Canadian while her husband was abroad. "It was the simple things," he says. "For pocket money, my brothers and sisters used to get a shiny shilling, while my father would press thrupence, or two scrap coppers, into my palm. Whenever the family went out for the day, I was always the one given the smallest ice cream or the fewest sweets."

For his mother, parenthood was a difficult balancing act. She stayed with her husband right up to his death two weeks ago, but it was never easy. Time and again, her wartime indiscretion was thrown back at her.

Says Mr. Langstone: "My mother had to be careful what love and affection she showed me in front of my English father. Otherwise he might take it out on me.

Usually, it was a quick, snatched cuddle here and a few quiet words of praise there. That was all I ever saw."

It was not until two years ago that mother and son talked things through. Some of Mr. Langstone's lifelong questions were answered, but not all: "I still wonder what things would have been like if my mother had just gone off with this Paul. Perhaps we would have had a better life. It'd be nice to know."

He also needed to hear what his siblings knew. They remain as close as ever, but until this year the Langstone children swapped only happy stories from the early days.

When Peter finally began asking questions he found that even his older brothers and sisters had only foggy recollections of the things that had so affected him: "I seem to have the longest memory in the family, maybe because it was a much more poignant thing for me. All they remember is that our father spoiled his youngest daughter rotten."

Ian Burke was born in Winchester, Hampshire, in 1943. Soon after his Canadian father scarpered, his mother found a British husband and moved to Bristol. Mr. Burke always suspected that part of the story was being withheld. Earlier this year his suspicions were confirmed. "After years of being very fidgety on the subject, my mother finally told me this February that my father had been a Canadian," he says. "Even after all that time, it really shook me."

Since then, Mr. Burke, now a dentist in Bristol, has learned that his dad died in 1962. But he is now in touch with a half-sister in Ontario.

That Mrs. Burke took nearly fifty years to disclose her secret is far from unusual. Many war babies are just finding out about their Canadian roots because their mothers are now in their late sixties and seventies and are facing the choice: talk or take it to the grave.

Other war babies have known longer, after stumbling on the truth by accident. Looking through a forbidden drawer at the age of fourteen, Julia Pomeroy came across papers showing she had been put up for adoption by a Canadian father and a British mother in Southport near Liverpool. She told no one. Over the years, she clung to the hope that having her own children would one day set her mind at ease. Later, she had an illegitimate child, whom she gave away; then she married and had a family in the 1960s. It was no solace. Says Mrs. Pomeroy: "I'd convinced myself that a husband and children would be enough to satisfy something that was missing in my life. When it wasn't, I began hunting for my parents."

Having grown up in Cheshire, Mrs. Pomeroy now finds herself, by chance, living in Kiddminster, Worcestershire, not far from the home of the birth mother she traced several years ago. They do not speak to each other. Says Mrs. Pomeroy: "She has built up a respectable persona and illegitimate children just don't fit into it."

However, her mother has provided some information about her Canadian lover and made it known that he was shot down over Hamburg in 1942. The trouble is that the dates she gives don't add up. Convinced her mother is lying, Mrs. Pomeroy is looking for a Canadian father she thinks may still be alive.

How do you find a father who returned to Canada nearly half a century ago? If you have a name and a service number (many war babes have only a nickname to go on) then the Commonwealth War Graves Commission in Ottawa is the place to start. If he did not die in service, then the next step is coaxing addresses out of the Canadian government. According to Mrs. Graham, whose own group may be contacted at 77 Howdles Lane, Brownhills, Walsall, West Midlands, Britain, WS8 7PJ, telephone 0543 360526, that is like drawing blood from a stone.

"Canadian authorities still think as the Americans did before the court case. They feel that only the fathers have rights," she says. The case to which she refers was won by War Babes in U.S. courts last November. The judgment gave them the right to the last-known home city and state of former GIs. From there it is often a matter of leafing through U.S. phone books in British libraries or ringing international directories. Since the decision, there have been more than 500 reunions.

The Department of Veterans Affairs in Canada, on the other hand, is far more stingy with its files. Letters are forwarded to former servicemen (War Babes has many in the mail), but addresses are only released if the man is dead. To Mrs. Graham, the only way to achieve the same openness that prevails in the U.S. is through the courts: "As soon as I find a litigation group in Canada, we will begin organizing a similar lawsuit to the one we fought in the States."

The downside of all this, however, is that con men are climbing aboard the bandwagon. War Babes has been swamped by glossy brochures from detective agencies in Canada offering, in return for huge sums of money, to do things that Mrs. Graham does for free.

To be sure, many war babies have opted not to visit Blackpool because they want to avoid publicity that might embarrass relatives in Britain or in Canada. Mrs. Graham promises that as soon as a Canadian father says he wants nothing to do with any wartime offspring, War Babes will call off its search and advise the war baby concerned to do likewise. Discretion is the name of the game.

Certainly, that is the approach recommended by Pamela Watson (not her real name). After a fifteen-year search, she finally located her Canadian father, who was living in New Brunswick, in 1986. After a few awkward conversations and letters, she arrived for a visit. She believes that building up a relationship before the face-to-face meeting was the wisest thing she ever did: "One should never go bulldozing in anywhere. These men are all elderly and the worst thing to do is suddenly show up saying 'Accept me!' I mean, everybody has made new lives."

Her Canadian father has since died, yet a strong bond remains between Mrs. Watson and her newfound Canadian relatives: there are regular phone calls and fortnightly letters.

But there were pitfalls. For a start, Mrs. Watson got a very cold shoulder from one member of the New Brunswick family. She issues a caveat to war babies who reach the stage where they are ready to visit their Canadian fathers: "At first, you fly over and it's a big, big high. I had a marvellous time in Canada. But when I returned home, I was terribly confused and shaken. That dream that's been with you for so long, forty years for some, is now suddenly a reality and you have to deal with." Counselling, she warns, is essential.

If the American example is anything to go by, the prospects for Canadian war babies are hopeful. Groups tracing GIs report that, after the initial unease, nearly all American fathers are pleased to have been found.

Says Mrs. Graham, "Once the Canadian fathers hear these children's stories, hopefully they'll realize that the best thing for everyone is to come forward, even if only to say they wish to be left alone. After all, time is running out."

So it will be with some optimism that about fifty Canadian war babies drink the final toast tonight at the Savoy Hotel. For a start, they have the courage of numbers; every week a few more come out of the closet. If Glen Graham is right, there could be tens of thousands more on the way. Of course, there is also trepidation. Happy precedents are reassuring, but nothing can ward off the possibility that waiting at the end of the road is rejection or a death certificate. There is no easy avenue open to the war baby.

As much as possible, expectations are being kept to a modest, even light-hearted, minimum. Keith Biley is particularly easygoing: "You know, I really just want to say hello and how have you been?"

There are many family stories in Canada about World War II. In private memory, as well as in public, a defining national experience lives on.

My Father's Days

Rick Johnson

WHEN I WAS TWO YEARS OLD my father went to war with the Canadian Army. Nobody consulted me about the wisdom of his departure. Being only two feet tall, with a vocabulary of a few dozen words, I wasn't privy to decisions that would affect my life well beyond the age of innocence.

My father never returned. He was killed during the sputtering vestiges of the Italian campaign, two days before the First Corps of the Canadian Army began transferring to Marseilles, eventually to join their comrades in Holland for the final assault on Germany. He died on my third birthday, 22 February 1945.

I can't remember how I felt when told of his death, not knowing the meaning of the word. But as I grew in consciousness, his absence became a fact of my life—like being a boy and not a girl, or living with people who were my family and not somebody's else's. I came to realize I would never see him, but it wasn't something I could rationally get my mind around.

Because everybody else I knew had a father, I felt set apart, like one of the strange people hidden in back rooms or attics. It also meant I didn't have an obvious and recognizable identity: I didn't belong to Dr. X or Shift Boss Y. However, I did have a privileged spiritual link. While my classmates uttered abstractions during the daily rote muttering of the Lord's Prayer, I had a picture in my mind of "Our Father, who art in Heaven," to whom I spoke with filial longing.

I have only two distinct memories relating to my father, fleeting moments, frozen in time, marking the beginnings of my self-conscious life. They're not entirely visual, more like complex recollections of feeling and form, shadowy yet substantial.

In the first, I am running with my mother on a gravel road alongside a railway track. Beyond the track rises a hump of bare rock sparsely shaded by frail trees with brilliant leaves. My arm is stretched up in the grip of my mother's hand and as we run

I trip and tumble on loose stones. I feel as if I am spinning at the end of her arm, with the wind hissing in my ears. Then a large form swings me giddy onto his shoulders, which feel rough and bristly against my legs. He hands my mother his kit and carries me.

In the second, I am standing at a window almost opaque with frost, trying to see into the backyard filled with mounds of snow. A man has just come to the door with an envelope for my mother. Now the house is filled with sobbing.

Thirty-three years after the telegram came, I sat on my father's grave in the Coriano Ridge War Cemetery near Riccione, a small beach resort on the Adriatic coast. There he was: Pte. Elmer Roland Johnson, D144615, Loyal Edmonton Regiment, age twenty-seven. Plot ten, row D, grave nine.

My father had been among the Canadian troops defending a twenty-seven-mile front, part of which ran along the Senio River, west of Ravenna. Between August and November 1944, the Allied forces had pushed the Germans, in some of the most vicious fighting in the Italian campaign, from the Gothic Line—the enemy's last significant defensive position before the southern entrance to Austria and Germany. However, a combination of rugged terrain, bad weather, lack of reinforcements and supplies, and tenacious German resistance stopped the Allied advance. With the advent of winter, the war became static, reminiscent of World War I. Between December and April both sides were dug in, making preparations for the spring offensive. Although neither side was on the move, each maintained an aggressive defence to sustain morale.

According to the *Official History of the Canadian Army*, the enemy's proximity warranted constant battle conditions:

> Frequently the German slit-trenches were only a few yards from the Canadian positions. In such cramped quarters patrol clashes and fire fights came often, and in the intervening lulls inventive minds improvised new weapons of war or devised unorthodox uses for existing ones. . . . The Seaforth produced the "V-2"—a large catapult made from the inner tube of a car tire, capable of throwing a No. 36 grenade fifty yards. . . . Some experimenters had filled a motor car with high explosives and sent it careering down the floodbank into an enemy post.

The Germans did the same.

My father was with D Company of the Loyal Edmonton Regiment, which was stationed along the floodbank of the Senio River. The enemy was on the other side, a distance of perhaps fifty feet. On the evening of 21 February 1945, the *Regimental History* says, "A barrel of high explosive was trundled over the crest of the floodbank and descended on the Loyal Edmonton outpost. Three men were injured." One was my father. He received severe blast and concussion wounds to the head. He was immediately taken to a British general hospital, where he died several hours later, never having regained consciousness.

Two days later, the Canadians fought their last battle in Italy. Two German companies of the 362nd Division attacked the Seaforth and Loyal Edmontons, and were repulsed. By 25 February the last of the Canadians in that area were withdrawn in Operation Goldflake.

My father was buried in Miramare, between Rimini and Riccione, and later reburied in the Coriano Ridge War Cemetery, when the Commonwealth War Graves Commission gathered the temporarily buried soldiers and created the official World War II cemeteries.

I don't know why it took me thirty-three years to get to my father's grave. As a child, my imagination was galvanized by the war and my father's part in it. I kept a cache of his personal effects sent home after his death. Every Remembrance Day I paraded with his medals around the bedroom. By the time I got to high school, I had a larger collection of books on the war than the local library. However, actually going to Italy to see his grave never seemed to be an issue in our family. In the fifties, Italy was a distant place; during the sixties I was too busy with life to think of the dead; by the seventies I had forgotten my childhood preoccupations.

At thirty-six it suddenly seemed important to go. I didn't hear a voice one morning saying, "You will now go to Italy." But I began feeling a yearning to know what the grave looked like; and soon the yearning became a palpable need. However, I still didn't think of a trip to Italy as a pilgrimage. I planned a holiday to see the wonders of Florence and Venice, Siena and Perugia, with a side trip to Coriano Ridge. My priorities hadn't yet fallen into order.

In England I began getting intimations of something more important than merely a holiday and a sentimental journey. I called the Commonwealth War Graves Commission for information about the best way to reach the cemetery. A kind of soft-spoken man took my father's name and went to look in the files. In a few minutes he returned and said, "Yes, Johnson, E.R., Coriano Ridge Cemetery. Plot ten, row D, grave nine. Now, this is the route from Riccione. . . ." Immediately, unsummoned tears poured from my eyes. It was as if someone inside me was weeping, using my tear ducts.

I quickly arranged to have the documents sent to my London address, hung up, and tried to come to grips with my spontaneous outburst. It was obvious that my recent yearning-cum-palpable need was more than the desire to have my curiosity quenched. I was having intimations of an inner life clamoring to be made known. The voice of the telephone had been a witness, an objective, external confirmation that my father had existed. The sudden proof of his existence invoked a response in me that lay deeper than the happiness I felt in finally going to the grave. I felt elation—a barrier had been crossed—and foreboding. I was frightened by a buried part of myself that now chose to come into consciousness.

Another incident gave further proof that my trip was meant to satisfy more than curiosity about a grave in rural Italy. On the train from Paris to Pisa I shared a compartment with a middle-aged couple who were also travelling from England to Italy. Husband and wife, they were going to visit her family's villa and their remaining relatives. I was stunned when I learned the family villa was located a few miles from the area where my father was killed. In fact, the woman had lived her teen years through the war. She had witnessed the kind of fighting that had claimed my father. And the villa in which she grew up had been a microcosm of the Italian campaign.

She presented a wry account of the fate of the villa. When the Germans came, they commandeered her home and occupied it for two years, relegating her family to a back room. She said the officers who lived in the house treated her family well, but in the winter they burned the furniture as fuel. When the Allies came, they also used the villa, with first British and then Polish troops passing through. The British allowed her family a few more rooms, but cut down the trees in the garden to build a bridge. It was the Americans who bombed the villa itself. She met her Polish husband, with whom she was now travelling, during the Polish occupation of the villa.

Meeting this couple was a "synchronicity"—a Jungian term for coincidental events having personal psychic value. The voice on the telephone in London had been one kind of witness to my past; this couple was another. With two incidents I gained assurance that the past was palpable. If my father had been real, then what I was beginning to discover in myself was real, had to be recognized and brought into conscious life.

When I got to Riccione, I decided to walk the three miles to the cemetery instead of taking the bus from Rimini, wanting to approach the site gradually. I didn't want it to appear suddenly and have to scramble to be let off. I also wanted to get a sense of the countryside, something I would miss peering through the window of a moving vehicle. I believed, finally, that I was on a pilgrimage; and a pilgrimage requires effort, a sensory preparation as well as a spiritual one.

The road first passed through postwar suburban Riccione. Except for the terracotta roof tiles, it was indistinguishable from Canadian suburbs. However, soon the landscape became rural, meandering through gently undulating, intensively cultivated fields of wheat, grape vines, and olive groves. I gathered brilliantly coloured poppies and purple and white wildflowers to put on the grave. The morning was hot, with a hazy, pale sky. After walking for several dusty hours, I stood on a small ridge and looked into a shallow valley at the cemetery.

I remained there, fixing the scene in my memory and trying to focus my thoughts and feelings so that later I could recall that first view exactly and wholly. However, from my vantage, the setting appeared incongruous, and the incongruity intruded between me and my feelings. I expected a military burial site to have regimented rows of headstones and a simple cross monument—the Cross of Sacrifice, with its superimposed bronze sword. But I wasn't prepared for the lush and decorous orderliness of the grounds—the English-country-garden beauty—absurdly surrounded by acres of Italian farmland alive with families cultivating their crops.

I found plot ten, row D, grave nine. When I sat on the manicured lawn over the grave, I tried to open myself completely to the moment. I didn't want it to be blurred by sentimentality. But it was hard to commune with just a name on a marble headstone. And my conscious memories and feelings were too vague to be brought forward to heighten my immediate responses. I was distracted from my solitary vigil by the formal beauty: the orderly rows of grave markers, the geometrically patterned plots, the opulence of many-coloured flowers planted along the rows, and the cool shade and shadow of cypresses and weeping willows.

There was an irony in this orchestrated beauty. How many of these 2000 dead had had access to such splendour when they were alive? My father had been a gold miner in northwest Quebec. He had gone to the newly opened mines to escape the vicissitudes of the Depression. Cut out of the Precambrian Shield, the mining town of Perron, where I was born, consisted of a headframe and a huddle of wooden houses surrounded by limitless miles of coniferous trees, rock, and muskeg. It was tortured by blackflies and mosquitoes in the summer, and frigid in winter. In contrast, this cemetery gave a glimpse of paradise.

It demanded a theatrical response. I felt there should be a parting of the heavens, a lightning bolt and crash of thunder. I was confused. More than thirty years of anticipation were involved in this moment, but I couldn't give it clarity. Then, one of the young Italian gardeners gathered my poppies and wildflowers, put them into a tin of water, and gently placed them on the grave. His spontaneous act of kindness brought my attention back. I noticed for the first time a flight of bees nudging and clinging to the delicate, bobbing flowers beside the headstone. Everything clicked into place. "I am because of him, and we are here together, finally."

As I felt a great peace pass over me, the cemetery as a whole took on greater value. I could be there because many others had been concerned for both the living and the dead. Had records of the dead not been kept, and these cemeteries not acquired, families would never know the ultimate fate of their men and women missing in action. It would be infinitely sad to see a faded, teetering cross sticking from a pile of weeds in a ditch; or to be told that somewhere under a high-rise building lie the remains of Canadian troops. I am comforted to know my father is buried in a place that is constantly cared for.

Back in Canada, the trip to see the grave seemed not to be an end to years of curiosity but a new beginning. I wanted to know more about my father, to know more about myself. The witnesses—the voice on the telephone, the woman on the train and the young gardener—helped me to feel the substance of a relationship that needed to be uncovered. For the first time I understood that my father and I had affected each other's lives before he went away. Now I know the power of that relationship. It had not disappeared, even though it had been breached before I was conscious of it at all. What had started as a trip to satisfy a lifelong sense of wonder was shifting into another kind of journey.

However, when I asked my uncles to tell me what my father was like, they lapsed into a strange reticence. Instead of giving me insights into his character, they told stories and anecdotes. Nobody else would say much more. When I broached the subject, I got shuffling feet, clearing of throats, a few clichés: "Ah, he was the best of the bunch" or "Yes, your father and I were good friends. . . ." It wasn't that people didn't care or were embarrassed. Most did not have the sensibility or the vocabulary to express what they wanted to say. They spent hours trying to tell me they couldn't tell me what I wanted to know.

Fortunately, my mother had saved all the letters my father had sent, from the time he joined the Army until his death. She gave them to me. Although laconic, they are my legacy, a map of his heart and mind during the last year of his life. They record the human face of war and reflect the banality and boredom of much of military life outside the battlefield. They do not say much about his inner life—his feelings and imagination; he didn't have a poet's powers of observation. But they do reveal his deep concern and love for his family and friends.

He never mentioned the abstract words we are supposed to associate with war: sacrifice, honour, duty. He did not write of Hitler or of the defence of democracy. His only reference to what he was doing came in a little postscript to me:

Hello son, I got your little letter today and you made me very happy and lonesome. I hope you are taking good care of Mummy and Leeny while Daddy is away. I am coming home after I have spanked all the Germans.

He didn't know he wouldn't come home, and therefore left many details of his experiences unsaid until his return. I wish he had elaborated on some of them.

For instance, on 15 December 1944, he wrote:

I suppose you have wondered why I never wrote to you on the boat but it was just about impossible to write as it was so darned crowded. It really was terrific. I'll tell you all about it when I get home.

Earlier, on 10 December, he wrote:

Here I am in London on a 36 hour pass and it is quite an interesting place. I just wish you could be here with me. We have not had much time to look around as we came in quite late yesterday afternoon. But we have been to Piccadilly, Charing Cross and Trafalgar Square. I wish we had more time to spend here. Would like also to go to St. Paul's Cathedral but don't know if I'll get there today. It's hard to find your way around here the first time and there is a lot of underground travelling by electric trains. We slept in an air raid shelter last night and it was pretty good. I'll sure have a lot to tell you when I return.

No matter where my father was, in training camp in Canada, in England, or in Italy, he was chiefly concerned about his wife and family. I suppose he kept his letters from becoming too personal to save the people at home from worry. By wondering about his children and speculating on their growth, he avoided issues that would reveal his fears and anxieties. He wrote in his last letter, 17 February 1945:

How are our little children? I hope you are all in the best of health. Just imagine, another five days and Ricky will be three years old. And Leeny will be one year old. I wonder how old they will be when I get home.

Five days later he was dead. The telegram we received is a cruelly terse announcement:

Deeply regret D144615 Private E.R. Johnson has been officially reported to have died twenty second February 1945 as a result of blast wound to head with concussion received in action stop you should receive further details by mail direct from the unit in the theatre of war stop to prevent possible aid to our enemies do not divulge date of casualty or name of unit.

We did receive further information from the front. In time, letters arrived from the commander of D Company and the principal matron of the British hospital. Both made the point that my father had received very severe head injuries and had remained unconscious until his death soon after being admitted to hospital. Although obviously form letters, at least these voices had names. They did give a human veneer to an impersonal process.

For a few years after reading the letters, the telegram, and other official documents, I assumed that I had reached the end of my journey. I had travelled to see the grave; I had pieced together some of the last months of my father's life; and I had discovered a latent element in my character that had been influenced by my truncated relationship with him. I was saddened because I felt I would never get to know completely what he was like, or the exact nature of our relationship. I wanted to give a finer tone to the feelings within myself that were beginning to surface. But I couldn't be sure they weren't merely aberrations in emotional behavior galvanized by approaching middle age.

However, a few months ago I was able to extend both my knowing and my feelings. One November morning I was called by an uncle, my father's youngest brother, who told me about a man living in a Toronto suburb who had been in the Army with my father. This man had been discovered by a friend of the family who made a habit of stopping for coffee at a particular restaurant on his trips to and from Sudbury. On these occasions he usually chatted with one of the owners. When talk turned to travel and friends, Louis Filipovic, the restaurant owner, said he had served in World War II with an Elmer Johnson who had been killed. He said he was my father's best friend and closest companion during the last year of his life. They met just after their initial Army medical and were inseparable until my father's death. Louis told me, "We lived together; we went through basic training at Farnham; we went to Nova Scotia and

Aldershot [England]; we were together in Avellino [Italy]; and they took us right to the front together."

When I went to see Louis, I was anxious about whether he would want to speak to me. But Louis seemed to intuit my needs and he responded with candour. He brought coffee to one of the booths in the restaurant and we talked openly and freely about our feelings toward my father.

He spoke with affection about their adventures, relating the usual stories of basic training and glorious drunken moments. But he also revealed a profound male closeness with my father—something that perhaps is only fostered during wars, when gratuitous death challenges and heightens fear and love. Louis spoke of my father as seen through the eyes of friendship, a facet that nobody else could offer. "We were always together, your daddy and me. God, I felt so bad when the padre told us he was dead. Your daddy was a good man. Oh, he was a good man really. He was always talking about the family. He was always talking about home."

Louis also helped fill in some of the gaps in my father's letters. About the boat trip to England: "The boat was a converted banana boat from the Caribbean. It had a big, big belly—you know, wide, very wide. They just converted it to carry troops. There were two or three decks all filled with hammocks. We were all packed in like sardines. You used to eat once or twice a day. There were no tables. You got your food and ate it anywhere."

He remembered the Senio River dyke. "It was so close. We were on this side and they were on the other side. And at night the enemy used to prowl and come over and roll barrels of dynamite containing steel, razor blades, and everything else. During the day you wouldn't dare stick your head out. One night they rolled down a barrel and that's how your daddy got killed. I don't think we were there for more than a week. God, he was killed in such a short time."

Louis also recalls one irony. "Your father kept saying, 'I don't think we will every go back home.' Honest to God, many times. I would say to him, 'Come on, for God's sake, you never know.' "

And that's what I'm left with as well. I'll never know my father, nor will I really understand the inner urgings connected with his memory. I'll always wonder how different life would have been, or the kind of person I might have become as his son, had he returned. Knowing only the void his absence left, I can't feel any pride that he fell so that others could live.

I also realize there is nothing to be gained in self-pity. I have bridged some of the gap between my current self and the relatively uncharted first two years of my life. I believe the impetus to do so came from a germ planted by my father that began to influence me when I started to feel the need to see his grave. Since then it has guided me into the past and into myself. In a sense, my father never really died; he has lived on through me. I have been the guardian of his bequest—a love transcending time and distance.

Appendix A: Public Opinion

Public opinion polls became part of everyday life in Canada during World War II, and an important weapon in the arsenal of the planner. As elsewhere, polling opened up new opportunities for politicians and bureaucrats to both comprehend and influence what the public thought. Big government and information science went forward together. The Gallup Poll was taken in Canada, beginning in 1941, by the Canadian Institute of Public Opinion (CIPO), an offshoot of the American Gallup organization. The institute's polls were published in newspapers that subscribed to its services. The following data are taken from increasingly sophisticated polls conducted throughout the war by the CIPO.

Opinion on the War

Are you satisfied with Canada's war effort? (13 Dec. 1941)*

Before Japanese attack:

Satisfied	61%	Dissatisfied	35%	Undecided	4%

Breakdown:

	Satisfied (%)	Dissatisfied (%)
Conservative Party	54	46
Liberals	71	29
In British Columbia	34	66
All other provinces	66	34

Do you think Canada will have to adopt selective service for its manpower, including compulsory overseas service before the war is over? (23 Dec. 1941)

	Will Adopt (%)	Will Not (%)	Undecided (%)
Before Japanese war	60	29	11
After Japanese war	67	25	8

*The date given is the date the poll was published.

In Quebec:

Expect compulsory overseas service before the end of the war	41%
Do not expect it	48
Undecided	11

Do you think that a Japanese attack on Canada's west coast is likely within the next year? (27 May 1942)

Yes	56%
No	35
Don't know	9

Do you think the soldiers who return from this war should be treated more generously than the veterans of the last war? (4 July 1942)

More generously	66%
Would not treat more generously	21
Undecided	13

Do you think Canada is doing all she can to help win the war? (13 Oct. 1943)

	August 1942 (%)	Today (%)
Yes	54	71
No	41	21
Undecided	5	8
French-speaking Canadians:		
Yes	89%	84%
No	8	9
Undecided	3	7

A great many Canadian soldiers are marrying girls in Britain. Do you approve of this or not? (10 May 1944)

	Approve (%)	Disapprove (%)	Undecided (%)
Total	46	41	13
Men	60	40	*
Women	47	53	*
Quebec	27	61	12
Rest of Canada	54	33	13

* Undecided group eliminated in sex breakdown.

Do you think that women who join the armed forces should or should not receive the same rate of pay as men who join the armed forces? (31 May 1944)

Should get the same pay	57%
Should not get the same pay	34
Undecided	9

By sex:

	Men (%)	Women (%)
For equal pay	53	60
Against equal pay	38	30
Undecided	9	10

Now that it's all over, do you think the Allies should or should not have used the atomic bomb against Japan?

Should have used bomb	77%
Should not have used it	12
Undecided	11

Opinion on Domestic Matters

Are you in favour of labour unions? (17 Dec. 1941)

Favour labour unions	63%
Do not favour	23
Undecided or no opinion	14

Should strikes be forbidden in war industries, or should the workers in those industries continue to have the right to strike? (17 Dec. 1941)

Strikes should be forbidden in war industries	78%
Strikes should not be forbidden	17
Undecided	5

Do you think the government should have the power to decide which men are to be used in industry, which men are to be used in farming, and which in the armed forces? (20 Dec. 1941)

Think government should have the power to allocate manpower	72%
Think government should not	20
Undecided on the question	8

In general, do you approve or disapprove of Mackenzie King as Prime Minister? (30 Dec. 1941)

Approve	66%
Disapprove	34

If women take the place of men in industry, should they be paid the same wages as men? (16 Feb. 1942)

Yes	78%
No	14
Undecided	8

By sex:

	Men (%)	Women (%)
Yes	71	85
No	20	7
Undecided	9	8

If the government should start a national health plan, would you be willing to pay a small part of your (or your family's) income every month so that you and your family would receive medical and hospital care whenever you needed it? (8 April 1942)

Would be willing	75%
Would not be willing	18
Undecided	7

Do you think Canada would be fighting in this war if she were completely independent and not a part of the British Empire? (19 Aug. 1942)

	English Canadians (%)	French Canadians (%)
Yes, would be fighting	81	33
No, would not be fighting	14	59
Undecided	5	8

Since the war started, the government has taken a bigger and bigger share in the control of business, industry, and agriculture. Some people say this control should continue after the war. Do you agree or disagree? (15 Aug. 1942)

	English Canadians (%)	French Canadians (%)
Agree	48	37
Disagree	41	51
Undecided	11	12

After the war, do you think women should be given equal opportunity with men to compete for jobs in industry, or do you think employers should give men the first chance? (21 April 1943)

	Total (%)	Men (%)	Women (%)
Equal chance	24	21	27
Give men first chance	72	75	68
Undecided	4	4	5

Which of these would you like to see Canada do after the war: 1. Decide for herself how she will deal with other countries in the world, or 2. Join with the other dominions and Britain in deciding one foreign policy for the whole empire? (25 March 1944)

	Decide for herself (%)	Join with dominions (%)	Undecided (%)
Total	47	46	7
Quebec	70	21	9
Rest of Canada	39	55	6
By age:			
21–29 years	58	37	5
30–49 years	48	45	7
50 years and over	39	54	7

It is suggested that the government should pay a family allowance of between $5 and $8 per child every month to families in the lower income group. Do you think this is a good idea or not? (2 Aug. 1944)

	Quebec (%)	Rest of Canada (%)
Good idea	81	57
Not good idea	12	35
No opinion	7	8

By age:

	21–29 years (%)	30–49 years (%)	Over 50 (%)
Approve	72	63	57
Disapprove	19	30	35
Undecided	9	7	8

Asked of young Canadians between the ages of 15 and 24 years:

After the war, would you like to see many changes or reforms made in Canada, or would you rather have the country remain pretty much as it was before the war? (26 Aug. 1944)

	Youth (%)	Adults (%)
Want changes	62	71
No changes	26	23
Undecided	12	6

Appendix B: Tables

Enlistments

	Male	Female
Navy	106 522	7 126
Army	730 159	21 624
Air Force	249 662	17 467
Nurses		4 439

Source: Directorate of History, Department of National Defence.

Casualties

	Killed in action	Died from other causes	Wounded in action	Prisoner of war
Navy	1 533	491	319	87
Army	17 682	5 235	52 679	6 433
Air Force*	13 498	3 603	1 416	2 475
Nurses	1			

*The Air Force casualty total includes 4 RCAF (Women's Division) members killed in action and 3 died from other causes.

Source: Directorate of History, Department of National Defence.

Marriages and Divorces in Canada

	Marriages	Divorces
1939	106 266	2073
1940	125 797	2416
1941	124 644	2462

	Marriages	Divorces
1942	130 786	3091
1943	113 827	3398
1944	104 656	3827
1945	111 376	5101
1946	137 398	7757
1947	130 400	8213
1948	126 118	6978

Source: F.H. Leacy, ed., *Historical Statistics of Canada* (Ottawa, 1983).

The Civilian Labour Force*

	With jobs	Non-agricultural	Agricultural	Jobless
1939	4120	2741	1379	529
1940	4184	2840	1344	423
1941	4271	3047	1224	195
1942	4434	3295	1139	135
1943	4491	3373	1118	76
1944	4485	3349	1136	63
1945	4447	3303	1144	73
1946	4738	3467	1271	124
1947	4862	3690	1172	92

*Numbers are in thousands.

Source: *Historical Statistics of Canada.*

Women in the Labour Force*

	Paid	Other than paid
1938	575	102
1939	575	111
1940	602	131
1941	683	117
1942	711	163
1943	849	335
1944	935	264
1945	923	270

	Paid	Other than paid
1946	808	81
1947	807	91
1948	826	88

*Numbers are in thousands.

Source: *Historical Statistics of Canada*.

Union Membership*

1938	382
1939	359
1940	362
1941	462
1942	578
1943	665
1944	724
1945	711
1946	832
1947	912

*Numbers are in thousands.

Source: *Union Growth in Canada, 1921–1967* (Ottawa, 1970).

Strikes and Lockouts

	Number	Days Lost
1938	147	148 678
1939	122	224 588
1940	168	266 318
1941	231	433 914
1942	354	450 202
1943	402	1 041 198
1944	199	490 139
1945	197	1 457 420
1946	228	4 516 390
1947	236	2 397 340

Source: *Historical Statistics of Canada*.

Federal Government Expenditure and Revenue*

	Expenditures	Revenue	Revenue from income tax	Revenue from corporation tax**
1938	$553	$502	$47	$85
1939	681	562	45	78
1940	1250	872	104	156
1941	1885	1489	296	321
1942	4387	2250	484	783
1943	5322	2765	698	740
1944	5246	2687	673	617
1945	5136	3013	687	645
1946	2634	3008	671	672
1947	2196	2872	670	591

* In millions of dollars.

**Corporation taxes include excess profits tax.

Source: *Historical Statistics of Canada.*

Further Reading

THE PRIMARY TEXT on Canadian politics and attitudes in the years leading to the outbreak of war is H.B. Neatby's *William Lyon Mackenzie King*, vol. 3, *The Prism of Unity 1922-1939* (Toronto, 1976). On pacifist attitudes, Thomas Socknat's *Witness Against War* (Toronto, 1987) remains the best account, while the sometimes complicated diplomacy between Canada and Britain, and between Ottawa and Washington is recounted in J.L. Granatstein and Robert Bothwell, "'A Self-Evident National Duty': Canadian Foreign Policy, 1935–1939," *Journal of Imperial and Commonwealth History* (Jan. 1975).

Prewar Canadian defence policy and the Armed Forces are examined in James Eayrs, *In Defence of Canada: Appeasement and Rearmament* (Toronto, 1965) and in Stephen Harris's, *Canadian Brass: The Making of a Professional Army 1860–1939* (Toronto, 1988). There is a chapter on the prewar Permanent Force and Militia in J.L. Granatstein's *The Generals: The Canadian Army's Senior Commanders in the Second World War* (Toronto, 1993), and material on the interwar years of the RCAF in W.A.B. Douglas, *The Creation of a National Air Force* (Toronto, 1986), the second volume of the official RCAF history.

There is still no modern official history of the Royal Canadian Navy's role in the war. The best scholarly naval studies are unquestionably Marc Milner's *North Atlantic Run: The Royal Canadian Navy and the Battle for the Convoys* (Toronto, 1985), and his *North Atlantic Run: The Royal Canadian Navy and the Battle for the Convoys* (Toronto, 1994). Equally problem-oriented is David Zimmerman's *The Great Naval Battle of Ottawa* (Toronto, 1989), which looks at the ways in which senior officers and politicians "impeded the development of high technology in Canada's wartime navy." Also very useful are two books of papers on RCN history: J.A. Boutilier, ed., *RCN in Retrospect 1910–1968* (Vancouver, 1982), and W.A.B. Douglas, ed., *RCN in Transition 1910–1985* (Vancouver, 1988).

The Royal Canadian Air Force's official history is now three volumes strong. Douglas's volume, referred to above, treats the wartime role at home. Brereton

Greenhous et al., *The Crucible of War 1939–1945*, volume 3 of the history, examines the Air Force's role abroad with a heavy focus (in discrete sections) on policy, the bomber offensive, fighters, air transport, and maritime air activities. The policy section focuses on "Canadianization," the effort to get Canadians serving together, while the bomber-offensive section is a controversial look at aims and results. The sole published study of the RCAF in Bomber Command is Spencer Dunmore and William Carter, *Reap the Whirlwind* (Toronto, 1991), a study of the RCAF's No. 6 Group.

The Army's official history is a model of what official history can and should be—judicious, balanced, honest. There are three volumes: C.P. Stacey's *Six Years of War* (Ottawa, 1955), which examined the home front, the Dieppe raid, and Hong Kong; G.W.L. Nicholson's *The Canadians in Italy, 1943–1945* (Ottawa, 1957); and Stacey's *The Victory Campaign* (Ottawa, 1960), an examination of operations in North-West Europe.

There are many books on aspects of Army operations and personnel. One of the very best is Col. John English's *The Canadian Army and the Normandy Campaign: A Study of Failure in High Command* (New York, 1991), an unsparing study, whose subtitle says it all. Equally impressive are Terry Copp and Bill McAndrew, *Battle Exhaustion: Soldiers and Psychiatrists in the Canadian Army, 1939–1945* (Montreal, 1990), and Daniel Dancocks, *The D-Day Dodgers: The Canadians in Italy, 1943–1945* (Toronto, 1991). Copp, the editor of *Canadian Military History*, a new journal published at Wilfrid Laurier University, also wrote *The Brigade* (Stoney Creek, ON, 1992), a study of the Fifth Canadian Infantry Brigade of the 2nd Division from its formation through to its disbandment after much fighting in North-West Europe. R.H. Roy published the heavily detailed but thoroughly reliable *1944: The Canadians in Normandy* (Toronto, 1984) to mark the fortieth anniversary of the D-Day invasion. Brig.-Gen. W. Denis Whitaker and Shelagh Whitaker produced the impressive *Tug of War* (Toronto, 1984) on the struggle to clear the Scheldt and on the impact reinforcement shortages had on the fighting soldiers. Another wartime officer, Jeffery Williams, treated the whole Canadian effort after Normandy in *The Long Left Flank: The Hard Fought Way to the Reich, 1944–1945* (Toronto, 1988). One useful memoir of the Italian campaign is Fred Cederberg's *The Long Road Home* (Toronto, 1985).

Dieppe and Hong Kong still sit like scars on the Canadian conscience. On Hong Kong, see Carl Vincent's *No Reason Why* (Stittsville, ON, 1981), a straight-out condemnation of government policy. On the ill-fated Dieppe raid of August 1942, the Whitakers' *Dieppe: Tragedy to Triumph* (Toronto, 1992), clashed head-on with Brian Villa's well researched and argued *Mountbatten and the Dieppe Raid*, 2nd ed. (Toronto, 1994), as both try to grapple with questions of responsibility, politics, and diplomacy.

There are countless other biographies and autobiographies of soldiers, sailors, and airmen, far too many to list here. Readers should be aware of Owen Cooke's *The Canadian Military Experience 1867–1983* (Ottawa, 1984), a very useful guide to the literature.

The best general account of the government of Canada's conduct of the war remains C.P. Stacey, *Arms, Men and Governments: The War Policies of Canada 1939-1945* (Ottawa, 1970). See also his *Canada and the Age of Conflict: A History of Canadian External Relations*, vol. 2, *1921–1947* (Toronto, 1981), and the relevant chapters of Robert Bothwell et al., *Canada, 1900–1945* (Toronto, 1987). The political history of the war period is surveyed in J.L. Granatstein, *Canada's War: The Politics of the Mackenzie King Government, 1939–1945* (Toronto, 1975). His other contributions to the history of these years include *The Politics of Survival: The Conservative Party of Canada, 1939–1945* (Toronto, 1967); *A Man of Influence: Norman A. Robertson and Canadian Statecraft 1929–68* (Ottawa, 1981); *The Ottawa Men: The Civil Service Mandarins, 1935–1957* (Toronto, 1982); with R.D. Cuff, *Ties that Bind: Canadian–American Relations in Wartime: From the Great War to the Cold War*, 2nd ed. (Toronto, 1977); and with J.M. Hitsman, *Broken Promises: A History of Conscription in Canada* (Toronto, 1977). Nationalist attitudes in Quebec during the war are dissected in Donald Horton, *André Laurendeau: French-Canadian Nationalist 1912–1968* (Toronto, 1992). For the legacy of the war artists, see R.F. Wodehouse, *A Check List of the War Collections of World War I, 1914–1918 and World War II, 1939–1945* (Ottawa, 1968).

The economic mobilization of the country is examined from the perspective of its central figure in Robert Bothwell and William Kilbourn, *C.D. Howe: A Biography* (Toronto, 1979). Two very informed economic studies are R. Warren James, *Wartime Economic Co-operation: A Study of Relations between Canada and the United States* (Toronto, 1949), and A.F.W. Plumptre, *Three Decades of Decision: Canada and the World Monetary System, 1944–75* (Toronto, 1977). Canada's important role in atomic development is described in Robert Bothwell, *Eldorado: Canada's National Uranium Company* (Toronto, 1984).

Canada does not yet have an equivalent to Richard Polenberg, *War and Society: The United States 1941–1945* (Philadelphia, 1972), but extensive work has been done on many social history topics. The remarkable changes that the war brought to the lives of women are examined in Alison Prentice et al., *Canadian Women: A History* (Toronto, 1988). Diane G. Forestell, "The Necessity of Sacrifice for the Nation at War: Women's Labour Force Participation, 1939–1946," *Histoire sociale/Social History* 22, 44 (Nov. 1989): 333–47, challenges previous interpretations of a key development. A collection that broke new ground in the understanding of the history of ethnic relations during the war is Norman Hillmer, Bohdan Kordan, and Lubomyr Luciuk, eds., *On Guard For Thee: War, Ethnicity, and the Canadian State, 1939–1945* (Ottawa, 1988). Two other insightful papers dealing with national security issues are Robert H. Keyserlingk, "'Agents within the Gates': The Search for Nazi Subversives in Canada during World War II," *Canadian Historical Review* 66, 2 (1985): 211–39, and Reg Whitaker, "Official Repression of Communism During World War II,"

Labour/Le Travail, 17 (Spring 1986): 135–66. The Japanese-Canadian experience is recounted in Ken Adachi, *The Enemy That Never Was: A History of the Japanese Canadians* (Toronto, 1976); Ann Gomer Sunahara, *The Politics of Racism: The Uprooting Of Japanese Canadians during the Second World War* (Toronto, 1981); and W. Peter Ward, *White Canada Forever: Popular Attitudes and Public Policy Towards Orientals in British Columbia*, 2nd ed. (Montreal, 1990).

Two books by James Struthers that have transformed knowledge of the history of the Canadian welfare state are *No Fault of Their Own: Unemployment and the Canadian Welfare State 1914–1941* (Toronto, 1983), and *The Limits of Affluence: Welfare in Ontario, 1920–1970* (Toronto, 1994). The reassertion of provincial power at the end of the war is highlighted in Marc J. Gotlieb, "George Drew and the Dominion–Provincial Conference on Reconstruction of 1945–6," *Canadian Historical Review* 66, 1 (1985): 27–47. Wartime discussion and planning for reform of medical care is well explained in C. David Naylor, *Private Practice, Public Payment: Canadian Medicine and the Politics of Health Insurance 1911–1966* (Montreal, 1986). For a survey of the origins and administration of the Veterans Charter by one of its principal architects see Walter S. Woods, *Rehabilitation (A Combined Operation)* (Ottawa, 1953). Irving Abella, *Nationalism, Communism, and Canadian Labour: The CIO, the Communist Party, and the Canadian Congress of Labour 1935–1956* (Toronto, 1973) gives a useful overview of the eventful history of Canadian unions in the war period. On the strike situation, Laurel Sefton MacDowell *"Remember Kirkland Lake": the History and Effects of the Kirkland Lake Gold Miners' Strike, 1941–42* (Toronto, 1983) is required reading. The connection between organized labour and the CCF is discussed in Walter D. Young, *The Anatomy of a Party: The National CCF, 1932–61* (Toronto, 1969).

Much work remains to be done on the impact of the war on Canada's regions, but a substantial body of writing exists. For Atlantic Canada see Ernest R. Forbes, "Consolidating Disparity: The Maritimes and the Industrialization of Canada During the Second World War," *Acadiensis* 15, 2 (Spring 1986): 3–27; Peter Neary, *Newfoundland in the North Atlantic World, 1929–1949* (Montreal, 1988); and R.A. Young, " 'And the People Will Sink into Despair': Reconstruction in New Brunswick, 1942–1952," *Canadian Historical Review* 69, 2 (1988): 127–66. Developments in the Canadian North are examined in Shelagh Grant, *Sovereignty or Security? Government Policy in the Canadian North, 1936–1950* (Vancouver, 1988) and Morris Zaslow, *The Northward Expansion of Canada 1914–1967* (Toronto, 1988). For events in Quebec see Paul-André Linteau, et al., *Quebec since 1930* (Toronto, 1991).

Credits

Extracts from Mackenzie King's Diary, 1–10 Sept. 1939, 26–27 March 1940, 27–28 April 1942, 7–8 May, 11 June, 6 and 15 Aug. 1945. Reprinted with the permission of the National Archives of Canada.

Speeches in the House of Commons. From Canada, House of Commons, *Debates*, 5th (Special War) Session—18th Parliament, Sept. 1939. Reprinted with the permission of the House of Commons.

Howard Graham, "Citizen and Soldier." From *Citizen and Soldier* by Howard Graham (1987), 99–101, 103–7. Used by permission of the Canadian Publishers, McClelland & Stewart, Toronto.

Gabrielle Roy, "A New Life Was Beginning for Them All." From *The Tin Flute* (Toronto: McClelland & Stewart, 1959), 267–74. Copyright: Fonds Gabrielle Roy. Reprinted with permission.

Timothy Findley, "War." From *Dinner Along the Amazon* by Timothy Findley. Copyright © Pebble Productions Inc., 1984. Reprinted by permission of Penguin Books Canada Limited.

Hugh Garner, "A War of Strangers." From *Storm Below* (Toronto: Collins, © 1949), 53–59. Reprinted with the permission of the estate of Hugh Garner.

Marc Milner, "Royal Canadian Navy Participation in the Battle of the Atlantic Crisis of 1943." Reprinted with permission of the publisher from *The RCN in Retrospect: 1910–1968*, edited by James A. Boutilier (Vancouver: University of British Columbia Press, 1982). All rights reserved by the publisher.

Patricia E. Roy, J.L. Granatstein, Masako Iino, Hiroko Takamura, "The Hong Kong Disaster." From *Mutual Hostages: Canadians and Japanese During the Second World War* (Toronto: University of Toronto Press, 1990), 62–74. Reprinted by permission of University of Toronto Press Incorporated. Copyright © 1990.

Raymond Souster, "Pictures From a Long-Lost World: Hong Kong, 1941." Reprinted from *Collected Poems of Raymond Souster* (1983) by permission of Oberon Press.

"Commando Raid on Dieppe." *Canadian Heroes* magazine, Public Record Office, Kew, AIR 38/20.

Mona McTavish Gould, "This Was My Brother." From *We Stand on Guard: Poems and Songs of Canadians in Battle*, ed. John Robert Colombo and Michael Richardson. Copyright John Robert Colombo and Michael Richardson, 1985. Reprinted by permission of the author and Gage Educational Publishing Company.

Farley Mowat, "The Worm." From *And No Birds Sang* (Toronto: McClelland & Stewart, 1979), 221–36. Reprinted with the permission of the author.

Earle Birney, "Turvey is Psychoanalyzed." From *Turvey* by Earle Birney (1949; 1976), 204–13. Used by permission of the Canadian Publishers, McClelland & Stewart, Toronto.

Bill McAndrew, "The Soldier and the Battle." From David A. Charters, Marc Milner, and J. Brent Wilson, eds., *Military History and the Military Historian*, reprinted with permission of Greenwood Publishing Group, Inc., Westport, CT. Copyright © 1992, Praeger.

Ruth Roach Pierson, "Wartime Jitters Over Femininity." From *"They're Still Women After All": The Second World War and Canadian Womanhood* by Ruth Pierson (1986). Used by permission of the Canadian Publishers, McClelland & Stewart, Toronto.

Walter R. Thompson, "Service Flying." From *Lancaster to Berlin* by Walter Thompson, Copyright © 1985 by Walter R. Thompson. First published in Great Britain 1985 by Goodall Publications Ltd and published in Canada by Totem Books, a division of Collins Publishers.

"Diary of the Royal Air Force Ferry Command, Gander, 8–23 December 1942." Public Record Office, AIR 38/3. Transcript of Crown-copyright record appears by permission of the Controller of H.M. Stationery Office.

John Gillespie Magee, Jr., "High Flight." From *The New Treasury of War Poetry: Poems of the Second World War*, ed. and with an intro. by George Herbert Clark (Boston: Houghton Mifflin Company, 1943).

Murray Peden, "Gelsenkirchen." From *A Thousand Shall Fall* by Murray Peden. Copyright © 1979 by Murray Peden. First published by Canada's Wings Publishing. Reprinted by permission of Stoddart Publishing Co. Limited, Don Mills, ON.

René Lévesque, "Dachau." From *Memoirs* (Montreal: Québec/Amérique, 1986), 101–3. Repinted with the permission of the publisher.

Joan Murray, "You'll Get Used to It." From *Canadian Artists of the Second World War* (Oshawa, ON: The Robert McLaughlin Gallery, 1981), 6–19. Used by permission of the author.

André Laurendeau, "The Plebiscite." From Philip Stratford, ed., *André Laurendeau: Witness for Quebec* (Toronto: Macmillan of Canada, 1973), 54–61.

F.R. Scott, "What Did 'No' Mean?" From *Canadian Forum* 22 (June 1942): 71–73. Reprinted with the permission of James Lorimer and Company Limited.

Roch Carrier, "Corriveau's Return Home." From *La Guerre, Yes Sir!* pp. 38–43, House of Anansi Press, 1970. Translation © 1970 by Sheila Fischman. Reprinted with the permission of Stoddart Publishing Co. Limited, Don Mills, ON.

Ralph Allen, "Going Active." From *Home Made Banners.* (Toronto: Longmans, Green & Co., 1946), 60–75.

William Kaplan, "National Security." From *State and Salvation* (Toronto: University of Toronto Press, 1989). Reprinted by permission of University of Toronto Press, Inc. Copyright © 1989.

Jeff Keshen, "One for All or All for One: Black Marketing in Canada, 1939–1947." A revised version of this paper will appear in the *Journal of Canadian Studies* 29, 4 (Winter 1994–95). Used with the permission of the author.

Michael Bliss, "Visible Hand: The Years of C.D. Howe." From *Northern Enterprise* by Michael Bliss (1987). Used by permission of the Canadian Publishers, McClelland & Stewart, Toronto.

Laurel Sefton MacDowell, "The Formation of the Canadian Industrial Relations System During World War II." Reprinted with permission of the publisher. From *Labour/Le Travailleur* 3 (1978): 175–96. © Canadian Committee on Labour History

James Wreford, "Kirkland Lake 1943." From *The Blasted Pine*, arranged and introduced by F.R. Scott and A.J.M. Smith, revised and enlarged edition (Toronto: Macmillan, 1967).

Raymond B. Blake, "Mackenzie King and the Genesis of Family Allowances in Canada, 1939–1944." Not previously published. Used with the permission of the author.

F.R. Scott, "W.L.M.K." From *The Blasted Pine*, arranged and introduced by F.R. Scott and A.J.M. Smith, revised and enlarged edition (Toronto: Macmillan, 1967).

Justice R.L. Kellock, "Report on the Halifax Disorders." From *Report on the Halifax Disorders May 7th–8th 1945* (Ottawa, 1945), 29–33, 59, 61.

Gordon O. Rothney, "Quebec Saves Our King." *Canadian Forum* 25 (July 1945): 83–84. Reprinted by permission of James Lorimer and Company Limited.

Doug Owram, "The Dominion–Provincial Conference on Reconstruction: The Limits of Success." From *The Government Generation: Canadian Intellectuals and the State, 1900–1945* (Toronto: University of Toronto Press, 1986). Reprinted by permission of University of Toronto Press Incorporated. Copyright © 1986.

Dean F. Oliver, "Canadian Military Demobilization in World War II." Not previously published. Used with the permission of the author.

Peter Neary and Shaun Brown, "The Veterans Charter and Canadian Women Veterans of World War II." Not previously published. Used with the permission of the authors.

J.D. Ketchum, "Home Won't Be Heaven Soldier." *Maclean's,* 1 May 1945, 5–6, 30–31. Reprinted with the permission of *Maclean's.*

Mordecai Richler, "Benny, the War in Europe, and Myerson's Daughter Bella." From *The Street* by Mordecai Richler. Used by permission of the Canadian Publishers, McClelland & Stewart, Toronto.

Carl Honoré, "Canada's Children of Love and War." *Globe and Mail*, 23 Nov. 1991. Reprinted with the permission of the author.

Rick Johnson, "My Father's Days." *Quest*, Nov. 1982, 19–20, 22, 23–25.

Photography for the Canadian War Museum by William Kent.

Index